BEFORE AMERICAN HISTORY

WRITING THE EARLY AMERICAS

Anna Brickhouse and Kirsten Silva Gruesz, Editors

Before American History

Nationalist Mythmaking and Indigenous Dispossession

Christen Mucher

UNIVERSITY OF VIRGINIA PRESS

Charlottesville and London

University of Virginia Press
© 2022 by the Rector and Visitors of the University of Virginia

All rights reserved
First published 2022

1 3 5 7 9 8 6 4 2

Library of Congress Cataloging-in-Publication Data
Names: Mucher, Christen, author.
Title: Before American history : nationalist mythmaking and indigenous dispossession / Christen Mucher.
Other titles: Nationalist mythmaking and indigenous dispossession.
Description: Charlottesville : University of Virginia Press, [2022] | Series: Writing the early Americas | Includes bibliographical references and index.
Identifiers: LCCN 2021054547 (print) | LCCN 2021054548 (ebook) | ISBN 9780813948249 (hardcover) | ISBN 9780813948256 (paperback) | ISBN 9780813948263 (ebook)
Subjects: LCSH: Indians of North America—Historiography. | Nationalism and historiography—United States. | Nationalism and historiography—Mexico. | Indians of North America—Antiquities—Collectors and collecting—History. | Settler colonialism—United States—History. | America—Antiquities.
Classification: LCC E76.8 .M83 2022 (print) | LCC E76.8 (ebook) | DDC 970.004/97—dc23/eng/20211122
LC record available at https://lccn.loc.gov/2021054547
LC ebook record available at https://lccn.loc.gov/2021054548

Cover art: G. Whipple, cover stamp from
John Delafield, *An Inquiry into the Origin of the Antiquities of America.*
Cincinnati: N. G. Burgess & Co., 1839.

S|H   **The Sustainable History Monograph Pilot**
M|P   Opening Up the Past, Publishing for the Future

This book is published as part of the Sustainable History Monograph Pilot. With the generous support of the Andrew W. Mellon Foundation, the Pilot uses cutting-edge publishing technology to produce open access digital editions of high-quality, peer-reviewed monographs from leading university presses. Free digital editions can be downloaded from: Books at JSTOR, EBSCO, Internet Archive, OAPEN, Project MUSE, ScienceOpen, and many other open repositories.

While the digital edition is free to download, read, and share, the book is under copyright and covered by the following Creative Commons License: CC BY-NC-ND 4.0. Please consult www.creativecommons.org if you have questions about your rights to reuse the material in this book.

When you cite the book, please include the following URL for its Digital Object Identifier (DOI): https://doi.org/10.52156/m.5619

> We are eager to learn more about how you discovered this title and how you are using it. We hope you will spend a few minutes answering a couple of questions at this URL:
> **https://www.longleafservices.org/shmp-survey/**

More information about the Sustainable History Monograph Pilot can be found at https://www.longleafservices.org.

For Amy Kaplan

CONTENTS

List of Illustrations xi
Preface: Unsettling the Moundbuilders xiii
Acknowledgments xvii
A Note on Terminology and Method xxi

INTRODUCTION 1

CHAPTER 1
Ordering the "Indian" Archive 19

CHAPTER 2
Storied Lands of the Old West 53

CHAPTER 3
Mexico Antiguo through Americano Eyes 91

CHAPTER 4
Nationalist Science and the Chronology of Dispossession 128

CHAPTER 5
Removal in the Antiquarian Archive 165

CHAPTER 6
An American Babylon in the Mexican Republic 205

EPILOGUE
After American History 243

Notes 249
Bibliography 327
Index 393

ILLUSTRATIONS

FIGURE 1. Orator's Mound, Yellow Springs, Ohio (c. 1890). Courtesy of Antiochiana, Antioch College. xiv

FIGURE 2. "Turn and Learn," Aztalan State Park, Aztalan, Wisconsin. Author's photograph, 2016. 2

FIGURE 3. Karl Nebel, "Plaza Mayor de Mexico," detail, *Voyage pittoresque et archéologique* (1836). 3

FIGURE 4. La Piedra del Sol, Museo Nacional de Antropología (INAH), Mexico City. Author's photograph, 2016. 4

FIGURE 5. Giovanni Francesco Gemelli Careri, "Siècle des Mexiquains," *Voyage du tour du monde*, t. 6 (1719). Courtesy of the Bibliothèque Nationale de France. 33

FIGURE 6. *Codex Boturini* (c. 1530), detail. Courtesy of el Instituto Nacional de Antropología e Historia (INAH), Mexico. 34

FIGURE 7. José Joaquín Granados y Gálvez, *Tardes Americanas* (1778), pl. 1. Courtesy of the John Carter Brown Library, Brown University. 44

FIGURE 8. Francisco Javier Clavijero, "Il Tempio Maggior di Messico," *Storia antica del Messico* (1780), t. 2 pl. 1. Courtesy of the John Carter Brown Library, Brown University. 74

FIGURE 9. Benjamin Smith Barton, *Observations on Some Parts of Natural History* [. . .] (1787). Courtesy of the John Carter Brown Library, Brown University. 87

FIGURE 10. José Antonio de Alzate y Ramírez, "Plano de Tenochtitlan" (1789), detail. Courtesy of the Bibliothèque Nationale de France. 106

FIGURES 11a and 11b. Antonio de León y Gama, *Descripción histórica y cronológica de las dos piedras* [. . .] (1792), pls. 1, 2. Courtesy of the Kislack Collection, Library of Congress. 119

FIGURE 12. "Sala 1," el Museo del Templo Mayor (INAH), Mexico City. Author's photograph, 2016. 127

FIGURE 13. Alexander von Humboldt, "General Chart of the Kingdom of New Spain [. . .]" (1804), detail. Courtesy of the Library of Congress. 130

FIGURE 14. "Great Body of Clay," *Memoirs of the American Academy of Arts and Sciences* 3 (1809), f. 2. Courtesy of the Biodiversity Heritage Library and Missouri Botanical Garden. 170

FIGURE 15. Caleb Atwater, "Ancient Works at Circleville Ohio," *Archaeologia Americana* (1820), pl. 4. Courtesy of the Library of Congress. 176

FIGURE 16. Sarah Clifford, "Triune Idol" (c. 1820). Courtesy of the American Antiquarian Society. 180

FIGURE 17. Abner Reed, "Map of the State of Ohio, including the Indian Reservations Purchased and Laid out into Counties and Townships in 1820," detail. *Archaeologia Americana* (1820). Courtesy of the American Antiquarian Society. 199

FIGURE 18. North Bridge Street Mound, Chillicothe, Ohio. Author's photograph, 2018. 204

FIGURE 19. Title page, *Colección de las antigüedades mexicanos* (1827). Courtesy of the Newberry Library. 231

FIGURE 20. Ricardo Almendariz, *Colección de estampas copiadas de las figuras originales* (1787), pl. 23. Courtesy of the Kislack Collection, Library of Congress. 237

FIGURE 21. "Table Cross." Courtesy of the American Philosophical Society. 239

PREFACE: UNSETTLING THE MOUNDBUILDERS

I want my ink to bellow—
Where is this ground unstained with blood?

—Laura Da', "American Towns," 2015

I grew up on Shawnee and Miami homelands, a descendant of European settlers looking to escape their former lives. I do not know why they made their journeys, nor why they settled where they did; I do know, however, that my ancestors benefitted from established and emergent systems of labor, credit, and kinship as well as settler colonial modes of domination that included Indigenous eviction and erasure from the lands on which they settled. Uninvited guests who never left, my relatives grew deep roots in places I still think of as home. Their experiences comprise wholly conventional settler events: the claiming of a homestead, naming of a road, marking of boundaries with fence posts and burial plots, the tallying and settling of debts with neighbors, landlords, and savings banks. Their few acknowledged connections to Indigenous peoples were filtered through dishonorable mascots and town seals, as well as—on one side—an indistinct sense of pride in our distant cousin Davy Crockett.

Although my school fieldtrips included visits to important Shawnee and Miami sites like Cedar Bog, Buckeye Lake, and the Johnston Indian Agency, the lessons largely centered on "natural history." In good weather, I would walk a few blocks with my schoolmates to the local nature preserve, where we studied swamp cabbage, jack-in-the-pulpit, and box turtles, passing several "Indian mounds" on our way. These registered as much a part of the landscape as the nearby limestone caves and rusty mineral springs. Despite becoming a "junior naturalist," I little recognized the earthen architecture around me as much older than any other history I knew of the Midwest. Nor did I have any sense of my location in Native space—let alone Shawnee or Miami place-worlds—despite always knowing myself to be in rural Ohio and, especially during the first Gulf War, in the United States of America.[1] Then, I did not understand how the

FIGURE 1. Orator's Mound, Yellow Springs, Ohio (c. 1890). Courtesy of Antiochiana, Antioch College. This burial mound was reportedly used as a speaking platform by Daniel Webster and Edward Everett Hale. Excavated and emptied in the 1970s, the remaining structure is now being reabsorbed by the forest.

violence of war, occupation, and displacement centuries-over had enabled my incipient patriotism, nor how internalized dispossessive logics overwrote deeply held Indigenous histories with fables about "First Ohioans."[2] Really, I knew little outside what Lenape scholar Joanne Barker has referred to as "settler colonial thought and reality."[3] Even then, my very concepts of history, time, and space had already been constricted by the teachings of "colonial permanence," nationalist liberalism, and settler futurity.[4]

If the settler project disciplines Indigenous homelands, histories, and empowered objects into properties, legends, and antiquities—and above all, into a past that is *settled*, in all of its preterit force—then the practice of *unsettling* the settler-produced past disrupts the imaginaries and epistemologies that petrify and extinguish Indigenous presents and futures. *Unsettlement* calls on settler and settler-educated scholars to relinquish the dispossessive intellectual legacies of their academic inheritance, which involves "decenter[ing] settler perspectives"—especially whiteness—and upsetting those easy ways of knowing and living that maintain settler futures at the expense of Indigenous ones.[5] In their influential 2012 article, "Decolonization is not a metaphor," sociologists Eve Tuck (Unangax̂) and K. Wayne Yang remind readers that decolonization is unsettling—uncomfortable—because it challenges the structure of property-holding at the heart of colonization.⁶ But decolonization, they explain, "is not a metaphor for other things we want to do to improve our societies." It is instead a serious call for the restoration of "Indigenous land and life."⁷ While I see the unsettling of American history as a practice in support of Indigenous futures, engaged in solidarity with Indigenous resurgence and necessary to the land-rendering demanded by decolonization, *Before American History* is unsettling rather than decolonial.⁸ That is, it seeks foremost to unsettle the quotidian, dispossessive ways of knowing the past that have been and are being enacted by settler scholars on Indigenous lands in the name of American history and American futures.

Often non-Indigenous people say that they "never learned" Native history.⁹ But I *was* taught to be a settler—how to think like one, how to see like one, how to take up space like one—even if the curriculum was never explicitly assigned. It is through the process that some Native American and Indigenous studies (NAIS) scholars call "colonial unknowing" that settlers have *learned* not to understand their lives or the life around them in relation to indigeneity.¹⁰ For settlers, unlearning the unknowing means recognizing our ways of living as themselves learned and practiced, especially in those most mundane, "innocent," or "natural" of situations. This book attempts to unlearn that "unknown" history—and thus to unsettle the past as I once knew it—before "America."¹¹

ACKNOWLEDGMENTS

I've lived with this project for so long and amassed so many obligations that these words can only begin to express my gratitude. The research and writing for this book was done on myriad Indigenous homelands including Wabanaki, Nipmuc, Susquehannok, Lenape, Shawnee, Miami, Potawatomi, Odawa, Ojibwe, Baxoje, Chiwere, Notoway, Piscataway, Cherokee, and Nahua lands. I gratefully acknowledge these lands' peoples and I thank them for hosting and teaching this uninvited guest. I am grateful for the financial support provided by Smith College, the National Endowment for the Humanities, the American Antiquarian Society, and the Newberry Library, which made this publication possible.

Although much of the work for this book happened after graduate school, my time at Penn English laid its foundation. To my cohort and fellow students who made the intellectual world in Philadelphia so vibrant, my million thanks: Kate Aid, Raquel Albarrán, Dave Alff, Avi Alpert, Sari Altschuler, Jarrett Anthony, GerShun Avilez, Rachel Banner, Marina Bilbija, Cal Biruk, Julia Bloch, Larissa Brewer-Garcia, Ashley Cohen, Sarah Dowling, Jeffrey Edwards, Stephanie Elsky, Scott Enderle, Shonni Enelow, Laura Finch, Ellery Fouch, David Gardner, Isabel Geathers, Matt Goldmark, Sarah Mantilla Griffin, Chris Hunter, Emily Hyde, Ren Heintz, Jen Jahner, Adrian Khactu, Greta LaFleur, Grace Lavery, Jeehyun Lim, Phil Maciak, Cliff Mak, Mel Micir, Vanessa Mongey, Rachael Nichols, Emily Ogden, Joshua Ratner, Jessica Rosenberg, Courtney Rydel, Ana Schwartz, Jill Shashaty, Laura Soderberg, Emma Stapely, Lucy Swanson, Mecca Jamilah Sullivan, Chris Taylor, Lindsay Van Tine, Megan Walsh, Emily Weissbourd, Sunny Yang, and Jason Zuzga. I am so grateful for Poulomi Saha, who stayed with me through it all. A course with Bethany Schneider changed my trajectory, and David Kazanjian and Amy Kaplan helped me follow the new path. David was an indefatigable advisor and has been a true mentor and friend, opening doors I didn't know existed, tolerating my stress-noodle, and skilled in the ways of cross-continent tag. Amy always knew when she saw my best work, and I wish I could have shown her this. Thank you to my committee, David, Amy, Max Cavitch, Yolanda Padilla, and María-Josefina Saldaña-Portillo, for your indispensible feedback, support, and patience with my footnotes. Thanks too go to Nancy

Bentley, Warren Breckman, Jed Esty, Michael Gamer, Steven Hahn, Tsitsi Jaji, Suvir Kaul, Ania Loomba, Heather Love, Jo Park, John Pollock, Peter Stallybrass, Dan Richter, Salamishah Tillet, Edlie Wong, and Chi-ming Yang. I also thank the McNeil Center and the Wolf Humanities Forum for their support.

To the amazingly accommodating archivists, librarians, and support staff at the American Antiquarian Society, American Philosophical Society, Archivo General de Nación, Bentley Historical Library, Biblioteca Nacional de Antropología e Historia, Bowdoin Library Special Collections, Library of Congress, Missouri Historical Society, Morgan Library, Newberry Library, New-York Historical Society, Smith College Circulation, ILL, and Special Collections, the Smithsonian Archives and Libraries, University of Pennsylvania Libraries and Special Collections: thank you. Scott Sanders at Antiochiana and Mike Kelly at Amherst Special Collections will always deserve an extra shout-out. Thank you also to Brad Lepper and Tim Jordan at Ohio History Connection.

As someone who works at the overlap and intersection of many disciplines and subfields, I have had the pleasure of making friends and finding mentorship in many corners. Many thanks go to the organizers and members of the AAS "Histories of the Indigenous Book" seminar, where I met kindred souls and made fast friends, including Angie Calcaterra, Ashley Cataldo, Paul Erickson, Drew Lopenzina, Mark Mattes, Dan Radus, Phil Round, Kim Toney, Kelly Wisecup, Hilary Wyss, and Nan Wolverton. I was supremely lucky to return to the "Generous Dome" with Jim Casey, Elizabeth Eager, John Garcia, Sebastian Herrmann, Tyesha Maddox, Whitney Martinko, Don James McLaughlin, Kappy Mintie, Sharada Balachandran Orihuela, Hunter Price, Wendy Roberts, Len von Morze, and Clay Zuba. At the Newberry Library, the company and fellowship of Chelsea Blackmore, William Brooks, Susan Gaylard, Kara Johnson, Kat Lecky, Erin-Marie Legacey, Suparna Roychoudhury, Miriam Thaggert, Cynthia Wall warmed the Chicago winter. The year I was on fellowship changed my project and gave me an incomparable set of new intellectual companions, including Seth Cotlar, Patrick Del Percio, Leon Fink, Melissa Gniadek, Heather Kopelson, Patricia Marroquin Norby, Coll Thrush, Caroline Wiggington, and Seonaid Valiant. I thank both the American Antiquarian Society and the Newberry Library for their generosity, as well as the National Endowment for the Humanities and Lloyd Lewis Memorial Fund.

Thank you to Sean X. Goudie, Priscilla Wald, Thomas Beebee, Hester Blum, the Center for American Literary Studies at Penn State, and my fellow first First Book Institute members: Adrienne Brown, Todd Carmody, Danielle Heard, Samaine Lockwood, Ted Martin, Sarah Juliet Lauro, and Sonya Posmentier.

Thanks to Laraine Fletcher and George Scheper for organizing the "Native Grounds" NEH Seminar at the Library of Congress and introducing me to Christina Giacona, Lindsey Kingston, Adriana Link, Kenlea Pebbles, and Cristina Stanciu. Thank you also to Heike Paul, Margaretha Schweiger-Wilhelm, and the Bayerische Amerika-Akademie as well as Nuremberg participants Melanie Eis, Eve Eure, Liana Glew, Andrew Hnatow, Amber Rose Johnson, Mark Kelley, Mahshid Mayar, Spencer Tricker, and Cecily Zander for timely interventions, long walks, and supportive hugs. I thank my super collaborator Gesa Mackenthun for her rigor, warmth, and consolation. I thank Amy Greenberg and Ari Kelman for the invitation to join the C19 Settler Colonialism seminar as well as Rick Bell and Holly Brewer for welcoming me to the Washington Early American Seminar. Thank you as well to colleagues and community at the Tepoztlán Institute for the Transnational History of the Americas.

Smith College has given me countless opportunities to grow into the scholar I want to be. I thank my students and advisees, including top research assistants Illaria Dana and Celeste Clerk, and the colleagues and friends who helped me find my place, including Jeff Ahlman, Lisa Armstrong, Carrie Baker, Chrissie Bell, Brigitte Buettner, Darcy Buerkle, Floyd Cheung, Jay Garfield, Michael Gorra, Jennifer Guglielmo, Ambreen Hai, Lane Hall-Witt, Michele Joffroy, Connie Kassor, Alex Keller, Elizabeth Klarich, Daphne Lamothe, Mehammed Mack, Jen Malkowski, Liz Pryor, Jeff Ramsey, Daniel Rodríguez, Shani Roper-Edwards, Vicky Spelman, Andrea Stone, Michael Thurston, Lester Tomé, Susan Van Dyne, and Fraser Ward. A special thank you to Pinky Hota, Laura Kalba, and Andrea Moore, who lifted me up and carried me along. Without the care, collaboration, and guidance of Dana Leibsohn, Kevin Rozario, and Steve Waksman, I would be lost. The Jean Picker Fund generously funded course releases and research materials, as did the Kahn Liberal Arts Institute.

I have learned more from the Five College NAIS group than I could ever say. I thank Lisa Brooks, a model reader and mentor, as well as Sonya Atalay, Paul Barton, Kathleen Brown-Pérez, Christine DeLucia, Rae Gould, Jennifer Hamilton, Alice Nash, Bob Painter, Mary Renda, Neil Salisbury, Kiara Vigil, Ron Welburn, and Ashley Smith. I also send thanks to Hiba Bou Akar, Nusrat Chowdhury, Jennifer Fronc, David Hernández, Hannah Holleman, Fran Hutchins, Vinayak Ramanan, and Uditi Sen.

Without Kate Aid, developmental editor extraordinaire, I would never have found the project's threads or pulled them into the right shape. Nadine Zimmerli is the most insightful, supportive, and patient editor, and she always knows just what to send and say. Thank you to the generous series editors at the University of Virginia Press, Anna Brickhouse and Kirsten Silva Gruesz, and to kind and insightful readers Robert Gunn, Erica Panni, and an anonymous UVA Press reader. Thank you also to the Andrew W. Mellon Foundation, the Sustainable History Monograph Pilot program, and Longleaf as well as Kay Banning, Bridget Fountain Manzella, Ihsan Taylor, Sherondra Thedford and Lisa Stallings.

So many colleagues have made the Chesapeake a home-away-from-home, including Karen Caplan, David Freund, Julie Greene, James Maffie, Nancy Raquel Mirabal, and David Sartorius. Julie, Jim, and Sophie F. M. Maffie sustained me before and during the pandemic, and I couldn't have found a better pod. To Lesley S. Curtis, Cord Whitaker, and L, friends of my heart: mèsi. I couldn't be more grateful to Penny Von Eschen for her guidance, love, and taste in wine. Thanks to Karen Miller, a fantastic reader, and a fierce cook. Thank you to Suzi Linsley, who accompanied me through the dark and the light, and to Michelle Boisseau, who always made sure I was loved and fed. Thank you to my family: Kevin and Z Jones, Pat McKane, Charles Osborn, Jan Shanahan, Bob, Jess, Kate, and Laura Woods; to my grandparents, godparents, aunts, and uncles who have given me the gifts of plants, birds, history, storytelling, and fine detail; to my brothers Mike and Stephen, who help me laugh and remind me to pay my bills on time. Thank you to Evangeline Heiliger and Q, whose presence and love has made my life cozier, sillier, and more beautiful. Thank you to my parents, Chris and Cynthia, with whom I've visited countless historical sites, who are always ready for more, and who have already given me everything. And to my love Colleen Woods, who has lived with this book for almost as long as I have and whose words and ideas are all over it, who has traveled with me to visit mounds and museums and bookstores around the globe: I'm stuck on your heart.

A NOTE ON TERMINOLOGY AND METHOD

A transhistorical and hemispheric scope presents problems of terminology. In this book "North America" refers to the landmass containing both New Spain/Mexico and the United States, respectively differentiated by their relative northerly and southerly positions. Relatedly, I refer to Americas-born Europeans (whether Spanish, British, etc.) from northern North America as "creoles" and southern North America as "criollos," a roughly similar identity in the period. The neologism "criollo-americano" is meant to reference a transitional, politically autonomous identification among criollos in late New Spain. For convenience, when I refer to Indigenous communities continent-wide and without regard to specificities (tribal, ethnic, national, or otherwise) I use "Indigenous" or "Native." Otherwise, I strive to use communities' self-appellations, with reference to conventional scholarly names for clarity. One case is worth elaborating: despite the term's ubiquity, I use "Aztec" only in reference to the "Aztec Empire"—i.e., the Triple Alliance of Tenochtitlan, Texcoco, and Tlacopan—a polity that lasted from 1428 to 1521 CE. The ancestral Nahua peoples of Aztlán I identify as "Aztecas": according to tradition this was their name before the sibling groups divided and arrived in the Mexico Valley. Their descendants are called by ethnonational names before 1521 (i.e., Mexica, Acolhua, Tepaneca, etc.) and identified as Nahua (the large Nahuatl-speaking family) afterward.[1] Where possible I retain Indigenous terminology, capitalization, conventional singular and plural usages (i.e., teocalli, s., and teocalme, pl.), and avoid italics. I retain period orthography in English, Spanish, and French. In terms of chronology, I deploy "ancient" to designate Indigenous deep time and "distant" to name the millennia before the conceptualization of "America," roughly 500–1500 CE, a choice further explained in the introduction.

Although most primary and secondary sources refer to the imaginary race of earthworks-creating people as "Mound Builders," I employ "Moundbuilders" to avoid confusion with actually existing mound-building peoples. I recognize that there are vast differences in region, culture area, and chronology that I am eliding in my synthetic account of earthworks and mounds.[2] Moreover, archaeologists often reserve the term "mound" for individual conical, rounded, or flat-topped structures and deploy "earthworks" for the extended earthen architecture forming walls, trenches, and related shapes. A notable exception is "effigy mound," which refers to earthworks resembling specific beings. While acknowledging this complexity, I also recall that many of these technicalities originate in the context under study.

Introduction

the archive was never inanimate
the archive was never dead
the archive was never yours.

—Deborah A. Miranda, "When My Body Is the Archive," 2017

IN SOUTHERN WISCONSIN, NOT far from the capitol at Madison, three large platform earthworks sit on the central plaza of a state park now known as Aztalan. The well-tended earthen architecture and "prehistoric Indian stockade-protected village" site are located about ten miles upstream from the town of Fort Atkinson, where the Black Hawk Tavern, Black Hawk Senior Residence, and high school mascot quietly understate the area's brutal history.[1] The state park mainly attracts fishing enthusiasts, schoolchildren, and offbeat tourists who come to marvel at the seemingly inexplicable mounds of terraced earth. In the parking lot, a plaque on polished pink granite announces Aztalan's 1964 designation as a National Historic Landmark, awarded by the US Department of the Interior for its "exceptional value in commemorating and illustrating the history of the United States."[2] Another sign announces plainly, "Indian people lived at Aztalan between A.D. 900 and 1200," although a laminated land survey from 1850 provides no connection between the site's former residents and its remarkable landscape.[3] Across the grassy plaza, a self-powered "Turn and Learn" audio guide gives lessons in mystery rather than clarity: "around 1300 A.D., the people of Aztalan, like their relatives at Cahokia, simply vanished."[4] *Why* the presence and alleged disappearance of Azatlan's people—at least five hundred years before 1776—illustrates the history of the United States is left unsaid.

The Turn and Learn narrative, in which Aztalan's inhabitants and "their relatives" at Cahokia farther south—or indeed any number of peoples across the continent—"simply vanished" is strikingly similar to the one that originally occasioned the site's unusual name almost two hundred years before. After the treaty ending the Black Hawk War of 1832, an influx of white settlers rapidly surveyed the grounds, founded their villages—such as Fort Atkinson in 1836— and bestowed new historical narratives on the Ho-Chunk, Dakota, Menominee,

FIGURE 2. "Turn and Learn," Aztalan State Park, Aztalan, Wisconsin. Author's photograph, 2016.

and Anishinaabeg homelands.[5] The same year the Territory of Wisconsin was incorporated into the United States, 1836, rumors of square-topped "mounds" and disintegrating wooden palisades began to circulate across the new white settlements. Milwaukee's Nathaniel F. Hyer, "Counsellor at Law and Land Surveyor," traveled almost fifty miles westward to see the handiwork for himself.[6] Hyer's map and account, which ran in US newspapers from February to June of 1837, ignored any connections with contemporary Indigenous communities (or concurrent settler aggressions) in favor of a narrative about "the people inhabiting the vale of Mexico."[7] For in Wisconsin's misappropriated soil, Hyer saw evidence of an ancient, continental people whose history was apparently important to contemporary settlers. Indeed, believing the structures to have been built by "ancient Aztecs," Judge Hyer named the site for the traditional Azteca homeland, Aztlán.[8] His misspelling—Aztalan—remains to this day.

As they presumably did in the late 1830s, the mounds at Aztalan presently bear some resemblance to the immense teocalli (temple) at Cholula near Puebla, Mexico, and to the Pyramids of the Sun and Moon at Teotihuacan, near Mexico

FIGURE 3. Karl Nebel, "Plaza Mayor de Mexico," detail, *Voyage pittoresque et archéologique* (1836). Courtesy of the Newberry Library. The Sun Stone is visible just behind the cross.

City. Hyer had likely seen engravings of Cholula—circulating since at least 1810—and perhaps images of the Teotihuacan or Tenochtitlan temples as well.[9] In fact, it was quite commonplace in nineteenth-century US literary and popular outlets to associate the Mississippi Valley "mounds" with "Aztec" history. This was the case even before 1821—the year of Mexican independence as well as the year US citizens began settling in Tejas—when Michigan Territory's governor Lewis Cass wrote of his certainty that the mounds' builders were the "progenitors of the Mexicans."[10] Long before Aztalan got its name, the archive of "Mexican" antiquities was assisting settlers in staking claims to Indigenous spaces and vanishing Indigenous ancestors for the sake of illustrating "American" history.

At the same time, in independent Mexico, the "Aztec Calendar Stone"—which had been unburied from Mexico City's main plaza in 1790—gazed out from the western wall of the Metropolitan Cathedral, visible to anyone who shopped in the market, worshipped at the baroque chapels, or visited the nearby palace. By the 1830s this monument—the "Piedra del Sol" (Sun Stone) as it is more commonly known—was recognizable far and wide. In addition to a

FIGURE 4. La Piedra del Sol, Museo Nacional de Antropología (INAH), Mexico City. Author's photograph, 2016.

lithograph included in Baron Alexander von Humboldt's transatlantic bestseller *Vues des Cordillères et monumens des peuples indigènes de l'Amérique* (1810), the Hamburg artist Karl Nebel—who lived in Mexico from 1829 to 1834—published two views of the stone in his *Voyage pittoresque et archéologique* (1836), copies of which were soon available in New York, Philadelphia, and Mexico City.[11] Today the Sun Stone serves as the centerpiece of the Museo Nacional de Antropología in Mexico City's Chapultepec Park.

Over the intervening years, the Sun Stone became an icon of Mexican national identification with the "Aztec" past, appearing as souvenir statuettes, on picture postcards, coins, jewelry, and, famously, on Mexico's 1998 World Cup soccer jersey. While this replication enshrines the archaeological past as a crucial element of the Mexican present, it also effectively effaces currently living Indigenous peoples from the greater Mexican polity, just as the Sun Stone's relocation to Chapultepec displaced it from the historic city center.[12] Although Mexico counts more than twenty-five million Indigenous residents today—over a million in the vibrant capital alone—the nation's most identifiable expression of indigeneity is carved in stone and kept behind museum doors.[13]

The different ways in which Mexican and US histories locate themselves vis-à-vis Indigenous pasts depends on their shared, but differently experienced, beginnings in conquest, slavery, colonialism, and imperialism, as well as the different significations of land, labor, and citizenship to the national project.[14] In the United States, where archaeological artifacts have long been used to argue that Native peoples were not autochthonous New World populations, Indigenous histories have been overwritten by an empiricism that provided the beginnings for American anthropology.[15] In New Spain—and later the Republic of Mexico—America's antiquities gave criollos (Americas-born Europeans) an imperial yet non-Hispanic past upon which to base their own sovereignty claims. Yet as different as these national trajectories are, the two countries are united in a mutual project of settler nationalism, and both deploy "American antiquities"—like the Aztalan earthworks and "Aztec Calendar"/Sun Stone—to that end.[16]

As epitomized by the Sun Stone, indigeneity in Mexico has long been figured as ancient, monolithic (literally expressed in stone), and "Aztec" but also tied to mestizaje, the ideology of mixed Indigenous-European ancestry so central to twentieth-century, post-Revolutionary Mexican identity.[17] In the 1940s, Mexican poet Octavio Paz expressed this sentiment, writing: "Any contact with the Mexican people, however brief, reveals that the ancient beliefs and customs are still in existence between Western forms."[18] More recently, Latinx literary critic Nicole M. Guidotti-Hernández identified "the dead Aztec as the foundation of the Mexican Nation."[19] In the United States, on the contrary, indigeneity is referenced more often than not in the past tense of pilgrims and pioneers, during debates over slurs and mascots, or is replaced altogether by dates more symbolic of catastrophe than continuation (e.g., 1492 or 1830). In other words, whereas Mexican citizens typically have been encouraged to imagine their national history as linked to select Indigenous precedents, US citizens have been incentivized to "play" with, overwrite, and ignore Indigenous pasts.[20] While the forms of indigeneity circulating in each national space are usually considered on their own terms, creating North American national histories has meant misappropriating Indigenous pasts across misappropriated lands, continent-wide.[21]

For much of their early national periods, the histories of Mexico and the United States depended on one another: the writings, images, cabinets, museums, and libraries of both "Aztec" and "Moundbuilder" archives relied on interrelated networks of collectors and collections as well as many of the same methods and assumptions. Settler nationalism did not form in isolation but rather was enmeshed in preexisting colonial contexts. Crossing borders, languages, cultures, and political differences, early US and Mexican processes of historical knowledge production interacted with, adapted, and fabricated Indigenous histories of the shared continent. This is not to say that the processes were the *same*, but rather that they were interrelated and co-constituted.[22] But while the United States and Mexico shared the same *strategy*, they used different *tactics* in their nation-building efforts, and those too were exchanged and repurposed across a vast network of transamerican elites whose loyalties sided with the settlers—not Indigenous peoples—of North America.[23] Nonetheless, the historiographic, scientific, and museological methods developed and exchanged by creole and criollo elites on either side of changing American boundary lines produced strikingly similar initial results: the successful establishment of settler nations on lands taken from Indigenous stewards.

Before American History reveals the complex transamerican interactions crucial to the process of narrating European colonies into nineteenth-century American nations. Recovering the asymmetrical material and intellectual exchanges across New Spanish criollo patriots, US scientists, and Mexican letrados (educated elites) in the late eighteenth and early nineteenth centuries reveals their commonalities and shows that settlers' historical work epistemologically and ideologically enabled and depended on denials of past and present violence against the Indigenous peoples of North America.[24] *Before American History*, therefore, seeks to understand America's historiography—Americans' history writings and writings about America's history—as a means of discursive control negating Native sovereignty claims and "place-based autonomy," effacing Native lives, and creating settler attachments to the land through the materiality of Indigenous pasts.[25]

In making a connection between the literal touchstone (Sun Stone) of Mexican history and the Mississippi Valley earthworks (mounds), this book details the process by which eighteenth-and nineteenth-century Euro-American nationalists wrote Indigenous pasts out of US and Mexican histories and lands to create an "American antiquity," and it demonstrates that Indigenous dispossession from both land and history are co-constitutive of the two North American settler republics. What is more, *Before American History* places discussions of past-making and transnational circulation into conversation with accounts of Indigenous displacement and settler land policy to make clear that these seemingly distinct bodies of nationalist mythmaking were already informing each other well before the US-Mexican War. Yet this overlap of intellectual networks and material sources, shared practices of history-writing and archive-making, common struggles over sovereignty and systems of extractive labor, and the inextricability of Indigenous dispossession from nation-formation are often overlooked in the separate national historiographies.²⁶ Aztalan, for example, is rarely considered alongside Aztlán.

By following hemispheric imaginings, narratives, and materials of "American antiquities" as they circulated across the continent—and by attending to the epistemological and material consequences of historical knowledge production—this book is committed to analyzing the two nations in relation rather than in comparison, while at the same time holding them both in Native space.²⁷ That is to say, in writing a connective, relational history, I attempt to reorient American antiquity within a transamerican network of relationships. And because of this relational approach, the book is in many ways a social history of ideas rather than a traditional intellectual history; it is an account of epistemology "in the making," one focused on methods, sources, social formations, networks, and circulations. Judge Hyer's construction of Mexican antiquity in Wisconsin, for example, belongs to a long tradition of settler writing, surveying, and mapping techniques intended to capture, transform, and spread certain kinds of information about Indigenous histories even while displacing other local knowledges. Hyer's Aztlán-Aztalan mistake, moreover, reveals the contingency and capaciousness of the developing archival structure of American settlement and dispossession that had consequences on a continental scale.

The source for Hyer's spelling error exposes the widespread circulation of settler-nationalist logic in nineteenth-century North America. The mistake originally appeared in Albany saddlemaker Josiah Priest's bestselling *American Antiquities and Discoveries of the West* (1833), a miscellany of antiquarian knowledge that moves from theories of the "Deluge" and "Lost Tribes" to examinations of mastodon skeletons, hieroglyphic analyses, and reports of "Mongol Tartars" living on the American West Coast.²⁸ Accounts of earthworks and other "aboriginal fortifications" share space with the "Tradition of the Mexican natives respecting their migration from the North," a "Mosaic history found among the Azteca Indians," and an illustration of the Sun Stone.²⁹ Although seemingly a work of unparalleled eccentricity, Priest's volume is in fact a carefully, if opaquely, argued history interpreted along the lines of Christian millennialism and civilizationist supremacy. His *American Antiquities* deftly incorporates earth science, ethnology, biblical exegesis, and antiquarian speculation—all as "American antiquities"—into a body of "Evidence that an Ancient Population of Partially Civilized Nations, Differing Entirely from Those of the Present Indians, Peopled America." These invented ancient Americans built the mounds in New York, Ohio, Illinois, and Wisconsin before going south to Mexico.

If the shared processes of settler nation-building hinge on the elimination of real Indigenous peoples from national territory, they also depend on settlers' disavowal, distancing from, and ignorance of that very work.[30] Aztalan. The Sun Stone. *American Antiquities*. These all exemplify a common but often unrecognized archive of American past-making in which indigeneity and Indigenous dispossession are crucial yet unnoticed. Many of these same American antiquities today still sit at the core of early Americanist scholarly work, yet their dispossessive power is typically undetected thanks to Americanist scholars' deep training in "colonial unknowing," an expertise in ignoring the interconnections of Indigenous and settler histories that absolves responsibility for the ongoing consequences of colonization.[31] This book looks to emphasize the interconnectedness of Indigenous and settler histories, to expose the Americanist archive's settler national power, and to situate Americanist scholars within a matrix of recognition and responsibility for the lasting effects of "American antiquity."

To do so, *Before American History* extends the framework of settler colonialism across North America to make visible the foundational methodologies, materials, and mythologies that have created an American history out of and overtop Indigenous worlds. This is not a history of inevitability but is instead an account aiming to reveal the epistemological tricks that have made settler colonial projects in North America—when seen at all—appear as inevitable, as settled fact.[32] Enriching my training in comparative American, historicist, and material text literary studies with materials and methodologies from intellectual history, ethnohistory, cultural studies, and Native American and Indigenous Studies (NAIS), I create a new story about old materials, one that recurs, revises, and revives. It is an attempt to create what Abenaki scholar Lisa Brooks calls pildowi ôjmowôgan, a cyclical, relational, new mode of history making that unsettles the familiar American past.[33]

Unsettling the Archive

Before American History addresses how antiquarians and historians imagined a period earlier than—*before*—US and Mexican history, an era frequently called "American antiquity." North American settler elites used antiquarian knowledge—in forms archival, historical, archaeological, and epistemological—to displace "ancient" Indigenous pasts and thereby create *ante*-colonial—that is to say, *before* as well as *against* European colonialism—histories.[34] Embracing the homophone, settlers' "ante-colonial" work hinged on a denial or disguising of the colonialism still inherent in the national project. The libraries, museums, and scientific cabinets that house "Indian Implements" or Indigenous manuscripts alongside fossils, minerals, and stuffed animals reveal the epistemic contours of historical knowledge created and held by this larger North American settler archive of the "ante-colonial" past. The historiographic processes used to create and engage the archive included "discovering," describing, recording, producing, collecting, and displaying Indigenous pasts as "American antiquities." The items considered "antiquities"—such as Indigenous-made sculptures, tools, manuscripts, and earthworks—still carry the violence inseparable from their transformation into evidence of the past. These "amateur" historians' foundational archives, collections, and writings, made before American historiography *per se*—before even the "romantic" scholarship of George Bancroft or Manuel Orozco y Berra—were essential to the production of "modern" American history.[35]

This book approaches the archive of American antiquities as both physical space and epistemological configuration, as both actor and effect. When I refer to the "archival structure of settlement," I am referring to the ways that physical and intellectual archives enact, structurally, Indigenous dispossession, while also being themselves the artifacts of the settler national project. Illustrating the epistemological and material circumstances from which archives, histories, and national myths were created exposes them as ideological prerequisites to the establishment of settler nations. In some senses, an archive's agential power is apparent in its make-up, which reveals that the same knowledge systems denying Indigenous historicity often also rely on Indigenous-made materials for their own legitimacy. At Monticello, for example, Thomas Jefferson's Book Room was supplemented by the separate Indian Hall, which displayed a collection of sculptures, paintings, and maps as well as minerals, fossils, and Indigenous artifacts. Mexico's National Museum inherited New Spain's Indigenous manuscripts rather than its National Library, even though both were founded at the same time.[36] The collections of Miami vocabularies in Philadelphia and "Mexican" antiquities in Madrid speak to the imbrication of state, economic, and archival formations; that Indigenous descendants should have to leave their homelands to visit heritage items or ancestors speaks to the continuing material and psychosocial damage of these American archives. Similar examples of the archives, libraries, and materials that serve as loci of the settler colonial project—producing and reproducing dispossessive power that often goes unchallenged—appear throughout this book.[37]

To begin the reframing and healing work of returning peoples, knowledges, and artifacts to their "original Indigenous intentions," Abenaki anthropologist Margaret M. Bruchac suggests attending not to "artifacts" themselves, but instead to collectors and the context of collection.[38] Following Bruchac, *Before American*

History situates settler collectors—antiquaries, historians, artists—within their intellectual and ideological networks so as to identify the processes that produced Indigenous materials as "artifacts" severed from their "original Indigenous intentions." It reveals the collectors and contexts of collection as indispensable to the uneven and ongoing—not discrete and finished—processes of settler colonialism and it seeks to "restore" those so-called artifacts in small ways by holding the settler national histories that rely upon them accountable to the Native communities upon whom their dispossessive powers continue to act.[39] In other words, this book seeks to construct a new context for the empowered objects, peoples, and places so often refigured as artifacts in the archives of American antiquities.

The main components of *Before American History*'s own archive are primary printed texts from the late eighteenth and early nineteenth centuries, ones that describe or reproduce "American antiquities" as history's "proof." In the period, artifacts were presumed to contain inherent and incontestable explanatory information: an "artifactual" text, therefore, renders the objects of their description into the "facts" of history.[40] Most artifactual texts sought to simulate the experience of antiquarian collecting, often reproducing the "antiquities" in word and image on the page, the volumes then becoming collections themselves. Paradigmatic is Josiah Priest's *American Antiquities and Discoveries in the West* (1833), which in its inexpensive and ubiquitous editions made knowledge of "Aztec" and "Moundbuilder" pasts—and their interrelation—widely accessible to US readers like Nathaniel Hyer in Wisconsin Territory. A more rarified example is the eccentric compilation created by the wealthy Cincinnati banker John Delafield, *An Inquiry Into the Origin of the Antiquities of America* (1839), with its full-scale lithograph of an "Aztec map, or hieroglyphic history" (the *Codex Boturini*) supposedly proving "all the antiquities of America were built by ... the race known to us in Mexico and Peru."[41] Artifactual texts also appeared as manuscripts and museum inventories, as letters in magazines and essays in the publications of learned societies. Unlike earlier antiquities compilations—such as Carlos Sigüenza y Góngora's library or Cotton Mather's *Curiosa Americana* project—artifactual texts—particularly those that engendered and sustained "Aztec" and "Moundbuilder" pasts—were largely focused on negating Indigenous claims to the continent and its histories.

Uncovering American Antiquities

By the second half of the eighteenth century, readers in the British and Spanish Atlantic would have had a hard time avoiding the topic of "antiquities," whether in the form of architecture, artifacts, or ancient written documents. Already in the sixteenth and seventeenth centuries British antiquaries such as John Leland, William Camden, and William Dugdale were studiously examining "monumental" temples and tombs (or "barrows") on their home islands.[42] The Society of Antiquaries in London published descriptions of Roman-era sites, buildings, and artifacts in *Vetusta monumenta* (1718). By the middle of the eighteenth century, European publications were devoted to illustrating "antiquities" from Greek, Egyptian, and Roman times, and their coverage soon expanded. Literary journals referencing an "ancient city, uncovered" were not uncommon nor were descriptions and engravings of scenes from India, Dorsetshire, or the Scottish Highlands. These antiquities were all largely known in their textual form, portrayed in accounts that usually paired visual and verbal description to produce an artifactual chronology that visualized historical change over time.[43]

In the eighteenth century antiquities also took on an association with the subterranean thanks to the excavations at Herculaneum and Pompeii, then part of the Spanish Empire. The Neapolitan digs—meant to recover art objects for wealthy patrons, such as the future Charles III—promised to make visible the traces of an otherwise invisible past, to resurrect memories that seemed lost.[44] The resultant collections established certain standards for identifying, arranging, and describing the uncovered objects as well as representing them in print.[45] The Vesuvian excavations uncovered perfect illustrations of the chasm between the "Ancients and Moderns," while the neoclassical decorative vogue became an aesthetic way to reconnect the eras, as did the increasingly familiar activity of unearthing and displaying "antiquities." Successfully rescuing—and representing—relics from a first-century CE disaster (the eruption of Mt. Vesuvius) suggested that unexpected monuments of history could be located elsewhere as well.

Contemporaneously, changes to methods of history writing emphasized the past not as an independent, annalistic series of incidents but rather as events connected by secular causality and ordered into epochs separated by complete change.[46] In particular, with the revolutionary "breaks" of 1776 and 1789—epochal events that announced new eras—time's fissures became more apparent.[47] Yet in part, this developing consciousness of temporal fragmentation—which would later be smoothed by the narrative powers of nineteenth-century "romantic" historians—was due to the new temporal conceptualizations emerging under colonialism itself.[48] When faced with the immensity of American lands and histories, Europeans' spatial and temporal limits were stretched to breaking; they had no cognitive frame in which to comprehend—let alone people—the continent's far reaches of space and time.[49] The causal chronology so fundamental to "modern" historical consciousness—seriality—largely resulted from this collision of European exegetical time with the antiquity of Indigenous history.[50]

To criollo and creole settlers in the Americas, glorifying "American antiquity" became a way of asserting intellectual, economic, and political dominance. For the Atlantic intellectuals who increasingly quarreled over questions of superiority and sovereignty, preserving the chronology of the Old Testament became less important than uncovering a past that favored one side over another. If European excavations had taught them how to illuminate the undocumented past—which seemingly had disappeared into complete oblivion but really remained, invisibly, in the present—then excavating in the Americas promised a treasure of "lost" peoples and worlds now potentially "discoverable."[51] Moreover, establishing the existence of "antiquities" on a previously unknown landscape of indeterminate age would prove that the "New World" was, in fact, old. Thus, by the late eighteenth century, settler-scholars were using the techniques of European antiquaries, chorographers, and chronologists to accumulate and analyze materials with which to write their own histories of America.[52] But the necessity of declaring the continent's "ancientness" while denying the antiquity of its peoples was driven by legal necessity, not just pride. However, this transatlantic intellectual "quarrel"—in which the narration and interpretation of antiquities were central—has long served as a distraction from the main objective of inter-imperial and postcolonial struggles: securing Indigenous land for American settlers.

In English and Spanish (Roman) property law, title awarded by dint of possession since ancient times was called "aboriginal title."[53] That is, the first recorded peoples in an area were deemed its indigenes and awarded legal possession of the land. For this reason, the identity of the continent's original peoples and where they—and *their* antiquities—originated carried considerable legal and political, not just intellectual, weight.[54] Therefore, for the timeline of American antiquity to become an aid against—not for—Indigenous claims to the continent, Indigenous claimants had to be found *not* "aboriginal." This was accomplished by arguing that they had not been in the Americas since its antiquity and could therefore not have held possession of the land first. Even those scholars who believed in the "ancientness" of the Americas seldom credited Indigenous populations with existing there before the ninth century—rather late on the scale of Christian chronology—meaning there was plenty of time for a prior occupancy. Moreover, as each eon that the annals of rocks, fossilized bones, or vanished riverbeds added to the age of the universe increased the scope of History, the horizon of Indigenous pasts—as documented by "artificial" (or "artifactual," i.e., human-made) antiquities—remained one thousand years. Although in theory, all archaeological objects should have exhibited the same evidentiary power, in practice Indigenous-made artifacts were not seen as testifying to the long duration of Indigenous occupation of the Americas.

Although using Indigenous artifacts and chronologies differently, nationalists in both Mexico and the United States sought to demonstrate a limited timeline of the Indigenous past. In Mexico, the official Indigenous past—no matter where or when it began—built to the height of the Aztec Empire but fell with Tenochtitlan in 1521, after which the "real" Indigenous peoples of Mexico—and thus rival claimants to the throne—were considered to be gone. In the US, where nationalists were constantly searching for "evidence" to "prove" that "the Present Indians" were not aboriginal, settlers invented histories that linked "American antiquities" to overwhelmingly fantastical aboriginal origin stories. They assiduously filled "prehistoric" space with myths about Moundbuilders, Japanese colonies, Welsh royalty, and lost Israelites, purposefully leaving no space for Native ancestors or property claims. With these myths, settlers were able to reassign the identity "aboriginal" and thereby obviate any legal claims to American lands based on aboriginality.[55] In both cases, finding no legitimate claimants to the land, the settler nations were free to stake their own historical and territorial claims to North America.

Revealing the Settler-Colonizing Trick

Territory is not the same as land; land, as Yankton Dakota scholar Vine Deloria Jr. wrote, is the "relationships of things to each other."[56] Shawn Wilson (Opaskwayak Cree) echoes the importance of relationality when understanding land, explaining that Native peoples' identities are "grounded in their relationships with the land . . . we *are* the relationships that we hold and are part of."[57] Territory, however, is land stripped of that relationality and transformed (or alienated) into property in soil; it is governable and in the possession of a controlling power.[58] At the core of settler colonialism is the desire for, acquisition of, and ongoing maintenance of land *as territory*, a process Australian anthropologist Patrick Wolfe referred to as "territoriality."[59] Territoriality is the making of territory from land; territorialization, as I use it here, is the extension of state power over autonomous populations on those lands. This process necessarily implies the wrenching of land and sovereignty from Indigenous peoples and its transfer to settler states—Indigenous dispossession—as well as the elimination of Indigenous bodies from the polity.[60]

Dispossession is a condition "characterized by a privation of possession" that retroactively figures land as alienable property destined for territorialization.[61] This recursive process is always already meant to confine and expel those Indigenous "occupants" brought under settler jurisdiction, the very definition of "occupation" used as a weapon.[62] The wrenching of land and sovereignty is also the destruction of Indigenous self-determination, identity, and relations.[63] It is in this sense that Mohawk scholar Audra Simpson has explained settler colonialism as "an ongoing structure of dispossession that targets Indigenous people for elimination."[64] The mere existence of Indigenous persons and polities in North America challenges the exclusive sovereignty and absolute property of the state. Native elimination—carried out through murder, systemic oppression, and dehumanization—includes the destruction of Indigenous ways of being and knowing in time and space as well as the treating of Native histories as inconsequential or nonexistent.

Yet the specific mechanics of settler colonial nationalism operationalized in the United States and Mexico *conceal* territoriality—and therefore dispossession—which in turn causes it to seem *as if* state power is only interested in administering populations rather than in possessing land. This is manifest, for example, in the relocation of Native peoples to reservations, which, at its base, is a mechanism for maintaining and naturalizing territorial control rather than protecting Native interests.[65] The concealment of territoriality—and therefore Indigenous annihilation and dispossession—is effected in large part by ignoring or disavowing the fraud and violence at the core of American property relations.[66] Equally, it is accomplished by insisting on the minimizing effects of time and by playing semantic games with "possession," "occupation," and "aboriginality."

Drawing from literary scholar David Kazanjian's concept of the "colonizing trick," I argue that settler colonialism conceals itself in plain sight, in the lessons of ignorance and unknowing. Giving away the trick of settler colonialism means unmasking the crucial issues of land and sovereignty concealed by settlers' *dispossessive* investment in American history and American territoriality.[67] In the United States the trick was revealed—just for a moment—by the Supreme Court's 2020 ruling on *McGirt v. Oklahoma*, after which news outlets announced that non-Natives in Tulsa and Oklahoma City awoke to find themselves "on Indian land." The trick, of course, concealed that they had *always* been "on Indian land." Legal experts reassured shaken Sooners, and even the Muscogee (Creek) Nation had to confirm that the decision did not instate Creek rule (far from it!) and that "private land" was safe from seizure. Within a few days, "Indian land" was once again cloaked in its US disguise. The *settler*-colonizing trick is territorialization presented as liberal democracy, "America" as self-evident and eternal, its sovereignty and right to territory unquestioned.[68]

The settler-colonizing trick, I believe, is the main reason it is so difficult to ascertain the workings of settler colonialism in Mexico. There, as the old argument goes, it is about labor, not land. Indeed, conventionally Mexico's absence from the list of settler-colonial nations is ascribed to past policies of tribute and enforced labor rather than land seizure, conditions often identified as "colonial" rather than "settler colonial." However, the Spanish and Mexican systems for controlling Indigenous labor—from the encomienda, repartimiento, latifundio, and hacienda systems—have always tied labor and land together (what Chickasaw scholar Shannon Speed has called the "land-labor system").[69] And while independent Mexico largely (but not entirely) concentrated on maintaining rather than acquiring land—by depending on Hispanicization and blanqueamiento (whitening) rather than "expansion"—its version of territorial control nonetheless relied on Indigenous dispossession as well. What is more, some of the resistance to connecting Mexico and settler colonialism traces to a cultural imaginary defined by criollo patriots in the eighteenth century and elaborated by Mexican nationalists in the nineteenth. Their understanding of cultural "mixing"—mestizaje—in which, as historian Enrique Florescano put it, Mexico "stopped being only Indian to become Creole and Mexican," serves as the "trick."[70] In fact, the popular belief that Mexico was a mestizo nation from the 1810 Grito de Delores accompanies a later valorization of the Indigenous past.[71] The twentieth-century ideology of the raza cósmica—a post-Porfirian idea that Mexico is overall a mestizo state—has further obscured the ways in which the processes of settler colonialism rely on the expropriation of Indigenous bodies and Indigenous lands.[72] The myth of mestizaje de-territorializes Indigenous peoples by figuratively forgetting them, placing their lives outside the specificities of history, economics, or culture.[73] Mestizaje stands, allegorically, for the durability of the Mexican national project as an atemporal and inexorable phenomenon.[74] Studies that examine the nationalist imperative toward mestizaje have well demonstrated the ideology's participation in the erasure of Indigenous subjectivities and its facilitation of the state's appropriation of Indigenous resources.[75]

Mexico's mestizo myth has its more explicit twin in the US's "vanishing Indian," which is most recognizable in narratives where Native peoples are doomed to move westward or perish in the face of "modernity."[76] In these stereotypical portrayals Native peoples are either irrelevant, out-of-place relics or already "extinct," in both ways absented from national histories of race-making.[77] White and mestizo supremacies—which provide crucial ideological support for liberal settler nationalism—insist on the abjection of Blackness and Black lives as well as the erasure of Indigenous bodies, polities, and temporalities.[78]

These temporalities are never placeless. Rather, as anthropologist Keith Basso learned from working with Ndé (Western Apache) elders, "place-worlds" are "a particular universe of objects and events . . . wherein portions of the past are brought into being."[79] Place-worlds are created by situating historical material in its place, by "fashioning novel versions of 'what happened here.' . . . Building and sharing place-worlds, in other words, is not only a means of reviving former times but also of *revising* them."[80] I seek to revise relatively well-known episodes of American history by reviving their place-worlds, that is, replacing their *landed* context—which is also always the context of struggles over Indigenous sovereignty and humanity—to disrupt the dispossessive trick of territorialization.

Revising and Reviving

The histories engaged in this book operate according to at least two time horizons: the *distant*—which is to say the past of the last fifteen hundred years or so—and the *ancient*, a period often referred to as "time out of mind." I offer "distant" for the period c. 500–1500 CE so as to synchronize Indigenous timelines across the constraints of nationally bound temporal and culture-area categories (i.e., "Mississippian," "Mesoamerican," "Ancestral Puebloan," etc.).[81] For even deeper histories, I borrow the term "ancient" from Pawnee archaeologist Roger Echo-Hawk, who has written of the "deep time" memories of thousands-year-old events in a period he calls "ancient American history."[82] Changing the dominant terminology of temporality is important as well, as it is a primary mode through which settler epistemologies conceal the dispossession of Indigenous peoples from their pasts.

This book shuttles between past and present but also across pasts distant and deep in a challenge to conventional chronology's routine smoothing of these textured temporalities.[83] Inspired by Michi Saagiig Nishnaabeg scholar Leanne Betasamosake Simpson, my transhistorical writing practice seeks "a way of living in [a . . .] presence that collapses both the past and the future."[84] Indeed, one of the many pernicious effects of settler histories is the way they retroactively empty the continent, erasing the multifaceted communities stretching over vast spaces and ignoring the complex temporal negotiations of past—as well as present and future—Indigenous peoples.[85] Literary scholar Scott R. Lyons (Ojibwe/Mdewakanton Dakota) explains that Indigenous historical thinking means seeing the dynamic unfolding of different times in common spaces.[86] He cautions against thinking of Indigenous timekeeping as *either* linear or cyclical, suggesting instead to consider it as characterized by movement and diversity. For Anishinaabe historian Michael Witgen (Red Cliff Ojibwe), understanding past-making on Indigenous terms requires thinking about the concepts of "past" and "history" in culturally and tribally specific rather than Western historiographic terms. It means thinking through past events in ways that look forward as well as back and considering how the past changes materially, epistemologically, and cosmologically in reference to present and future Indigenous worlds.[87]

Settler colonialism is not just a "problem" of time or one of space—with the acquisition of land at its center—but a problem articulated at their intersection.[88] Whereas cultural studies scholar María Josefina Saldaña-Portillo has asked how some national geographies in the United States and Mexico have come to be marked as "racialized landscapes"—with the United States perceived as "nonindigenous space atop Mexico as indigenous space"—this book asks how indigeneity has come to be *spatialized* in Mexico but *temporalized* in the United States.[89] That is to say why it is, discursively, that there *are* "Indians" *there* (Mexico) whereas there *were* "Indians" *here* (the United States).[90] A key insight into this intersecting problem of space *and* time comes from Lenape scholar Joanne Barker, who explains that dispossession is not "done" but "doing": its temporal continuation is enabled by the view that Indigenous dispossession is a fait accompli.[91] Lands stolen in the past—and the pasts stolen from the lands—remain stolen in the present. The settler archive exists on stolen space, in stolen time, its existence ensured by naturalizing both conditions as self-evident or "givens."[92]

Before American History spans the 1780s to the 1840s, but all of its chapters are also enmeshed in deeper—distant and ancient—pasts, layered like the mounds and the pyramids, many existing at once. While roughly chronological, each chapter also considers present-day reiterations and reactivations, recalling the ways in which some histories—those of violence as well as regeneration—are not linear. The chapters, episodic and recursive, return to touchstone moments to tease out changes in significance and meaning over time and space. Key figures, places, and materials recur and reappear across the book.[93] This method not only highlights materials that became influential in both nations' settler histories, it also reflects the era's intertwined, relational networks of scholarship and culture.

The first two chapters, set in the late eighteenth century, outline key early archives of America's past to address the ways settlers replaced Indigenous meanings and intentions with their own versions of American antiquity.[94] Chapter 1 focuses on Milanese lawyer Lorenzo Boturini Benaduci's "Indian Museum" and engages the first major criollo history to be constructed from it, Francisco Javier Clavijero's *Storia antica del Messico* (1780). Chapter 2 follows Boturini and Clavijero via the US writers who relied on them—Thomas Jefferson, Benjamin Smith Barton, and William Bartram—to elaborate a "migration theory of American history" first created in New Spain.[95] The second pair of chapters examines settlers' visual and scientific methods for writing American history by revising the methods set forth in the previous two chapters. Chapter 3 analyzes criollos José Antonio de Alzate y Ramírez's and Antonio de León y Gama's descriptions of the built and archaeological environment of Mexico City, introducing the thematics of excavation and cohabitation as temporal imaginary. Chapter 4 looks into Benjamin Smith Barton's natural history research to detail how the "Moundbuilder myth" emerged from extracted Indigenous knowledges and the professionalization of US science. The final two chapters present settler techniques of "excavatory envisioning" that transform Indigenous homelands and burial sites into historical artifacts and dislocate present from past Indigenous communities. Chapter 5 centers the physical archive of Ohio Valley earthworks as preserved in the first volume of *Archaeologia Americana: Transactions and Collections of the American Antiquarian Society* (1820), showing the inextricability of US Indian policy from the nationalist antiquarian project.[96] Chapter 6 analyzes the popularization of Maya "hieroglyphics" during the first Mexican Republic (1824–1835) to shed light on the ongoing struggles over sovereignty that are often obscured by conventional archaeological attention to "lost" cities. All six of the chapters follow the Sun Stone and the earthworks—and their associated "Aztec" and "Moundbuilder" archives—as they take on new meanings and revisions within and among chapters, crossing temporal, spatial, national, and written lines.

A "before" implies an "after." Settler nationalists used the past to inhibit Indigenous futures, to make an "after" seem impossible and their successes appear inevitable. Yet the early architects of the United States and Mexico also easily envisioned the end of their own nations, which they nearly met a handful of times. The epilogue of this book, therefore, attempts to draw out the implications of American antiquity for the future in an age of climate apocalypse, social justice protest, and rising nationalism, but most especially of Indigenous resurgence.[97]

CHAPTER 1

Ordering the "Indian" Archive

What threatens white people is often dismissed as myth.
I have never been true in America. America is a myth.

—Natalie Diaz, "The First Water is the Body," 2018

Thus they have come to tell it,
Thus they have come to record it in their narration,
And for us they have painted it in their codices,
The ancient men, the ancient women.
They were our grandfathers, our grandmothers,
Our great-grandfathers, great-grandmothers,
Our great-great grandfathers, our ancestors.
Their account was repeated,
They left it to us;
They bequeathed it forever
To us who live now,
To us who come down from them.
Never will it be lost, never will it be forgotten,
That which they came to do,
That which they came to record in their paintings:
Their renown, their history, their memory.

—Alvarado Tezozómoc with Chimalpahin Quauhtlehuanitzin,
Crónica Mexicayotl (c. 1600)

IN 1601, JUAN DE OÑATE Y SALAZAR, the conquistador and colonial governor of Santa Fe de Nuevo México, led an entrada (expedition of conquest) across the prairielands currently known as Kansas and Oklahoma.[1] Three years before, Oñate—whose wife was a direct descendant of both Hérnan Cortés and Motecuhzoma Xocoyotzin—traveled northward from the Kingdom of New

Spain, looking to make his fortune by finding a city as prosperous as México.² As early as 1529 another Spanish conquistador had learned—likely from the Nahua soldiers under his control—of seven northern cities where the cotton-clothed inhabitants were all rich in turquoise and gold.³ In the 1540s, conquistador Francisco Vásquez de Coronado attempted to locate those cities; he voyaged as far as a river now called Arkansas. In the 1560s, another conquistador crossed what is currently the state of Chihuahua to continue the search, noting ruins of "casas grandes" (great houses) but no golden cities.⁴ The impulse for these entradas likely grew stronger due to Nahua accounts of the Aztlán migrations and the seven caves of Chicomoztoc, locales the conquistadors sought under names including "Cíbola" and "Quivira."⁵ Three decades later, by brutally crushing opposition in lands optimistically dubbed "New Mexico," Oñate's forces occupied regular outposts among the extensive pueblos (Indigenous villages), while the conquistador continued his search for gold. After ordering the siege and destruction at Acoma Pueblo—but before Spanish officials banished him for his cruelty—Oñate and his soldiers pushed east.⁶

Beyond the mountains, plateaus, and mesas of the Puebloans, and across the Llano Estacado and shortgrass prairies of Apachería, Oñate's forces eventually came to a "Gran Población" (large settlement) called Etzanoa, located at the confluence of rivers now called the Arkansas and Walnut in what is currently Kansas. Oñate's forces raided a nearby rival settlement; there he abducted a "Quiviran" man of Kitikiti'sh (Witchita) heritage, who was afterward sent to New Spain for questioning.⁷ In Mexico City, Spanish authorities instructed "Mjguel Yndio" to draw a map of his homelands and to calculate distances between towns and landmarks.⁸ Communicating with kernels of dried corn and a form of Plains Indian Sign Language (PISL), the captive complied. He drew lines for roads and rivers, "some of them winding and others straight," signified pueblos with shapes resembling Wichita council circles, and he placed the great Etzanoa at the center.⁹ But Miguel's map confused his Spanish interrogators. The map was not a territorial survey as expected but instead a depiction of relationships between different council houses, with Mexico City placed in relation to Miguel's birthplace and the rest of the world he knew. He had been expected, however, to provide directions to the Seven Cities of Gold.

Not only did Miguel's map indicate no golden cities, but it made no sense to the Spanish interrogators, with their European conventions of time and space. Nonetheless, they included the *Mapa diseñado por Miguel* in their report about Oñate's genocidal acts against the Pueblo peoples, Miguel's handiwork retained almost as an afterthought rather than as documentation of Indigenous history.¹⁰ More interested in gold and souls than Plains history and cartography, the Spanish officials misinterpreted the map in 1602 and their archival heirs would continue to do so for centuries. Over the years, settlers came to believe that Miguel's homelands were empty grasslands "plagued" by violent migratory peoples and lacking in the signs of "civilization" denoted by permanent structures such as those in Mexico and Peru. When the United States took the Great Plains in the nineteenth century, and Miguel's Wichita and Caddoan relations were chased from their homes—bison, gardens, and lives destroyed—their history was dismissed as the insignificant legends of wandering "wild Indians."¹¹ Almost four centuries would go by before Miguel's knowledge would outweigh settler perceptions of the area as terra nullius (empty land), although his map had made clear—even if the settlers could not understand—that the Plains were far from "empty."

Recently, using the resources of PISL and Indigenous cartography, retranslated Spanish documents, and remote sensing technology, US archaeologists followed Miguel's map to a site, likely Etzanoa, that was once a twenty-thousand-person metropolitan area near current Arkansas City, Kansas. The scholars date the city to the middle of the last millennia—roughly the same period as Tenochtitlan—about six hundred years before the present. One account explained that the findings "would make Etzanoa the second-largest prehistoric settlement ever found in North America after Cahokia," located across the Mississippi from St. Louis.¹² Almost overnight, "rural Kansas" transformed from a "fly-over" location littered with arrowheads and potsherds into an important site of World Heritage.¹³ "Everything we thought we knew" about Plains antiquity, summarized the lead archaeologist in 2018, "turns out to be wrong."¹⁴

While Miguel's map may have reordered history for Kansans, the update changed little in the daily lives of Wichita and Affiliated Tribes members, who warily watched the activity in their homelands from two hundred miles away at their tribal headquarters in Anadarko, Oklahoma. While settler Kansans boasted about a grand past no longer just "a vast empty space populated by nomadic tribes following buffalo herds" and looked forward to increased tourism, the Wichita and Affiliated Tribes' Cultural Program planner Gary McAdams, quite modestly, hoped his "ancestors may finally receive their due for the accomplishments of the great civilization they were able to establish in the present state of Kansas during the 14th and 15th centuries."¹⁵ McAdams's careful optimism was tempered by the fact that, for hundreds of years, settlers have ignored the past that Kitikiti'sh people have always known, even when it was documented in their own settler archives.

The story of Miguel's map is not only about archaeological success, the joy of archival recovery, or the affirmation of traditional Kitikiti'sh history: it also tells of the epistemological and material consequences of an archival structure of settlement in which *what* counts as a source, *where* it is located, *who* interprets those sources, and *how* they do so have profound, intergenerational effects on real human lives. It demonstrates a history in which Indigenous knowledge—even when fixed into settler forms (the dictated map)—was rendered unbelievable or invalid until confirmed by settler scholarship.[16] That Miguel's reinterpreted map and its archaeological outcomes have suddenly repopulated the distant-era Plains also shows the power of Indigenous-authored texts to transform not only the dominant narratives of the past but also the circumstances—epistemological, political, economic—of the present. How many similar stories are contained by the settler archive?

This and the following chapter examine key "Indian" archives built by criollos and creoles in the mid-to late-eighteenth-century Spanish and British worlds, collections created at a time when competing Atlantic powers were looking to expand and consolidate their bases of colonial knowledge. Just as Crown officials had hoped to access and transform Miguel's knowledge into a literal treasure map, eighteenth-century criollos and creoles worked to compile and transform Indigenous knowledge into settler forms, eventually weaponizing that knowledge by making it into evidence of American—not Indigenous—"antiquity," their idea of the time before Europeans invaded the "New World." Recent scholarship has focused on the roles of Indigenous and Spanish or criollo agents in assembling what has variously been termed the "creole" or "criollo archive," the "cacique-criollo archive," and the "annals of Native America."[17] The focus of the current chapter is on the "Indian" archive, that is to say, the compilation of past-related materials that came to constitute—for eighteenth-century settlers in New Spain—"Indian" rather than European history. In both this chapter and the next, I suggest that the "Indian" archive's structure of settlement was defined by a misappropriation of serial migration histories and a preoccupation with creating settler connections to the land.

This chapter shows the importance that Spanish officials and clerics—as well as Nahua individuals and communities—placed on narratives of origin, migration, and home when selecting and creating archival materials. Indeed, the first step in the process of weaponizing American antiquity was the identification of certain Indigenous "monuments"—a flexible term—as records of history, and as items worthy of inclusion in their "Indian" (as opposed to Indigenous) archive. Europeans and Americans amassed Indigenous-produced items of all kinds—including documents such as Miguel's map—into this "Indian" archive, and from these they also began to write their own "Indian" histories. Early colonial histories, which regularly included references to Azteca pasts and were often composed in conversation with Nahua collaborators, provided the frameworks into which later criollo historians would archive and interpret American antiquity. For example, Franciscan missionary Toribio de Benavente (called Motolinía) identified a series of ancient peoples supposed to have migrated to Central Mexico before the Mexicas—including the "barbarian" Chichimecas—in his *Historia de los indios de la Nueva España* (1565).[18] Similarly, Jesuit missionary José de Acosta noted in his *Historia natural y moral de las Indias* (1590) that the Chichimecas were the "ancient and first residents of the province we call Nueva España," explaining that subsequent settlers had issued from a "very remote land to the north, where a kingdom that has been called Nuevo México was recently discovered." This included one province called "Aztlan, meaning Place of Herons, [and] the other Teuculhuacan, meaning Land of Those Having Divine Grandfathers."[19] This context of migration was important to Miguel's map as well as so many other monuments included in the "Indian" archive. If the first step is compilation, then the second step in transforming Indigenous knowledge into American "antiquity" was the fixing of Indigenous sources into European-style chronological migration histories, stories of sequential replacement that ultimately aided settlers' inter-imperial struggles.

The present chapter centers on what is arguably the most influential archive of Indigenous knowledges assembled in the eighteenth century: the "Museo Histórico Indiano" (Indian Historical Museum) of Milanese lawyer Lorenzo Boturini Benaduci. His enormous collection would be referenced by most of the eighteenth century's succeeding scholars.[20] Now frequently called the foremost scholar of colonial Indigenous documents, Boturini had initially sought to compile an altogether different kind of archive during in his voyage to New Spain, one that would document the Moctezuma family encomienda (colonial land and labor grant) and help recover lapsed income.[21] The present chapter also examines how Boturini's composite "Indian" archive was used by later historians, especially by the exiled Jesuit Francisco Javier Clavijero, to create American—neither "Indian" nor Indigenous—history.

Unlike Clavijero's writings, Boturini's "Indian" archive is inflected with what historian Danna Levin Rojo has called an "Indian imaginary," meaning that its contents maintain Indigenous experiences and conceptualizations of the past and present in addition to settler colonial ones.[22] This is due, in part, to the fact that the early Spanish settlers looked to their Nahua students and congregants to learn how to place American antiquity within their universal Christian cosmology: much of Boturini's collection comes directly out of these interactions. Moreover, given that the repossession of encomienda lands provided this structure for the collection, it is no wonder that Boturini's museum was used in the service of imperial—and then criollo—land claims. The "Indian" archive's structure of settlement—both Mexica and Spanish—adheres in both Boturini's Museo as well as in the historical narratives that issued from it, such as Clavijero's, revealing the archive's enduring dispossessive power in New Spain and its afterlives of dispossession elsewhere.[23]

Settling the Hispanic Civitas

The main structure of Indigenous communities in pre-invasion central Mexico was the altepetl (pl. altepeme). This spatial arrangement, glossed by historian James Lockhart as a "territorial metaphor," both references a sovereign polity (city-state) of bounded territory as well as an ethnic community.[24] When the Spanish arrived in the Mexica capital of Tenochtitlan in 1519, they witnessed the height of the "Triple Alliance" or "Aztec Empire," the political union of the altepeme Texcoco, Tlacopan, and Tenochtitlan, dominated by the latter.[25] The vast capital was laid out according to Mexica spatial and social principles; the new architectural and epistemic ideals that Cortés and his Spanish entourage brought with them—in which cities were arranged orthogonally to promote good moral and civic order—became the rule after 1521, however, when the victorious conquistador ordered a gridded colonial city built atop the Mexica site.[26] The earliest Spanish settlers were made encomendados by the Crown, which awarded them encomiendas (land grants) along with the unlimited labor of the Indigenous populations there. At this time, the new cabecera (head town) and cacicazgo (Indigenous leadership) systems still resembled the altepetl in terms of land distribution, leadership, and the rotation of public duties.[27] Although the encomienda system was largely phased out in the mid-sixteenth century, Indigenous laborers were still required to work for "public benefit" and paid small wages.[28] All across the lands they called New Spain, the Spanish forced Indigenous peoples and spaces into similar colonial structures.

With these changes came a strenuous civic and social separation of Spanish and Indigenous worlds known as the "república de españoles" and "república de indios."[29] The Law of the Indies' codified system of spatial segregation resulted in different trazas (zones) for Spanish and Indigenous residents, different parishes, and different legal and financial structures, among other things. For example, Indigenous residents of Mexico City were not allowed to live in the central Spanish traza, which was fortified and separated from the Indigenous neighborhoods by a canal and ditch.[30] By the late sixteenth century, formerly separate pueblos (Indigenous towns) across New Spain were resettled into reducciones (congregations); new cities for the congregations were arranged in grids, with "left-over" lands parceled out to other Indigenous or castas (mixed-race) families.[31] This system targeted Indigenous spatial and indentity practices by condensing Indigenous communities and relocating them elsewhere, resulting in mixed-ethnicity pueblos.[32] Especially in the seventeenth century, congregations were relocated into the rural cities that had been established next to presidios (forts) or mission towns.[33] Forcing Indigenous peoples into condensed "urban" settlements was meant to bring the otherwise "barbarous" subjects to "reason" through physical reconfiguration. Indeed, the Hispanic model of civitas, which worked according to a deterministic logic wherein "indios bárbaros" (barbarous or noncooperative Indigenous subjects) became "indios de razón" (civilized or Hispanicized), was supposed to be the best way to control the spirituality, labor, reproduction, health, and tribute of the Crown's new Indigenous subjects.[34]

Not only did this system of spatial control change Indigenous peoples' relationships to their homes and home communities, it also altered patterns of land use and land occupancy, thereby likewise changing the environment and creating a new "emptiness" across landscapes where that had previously not been the case. Moreover, it meant that conquistadors like Coronado and Oñate or even mendicant Franciscan priests imagined the Indigenous present as having declined from an urban and "civilized" past as represented by places like Tenochtitlan and Quivira into a nomadic, "barbarous" one.[35] Despite the fact that European incursions into Native homelands had created the conditions of "barbarism"—wars, abductions, expulsions, and campaigns of annihilation—America's Indigenous peoples were often designated as "barbarians," a term that was also relative to a group's allegedly "nomadic" (as opposed to "settled" or "civilized") lifestyle.[36]

Spanish spatial practices were not only about territorial acquisition: they were also meant to divest Indigenous peoples from their specific identities and sovereignties. This process of dispossession was assisted, intellectually, by the labeling of some Indigenous groups as "civilized"—and potential Spanish subjects—whereas others became barbarous enemies of the state to be "pacified" or annihilated. Scholars Alfredo López Austín and Leonardo López Luján point out that sixteenth-century Spanish documents frequently used the term "Chichimeca" for peoples from lands to the northwest of the Mexico Valley—areas locally referred to as "Chicimecapan, Teotlalpan, Mictlampa, or Tlacochcalco"—and by extension Spanish colonists employed it as a pejorative catchall synonymous with "bárbaros" (barbarian) rather than as an ethnically specific term.[37] Although all "unpacified" Native groups were designated as "indios bárbaros"—and the peoples to whom it and "Chichimeca" referred changed according to currents of continental trade and war—terming those lands in the north "Grand Chichimeca" by drawing from Nahua migration histories both followed the idea of Hispanic civitas and indexes the particular political and historiographical battles of the first two hundred years of colonization.

Because the Triple Alliance had been led by Nahuatl-speakers—which the Spanish-allied Tlaxcalans were as well—the settlers spatially "civilized" these groups first. While so doing, they also assumed some Nahua biases, such as the presumption that Nahuatl-speaking peoples were superior to "Otomí" (meaning generically Oto-Pamean-speaking) and Maya groups. As a result, non-Nahua pupils were largely excluded from the early colonial educational structure.[38] For this reason, most of the documentation settlers initially collected related to the lives of "civilized" Nahuas from the Valley of Mexico.[39] These Indigenous groups largely became known to the settlers as "indios de razón"; this was in contrast to the "uneducated" others, usually located outside central Mexico.

Unlike the indios de razón—mainly central Mexico Nahuas—whose "progress" toward Hispanicization supported the success of New Spain (especially in the frontier colonies), Chichimecas or bárbaros were seen as a threat to the Catholic kingdom. When Spain invaded the northern areas often referred to as "el Gran Chichimeco"—present-day Sinaloa, Sonora, Durango, and Chihuahua—it sent "pacified" central Mexico groups (e.g., Hñähñus) as well as indios de razón as frontline fighters and colonists.[40] Those groups who resisted Spanish rule—especially those in the north like the Yoeme (Yaqui), Yoreme (Mayo), Akimel O'odham (Pima), and Ndé (Apache)—were all referred to as indios bárbaros, a term that indexed their "enemy" status.

The forced processes of relocation and resettlement furthermore echoed, in Spanish and criollo ears, the migration stories they were learning from Indigenous scribes and nobles. Spanish and criollo scholars learned from marveling at the glories of Tenochtitlan that the Nahuas' "Chichimeca" ancestors had eventually became "civilized," confirming the processes of conversion and declension.[41] These migration histories helped settlers to distinguish the "civilized" from the "barbarous," and it was easy enough to describe the process of Hispanicization as parallel to the Nahuatl-ization of the Chichimecas: that is to say, Indigenous sources were made to speak to Spanish concepts of civility and barbarism, which were recoded as predictions of Hispanicized indios de razón defeating or converting the "wild" indios bárbaros who refused to live according to Spanish models.[42] While this solidified the promise of transformation, it also reified the contemporary hierarchy of "civilized" over "savage" groups, thereby giving cover to the ever-expanding ambition of settlers who, by the sixteenth century, had already pushed far into northern and southern lands filled with resistant "enemies."

Compiling the Nahua Archive

Before the sixteenth-century European invasion, Mexica tlacuiloque (artist-scribes, s. tlacuilo) recorded aspects of their solar and sacred calendars, their annals, and other civic records on paper, cloth, and vellum.[43] The tlacuiloque who made and elites who used these manuscripts did not separate out "calendrical" from "historical" or "devotional" genres but instead employed their own conceptual categories for recording and performing knowledge.[44] After the invasion, however, the Spanish named the documents by material and generic form, using terms such as tira (cloth strip), lienzo (canvas), codex (if considered book-like), or mapa (any Indigenous-made manuscript).[45] Although many Indigenous documents were recognizable to Europeans as "Bookes," they were also perceived as potentially dangerous because intrinsically related to non-Christian religions.[46] Thus alongside the wooden and stone carvings they identified as "idols," sixteenth-century Spanish agents destroyed most documents of paper and animal hide; those few spared were largely sent to Europe as curiosities. Because the Spanish invasion began on the Gulf coast but was centralized in the Valley of Mexico and on the southern plateau, the cultural monuments in those communities that the Spanish invaders encountered first—largely Maya, Mexica, Ñuudzahui (Mixtec), and Hñähñu (Otomí)—suffered heavily. In fact, only a few Maya and Ñuudzahui documents made before the invasion still exist; no Mexica ones do.[47]

Because Indigenous cosmologies do not operate in ways familiar to settlers, correlating Mexica timekeeping systems with European ones became a specific concern of the scholars interested in documents of Indigenous history and religion. Manuscript calendars—tlapohualli (meaning both count and story)—were of particular interest to Atlantic scholars because of their own efforts to establish a universal chronology, although the documents were also eyed with suspicion for their supposed connection to Indigenous religions.[48] Often these were round documents inscribed with days and years—and which appeared to resemble Greco-Roman zodiac charts and medieval wheels of fortune—called calendáricas, calendarios, or sometimes ruedas (wheels) by the Spanish.[49] One of the first "wheels"—in actuality more of a square—seen in Europe appeared in the mid-sixteenth-century *Codex Mendoza*, a written compilation that also included Mexica tribute records and annals, which English antiquary Samuel Purchas reprinted in 1624 with the explanation that seeing the "weeke of yeares after the Mexican computation" made it easier to understand the "Mexican historie[s] in pictures."[50] Atlantic scholars were especially attentive to two temporal concepts: the fifty-two year xiuhtlapohualiztli ("half-century" bundle) and the longer cycle of ages.[51] In his *Historia natural* (1590), for example, José de Acosta wrote that the "New Fire ceremony" celebrated the turn of the tlapohualli (wheel count and story) and ended the cosmic fifty-two year cycle, noting that the "wheel" itself was an expression of the Indigenous "cleverness and skill" that enabled their knowledge of antiquity.[52] Settlers like Acosta, however, largely saw the tlapohualli only as counting devices or "cuentas" enabling accounts of "their antiquities," but not as documents integrated with other genres and uses. In fact, many of the calendarios collected by Europeans and criollos were cosmic account books inherently related to other topological, embodied, and inscribed sources, including "quotidian" texts like genealogies, land documents, and civil transactions.[53] Indeed, Mexica tlapohualli—often but not always in wheel-shaped forms—did not keep time (or history) on their own but were instead part of a multimodal, performance-based system for maintaining knowledge of the past.[54]

The Mexica world, writes historian Camilla Townsend, was "a shifting, constantly altering world, one in which Mexica peoples had to work to keep balance."[55] This movement is reflected in the cyclical intertwining of the 365-day solar year and 260-day sacred year that form the xiuhtlapohualiztli or fifty-two year "bundle."[56] Each individual year within the xiuhtlapohualiztli is named with a combination of the "trecenas" (thirteen-day cycles) of the tonallapohualiztli (ritual year) and the four "year-signs," Tochtli, Acatl, Tecpatl, and Calli (Rabbit, Reed, Flint, and House).[57] These years all work in tandem with the ceremonial cycles of the eighteen vientenas, the twenty-day cycles or "months" of the cempohuallapohualli (solar year). Although each date within the "bundle" is unique, regardless of their position on the calendar, all dates with the same names—day names, vientena names, or year names—are connected to dates of previous and future eras.[58] The overall sense is one of mobility, and Mexica experts relied on "books" and "wheels" to guide their understanding of the cosmos and keep it in balance with proper observances; i.e., the position of celebrations depended on what the tonalamatl (book of feasts) or xiuhámatl (book of years) advised. Understanding the outlines of Mexica temporality provides a better sense of the dispossession inherent in the misappropriation "calendar wheels."[59]

Prior to invasion, youths from the nobility were trained to become scribes and leaders at specialized calmecac academies. Afterward, when Spanish missionaries established colleges and seminaries as part of evangelization, they drew from the pool of calmecac pupils, meaning that the missionaries largely interacted with Nahuatl-speaking (Nahua) students of noble Mexica, Acolhua, Tepaneca, and Talaxcalteca descent. At the Franciscan Colegio de Santa Cruz de Tlatelolco—founded in 1533—multilingual students from Tenochtitlan and Tlatelolco translated Spanish texts for Indigenous audiences and taught Nahuatl to the faculty, their efforts enabling the friars to compile vocabulary lists and grammars as well as extensive information on Nahua lifeways.[60] Most of the resulting Franciscan texts were bilingual and often tri-scriptural; that is, scribes and interpreters frequently translated iconic script into alphabetic words—in Nahuatl and Spanish—on the same page.[61]

Even after Spanish schools replaced the Indigenous ones, Nahua pupils continued to train as tlacuiloque, becoming skilled in writing both iconic and alphabetic Nahuatl.[62] Thus Indigenous scholars of the sixteenth century and beyond retained their representational practices and continued to make historical records—albeit ones reinterpreted for the new colonial situation—during the Spanish occupation.[63] Moreover, some of the destroyed documents were remade. Indeed, Indigenous intellectuals produced and compiled records—including genealogies and land records—both on their own and in collaboration with Spanish settlers, and these writings helped in some ways to mitigate the transformation of Indigenous identities in the early colonial period. These multicultural Nahua scholars thus became the intermediaries between the Spanish and greater Indigenous worlds.[64] Indigenous intellectuals who spoke Spanish, were baptized with Spanish first names, and adopted Spanish dress—indios de razón—frequently sought to maintain their leadership status within the new colonial hierarchy by becoming caciques (Indigenous governors) of the separate Indigenous pueblos and cabeceras and even produced new documents to ensure their position within the colonial system.[65] Some of these sixteenth-century bilingual documents remained at the Spanish colleges and seminaries where they had been produced. Others, like the *Oztotipac Map* of Texcoco, were legal documents and were therefore kept in the court files.[66] Still others were given as gifts or accepted in lieu of payment.[67]

During the first century of Spanish rule, Nahua and mestizo leaders commissioned "dynastic genealogies, histories, and maps, for themselves as well as for the Spaniards."⁶⁸ These were iconic and alphabetic, and sometimes, both. For example, during the sixteenth century Mexica noble Fernando Alvarado Tezozómoc and Tlaxcalan mestizo Diego Muñoz Camargo produced important alphabetic histories, such as the document now called the *Crónica mexicayotl*.⁶⁹ In the next generation of scholars was the Tenocha-Tetzcocatl mestizo historian Fernando de Alva Cortés Ixtlilxóchitl, who was commissioned by the Spanish Viceroy to write local histories and who collected and authored an array of documents to do so.⁷⁰ One of these became known as the *Relación histórica de la nación tulteca* (c. 1600), written about a people to whom Ixtlilxóchitl traced his own descent. His contemporary, Chalco noble Domingo Francisco de San Antón Muñón Chimalpahin Quauhtlehuanitzin, maintained a diary, annals, and first-person testimonies in alphabetic Nahuatl as well as a version of *Historia de las Indias y conquista de México* (1552) by the Spanish chronicler Francisco López de Gómara.⁷¹ These and other Indigenous elites were the hands behind the sixteenth-and seventeenth-century Indigenous documents that later ended up in criollo libraries and museums.

Assembling the Altepetl Archive from the Ground Up

One effect of the spatial practices of encomienda and reducción was a proliferation of land-claim records in the sixteenth and seventeenth centuries as Indigenous pueblos sought relief through the courts.⁷² Under the two republics system, caciques, nobles, and entire pueblos adopted the legal tools of the "Indian Courts" in a "pragmatic response to dispossession and disempowerment."⁷³ Early lawsuits often had to do with patrimony and inheritance and, not infrequently, one Indigenous claimant opposed another. Sometimes claimants came from different ethnic groups, and sometimes pueblo sued pueblo, the latter suits tending to revolve around disputed land or communal labor rights.⁷⁴ This "indigenous juris-practice"—as historian Yanna Yannakakis calls it—frequently incorporated traditional practices including the use of oral testimony and iconic documents as evidence.⁷⁵

Many of the genealogies and títulos de tierras (land documents) submitted in these legal proceedings had been created to secure the Indigenous elite's hold on community leadership and the administration of pueblo lands, roles they had adopted to succeed within the colonial order.⁷⁶ Nahua nobles frequently made their claims on the basis of título primordial, that is, possession held since time immemorial as recognized by the larger community. The term "título primordial" (primordial title) itself implies a claim that has always existed, and indeed claimants often attempted to demonstrate their lineage and patrimonial holdings dated to the beginning of time. From this example, other claimants also learned that the most successful land suits were those that traced landholdings by descent (in the case of nobles) or altepetl (in the case of pueblos) and included documentary evidence.[77] Indigenous documents, including primordial titles and geneologies, frequently narrated how an altepetl came to be, which is to say, how particular communities came into their identity and became embedded in their place.

Traditionally, land records were written in iconic script, compiled with reference to oral tradition and the affirmation of the huehuetque (elders) or groups of respected citizens. Individual possession and inheritance were guaranteed by oral histories and also recorded in ink.[78] Colonial officials often confirmed possession by consulting community members and iconic records.[79] They tended to trust the latter, at least in the sixteenth century, because they were written iconically—not alphabetically—and therefore assumed to have been made without clerical oversight.[80] Crown authorities also believed—incorrectly—that iconic documents were the least "Hispanicized" and therefore most ancient. Paradoxically, the same iconic Indigenous texts used in colonial courts could also be seen as signs of failed or unfinished conversion, suggesting barbarism, apostasy, and even sedition.

Historian Ethelia Ruiz Medrano has shown that scribes in pueblos throughout the colonial period frequently copied or remade historical documents to support land-holding rights and sovereignty claims.[81] Indeed, the practice of making colonial titles for court sparked an iconic revival, as scribes sought to evoke the earlier iconic writing style and thereby index the authenticity of pre-invasion documents strategically set in a primordial, indefinite past."[82] Into the later part of the sixteenth century, many of the iconic texts would contain multilingual or multiscript glosses. The colonial archive is filled with documents used to settle lawsuits, including genealogies, tribute documents, and property descriptions, some of which even included explicit calculations, measurements, and boundary delineations.[83] These forensic documents went through the institutionalized steps of production, translation, and notarization, only to be stored in colonial court records offices, private hands, and pueblo archives.[84] These were also the kinds of documents eventually held in Boturini's museum.[85]

After a conspiracy in the 1560s and a failed rebellion led by the grandson of Motecuhzoma Xocoyoltzin in 1576, Philip II prohibited all "superstitious"—that is to say, Indigenous—texts in the viceroyalty.[86] Spanish authorities considered them anti-Catholic and, therefore, seditious. For their own safety, the

Indigenous scribes and historians drew hard generic lines between the "mythic" past of origin stories—narratives that Spanish authorities might consider "diabolical"—and the "historic" past documented by land transactions. Indigenous scribes and historians also maintained their histories by adopting forms that the Spanish more readily identified as secular: migration histories, tribute rolls, and historical relaciones.[87] Calendar "wheels" and land-related mapas—some of the most interesting records in Spanish eyes—were also seemingly safely secular.[88]

Late-sixteenth-century prohibitions and adaptations—alongside changes to the Indian courts, the renewed power of the Inquisition and, especially, a series of devastating epidemics that significantly limited the number of trained tlacuiloque and nahuatlatos (interpreters)—created a scarcity of new iconic documents after the sixteenth century. According to literary historian Anna More, these documents were increasingly regarded as esoteric after this period.[89] Yet in the face of strengthened anti-Indigenous regulations in the late seventeenth century, select criollo scholars—like Carlos de Sigüenza y Gongora and Augustín de Vetancurt—still continued to collect and write about Indigenous history.[90] This next generation saw the "calendars," in particular, as important astronomical texts and evidence of important scientific accomplishment on the part of the Mexica, evidencing extremely detailed understandings of time and the heavens. The criollo antiquary Sigüenza was so interested in the question of Indigenous time and astronomy that he dedicated an entire work to the calculations of the "Mexican calendar."[91] In his unpublished *Ciclografía Mexicana* (c. 1680s), Sigüenza described the process by which he determined European dates for Indigenous historical events by observing astronomical occurrences—comets and eclipses—and using these to correlate the timekeeping systems. In this way he not only provided a European-style chronology for Indigenous histories, he also gained insight into the workings of Mexica calendrics.[92] *Ciclografía* is an example of criollo scholars' interests in Indigenous history, astronomy, and timekeeping, as is Sigüenza's voluminous library of Indigenous documents.[93] Sigüenza, who died in 1700, willed his massive archive to the Jesuit Colegio Máximo de San Pedro y San Pablo in Mexico City, where his collection remained unseen for decades.[94]

Aside from those willing to risk the Inquisition, only a limited number of scholars in New Spain would consult the sixteenth-and seventeenth-century Indigenous materials again—the títulos, genealogies, histories, etc.—before the middle of the eighteenth century. By then, most settlers regarded Indigenous documents, in their alleged rarity, as antiquarian curiosities rather than reliable historical records. Yet after the Neapolitan traveler Giovanni Francesco Gemelli Careri—to whom Sigüenza showed Indigenous documents during his visit to

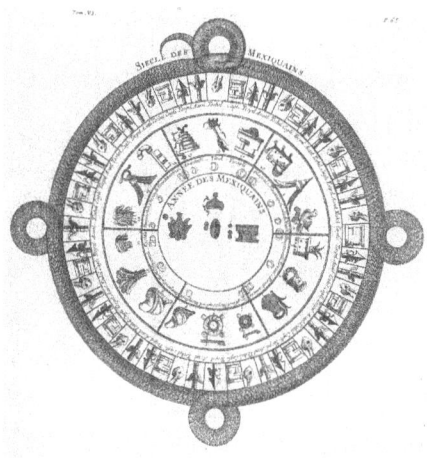

FIGURE 5. Giovanni Francesco Gemelli Careri, "Siècle des Mexiquains," *Voyage du tour du monde*, t. 6 (1719). Courtesy of the Bibliothèque Nationale de France.

New Spain in the 1690s—included an approximation of Sigüenza's calendario or "Mexican Century" in the sixth volume of his *Giro del Mondo* (1699), this would change.[95] Published first in Naples then London (1704) and Paris (1719), Gemelli's "Mexican Century" marked an important moment of European engagement with Indigenous time and heralded the beginning of concentrated criollo attention not just to Mexica calendrics but also to the "Mexican" history preserved in similar "monuments."

Making Paper Monuments into an Archive of the Antique Past

Lorenzo Boturini Benaduci, a lawyer from Milan—a Duchy then ruled by Spain—originally traveled to New Spain in 1736 to collect lapsed payments for a descendant of Motecuhzoma and to evangelize with the monies he recouped.[96] While in New Spain, however, Boturini became intrigued by the adoration of the Virgin of Guadalupe and began to research its origins and champion its wider adoption. Within his first year he was also compiling documentation in support of another project: writing a new history of America "founded on the indisputable Monuments of the very Indians."[97] His identification of Indigenous records as "monuments" implied that they were "pieces or types of histories that have come down from the ancients about past events," valuable for their ability to recall the past.[98] In the place of more conventional comparative philological, legal, or religious methods, he "found no other light, no other calm, no other

FIGURE 6. *Codex Boturini* (c. 1530), detail. Courtesy of El Instituto Nacional de Antropología e Historia (INAH), Mexico. Detail shown is from the beginning "episode," in which the Nahua ancestor paddles from Aztlán to Colhuacan in year 1 Flint.

port than in the histories of the Indians themselves."[99] Boturini's pledge to address the question of Indigenous origins "according to the same monuments of the Indians that they left us in their histories" reveals an almost heretical admiration and preference for Indigenous texts, a sentiment shared by few of his contemporaries.[100]

Mapas comprised the bulk of what Boturini believed to be "the histories of the Indians themselves." Yet to most European and many criollo eyes, mapas were nonsensical and far removed from the useable documents required to write proper histories: an early Spanish dictionary even defined the term as "anything outlandish and bizarre in its [out]line."[101] "Mapa," a word used by Europeans for all nonalphabetic manuscripts, is an extension of "map" or "chart" in the European cartographic sense, but it was deployed whether or not the documents in question were cartographic (indeed, cartographic "maps" are only one particular kind of nonalphabetic mapa).[102] The majority were made by anonymous scribes, elders, and other community record-keepers. These included annals, landholding records, songs, and property petitions as well as "mapas genealógicos" and "mapas geográficos."[103] One that appeared to be a combination of the latter was the *Tira de la Peregrinación* (also known as the *Codex Boturini*), which depicted Mexica origins over twenty-three pages of carefully delineated sequential "episodes." Boturini described it as a "pictorial document on Indian paper with folds like those of a piece of cloth" when "stretched out like a strip," and it contained tribute and geographical as well as cosmic information.[104] Other important records of Mexica migration accounts such as the *Mapa Sigüenza* and *Codex Azcatitlan*—which Gemelli likewise reproduced—also served to establish genealogies, identities, and sometimes tributary rights.[105]

Boturini collected "calendars" as well—although he was not restricted to round ones—including the Tlaxcalan *Tonalamatl de Aubin,* a rendering of divinities and feast days that takes a screen-fold form.[106] Some mapas also seem to be largely prosaic records of daily life: for example, the *Códice del Tecpan de Santiago Tlatelolco*, c. 1580, is a proposal and sketch for a new tecpan (Indigenous government building or palace) in Mexico City, an ordinary administrative document, albeit with Nahuatl glosses and Nahua aesthetics.[107] Boturini's collection also included "maps" in the cartographic sense, such as the *Plano de Tenoxtitlan*, a partial map of Tenochtitlan made on amate paper c. 1565 that shows land parcels, chinampas (floating gardens), and canals as well as buildings and the identities of landholders in each calli or "house" plot.[108] Not merely about spatial organization, one side of the *Plano* depicts a lineage of tlatoque (rulers) from Itzcoatl (reign 1427–1440) to don Luis de Santa María Cipactzin (reign 1563–1565), showing the Mexica city's organization not only spatially but politically and ethnically as well.[109] If, as art historian Barbara Mundy has surmised, this document was produced to support Indigenous rulers' attempts to maintain their hold on tribute lands, the combination of land and dynastic information demonstrates the document's necessary multimodality.[110]

Textual evidence hints that Boturini knew the Mexica system of chronology to be inseparable from the way Mexica history was both understood *and* recorded, and suggests he had some sense of the mapas' mobility and multimodality.[111] Boturini also seems to have taken some of "their own concepts" to heart in dividing American time into three ages: "Divine," "Heroic," and "Human." Although he wrote of the similarity to the "Egyptian" and "Roman" divisions of time, the structure is also reminiscent of the cyclical Five Ages of the Five Suns.[112] He recognized the inseparability of the structure of ages from that of the histories—as well as the correspondence of "well-ordered chronology" to geography—even if this was masked by the conventionality of his generic organization, some of which reflected the protective measures of Indigenous scholars.[113] Subsequent criollos routinely missed the importance of the "calendar" to the very form of the Mexica past and violated the Mexica value of movement by attempting to locate absolute beginnings and endings rather than explicating an event's cosmic typology.

Boturini was not entirely iconoclastic. Like his predecessors, he retained a thoroughly Catholic understanding of the structure of universal history.[114]

Accordingly, he identified and arranged the contents of his museum according to conventional European genres such as "Histories" and what he called "Kalendarios," even though this was a profound misunderstanding of the documents' interdependence and a misreading of how the texts were used in their social context. Misinterpretations on the part of future scholars, however, can partly be attributed to how Boturini arranged his museum—where the calendars were categorized separately as "Natural," "Civil," "Astronomical," and "Ritual"—which masked how they worked together. Boturini's catalog also specified categories as "European" or "Indian" separated out by ethnicity ("Mexican history," "Toltec history," "Chichimeca history," etc.). The "Indian" group was largely comprised of materials written by Nahua intellectuals such as Ixtlilxóchitl, Tezozómoc, Muñoz Camargo, Chimalpahin, and Cristóbal del Castillo and their elite origins meant that Boturini's museum privileged the pasts of their own ancestors (such as the Tolteca, Chichimeca, Tepaneca, Mexica, Tlatilulca) over other aspects of "Indian" history, lending Boturini's museum a decidedly pro-Nahua, indios de razón bias that later historians were unable to detect and would misappropriate as "Mexican."[115]

Some mapas were well traveled before coming into Boturini's hands. He described, for example, a "Chicimeca mapa" from Sigüenza that originated with Fernando de Alva Cortés Ixtlilxóchitl, who apparently had "used it to write the history of the same empire," his *Historia chichimeca*.[116] Boturini's critics, however, sneered at the fact that many were written on European-made paper, causing them to question whether they were even "ancient" or "indisputable monuments" at all.[117] But what mattered most to Boturini was the records' content, not necessarily their authenticity. Indeed, while Boturini did collect original documents, he also made copious copies—and helped himself to more than a few—of manuscripts in the Catholic libraries, particularly the Ixtlilxóchitl-Sigüenza collection at the Colegio de San Pedro y San Pablo.[118] Boturini's move away from European antiquarianism—which focused on debating the existence and legitimacy of Indigenous documents—toward an understanding of them as "monuments" and archival records in and of themselves signals the change in historiographical practice that his work made possible for later criollo historians.

Boturini's project was not merely one of recovery and reappraisal: it also instigated a vast epistemological shift in these documents' framing. Turning iconic accounts into interpretable alphabetic narratives relied on processes of sorting, arranging, and ordering, a fixing of Indigenous texts into European cosmological frameworks to enable authoritative interpretations.[119] These frameworks, in their prioritization of chronology and progressive linearity, tended to miss the Indigenous "cosmovision"—especially the importance of continual movement and multimodality—transforming the records into something other than what they were originally meant to be and do.[120] Nonetheless, it was through his Museo Histórico Indiano—and not only its collection—that Boturini made it possible for later historians to use Indigenous documents to construct new histories of the American past because he made these documents legible as interpretable sources.[121] Boturini's collection and his understanding of mapas as interpretable enabled one of the most important historiographic innovations of the period: the reevaluation of Indigenous documents as historical materials, a return to the way these documents had been seen by Europeans in the sixteenth century.

ALTHOUGH NOT CRIOLLO himself (but still a Spanish subject), Boturini engaged in two projects that became seen as the very essence of criollo patriotism: the championing of Guadalupe and the appreciation of Indigenous documents.[122] Madrid, however, saw Boturini's work as a challenge to the Crown's authority: he was imprisoned in 1743 and his property was impounded in Mexico City's Caja Real.[123] By the time he was arrested, Boturini had amassed 319 items for his collection. It included rare texts in Nahuatl and Spanish as well as the kinds of Indigenous documents already popular in Europe: maps, calendarios, and *"otros diferentes monumentos."*[124] At the insistence of the Crown, Boturini made an inventory of his collection—from memory—while in prison. The result became his *Catálogo del Museo histórico indiano del cavallero Lorenzo Boturini Benaduci*, appended to the outline of his projected fifteen-volume history of North America, *Idea de una nueva historia general de la América septentrional* (1746).[125] He hoped the descriptions of riches would persuade the king to return his valuable "Indian Historical Museum."[126] But the materials never were restored to Boturini, and his museum only ever existed again in printed form. It would be almost four decades before the usefulness of these documents registered with the Crown, at which point authorities in Madrid repeatedly requested Boturini's collection, still housed in Mexico City.[127]

Boturini stands as a liminal figure, neither fully operating according to colonial nor criollo archival practices. Yet his Museo Histórico Indiano demonstrates a crucial initial stage in criollo historical thinking: it shows an understanding that, with assiduous collecting and interpretive efforts, the historical information held by Indigenous "monuments" could become knowable to non-Indigenous experts.[128] Thanks to his *Catálogo*, successive historians on both sides of the Atlantic would possess concise descriptions of extant Indigenous texts; thanks to the confiscation, historians in Mexico City had an expanded archive of "Indian" records for reference. Boturini's work began a change in historical methodology that would influence a generation of criollo historians to come.

Mapping Meaning and Migrations across New Spain

During the 1730s, when the non-Indigenous population of New Spain was booming, the new Bourbon monarchy encouraged programs of privatization and Hispanicization, thereby increasing the pressure on hard-defended Indigenous lands. Concurrently, the viceregal government was shrinking communal holdings and dissolving or privatizing church assets (which often were Indigenous assets) in the name of modernization, placing additional financial stresses on Indigenous communities. The increasing pressure meant pueblos' more active reliance on historical documents—some of which had been made under similar conditions two centuries before—but these circumstances also meant that land-related documentation was no longer adequate to keep patrimonial lands and pueblos intact.[129] At this same time, a series of events prompted the mass movement of Indigenous populations from rural pueblos into the cities or, alternately, farther out beyond Spanish influence, leaving some settlements to seem "abandoned" or "empty," an effect long attributed to disease alone.[130] Modernization efforts and the previous century's reducciones as well as a series of droughts, epidemics, and other crises all challenged pueblo self-sufficiency and altered demographics across New Spain.

Pueblos faced particular pressure from settlers who wanted their lands and waterways for agriculture and mining; as cattle ranching became economically profitable and mines closer to the capital ran dry, settlers eagerly looked to seize lands in Sonora and northward. During the period lasting roughly 1700–1740, the Crown entered into a "pax colonial" with whichever northern Indigenous communities would provide miners and fighters for wars with the omnipresent indios bárbaros; it encouraged the founding of satellite communities across the contested frontier.[131] These Hispanicized Indigenous colonies were deliberately installed to serve as buffers against the broncos (wild ones) and the resulting "peace" afforded settlers increased ease of movement outside the capital. Moreover, Spanish (and Hispanicized Indigenous groups') encroachment into the "empty" interior lands extended the networks into and through which additional settlers could move.

Boturini obtained many of his materials as a direct result of travels through New Spain's countryside in the late 1730s and early 1740s. Indeed, when Boturini traversed the "extensive lands" of New Spain, caciques would allegedly show the "ancient pictures" to him during his visits, as he reported they did at Huejotzingo.[132] Some offered them as gifts or for sale. Boturini later boasted of his ability to obtain such documents, explaining in 1746 that there were still "many more by Indians" available for collection.[133] Given this timing, it is highly likely that many of the records Boturini acquired were originals or copies of documents already used (or never used) to defend patrimonial landholdings or pueblo status. The mapas about land and genealogy by far outnumbered calendars or other kinds of iconic documents Boturini held. In fact, in his attempt to convince the authorities to return his collection, Boturini had underscored its value to the empire by recalling that his mapas had once been used to settle land claims. It is "on a genuine understanding of the said pictorial documents, [that] many acts of possession and property and frequent verdicts depend," he insisted on the final page of *Idea*.[134] His very collection was the result of Indigenous dispossession and Indigenous efforts to stop it, its very structure defined by the project of settlement.

Unlike his successors, Boturini had visited the sites where many of these texts originated—witnessing the context of dispossession that provided the archival structure of settlement—which also gave him a specific appreciation of the Nahua conceptions of space and time as they related to interpretation. In his later outline, Boturini would provide a prolonged explanation of the counting, naming, and cycling of Mexica time because he found it so crucial to understanding the monuments he collected.[135] Indeed, it was the "Indian solar cycle," Boturini insisted, that made Mexican history so "excellent," with its precise arrangement that reiterated the different ages (or Suns) of the past.[136] It was also during his years spent among Indigenous communities that Boturini learned that the documents themselves did not hold entire histories: they were only outlines to be filled by scribes and performers. But Boturini did not have access to those meanings, for knowing Nahuatl was not enough: whether or not he spoke or read Nahuatl, he would not have been able to "arrive at their true meaning" without Indigenous collaborators because he had not been trained in the scribal traditions as taught in the elite calmecac schools or, later, passed down in families.[137] Nonetheless, Boturini's experience had helped him learn how to read the documents somewhat, and he became certain of his own ability to translate them into European-style histories.[138]

The very first step in translating mapas was to transform iconic script into alphabetic words and Arabic numbers. At its simplest level, this meant identifying what the Nahuatl images *seemingly* looked liked to him—for example, a serpent, a hill, a headdress—and assigning an assumed Spanish equivalent. After tracking patterns through processes of collation and comparison, more complex meanings emerged: a feathered headdress in proximity to a human figure, for example, translated as "ruler" and not simply "headdress." For numbers and dates Boturini followed Sigüenza's chronological system, which depended on matching events from the "cartographic histories" with those appearing in the "calendars."[139] He similarly identified specific locations by translating altepetl names—often denoted by the calli (house sign) modified by a name-bearer sign—and matching indicated features to known geographies.[140] In this way, Boturini translated the mapas' imputed meanings into European chronological, cartographical, and narrative concepts.

Following the mapas, Boturini compiled an account of ancient American history. He explained that the documents relayed that the Nahua people were part of a series of migrants from the north who came into lands occupied by the Toltecs—the latter the first peoples to cross to the Americas from Asia and whose descendants retained memories of the Flood and Tower of Babel, which they commemorated by constructing the "famous hill" of Cholula.[141] The migrants had thereby left proof of the historical truth of their journey across the land.[142] The *Codex Boturini*, for example, shows "the departure of the Mexicans from the island of Aztlán and their arrival at the continent of New Spain, with the dwellings they constructed in each place, and their years signified with their characters, and at the end, the wars that they waged in the service of Cocoxtli, king of Culhuacan."[143] The mapas instructed Boturini to cross-reference and prioritize names, geographic features, and the built environment in his translation efforts.

According to Boturini, the Nahua people were part of a fourth wave of northern migrants into the lands first occupied by the Toltecs, who founded the powerful "empire of Tula" in the Toluca Valley. Based on his translations, Boturini believed most Toltecs had abandoned the valley after a great catastrophe.[144] After their demise, Boturini explained, only a few survivors stopped in central Mexico, while the rest continued to Guatemala and the Yucatán.[145] The second arrivals were the "Olmec and Xicalanco Indians," who initially settled near Puebla but according to Boturini later "abandoned the land [near Puebla], perhaps going to the kingdoms of Peru and the other windward islands."[146] The next were "the settled Chichimeca nations (as distinguished from the nomadic Chichimecas who nowadays live in the mountainous area and make continuous raids against peaceful Indians and Spaniards and eat the human flesh of their enemies)," who migrated because "there was no room in the ancestral territory because of its large numbers."¹⁴⁷ The "settled" Chichimeca leaders soon sent their children to learn "Toltec" ways, including how to "speak clearly" in Nahuatl, the Toltec language, after which they became Tolteca-Chichimecas.¹⁴⁸ After displacing Nahuatl-speaking "Toltecas" but learning their language and culture, all subsequent Chichimec groups in the Mexico Valley spoke Nahuatl.¹⁴⁹ The processes of migration, displacement, and language change differentiated the groups as they migrated: in Aztlán the Aztecas were originally chichimecoytl, "barbarian language-speaking" (as opposed to Nahuatl- or "clear language"-speaking).¹⁵⁰ Finally, while the Chichimeca prospered in the Toluca Valley and elsewhere, the Mexica, "another warlike and glory-seeking nation reached the lake of Chapultepec, which ... would rule the others."¹⁵¹ The entire narrative was based on dispossession and replacement through successive settlement cycles.

Boturini's wave theory of migration—Toltec, Olmec/Xicalanco, Chichimec, and last Mexica—reflected the importance that Nahua history placed on locating its Toltec-Chichimec ancestors in a direct lineage through language and the built environment, but it also related to the ethnic and linguistic differences he encountered on his travels.¹⁵² That Boturini located Toltecs in the Yucatán and Guatemala (Maya homelands) and Olmecs/Xicalancas in the Puebla-Tlaxcala Valley (Tlaxcala, Mixtec, Zapotec, and others' homelands) indicates some level of sensitivity to the great diversity of peoples living within the lands nominally claimed by Spain in the eighteenth century. Moreover, his emphasis on the centrality of migration, displacement, and language change provides a longer, imperial history responsive to the acculturationist pressures of mid-eighteenth-century New Spanish expansionism by pointing northward and toward the violence inherent in Spanish searches for Mexica origins.

Locating Barbarians in the North

At the time Boturini was analyzing his documents, the viceroyalty was attempting to maintain its settlements in the "interior provinces" of Coahuila, Tejas, Sonora, Sinaloa, and Nuevo León against the indios bárbaros. Although these groups were a changing array of peoples affected by the larger currents of continental trade and war, their commonality was their opposition to the Spanish invasion and settlement in their homelands. Throughout the early eighteenth century, peoples such as the Akimel O'odham (Pima), Comcáac (Seri), Yoeme (Yaqui), Nʉmʉnʉʉ (Comanche), and Ndé (including Gileño, Mescalero, and Lipan Apache groups) repelled Spanish domination. Their resistance required the conscription of more and more "pacified"—allied Indigenous—fighters into the Crown's forces.¹⁵³ Indigenous groups who sued for peace were forced to relocate to the presidios, where they were surveilled and forced to labor and fight other Indigenous groups.¹⁵⁴ As the century advanced and more settlers moved to the north, the Spanish and allied fighters and the Indigenous peoples they designated as indios bárbaros increasingly came into conflict, triggering an even greater militarization of the northern lands.¹⁵⁵

Boturini knew nothing of the northern lands or peoples in the place he believed to be Aztlán: across the Gulf of California near the Colorado River delta. This area included the O'odham homelands then also called Pimería Alta (currently Sonora and southern Arizona) and parts of Apachería and Pueblo lands then and now called New Mexico. The constant warring meant Boturini would not travel there, despite his clear interest, but that did not stop him from pursuing his Mexica history. Instead, Boturini relied on old Franciscan texts to supplement his narrative, including an unpublished manuscript, *Luz de tierra incognita de la América septentrional* (c. 1720)—written by a military captain who had been on northern entradas in the early 1700s—and diaries from the Jesuit father Eusebio Kino—who led an entrada in 1697—that documented his "discovery of the [source of the] Río Grande [Colorado River], adjacent to the Sea of California, and the peaceful state of the provinces of Pimería and Sonora."¹⁵⁶ Combining these Spanish records with what he had already learned of Mexica migrations from the mapas convinced Boturini that he could demonstrate a clear trajectory from Aztlán to "California," Sonora, and New Spain:

> In all the pictorial documents of the Mexican nation and others that accompany them, which I have in my archive, their first arrival is depicted at the town of *Culhuacan*, which means *the town of the serpent*, which is the first on the continent and is situated in front of the said California in perspective almost to the end of the peninsula itself, only separated from it by a branch of the South Sea. The Mexicans crossed this strait with other nations in boats...and that is how they depict it on their pictorial documents.¹⁵⁷

Even though the migration narrative he wrote was one he allegedly read on the mapas, his framework for understanding it was necessarily triangulated through Christian and European cartographic and aesthetic epistemologies. That the calli for Culhuacán—which looks bent over on the *Codex Boturini*, perhaps like a snake—should more correctly translate to "place of those with ancestors" and not "town of the serpent" as he wrote reveals the limits of Boturini's Nahuatl and his knowledge of Nahua history (the town in question is now Culiacán, in Sinaloa).

Nonetheless, Boturini's work enabled the study of Indigenous materials as evidence to argue for (or against) the relative civilizational status of descendant communities in the north.[158] The extreme emphasis on *some* Indigenous groups' alleged degrees of "civilization" or "barbarism"—the latter always portrayed as lawless cuthroats posing a threat to national peace and security—reveals the inextricability of the civilized/barbaric concept from the settler colonial project. Using the same civilized and barbaric binary, criollos continued to contrast "ancient" Mexicans—not in time but in supposedly "civilized" behavior—with the "uncivilized" foil of indios broncos from "the north."[159]

After France turned nominal control of "Louisiana" over to Spain in 1763, the Crown suddenly faced an even larger territory of bárbaros, including Wazhazhe (Osage) groups.[160] In 1776 Carlos III carved the northern frontier lands into a military-controlled semi-autonomous administrative jurisdiction answering directly to the Crown, the "Provincias Internas del Norte"; its new commandante-general Brigadier Teodoro de Croix spent four months in Mexico City examining documents relating to the north in the viceregal archives—including the "Indian" archival materials—in preparation for his mission.[161] His studies no doubt shaped his understanding of tribal differences and diplomatic alliances and likely led him to encourage war against Ndé (Apache) groups and coerce alliances with others.[162] For, by the second half of the eighteenth century, Spain considered Apaches "the most ferocious, vindictive, and irreconcilable" of all northern Indigenous groups, and they formed their policy accordingly.[163] No matter the new enemy, New Spain's answer to its "wild Indian problem" in the eighteenth century was military reinforcement of the presidial line, the violent repression of uprisings, cultural denegration, and "systematic extermination" of the alleged "barbarians."[164]

During this time of increasing Spanish-Indigenous conflict the Franciscan priest José Joaquín Granados y Gálvez wrote his *Tardes Americanas* (1778), which staged a dialogue between an "indio" and "español" to insist, via the splendor of the Indigenous past, on the importance of the social unity of European and "Indian" (that is to say, the composite and largely imaginary) populations to the colony's success.[165] *Tardes Americanas* referenced "various monuments" of "Historia Indiana"—including the writings of Ixtlilxóchitl and other seventeenth-century Mexicanists—and included illustrations of a calendar wheel and Mexica migration narrative, the latter contrasting sedentary "Tultecas" with nomadic "Chichimecas."[166] It is hard to miss the contrast of "barbarous" and "civilized" in this account of history or its lessons on the present importance of uniting criollos and indios through Hispanic "civilization," all enabled by Boturini's earlier work.

FIGURE 7. José Joaquín Granados y Gálvez, *Tardes Americanas* (1778), pl. 1. Courtesy of the John Carter Brown Library, Brown University.

The documentation available to Boturini in the middle of the century—as well as the increasing interest in documenting Mexican "civilization"—was directly connected to the barbarity-civilization binary, which itself was borne out of attempts to expand the lands and resources of the Spanish Empire, while shrinking the power of alternative configurations of territory such as the altepetl and Kónitsaahii gokíyaa (Apachería).[167] In compiling, documenting, and describing his museum, Boturini made available an archive not of Indigenous history but one of "Indian" history; that is, his archive is structured by the settler colonial struggles over land and sovereignty that led to the creation of a racialized "Indian" identity in New Spain. And by the time the Crown finally called up Boturini's collection—in the 1780s—violence was no longer the Viceroyalty's lone tool for seizing control of territory: thanks to Boturini's efforts in the 1740s, the new weapon was ancient American history.

Transforming Indigenous Knowledges into Settler Forms

Throughout the centuries of colonial expansion, Spain held information about its colonies close.[168] It was Boturini's inventory and a few other eighteenth-century publications—mainly from Mexico City—that finally afforded the non-Spanish world a glimpse of ancient America. Using these, the Scottish historian William Robertson became one of the most important English-language disseminators of Indigenous texts.[169] His *History of America* (1777) drew not only from published accounts and European archives but also descriptions provided by Boturini. Although partial, Robertson's *History* set a standard for using Indigenous-authored materials in European accounts.[170] But, laden with anti-Spanish "Black Legend" tropes, the work unsurprisingly was received unfavorably in Madrid and Mexico City.[171]

In response, the Royal Geographer of the Indies Juan Bautista Muñoz y Ferrandis was tasked with writing a "historiographical defense of Spain and Spanish colonialism."[172] For his new American history, Muñoz asked to see all of Spain's related records. The results laid the basis for what became the Archivo General de Indias in Seville, which continues to serve as the central repository for historians of the Spanish Empire.[173] Muñoz's work spanned the 1780s and 1790s, and he admitted sparing "neither time nor pains, to amass, and digest all the materials that could possibly be collected."[174] When *Historia del Nuevo Mundo* (1793) appeared in English in 1797, Muñoz's translator predicted it would overtake Robertson's *History*, due to Muñoz's unparalleled "access to a vast number of documents and original papers, which lay buried in dust and oblivion, unknown to the Doctor [Robertson], or to anyone else, till our author called them into light and order."[175] Yet much like his rival Robertson, Muñoz also discounted the Indigenously-produced records, preferred Spanish authors, and did little to reclaim ancient America for Spain.[176]

The criollo historian Francisco Javier Clavijero, who lived in New Spain for the first half of his life, also intended to write a new history of America. In Mexico City he consulted the growing "Indian" archive, including Sigüenza's library, still housed at the Colegio de San Pedro y San Pablo. In 1759 Clavijero described its contents as "paintings, containing chiefly the penal laws of Mexicans."[177] He also viewed many of the materials amassed by Boturini which, still impounded, were then held at the Royal and Pontifical University in the viceregal palace.[178] Clavijero was expelled from the continent in 1767 along with his brother Jesuits, and he ended up in the Papal States surrounded by other exiled clerics from Spanish America.[179] Far from the subject matter he had studied for so long, Clavijero turned to Boturini's paper museum to continue his work.[180] Thirteen years later, Clavijero published a four-volume history of ancient Mexican history in Italian, *Storia antica del Messico* (1780).

Unsurprisingly, Clavijero's text drew Spain's instant condemnation, largely for its unauthorized, pro-Indigenous perspective. Like Robertson's *History*, it was banned across the empire, although by 1784 copies of *Storia antica del Messico* appeared in Mexico City. Three years later, an English translation was published in London.[181] There, reviewers portrayed Clavijero's work as a "necessary companion" to Robertson's and "the most correct and probable relation which has been published."[182] Robertson, however, critiqued Clavijero's *Storia* as derivative, claiming that it relied too much on the writings of Franciscan chronicler Fray Juan de Torquemada and Boturini's *Idea*.[183] Yet Robertson's assessment overlooked what Clavijero's text did *differently* from its predecessors: not only did this new narrative of ancient America rely on primary Indigenous sources, it also brought Spanish and Indigenous sources together in a way that gave voice to the latter in explicitly patriotic criollo tones.

Not only had this criollo historian learned to read Indigenous documents—aided by having learned Nahuatl while teaching at Jesuit seminaries—Clavijero even claimed to "have read and examined every publication which has appeared hitherto on the subject."[184] "I have studied many historical paintings of the Mexicans; I have profited from their manuscripts, which I read formerly in Mexico [City]," he recounted.[185] This material came from "histories and memoirs written by the Indians themselves," not from European authors.[186] Clavijero also claimed to have previously "conversed with the Mexicans, whose history I write," which allowed him an intimacy unparalleled by his European counterparts. Histories written by non-Americans, he complained, were riddled with "a thousand blunders in the interpretations, arising from total ignorance of antiquity, and the Mexican [Nahuatl] language."[187] Clavijero's *Storia* aimed to amend the errors of American histories composed without reference to ancient Indigenous pasts.[188] He singled out Robertson for his especial ire, firing back at the Scottish historian's dismissal of Indigenous texts by charging that they were only useless to "those who do not understand the characters and figures of the Mexicans, nor know the method they used to represent things," as texts in English or Spanish would be to those who did not know the language.[189]

Clavijero transformed the narration of American history by applying to it the category of "ancient" (antica), rather than collapsing all preinvasion past into an empty moment awaiting European fulfilment.[190] But of course, as much as Clavijero was an American apologist, and as familiar as he was with Nahua sources, his own understandings were shaped by the "Indian" archive and its structure of settlement. Indeed, Clavijero's entire construction of "ancient Mexico" relied on proving Mexican "civilization" and providing foils of "barbarism." That is to say, Clavijero had to demonstrate not only that Indigenous records were useable as historical documents but also that the documents reflected a high level of social sophistication on the part of their authors. To do so, *Storia* prioritized accounts written by elites of Nahua lineage, emphasizing the noble, reliable, and *alphabetic* origins of much of his information.[191] Evident as it had been to Sigüenza, Gemelli, and Boturini, it was also clear to Clavijero that the Indigenous documents sometimes called "calendar wheels" were proof of Mexica "civilization."[192] But whereas Boturini had narrated the five-age structure of Mexica history in his *Idea* to demonstrate its "excellence," in *Storia* Clavijero explicitly connected the cosmological structure provided by the calendrical and cartographic documents to the history of Mexica settlement.[193] The wheels and books of days also served as evidence of the indios de razóns' transformation; for criollos, explicitly, it proved the significance of the Mexica people whose home they claimed and whose own conversion to Spanish "civitas" perfected their migration to "civilization."

Ultimately, it was Clavijero's ability to produce a chronological, linear narrative from the mapas that made his method so useful to settler historiography. In particular, the migration accounts Clavijero consulted facilitated his plotting of the "Migration of the Mexicans to the country of Anahuac" across space and time in the orthogonal terms of the Spanish Empire.[194] Following Boturini's lead, Clavijero translated the *Codex Boturini*'s toponymic images into the alphabetic place names of ethno-national settlements—Azcapotzalco, Xochimilco, Chalco, etc.—which were also extant Central Mexico cities and neighborhoods, locatable on eighteenth-century maps. Likewise, Mexica chronologies became linear ones. With the help of Sigüenza's *Ciclografía Mexicana*, Clavijero translated the year of departure from Aztlán—Ce Tecpatl or 1 Flint—into the Julian calendar, writing that the "Aztecas or Mexicans . . . lived until about the year 1160 of the vulgar era, in Aztlan, a country situated to the north of the gulf of California, according to what appears from the route they pursued in their migration, and the conclusions made by the Spaniards in their travels towards these countries."[195] The result was a cohesive, chronological migration narrative written in European historiographic and cartographic form.

Clavijero emphasized the importance of the migration framework through his terminology. The word "Azteca" adapts the Nahuatl plural, aztecah (s. aztecl), meaning peoples from Aztlán, the Mexica homeland. Clavijero, however, applies it as a name for all of the different Nahuatl-speaking groups who migrated to Central Mexico in the twelfth century regardless of the national identifiers (Tolteca, Chichimeca, Mexica, etc.) employed in the traditional histories.[196] These tell that when the "Aztecas" arrived in Anáhuac, they were instructed by their patron god Huitzilopochtli to rename themselves "Mextli," denoting their separate ethnicity; later, the Mexica group would split into Tenocha and Tlatelolca factions, founding México-Tenochtitlan and México-Tlatelolco. Yet, in *Storia*, Clavijero uses the terms Mexica(n) and Azteca interchangeably.[197] Clavijero's "ancient Mexicans" were thus synonymous with all of Aztlán's people, who themselves were synonymous with the subjects of the temporally determined "Aztec" political regime (1428–1521), a choice which extinguishes Nahua political and ethnic difference and forecloses a deeper timeline. Moreover, his synonymous use of "Azteca" and "Mexican" for "indio" effectively erased non-Nahuatl-speaking groups from the political category of "Indigenous." Whereas his predecessor Boturini had effectively retained "indio" as a political rather than an ethnic category—i.e., Hnähñu (Otomí), Ñuudzahui (Mixtec), Maya, etc. were all "Indian"—with Clavijero non-Nahua pasts disappeared from ancient history.

Because the archive from which Clavijero worked was primarily comprised of accounts written by Nahua nobility, it was structured to overlook other histories. Clavijero even confessed to "not here mention[ing] those authors who wrote on the antiquity of Michuacan, of Yucatan, of Guatemala, and of New Mexico; because, although many at present believe all these provinces were comprehended in Mexico, they did not belong to the Mexican empire, the history of which we write."[198] Recognizing a popular misunderstanding—that "Mexico" and "New Spain" were synonymous—Clavijero insisted instead on a smaller political territory for "ancient Mexico." In emphasizing the historical context of the terms, however, Clavijero exacerbated the problem: the history of the "Mexican Empire" (Triple Alliance) became the only ancient American history there was. Moreover, by making all "Aztecas" into "Mexicans," Clavijero gave Mexico City's residents—whether Indigenous or criollo—a particular stake in this partial account.[199]

Traveling from Mexico to California

Migration and land was central to criollo historiography in the eighteenth century in part because criollos traced themselves to the first Spanish settlers of New Spain—the "pobladores antiguos" or "old settlers" of 1521—and they saw parallels to their own history in these migration narratives. For Clavijero, tracing the Mexica migration from Aztlán to the Anáhuac Valley was a central concern, key to which was the ability to locate Nahua ancestral landmarks within a geographical framework that Europeans understood.²⁰⁰

Most of the traditional sources pointed northward, but Clavijero, like Boturini, was short on northern Indigenous sources. Even from exile, Clavijero lamented "the furious incursions of the Apachas and other barbarous nations [that] had kept him from investigating any further."²⁰¹ Much like Viceroy Gálvez had seen Apaches as obstacles to the future of New Spain so did Clavijero view alleged indios bárbaros as obstacles to writing Mexica history. Nonetheless, Clavijero managed to plot the migration route through exactly those northern lands the Crown was struggling to take or defend. For Clavijero, as for agents of the Spanish Crown, patriotic progress was as inseparable from Indigenous annihilation as the history of ancient America was inseparable from histories of Indigenous dispossession and struggles over sovereignty.

As Boturini had done almost forty years earlier, Clavijero also turned to Spanish reports of "travels from New Mexico towards the North" to supplement the missing records and geographies.²⁰² These sources included sixteenth-century "charts" as well as writings by Torquemada, Boturini, and Robertson, diaries from Father Kino and a map he made in 1701 that, unconventionally, depicted Baja California as a peninsula rather than an island.²⁰³ Published widely in Europe, Kino's map had great influence on Clavijero's understanding of Pacific geography. Clavijero also referenced Boturini's description of the *Codex Boturini*—which showed "the departure of the Mexicans from the island of *Aztlan* and their arrival at the continent of New Spain, with the dwellings they constructed in each place"—and this source, if not the document itself—informed his attention to the position of rivers, water, and built environment when determining physical locations.²⁰⁴

Clavijero implied that, like the "civilized" people they were, the Aztecas had left permanent structures along the way to Lake Texcoco such as the "Casas Grandes" in the Sonoran desert, noted by Kino in 1694. Indeed, a location marked "Casa Grande" is clearly depicted on Kino's 1701 map of New Mexico—at the banks of the Gila River near areas marked "Sobaipoxis" (O'odham Sobaipuri) and "Apaches"—and located "more than two hundred and fifty miles distant from the city of Chihuahua" on the eastern side of the Gulf of California.²⁰⁵ The constructions there, Clavijero later remarked, were in the style of "the inhabitants of New Mexico," which suggested Puebloan peoples also somehow comprised the Nahua narrative, although Clavijero does not make the connection with descendant peoples clear.²⁰⁶ By Clavijero's time, Casa Grande (Great

House)—today a US national monument within the borders of Arizona—was located closest to the defensive presidio San Felipe y Santiago de Janos, by the 1760s an important anti-Apache campaign base in Chihuahua province.[207] Only five years before Clavijero's *Storia*, Juan Bautista de Anza (later governor of New Mexico) had stopped to measure the Casa Grande ruins on his way to Alta California—amidst Spain's violent war against Apaches—because it had been so widely discussed as a stop on the Mexica migration route.

Clavijero produced the following section of the migration history by locating the narrative on a grid of parallels and meridians, enabling anyone to trace the path across European maps and effectively bringing Mexica history—as well as all of the northern lands—into Hispanic civitas:

> Having passed, therefore, the Red [Colorado] River from beyond the latitude of 35, they proceeded towards the south-east, as far as the river Gila, where they stopped for some time; for at present there are still remains to be seen of the great edifices built by them on the borders of that river. From thence having resumed their course towards the S. S. E. they stopped in about 29 degrees of latitude, at a place which is more than two hundred and fifty miles distant from the city of Chihuahua, towards the N. N. W. This place is known by the name of *Case grandi*, on account of an immense edifice still existing, which, agreeably to the universal tradition of these people, was built by the Mexicans in their peregrination.[208]

Clavijero integrated the spatiality of the mapas within the 1701 map: it provided specific landmarks for the itinerary—the Colorado and Gila Rivers, Chihuahua, "Case Grandi"—as well as standardized distances and precise cardinal and latitudinal directions. His account of the migration continues over Quechan (Yuma), Yoeme (Yaqui), Yoreme (Mayo), Opata, Rarámuri, and O'odham lands, although these peoples are unremarked. Clavijero does narrates the Aztecas' three-year stop at "Huicolhuacan, at present called Culiacan" where the Mexica patron Huitzlipochtli appeared; he also recalls the fissuring of the "seven tribes" at Chicomoztoc, twenty miles south of Zacatecas.[209] At that place Clavijero noted the "remains of an immense edifice" referred to as "La Quémada." This site was supposed by "the ancient inhabitants of that country" to be "the work of the Aztecas in their migration," who from thence crossed the mineral rich altiplano to Tula and on to Anáhuac.[210] Clavijero's entire narrative inscribed ancient Mexica history over most lands then claimed—and under siege—by Spain without giving any mention to the ancestors of Spain's current enemies.

As contests over land and sovereignty with imperial and tribal rivals peaked toward the end of the century, so did criollos' interest in causal chronology and migration, especially those journeys that traced to Aztlán. Not incidentally, tracing the migration route also illustrated that ancient Mexicans—and therefore current-day Nahuas—were not indigenous to the Anáhuac Valley. By then, however, the "Indian" archive already contained all of the materials criollos needed to create a new ancient history for their continent. Boturini's museum had built this "Indian" archive on the grounds of colonial relocation, settlers' wealth-driven curiosity about Aztlán, and both Nahua and settler interest in migration and settlement histories.

As the authorized "monuments" of an enlightened Mexican past were created, organized, and then celebrated by criollos, they became tools for criollo dominance, particularly in the glorification of a civilized "Azteca" past versus a vilified, "barbarous" Indigenous present. That is to say, Boturini's discussion of altepetl origins and Clavijero's mapping of Mexica migration over time and space provided entry points for criollo successors who were more explicitly interested in the imperial dimensions of lands to the north, where nomadic "barbarians" had displaced their civilized predecessors. Following Clavijero, New Spain's next generation of criollos would lay claim to their patria by representing Indigenous peoples either as "pacified" remnants of "ancient" settlers or threatening "barbarians." By creating and controlling the alternative historical monuments from which New Spain's history was written—and authorizing only these—criollos represented their homeland not as a place of insignificant "wild Indians" but one of significant, world-historical value.

In the 1780s and 1790s, as imperial competition between Spain and Britain came to a head with the "Nootka Affair," and with US-Spanish disputes over Mississippi navigation and access to the lands and waters of Florida and Louisiana, New Spain's criollos helped the Crown exert its sovereignty through recourse to Mexica history. Criollos' recourse to history helped the Crown's agents—like Anza or Croix—understand the geography and peoples they attempted to subdue. In establishing further chronological histories, these next historians would emphasize civilizational seriality in their attention to migration: descendants replacing ancestors, migrants replacing locals, empires replacing kingdoms. This sequence disguised settler acts of anti-Indigenous violence as necessary acts of imperial defense.

Conclusion

In 1785, with Spain still interested in securing the Pacific, New Orleans's governor general Esteban Rodríguez Miró proposed holding the Missouri River as the easiest way to ensure Spanish dominance. He sent the Crown a description of regional geography that brought together New Mexico, Quivira, and a place he called "Teguayo"—near Aztlán on the West Coast—which made it seem as if these locations were close to each other and easy to conquer. He explained that by tracing the chain of mountains "that starts from Santa Fe, a little to the east of it and which goes to the province of Quivira"—retracing Oñate's route—the Spanish could reach the Missouri, which flowed "as far as the other chain of mountains which passes between the Colorado River and the province of Teguayo."[211] In other words, from a base at Quivira Spain's forces could line the Missouri west to the Rocky Mountains and on to the Pacific, forming a natural presidial line across almost half of the continent. While his unrealistic geography implies that the Plains, Rockies, and Great Basin were empty and far smaller expanses than they are, it also reveals that Miró's sense of spatiality was, in 1785, still shaped by Mexica migration and the search for Aztlán.

Over two centuries later, Kansans would be shocked to learn that their homelands had been a center of "civilization" at the turn of the last millennium. Thanks to a historical inheritance largely traced to New Spain and Mexico, it has been the US Southwest—not the Midwest—that is consistently identified with "ancient" Indigenous glories in the United States. Yet when the conquistadors arrived on Mogollon, Hohokum, and ancestral Puebloan lands, they imagined them filled with Nahua ancestors. They had envisioned discovering a new México and sought to replace the local indios bárbaros with indios de razón living Spanish lives in Spanish cities. Today, maps of the Four Corners region testify to that enduring history, with places named "Aztec Ruins" in New Mexico or "Montezuma Castle" in Arizona. That there is also a Montezuma, New York, and a Toltec, Arkansas signals that British and US creoles too came to understand Indigenous history in terms of "ancient Mexico."

CHAPTER 2

Storied Lands of the Old West

*In the beginning, some say the Choctaw people
came up out of the mound at Nanih Waiya singing....*
Issa hal-a-li haa-toko Ik-sa illok isha shkee
Because you are holding onto me I am not dead yet.

—LeAnne Howe, "Homeland," 2014

IN 1790 MASSACHUSETTS HISTORIAN Jeremy Belknap sent a letter to the *American Museum*—Matthew Carey's popular Philadelphia magazine—in an attempt to account for the origins of America's Indigenous populations.[1] Belknap disagreed with environmental determinists like the French naturalist Buffon, who believed that regional climate rather than migration and ancestry accounted for global diversity.[2] Buffon reasoned that if the people of Mexico and Peru "reckon[ed] only two or three hundred years from the time that they were first assembled together" then the Americas could not be much older, sparking the transatlantic debate over continental superiority known as the "querelle d'Amérique."[3] Belknap's letter signaled his partial agreement that America's "population may be more recent" than Europe's, but also challenged Buffon's chronology by introducing the "Toltecas," who according to "the late historian of Mexico, abbé Clavi[j]ero" had arrived in Mexico around 650 CE. Thus, even if it was younger than the Old World, Belknap's homeland nonetheless held over a millennium of history. Belknap's reliance on the timeline of criollo historian Francisco Javier Clavijero reveals his true purpose: not to quarrel over chronology but instead to insist that marking the difference between "those celebrated empires" of Mexico and Peru and "the wild wanderers in the more northern regions of this vast continent" was crucial to understanding the continent's past.[4]

Like much of his hemispheric cohort, Belknap supported the idea that America's Indigenous peoples had originated elsewhere—"the desarts of Tartary" in Siberia or among the Pacific islands—a collection of ideas known as the "Asiatic origins" hypothesis. Indeed, by the late eighteenth century, most Atlantic scholars assumed America's indigenes had originated in "Asia," a capacious geography that ranged from northern Africa and the Holy Lands to Turkey, Russia, and China. But by drawing on Clavijero's work, Belknap located the ancestral Toltecs (whose descendants went south to Mexico and Peru) in *east* Asia, whereas northern Indigenous peoples' ancestors came from "the immense forests of the northern parts of Asia."[5] This distinction implied that southern and northern American peoples were *completely* different from one another—not due to time, climate, continental novelty, or other conditions of racial mutability—but because the populations belonged to different geographically-fixed "stocks."[6] Thus Belknap found his answer to human variety—adapted from the practice of animal husbandry and continental race theory—in migration.[7] While accounting for differences in the "degree of improvement" of America's peoples had long perplexed settlers, in the 1780s and 1790s criollo writings on migration such as Clavijero's cleared the way for accounts of American antiquity in the United States.[8]

In the same issue of the *American Museum*, the lexicographer Noah Webster addressed a different question of origins: those of the curious "fortifications" in the Ohio Valley.[9] As missionaries and traders increasingly crossed the "Endless Mountains" in the second half of the eighteenth century, accounts of the earthworks there had made their way to ears and eyes back east. In 1772, Presbyterian missionary David McClure had noted a "Tumulus about 12 feet high, in the form of a Pyramid, I saw at Logs town [Shawnee-Seneca-Lenape town of Chiningue], which was once the seat of Indians."[10] McClure guessed that the several "fortifications" on the Muskingum River "were built from defense," but noted little to betray "much knowledge of architecture or civilization" locally.[11] Three years later, the English trader Nicholas Cresswell visited a sixty-foot-tall mound near "Grave Creek," named after the local "Indians' tradition" of a great battle in which many had been killed, the immense "Grave" allegedly "raised to perpetuate their memory."[12] Like McClure and Cresswell, many eighteenth-century travelers and traders located the earthworks' origins in defensive architecture, made—as Cresswell supposed—by "a race of people superior in military knowledge to the present Indians."[13] Consistently termed "antiquities" by the 1780s, theories about the earthworks' origins and purposes abounded.[14]

In the *American Museum*, Webster—who formerly believed the mounds to have been made by Hernando de Soto during his 1539–1542 entrada—announced a revision of this Spanish hypothesis in light of ancient Mexican history. Writing "that the Southern Indians, in Mexico and Peru, are descended from the Carthaginians or other Mediterranean nations, who found their way to the continent at a very early period," Webster suggested the earthworks were constructed for protection when their homelands were invaded by "Northern Indian" newcomers. In "the contest between these different tribes or races of men," Webster explained, the intruders drove "the more ancient settlers from their territory" and left the mounds as witness to the usurpation.[15] For Webster, earthworks were the archives, but migration provided the means to interpret them as records of a mound-building "race."

Criollo historians provided the method by which US nationalist historians such as Webster and Belknap could narrate ancient American history, which confirmed what US settlers thought they already knew: that the builders of the earthworks were the same "Southern Indians" who had made the Mexican mapas, but they were *different* from existing Native populations in the north. While nationalists proposed both migration and stadial acculturation to account for this vanished population, Mexican migration narratives were especially useful because they established a procession of settlement (Toltec, Chichimec, Mexica, etc.) that also helped US nationalists conceptualize northern migration in terms of seriality.[16] By compiling criollo histories alongside interpretations of earthworks and northern Indigenous traditions of migration, US nationalists—like Belknap, Webster, Thomas Jefferson, and Benjamin Smith Barton—constructed an "Indian" archive of their nation's own: the "Moundbuilder myth."[17] The early imprint of this myth is traceable in Barton's *Observations on Some Parts of Natural History* (1787), which demonstrates how criollo and Spanish American scholarship on Mexica chronology offered methods for examining Indigenous history—accounting for population movement, population size, and, potentially, population demise—in a way that helped US settlers explain earthworks to their own advantage.

Moreover, US settlers found that this new, sequential American history was useful in stabilizing their fragile land claims. Assertions of relative "priority" on the land were forwarded through the creation of imaginative accounts that—explicitly or not—delegitimized Native aboriginal claims, a process that White Earth Ojibwe historian Jean O'Brien has in other contexts called "firsting."[18] Layered overtop the well-documented ideology of "vanishing"—the idea that contemporary Native peoples were destined to "vanish" in the face of colonization—"firsting" finds one of its most recognizable expressions in the Moundbuilder myth, which attempts to establish juridical as well as moral justifications for the settler occupation of North America.[19] These histories are enabled by and reinforce the ideology of serial occupation, a historiographical technique that strategically undermines Indigenous peoples' "aboriginal title."[20] In the nineteenth century, those origin theories that depended on seriality—spread as Moundbuilder myth—would become authoritative, self-evident historical expressions of what literary scholar Mark Rifkin has called "settler common sense."[21]

Almost every Moundbuilder account centers the alleged disappearance—whether killed or chased away—of the mound-building peoples and their absolute lack of descendants. Over the span of a century the origins of the Moundbuilder "race" changed: Barton, in 1787, believed they were Viking-descended "Toltecs." For Belknap, the Moundbuilders were a "race" of people whose ancestors had originated in the "East"—China or Japan—and moved through the Mississippi Valley on their way to Mexico. Webster, who first believed the Moundbuilders were Spanish conquistadors, later changed his mind to propose a Carthaginian origin instead. Others suggested Malaysians, Israelites, and Lamanites.[22] Notwithstanding identity, the mythology's basic structure—in which aboriginal mound-building people were racially distinct from and antecedent to contemporary Natives—remained intact into the twentieth century. This process of conjuring an imaginary Moundbuilder race as different from, superior to, and *previous to* America's Indigenous peoples was a strategy for dominating and displacing Indigenous peoples and polities in the service of securing a future for the United States.[23] It likewise partakes of larger discursive processes to produce racially homogenous—and theoretically more governable—populations in the eighteenth century, such as the consolidation of the category "Indian."[24]

In the chapter that follows, I trace eighteenth-century US nationalists' misappropriation of Nahua history via criollo accounts of the Mexica past—especially accounts of serial and racialized migration—to construct an ancient history for the United States. As in New Spain, settlers in the United States learned to deploy "American antiquity" to claim American pride and property. Land speculators eager to lure investment for western land ventures used "antiquities" as a marketing strategy to line their pockets.[25] To the landed and moneyed creole elite, the earthworks represented potential arms with which to battle European chauvinists.[26] Eighteenth-century writings by McClure, Cresswell, Barton, Webster, Belknap and others exemplify the structure of settlement comprising the "Indian" archive in the US, one formed by men engaged in war, prospecting, evangelizing and, especially, negating Indigenous sovereignty and transforming Indigenous homelands into wealth-producing property.[27]

Like the Spanish visions of golden cities, many settler versions of ancient American history were informed—or misinformed—by Indigenous traditions and perspectives. Indeed, in the early United States, the misappropriation of Indigenous traditions and the perpetuation of Moundbuilder mythology went a long way to naturalize and support the US-led campaigns of deprivation, dispossession, and terror already underway in Native communities east of the Mississippi.[28] But this chapter also suggests that Moundbuilder mythology came not only from Indigenous imaginaries and scientific discourse—derived from transatlantic ideological struggles over the historical "value" of the New World—but also emerged from the context of stolen land and labor guised as the "right to happiness."[29] The economic, demographic, and administrative precariousness of the early US republic—with its contemporary inter-imperial rivalries with Spain and powerful Native polities—highlight the practicality of "antiquity" as a political as well as intellectual instrument to ensure settler national success.[30] The Moundbuilder myth is a cultural trace of the work of settler statecraft, its technologies of historical reconstruction migrating from New Spain to the United States.

Creating Moundbuilder Monuments

Just as Clavijero used his understanding of Mexica history as a rhetorical weapon against European chauvinism, settlers in the United States wished to do the same. They, however, valued the "Indian" materials around them much less than Clavijero had valued Nahua documents. Many, like American Academy of Arts and Sciences' president James Bowdoin, believed "it would be in vain to search among them [Native peoples] for antiquities."[31] And, unlike in New Spain, settlers in the US seldom recognized Native-authored historical sources as such. When they did, say, witness wampum protocols, colored poles, or bark inscriptions, they saw them as nothing more than aides-mémoires. In a now well-known passage of his *Notes on the State of Virginia* (1787), Thomas Jefferson professed to "know of no such thing existing as an Indian monument: for I would not honour with that name arrow points, stone hatchets, stone pipes, and half-shapen images."[32] For Jefferson's part, it is not that he doubted the existence of "Indian monument[s]" per se—as in tombs or commemorative structures—but instead that he assumed Indigenous peoples, lacking "civilization," could not exhibit the labor and social organization of "advanced society." To Jefferson, "civilized" peoples left complex traces of their presence. Hatchets and pipes were everyday objects, not monumental structures befitting history. Moreover, those few US settlers who did believe Native peoples maintained historical monuments usually doubted their reliability. Irish trader James Adair, for example, suspected the imprint of "the innovating superstitious ignorance of the popish priests" on the Chickasaw traditions he learned.[33]

But earthworks—"the Barrows, of which many are to be found all over this country"—were something else.³⁴ To Jefferson, barrows *were* monuments "[o]f labor on the large scale."³⁵ Others, like the botanist William Bartram—who in the 1770s witnessed earthen architecture across Cherokee, Creek, and Seminole countries—also saw in the mounds "many very magnificent monuments of the power and industry of the ancient inhabitants of these lands."³⁶ *The Columbian Magazine* from July 1789, for example, proclaimed the western earthworks were evidence that "this country was once inhabited by a civilized and martial people."³⁷ Likewise, in 1791, US Army officer and western settler Jonathan Heart concluded that the Moundbuilders were evidently "not altogether in a state of uncivilization," for to have been "made to contribute to the carrying on [of] such stupendous works," he reasoned, they "must have been under the subordination of law, a strict and well-governed police."³⁸ That mounds were the monuments of a once great—and necessarily agrarian, heroic, and hierarchical—civilization became, by the late 1780s, the most popular interpretation. Yet with (supposedly) no record of such civilizations, earthworks disrupted settlers' reigning philosophies of world history. US savants found the idea that contemporary Native peoples had constructed the earthworks unthinkable: their assumptions about the hierarchy of civilizations meant that permanent structures (signs of agriculture and commercialism) and Native peoples *could not* match. Thus, inventing a more "advanced" people—the Moundbuilders—not only upheld the priority of settler land claims but also kept the Enlightenment episteme intact.³⁹

One of the most influential structures for understanding human history at the time, based on the theorizations of Scottish philosophers, was that of stadialism. This theory held that all the world's peoples progressed through successively organized stages of society. According to economist Adam Smith, people were first hunters, then shepherds, farmers, and finally commercial actors.⁴⁰ Scottish stadialists believed all populations capable of progressing toward "civilization," but equally they were all liable to regress toward "barbarism." A peoples' civilizational "stage" was also indicated by the lack (barbarity) or presence (civilization) of permanent, human-made structures, the latter allegedly signifying a level of prosperity enabled by a "mastery" over nature.⁴¹ As in most iterations of stadial theory, Smith placed significant emphasis on "nomadic" (the first two stages) versus "sedentary" (the latter two) subsistence, meaning that civilizational mobility was tied directly to a society's mode of food procurement and exchange. In most scholarly accounts, stadialism has been used to explain extra-Americas origins hypotheses.

Scholars in the continent's northern stretches, influenced by their Spanish counterparts—especially José de Acosta and Bartolomé de las Casas—similarly placed Indigenous origins across the Atlantic or Pacific.[42] The latter, termed the "Asiatic origins" hypothesis, was ubiquitous in late eighteenth-century criollo work including Boturini's and Clavijero's writings as well as northern travelers' reports.[43] The British traveler Jonathan Carver, for example, found the "suggestion that the continent was first peopled from Siberia to be the most convincing hypothesis."[44] After British captain James Cook's transpacific voyages (1768–1779), new maps emphasized the physical proximity of the two continents, casting geography itself in support of America's Asian origins. Moreover, contemporary scholarship on the customs and languages of Mongolia, Manchuria, Turkestan, and Siberia—"Great Tartary"—especially by Orientalists William Jones and Peter Simon Pallas seemed to provide further corroboration. By the 1780s, the idea that the original "Americans" had migrated from Asia—probably across "Bhering's Straits"—was the prevailing explanation for the original peopling of the New World.[45]

Searching for American Autochthones

The "Asiatic origins" hypothesis reveals that US conversations of originality, race, and migration at the end of the eighteenth century revolved not around autochthony—true human origination—but instead around *aboriginality*, which was a matter of priority in succession. Although "aborigine"—like "indigenous" and "native"—eventually came to designate the pre-invasion populations of the Americas, *priority* of occupancy does not imply absolute *origin*.[46] According to the Book of Genesis, all humanity originated with Adam and Eve, the two first people who had been formed from the earth by God. After the great Deluge all humanity was limited to Noah's line, and with the fall of the Tower of Babel Noah's descendants were scattered across the earth. That is to say, the assertion that a population was "aboriginal"—"ab origine" or "from the beginning"—did not mean they had "sprung up" ex nihilo but instead that they were the "first inhabitants" of a vacant, postdiluvian landscape.[47] In English, the word was first used to designate the peoples coming from Latium (Rome) and extended to refer to any location's earliest populations (as documented by Christians). These peoples were considered to hold the location's "aboriginal title," a legal construct in British colonial and then US national law.[48]

Atlantic science, like law, was also structured on this Mosaic narrative of monogenesis: i.e., that all peoples were issue of Eden's clay. If America's indigenes were aborigines rather than migrants they could not be part of the Adamic family, which would contradict the ontological frame of Judeo-Christian scripture. It implies the creation of multiple pairs of humans across the globe, a heterodoxy that became commonplace in later nineteenth-century US race thinking—especially among slavery's apologists—but enjoyed little support before the century's turn.[49] Believing that they were "in strict language the aborigines of the soil," therefore, was a heresy only a minority—like Voltaire, Montesquieu, and Hume—entertained.[50] Skirting the scriptural challenge, criollo scholarship on Mexica origins and Indigenous migration provided US nationalist historians the means to establish America's Natives as immigrants, not autochthones, a process Chickasaw literary critic Jodi Byrd has termed "originary racialization" because it established "race" based on supposed foreign origin.[51] Indeed, an important strain of race thinking in the late eighteenth-century United States emphasized a fixed, continent-based theory of racialization supported by Linnaeus's *Systema naturae* (1735), Blumenbach's anatomical studies, and Lord Kames's *Sketches on the History of Man* (1774), which sought to document race as species-level difference across human beings.[52]

While seemingly not a debate about settler land claims, debates over methods of natural history, especially the practice of taxonomy—which classified organisms according to hierarchies of relation—were closely related to discussions of American antiquity.[53] The Linnaean language of genus and species was particularly helpful, as when some plants and animals were designated as "native" or "indigenous" species in contrast to those imported from their own "native countries." This enabled Atlantic scholars to imagine the relationship of population to location and thus explain human diversity as fixed according to geography rather than transformed by forces such as the environment (often also linked to geography).[54] Indeed, as demonstrated by Belknap's letter, continental migration waves were key to the ways in which race was beginning to be conceived in the United States.[55]

While stadialism was largely compatible with ideas about Asian origins, it makes an uncomfortable fit with the Moundbuilder myth.[56] Consider, for example, when Jefferson wrote of an "immoveable veil" of Blackness that was "fixed in nature" in his *Notes on the State of Virginia*.[57] Although he also wrote—in the same passage—of an assimilationist admiration for the "fine mixtures of red and white," this strongly essentialist Black-white racial binary essentially rejects the kind of racial mutability proposed, at least theoretically, by stadialism.[58] Moundbuilder narratives of serial migration relying on "Asiatic origins" therefore reveal the beginnings of a mode of race thinking, in operation from the settler nation's earliest days, that would later come to be called "scientific racism." The hypothesis itself—not the same as stadialism, although borrowing from it—is an expression of an emergent racial philosophy that anchored settler-nationalist historiography.

Today more commonly called the "Land Bridge" thesis, in the eighteenth and nineteenth centuries the Asian origins hypothesis mapped onto fantasies of inevitable continental domination: connecting the continent's Indigenous residents to Asia shortened the distance from Philadelphia to the Pacific, while also laying claim to all the land in between.[59] Moreover, this hypothesis became the most convincing explanation for the peopling of the Americas because it strengthened the argument for *racialized* migration. Its point was not necessarily to prove "Behring Strait" or even Atlantean narratives, but instead to deploy serial migration as a mechanism through which to create—through the guise of explanation—racial difference.

Most Americanist scholarship has acknowledged the influence of continental racial theory and Linnaean classification but also assumes that US naturalists employed a stadialist understanding of human history in the eighteenth century that was then supplanted by scientific racialism in the nineteenth century.[60] But in the United States, the interpretation of absolute (racial)—rather than relative (civilizational)—difference between the Moundbuilders and contemporary Native peoples betrays a significant divergence of late-eighteenth-century racial thinking in the United States from that of the rest of the Atlantic world. The narratives that eighteenth-century US nationalists created about earthworks and Moundbuilders both relied on and produced a model of historical change that posited unidirectional, linear succession. Theirs was not a question of one population *transforming* into another (now called "coalescence" or "ethnogenesis"), but rather one of usurpation and serial replacement.

Surveying Land and Securing Property

When representatives from the new US government negotiated peace in Paris after the war with Britain no Indigenous delegates were invited, even though Native nations had served as allies on both sides. With the 1783 treaty, Britain signed over the territory it had promised to maintain as a perpetual "Indian Reserve," the boundary for which—known as the Royal Proclamation Line—roughly ran along the chain of the Appalachians. In exchange for the recognition of US independence and sovereignty, the new nation agreed to repay private British debts, creating even more of a financial strain on the already struggling republic. One solution was to raise revenue by transforming the formerly reserved lands into real estate.[61] Land was property—or more properly, credit—abstract and valuable. In March 1784, Jefferson debuted his proposal for the temporary governance of the entire "Western territory," revealing that the nationalists had no intentions of sticking to the former British-Native boundaries. When Virginian Arthur Lee was offered a position as a commissioner to treat with Native nations he knew it was an important charge because "The only adequate fund I can conceve for the payment of our debts, are our western Lands."[62] Along with general Richard Butler, Lee headed to Fort Stanwix, New York in 1784, with instructions to "secure a large purchase from the Indian Nations."[63] Butler had gained experience negotiating with Lenape and Shawnee representatives during the war, and Lee had previously been a diplomat in France. Lee was also a member of the Continental Congress's committee on Indian affairs tasked with studying western land policy.[64] At the treaty council's conclusion in late 1784, Lee reported to Washington his hopes that "the laying off of that [Ohio] country may commence in the Spring" with increased US fortunes to follow.[65]

During the negotiations, the commissioners insisted the Six Nations cede lands north and west of the old British line. This resulted in a new US-Native border running from Oswego on Lake Ontario to northern Pennsylvania—including "the carrying place & the fort of Niagara," which was crucial to US transport, trade, and security—and down the Ohio River.[66] Even though the Ohio River would become the new border, the United States still asserted preemptive rights to the huge swath of Indigenous home and hunting lands northwest of the Ohio River, lands that Jefferson and others had already made plans to divide with the Land Ordinance of 1784.[67] For the negotiations, Jefferson suggested Native nations be "induced to part with" these western lands, encouraging the US agents to use coercive tactics if necessary.[68] While the commissioners treated with the Six Nations first in seeming recognition of the confederacy's lasting diplomatic influence, the 1784 treaty at Fort Stanwix also followed another of Jefferson's specific instructions: "to treat with every tribe at different times and places" so as to divide them against one other.[69] Indeed, Butler and Lee had been instructed to "countenance every disposition in any one of the six nations to treat and act separately and independently of their confederacy," although ultimately the Longhouse stayed united.[70] Recognizing the new nation's still fragile position, Jefferson moreover warned the commissioners against gathering multiple nations together because such meetings had "a tendency to generate combinations for the purposes of war." The United States was concerned with weakening, not facilitating, Native confederacies.

Following their instructions, commissioners Lee and Butler traveled to the Ohio country from New York through the newly "opened" Pennsylvania backcountry to the former Lenape village of Saukunk—at the confluence of the Ohio and Beaver Rivers—where they planned to hold a council under the protection of the federal army.⁷¹ Backed by rifles and bayonets, Lee, Butler, and notorious "Indian fighter" George Rogers Clark—who was the "Principal Surveyor of Bounty Lands"—met with "Sachems and Warriors of the Wiandot, Delaware, Chippawa and Ottawa Nations" at Fort McIntosh to propose restoring the status quo ante bellum in exchange for their homelands east of the Cuyahoga River and south of a line drawn across to Fort Pickawillany (near the current-day Ohio-Indiana border) on the Miami River.⁷²

Next, the commissioners invited the Shawnees to a separate treaty council "for the double purpose of procuring peace and extinguishing rights to the territory lying between the Great Miami & the Missisippi."⁷³ When Butler, Clark, and General Samuel Holden Parsons (replacing Lee) went to Fort Finney—at the mouth of the Great Miami, not far from what is currently Cincinnati—they were accompanied by a sizeable Wyandot and Lenape contingent, a sign of their new alliance.⁷⁴ The Shawnees, however, rejected the US proposals and excoriated the commissioners for their divisive tactics, writing that they "ought to know this is not the way to make good on lasting peace, to take our Chiefs prisoners, and come with Soldiers at your backs."⁷⁵ They allegedly presented a strand of black wampum, protocol for war. Destroying it, Butler retorted: "this country belongs to the United States—their blood hath defended it and will forever protect it."⁷⁶ Under clear threat of violence, the assembled Shawnee representatives eventually signed, "acknowledge[ing] the US to be the sole and absolute sovereigns of all the territory ceded to them by the Treaty of Peace." The so-called peace stripped Shawnees of their Scioto and Ohio River valley lands and "assigned" them territory in what is currently Indiana, shared with their Miami neighbors.⁷⁷

In May of 1785 Congress formally adopted the new Land Ordinance to turn the millions of legally vacated acres into national funds.⁷⁸ Initially there had been the question of how to sell land few US purchasers had ever seen and some brokers never would. The answer was provided by geographer Thomas Hutchins, who with triangulation, a surveyor's plumb, and Gunter's chains would grid the territory into a regularized system of square-mile lots. An improvement on the British system of metes and bounds—which required intimate knowledge of the landscape—Hutchins's orthogonal system could be externally imposed by people who knew little of the land and, importantly, purchased by those knowing nothing more than an assigned number. The area ceded at Fort McIntosh would comprise the first sets of north-south ranges or "townships," standardized into thirty-six units of one-square-mile lots (640 acres).⁷⁹ To implement Hutchins's system, however, the lands had to be surveyed to set meridians—baselines—for the grid. This initial stage of the first Public Land Survey was set to begin with the first seven ranges in the fall of 1785.[80]

In October of 1785 the First American Regiment, guided by Lieutenant Colonel Josiah Harmar, moved away from their former headquarters at Fort McIntosh to new quarters at the confluence of the Muskingum and Ohio Rivers. The new position was even more advantageous: the Ohio was the vital riverway to points east and west while the Muskingum led to Lenape towns upriver and after a short portage to the Cuyahoga River with its important intertribal settlements and trading post on Lake Erie.[81] Moreover, just across the Muskingum River sat a complex of earthworks later described by Philadelphia naturalist Benjamin Smith Barton as "remarkable remains"; it was at this same strategic juncture that federal troops constructed the stockade that would later bear Harmar's name.[82] Supposedly built to surveil squatters and enforce the Ohio River boundary, the new fort also reassured settlers and encouraged immigration.

The Ohio Company of Associates, comprised of Revolutionary War veterans and members of the Society of the Cincinnati, was founded in March 1786 by General Rufus Putnam, Brigidier General Benjamin Tupper—both of whom assisted Hutchins with the Seven Ranges survey—Reverend Manasseh Cutler, Samuel Holden Parsons, and Winthrop Sargent.[83] As the survey was nearing completion in 1787 the company made a contract to purchase 1.5 million acres of Ohio lands adjacent to those first seven ranges. The following year the Ohio Company built the town of Marietta on those lands, their site located just across the Muskingum River from Fort Harmar.[84] Naming their new town "Marietta," in recognition of the French queen's support for the American War, the company's members symbolically wrote the most historic moment of their own lives—the Revolutionary War—over a place already covered by "mounds, not natural, but made by the hand of man."[85] Fittingly Marietta, the United States' first official civilian outpost in the occupied territory northwest of the Ohio, took over the earthworks there as well.

Mapping Ohio Antiquity

One of the many settler-colonial ideological constructions that encouraged the gradual usurpation of Native land was the conviction that the area across the river—the Ohio country—was largely empty.[86] Texts such as Lewis Evans's influential 1755 map and pamphlet—which described the area of "the Ohio and its Branches" as formerly occupied by the "Erigas," of whom "the far greater part have been extirpated, some incorporated into the Seneca, and the rest retired beyond the woodless plains over the Mississippi"—imparted the sense of shifting, impermanent populations.⁸⁷ Popular renditions of "Indian traditions" detailing great battles and rumors of "extirpated" races reinforced the idea of Ohio lands emptied by war and scarcity. The belief that the word "Kentucky" translated as "Dark and Bloody Ground"—claimed by Daniel Boone and popularized by John Filson's *The Discovery, Settlement and Present State of Kentucke* (1784)—furthered terra nullius convictions.⁸⁸ This ideology of an empty country was powerful, as were the narratives that supported it: for every account of warfare further naturalized the appearance of new forts, the symbol of settler primacy on the land.

Settlers tended to encounter earthworks located at strategic sites such as confluences, bluffs, and portages, and thus their accounts almost always portrayed earthworks as fortresses and redoubts. Only occasionally were they pictured as property markers, outlooks, or astronomical observatories. In fact, almost every settler who looked at the earthworks saw war. Trader James Adair, for example, saw in earthworks military "breastworks" and "forts of security against an enemy."⁸⁹ Missionary David Jones, who visited Shawnee villages along the Scioto in 1772–1773, surmised that the ancient inhabitants had erected the earthworks as their defensive "denier resorts" in times of war.⁹⁰ Similarly Reverend David McClure, noting a "large Indian fortification" near Ligonier, Pennsylvania, in January 1773, wrote of learning from "an Indian, Joseph Wapee, who informed me, that the forts in the Ohio country were places of retreat and defense, made by the ancient inhabitants, against the Catawbas. This probably he received by tradition from his ancestors."⁹¹ The tradition that Wapee—a Christian Lenape man—transmitted to McClure likely reflected ancestral accounts learned further east as well as those Wapee had heard since his community moved to the war-torn region. In 1775, Moravian missionary David Zeisberger recorded a similar hypothesis: "Long ago, perhaps more than a century ago, Indians must have lived here . . . who fortified themselves against the attack of their enemies . . . no one knows to what nation these Indians belonged; it is plain, however, that they were a warlike race."⁹² These accounts of the landscapes of war were overwhelmingly written by missionaries, surveyors, speculators, or military men, almost all of whom were located in the western country because of the war over land.

Although some observers like missionary David Zeisberger allowed that the earthworks may have been built by the ancestors of contemporary Indigenous peoples, most did not. When surveyor John Filson identified "several ancient remains in Kentucke" in the 1780s, he interpreted the alleged fortifications as proof that "this country was formerly inhabited by a people different from the present Indians."⁹³ Filson was also careful to note that it was "well known, that no Indian nation has ever practiced the method of defending themselves by entrenchments."⁹⁴ These settlers' martial earthworks interpretations were not just rhetorical: these men *were* militarizing the landscape and engaging in warfare. And even if the identity of the earthworks' artisans was ambiguous, the lesson was always the same: the lands had been conquered once and therefore could be conquered again.

In 1775 Boston's *Royal American Magazine* printed Jones's report of "an old FORT and INTRENCHMENT in the Shawnaese country" along with an engraved "Plan" which, in identifying a "circular parapet and ditch, surrounding a pyramid of earth," illustrated his imagined scene of constant war.⁹⁵ The circular stockade, Jones proposed, "might probably be the place where the Indians put their provisions . . . in time of danger, or their women and children in the time of an engagement." The square form he described as a fort was protected by regular gates and an "eminence of 4 or 5 feet high, upon which appears to have stood a castle."⁹⁶ Jones remarked that the earthworks "are not all built alike, for some are circular, some in the form of a half moon, and others square," but that the "present Indian inhabitants were not the builders, and they can give us no satisfactory account who were."⁹⁷ His diagram is one of the first sources from which US readers learned how earthworks looked and how to see them as the ruins of war.

Draining the Common Pot

In 1785, nineteen-year-old Benjamin Smith Barton journeyed with Thomas Hutchins's Seven Ranges surveying party, which comprised Barton's uncle the astronomer David Rittenhouse and additional surveyors Winthrop Sargent, Andrew Ellicott, and Ellicot's son Joseph.⁹⁸ In late summer, retracing the path of Seven Years' and Revolutionary War fighters, the party descended the river from Redstone to Fort Pitt and then traveled about thirty miles down the Ohio past the Beaver River—where Fort McIntosh was located—to Little Beaver Creek, where the Pennsylvania state line met the Ohio River. Their survey began there on September 30, 1785, but the team's work was suspended a little over a week later due to the "threat of Indian hostility" on the Tuscarawas River, fifty miles away.⁹⁹ Rittenhouse immediately turned back, missing any opportunity to examine the landscape's earthworks for their connection to the heavens; his nephew Barton, however, set out on a tour with Joseph Ellicott.

The pair first headed to "Cayahoga-town," the Wyandot and Moravian Lenape village near Lake Erie, and while there he noted seeing "a number of circular, and irregular tumuli."[100] Barton had become attuned to earthworks even before reaching Cuyahoga. In fact, Barton noted the presence of "ancient works" all along the way.[101] At the "Red-Stone Settlement" on the Monongahela River, for example, he saw "mounts, or tumuli, or different heights" and recorded that there, "and, indeed, in many other parts of this western country, there have . . . been discovered a considerable number of artificial earthen walls, which are commonly known by the name of Indian Fortifications."[102] From Lake Erie Barton and Ellicott headed along "the Cayohoga-path" to Kuskusky, "or more properly, the remains of an Indian town, of that name."[103] This was the old Lenape town on the Beaver River that had been destroyed 1778, its few residents—mostly women and children—killed by US forces. The recentness of violence and mourning were written onto and into the land; however, Barton failed to connect this recent history to his observations of earthworks and other ceremonial elements of the landscape he witnessed on his trip. From Kuskusky he returned to Fort Pitt and then crossed his home state to arrive back in Philadelphia in late 1785.

THE TERRITORY THROUGH which Barton and Ellicott passed long served as refuge to migrants pushed from greater Anishinaabewaki, Lenapehoking, Wendake, as well as Haudenosaunee and Chesapeake lands by Indigenous warfare in the seventeenth century and the settler wars of the long eighteenth.[104] That Barton recorded in his journal seeing "nine Indians" at Cuyahoga Town in 1785, however, implies that the area's Native residents had otherwise kept their distance on preceding legs of the trip.[105] During this time of constant war, Native communities leveraged their intimate knowledge of the land—its swamps and prairies, its lookouts, limestone overhangs, and hidden water-crossings—to keep themselves out of settler sights.[106] This strategy, however, often reinforced settler assumptions that the country was empty. But the large number of British forts there—many of which US forces later took over—belie claims that these lands were vacant.

Already by the late seventeenth century, Council of Three Fires (comprising Ojibwe, Odawa, Potawatomi), Michi Saagiig (Mississauga), and Wyandot peoples were living south of Lakes Erie and Michigan, escaping colonialism-fueled wars to the north. Shawnees—who knew lands north and south of the Ohio as home and hunting grounds—had begun returning to the Ohio Valley by the 1730s.[107] By the mid-eighteenth century, Ohio's waterways were also host to Lenape, Mahican, Myaamia (Miami) and Haudenosaunee groups as well as a small number of Mvskoke (Creek), Cherokee, and other Eastern kin. Near the French trading post at current-day Cleveland in the 1740s, for example, lived a multiethnic population of Anishinaabeg, Haudenosaunee, and Wabanaki relatives.[108] Indeed, by the time Lewis Evans published his 1755 map detailing the vanished "Erigas"—as well as the "present, late, and ancient Seats of the original Inhabitants"—Ohio lands and waterways were important centers of returning extended kin and interethnic communities; the mix of peoples also included settler captives and adoptees.[109]

In the 1750s, French and Anishinaabe attacks at the Miami village of Pickwaawilenionki, or Fort Pickawillany, presaged the violence and divisiveness of the Seven Years' War.[110] Much of the conflict was rooted in the struggle to control Ohio lands. And unlike predominantly French habitants (settlers) farther west, British settlers—especially Virginians—were largely anti-Indigenous separatists.[111] In 1763, an anti-settler uprising led by the Odawa leader Pontiac—following the Lenape prophet Neolin—triggered a punitive anti-Indigenous campaign along the Ohio, Muskingum, and Tuscarawas Rivers by British forces.[112] After the vigilante Paxton Boys killed twenty Susquehannock (Conestoga) people in Conestoga and Lancaster, Pennsylvania in 1763, survivors sought asylum with Seneca, Cayuga, and other fellow Iroquoian-speakers already living in Ohio, ultimately forming a coalescent people often referred to as "Mingo" or Ohio Seneca.[113]

In the 1770s, Moravian Lenapes from along the Siskuwahënèk or Susquehanna—as well as neighbor Susquehannock, Minsi Lenape, Shawnee, and Mahican groups—resettled along the Beaver River in western Pennsylvania and the Muskingum and Tuscarawas farther west.[114] Some joined Shawnee kin along the Scioto River and others went to live with Wyandot relatives near Lake Erie. Facing pressure from the north and east, many Inoka (Illinois) groups—a loose confederation of allied and related peoples including Miamis, Peorias, Kaskaskias, and Cahokias—joined with their relations down the Mississippi, while some consolidated in what is currently Indiana and Illinois.[115] Further south—in the spatiotemporal region now called the "Mississippian Shatter Zone"—Chickasaw, Creek, Choctaw, and Natchez peoples coalesced and regrouped their communities even as French, British, and Spanish settlers pressed ever nearer.[116] Indeed, the series of European imperial shifts in the region—from Spanish and French to British, Spanish, and American—saw concomitant changes in Native confederacies, loyalties, and mobility patterns as well. In the eighteenth century the western country was a crucible fired by colonization, disease, ecological change, and inter-imperial warfare; the results were populations who adapted, some by moving and some by staying in place, even if their presence was not always registered by settlers.[117]

Yet many settlers knew to expect violence if they invaded Native lands, which causes any assertions that they were settling on unoccupied lands to ring false.

And indeed, as British settlers invaded western lands to stake their "cabin rights" in the 1760s and 1770s, Ohio country's Native residents met them with constant opposition, deploying rumor, chaos, and the settlers' own anxieties to their advantage.[118] When the trespassing Virginian Ebenezer Zane settled on Wheeling Creek in 1769, for example, he already knew to build himself a blockhouse.[119] Forts and blockhouses constructed across the region recall that settler-Native violence was expected in the Ohio country, and that the settlers' answer was to advance rather than retreat.[120]

In response, Indigenous defenders conducted periodic strikes on white settlements, burning cabins and gristmills, killing livestock or people, and taking hostages; reports of war and violence were constant news in the East, inescapable lessons in the dangers of western occupation. Like their English predecessors in the seventeenth-century Northeast, Ohio country settlers also failed to detect the "decentralized character of the Indigenous military effort[s]" as strategies for community security, seeing instead revenge-based expressions of "savagery" against innocents.[121] And like their colonial sibling Spain to the south, British Crown forces constructed military fortifications to hold their territorial line and protect vanguard settlers. Unlike Spain, however, Britain did not officially organize outlying colonies: private subjects took care of that.[122] It was in this context of naturalized conflict that settlers consistently perceived the earthworks as "dernier resorts."

When Barton arrived at Kuskusky (now called New Castle, Pennsylvania) in 1785, the wounds of war were still fresh. Barton did not, however, reflect on the connection between his presence on the surveying tour and the prevalence of burial grounds and empty villages. He observed, sterilely, an array of graves "enclosed by a fence of pales, nailed to cross sticks" and a post on which "there were some marks, unintelligible to me, made with red paint."[123] Near the post and palisaded cemetery Barton also saw "a child's grave, which appeared to have been recently made. It was shaped like those in our grave-yards," next to which someone had placed a cradleboard, perhaps left during the funeral feast to hold the child on the journey to the next world.[124] In traditional Lenape communities, a post covered in olàmàn (sacred red ochre) was left to mark the burial spot of a man; a marker shaped like a cross with diamond shapes at the top and ends was meant for women. That Barton saw these kinkinhikàn (grave markers), which are usually left to rot, and the cradleboard points to the site's rather recent occupation by Lenape traditionalists, and to obviously recent deaths—including of women and children—in the community.[125] Yet to the extent that Barton was moved by this devastating scene, he only noted "with respect, the attentions of our Indians to the relicts and the memory of their dead."[126] He made no notes as to why Kuskusky was such a scene of mourning.

During the US War for Independence, Patriot and Royal (British, French, and Spanish) forces attacked Indigenous allies, and Indigenous communities attacked each other.[127] Lenape communities in the Tuscarawas and upper Muskingum River valleys saw widespread destruction.[128] Their villages were closest to Fort Pitt, and their leaders were split—largely along clan lines—on the question of neutrality or allegiance.[129] Yet neither decision promised protection: in 1777, militiamen murdered the pro-Patriot Shawnee leader Cornstalk; the Patriot-allied Lenape leader Koquethagechton (Captain White Eyes) was murdered the following year.[130] In 1778 the mother and brother of Lenape leader Konieschquanoheel or Hopocan (Captain Pipe)—who had initially remained neutral—were killed at Kuskusky. In 1781, US forces destroyed the important neutral Lenape town Coshocton on the Muskingum River. In 1782, members of the Pennsylvania militia massacred fifty-seven Moravian Lenape adults and thirty-nine children at Zeisberger's Gnadenhutten village.[131] To escape the indiscriminate violence, Lenape communities fled to the Sandusky River area and their Wendat (Wyandot) allies.[132] Shawnee towns along the Scioto and Mad Rivers suffered during the war as well: when George Rogers Clark led campaigns in 1778 and 1780 his forces deliberately laid waste to Shawnee homes and cornfields along the way.[133] At this time Shawnees also began concentrating farther north and west, largely along the Sandusky, Auglaize, and Maumee Rivers at the heads of the Scioto and Great Miami. Some departed the Ohio lands altogether, heading across the Mississippi to Spanish-claimed Luisiana and Tejas.[134] Nonetheless, Ohio's peoples still desired to continue living on the lands north of the river, to hunt and tend their old grounds: they had been given the Ohio country to share as a "Common Pot," and many wished to eat again with the same spoon.[135]

THE POLITICAL SITUATION in the Ohio country worsened after Barton's journey west. Far from inhabited by only "nine Indians," the area where Barton had just been was not "empty" or "abandoned": on the contrary, the region was abuzz with negotiations and strategy deliberations with extended diplomatic protocols that hardly registered to US contemporaries. In 1786, at the mouth of the Detroit River—that important waterway between Lakes Erie and Michigan connecting Haudenosaunee and Anishinaabeg relations to their southern kin— at the Wyandot village of Brownstone, located just across the water from the important Miami, Wyandot, and Delaware council houses on Erie's southern shore—the United Indian Nations held a "Confederated Council Fire" to discuss the necessity of acting in common to protect their ancestral homelands.[136] Later, the Mohawk leader and envoy for peace Thayendanegea (Joseph Brant) recalled the Council's precedent by describing how their ancestors had once placed a "Moon of Wampum" with four paths in the four directions at the country's center, a message that showed the connections between all peoples.[137] "A dish with one spoon"—which symbolized their shared fortunes—"was likewise put here with the Moon of Wampum," he recalled, the action "show[ing] that my sentiments respecting the lands are not new."[138] On the contrary, the 1785 treaty at Fort McIntosh and 1786 treaty at Fort Finney were perfect illustrations of the divisive behavior that Jefferson had encouraged and the Confederates condemned.[139] Not having been issued in the "general voice of the whole confederacy," these agreements were invalid.[140]

The United Indian Nations sent a speech to Congress—penned by Brant—stating their "sincere wishes to have peace and tranquility established between us," but insisting no US surveyors or settlers would be allowed to parcel up the lands audaciously being called the "Northwest Territory."[141] In response, Congress informed the Northwest Territory's governor Arthur St. Clair that the treaties "must not be departed from" and that he should "not neglect any opportunity that may offer, of extinguishing the Indian rights to the westward, as far as the river Mississippi."[142] Congress continued to sell lots, surveyors continued to map them as part of the United States, and settlers continued to access a growing repertoire of myth to justify their presence across the Ohio River. But unless the Ohio River boundary was restored, the Confederates held, "no peace would take place."[143]

Finding Mexico on the Ohio

Having returned from the Fort Finney council in April 1786 with ample sense of Ohio Valley lands, General Samuel H. Parsons wrote Yale College president Ezra Stiles to describe the "lines of circumvallation" made in the soil at the confluence of the Muskingum with the Ohio, sending a sketch along with the letter.[144] This was just where the Ohio Company wished to purchase land and establish their settlement. Stiles passed the letter and map on to Jefferson—then in Paris—to notify him that Parsons had allegedly found bricks among the earthworks and that these, along with the "Earthen Ware dug up in the Kentucky country, show that there have been European or Asiatic Inhabitants there in antient ages, altho[ugh] long extirpated."[145] Jefferson rebuffed the news as stadialist impossibility, writing that Native peoples across the Ohio were "in the hunter state." If Parsons had really found bricks, they must have been made by some other, more "civilized" peoples.[146]

Employing Scottish Enlightenment methods of "conjectural history" that applied the stadial model of "civilization," settler scholars like Jefferson and Stiles proposed multiple "theories" about the supposed Moundbuilders in attempts to preserve their beliefs about human "progress."[147] In this process they frequently resorted to analogy: considering America's built environments as Roman structures or Indigenous writings as Egyptian hieroglyphics gave them a way to see Moundbuilder "civilization" in ways parallel to those they already knew.[148] The work of William Robertson—the Scottish historian who had used, among other sources, Boturini's museum to write his *History of America* (1777)—first prompted US settlers to seek out these hemispheric similarities.[149] Robertson had suggested—as had Boturini and Clavijero—that Mexica migrants had left physical proof of their original itinerary across the continent, such as the site of Casas Grandes, and perhaps had practiced their monumental architecture until arriving in the Anáhuac Valley. In the United States, readers understood this as applying to the earthworks, which were perhaps ruins of "their various stations as they advanced from this [northern country], into the interior provinces."[150] As the highest expression of their skill, the migrants constructed a grand capital, Tenochtitlan, which they filled with impressive teocalme (s. teocalli), or "temples." Thus, in their search for appropriate analogies, settler-scholars drew connections not only between western earthworks and the "Old World" but also to the "temples" of ancient Mexico.[151]

Until the publication of Robertson's *History*, however, there had been few images of Mexican teocalme in English-language publications. But after Robertson included depictions of two stepped, pyramidal forms that he claimed "exactly resembled" the famous "great temple" at Tenochtitlan—of which he also included an engraving—these forms became much better known.[152] Moreover, Robertson's description of the "considerable" teocalli at Cholula—that appeared "now like a natural mount, covered with grass and shrubs"—opened interpretive possibilities for identifying both stepped-stone pyramids *and* vegetation-covered "natural mount[s]" as Mexican architecture.[153] To US eyes, Mexico's teocalme resembled earthworks in their perfected form.

In April 1787, Secretary of Congress Charles Thomson wrote to Jefferson regarding a letter from Judge John Cleve Symmes, formerly of New Jersey. Symmes, like many settlers, had traveled to the Ohio River region to prospect for land. In his letter, Symmes referred to migration history and "the tradition, which Doct. Robertson says prevailed among the old Mexicans, that their Ancestors came from the northward about the 10th century."[154] Symmes referred to the cycle of "successive migrations from unknown regions towards the north and northwest" and then to the Mexico Valley as recounted in Robertson's *History*.[155] These migrations were comprised, per Robertson, of "small independent tribes, whose mode of life and manners resembled those of the rudest savages," whom he identified as "Chichimecas" and "Otomies"—"a fierce and uncivilized people"—before being replaced, in the thirteenth century, by "a people more polished than any of the former"—Mexicas—migrating "from the border of the Californian gulf."[156] Robertson's narrative of successive migration (Chichimeca, Otomí, Mexica) provided Symmes a way to differentiate between different kinds of ancient peoples, some ruder and some "more polished" than others.

Robertson's illustrations provided a visual template for identifying "Mexican" architecture in the United States.[157] Using this reference, Symmes promised to "shew from relicks [earthworks] still remaining that they [the Moundbuilders] went [to Mexico] from the country bordering the Ohio."[158] As one example, Symmes described the mound at Grave Creek and others nearby as "Extraordinary temples" that were "exactly correspondent to the Mexican temples" in Robertson's book.[159]

But if Robertson provided the initial Mexican analogy for US settlers, Clavijero made the compairison canonical. For readers on both sides of the Atlantic— an English translation of *Storia antica del Messico* was published and reviewed in London in 1787—Clavijero's history provided visual and written descriptions of "Mexican" landmarks that complemented those in Robertson's history.[160] These included an engraved image of the stepped teocalli of Tenochtitlan and a written description of the "pyramid" at Cholula, up which, he noted, one "may ascend to the top by a path made in a spiral direction." Evoking both the ziggurat (of Babel) and the mount (of Ararat), Clavijero specified that Cholula was presently "so covered with earth and bushes, that it seems more like a natural eminence than an edifice." Clavijero also borrowed—from Gemelli's approximation of the *Codex Sigüenza*—a detail of the Tenochtitlan altepetl topped by bird and branch, mixing the Mosaic and Mexica narratives even further.[161] These illustrations would help settlers learn to identify their own surroundings in terms of Mexican history.

For example, in 1786 a soldier stationed at Fort Harmar drew a plan of the earthworks at the site that would become Marietta, the first US town in the Northwest Territory and evoked, if not relied upon, the Mexican architectural precedent in his sketch.[162] The image depicted two square structures, one larger than the other, with regularly spaced dashes and dots representing earthen walls

FIGURE 8. Francisco Javier Clavijero, "Il Tempio Maggior di Messico," *Storia antica del Messico* (1780), t. 2, pl. 1. Courtesy of the John Carter Brown Library, Brown University.

and mounds, evoking the images of Cholula (circle) and Tenochtitlan (square). He later lamented that the drawings were "not so accurate as I could now wish they had been" because settlers had already begun clearing and leveling the site by the time he drew it.[163] Nonetheless, the shapes and contours on his early map were clear. Later, he also described the earthworks at Grave Creek as "squares and circular redoubts, ditches, walls, and mounts," still sounding echoes of Cholula and Tenochtitlan.[164] In May 1787 his illustration of Marietta's earthworks appeared in the first volume of the *Columbian Magazine*, thereby spreading knowledge of the region's wonders across the eastern seaboard.[165] In 1788, when Rufus Putnam created a new map of Marietta, he included an inset portraying "the great Mound"—"Conus"—as a small, conical mountain, not unlike Cholula or Clavijero's figure of the Tenochtitlan altepetl.[166]

It is difficult to overemphasize the impact of Clavijero's work in terms of expanding settler conceptions of ancient American history, especially in confirming migration as a suitable method for historical reconstruction.[167] By 1789, Jefferson remarked that Clavijero's book was "assuredly the best we possess."[168]

Geographer Jedediah Morse recommended Robertson and Clavijero as "the best history of South America and Mexico," mentioning that Clavijero's sources provided records back to 1325 CE.[169] Harvard librarian Thaddeus Mason Harris, who later relied on Clavijero extensively in his *Journal of a Tour of Ohio* (1805), named the Jesuit's history "one of the most valuable works that has ever been published on the subject of America."[170] Indeed it was from Clavijero that Harris learned the first peoples in the New World were the Toltecs; Harris would later argue that Toltecs had built the mounds as defensive structures.[171] In fact, Clavijero first introduced the words "Toltec" and "Aztec" into the English vocabulary, thereby giving names to peoples who had previously been chronologically impossible, unnamable, and thereby unthinkable.[172]

Settlers became convinced of the Moundbuilder myth through visual comparison, but it was not simply that earthworks and teocalme looked similar in structure: Robertson's and Clavijero's migration accounts led scholars like Symmes—future father-in-law to William Henry Harrison—to conclude that "the ancient inhabitants of this part of America were *exactly the same people*" as "those who found their way into the Mexican territory, about the tenth century."[173] So widespread was this belief that by 1789 a settler near Wheeling, Virginia had concluded that he could "form no other conjecture than that the ancient Mexicans, who were much more civilized than our Indians, had settlements formerly on the Ohio and its branches, but not liking their situation, have retired to the southward."[174] Yet this attention to Mexican history came at a cost. To some US readers, criollo scholarship accentuated the supposedly "immense chasm" between ancient Mexicans—possibly the mounds' builders—and those northern populations to whom historian Robertson referred as "the savage tribes of America."[175] Indeed, the visual resonance of Babylonian ziggurats, Egyptian pyramids, Mexican teocalme, and western earthworks prompted US viewers to ask whether the mounds had been created by a "civilized" ancient people who they could not imagine were relatives of the "rude" Indigenous nations currently living in the United States. Moreover, the closer any Indigenous monuments seemed to resemble "Old World" structures the more evidence they seemed to lend to theories that the Americas had originally been populated by long-gone overseas immigrants. After leaving Marietta, Reverend Manasseh Cutler speculated that the earthworks there had resembled temples because they marked sites of worship and, "like the charnel houses in Mexico," contained "the skulls of the sacrifices."[176] He made these deductions by "comparing their form and situation with the places of worship in Mexico and other parts of the country":

Their temples were generally erected and their idols placed on natural or artificial elevations, with gradual ascents. If the Mexican tribes, agreeably to their historic paintings and traditions, came from the northward, and some of them, in their migrations, went far to the eastward it is not improbable, that either some of those tribes or others, similar to them in their customs and manners, and who practiced the same religious rites, were the constructors of those works.[177]

Cutler imagined that the Moundbuilders had "erected their temples, placed their idols, and offered their sacrifices" atop the earthworks and he therefore saw signs of "idolatry" all around the city he helped found: in the "walls and mounds of earth, in direct lines, and in square and circular forms."[178] Perhaps the belief that the surrounding grounds had been the scene of unholy sacrifice and idolatry eased his conscience. Believing the Moundbuilders were Mexican idolaters or that the entombed had been victims of sacrifice allowed for their remains' disturbance to become expressions of Christian righteousness.

The settlers' tendency to identify earthworks as teocalli, "Indian graves," or "ancient fortifications," reveals a contrast of space and time that was shaped by Mexica history as well as indecision about where Ohio's aborigines "belonged" on the settlers' civilizational schema. In the late 1780s the scenario in which the ancestors of one aboriginal group had become "civilized"—like the Tolteca-Chichimeca-Mexica—became increasingly plausible in relation to the United States, especially when also considering criollo accounts of the so-called "degeneration" of the Spanish empire's Indigenous residents. This also worked to separate ancient "Ohioans"—truly the peaceful, refined southern indigenes—from those migrant invaders who took over their lands.

IN THE LATE 1780s, white settlement of the Ohio country skyrocketed while violence continued apace.[179] In 1789, Secretary of War Henry Knox sent a series of reports to Washington pertaining to "discontented Indians." His first relayed notice of several squatters killed on the Ohio frontier "by small parties of Indians, probably from the Wabash country," deaths that were answered by Kentuckians who "destroyed a number of peaceable Piankeshaws."[180] Piankeshaws—Miami relatives—were formally US allies, and the betrayal did little to convince the region's other Native peoples of their white neighbors' peaceful intentions.[181] These "events on the frontier," Knox foreshadowed in 1789, "will deeply injure, if not utterly destroy, the interests and government of the United States in the Western Territory."[182] This dire message was reiterated in Knox's second report, which was dedicated to the situation of the "Creeks on the Alabama and Apalacicola Rivers," then engaged in a "serious war" with the state of Georgia, which was selling their lands. North Carolina was similarly disrespecting the Treaty of Hopewell (1785) made with the Cherokee Nation.[183] As in the northwest, Knox predicted the conflict would draw the Cherokees, Choctaws, Chickasaws, Creeks, and Seminoles into a "union as firm as the six Northern nations"—i.e., the "Iroquois Confederacy." He likewise warned that Spain was "endeavor[ing] to form and cement such an union of the Southern Indians."[184]

Initially, the United States understood the "Northern," "Western," and "Southern" nations to be politically different units that had more to do with imperial alliances than Indigenous politics: Haudenosaunee alliances with Britain, Mvskoke (Creek) alliances with Spain, and to a much lesser extent, Illinois (including Miami) and Anishinaabeg with France. Knox's War Department had inherited two Indian superintendencies based on the north-south division of the Ohio River, which placed Western and Northern nations together.[185] This administrative arrangement, however, seems to have been not only about alliances but was also based on—as revealed by Belknap's 1790 letter in the *American Museum*—a sense that *some* Native nations in the South were, potentially, more "civilized"—or more open to "civilization"—than others.

If ancestors of certain groups of "modern Indians of North America" had invaded and warred with the peaceful earthworkers—whose descendants eventually became the nations of the South, Florida, and New Spain—then the current-day "invaders"—the US settlers—were simply avenging the memory of the wronged first groups. In this sense, proper veneration for the ancient inhabitants called for the complete routing of their successors. Moundbuilder narratives were useful for western settlers as well as eastern investors because it helped them believe their actions—however bloody—were following the well-established, natural cycle of migration, conflict, and settlement recounted by criollo historians.[186]

Ordering Aboriginality

To secure their rights to occupation and legal title, US settlers needed to trace the legitimacy of their occupation to one of three possessive acts: conquest, contract, or priority. The Spanish and British empires had justified their territorial claims by fiat, conquest, and contract: Spain had gained its right by papal pronouncement while Britain based its claims on "discovery."[187] Devoid of either Crown or Church authority, the United States required new justifications to ensure their rights. Options included war and diplomacy, "fair and bona fide purchases," as Secretary Knox put it, and legal machinations.[188] Moreover, Knox believed war would financially ruin the new nation, and so he worked with Congress to develop an Office of Indian Affairs within the War Department, with the aim of pursuing diplomacy through trade.[189] Knowing the ideal of liberty would be hard to uphold in the face of land usurpation, Knox also theoretically supported a policy of "fair" compensation for land. Congress, in fact, in 1788 had set aside monies "for the purpose of extinguishing the Indian claims to lands they had ceded to the United States, and for obtaining regular conveyances of the same."[190] However, Knox deemed paying a "fair price" too costly for the empty federal treasury. The most economical solution to the problem was thus calling into doubt contemporary Indigenous peoples' priority of occupation and thereby their right to "aboriginal title."[191] This was despite the fact that Congress in 1788 had already recognized "the Indian right to the lands they possess."[192]

If, according to the precedent set by Roman law, the earliest-known inhabitants of an area were recognized as holding *original* claim to it—"aboriginal title"—then identifying a location's original occupants was necessary to "clear" the title so as to alienate the land as private property. This means that if settlers proved Native peoples were *not* aboriginal—legally—then Native claims to the legal right of possession would be invalidated. Yet establishing US legal priority depended less on courtroom argumentation and more on the creation and circulation of narratives in which peoples and events were ordered serially, creating a form of *relative* originality that marked who came "before" rather than who was absolutely "first." In other words, modern Indigenous populations would have no legal claim to title if a *previous* aboriginal people had preceded them. The issue of identity was moot.

Another option was for settlers to insist that Native peoples had invalidated their aboriginal title by not using their lands "properly," i.e., in a manner that settlers deemed "civilized." This opinion found support in international law. In 1758, the Prusso-Swiss jurist Emmerich Vattel argued that Spain's campaigns of conquest in Mexico and Peru had been "notorious usurpations" of established polities' sovereignty. Due to this, Spain's claim on Spanish America was void.[193] Yet in northern America, he explained, the populations "range over rather than inhabit" the land and by their "idle life" they "usurp" more land than they would with "honest work."[194] In British North America Vattel found it "very legitimate" if "more industrious" nations would "come and occupy part of those lands" otherwise home to "ranging" (i.e., nomadic) peoples.[195] Vattel thus set different legal operations for possession in the northern and southern portions of the American continent, as based on the stadial discourse of relative "civilization."

Following this approach, the 1788 article "A Few Observations on the Western and Southern Indians" appearing in Hartford's *Connecticut Courant* argued that the "Western Indians"—such as the Miami—were descended from the Lost Ten Tribes of Israel while "Southern Indians," like the Creeks, traced their lineage to Mexico and thus back to Asia.[196] This argument implicitly located Western and Southern peoples differently on the scale of civilization, but it was due to their supposed place of origin, not their behavior. Ultimately neither were "aboriginal" to the American continent. In adapting this differential legal structure, US nationalists made the invalidation of aboriginal title dependent not on potentially subjective assessments of stadialist behavioral difference—"idle" versus "honest" living—but rather on supposedly objective racialized difference. American peoples north and south—Moundbuilders and "barbarians"—were *racially*, as well as civilizationally, distinct.

When settlers sought to prove that the mounds had been built by peoples *as civilized as* ancient Mexicans—or, even further, that they *were* ancient Mexicans—they were separating the Moundbuilder "race" from contemporary Native peoples, dubbed the "Indian" race. This discursive creation of separate "Moundbuilder" and "Indian" racial populations was a technique of statecraft that had aided colonial governance since the seventeenth century.[197] It was a method of grouping people—by language, geography, etc.—who otherwise tended to exist in their own polities and arrangements, for the convenience of the state.[198] Thus the new United States conceived of all Indigenous peoples as uniform—and therefore governable—subpopulations of "Indians" to better allow for diplomacy, treaty making, and title transfer.[199] In a more quotidian sense, US settlers saw Indigenous peoples not as holding particularized identities but instead as monolithic "Indians" who were either enemies or allies, and whose hold on the land came not from aboriginal title, but—like Europeans'—from conquest.[200]

Refilling the Dish with One Spoon

In the years after the great droughts of the mid-twelfth to thirteenth centuries, the large-scale movements of Native ancestors was part of a series of relocations and journeys home.[201] Caddoan-speaking ancestors of Great Plains peoples moved further northward; Mississippian peoples largely moved south; Central-Algonquian/Illinoian-speaking Inoka and Myaamia ancestors emerged from the waters and spread south to the kaanseenseepiwi (Ohio River), west to the mihsi-siipiiwi (Mississippi River), and east to the ahseni siipiiwi (Great Miami River).[202] Before this, Dhegiha-Siouan-speaking ancestors had left their homes along the kaanseenseepiwi and headed to the Mississippi.[203] The U-ga'qpa

(Quapaw) would go downstream, while the U-man'-han (Omaha) traveled against the current toward their powerful Ho-Chunk, Chiwere (Otoe), Niúachi (Missouria), and Baxoje (Iowa) kin.[204] The Wazha'zhe (Osage)—Children of the Middle Waters—stayed on the Missouri peninsula.[205] This was a time of war and alliance, exchanges of captives, relatives, and protocols like condolence and calumet ceremonies, the movement of corn, beans, and squash.[206] Connections from the arterial waters stretched out like a spider's web, connecting peoples, ideas, and powerful objects throughout the continent.

Center and south to the Gulf, Caddoan, Atapakan, Muskogean, Natchez, Algonquian, and Iroquoian-speaking relations as well as others inhabited, built, and maintained a vibrant, storied, and negotiated landscape.[207] Some communities moved through the Mississippi watershed as refugees, exiles, and emigrants, impelled by the forces of war, climate, prophecy, or choice. Along the way, older sites were abandoned for new ones, and some topological and embodied knowledge of origins and lifeways went dormant.[208] Sometimes migrants had first-hand knowledge of their adopted lands; sometimes they only knew what they had learned from neighbors and new kin. Yet even as they made radical adjustments to their new worlds, memories of origins, homelands, and ancestral knowledges continued to guide and shape the Native peoples of Turtle Island.[209] They brought it with them, as when Sky Woman brought seeds down to Earth, or Beetle brought up mud from under the seas.[210]

For these and many reasons, Indigenous histories of the middle continent are often structured according to timescapes of movement and change, and this is especially true of the Mississippi watershed.[211] In this context, the goal is never to arrive *somewhere* as much as it is to arrive some *place* as *People*. Indeed, the direction of movement matters little because the destination is ontological. As Indigenous philosopher Niamachia Howe explains, "original People" is an "expression to distinguish us from all the rest of the surrounding life forms and not to mean *the* People in an ethnocentric sense."[212] Instead, it is in the sense of human beings created in situ, in the homelands created for them. "[I]f one seeks to understand Haudenosaunee history," writes Mohawk scholar Susan M. Hill, "one must consider the history of Haudenosaunee land.... we are born from the land and our bodies will return to it when our time on the earth is done, land serves as the primary focus of our identity."[213] In this way, Mohawk and other Haudenosaunee peoples belong *to* as well as issue from the land.[214] In some cases, the People gain new aspects of their identities from new environments. As Tuscarora historian David Cusick recorded in 1826, in the early days of the Longhouse family, languages changed after each group settled in the places appointed by the Holder of Heavens.²¹⁵ As Howe explains, the Niitsítapiiksi (Blackfoot) creator Naapi "shapes the homeland landscape and [the Peoples'] consciousness concurrently."²¹⁶ The People move through their homelands as they, in turn, are created of them.²¹⁷ Indigenous histories of emergence not only record pasts, but they also serve as sets of "storied practices" through which to rebirth Indigenous identities in the present.²¹⁸ Narrative, architectural, ritual, and bodily movements all enact the reciprocal, constituitive relations of people and land: across human and more-than-human elements and the landscape sacred and storied.²¹⁹

Some traditions specifically emphasize migration and contain memories—of transition, hardship, and violence—that emphasize movement and transformation as continuity.²²⁰ Choctaw tradition, for example, tells of the two brothers—Chata and Chicksah—who originally led their family east from western lands. Ojibwe traditions also maintain their Great Migration tradition of moving from east to west along the Great Lakes.²²¹ The Shawnee tradition of crossing the sea to reach a river at the center of Turtle Island is another of these emergence teachings.²²² After a long journey underground, the Alabama and Koasati (Coushatta) people emerged from opposite roots of the Tree of Life, near the Alabama River.²²³ A Miami tradition holds that mihtohseeniaki ("born of the soil")—the People—first "sprang up" at saakiiweeyonki, also known as the "Coming Out Place."²²⁴ In coming out of the water and onto the land, the People emerged.²²⁵ Emergence is cosmogenesis, not polygenesis.

Northern North American Native peoples frequently place their knowledge about earthworks within traditional origin histories, many of which posit Native peoples' emergence from the sky, land, or waters. For example, Dawnland and Great Lakes peoples tell versions of what is sometimes called an "Earth Diver story," in which the Earth was created amidst the waters from mud deposited on the shell of a turtle to catch the Woman Who Fell from the Sky. Some earthworks are thought to recall the Turtle's shell and recapitulate that teaching. Choctaw history recounts emergence from the Mother Mound, Nanih Waiya.²²⁶ Constantly being made and remade, the great mound still calls Choctaw people home to participate in creation, emergence, and as Choctaw scholar LeAnne Howe explains, holding the People together.²²⁷ These traditions cannot be separated from their lands, as the People cannot be emptied from them.

The insistence that the Ohio country or the West more generally was empty, however, was a discursive weapon in the settler battery. In this way, asserting that there was no Indigenous knowledge of the earthworks—as, for example, Manassah Cutler did when he stated that "the present natives retain no tradition" of them—also implied there was no long history of Indigenous peoples on the land.²²⁸ Settlers applied their colonial-era observations of devastation or depopulation to eras before the colonial period to propose an empty continent, a vacancy hypothesis seemingly independent of colonial forces. For, if the Ohio lands (or elsewhere) had already been emptied *before* settlers got there, then—if not a providential sign, as the Pilgrims interpreted the destruction of Patuxet village—at least the "clearing" was not the settlers' *fault*. These lines of thinking held well into the twentieth century: for example, the "Vacant Quarter" hypothesis suggested the upper Mississippi watershed and lower Ohio Valley were entirely "depopulated" from 1450 to 1550 CE without really engaging why or how what settlers saw as (a lack in) permanent population was on a much shorter timeline than Indigenous chronologies.²²⁹ Historiographically, this particular "settler move toward innocence" not only denies Indigenous peoples' agency in their own destinies but also fundamentally validates the finders-keepers premise of settlement.²³⁰ More recent histories and amplified Native voices, however, have made it clear that the lands were never abandoned but instead were densely but flexibly networked and scored with trade, kinship, and cosmic hubs.²³¹

What settlers interpreted as Native peoples' lack of knowledge about the past was often the result of not asking the right questions. For example, when settlers asked "Indians" if they had made the earthworks the response was often "no," at least partially because they did not understand themselves as "Indians" but instead as a specifically located People. Their answers were not the same as confessions that the earthworks had not been made by "Indians," although they were frequently taken as such. Rather, respondents were often disclosing that they *themselves*, or their close relatives, had not made the earthworks, not that *no* Native peoples had. Miamis, for example, do not claim to have created the Great Serpent Mound, but they do maintain a duty to care for it.²³² Similarly, Shawnee, Lenape, Potawatomi, Wyandot, Seneca, and other groups respect the earthworks of the Ohio country as the sacred creations and homelands of their ancestors.²³³

Nonetheless, by the time Europeans arrived on the Mississippi in the sixteenth century they were only dimly aware that its watershed was such a lively and storied space.²³⁴ Although Ponce de León (1513), Alonso Alvarez de Piñeda (1519), Pánfilo Narváez (1528), and Hernando de Soto (1539–1542) all came into contact with peoples actively making and using mounds in "La Florida," these Spanish conquistadors left no written descriptions of the earthen structures. Moreover, Black Legend dismissals meant that English and French readers tended to doubt the validity of the conquistadors' reports into the eighteenth century.²³⁵ Nor did the French Jesuits take any notice of earthworks during their seventeenth-century missions up and down the Mississippi, even though around 1700 Father Jacques Gravier reported seeing "old outworks" at the mouth of the "Akansea" when he camped at a place called "Kaowikia" (Cahokia).[236]

US settlers had only a certain degree of tolerance for historical lacunae. Used to the grand histories recounted as annals and chronicle they focused on documenting event to event, not necessarily the relationship between or among events. Historian Jacob F. Lee has explained that early US nationalists "considered the 600 years between the collapse of Cahokia [c. 1250–1350 CE] and the rise of the United States as little more than a footnote" in American history. The missing ancient and distant context was thus doubly disconnected from the forces leading to the migrations and population changes over those six hundred years.[237] Moreover, settlers' insistence on following the "rise and fall" of ancient Mexico therefore reveals the importance settlers placed on empires—their own included—to structure a pre-US timeline that largely started in the seventeenth century and sped to 1776.[238]

Originating American Emergence

Most traditional accounts identify earthworks as indisputably Native made, which settlers could have—but overwhelmingly did not—take as proof of Indigenous aboriginality. Indeed, many Native interviewees even affirmed to settlers that the earthworks had been made or used by their own people. In 1788, for example, Presbyterian missionary Samuel Kirkland recorded a Seneca tradition explaining that the "fortifications" across Seneca lands had been "raised by their ancestors in their wars with the western Indians, three, four, or five hundred years ago."[239] Similarly, in 1790 George Rogers Clark recalled learning from Kaskaskia leader Jean Baptiste Ducoign that earthworks in the Illinois country were the labors of Ducoign's ancestors.[240] A quarter-century later, the Shawnee Prophet stated that the Ohio Valley's fortifications had been "erected by their forefathers for defense" on their way across Turtle Island from the sea to the river.[241] Yet even when Native peoples *did* offer information on the earthworks, settlers often deemed it too fabulous to be reliable. Over time, traditional Indigenous knowledge became equated with gossip, superstition, or folklore; some settlers even fabricated their own "Indian accounts," the tall tales becoming a recognizable faux-folkloric genre in their own right.[242] Over and over, settlers misheard or misunderstood Natives' own explanations of their origins. As a result, they wrote interpretations framed within settler epistemologies that shored up, rather than challenged, their previous hypotheses.

Misunderstood and secondhand accounts of Indigenous traditions strengthened the idea that Natives were not aboriginal and that they had exterminated their predecessors in bloody battles. One such example ran in the September 1789 issue of the *Columbian Magazine*, providing rich fodder for easterners' imaginations.[243] It was an account of Moravian missionaries John Heckewelder and Abraham Steiner visiting David Zeisberger's mission at Petquotting (later renamed New Salem) in present-day Erie County, Ohio. The two missionaries were there on business regarding the former Moravian Lenape settlements along the Tuscarawas River that had been destroyed during the Revolutionary War. In his account, Steiner wrote of speaking with local people about the "fortifications" there, and he included a draft of "a plan of two old fortifications, supposed to have formerly been made by the Indians."[244] Their orientation, he thought "ma[de] it appear, as if two enemies had been opposed to each other, and that at different attacks, numbers were killed, and afterwards buried near the works, the place of the slaughter."[245] Similar writings naturalized the military landscape of the Ohio country and made it seem as if the land had always been contested, emphasizing (or at least contextualizing) the "barbarity" of its current residents, the story of which was inscribed on the landscape.

The turn of the century also saw an explosion of fables about *white* Moundbuilders, which literary scholar Edward Watts has called stories of "primordial whites."[246] Tales of "Welsh Indians" were so popular they inspired English Romanic poet Robert Southey's epic, *Madoc* (1805), much of which is set in "Aztlán" (it was published as a colonization fundraiser) as well as stories of ancient colonists from Judea, Atlantis, or Scandinavia.[247] These myths were routinely accepted as scientifically plausible and even probable.[248] Although there was much disagreement over the details, ultimately all of these hypotheses met at one radical point: America's Natives were not, at root, native to the Americas.

Nonetheless the imprint of Indigenous communities' own histories and teachings on settler ideas about earthworks is particularly visible when it comes to migration; there are also tracings in stories of previous peoples and crises over shared resources.[249] Ojibwe scholar Scott R. Lyons's relation of the Great Migration, for example, includes some of the elements that were misappropriated for the Moundbuilder myth. His twenty-first-century version of the teaching begins with all Anishinaabeg peoples living in one large group along North America's eastern coast. After being told to move west, their path and destination was revealed in prophecy, dreams, and visions: home on a turtle-shaped island.[250] Meeting with different peoples along the way, different factions emerged and stayed behind at each stop. Some left inscriptions in rocks to mark their passage

(Lyons does not mention earthworks), still visible today.²⁵¹ Lyons stresses that each new community or people *supplemented*, not supplanted the old, thereby creating diversity, not replacement. "The Great Migration continued," he concludes, "always leaving in its wake new peoples and new communities scattered along the St. Lawrence [Riverway] and the Great Lakes."²⁵² For Lyons, this story teaches about moving away from "undifferentiated singularity" and toward localized and differentiated identities. It is not about war or displacement—although though these events are included in his telling—but about *becoming*.

Similarly, Ho-Chunk (Winnebago) traditions emphasize that about nine-hundred years ago the great family of Chiwere-Siouan-speaking ancestors moved south and west from east of the Great Lakes and Ohio Valley. Some Ho-Chunk ancestors stopped while their relations continued on to the Mississippi, staying first at a large lake and then spreading out to the eastern shore of Lake Michigan around what is currently called Green Bay.²⁵³ Like Lyon's narrative, this too is about movement and creation, not defense or usurpation.

Settler-scholars, however, imagined migration as unidirectional and merely functional, accounting for movement from there to here. They wanted to trace migration itineraries physically across territories, using cardinal directions and longitudinal coordinates. They attempted to connect point to point as plotted in the collected traditions but failed to consider coalescence, scattering, coming-back together, pilgrimage, kidnapping, adoption, adaptation, or any other ways that a people move and change over time. More generally, settler understandings of migration were usually colored by their experiences as the descendants of European migrants. Unlike their Indigenous or African neighbors, most upper-to-middling creoles and criollos had a traceable family history relating European metropole and American colony. Settlers' own ancestral histories profoundly constrained their concepts of origins, migrations, and history. And just as criollos narrowed the fundamentally Nahua character of Boturini's archive to its purely "Mexican" aspect, so too did the process by which US settlers created this "Mexican" history become a way to deny, displace, and misappropriate the Indigenous knowledges already in their "Indian" archive.

Trailing the Toltecs

By the time the first section of the Public Lands Survey was finished, Benjamin Smith Barton was just completing his own project on America's earthworks, *Observations on Some Parts of Natural History: To which is Prefixed an Account of Several Remarkable Vestiges of an Ancient date which have been discovered in different parts of North America* (1787).²⁵⁴ Publishing the text while living abroad in Britain, Barton claimed it his patriotic duty to inventory "American antiquities" for European readers, and *Observations* sought to show that the earthworks of the West did not disrupt what was already known of world history.²⁵⁵ He began the project while at medical school in Edinburgh, where phylogeny and Linnaean taxonomy reigned supreme and William Robertson was one of his tutors. There, the Philadelphian brought to his studies an interest in American origin debates as well as American bodies, writing earlier essays on the "Natural History of the North American Indians" and another on "American albinos," explaining his choice of topics by admitting the "History of the Savages...of his country [had been] a favourite study [of his] for some years."²⁵⁶ In these scholarly disquisitions, Barton attempted to account for human diversity—in one by arguing that "America was principally peopled from Asia"—and through this laid a foundation for his later work.²⁵⁷

Observations attempted to amass and relay enough "facts" to support Barton's conventional conclusion that the "Remarkable Vestiges" of his home continent had been made by "a people differing in many respects, from the present savage nations in America." To do so, he consulted largely the same corpus of travel writings—Kalm, Carver, Filson—that had informed most settler writings about earthworks to that point.²⁵⁸ Barton was, however, also able to add his own firsthand descriptions thanks to his experiences in 1785.²⁵⁹ Additionally, he included a plate detailing the Muskingum River earthworks at the site not yet named Marietta, which had been made from the sketch of a colleague and was likely the earliest depiction of the site seen across the Atlantic.²⁶⁰ As Rufus Putnam's map would a year later, Barton's engraving also indicated that a large, conical "Pyramid...considerably resembl[ing] some of the eminences which have been discovered near the Mississippi [Natchez]" was located at the confluence of the Ohio and Muskingum.²⁶¹

Only mildly successful, *Observations* circulated throughout the nineteenth century as proof of the western earthworks' antiquity as well as the alleged inability of local Native peoples to answer for their presence. Of the "stupendous eminence composed of huge quantities of earth" at Grave Creek, for example, Barton wrote: "Notwithstanding all the inquiries which have been made, the oldest INDIANS are incapable of giving any account of this curious ANTIQUITY."²⁶² He came to the conclusion that the Ohio Valley earthworks were not "Indian" at all. For this reason, despite *Observations*'s relative obscurity, the publication is sometimes identified as an originary event for the Moundbuilder myth.²⁶³ However, Barton's *Observations* is perhaps more important to the

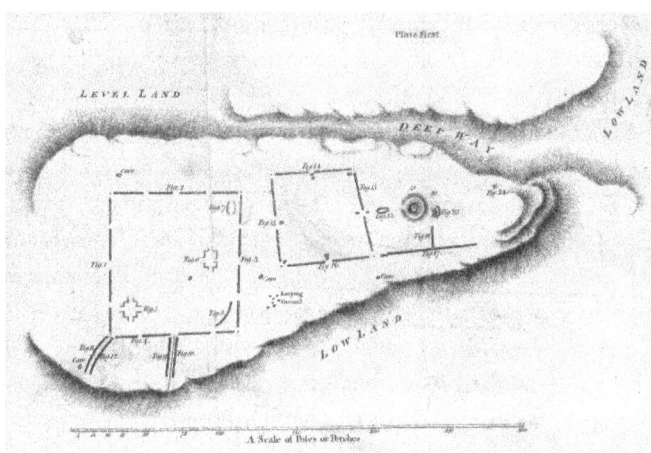

FIGURE 9. Benjamin Smith Barton, *Observations on some parts of Natural History* [...] (1787). Courtesy of the John Carter Brown Library, Brown University.

longevity of the Moundbuilder myth in another way: because toward the end of its writing, Barton began to read criollo history. And it did not take him long to connect records of earthworks at Natchez with accounts of earthworks along the Ohio at Lexington and on the Muskingum to structures in Clavijero's *History of Mexico*.[264] He summarized on the publication's last pages: "if we consider the eminence near the mouth of GRAVE CREEK and those on the MISSISSIPPI, as the workmanship of any of the MEXICAN or other nations, we cannot but view the fortifications in the same light."[265] "I am also of opinion," he continued, "that the very remarkable remains at LEXINGTON, and those at the river MUSKINGUM, are to be attributed to this people likewise."[266] "I think there can be little doubt that they have been constructed by the same people, and for the same purposes" he appended to the forthcoming book.[267]

Drawing from Clavijero, Barton speculated that the earthworks had been made by Viking-descended "Toltecas" along their trail from the Labrador Peninsula south to "the vale of MEXICO."[268] He was satisfied that "the fortifications and eminences" in the Ohio country "were constructed by the Toltecas, or some other Mexican nation" that had passed through the Ohio Valley on the way to Cholula and Tenochtitlan and that the earthworks provided an illustrated chronology of this migration.[269] Thanks largely to his exposure to the criollo migration model of history, Barton eventually gathered the data he needed to "deduce an inference of no small importance in the early history of NORTH AMERICA": that "Americans are of Asiatic origins."[270] Barton determined that the earthworks mapped an itinerary of migration, and he realized that he had only to seek the traditions that would confirm these paths and then lead to the origin of America's Native populations.

Even after *Observations* went to press, Barton continued to develop his Mexican mound hypothesis. Having previously learned from his fellow Philadelphia naturalist William Bartram that there were "artificial mounds or terraces" at almost every "ancient Indian town" in the South, Barton wrote to ask Bartram's help in expanding the scope of his just-published work.[271] Receiving no answer at first, Barton wrote again in February 1788, asking once more after the "several artificial mounts or eminances, which you saw in the course of your travels." This time, Barton also inquired about migration, asking if Bartram had come across "any traditions concerning their Origin,—their Progress, or Migrations, which you think worthy of notice?"[272] As with many of their contemporaries, both Barton and Bartram understood migration in terms of seriality and European historical concerns: wars, death, and the succession of political formations. Barton and Bartram imagined that history was shaped by lineal succession—based on the assumption of an empty continent peopled in successive arrivals and invasions—and applied this intellectual framework to interpretations of Native origins. Barton, for one, did not consider that the *places* themselves mattered to the histories.[273]

In 1789, after he returned from Edinburgh to Philadelphia—where he became professor of natural history and botany—Barton proposed writing another volume, much expanded, on the "Various Remains of Antiquity."[274] With this work Barton planned to devote a large amount of his research to migration accounts, some of the first of which he had obtained from Bartram, and which gave further credence to the idea that the Native peoples of North America had always come from elsewhere. That year, although US agents attempted diplomacy again, settlers still refused to temper their sense of entitlement to Ohio Valley lands.[275] In 1790, the US Army attacked the council fire of the Western Confederacy, ensuring war.[276] After four years of fighting—most battles of which the US forces lost—the Western Confederacy was eventually beaten at the Battle of Fallen Timbers. Afterward, the new boundary line definitively barred the region's Native communities from their homelands along the Ohio River, separating them from landscapes inscribed with their histories recent and ancient.

OVER THE PAST millennia, the Ohio and Mississippi River valleys' peoples covered their homelands with ceremonial and commonplace markers: earthworks in the significant shapes of circle and square, enclosures, ditches, and stone mounds. Up near the Mississippi's source, the earth crawls with turtles, muskrats, and horned serpents, the doodemag of the Great Lakes and manëtuwàk of the Woodlands.[277] To the south, the Kentucky and Tennessee Rivers—which feed the Ohio and run to the Mississippi—lead to the Cumberland, Hiawasee, Coosa, and Tombigbee, watering Chickasaw, Cherokee, Creek, Choctaw, and other southern peoples' lands, where flat-topped pyramids, terraces, and gentle earthen swells follow the waters to the Gulf. The Ohio lands are the meeting points of north and south, east and west, just as depicted by Brant's "Moon of Wampum." Along the beautiful waters the persons—both human and more than human—and the worlds above and below coexist in rich, reciprocal, and overlapping sociality, the land of many peoples and languages that the Shawnee leader Tecumtheth (Tecumseh) would call "kwaw-notchi-we au-kee," "beautiful country."[278] In shaping their homelands, eastern Indigenous peoples have transformed these landscapes into an ongoing record of Native history. As Choctaw critic LeAnne Howe writes, they have "emplotted the land with meaning."[279] Because settler theories of history prioritize events over relationships, however, earthworks are still read as fortifications or graves rather than as embodied practices of world-making and reciprocal renewal.[280]

Instead of Mexican pyramids, the US nationalists might more fruitfully have concentrated on Mexican cosmology. Perhaps this would have enabled them to see the earthworks as landscapes that reflect the cosmos and enable celestial rituals of renewal. The squares for the Middle World of Earth and the circles for the Sky World: soil environments complemented by nearby rivers and seasonal trenches for the World Below.[281] Some of the earthworks in the beautiful land flood seasonally, mirroring the destruction wrought by the Lenape manëtuwàk Màxaxkuk (Great Serpent) as Pèthakhuweyòk (the Thunderers) wash away violence with rain.[282] When the waters subside, the earthen peaks rise from the water just as Tëmàskwës (Muskrat) surfaces with dirt to be carried on the back of Tahkox (Turtle).[283] Such is the case near Wheeling, West Virginia, where the majestic "Grave Creek" earthwork still rises high from the ground. In what is currently Peebles County, Ohio, Màxaxkuk swims the earth, absorbing the power of an ancient meteor. At the earthworks complex in what is currently Newark, Ohio, the Great Circle—once an attached circle and square until bisected by farms, canals, railroads, and roadways—has ditches meant to hold water and reflect original teachings. Located between Raccoon Creek and Licking River, these earthworks could once be reached from either the Ohio River or the Great Lakes.[284] The Great Circle leads to an eight-sided earthen enclosure, now called the Octagon, that tracks the movement of Nipaii Kishux, the Moon. Its shape marks the heart of the four directions and recalls our shared history on Amankitaxkwâwikan'ànk, the Place of the Great Turtle's Back.[285]

Although they began with the assumption there was little in the way of "ancient" history for their new nation, US settlers ended the eighteenth century with an entirely revised set of ancient populations and historical chronologies. This was accomplished by overwriting the land's history with mythical Moundbuilders, migrations, and inevitable alienation. Using the criollo histories of New Spain, especially the method of establishing chronology from monuments, US settlers misappropriated earthworks to support the political, legal, and territorial aims of their new nation. In these settlers' "Indian" archive, flickers of traditional knowledge sparking in narratives about Grave Creek, Cahokia, or elsewhere were turned into sequences of dispossession, replacement, and loss rather than stories of movement, continuity, and renewal.

CHAPTER 3

Mexico Antiguo through Americano Eyes

Truly we can assert that,
although some want us to disappear,
we Nahuas continue to live,
we Nahuas continue to grow.

—Joel Martínez Hernández, "Quesqui Nahúamacehualme Tiiztoqueh?," 1983

Everywhere that meets the eye,
everywhere you look you see
the remains of their clay vessels,
their cups, their carvings,
their dolls, their figurines,
their bracelets,
their ruins are all around
truly the Toltecs once lived there.

—*Cantares mexicanos*, c. 1580

IN THE SECOND HALF of 1790, workers repairing Mexico City's central Plaza del Palacio unearthed two enormous basalt boulders. The first, uncovered in August and located just south of the viceregal palace, was a three-ton, eight-foot, "curiously carved" statue identified by a palace guard as an "idol from pagan times."[1] Given its striking ornamentation of serpents, skulls, and dismembered hands, other viewers agreed that it was one of the so-called ugly "ídolos" formerly worshiped in Tenochtitlan and buried during the early days of the Spanish invasion.[2] Another massive statue emerged that December, located only a short distance from the first. This one was a twenty-ton disc of inscribed, greyish-brown volcanic rock measuring twelve feet across. On its sculpted surface two concentric rings of ovals and an inner quincunx included a humanlike face with outstretched tongue. Some guessed it was a Mexica ceremonial object, perhaps a cuauhxicalli or temalacatl, while others suggested a sundial or "calendario Azteca." Because they were determined to be relics of a former era—not necessarily because they were especially old—the carved stones were called "piedras antiguas."

For the first few weeks, the stones were left where they had been uncovered, on full display in the city's center, a temporary deviation from the capital's rhythms of renovation and modernization. A few months after their emergence, Viceroy Revillagigedo and the provincial intendent-corregidor declared both pieces to be "precious monuments emitting the light that elucidates the Indian people during the time before the Conquest."[3] Revillagigedo ordered their preservation in perpetuity. Not long afterward, the statues were noticed in two local periodicals—the *Gazeta de México* and *Gazeta de Literatura de México*—where they were folded into the contemporary discussions of antiquity, science, and patriotism crossing the Atlantic.

In the 1780s and 1790s, criollos—whose own identity within the Spanish imperial world was in flux—began to experiment not just with ways to document and interpret New Spain's Indigenous past but how to inhabit it as their own.[4] By the late eighteenth century, Enlightenment ideas about art, science, and political economy from Madrid, Paris, Edinburgh, and Philadelphia were prominent topics in Mexico City's homes and public places.[5] The capital's letrados were particularly influenced by Scottish political economy, Rousseau's theories of "natural rights," and the revolutionary rhetoric coming from the United States and France.[6] Criollos increasingly saw themselves as culturally, if not politically, separate from Iberian Spain and by the 1790s autonomist movements were already afoot in some parts of Spanish America (with London and Philadelphia emerging as important centers of transamerican collaboration).[7] It was at this point that the criollos of Mexico City began to consider the piedras antiguas and other Indigenous architectural features—as opposed to just written documents—as anchors for a new ancient American history.

Scholars have frequently interpreted the piedras antiguas as emblems of "creole patriotism," the movement among New Spain's criollos to construct a cultural and political identity apart from that of Europe.[8] For years, New Spain's criollos had been impatient to disprove European accusations of American inferiority.[9] An entire subfield of what historian Jorge Cañizares-Esguerra has called "clerical-creole historiography" was dedicated to renovating America's reputation: this included the work of Boturini and Clavijero.[10] In these piedras antiguas, criollos saw the physical proof they sought to secure America's importance within the Spanish Empire: obvious evidence of the great civilizational heights attained in American antiquity. Despite the fact that the "ugly" first statue reminded criollos of the "fallen" situation of New Spain's non-Christians, the second made evident—to them—that the past concealed beneath their feet was on par with that of Egypt or Greece. Indigenous history thus became a way for criollos to confront European and Hispanic cultural and political hegemony, while expressing their amor patriae during uncertain times. Not unlike their counterparts in the United States, New Spain's criollos attempted to access Mexican history as part and parcel to controlling access to the land, especially as the base of their patria shifted from Europe to America.

MUCH OF THE scholarship on science and empiricism in nineteenth-century Mexico focuses on the ways that Atlantic Enlightenment figures examined Indigenous history anew only *after* Mexican independence.[11] These accounts often credit Prussian naturalist Alexander von Humboldt with the "rebirth of . . . interest in the pre-Hispanic history of Mexico."[12] But criollo eyes were already fixed on that past, and even Humboldt's own work reflects this. Moreover, as Humboldt certainly knew, Europeans were not the only peoples in New Spain interested in figuring the past for present concerns. While much has been made of the use to which Mexican history was put during the War for Independence (1810–1821)—especially in patriots' evocations of Mexica emperors and the choice of the country's new name—the "Mexico" conjured by that Revolutionary cohort had already been solidified by a previous generation. The work of criollos like Francisco Javier Clavijero, Antonio de León y Gama, José Antonio de Alzate y Ramírez, and Guillermo Dupaix described Indigenous history as a nameable, visual archive—one on paper and in stone—and as their patria's Mexican past.[13]

The stones' 1790 appearance provided criollos material for visualizing themselves as rooted "americanos" rather than as deracinated Europeans, as well as the perfect occasion for criollos-americanos to refine a specialized visual and architectural language through which to develop an americano historiography.[14] "Description"—a method of "writing as if drawing" ("como si la dibujara") in which the visual was fixed into a verbal frame—lay at the root of the criollo belief that they, exclusively, could turn Indigenous materials into Mexican history.[15] Similar to other processes of knowledge production, description—which involves choices of perspective, selection, emphasis, and exclusion—was an effective tool for establishing interpretive supremacy over Indigenous pasts. Moreover, criollos like Alzate and León y Gama emphasized the importance of describing "Indian antiquity"—visiting the stones at the Pontifical University or trekking to see Xochicalco—based on firsthand experiences. To stress the importance of empirical objectivity, they augmented their historical descriptions with visual representations, in words and images.

Yet these 1790s criollo-americano projects depended almost entirely on a version of "Mexican history" learned from the criollo rather than Mexica or Nahua archive and were furthermore disconnected from—and dismissive of—living Indigenous peoples. As if they were making paper tracings, criollos-americanos copied historical materials in all of their detail, transforming them from three-dimensional into two-dimensional descriptions, while their claims of descriptive verisimilitude only hastened the transformation of Indigenous words and views into possessable, interpretable, historical evidence.[16] And although criollos-americanos often worked with Indigenous informants and their descriptions often derived from sources produced by Indigenous authors, the "Mexican" history they produced kept Indigenous populations at a distance from the pasts that criollos-americanos copied to keep for their own.

Although the recovery of the piedras—there were eventually seven in all—usually marks the beginning of criollo nationalist interest in Mexican antiquity, the island city of México had long been a center of antiquarian activities. When Cortés and his forces arrived in Tenochtitlan, they were met with a display of objects from many eras and locations as well as an urban landscape self-consciously modeled to reiterate Mexica concepts of time and power.[17] Of course, the conquistadors neither identified the Mexica temporal, spatial, and architectural configurations as techniques of governance, nor as expressions of what art historian Byron Hamann calls "cohabitation."[18] Later, as criollos and criollos-americanos studied Mexica cosmology, they too failed to understand the importance of "cohabiting" temporalities to Mexica power.

Whereas their descriptions *seemed* to combine past and present, really criollos-americanos created an effect of past-in-present that was different from acknowledging the ways in which Indigenous temporalities continued to operate in the present. Indeed, criollo-americano visualizations required portraying the cohabitation of past with present only aesthetically, as a superficial rather than cosmic reality. In this way, the antiquarianism practiced by criollos-americanos in Mexico City—with its determinedly European structure despite its American façade—became a practice that saw Indigenous monuments like the piedras not as "witnesses" of the past but as resources for keeping history in an anterior, aestheticized past as opposed to the present moment of New Spanish modernization. Criollos in New Spain saw contemporary indios as, at best, "semi-rational" and "semi-civilized" and certainly incompatible with criollo modernity.

Eradicating Indigenous ethnic identity—largely through Christian conversion and spatial reconfiguration into the Spanish civitas—had long been the goal of

New Spain's designers. Their project relied on the assumption that the Hispanic city would "civilize" and eventually assimilate the kingdom's Indigenous residents. This was tactical, as well as ideological, for cross alliances and in-fighting among Tenochtitlan's Tlatelolca, Acolhua, and Tenochca elite threatened to scuttle Spanish power.[19] Initially, when Hernán Cortés refigured the political landscape of Tenochtitlan, his reorganization still acknowledged the power of the Mexica past for the Nahua present. For example, he moved directly into the former palaces of huey tlatoani Axayacatl (reign 1469–1481), thereby creating an explicit connection between Mexica and Spanish rulers.[20] Ultimately, however, Cortés ordered the remaining structures of the imperial city razed, just as he had ordered Cuauhtémoc, the last Mexica tlatoani, executed. The conquistador had a church constructed and a large open plaza—later called the Plaza del Palacio—installed over Tenochtitlan's main Templo Mayor complex. These spatial rearrangements marked the city's Spanish traza (zone) as the seat of colonial power by misappropriating the power of the city's Mexica core.

Demonstrating Spanish dominance over Indigenous spaces and bodies, Cortés and his successors compelled the capital's indios (no longer ethnically distinct) to construct the new colonial city.[21] Countless Indigenous laborers died, testified the chronicler Motolinía, "some hit by beams, others falling from heights, and others buried beneath the rubble of the buildings that were being destroyed and replaced, especially when they demolished the main pagan temples."[22] By the mid-sixteenth century, a church and Cortés's new palace—built with the stones of Motecuhzoma's destroyed residences—covered the rest of the formidable ceremonial complex, literally burying the "pagan" past along with the Indigenous bodies.[23] In the sixteenth and seventeenth centuries, while Spanish officials across the kingdom placed churches and chapels atop "pagan temples"—such as the Santuario de la Virgen de los Remedios built on Cholula's Tlachihualtepetl pyramid in 1594 or the Chapel of Roses placed atop the summit of Tonantzin's Tepeyac Hill in 1666—to stamp out "idolatrous" lifeways, hasten salvation, and ensure Spanish control over the present by erasing the past, what they did not realize is that this is also how Mexica rulers had used space and time to shore up their own power more than a century before.[24]

Conventional wisdom holds that by the eighteenth century, the Mexica past had been long forgotten. A new cathedral and rebuilt viceregal palace dominated the north and east ends of the busy Plaza del Palacio, its pavers completely concealing Tenochtitlan's foundations and—often flooded—waterways. The popular tianguis (market), tecpan (Indigenous government building), and Indigenous parish San José de los Naturales—beating hearts of Indigenous continuity in the city—were kept blocks away from the colonial power center. If the most notable sign of indigeneity was the "persistence of traditional religious beliefs," then other signs of continuing Indigenous identities and practices must have been too subtle or dangerous to be obvious to criollos.[25] Mexico City's Indigenous population nonetheless maintained a temporal and spatial distinctiveness—despite both segregation and integration orders—and their visible presence ultimately posed an ideological threat to Spanish sovereignty.[26] The piedras antiguas of 1790, in this sense, are usually considered to physically embody a resurgence of Mexico City's "forgotten" Indigenous past.[27] Certainly, however, México's archive of Indigenous history—a project that stretched back hundreds of years—did not originate in 1790.

And neither the stones' aesthetic nor their reappearance was a complete surprise to those criollos-americanos already drawing from Mexica, Nahua, and colonial archives to create an American past of their own.[28] In fact, by the 1790s, New Spain's capital city was studded with physical elements of pre-invasion history. Yet as in the previous century, settler confusion or misunderstanding of Indigenous temporalities and what counted as "religious" shaped the criollo-americano archive and their interpretations of ancient American history. The tensions inherent in criollos-americanos' attempts to describe Indigenous pasts that were *not* "idolatrous" came to the surface in 1790, as the growing requirement of secularism among Atlantic scholarship and an attenuating relationship to the secularizing Crown caused the predominantly Catholic criollos-americanos to miss (or avoid) the cosmological histories stamped on the city's piedras themselves.

This chapter returns to the Mexica pasts that Cortés and his cohort banished underground, but that criollos-americanos would work so hard to bring to light. Yet in studying what they believed to be remnants of a vanquished past, criollos-americanos missed the multiplicity of temporalities and cosmologies that enabled the lived space of Indigenous life in Mexico City to remain, allegedly hidden in plain sight. The consequence was the justification of policies and everyday actions that denied the priorities of living Indigenous peoples in New Spain, revealing that Indigenous dispossession was inevitable to criollos-americanos' vision of the modern New Spanish landscape.

Balancing and Cohabiting with the Ages

Mesoamerican archaeologists believe that over thirty-five hundred years ago, in the Gulf lowlands of the slender isthmus currently occupied by the Mexican states of Veracruz and Tabasco, lived the people Nahuas later called "Olmecas."

There, and along the central Coatzacoalcos River, these Olmecas built towns with pyramids and ballcourts, raised corn and beans, developed a timekeeping system, wrote on stone tablets, and carved colossal basalt busts.[29] Their markets circulated with precious jade, obsidian, turquoise, and marine shells, objects that connected them to communities far across land and water.[30] Farther north and inland—but at roughly the same time—the city-state of Cuicuilco, located on the southern shore of Lake Texcoco, dominated the central Mexico basin. After Cuicuilco was destroyed by the volcano Xitle, a rival city north of the lake rose from the ashes: this was the place the Nahuas would call "Teotihuacan" or "the place of the people who had become gods."[31] Olmecas, Cuicuilcas, and Teotihuacanos, among others, left testimonies on the land in the form of their structures, carvings, and votive objects, their physical traces regularly encountered, collected, and narrated by Nahuatl-speaking migrants and others who moved into the central part of current-day Mexico. For the most part, Nahua historians referred to any of these "civilized" predecessors, "los antiguos"—real and fictive ancestors—as "Toltecas," a name from the Nahuatl for "artisan."

The arrival of the migrant Mexica in the central basin was preceded by the occupation and invasion of Nahuatl-speaking kin from the north. By 1428, however, the denizens of Tenochtitlan—Mexicas who had allied with Tepanecas from Tlacopan and Acolhuas from Texcoco—defeated the once-preeminent altepetl Azcapotzalco to rise to dominance, their trebled power expanding for almost one hundred years.[32] The Triple Alliance forces would eventually extend southeast to areas in the current Mexican states of Puebla, Veracruz, Chiapas, Oaxaca, and to the edge of Michoacán in the west.[33] Mexica rulers used their might to amass los antiguos' items—carvings, figurines, obsidian, jade, turquoise pieces, etc.[34] At the imperial complex on Chapultepec Hill, Motecuhzoma I installed plants, animals, and objects from across the Mexica domain. Meant to emphasize the enormity of Alliance tribute lands, Motecuhzoma's encyclopedic zoological and botanical gardens designated Tenochtitlan as the center of the Mexica political universe. The architecture, artifacts, and imagery from antiguo (former) eras on display designated it as the cosmic center as well.

Mexica historical protocols—cosmic, scribal, aesthetic, and archival—literalized Mexica power in a way that was visible to—and could hardly have failed to impress, and perhaps intimidate—the Spanish invaders.[35] But when Europeans arrived in the Mexico Valley they were largely unaware of how the "Toltec" and other antiguo places and pieces were used to Mexica ends. Spanish scholars like Sahagún recorded songs, commissioned chronicles, gathered mapas, and copied "hieroglyphics," seeking to document Toltec existence as historic rather than cosmic. From this base, Europeans and later criollos fixed storied spaces and cosmic beings based on materials that were sometimes themselves interpretations meant to legitimate Mexica rule.

Current-day scholars have described the Mexica reuse of antiguo items as "Aztec antiquarianism" or "indigenous Mesoamerican archaeology," the latter clarifying it as not a uniquely Mexica practice. These terms, however, inaccurately imply that the materials were considered *old*, rather than merely from a distant world, or that they were used to *study* the past in a way analogous to Western archaeological practices.[36] Remnant antiguo objects, however, mark not an *absolute* break between past and present—as in Western versions of archaeology or antiquarianism—but instead enable the cohabitation or deliberate intermingling of different temporalities. Antiguo items—usually considered "inanimate" by Westerners but considered by the Mexica as animated with teotl (cosmic power)—live in the present as well as being from the past.[37] Thus Mexicas experienced traces of previous worlds not as "ruins" but as living aspects of los antiguos (ancestors) that connected them to distant but still-visible pasts.

For example, the Mexica adopted Toltec iconography and sculptural aesthetics—such as deploying the reclining chacmool figure in their own temple complexes—and incorporated powerful materials—such as tezontle (volcanic stone) from Mount Xitle, the volcano that had destroyed Cuicuilco—in the statues and buildings of Tenochtitlan.[38] And when Motecuhzoma I's rule ended in 1469, Mexica-style monumental sculptures could be found across central Mexico and toward the southeastern coast—over all of the tribute lands—many of which were constructed to displace gods other than the Mexica patron Huitzilopochtli.[39] In this way Mexica dominance was enacted over and on the land.[40]

Even after the Spanish invasion, Nahuas saw the landscape around them as inextricably tied to the cosmic stories that gave meaning to their pasts and presents. With Franciscan missionary Bernardino de Sahagún, sixteenth-century Nahua students recorded how los viejos (elders) told of the earliest peoples, obscured by the mists of time, who had lived in a northern place called Tamoanchan, "Land of Rain or Mist." Sometimes the people of Tamoanchan—supposed to come from the rubber lands of the Gulf coast—were called olmecah (s. olmecatl), "rubber people," and sometimes toltecah (s. toltecatl), "artisans."[41] The elders remembered them because "everywhere you look you see the remains of their clay vessels, their cups, their carvings, their dolls, their figurines, their bracelets, their ruins are all around."[42] A song, included in a collection now called the *Cantares mexicanos*, spoke of a great metropolis or tollan (place among the reeds), where "[i]n a certain era which no one can reckon, which no one can remember there was a government for a long time."[43] It recalled how power, knowledge, and prestige were afterward transferred to Teotlapan, "Land of the Gods," where another tollan—Teotihuacán—was built by giants. The giants dedicated their immense stone pyramids to the Sun (Tonatiuh) and the Moon (Coyolxauhqui). Other tollans—Xicocotitlan, Tula, and Tlalchihualtepec (Mountain of Unfired Bricks)—featured massive stone pyramids as well, the latter dedicated to the feathered-serpent deity Quetzalcoatl.[44] Of these great tollans, all eventually destroyed, the *Cantares* recount: "truly the Toltecs once lived there."[45]

For the Mexica and their descendants, creation from destruction was a pattern with cosmic precedence. Mexica teachings held that at the conclusion of each age, the old world is demolished and a new one is created along with new creatures and new landscapes. Different Suns (ages) are linked to transformations—in landscapes and beings—of cosmic power, teotl. The rulers' deliberate rewriting and reworking of the past balanced the universe according to these Mexica principles: new days result from struggles amongst the Sun (Life) and Moon (Death); new ages result from struggles between the patrons of the four cardinal dimensions (North, South, East, West).[46] The implosion and recreation of days and ages are the result of cataclysmic change and subsequent rebalance brought by the gods and steadied by ceremony and just leadership.

Nauha students also recorded traditional stories and teachings that recalled the previous ages and how each had met its end.[47] An account included in the *Annals of Cuauhtitlan*, also recorded around 1570—likely by one of Sahagún's students—tells that the first and earliest age, called the Sun of 4 Atl (Water), came to an end when the world was flooded and all the inhabitants became fish.[48] The second age—the Sun of 4 Ocelotl (Jaguar)—was ruled by Tezcatlipoca (Smoking Mirror), patron of the north. This world, the Age of Giants, ended when mighty jaguars devoured the Sun. Next came the Sun of 4 Quiahuitl (Rain), ruled by Tlaloc, god of rain and lightening. During this age it rained fire and the earth was covered in tezontle; Quetzalcoatl (Feathered Serpent) formed humans from this world's ashes. At the end of the final Toltec era, the Sun of 4 Ehecatl Quetzalcoatl (Wind), the humans were transformed into monkeys and swept into the mountains by a hurricane.[49]

While the Toltecs had maintained a system of Four Suns, the Mexica added a fifth, the Sun of 4 Ollin (Movement). This age was ruled by the god of the east, Tonatiuh (associated with the Mexica solar god, Huitzilopochtli), also known as Ollin Tonatiuh (Solar Movement). An account recorded in the *Florentine Codex* places the beginnings of 4 Ollin in flames, when the gods at Teotihuacan invited the ordinary person Nanahuatzin to immolate himself to bring forth the dawn.⁵⁰ According to another version, after Huitzilopochtli was born, his siblings attacked their mother Coatlicue (Serpents, Her Skirt) at Mount Coatepec (Serpent Mountain).⁵¹ Huitzilopochtli vanquished his four hundred cloud-serpent brothers (Centzonhuitznahua) and transformed them into stars. His sister Coyolxauhqui became the Moon and Huitzilopochtli took the form of the Sun (Tonatiuh). Every night, during the long period of darkness between dusk and dawn, Huitzilopochtli reenacts this epic battle with his siblings. As indicated by its name, the Fifth Sun is expected to end in earthquake, famine, and upheaval.⁵²

Ensuring the cosmos remained balanced when passing from one age to the next required certain precautions, and each end of the fifty-two-year cycle requires specific protocols as well. These actions, such as the "New Fire" or "Binding of the Years" ceremony—which welcomes the new Sun through the ritual extinguishing of the old fire at dusk and lighting of a new fire at dawn—were dictated by prophecy and divine instructions as recorded and performed by the tlacuiloque and other ritual experts. In preparation, animate or votive objects from the former Sun (or antiguo times) were broken and discarded or buried. Those selected to persist into the next age—called "pre-Sunrise" objects because they belonged to the time before the current Sun—were repaired and readied for their new roles.⁵³ The extinguishing of fires at the beginning of the New Fire ceremony not only evoked the diurnal solar year and the Sun cycles but also Huitzilopochtli's birth, and therefore, the rise of Mexica power.⁵⁴ On this occasion, the previous fifty-two years are "bound up" by the ceremonial recitation of the "bundled" records.⁵⁵ All years are covered—often by multiple performers—and the retellings emphasize the most relevant stories and events.⁵⁶ Thus the New Fire ceremony, reminiscent of Nanahuatzin's sacrifice, is a form of embodied historical record keeping, compressing the events of many eras into one evening.⁵⁷

Mexica leaders recreated their world to emphasize the new Mexica age. Under the rule of tlatoque (s. tlatoani) Itzcoatl (reign 1428–1440) and Motecuhzoma I (reign 1440–1469), the Mexica-Tenochca capital's gridded layout, causeways, canals, and doubled Templo Mayor dedicated to Huitzilopochtli and Tlaloc were expressly constructed to recreate the cosmic arrangements of Aztlán and the tollans.⁵⁸ Starting with Itzcoatl, the tlacuiloque (professional scribes) produced new records centering Huitzilopochtli, presenting history from a Tenochca-Mexica perspective and instantiating Tenochtitlan's rule as the beginning of a new life.⁵⁹ Whereas previous ages had belonged to Olmec, Teotihuacano, Chichimec, or Toltec peoples, the current Sun belonged to the Tenochca-Mexica, in the present and the past.

When rulers like Motecuhzoma I gathered olmecah and toltecah statues, ceramics, and masks, these pre-Sunrise items were not just meant to recall illustrious forebears or evoke the cycle of ages: they were a technique to harness these items' teotl.[60] Pre-Sunrise items reiterated cosmic history and visualized the cosmic balance of power; incorporating them into the Tenochca-Mexica world had the effect of placing the Triple Alliance in an auspicious position in the spiraling sacred cycle of time.

ALTHOUGH THE SIXTEENTH- AND seventeenth-century Franciscans and Jesuits were careful to investigate and document Indigenous lifeways in their own style, access to—or expressions of—antiguo Mexico were seen as dangerous to Spanish eyes. "Pagan" materials were still subject to seizure: those not exported were locked away in royal treasuries, out of sight of reportedly impressionable Indigenous viewers.[61] Yet as mapas depicting "idolatrous" scenes and "ugly" stone "idols" (god images) and other votive figures were publicly destroyed—whether forcibly or voluntarily—others were secreted away inside houses, caves, or buried underground, many still in Mexico City's center.[62] Unlike pre-Sunrise objects, these items were usually interred whole because breaking them would cause them to become unstable. In one piece, their power was still useful in the new colonial age. In this way, Nahua peoples maintained the cosmic balance as best they could, creating continuity with los antiguos.

Thus, despite colonial-era efforts to displace and replace Mexica society, the old city still lived beneath the new one, its innumerable pre-Sunrise (antiguo) objects testament to an ongoing cosmic historicism. When Indigenous families left their segregated districts and moved into the traza for work, often living with Spanish families, they became even closer to the "idols" that had been built into exterior walls or secreted away inside.[63] Thus the god images and other powerful items inside the plaster of their homes or under the pavement continued to enable the cohabitation of Mexica past with the Nahua and settler presents.[64] In the late eighteenth century, as criollos-americanos turned to antiguo objects for their own needs, they further enabled that cohabitation.

Visualizing Antiguo Mexico

Despite the growing restrictions on Indigenous studies in the late seventeenth century, some criollo scholars still turned to structures and sculptures—both above and below ground—to demonstrate the antiquity of Indigenous peoples in the Americas.[65] Carlos de Sigüenza y Góngora, for example, performed a partial excavation of the Pyramid of the Sun at Teotihuacan in 1675.[66] Boturini went to Teotihuacan, too, likely bringing a few pieces back to his museum.[67] The well-publicized excavations in the Spanish Kingdom of Naples and arrival of the celebrated *Le Antichità di Ercolano eposte* (1757–92) volumes—which contained illustrations of the king's Herculaneum collection at Portici—caused a stir in Mexico City, further encouraging landowners and savants to amass their own collections of antiquities.[68] Elite hacendados who searched for bits of hidden history—or, more accurately, ordered Indigenous bondspeople to do so—not infrequently turned up caches of statuary, pottery, or funerary remains on their vast landholdings, sometimes broken, sometimes whole. While the neoclassical style inspired by the Vesuvian excavations resulted in a profusion of decorative candelabras and laurel swags in Europe, householders in New Spain took their decorative cues more locally, crafting cornerstones, baptismal fonts, and patio walls out of unearthed Indigenous sculptures, placing the massive monuments from the past on display.

In 1786, criollo mathematician José Antonio Alzate y Ramírez in Mexico City received a letter from his colleague José Francisco Ruiz Cañete, which described a beautifully carved stone slab recovered from the rancho belonging to his family northeast of the capital.[69] Ruiz explained that, not wanting to leave the carving behind, he had ordered the "Indios Carpinteros" at the rancho to dismantle, relocate, and reassemble it as a sluice box ("la caxa de un Placer"), an exceedingly pedestrian use for such an allegedly exceptional stone. Ruiz also described encountering a "very ugly" statue that he did not take home, one he identified as an "ídolo" in human form, missing its head and arms. Ruiz recalled that over the years many such pieces had been taken from the rancho and used as material for outbuildings, courtyard pavers, or decoration.[70] In his great-grandfather's days, he remembered, a disinterred stone lion had been affixed to a font of holy water.[71] The previous proprietors had engaged in a process of selective secularization, wherein certain Indigenous elements were deemed aesthetically pleasing and valuable (i.e., the sacred jaguar became a heraldic lion) while "ugly" god images were rejected as "idols" and therefore left in place.

Ruiz's account demonstrates the ubiquity of Indigenous statuary on view in eighteenth-century New Spain, almost all of which—like his sluice box—were the result of Indigenous laborers doing the work of excavation and transportation. Indeed, almost every broken ídolo installed in the walls and patios of New Spain had been placed there by Indigenous hands. In Mexico City, for example, fragments of the Templo Mayor went into the city's first Catholic church, which Cortés had placed at the intersection of Tenochtitlan's four altepeme as a stony declaration of Spanish power. Likewise, pieces of Motecuhzoma's palace became building stones for the viceregal complex. During the late eighteenth-century canal renovation project workers reportedly broke and reused unearthed monuments to repair the flood-prone plaza. These structures, as much a display of Indigenous presence as they are of criollo and Spanish visions of the ancient past, were literally built *from* Indigenous materials *by* Indigenous people. Ruiz thus provides a lesson in how to see in New Spanish architecture an ongoing system of extractive labor and a reiteration of Cortés's original project in which Indigenous subjects were forced to dismantle their own history but which, at the same time, kept that past close at hand.

Ruiz's letter also hints at a network of criollo-americano antiquaries extending outside the capital city, a patriotic cohort who discussed the Indigenous past in terms of beauty, utility, and historicity. Whereas the previous generation of criollos had prioritized the recovery and translation of manuscripts, this one increasingly utilized the material world to construct their histories. Criollos-americanos like Alzate and Ruiz were learning to read paper documents and landscape features as parallel texts. Moreover, they began to consider the Indigenous materials as records not only of the past—as in proof that "it" happened—but as interpretive sources from which to learn *about* the past as well. Gradually, criollo-americano past-making practices shifted from that of typical antiquarianism—accentuated by the self-evident "pastness" of accumulated physical artifacts—to that of historiography: that is to say, the creation of a past through expert description and interpretation.[72]

By the end of the eighteenth century, criollos-americanos had created a circuit of "must-see" archaeological sites. Although they knew of the interest Clavijero and his predecessors had shown in the supposedly Mexica structures in the north, these criollos-americanos kept their eyes largely focused on the kingdom's tollans or toltecatl sites in the center and south. Some of the first to receive their descriptive attentions were Cholula, El Tajín (Paplanta), and Xochicalco. But Mexico City was really where the criollo vision of the Mexica past was clearest.

Seeing the City under the City

In 1769, Alzate had been selected to lead the Archdiocese of México's spatial organization project called "secularization," that is to say, the integration of segregated Indigenous and Spanish parishes. According to the sixteenth-century principle of the "república de indias," Indigenous residents of the capital lived apart from the Europeans, who occupied the center of the city or traza.[73] Initially, all of the city's Indigenous residents had been confined to a single parish, San José de los Naturales, but after 1560 six Indigenous-only parishes (known as "doctrinas de indios") were installed across the city's four quarters. Congregational separation was meant to facilitate evangelization, tribute collection, and the administration of the forced labor drafts as well as surveillance; after the 1692 uprisings, the segregation lines were redoubled.[74] Despite migration over the course of the eighteenth century, Indigenous residents were still compelled to belong to the doctrina where they used to live. Among other things, this caused a crisis of funding: for if Indigenous residents attended parishes outside of their home neighborhoods, the local parishes were deprived of their tithes. Alzate was called upon by Archbishop Lorenzana to study the problem and to propose a system for dissolving the caste-based spatial segregation. Although the project itself ended in 1772, Alzate did not stop learning about the city's Indigenous history.

Before the Spanish takeover, Tenochtitlan had been comprised of four political divisions—the altepeme Moyotlan, Teopan, Atzacoalco, and Cuepopan—each separated by canals and causeways running from the city's ceremonial center to territories across the lake.[75] The Spanish would later term these divisions "parcialidades," (quarters) and would preserve their boundaries and names: thus the initial quarters of Mexico City were San Juan Moyotlan, San Pablo Teopan, San Sebastián Atzacoalco, and Santa María Cuepopan (later Santa María la Redonda).[76] In México-Tenochtitlan, residents belonged to a specific politico-ethnic enclave of a given parcialidad, units called "tlaxilacalli" or "calpolli" (later called "barrios" by the Spanish), which each had separate leadership, duties, patron gods, and specific monumental architecture.[77] The new Spanish city's administrative barrios (neighborhoods) largely followed the spatial arrangement of the old ethnic units, which in turn allowed for a level of Indigenous control and continuity. Thus, with Indigenous life and identity still centered in the altepetl and its internal divisions in the sixteenth and seventeenth centuries, many of the ethnic identity groupings and subgroupings were sustained—spatially and in other ways—into the later colonial period.[78] México-Tenochtitlan's placenames, too, endured, as the pastor of San José de los Naturales, Friar Agustín de Vetancurt, documented in the late seventeenth century, and some endure today.[79]

In 1789, Alzate began to revisualize the former Indigenous city. Alzate had prior cartographical experience: in 1767, he had copied a map depicting the Pacific coast of New Spain, which he updated into a map of southern North America the following year.[80] This map is noteworthy for the fact that it places most Indigenous peoples and places far to the north of Mexico City, not inside central New Spain.[81] According to historian Matthew O'Hara, Alzate "believed there were few true Indians left in urban areas" and that "pure Indians" only lived in the countryside, such as on the hacienda where Alzate grew up. Thinking that real Indigenous presence in Mexico City was a thing of the past, Alzate proceeded to look for it in the past.[82] He pursued his social-mapping project with reference to important archival antecedents: Sigüenza's map for the strengthening of segregation after 1692; Vetancurt's records of Indigenous placenames in *Teatro mexicano* (1698); and another map, held among Boturini's materials: *El Plano de Tenoxtitlan*.[83] Alzate also had prior experience with Nahuatl and put particular stock in Indigenous languages as keys to Indigenous worlds. From his work on the papers of sixteenth-century Spanish naturalist Francisco Hernández de Toledo, for example, he had learned that Nahuatl plant names were a vast "storehouse of knowledge."[84] As Alzate walked Mexico City's streets, he could still perceive the borders and identities of México-Tenochtitlan's neighborhoods as noted on his sources.[85]

Using these words and examples, Alzate would create a new map of the old city in 1789. This reconstruction project was necessary, he believed, because "the Mexican denominations will promptly be destroyed ['exterminando']" and preserving the names would provide "much knowledge of this part of history."[86] Using a 1778 map of the contemporary city, Alzate overlaid what he had learned about the spatiality of Tenochtitlán, showing the sixteenth-century ethnic organization in eighteenth-century space.[87] In a cartouche at the bottom of the sheet Alzate explained his map as meant "to give a sense of the people of ancient [antiguo] Mexico," certainly implying that "the people" otherwise had no such sense.

Alzate's 1789 map outlined the borders of Tenochtitlan's altepeme and sixty-nine of its tlaxilaclque, providing boldface numbers for the latter to index their Nahuatl names and Spanish translations. To better visualize the original quarters, Alzate outlined them in yellow, blue, red, or green, superimposing Nahuatl names across the old altepeme.[88] These colors were not haphazard; they emulated the yellow causeways, blue canals, and red teocalme on the *Plano de Tenoxtitlan*.[89] The city's ceremonial center, overlaying the Spanish traza, was outlined in yellow and annotated in red: a manacle points to the Templo de Huitzilopochtli and a star locates the Palace of Axayacatl, Motecuhzoma's (and Cortés's) former seat.[90] Alzate certainly did not provide every neighborhood name—perhaps this was because Mexica cosmological names were not usually bestowed on churches (likely for reasons of "idolatry"), and many by the 1780s were no longer in (public) use. Yet the volume of Indigenous toponyms listed in the key is nonetheless striking.[91] Indeed, the entire execution implies that Alzate attempted to create something resembling a mapa antiguo.

FIGURE 10. José Antonio de Alzate y Ramírez, "Plano de Tenochtitlan" (1789), detail. Courtesy of the Bibliothèque Nationale de France. Map is shown without legend or cartouche.

Marking the borders of quarters and neighborhoods were important civic functions in Mexica society and were reserved to a special class of elders who occupied the Huehuecalco (House of the Elders), the seat of social history in Tenochtitlan.[92] Alzate numbered the quarters in such a way as to follow the counterclockwise priority of altepetl responsibilities (which set the order of duties performed for the huey tlatoani or great ruler). Preserving that social spatial order, Alzate started with Moyotlan, the most important quarter and heart of the Indigenous city, where the Huehuecalco was located.[93] Thus in creating his mapa, Alzate took on the role of a tlaxilacalli elder, recalling who belonged where and why. He visualized duties and identities spatially, and his map allowed non-Nahuatl speakers to think that they, too, could do the same. Whereas previous maps performed what art historian Barbara Mundy terms "cartographic effacements," Alzate's 1789 map made the Indigenous city highly visible.[94]

Yet Alzate sought only to preserve that which he understood as historical and geographic, not cosmic.[95] Perhaps for this reason, most names on Alzate's map seem straightforward: Tzapotlan (Sapote Tree Place), Tecpancaltitlan (Next to the Tecpan), Teocaltitlan (Next to the Temple), Tequezquipan (Place of Much Salt), Tomatlan (Tomato Place). Likely, however, those translations were just the first-level meanings he was able to discern with his limited grasp of the language. For example, while Alzate noted the location of two "Places of Serpents" (Coatlán), he did not connect them to Coatlicue (Huitzilopochtli's mother) or the beginning of the Fifth Age, which would have required a more metaphorical interpretation. Similarly, Alzate's map provided no explanation for why Hueipantonco is the "Land of Great Things," implying that the higher-level meaning—at least—was lost on him.[96] While purporting to provide "a sense of the people of ancient Mexico," the map instead described a Mexica topography—rather than Nahua ontology—that may no longer have held literal relevance (such as number forty-one, "Where They Twist Ropes"). Nonetheless, because many of the new churches and chapels retained their Nahuatl names into the eighteenth century, Alzate assumed they were continuous with toponyms of the past.[97] In some ways this was true, due to the symbolic importance of parishes to community life.[98] Having physically built most of the doctrinas' churches and chapels—as well as funded their construction—Indigenous communities made the buildings and interiors into "a type of communal spiritual capital."[99] These spaces adapted tlaxilacalli identity and functioned to cohere an ethnically and spatially specific Nahua identity throughout the eighteenth century.[100] Alzate's knowledge of the locations, however, came not from Indigenous residents themselves—whom he believed no longer existed—but from the "Indian" archive, which preserved a past rather than present record of Indigenous México.

Alzate's reconstructed Tenochtitlan was a colonial artifact that perpetuated colonial interpretations of Nahua space. In this sense, even the map's recovery of literal place and practice still results in an effacement of contemporary belief and existence. Nonetheless, because the spatial arrangement of lots and neighborhoods as well as the distribution of monumental architecture and sacred sites enacted the Mexica migration history—which sixteenth-century historian Tezozómoc recalled was dictated by Huitzilopochtli himself—the preservation of these spaces into the colonial era meant the preservation of that living narrative.[101] Moreover, because it was at the level of the altepetl and its subdivisions that the duties and identities of an individual Mexica person would have become socially legible and because tlaxilacalli identities comprised a "crucial part of residents' sense of themselves in the city," Alzate's map did—by extension and by accident—repopulate a Nahua city, even when one criollo-americano had learned to visualize, but not see, it.[102]

Observing the Empire's Archive

The renovations that revealed the piedras antiguas in 1790 were part of a larger program of imperial revitalization pushed onto the colonies from the imperial center.[103] The Bourbon kings Carlos III (reign 1759–1788) and Carlos IV (reign 1788–1808) pursued "modernization" agendas that advanced infrastructural, secularization, and economic reforms, including new "scientific" forms of labor management, population control, and resource extraction.[104] Spain's power over its overseas kingdoms had wavered a century before—exemplified by the 1692 "tumulto de los indios"—but the imperial grip had been progressively tightening ever since, particularly renewed in the eighteenth century by an influx of American raw material to the Iberian Peninsula and changes in reigning power.[105] The new Spanish court, in the thrall of Enlightenment theories of science and governance, was eager to enact them in the Americas.[106] In New Spain, the imperial government enforced new fiscal policies (including new Royal monopolies, taxes, and increased exports), installed standing armies, and reorganized the kingdom into twelve new "intendencies" (districts).[107] Whereas formerly most of the colony's bureaucratic posts had been held by American-educated, religious criollos, these positions were increasingly filled by secular "peninsulares" who looked to bring the colony under closer Spanish oversight.[108] The Crown also attempted to mitigate Church power by seizing Church property, expelling Jesuits, and encouraging the appointment of European rather than mendicant (usually criollo) parish priests.

The Crown also sponsored long distance expeditions to sites of scientific, historical, and economic interest around and beyond the empire. Beginning with the 1768 Franciscan explorations of what became Alta California and the 1779 Bodega y Quadra excursion to "Puerto de Santiago"—presently Port Etches, Alaska—overseas voyages brought Madrid new information about the world while attempting to lay claim to Pacific lands ahead of Russian and British competitors. In 1789, Carlos IV backed Alessandro Malaspina's famous "Voyage of Discovery" that sailed the Pacific for five years and gained an enormous amount of intelligence as well as territory and "natural resources."[109] On the mainland, the Crown sponsored an official exploration of the reportedly ancient ruins in the Kingdom of Guatemala near the village of Santo Domingo de Palenque as well as the Expedicíon Botánica al Virreinato de Nueva España (1787-1803) led by Spanish physician Martín Sessé y Lacasta and accompanied by botanists José Mariano Mociño (criollo) and Vicente Cervantes (Spanish).[110] The Sessé-Mociño team set off to explore areas near Cuernavaca and Acapulco before turning northward to the provinces of Michoacán, Guadalajara, Sonora, and Sinaloa in 1790.[111] By 1792, Mociño was sailing off the coast of current-day Alaska, writing about the lands, plants, and peoples he encountered in his 1794 *Noticias de Nutka*. As many of the Crown's exploring and military activities—often led by Europeans—focused on New Spain's borderlands, soon New Orleans, Pensacola, and San Francisco threatened to eclipse Mexico City as the center of New Spanish intelligence.

With the rapidly shifting alliances of the late eighteenth century and Crown attention drawn to farther-flung territories, Mexico City's criollos realized the potential for their political and intellectual marginalization as well: for while administrative power was still coming from Madrid, the balance of intellectual power seemed to be moving north and eastward.[112] Already, the US capital of Philadelphia had become a cosmopolitan hub for science, especially thanks to the preeminent American Philosophical Society, founded by Benjamin Franklin in 1743. Increasingly those Spanish subjects in Havana or Madrid who could have come to México headed north instead.[113] Criollos-americanos, too, looked abroad rather than at home for intellectual inspiration. Yet increasing marginalization also pressed criollos-americanos to express their expertise over the lands of their birth in the scientific lingua franca of the Atlantic: observation and description. Long an important component of natural philosophy, by the mid-eighteenth century "scientific observation" was a practice and form of knowledge in its own right, and criollos-americanos readily took it up to maintain a say in transatlantic conversations.[114]

Although European naturalists and cartographers could easily observe and describe peoples, landscapes, and plants seen on their expeditions, their access was limited to that which was in the present moment and close at hand. Both criollos-americanos and Europeans vied to gain and maintain interpretive authority over the records of Mexica history, of which Boturini's collection was emblematic. These materials comprised, mainly, the "cacique-creole archive" that had been written or assembled by Indigenous historians (such as Alvarado Tezozómoc, Ixtlilxóchitl, Chimalpahin, etc.) and mapas that had become part of—or were products of—colonial administration.[115] Thus the opportunity for first-person observation enabled by criollos-americanos' physical proximity to American materials—as well as their ability to transcribe, translate, and transmit those sights abroad—became a prominent way of asserting their authority and ownership of New World information, especially of knowledge about the past. To capitalize on their new position, criollos-americanos emphasized the importance of their direct access to original physical monuments and reproduction from eyewitness, not exegesis. In this way, criollos made sure that *they* were the experts; theirs was an acquisitive, possessive visuality that occluded other sightings of the past.

In the 1780s and 1790s, prominent criollos-americanos in Mexico City organized periodicals and salons to disseminate the newest scientific developments from Europe, the United States, and South America and to circulate their own first-hand observations across the Atlantic world.[116] Due to the high patriotic stakes, criollos-americanos were keen to challenge foreign interpretations of New Spain with their own descriptions of "Mexican antiquities"; indeed, they were particularly interested in disseminating correct—or at least favorable—interpretations of American materials.[117] In 1788, Alzate founded the magazine *Gazeta de Literatura de México*, which over its seven years in print became the mouthpiece for European-inspired, Enlightenment-era scientific and political writings.[118] In its inaugural issue, Alzate announced the magazine's commitment to detail "the few antiquities that remain of the Mexican nation" and to conserve "in writing the irrefutable records that serve as an index to the genius, character, and customs of the Mexican nation," making clear the connection between historical description and criollo patriotism.[119] Although a supporter of the Bourbon renovation projects, Alzate worried that New Spain's "ancient" history would be forgotten in the push for modernization.[120] He thus highlighted the need to preserve antiquities through description because if otherwise, "in the short span of a century, scarcely any records will still be found."[121] Connectedly, Alzate promised to include engravings of the antiquities in the magazine, "if the printing costs [could] sustain it."[122] The organization of this field of readers resulted in increasing interest in criollos reproducing and interpreting the colonial archive for themselves.

Until the publication of Clavijero's *Storia antica del Messico*, the Crown and its viceregal agents had been largely ambivalent about the "Indian" archive in New Spain. Boturini's materials had been seized, after all, largely in consequence of his support for the Virgin of Guadalupe and his allegedly unauthorized presence, not because of the danger—or value—of his collection's contents. In 1780, however, the Spanish Crown issued the first in a series of royal orders to remand all colonial records—including Boturini's—to Spain.[123] This assertion of royal prerogative to claim any records from "the Indies" targeted the very materials and themes that criollos-americanos believed was their own heritage. In response, throughout the 1780s and 1790s, a team of Mexico City americanos—comprised of Mariano Fernández de Echeverría y Veytia, Diego García Panes, José Joaquín Granados y Gálvez, and Antonio de León y Gama—worked to "take copies" of the records for their personal collections.¹²⁴ The copying they performed—not just the reproductions made to keep paper documents in the country but also those copies made of archaeological artifacts—prioritized both criollo-americano eyewitness *and* possession. When, in 1791, Boturini's collection was again inventoried and the entire holdings of the Royal and Pontifical University transferred to Madrid the following year, this seemed to confirm Mexico City's antiquaries' fears of losing their patria's treasures forever.¹²⁵ Thus the americanos' replication of the viceregal archive was a deliberate gesture through which to claim Mexican heritage as well as Mexican title on criollo grounds.¹²⁶ León y Gama, who served on the high court and in the viceregal Secretariat, had exceptional access to the archive of colonial records that made him a particularly important node in the Mexico City network of criollo knowledge production. He even hired an artist to copy records for a year and a half in an effort he described in 1796 "to prevent the Mexican monuments from leaving here"—if not in form—then at least in content.¹²⁷

In some ways, the conspiracy worked: although many of the Boturini materials ultimately left Mexico for Spain—as well as France, Britain and the United States—at least four copies of the collection were in existance by the end of the 1790s. This criollo-americano version of the "Indian" archive—many steps away from the supposedly forgotten "pre-Hispanic" past they were assumed to represent—became "a substantial element of what is today Mexican historiography."¹²⁸ The new archive, both in Spain and across the Atlantic world, was a thoroughly transformed version of the Indigenous past as *americano* history.

Publishing Possessive Visuality

The transformation of physical Indigenous materials into printed paper records would become the hallmark of criollo-americano description. Indeed, to ensure correct versions of American history, criollos-americanos added the crucial visual component of engraved illustrations to their verbal descriptions. Ultimately they described the past as much with pictures as with words. By adjusting and adapting the reigning conventions, criollo-americano observers became local examples of transitional *settler* visual regimes that included select aspects of Indigenous-built landscapes when describing American history.¹²⁹ While their visuality was certainly conversant with Western epistemological priorities and the politically and ethnically specific "visual appetite" that art historian Daniela Bleichmar has called a "Hispanic way of knowing empire," the criollo-americano model of visuality was expressly—and possessively—American in that it also mirrored the visuality of Mexica mapas.¹³⁰

Because descriptions or "copies" were, as León y Gama put it, attempts to keep the monuments in their possession, criollos-americanos valued technical accuracy in their reproductions. These late eighteenth-century scholars, however, were certainly not the first to illustrate ancient Mexican history, but the engravings in earlier Spanish chronicles had largely been narrative reconstructions rather than eyewitness depictions or testimonies. Boturini's *Idea*, for example, contained no images and only spare verbal description; Clavijero's illustrations were made in Europe and based on previously published images. The illustrations for antiquarian writings by criollos-americanos Alzate or Ruiz, however, were engraved contemporaneously from sketches taken on-the-spot and reproduced with the explicit promise of verisimilitude.[131] To this point, even if only the criollos-americanos were authorized to make the descriptions, it was nonetheless a patriotic imperative for all Spanish subjects to view them. This quasi-democratic impulse assumed that all (criollos) not only *could* know these materials but also that they *should*.

For this reason, the two important and criollo-run periodicals in Mexico City, *Gazeta de México* (the Viceroyalty's semiofficial publication, founded in 1784) and Alzate's *Gazeta de Literatura* (founded in 1788), frequently centered topics of transatlantic and hemispheric scientific, historical, and literary interest. An early issue of *Gazeta de México*, for example, described a cache of gigantic bones—tusks, shoulder blades, and femurs—unearthed during excavations at Mexico City's Tepeyac Hill quarry, fossils that the author related to the "Elephant bones" emerging in Siberia and Canada as well as those "in abundance on the banks of the Ohio River."[132] Another example appeared in the July 12, 1785, issue in which a government inspector named Diego Ruiz described his visit to the "Pirámide de los Nichos" at El Tajín (Paplanta) in the highlands near the Gulf coast (now Veracruz state).[133] Describing the structure's dimensions rather than its appearance—and counting its 1,075 steps—Ruiz included an idealized illustration depicting the site's main pyramid in a style reminiscent of the engraving of Teotihuacan used by Clavijero.[134] In so doing, agent Ruiz placed El Tajín within Teotihuacan's aesthetic—and therefore historical—lineage. This article notably increased criollos' and Europeans' desire to see El Tajín and to locate other structures within that Teotihuacano lineage as well.[135] And as Ruiz had done in 1785, in 1791 Alzate also provided a description and engraving of the pyramid at Xochicalco, similarly placing it on the criollo-americano circuit of the past.[136] In using Teotihuacan as a model against which to compare other Indigenous architectures, Ruiz and Alzate applied a Mexica sense of the Toltec past that was circulated, visually, in printed media. Not only were criollos-americanos describing the Mexica history around them: they were also recreating their own images of that past in the present.

Mapping Migration from the North

Alzate could not have missed Mexica migration history entirely while mapping Mexico City because afterward he redoubled his interests in locating Azteca origins, which had surfaced on the simple map he created for Archbishop Lorenzana's *Historia*—depicting Cortés's voyages and measuring the distance from Mexico City to Hawikuh (Cíbola)—as well as on his extremely detailed 1768 map of southern North America.[137] On that latter map, Alzate depicted not only the rivers Gila and Colorado, the Gulf of California, and Cíbola but also "Quivíra Fabulosa" and the place from which "the Mexican Indians left to found their Empire," the "Laguna de Teguyo."[138] In an article on Mexica origins published in his magazine, Alzate stated that the Mexica journey had begun when they "left the North, in the vicinity of the Tehuallo [Teguayo] Lagoon," and he identified the position at "41 degrees latitude and 265 and a half longitude," supposed to index Mowichat, or Nootka Sound, the site of contemporaneous territorial disputes among Spain, Britain, and the US.[139] Locating Mexica homelands in the Pacific Northwest, therefore, could potentially tip the scales of possession.

Relying on descriptions portrayed in Captain Cook's *A Voyage to the Pacific Ocean* (1784) and records of the 1775 Bodega y Quadra expedition, Alzate registered similarities between Nu-chah-nulth (Nootka) and Mexica peoples. For example, on plate forty-two in the atlas from Cook's *Third Voyage,* in an image of two sculpted pillars in a Nuu-chah-nulth dwelling—probably painted divider screens—Alzate detected a resemblance to "two pilasters sculpted with base-relief hieroglyphs" retrieved from the banks of Lake Texcoco at Pantitlan in 1767.[140] He concluded that if others also compared Mexican monuments to Captain Cook's illustrations, they too would "feel the oneness from sculpture to sculpture."[141] Alzate also noted a supposed similarity between Nuu-chah-nulth and Otomí women's clothing, and proposed—with unclear evidence—a similarity across language ("la lengua de los Nootcacos" and the "idioma Mexicano").[142] Not just an "interesting point in the History," to Alzate the connection meant that "Nootka" lands were once in Mexica (or even Otomí or Chichimeca) hands. To further support his hypothesis that New Spain's peoples migrated from Nootka, Alzate referenced traditions of migration allegedly held by all the "Naciones del Norte," not just the Mexica.[143] That these traditions were reliable indicators of a path rested on the fact that—as it had for Clavijero—the migrants had left physical records in the form of "antiquities which still remain," including "'casa grande' on the banks of the Rio Gila, and that of 'casas grandes' in the vicinity of the Presidio de Janos."[144] Alzate did not just transpose Mexica forebears: he transported all of central Mexican history northward.[145]

This conflation of disparate locations was not just cartographic imprecision: locating the Mexica homeland at 41 (and potentially also 49.5) degrees north amounted to a possessive tactic in the contemporary contest between Britain and Spain for the Pacific coast. Although his coordinates for the location of Mexica origins land in the water, a cross-comparison with those recorded by Mociño in 1792 gives a sense of what Alzate meant: N 41°33', W 127° instead of W 265.5° is still a location in the Pacific Ocean but it is not far from the California coast near the town of Klamath, within the current-day Yurok Indian Reservation.[146] This is also the spot that Juan Francisco de la Bodega y Quadra and Bruno de Heceta had renamed Trinity Bay in 1775. In fact, the Olekwo'l (Yurok) and Taa-laa-wa Dee-ni' Big Lagoon Rancheria is not far off from this site. It is therefore conceivable that "Tehuallo" (or Teguayo) is an approximation of "Tolowa" (or Taa-laa-wa), a Yurok name for the Dee-ni' peoples in the area.[147] Teguayo, the governor of New Orleans Esteban Rodríguez Miró reminded the Spanish Crown in 1785, was believed to be the location of Aztlán.[148]

Despite the inaccuracy of Alzate's directions, his intention is clear: to move Mexican origins north and locate Mexica ancestors in disputed Nuu-chah-nulth homelands. If, Alzate wrote in 1792, most of the Mexican monuments had not already been destroyed, then given the expanse of territory Alzate imagined the Mexica had once lived on, there would still be proof that Mexicans were once "one of the most powerful peoples in the world."[149] While Alzate would also insist that antiquities proved the "legitimate origin of Indians," by then he had already been thinking about the connection between Indigenous origins and Mexican monuments for some time; for Alzate, those connections were related to laying claim—linguistically, cartographically, and visually—to Indigenous homelands via Indigenous history.

Identifying Mexican History

In the late summer of 1790, the first piedra antigua was set aright in front of one of the viceregal palace doors, facing the former Plaza Mayor. The night it was hoisted up, onlookers immediately identified the stone as belonging to "the ancient temple of the Mexicans" once located on the site.[150] One guard remembered noticing that the statue was "without feet or head" and had a "skull on its back and another skull in front with four hands."[151] Some viewers speculated it was a statue of Huitzilopochtli; others insisted it was Tezcatlipoca.[152] To those familiar with Spanish rather than Mexica aesthetics, the statue's snakes, dismembered hands, and array of human skulls may have implied the themes of death and war and inspired descriptions of the statue as an "ugly idol."[153]

From his desk just steps away in the palace office, Antonio de León y Gama—one of the patriotic criollos-americanos working to copy New Spain's viceregal records before they disappeared to Madrid—had watched the excavation with particular attention. He believed that the monument would provide a correct understanding of "the Indians of this America," and for this reason approved of its display.[154] However, worried that the unrestricted exposure would subject it to the actions of "crude and childish people" and increase the damage already caused by extraction, León y Gama soon began to advocate for the piedra's protection and installation at the Royal and Pontifical University within the palace complex.[155] Before it was moved, however, he took "an exact copy of it, in order to keep it in my possession, as an original monument of Antiquity."[156] The fearsome "idol"—now commonly acknowledged as an image of Huitzilopochtli's mother, Coatlicue—was indeed sent to the University, where she attracted long lines of supplicants who left behind candles and various offerings in the courtyard where she stood.[157]

Yet despite this attention, in the December 13, 1790 issue of his *Gazeta de Literatura*, Alzate admitted with some surprise that no one had yet written of the piedra.[158] Four days later the second "grande lápida" was uncovered; Alzate printed a short notice in the new year's *Gazeta* and wrote about the topic again a few weeks later.[159] In these brief contributions, he identified the stones as part of the Plaza Mayor ceremonial complex, and he suggested that the second stone was a sacrificial or calendrical statue. Alzate also tentatively offered the identities of Huitzilopochtli, Tezcatlipoca, and Tlaloc for the first stone. Without expertise in the inscriptions, however, Alzate admitted his fear of looking for meaning where there was none to find (not, notably, where the meaning was merely not known to him).[160] Overall he proclaimed the task "not suited to his temper."[161] For Alzate, the statues posed a problem both of expertise and humility. But that did not keep others from seeking to know—and fix—what the stones "meant."[162]

A few months later, Alzate's brief writings on the piedras were critiqued in a letter to the *Gazeta de México*. The writer, styled "Ocelotl Tecuilhuitzintli," expressed his belief that the sculptures provided a much-needed opportunity to defend his American compatriots against European slander but that Alzate and his colleagues had failed to do so. To Tecuilhuitzintli, Alzate's failures indicated not merely a lack of knowledge, but a lack of direct, eyewitness observation. Tecuilhuitzintli identified the first statue as "Teotlacanexquimilli"—god of fog and obscurity—who was attended by the "shameful Venus" Tlazolteotl (Earth Lord) and Tlaltechtli (Filth Goddess), the "avenger of adulterers."[163] Those who had actually seen (or met) the statue, Tecuilhuitzintli continued, would never have mistaken it for the imperious Huitzilopochtli: "Everyone may have, Your Grace, the pleasure of meeting him [Teotlacanexquimilli] in the courtyard of this University, where he received me, Your Grace, this afternoon, standing, but without feet. The God of War, Señor Huitzilopochtli, is less courteous, and even if Moctezuma himself had entered [the courtyard] he would not have raised himself from his corner bench."[164] The amusing vignette made his point: had Alzate been led by Mexica priorities, he could never have made such an error in identification, which to Tecuilhuitzintli was an offense worse than European speculation. Indeed, he wrote, European detractors who "becloud our glories" were not nearly as treacherous as those who, though "born among us," nonetheless "shamelessly spread" misinformation.[165] The stone's true identity should have been obvious, chastised Tecuilhuitzintli, and Alzate's mistaken conclusions were a dereliction of patriotic duty.

Tecuilhuitzintli's emphasis on observation and description is itself telling, although not about the piedras' identities but instead about his own. Indeed, despite insisting that the first statue's identity was readily visible, Tecuilhuitzintli admits to taking interpretive cues from Boturini. In *Idea* and his museum, Boturini had identified a god-image in a passage repeated almost verbatim by Tecuilhuitzintli: "Teotlacanexquimilli, a dark bundle, or a god without feet or head, accompanied by Tlazolteotl, the shameful Venus, and by Tlateuctli, vengeful god of adulteries."[166] He also also confirmed that the second stone was indeed a "calendar"; he reported knowing that "the said sacrificial or meridian stone at least represents the Mexican months" from comparing their inscriptions to those on the mapas described by Boturini and Clavijero.[167] Despite what he saw as Alzate's errors, Tecuilhuitzintli's own identifications imply a studied rather than firsthand experience. Moreover, the limited opportunities to accomplish rarified antiquarian studies of the "Indian" archive betray Tecuilhuitzintli as criollo.

Accurately recognizing the specific iconography of the Mexica deities and inscriptions, as Tecuilhuitzintli alleges to have done, would have been almost impossible without some training in iconic Nahuatl as well as with the Spanish and alphabetic Nahuatl documents. Certainly, facility with spoken or alphabetic Nahuatl would have made understanding the iconic writing that much easier, and given his pseudonym Ocelotl Tecuilhuitzintli positioned himself as having an intimacy with Nahuatl language as well as Mexica cosmology. The pseudonym—which literally translates to "Jaguar Hummingbird-month"—ostentatiously evokes a Mexica naming practice. But nonetheless, because Nahuatl writing simultaneously relays visual, vocative, aromatic, and embodied concepts, reading its metaphorical and multisensorial dimensions requires erudite local knowledge and a lifetime of training.[168] Even if able to read on mimetic, conceptual, or phonetic levels, an untrained reader would still not be able to gather the text's entire meaning.[169] Tecuilhuitzintli must have had little sense of this, however, because he so forcefully asserts his absolute knowledge and thereby identifies himself even more clearly as a settler, not a Nahua, scholar. His letter demonstrates how the misappropriation of Indigenous concepts in criollo-americano history-making—on both material and epistemological levels—depended in large part on word *and* image. And although criollo historical methodology was potentially Nahua-inflected, it nonetheless ultimately asserted the primacy of Western over Indigenous knowledge frames.

Tecuilhuitzintli's "obvious" interpretation of the piedras antiguas implies something else as well, for the impulse to use Boturini's specific translation would only have occurred to Tecuilhuitzintli had he seen the image of Tlazolteotl (Earth Lord) carved into the underside of the piedra's base. But Tecuilhuitzintli specifically wrote that the stone was *standing* when he visited the University courtyard. For him to have known about the Earth Lord's presence firsthand he would need to have witnessed the statue when it was first excavated, because it was hoisted aright almost immediately. Or, he would have needed access to León y Gama's "copy." Coincidentally, the same month that Ocelotl Tecuilhuitzintli's letter was published, August 1791, León y Gama announced in the *Gazeta de México* that he had finished writing his treatise on the piedras antiguas and was looking for subscribers so that he could publish it along with detailed illustrations.[170] This he did not achieve, however, until the following year, when his "copy" became *Descripción histórica y cronológica de las dos piedras* (1792). It is therefore most likely that Tecuilhuitzintli was León y Gama himself, and that he had staged the letter to advertise the project for which he was actively seeking support.[171]

Tecuilhuitzintli—or León y Gama—like other criollos-americanos, increasingly put on "Mexican" identities toward the century's end, using Mexicanized pseudonyms or spellings, celebrating Mexican topography, and deploying Mexican iconography. Yet these were all academic exercises and certainly did not amount to an adoption—or valorization—of Nahua lifeways. Indeed, criollos-americanos were firmly Hispanic and their allegiance was to *their* homeland, New Spain. Their loyalty was not to living Indigenous communities but to self-interpreted "ancient" ones. For those like Tecuilhuitzintli, it was inconceivable that the heirs to Mexica glory could be the same people that criollos had deemed as "stupid Savages, destitute of common sense, without Laws, without manners, without a fixed Religion, and without any systems at all."[172] Tecuilhuitzintli used the pages of the *Gazeta de México* to claim his authority as a Mexican by birth and custom, not by lineage. Other criollos-americanos, he seemed to suggest, should learn to do the same.[173] By inventing "Mexican" ancestors from a "Mexican" archive, criollos-americanos bequeathed themselves all that they identified—or portrayed—as "Mexican" while simultaneously distancing "ancient Mexicans" from everyday indios living among them.

Seeing and Circulating the Stones

By July 1792, León y Gama was finally able to cover his costs and send subscribers copies of *Descripción histórica y cronológica de las dos piedras*.[174] By this time, the Sun Stone had been moved to the cathedral, where it was cemented into the building's western façade.[175] Anyone could stop to see the "Aztec calendar" on their way to mass or the crowded Parián marketplace. In fact, at least two of the seven stones were placed on public display. The people in Mexico City did not need León y Gama's help to see them, but with interest in the monuments expressed across New Spain (from Guatemala to the Philippines), León y Gama's *Descripción* made the piedras available, via his words and images, to an exclusive group of scholars and professionals across the Spanish realm, in a manner that was thoroughly americano.[176] For in his small volume León y Gama not only described the piedras antiguas in words but also translated them into large-scale copperplate engravings made by a local criollo-americano artist. León y Gama's *Descripción* was not about giving the people "an original monument of antiquity" but rather giving the *right* people the opportunity to see it *correctly*.[177]

As had been the case with his criollo predecessors, León y Gama's understanding of the stones focused primarily on the relation of chronology to migration. Using information collected by Boturini as well as the migration itinerary narrated by Clavijero, León y Gama developed a system for verifying migration dates that he called "my Indian chronology." A main conclusion of his *Descripción* was that the Sun Stone supported the hypothesis of Mexica migration from Aztlán to Anáhuac.[178] This was because Mexicans, descended from the Toltecs— who had invented the "century system" of record keeping—"did not forget the formula they learned from their elders and observed in Aztlan their homeland,"

FIGURE 11. Antonio de León y Gama, *Descripción histórica y cronológica de las dos piedras* [...] (1792). Courtesy of the Kislack Collection, Library of Congress.

León y Gama wrote.¹⁷⁹ The Sun Stone was scientific proof of their memory and evidence of the connection between Mexica and Toltec people.

For his part, León y Gama claimed to understand the piedras "perfectly" because his physical proximity and official position afforded him ample opportunity to compare the stone's inscriptions against archival documents.¹⁸⁰ But this does not mean that León y Gama was transparent with the source of his knowledge; indeed, like his alter ego Tecuilhuitzintli, León y Gama also emphasized the allegedly *obvious* meaning of the statues. This position was supported by his illustrations. One plate provided multiple views of the Coatlicue piedra, with the unmistakably reptilian head and necklace of severed hearts and hands rendered in exquisite detail. The Sun Stone occupied two plates, one dramatically shaded and the other in simplified relief marked with lettered points for easy identification. For León y Gama, the obvious visual heresy of the Coatlicue statue was counterpoised—in duplicate—by the domesticated Sun Stone's evident scientific value, made even more evident by the technical execution of the illustration.

Yet in his process of separating out seemingly religious (Coatlicue) from historical (Sun Stone) topics, León y Gama was himself unable to see the interrelation of the two piedras.¹⁸¹ Indeed, most of the European and criollo-americano witnesses had only ever seen the stones—or any painted or carved Indigenous items—as remnants of an otherwise extinguished idolatry. While León y Gama did not believe that the first piedra itself possessed "superstitious" power, he was concerned that it would recall vulnerable converts back to "paganism." For this reason, León y Gama bemoaned the lack of care taken "to conceal from the Indians whatever might induce them to remember their past idolatries that remained of the ancient history of this nation."¹⁸² In fact, all of the criollo-americano interpreters, including León y Gama—who admitted that he did not know how to tell "which figures pertained exclusively to religion, and which referred to their histories"—despite professions of mastery, failed to recognize the coexistence of the sacred and historic in these two carvings.¹⁸³

León y Gama's failure to bring together history and cosmology in his *Descripción* may have been a question of safety rather than epistemology: for although Spanish and criollos-americanos elites may have imagined themselves far removed from "pagan times" and well-justified in their possession of the lands on which Mexico City sat, the historiographic methods by which the piedras antiguas were identified, described, translated, displayed, and copied enacted a break between the settler and Indigenous Mexico City that was more absolute in fantasy than in reality. As emblematized by the indios who paid their respects to

Coatlicue at the University, the lines between past and present—before and after "conquest"—were not as clear as those drawn by criollos-americanos.

Uncovering Teotl in the Stone City

Even after the displeased padres ordered the enormous Coatlicue buried in the courtyard patio—clawed feet up—the visitations continued.[184] For the ordinary late-colonial Nahuas who visited her, she perhaps represented cosmic obligation or the era before the Spanish Sun. Yet to the Church fathers, she represented backsliding converts and evangelical failure.[185] Allegedly, the Coatlicue statue had been buried in response to her fearsome appearance, which explains why the much more benign looking Sun Stone was left on public display. In 1805, however, the Spanish Bishop of México Benito María Moxó y Francolí recalled that the Coatlicue had been buried because the "Indians showed a worrying curiosity to contemplate their famous statue."[186] The Coatlicue had supposedly been understood as threatening because of her appearance (severed hands, etc.), but as Bishop Moxó wrote, the threat she posed was actually based on the suspicion that she was still being used for ritual purposes.

The different itineraries of the two piedras highlight criollos' attempts to separate *secular history* from *idolatrous antiquity*. The first stone's identity as "an idol from pagan times" indicates its origin in a pre-Christian, superseded temporality; as such, its supersession needed to be signaled physically, i.e., by burial. This secular/idolatrous separation depended on an understanding of time that ordered past and present consecutively rather than concurrently, and any alternative temporalities challenged the supremacy and universality of the Crown's temporal realm. Replacement (or conversion) was imperative not only for personal salvation, but for the success of Catholic dominion. A failure to differentiate secular ancient history from "idolatrous" antiquity could also undermine the carefully constructed division between "ancient" and "modern" indios that upheld Catholic Spain's right to govern in the Americas. Thus, those Indigenous subjects who persisted in their "past idolatries" were both temporal aberrations and political threats to New Spain.

Criollo-americano interpretations of "secular history" required this strict distancing from "idolatrous antiquity" as well as a belief that monuments functioned with a single purpose: as calendars or land maps, for example. This is clear in the different ways that most criollos-americanos approached the Sun Stone and Coatlicue: one as history and the other as religion. Nahua cosmology, however, does not operate according to these divisions. All representations of Coatlicue and Coatepec evoke the Earth from which Huitzilopochtli emerged as well as his struggle with the Moon and Stars. With the centrality of Tonatiuh on its face, the Sun Stone celebrates 4 Ollin and therefore Huitzilopochtli's ascendance and the Mexica cosmic order. Indeed, any references to Coatlicue, Coatepec, Coyolxauhqui, or Huitzilopochtli index the events of Creation as well as previous destructions.[187] The stony Coatlicue also embodies the destruction of the old and the creation of the new, an agonistic creation of both Sun and Moon, the victory of the Mexica patron. The Sun Stone outlines an explicitly Tenocha-Mexica imperial account of history and time while the Coatlicue embodies a larger Nahua explanation of the cosmos—one that was not only visually cyclic, but generative, degenerative, and regenerative. They do not, however, hold separate histories.

Sixteenth-century missionary Diego Durán claimed that the stones at the Templo Mayor had been buried in 1521.[188] These stones, unlike the mapas, were in situ, deposited where their artisans' hands had left them. In its arrangement the Templo Mayor physically models Coatepec (and also Teotihuacan), the cosmic site of the beginning of the world. Thus, the place from which the Coatlicue and Sun Stone were excavated is not incidental; instead, it crucially positions them *both* within the parameters of 4 Ollin. And unlike the items ritually broken or buried before a New Fire ceremony, both of these piedras were interred relatively unscathed, maintaining their power from the previous—pre-Sunrise—era.

Whereas the Sun Stone's obduracy fixed time in the (now Spanish colonial) present, Coatlicue—despite her own durable surface—promised endless—and therefore eventual—change.[189] Perhaps Coatlicue was so important to the Indigenous penitents not (only) because she was sacred but because she was a visible reminder that the cosmos still operated on Nahua time. To León y Gama, the piedras antiguas only served to "show the lights that illuminated the Indian nation in the time before its conquest" but had no contemporary significance in Nahua lives.[190] To criollos-americanos (and Europeans) the stones looked like the past before the invasion. But the stones also revealed Indigenous power still flowing through the heart of the New Spanish city.

CRIOLLOS-AMERICANOS TENDED TO base their interpretations—whether secular or pagan—on apparent *use* rather than aesthetics. One stone was deemed ancient, astronomical, and "safe," while the other was contemporary, votive, and subversive. However, in the absence of "offerings," how would criollos-americanos have known how fifteenth-century Mexicas or eighteenth-century Nahuas used the stones? Would merely stopping to look—as encouraged by the Sun Stone's central placement on the Plaza—have registered as inappropriate? Or was there something about the particular form of "backsliding" that veneration for Coatlicue (or Tonantzin)—so close yet so far from Marian adoration—seemed to represent that was invisible to the Catholic criollos-americanos yet difficult for the (more secular) Spanish priests to overlook?

The potentially anticolonial use to which the stones could be put represented a clear political threat to Spain. Such is evidenced by the 1794 experience of Fray José Servando Teresa de Mier. In a sermon delivered atop Tepeyac Hill in December, Mier argued that the Virgin Mary had visited Saint Thomas there thousands of years before. This assertion was troublesome because it raised New Spain to an apostolic level equal to that of Spain and thereby called into question the Spanish right to dominate the Americas.[191] What is more, Mier asserted that the piedras antiguas—"more precious than all those of Herculaneum and Pompeii"—provided proof of the visitation. Their inscriptions, he claimed—although "all figured and symbolic"—detailed Saint Thomas as Quetzalcoatl meeting Mary as Coatlicue on that very hill.[192]

Mier's specific praise of the Coatlicue statue—which in his notes he referred to as "Flowery Coyolxauhqui [Moon], true Coatlicue de Minjó"—is even more interesting given the fact that this statue had been recently buried for attracting too much devotion. By the end of the eighteenth century, the Virgin of Guadalupe—who first appeared to Juan Diego atop Tepeyac in 1531—had been the official, papally sanctioned patron of New Spain for almost fifty years.[193] There had long been suspicion, on the part of Catholic authorities, that the Virgin gave cover to another adoration: that of Tonantzin. For Mexicas, Tepeyac was consecrated to Tonantzin ("our mother") a class of mother deities of whom Coatlicue is one; perhaps Nahua listeners found Mier's argument more convincing because of this.[194] Atop the sacred mountain, Mier collapsed all the female gods—Mexica and Christian—to serve as proof for his evangelization theory, using Mexica history—and perhaps even Mexica temporality—in the service of his patria. It is clear that the Spanish authorities had a sense of the sermon's potential resonance for the crowd: for the 1493 papal bull awarding sovereignty over the Americas to Spain was premised on the fact that there were no Christians already there. If the Coatlicue and Sun Stone were proof of Mexica Christianity, then the monuments were also an indictment of Spain's sword. For his audacity, Mier was expelled from New Spain the following year. A leading proponent of New Spain's independence, he continued to figure ancient Mexican history to support an autonomous Mexico in the years to come.

Envisioning Mexico Antiguo Everywhere

In 1791, the Luxembourgish dragoon captain Guillaume Joseph Dupaix arrived in Mexico City to serve in the viceregal military. He would remain in New Spain for the rest of his life, a naturalized criollo.[195] Soon after his arrival, Dupaix's interest in antiquities led him to investigate the city's Indigenous statuary. He also began visiting natural history cabinets, sketching Indigenous carvings, and amassing a collection of his own.[196] By 1791 the city was already home to at least eleven large private museums, mainly maintained by Europeans, capacious collections of specimens curious, artistic, natural, and rare.[197] The Spanish botanist Vicente Cervantes, for example, had a collection that included at least one "ídolo" and one "ídolito" as well as lithics, ceramics, bronzes, an encrusted mask from Tenochtitlan, a small marble head of a "rain god" (a Mixtec penate), an obsidian "espejo Moctezuma," and "two cartons of little artifacts."[198] A good enough draughtsman, Dupaix took copious notes and made detailed sketches of most objects he saw. In 1794, Dupaix created an album to document the extent of Mexico City's stone ornamentation, *Descripción de monumentos antiguos mexicanos*, which included engravings of nineteen sculptures in the city.

Dupaix's *Descripción* offers an additional way to visualize Mexico City's Indigenous past.[199] Its images and descriptions quickly circulated amongst interested criollos-americanos in the capital.[200] León y Gama, then working on a second part to his own *Descripción*, even borrowed some of Dupaix's illustrations for his work, arranging images of individual statues around a rendering of the Stone of Tizoc, which had been uncovered on December 17, 1791, exactly one year after Alzate first reported the piedras in the *Gazeta*.[201] Dupaix's text-and-image album reveals that by 1794, Mexico City had become a mapa of stone, a visual record of the city's reworked past.[202] The album physically marked the capital city as criollo-americano: that is, both American (the sculptures) and European (their placement), but not Indigenous.

The accumulation of private collections and the importance placed on collecting practices only intensified in early nineteenth-century New Spain, especially after Charles IV sent Dupaix on a Royal Archaeological Expedition in 1805–1807. In 1808, the viceroy organized a Junta de Antigüedades comprised of Mexico City's leading antiquaries to analyze the exciting results, although their attention was soon drawn away from the past by the turbulent political present.[203] A more immediate dissemination of criollo-americano intellectuals' claims to ancient history would come at the hands of an individual who would become the preeminent scientist of his time: Baron Alexander von Humboldt.[204]

While in the capital in 1803 the Baron met with a number of criollo-americano scholars, including Alzate and Dupaix. Impressed by the richness of the retired soldier's antiquities, Humboldt even chose to place a sculpture drawn from Dupaix's collection—the "Aztec Priestess"—as the first engraving or "monument" in his *Vues des Cordillères, et monumens des peuples indigènes de l'Amérique* (1810).[205] Engravings and descriptions of the "Calendrier Mexicain" and "Idole Aztèque"—by which many viewers outside of New Spain attained their first glimpse of the piedras antiguas were taken from León y Gama's *Descripción*.[206] Unfortunately, Humboldt had just missed meeting León y Gama in person—he had passed away in September 1802—but the traveler did attend the auction of the late antiquary's estate (where Humboldt picked up more than a few items).[207] Like the criollo-americano scholars he spoke to during his journey, Humboldt prioritized the Sun Stone over the Coatlicue because he saw its temporal and historical, rather than *cosmological*, significance.[208] Although Humboldt himself is usually credited with reinventing "pre-Hispanic history," Mexico City's criollos-americanos are the ones to whom Humboldt owed—and gave—credit.[209]

Even as Dupaix gathered "antiquities" across New Spain and Humboldt dreamed of seeing more monuments, artifacts of Indigenous life were far from being merely objects of the past. In 1805 Bishop Moxó described many of the monuments in his own collection including clay figurines acquired from "sympathetic Indians" in Tlatelolo—they had reportedly been presented to the bishop—as well as a singular new acquisition: "will you believe that I have in my collection . . . a piece of paper stained with countless drops of blood offered by these priests a few months ago to two ugly idols? Such is the cunning with which these natives seek at any risk to preserve what they call the immemorial custom of their forebears."[210] Moxó finished writing his *Cartas mejicanas* in 1805, meaning that he had obtained the offering sometime in 1804. When Humboldt visited New Spain in 1803–1804, the Coatlicue statue had been unburied for the occasion. Was the offer of blood made then as an act of balance and repayment? Even if not, Moxó's words make it clear that México's "ugly idols" had not lost their power.

In the monumental archive of "Mexican" history that criollos-americanos compiled, their eyes perceived the outlines of cohabiting colonial and Indigenous cities, which they focused into visions of ancient Mexico both in and on the landscape. The tezontle and basalt carvings, the Chapultepec teixiptlatl, the layout of the city's grid: all belonged to past and present. But by visualizing a Mexican past to fix into "Mexican history"—one that had little to do with indios' everyday life in Mexico City—americanos deemed non-Hispanic temporalities

FIGURE 12. "Sala 1," el Museo del Templo Mayor (INAH), Mexico City. Author's photograph, 2016. Foreground: a model of the city's historic center with the 1790 excavations represented in miniature in the left corner. Background: a panel celebrates the 1790 excavations using León y Gama's images.

as illegible, indeterminate, and ultimately, nonexistent. The way that they described—as well as traced, copied, and arranged—the piedras antiguas and other antiquities centered their own historiographic power. The "look of history" they created hid the ongoing power of the past they reproduced.

In the new century's early years, materials from Boturini and Clavijero's accounts of the Mexica migration continued to appear in the Mexico City press; so too did accounts and interpretations of the Sun Stone remain in the public eye.[211] In establishing the visual elements of Mexica history and claiming exclusive authority over reproduction and interpretation, New Spain's criollos-americanos made the control of history part of their struggle to control New Spain. Autonomists like Mier, now explicitly calling themselves "Mexicans," continued to underscore their commitment to ancient Mexico in their push for independence from Spain. Criollos-americanos knew who had made the monuments beneath and around them: *their* ancestors, the ancient Mexicans. Mexico City's past had not been forgotten; instead, it had been overlaid with a new, americano vision.

THE SUN STONE is one of the first sights greeting visitors to the Mexica Hall in Mexico's grand Museo Nacional de Antropología (Figure 4). The centrality of the piedra, which has been positioned upright against a gallery wall, gestures to the ongoing centrality of the Mexica past in the current age. Visually, the room is an overwhelming display of monolithic Mexica power, forever frozen as the people—although just one group in a long cycle and on a crowded continent—of Mexico's past.[212] That the Sun Stone and Coatlicue remain at the center of this important Mexico City institution attests to the ongoing power of "historical monuments of Indian antiquity" to provoke visions of "el antiguo México" both "then" and "now."

Exhibits at the Templo Mayor archaeological complex, near which the piedras were uncovered in 1790, are even more explicitly nationalist. These focus on the link between Indigenous monuments in the land and Mexico's national history. Indeed, an eighteenth-century image of the Sun Stone appears on a timeline there to represent a starting point for "a new nationalist conscience." The bilingual panel explains: "During the second half of the 18th Century, when the pre-Hispanic past seemed to be forgotten, the finding of objects and sculptures, together with the emergence of a new nationalist conscience, generated the rebirth of the interest in the pre-Hispanic history of Mexico."[213] The piedras antiguas, collections of antiquities, and Indigenous mapas all constitute a set of materials and methods through which americanos both fixed Indigenous monuments into "Mexican history" and enabled their imagery of the past to circulate as continental emblems of America's ancient history.[214]

CHAPTER 4

Nationalist Science and the Chronology of Dispossession

> *I imagine someone walking through the ruins of my house, years later when I am gone and anyone who knew me and my family and nation is gone and there are only stories as to what happened to us. Did we flee from an enemy, or die of famine or floods?*
>
> *The story depends on who is telling it.*
>
> —Joy Harjo, "there is no such thing as a one-way land bridge," 2000

ON HIS RETURN TO Europe in the early summer of 1804, the Prussian naturalist Baron Alexander von Humboldt—carrying a wealth of political, natural, and historical intelligence about the Americas—stopped in the United States expressly to meet with President Jefferson.[1] The recently completed Louisiana Purchase had placed a new emphasis on lands west of the Mississippi, and Humboldt knew he could be a resource to the illustrious Virginian. Already, Jefferson had commissioned his first "Corps of Discovery"—to ascertain the nation's new borders, survey its riches, and greet the Pacific—and would soon authorize others.[2] At the time, the most accurate geographical intelligence in US hands still derived from two French sources: one a 1718 map used to set the boundaries for the 1803 sale and the other from 1757, made by Louisiana naturalist Antoine-Simon Le Page du Pratz.[3] Humboldt, with his eyewitness observations and rare access to long-restricted sources documenting the continent's westward and Pacific stretches, was indeed welcome in Washington City.

Humboldt first disembarked at the old federal capital, Philadelphia. There, he made the acquaintance of numerous local naturalists including Benjamin Smith Barton and the peripatetic European emigrant Constantine Rafinesque. Humboldt was feted in Philosophical Hall and elected a member of the American Philosophical Society (APS) in July.[4] In addition to his maps, notes, and forty boxes of specimens—including a herbarium, minerals, and fossils—the traveler also brought a collection of "Mexican Paintings"—at least one of which had belonged to Boturini—as well as sketches by Dupaix and publications by Alzate and León y Gama.[5] Most of this he left in Barton's care when he went to Washington, and Barton presented the "Mexican Paintings" at the Society's June meeting in the Baron's absence.[6]

While at the President's House, Humboldt conferred with Jefferson and his cabinet, ultimately loaning his papers to secretaries Gallatin and Madison.[7] This included an invaluable "General Chart of the Kingdom of New Spain," which they copied. Humboldt's map provides detailed information about much of what had formerly been known as Spanish Louisiana. Along the right hand side it stretched from Chiapas—in the Kingdom of Guatemala—up the Gulf coast and north to the Arkansas and Missouri, while the left side traced New Spain's southwestern coast, followed the interior of Baja California, and reached up to N 42°, W 117°.[8] The hand-drawn copy, now held at the Library of Congress, also provides a hint as to the naturalists' conversation, which seems to have at least touched upon ancient Mexican history in the context of continental geography. For one, in a section of the map comprising today's Mexican states of Chihuahua and Durango appears an "X" labeled as "Casa grande Troisième démure des Aztèques" ("third stop of the Aztecs"), and a stretch along the Rio Gila is identified in English as the "Ruins of the great houses of the Aztèques."[9] These small details demonstrate, in a material sense, the continued connection of settler expansionism to the search for Aztlán and related attempts to document "Aztèque" migration as a key to American history.[10]

The materials Humboldt left in Philadelphia were not altogether unknown to APS members. Two years before Humboldt's visit, in 1802, the APS had received its first copy of León y Gama's pamphlet on the piedras antiguas, the gift plainly recorded as "sketches of two supposed Mexican Monuments." Barton had studied the text assiduously.[11] But until about 1804, most of the "western" collection on deposit at the APS or on display at Peale's came from the "west" of the Ohio Valley. However, with the significant changes to the nation's size and ambitions, scholarly interests also began to shift. In fact, only months before Humboldt visited the United States, a new American edition of Clavijero's *History of Mexico* had been published in Philadelphia, reenergizing discussions of the connections between ancient Mexican history and Indigenous peoples living farther west.[12]

Whether Barton was originally drawn to León y Gama's pamphlet due to its astronomical, horological, or explicitly Indigenous content is unclear. Because it arrived during a time in which US scientists were depending on astronomical

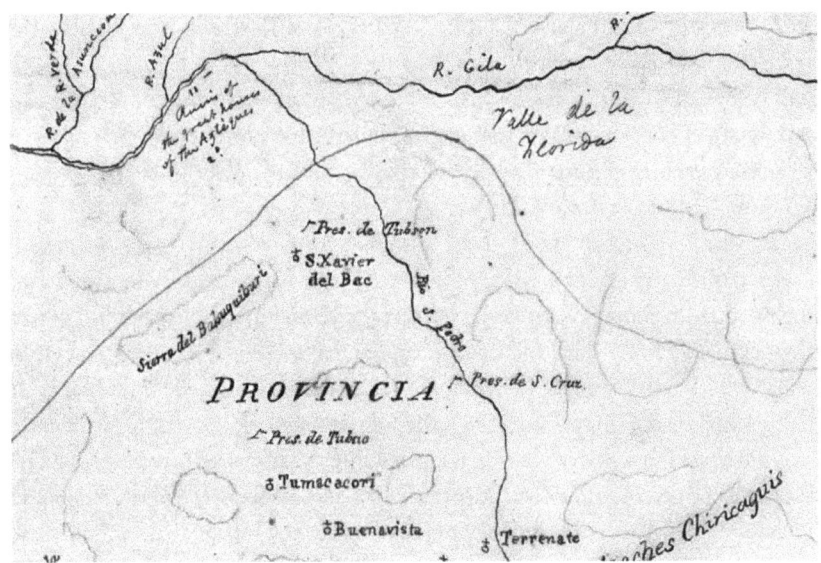

FIGURE 13. Alexander von Humboldt, "General Chart of the Kingdom of New Spain [...]" (1804), detail. Courtesy of the Library of Congress. "Ruins of the great houses of the Aztèques" is noted in the upper left.

knowledge in making land surveys, that too could have accounted for much of Barton's initial concern.[13] Yet it also could have held his interest because the pamphlet seemed to confirm the suitability of empirical, archaeological methods for recovering supposedly lost histories. When he later described the phamphlet to Jefferson—also the APS president—the Virginian considered it potentially "of real value" to their shared scientific endeavors.[14] León y Gama's pamphlet stood to prove its value in at least two ways: first, to answer Continental slander regarding the New World's age and cultural inferiority, which Barton, Jefferson, and León y Gama in Mexico City were duty bound to refute. Second, as a worthy testament to the antiquity of Mexica science, another important point to gain in the "querelle d'Amérique." Even more valuable than the fact that León y Gama independently confirmed anti-Buffonian historical arguments, however, was that his work demonstrated a methodological model for the use of archaeological evidence—particularly monumental "antiquities"—to reconstruct the American past.

Conventionally, Barton has been understood as an important figure in the early history of US science, and his botanical and zoological work are the typical foci.[15] His historical oeuvre—and in this category I include his botanical work as well as *Observations* (1787) and both editions of *New Views of the Origin of the Tribes and Nations of America* (1797, 1798)—is usually set apart from the botanical work, especially due to its association with the Moundbuilder myth. In this chapter, I argue that the criollo historiography imported from New Spain fundamentally powered not only this Moundbuilder myth but also the changing use of natural history in the United States. Whereas, in the 1780s, settler scholars including Barton had spent much of their time making the case for the *resemblance* of the western earthworks to structures in New Spain, by the turn of the century the push was to prove not their aesthetic *likeness*, but the actual *sameness* of their architects. By the early years of the nineteenth century, the emergent practice of fossil archaeology shifted the conventional scientific view toward articles *inside* earthworks rather than mounds themselves. However, the perceived evidentiary value of oral traditions—on migration, ecology, deep time, etc.—became increasingly marginalized as mere "myths and legends." Barton's efforts also became increasingly empirical, aided by the resources of Spanish America and a US intellectual culture shifting from amateur naturalism to standardized empirical science.[16]

In 1787, Barton had belatedly followed the guidance of Clavijero, his main access to Indigenous materials on the past. But after *Observations*, Barton began to consult Indigenous materials and knowledge-keepers directly. Whereas Barton's work for *Observations* had been based on his own eyewitness observation shaped by previously published sources, the research he compiled for *New Views* (1797) and his later textbook *Elements of Botany* (1803) widely relied on the contributions of others.[17] Barton accumulated materials via connections made through the American Philosophical Society, direct correspondence with US Indian agents, and interactions with Indigenous leaders visiting the federal capital.[18]

Barton both relied on what had already been written and what he could see and hear for himself. Alongside his earlier antiquities and newer language projects, Barton focused on collecting migration traditions from across the eastern half of the continent. In order to consider the continent's earthworks, languages, and traditions as suitable monuments upon which to build a new ancient history, however, they first needed to be translated—their dimensions and locations documented, explanatory traditions written down, vocabularies listed, recorded as facts, and *made* into historical records. Working from conventional travel and ethnographic accounts *as well as* living language speakers and oral traditions, Barton began the process of transforming Indigenous "myths" into American "facts."[19] Deeply influenced by his Scottish training in natural history, Linnaean taxonomy, and materia medica, Barton's scholarship would become increasingly empiricist over the next twenty-five years. The result was his transformation of living Indigenous teachings into inert, objective "data."

As Barton's "facts" (or "myths") were alienated from the lands and peoples to whom they belonged—extracted from larger systems of relationality—the resulting "data" became tools in the settler project of US permanency.[20] The results forged a link between antiquarian research and the extinguishing of Indigenous intellectual autonomy. Barton's engagement with traditional Indigenous knowledges—whether as "fact" or "myth"—served to reinforce boundaries not just between literature and history but also between Indigenous and settler perspectives on knowledge.[21] Both categories endorse epistemological hierarchies that violate and misappropriate Native knowledge either by alienating it as "fact" or disavowing it as "fable."[22]

Tracing migration accounts revolutionized Barton's approach to earthworks, and it was the migration model of historiography—which relied on a narrative of extra-continental arrival and movement for America's Indigenous peoples—that led Barton to develop his own theories of the continent's past, writing Indigenous history with Indigenous stories and objects that transformed Indigenous peoples and their histories into "data" for the settler colonial state. In this chapter, I show how the extraction of "facts" from Indigenous vocabularies, oral traditions, and ecological knowledge supported settlers' conclusions about Indigenous anti-originality—i.e., the idea that America's Native peoples were not indigenous to the continent. I argue that the very steps of scientific research that Barton practiced contributed to the intellectual and physical dispossession of Indigenous peoples in lands targeted by the United States: by helping private, territorial, state, and federal administrators confuse the issue of who had right to "aboriginal title."[23]

Traditionally, Barton's *Observations* and *New Views* are identified as progenitors of a myth that largely reached its peak after 1820. Yet contrary to the conventional assumption, the year Barton published his *New Views* is not the origin point for the Moundbuilder myth.[24] To be sure, 1797 marks Barton's development of an extractive historiographic method that brought together philological and naturalist study to follow Indigenous origins to ancient Mexico. Yet more importantly, *New Views* marked a significant change in the way that Barton sought and used the "facts" of the past because his data points indicate the strongly botanical and zoological orientation of his ideas about ancient history. Examining the Moundbuilder myth to detect its origins in 1797 obscures how it developed—and helped to develop—the settler colonial state continentally. Instead, this chapter looks to the centrality of Indigenous migration and emergence traditions—and the model of Mexica migration—to US nationalists' attempts to order world chronology and secure white settler sovereignty. It presents how Barton's historical work transformed earthworks, language, and traditional Indigenous knowledge into monuments for American history. In the United States, the writing of American antiquity was enabled through the shift in focus from oral, Indigenous traditions-based history to a data-driven "scientific" one. As an example, Barton began relying less on migration narratives and more on sources such as language or environmental knowledge that he could abstract and standardize.

With the growing importance of archaeological science, the roles of migration, emergence, and Mexico to the creation of the Moundbuilder myth receded from view; yet Barton's continuing interest in Indigenous timekeeping, even while considering the continent's archaeology, reveals the residual influence of criollo historiography—and misappropriated perceptions of Indigenous past-making—on early US technologies for reconstructing the ancient past. Restoring this context to his larger work places the "Moundbuilder myth"— which Barton indeed helped to circulate—within a longer, continental history of migration historiography that first turned on the concept of linear substitution or "seriality," and later, on conversions of Indigenous temporalities and relationships into scientific figurations of settler time.

Plotting Southern Migration

After reading parts of Clavijero's history, Barton became more interested in migration. Reflecting on that which he had learned about Mexica history, Barton began to research possible links between north and south. As a first step, he wrote his friend and fellow Philadelphian William Bartram, asking the botanist to send him migration accounts: "Have those tribes of Indians which you have visited any traditions concerning their Origin,—their Progress, or Migrations, which you think worthy of notice?—If they have, what are those traditions?...Have you any reasons for believing that any of the tribes of Indians, whom you have visited, are derived from either the Mexicans or the Peruvians?"[25] In his 1789 response, Bartram recalled that the Natchez had been the first to be pushed eastward by the Spanish from "a Region nearest to the border of the Empire of Old Mexico" and that they were followed by Chickasaws.[26] Next, a Mvskoke (Creek) group also left their "native land" to venture eastward "in Search of new & plentiful regions," and that party "crossed the Mississippi somewhere about the Chickasaw country below the confluence of the Ohio."[27]

Arriving from the western side of the Mississippi after their Natchez and Chickasaw kin, the Creeks battled local nations as they pushed eastward to Okmulgee Fields, which the "present generation of the Muscogulges [Mvskokes] say is the Ruins of their Camp and first Settlement."[28] There they defeated the "surrounding Indian Nations, which were then in the Spanish Interest, who they at length subjugated" and united into the Creek Nation, eventually sending out emissaries to the Spanish and English.[29] Last came the Choctaws, who crossed the river "in considerable force."[30] Bartram also told Barton that the Cherokees were "altogether a separate nation from the Muscoges, of much antienter establishment in those regions they inhabit." Barton had already suspected that that "the Six-Nation and the Cheerake are the same people," based on an unattributed Seneca account of a migration "from the vicinity of the Muskohge country."[31] He wanted to know more.

With Bartram's study of Mvskoke origins as his guide, Barton determined that Chickasaw, Choctaw, Natchez, and Creek nations all descended from "the same origin or country" due to the fact that "they all speak a dialect of the same country; and it is certain they all crossed the Mississippi from the west, as they say of themselves, and long since the Spanish invasion and conquests of Mexico."[32] These migration traditions and language profiles inclined Barton to believe that the "Mexicans ... were the ancestors of the nations known by the name of Choktah, Chikkasah, &c."[33] Thus he began to establish a geographic itinerary stretching from Mexico to Georgia.[34]

To support a broadly defined trans-Mississippi migration thesis, Barton extracted supportive information from Natchez, Six Nations, Mahican, and Narragansett histories gleaned from seventeenth- and eighteenth-century settler publications. His new task became identifying exactly which current-day peoples—Choctaw, Tuscarora, Seminole, etc.—were related to which ancestors, and to pinpoint the exact coordinates of their origins. Ultimately, the information he collected solidified his beliefs about the first Americans' migration from Asia to Mexico and the lands now occupied by the United States, providing an empirical basis for Indigenous anti-originality as well as an empirical basis for the United States' divisive and destructive Indian policy.[35]

Following Earthworks from Asia to Mexico

At the same time that criollo historians were charting the supposed migration paths of aboriginal Americans, scholars like Barton and Bartram were performing migratory work of their own. Traveling across territories, they amassed natural "data"—a word itself only newly employed to refer to a collective set of scientifically obtained information—often relayed in accounts of their travels. In the United States, both Barton and Bartram produced excellent examples of the writings literary scholar Mary Louise Pratt calls "civic description," but Barton's later writings were descriptions that relied on collections of previous "data" as well.[36]

In the mid-eighteenth century, data-gathering was epitomized by the work of Swedish naturalist Carl Linnaeus, who attempted to produce universal botanical accounts. His students, and the legions of naturalists he inspired, went on to "herbolize" around the globe, trekking across lands and among peoples largely not their own to bring back information, recoded as knowledge, to the centers of intellectual, economic, and political power.[37] At his teacher's urging, Linnaeus's student Pehr Kalm spent years in North America amassing information about the countryside and its inhabitants. Kalm's work, published in English in 1770–1772, was a major resource for Barton, a next generation herbolizer in his own right. Kalm's and similar "travel writings" contained a hodgepodge of recordings, descriptions, illustrations, vocabularies, cosmologies, and navigational intelligence.[38] Most were gathered through direct observation or conversations with inhabitants, Indigenous and settler. Sometimes the sources were clearly marked, although more frequently they were not.

By 1790—when he began to lecture on "the Philosophy and Nomenclature of Natural History" in Philadelphia—Barton was also well-versed in the natural history of Spanish America, having immersed himself in the writings of Hernández de Toledo, Acosta, Torquemada, and el Inca Garcilasco.[39] He was, in particular, interested in the history of Hernando de Soto's 1539–1542 journey across what is currently the US Southeast—reports of which were contained in Richard Hakluyt's *Virginia Richly Valued* (1609)—especially for descriptions of flat-topped mounds in Natchez territory.[40] Barton had also already read the unpublished version of William Bartram's 1770s travels—in which the botanist described seeing mounds being used in Creek towns—but when Bartram's *Travels through North and South Carolina, Georgia, East and West Florida, the Cherokee country, etc.*, was finally published in 1791 it lent Barton even more information about the spread of earthworks across southern lands.[41] As he updated *Observations* throughout the 1790s—in anticipation of another edition that never materialized—Barton turned away from earthworks as the subject of his inquiry and toward the method of using earthworks as evidence with which to test his migration hypotheses.[42] Earthworks, in other words, became corroborating facts in support of Barton's empirical analysis of migration.

Barton solicited descriptions of earthworks from people throughout his network. In 1791 he received a letter from Rev. Samuel Kirkland in Oneida that described earthworks in New York.[43] Two years later, the *New-York Magazine*—which had provided a "View of the celebrated Indian fortifications near the Junction of the Ohio and Muskingum Rivers" in 1791—detailed the exploits of "several gentlemen of distinction in the state of New-York, [who] made a tour through its western territory." Along the Seneca River south of Fort Oswego they had "discovered a remnant of ancient Indian defense," which seemed to them "unequalled perhaps even by the celebrated vestiges at Muskingum."[44] But Bartram was not only interested in the Northeast. In 1790, for example, he contacted his former acquaintance Captain Jonathan Heart—who had led the First American Regiment westward in 1785 and had been among the forces sent to protect the Seven Ranges surveyors the following year—to learn more about the Ohio earthworks. Writing from Fort Harmar in January 1791, Heart described earthworks on the Muskingum River, Grave Creek, Scioto, and those along the Little and Great Miami Rivers as well as mentioning others he had heard about on the Yazoo, Mobile, and Mississippi.[45] Barton also consulted a 1789 letter by William Morgan, brother of former Indian agent and speculator George Morgan, in which William described earthworks "most numerous and extraordinary in Extent & Construction" in Spanish Louisiana, noting that they were "very different from those found in the Ohio country."[46] In 1794 Winthrop Sargent, secretary of the Northwest Territory, described for Barton an "ancient Tumulus, or Grave, in the Western-country" and his letters formed the basis of the essay—published privately as *Papers Relative to Certain American Antiquities* (1796) and by the APS in 1799—in which Barton first definitively articulated his Mexican migration thesis.[47]

Barton began his 1796 essay with the assertion that the "ancient Tumulus" described by Sargent was evidence of the continent's occupation by a people who "had made much greater advances in the arts, and in improvement, than the present races of Indians, *or than their ancestors since our actual acquaintance with them.*"[48] He also, however, implied possessing proof "of the ancient strength and respectability of the ancestors of many of the savage Indian tribes who now inhabit the countries of America."[49] By this point, it was clear to Barton that the Ohio mounds not only resembled the mounds built by the Toltecs—which according to Clavijero, are "still to be seen in the neighbourhood of Cholula"— he suspected that they had been created by them, or their relatives, as well.[50] Although Barton had included references to Toltecs in *Observations*, at that time he believed the Moundbuilders to have been "Danes" (Vikings) from Greenland who became Toltecs after migrating south.[51] To 1787 Barton, these Viking-Toltec Moundbuilders were not the same as any of the continent's existing Native peoples; however, thanks to his ongoing research, Barton adjusted his initial conclusions. In this usually overlooked 1796 publication, Barton first proposed that the descendants of the Moundbuilders *still exist* among the continent's Indigenous peoples. He also determined that the "ancestors of some of the present races of Indians" on the continent's northern stretches were the "same people who constructed the extensive earthen fortifications, large conical and other shaped mounds, and other ancient works" in New Spain.[52]

Barton knew from criollo history that ruined structures had been discovered in the north by the "Aztecas, or Mexicans, in the progress of their migration from the northern country of Aztlan, to the vale in which they afterwards founded the capital of their empire."[53] He suspected that these structures were earthworks that dated from the earlier Toltec migration, which was said to have begun "towards the close of the sixth or the beginning of the seventh century of the Christian aera."[54] Barton argued that all of their ancestors commonly originated in Asia, a point allegedly proven by earthworks because their uneven distribution pattern—fewer along the Atlantic and more between the Alleghenies and Rockies—reflected a population distribution greater in the west than the east due to the original migration pattern from Asia.[55] Indeed, according to Barton the earthworks' prevalence in the "eastern-district" of the country only occurred because "[a]ll the eastern nations appear to have migrated from the west, from the north-west, or from the south-west."[56] The migration paths themselves, Barton claimed in 1796, were verifiable by the "actual march of many Indian tribes who now occupy, or who within the last two hundred years, did occupy, some of the countries east of the Alleghaney-mountains."[57] The mounds were his evidence.

Displacing the Wilderness Wars

As Barton was collecting materials for his study, the political forces of settler colonialism had not fully consolidated east of the Mississippi River. At the end of the eighteenth century, the United States shared at least two borders with Spain: La Luisiana to the west and Las Floridas to the south. Negotiating the southern border was particularly complex for these two settler empires in the absence of a major geographical divide like the Mississippi.[58] Tensions between the United States and Spanish Empire, as well as suspicions about spies and plots, ebbed and flowed as borders fluxuated and Spain repeatedly barred US access to the

Mississippi and port of New Orleans.⁵⁹ With no trading outlet to the East Coast, the US worried that western settlers would become Spanish subjects, meaning that the lands they lived on would remain under the sovereignty of Madrid.⁶⁰ In addition, many of the eastern Natives forced into crossing the Mississippi because of war in their homelands had become Spanish allies, reinforcing the War Department's fear of proxy involvement in the war across the Ohio.⁶¹ In the South, the United States attempted to avoid the kind of violence endemic north of the Ohio. Southern settlers, however, were committed to their occupation.

At this time, the United States relied largely on diplomatic negotiations rather than overt military force in the South.⁶² Key examples are the 1785–1786 Treaties of Hopewell made with Cherokee, Chickasaw, and Choctaw leadership, the 1790 Treaty of New York with the Creeks, and the 1791 and 1794 Cherokee treaties in which these nations accepted promises of peace with US settlers in exchange for settled boundaries.⁶³ Most included language such as that in the 1790 Creek treaty—that served "to extinguish forever all claims of the Creek nation, or any part thereof, to any of the land lying to the northward and eastward of the boundary herein described"—revealing an implicit recognition of aboriginal title through explicit efforts to abolish it.⁶⁴ The latter treaty, eventually signed in New York City by Hoboi-Hili-Miko (Alexander McGillivray), the powerful Upper Creek chief, required that the Creek Nation officially declare itself under US protection "and of no other sovereign whosoever," a clause aimed at nullifying preexisting Creek-Spanish relationships.⁶⁵ Similarly, the 1791 Treaty of Holston between the US and Cherokee representatives—which forbade US settlers from settling or hunting on Cherokee lands—also placed Cherokee peoples explicitly under US protection in an attempt to disrupt (or reinforce) prior Native-settler alliances.⁶⁶ Alongside the treaties, the United States brokered special arrangements—usually extra payments—to Native leaders to cultivate their loyalty.⁶⁷

To regulate the purchasing of land enabled by these treaties, Congress in 1790 passed the Indian Trade and Intercourse Act, which held that the US government—not private buyers—was the only lawful purchaser of lands from Native sellers. This was explicitly in response to Knox's interpretation of Native nations as foreign nations, and it meant that all profit from land transactions would go directly to the federal treasury. However, this policy was violated in at least two ways: first, private land agents simply disregarded it, often employing coercive or unjust measures when they did so. Second, using migration research such as Barton's—which called into question the ability of one particular Native group to claim aboriginality on specific lands—settlers would frequently dismiss, diminish, or ignore Native claims altogether.[68] Indeed, thanks to the migration model that Barton amplified, settlers tended to see land policies less as violations or usurpations and more as historically precedented property transfers. In this way, large swaths of land "changed hands" from Native signatories to manorial families, private speculators, and large syndicates such as the Holland Land Company. On the so-called "Yazoo lands" (now currently Alabama and Mississippi), private companies—with the support of the Georgia state government—speculated on lands in violation of many of the treaties negotiated with Choctaw, Chickasaw, Creek, Cherokee, and other southern leaders.[69] All this despite the federal interdiction; in fact, the federal system enabled dispossession and emboldened the states, since enforcement was essentially dependent on Executive support.[70]

While the US was largely able to negotiate peace treaties and land sales in the South, this was not the case in the West, where Mihšihkinaahkwa (Little Turtle), Weyapiersenwaw (Blue Jacket), and Paxkanchihilas (Buckongahelas) led a multiethnic war to end the US occupation.[71] Nor even farther north, where Britain still maintained strong alliances and forts along the Great Lakes in defiance of the 1783 Treaty of Paris. The fighting, which consumed the region and strained both Native and US diplomatic energies, was largely devastating for the outmaneuvered settler forces until August of 1794, when General Anthony Wayne destroyed Little Turtle's Village, kiihkayonki or "the Glaize"—the Western Confederacy's unofficial capital—and constructed in its place Fort Defiance.[72] A few weeks later, after the Battle of the Taawaawa Siipiiwi (Maumee) or Battle of Fallen Timbers, the United States officially declared an end to the long stretch of "Wilderness Wars" and seized roughly twenty-five thousand square miles of Indian Country.[73]

At the 1795 treaty council—attended by over one thousand people—Mihšihkinaahkwa objected that the large land cession unduly punished Miamis, explaining that the territory stretching from Detroit to the Ohio was myaamionki—the "Place of the Miami"—"the boundaries within which the prints of my ancestors' houses are everywhere to be seen."[74] He reminded Wayne that Miami lands had already been "disposed of without our knowledge or consent" at previous treaty councils. Moreover, the lands "watered by the Ohio"—that is, the lands along the Muskingum, Scioto, and Miami Rivers—were preferable to those that ran into the Great Lakes (Sandusky, Maumee, Cuyahoga) due to the richness of their soil and health of the hunting grounds.[75] Although they were allowed to hunt and fish in their old homelands, they were not allowed to live there. Later, the former Western Confederacy even offered to trade lands closer to the Mississippi in exchange for the US returning their hilly Ohio homes. The United States, however, was not interested.

More than eighty "sachems and war chiefs" signed the 1795 treaty document. General Wayne, accompanied by Adj. General Caleb Swan, interpreter William Wells, Wayne's aide-de-camp William Henry Harrison, and many others—affixed their names to the Greenville Treaty too.[76] In exchange, the US government pledged to relinquish claims to "all other Indian lands northward of the river Ohio, eastward of the Mississippi, and westward and southward of the Great Lakes and waters." These shared lands were to be inviolable Indian Country, save various "reservations," i.e., military enclaves meant to serve as US forts, trading posts, and way stations for US persons.[77] These reservations, generally located at crossroads, confluences, and other transitional spaces, were typically surrounded by multiethnic Native and métis communities. Many of them had been built during the wars as symbols of conquest: Fort Wayne, for example, replaced the important Miami capital at the confluence of the St. Joseph's and St. Mary's Rivers—and the portage between Lake Erie and the Ohio—kiihkayonki.[78] The military forts, certainly, reminded Native peoples that the United States would not hesitate to enforce their sovereignty.

The dictates of peace affected Native homes as well as livelihoods, something of which Little Turtle—from kiihkayonki—was well aware. For under the 1795 treaty, the United States would control two important portages connecting the Great Lakes to the Mississippi—Cuyahoga Town and kiihkayonki—and therefore all the traffic and commerce that went through them, placing Native hunters and traders at considerable disadvantage. While on paper the US pledged to respect the Confederacy members' sovereignties and stay out of the Northwest, the "reservations" show the promise was already rusted: settlers had no intention of staying on their side of the new dividing line, whether their inroads were made by occupation or economic dominance. But faced with the choice of land or life, all the gathered Lenape, Wyandot, Shawnee, Odawa, Ojibwe, Potawatomi, Miami, Wea, and Eel River signatories assented to part with their shared homelands.[79]

The Treaty of Greenville can be seen as one in a flurry of border-and migration-related agreements signed in 1794–1795. John Jay's treaty with Britain established a northern border with British Canada and solidified trading agreements in the Caribbean, a tricky matter while France and Britain were still at war.[80] Thomas Pinkney's treaty with Spain marked out the boundary with West Florida at the thirty-first parallel, running the United States' southern border straight through Choctaw and Creek lands in the Yazoo Valley.[81] These agreements articulated important aspects of Indian policy and land acquisition as well as US border security; they were also meant to shore-up political alliances for the new nation facing formidable challenges on all of its borders. This included the 1794 Treaty of Canandaigua. Signed by the Six Nations Confederacy, this treaty reiterated the US-Native border dictated at Fort Stanwix a decade prior that had penalized the Six Nations members—mainly Seneca and Mohawk—who had sided with Britain. The 1794 treaty also split the Haudenosaunee family, dealing slightly more favorable terms to Oneidas and Tuscaroras, who were both then largely located on the Oneida reservation. In these years, the US made clear to Native neighbors that peace could only be purchased with land.[82]

In 1797, surveyor Isaac Ludlow (who had completed some of the Seven Ranges Survey) blazed the line that now divides Ohio and Indiana, separating Indian Country to the north and west from settler lands to the south and east. While many Ohio Native communities were relocated and reestablished across the 1795 treaty line, others fragmented and coalesced elsewhere. Many destroyed sites were not rebuilt, such as the Wea town at the former French Fort Ouiatenon, now called West Lafayette.[83] Some installations over the line, like Fort Vincennes and Fort Wayne (formerly kiihkayonki), were occupied by US forces due to the treaty's reservation clause. Thus, an effect of redrawing the US border was also a redrawing of Native populations across space. With blazed and bent trees, mile markers, and scorched town sites, the land itself bore the scars of "peace."[84]

Phylogenizing Language

In the winter of 1798, French linguist Constantin François de Chassebœuf, comte de Volney, sat face-to-face with the great Mihšihkinaahkwa (Little Turtle) in Philadelphia. Only three years earlier, Little Turtle had signed the Treaty of Greenville; in late 1797 he traveled with his son-in-law Eepiihkaanita (William Wells) to address the 1795 treaty's consequences in the changed Ohio country.[85] In February 1798, Little Turtle reported to Congress and President Adams the murder of two Miami men at US hands at Vincennes and recalled the obligation under Article 9 of the 1795 treaty that both sides take measures "to preserve the said peace and friendship unbroken . . . to the satisfaction of both parties." He asked that the United States station an agent at Fort Wayne to keep the peace and ensure that treaty obligations were being met. Little Turtle also complained of white settlers "marking lands" where they should not and requested the boundary around Fort Vincennes be more clearly delineated so "that the Indians, as well as the whites, may know what belongs to them respectively."

Little Turtle's speech largely addressed his desire to safeguard the fragile peace, although the newspapers framed his memorial as a request for an "alteration of the Indian Line."[86] In fact, Little Turtle did request the return of a parcel of land around the Great Miami River. This, he explained, would "add greatly to our comfort and may prevent the inconvenience of having the White settlers so near to our principal Towns and hunting grounds." In exchange, the concerned nations had already agreed to grant the United States "an equivalent parcel between the Ohio and Mississippi."[87] But his motivations were keeping the peace rather than wholly upending the boundary agreement. Adams refused to engage the offer, responding that resetting the line would require a new treaty, which would likely entail further losses.[88]

Volney—who had been unable to speak with Little Turtle when he passed through myaamionki (Miami homelands) on a tour in 1796—was delighted by the occasion to do so in Philadelphia, not least because it would provide him "the mouth of a native to afford the true primitive words" of myaamiaataweenki, the Miami language.[89] Although Volney was clearly happy to meet such a celebrity— Little Turtle had been received in Philadelphia as "one of the most influential characters among the Indians north west of the Ohio"—he was most pleased by the opportunity to speak with the multilingual Wells.[90] Volney, author of *Les Ruines, ou méditations sur les révolutions des empires* (1791), collected world vocabularies because he believed languages were vital to understanding history.[91] Language could reveal a people's origins or—as he put it—how groups "sprung up at the beginning."[92] Words, he believed, represented the "most instructive and unerring of all the monuments of rude nations."[93] They were "living monuments of antiquity."[94] Mihšihkinaahkwa and Eepiihkaanita were thus perfect resources.

Volney, like his contemporary José Antonio de Alzate y Ramírez in Mexico City and many other scholars across the hemisphere and Atlantic, believed language—especially "primitive" languages, by which they meant supposedly static, non-European languages—was a vast "storehouse of knowledge."[95] Analyzing lists of nouns and common phrases let these scholars raid the depot of America's past.[96] Volney's colleague Thomas Jefferson had long held similar opinions, having asserted in his *Notes on the State of Virginia* (1787) that language presented "the best proof of the affinity of nations which ever can be referred to."[97] Barton too had spent the past decade collecting Native vocabularies, largely from conventional printed sources: James Adair for Cherokee, Chickasaw, and

Choctaw words; Antoine Le Page du Pratz for words in Natchez; "Mexican" and Mi'kmaq from Joannes de Laet; Massachusett from John Elliot's Indian Bible; Innu (Montagnais) words from Samuel de Champlain.[98] Like Volney, Barton also expanded his oral and aural sources, drawing from an expanded list of correspondents and sources cultivated through his personal contacts.[99]

Ten years after publishing his survey of the continent's earthworks, Benjamin Smith Barton brought forth a survey of its history and languages, *New Views of the Origin of the Tribes and Nations of America* (1797). In that decade's time, Barton had been compiling "whatever relates to the physical and moral history of the Indians, their traditions, &c." in addition to collecting "Indian words."[100] Over eighty pages in the resulting publication were comprised of these word lists. With this dataset, which he had compiled from "original manuscripts," Indigenous informants, and a hemispheric network of correspondents, Barton not only attempted to reverse-engineer Indigenous origins, he tried to lay an entire scientific base for the new nation's history.[101] This he explained in the essay (and dedication to Jefferson) that introduced his data.

Ultimately, it was the combination of language *and* migration traditions that allowed Barton to extract historical knowledge and complete his project.[102] Although Barton believed that most eastern Native peoples had migrated from elsewhere—they were possibly a "branch" of either the Mexica or Toltec families—he also believed that certain groups had been in place for so long that their languages, oral traditions, and ecological knowledge held important information about the past of their homes. Inspired by the work of Orientalists Volney, William Jones, and Peter Simon Pallas, language was an obvious means for ordering America's peoples.[103] Barton combed previously printed sources for the vocabulary he extracted—he described himself as having "borrowed," "procured," and "collected" the words—and then arranged them for the purposes of transcontinental comparison.[104]

But isolated words were not enough. Barton also spent much time studying in Bartram's Garden, and began traveling to look for botanical specimens, striking up long-distance correspondence with like-minded naturalists and collecting words along with migration traditions.[105] In a 1793 letter to the Moravian missionary Charles Gotthold Reichel, for example, Barton requested "the name of the veg[etable]s in the lang[uage]s of any of our indigenous tribes, as the Delawares, etc.," hoping his correspondent would send some of the Moravians' vocabularies.[106] Thus working from conventional travel and ethnographic accounts *as well as* living language speakers, oral traditions, and ecological observations, in

New Views Barton began the process of transforming Indigenous "myths" into the "facts" of American origins.[107]

Volney, impressed with *New Views*, would use its contents to argue that myaamiaataweenki (Miami language) was evidence of Asian origins in his travelogue, *Tableau du climat et du sol des États-Unis d'Amérique* (1803).[108] In 1804, Barton himself provided notes for the US edition of *Tableau* (which had been translated by another Philadelphian, Charles Brockden Brown), and the attenuated scholarly dialogue reveals their diverging views on Indigenous history. For his part, Barton insisted that language only demonstrated relationships between the "mouldering families of mankind," not "the real origin of the Americans." For that, Barton turned to oral traditions. However Volney, the philologist, dismissed traditions as unreliable and repeated the antiquated line that there was of "a total absence ... of [Indigenous] records or writings of any kind."[109] On the contrary, Barton the naturalist found the traditions indispensable. He emphasized "how correctly the Indians often preserve the memory of events, that had taken place at a period much beyond the period of one hundred years."[110] And like Clavijero, Alzate, and their contemporaries, Barton believed that collating Indigenous migration histories would allow him to establish a multipurpose dataset of information about the past. Yet more important than the migration points he gleaned from criollo histories was the example they set: the criollos believed the migration traditions were historical and their itineraries empirically demonstrable—not mythical—and Barton did, too.

In 1791, Barton requested and received a copy of Major Caleb Swan's journal, which included a sketch of the "Origin of the Muscogies, or Creek Indians."[111] Swan had already shared his journal widely. At the end of the 1790 treaty council held in New York City, Swan—now Deputy Indian Agent—accompanied McGillivray and "the Chiefs and warriors of the Creek nation" back to their southern homes. While there, he amassed intelligence for Knox at the Department of War, some of which came from McGillivray. According to Swan, McGillivray claimed that the Seminoles were "the original stock of the Creek nation."[112] The Upper Creek leader had also stopped in Philadelphia during his travels for the treaty negotiations in 1790, where he had likely met with both Barton and Bartram.[113] Barton had already learned from Bartram—whose information came from "Men of the best information and longest acquaintance with these Indians" (that is to say, settlers not Mvskokes)—that "Seminole" meant "wanderers, or lost people," and that Seminoles had arrived in Florida from the north before incorporating with the Creeks; after reading Swan's account, he wrote to McGillivray himself for clarification.[114] In Barton's July 1792 letter to McGillivray at his Little Tanasee (near current-day Montgomery, Alabama) home, Barton explained having "been, for several years, engaged in collecting materials for an history of the North American tribes, and intend[ed] to publish the result of my inquiries sometime in the course of the ensuing spring." But he was loath to do so without "some further information respecting that great confederacy, over which you preside."[115] It is unclear if McGillivray, who was also interested in natural history, replied.

All of these letters and resources made their way into *New Views*. In the publication itself, Barton differentiated his sources by using different typeface to indicate whether he had received words in print or aurally. All words printed in italics had been "taken from printed books, or have been communicated to me by my friends, in different parts of North America." Words in Roman type he had heard: whether spoken by a Native speaker, an interpreter, or an Indian agent.[116] All italicized words were unanimated specimens drawn from across the hemisphere, but the spoken words were only one step removed from a speaker's mouth. Barton's particular use of typeface allows readers to track entries that were the results of lived relationships, while also revealing just how much data Barton drew from correspondence with Indian policy operatives. Barton's aural research—which implied negotiated authority and multiple participants—thus draws a picture of the communities with which he had personal ties, whether Indigenous or settler. These words also reiterate the transformation of voiced, embodied knowledge from the 1790s Great Lakes and southeast into abstract and dispassionate data.[117]

Particularly evident in *New Views* is how Barton's theory of migration helped him detect family resemblances—genealogical or arboreal, not biological—in terms of language, "mythology," astronomical knowledge, and writing, all elements that criollos had taught him to recognize as aspects of highly civilized peoples. To visualize family relations in a way that illustrated his migration thesis, *New Views* provided lists of peoples and words, arranged in order of their supposed arrival in the New World. Here Barton applied his relational knowledge to his understanding of migration to supplement what he had learned from language alone. Using this method, Barton ultimately concluded that the Lenape peoples were the original descendants of the Toltecs, based largely on the evidence that other nations referred to Lenapes with the kinship marker "grandfather," implying both respect and obligation.[118] Except for the Six Nations, Wyandot groups, and the "southern tribes," Barton wrote, all other "Indian nations known to me on this side of the Mississippi call the Delawares their grandfather."[119] He had learned this, also, because Lenape migration traditons, which hold that all Algonquian-speaking peoples were originally one people in the past, emphasize change that nonetheless remembers family affiliation.[120]

Moreover, the diplomatic and treaty language conventionally used between colonial and Indigenous powers could not have been lost on Barton in formulating his arrangements: indeed, it is clear that he derived much of his sense of Indigenous socio-political networks from contemporary practices, speeches, and writings by Indigenous individuals such as Joseph Brant, Hendrick Aupaumut, and Little Turtle.[121] And his understanding was primarily kinship-based. When Barton reported that Lenapes call the Six Nations and Wyandots "uncles"—establishing their own relative seniority vis-à-vis non-Lenape Algonquian-or Siouan-speaking peoples—this also marked their difference from Iroquoian-speaking families.[122] Barton sought the "root" for each family tree, language that suited the naturalist. He explained, for example, how the Mahican "branch" related to the Lenape "limb" of a common ancestral tree.[123] His botanical language implied relative age—branches are newer shoots, whereas limbs and trunks are certainly much older growth—and with that also relative eras of arrival.

THE WORD LISTS collected by the likes of Barton, Volney, and Jefferson were largely comprised of nouns. Of his preprinted vocabulary list, Jefferson explained in 1799, he had carefully selected "such objects and nature as much be familiar to every people, savage or civilized."[124] The vocabularies' emphasis on nouns—highlighting naming, ordering, and analyzing—reflect an Enlightenment episteme that sought order and explanation.[125] Despite his relatively wholistic collection method, Barton's own choice to focus on nouns—not understanding the "verbifying" of Indigenous languages—turned the words into static data points, thereby missing the languages' vitality and movement. And as Michi Saagiig Nishnaabeg scholar Leanne Betasamosake Simpson cautions, "data created in dislocation and isolation and without movement" is not knowledge.[126]

The Siksikaítsitapi (Blackfoot) philosopher of science LeRoy Little Bear (Kainai) has characterized conventional vocabulary-collecting methods as an orientation toward measurement versus one of relationship.[127] As an example, he focuses on the English language's prioritization of nouns as abstracted isolates in space as compared to the prioritization of verbs in many Indigenous languages. He explains the latter as "action and process oriented" and "land based."[128] The noun-over-verb focus thus reveals what scholars have shown before: that the vocabularies enabled settler power via the isolation and dislocation of Indigenous subjects into data for study. The words become, as literary scholar Laura Murray has written, objects taken "out of people's mouths" rather than representations of living speech.[129] More than that, the translation of Native languages into European ones comes with epistemological and ontological costs: language is a "trick," explains Mohawk scholar Taiaiake Alfred, one that tricks Native peoples "into understanding their own personal identities as things."[130] Collection, translation, and analysis is thus also about dehumanization via abstraction.

Not dissimilar to the way that Barton had learned Linnaean taxonomy in terms of plant structure, and the way he taught it to a new generation of students at the University of Pennsylvania, Barton also broke down language into its constituent parts. (Indeed, the abstraction and focus required by the identification, naming, and analysis of Linnaean botany could also be understood as a power of territorialization, expressing an episteme that prioritized measurement over relationship.) By extracting key words and looking for radical, visual, and phonetic similarities, Barton concluded that most Indigenous languages were really "dialects" of one or two common American "stocks": one of these was "Mexican" and the other was "Delaware."[131] He later added a third, "Six-Nations." Barton arranged his words under each nominal heading according to an order he already assumed to be true, one based on the kinship relations he had already charted. While this would seem to preserve some measure of the relationship within groups, it misrepresents connections across groups. That is to say, the arrangement into three groups to illustrate discrete "waves" of immigration gives no sense of inter-group adaptation, adoption, or relationality. Yet producing a list of American peoples according to their relative order of migration to the New World did allow Barton to account for differences across "Delaware," "Six-Nations" and "Mexican" linguistic groups. Furthermore, by showing the alleged similarity of American "dialects" to Asian ones (he believed "Delaware" was really "Toltec" and "Asian"), Barton was able to furnish linguistic proof that geographically dispersed peoples were all effectively related to one of two (or three) groups, thus maintaining the idea of multiple migrations from Asia to America.[132]

In *New Views,* Barton took single words out of context and grouped them thematically to demonstrate commonalities across American languages. Whether encompassing large subjective concepts (God, Virgin, Bread), kinship (Mother, Sister, Wife), the natural world (Leaf, Fish, River), or the names of colors and directions, the extracted words were isolated and displayed as standardized nouns. Even human beings were anatomized into easily comparable parts: Head, Nose, Eye, Hair, Tooth, Belly, Skin, Blood.[133] Similarities visible in sets of common letters or morphemes seemed to confirm relationships Barton already thought existed.[134] Extracting and comparing these single words as data points allowed Barton not just to reveal family likenesses but also to determine geographic and chronological coordinates of origin. For example: because Barton considered the Lenape to be the "original people," his lists always began with "Lenni-Lennápe."[135] He had concluded that Lenape peoples were "of more ancient establishment in the country than many others," and this dictated the arrangement of his word lists.[136]

Barton's arrangement as plotted in *New Views* resulted in three seemingly ordered groups or "waves" of Indigenous migrants: clustered at the top were Lenape, Ojibwe, Munsee, Mahican, Shawnee, Potawatomi, Miami, Mississauga, Kickapoo, Piankashaw, Algonkian, Penobscot, Mi'kmaq, and Narragansett-Pequot (roughly all Algonquian-speakers); these were followed by Seneca, Mohawk, Onondaga, Cayuga, Oneida, Tuscarora, Kahnawake, Wyandot, Sioux, and Cherokee (Iroquoian-and Siouan-speakers). Last came the cluster of Creek, Chickasaw, Choctaw, Catawba, Waccamaw, Natchez, and Nahua (Muskogean-and Nahuatl-speakers).[137] Not incidentally, Barton's three groups map onto the three "Northern" (Iroquoian/Six Nations) "Western" (Algonquian/Miami/"Delaware") and "Southern" (Muskogean/Creek/"Mexican") political confederacies identified by Knox in 1789, even if these political divisions were simplistic, because there were Six Nations and Creek members of the Western Confederacy, etc. While Indigenous diplomats in the Ohio Valley were working to preserve homelands, alliances, and a fragile peace—the larger United Indian Nation (as envisioned by Mohawk leader Joseph Brant, for example) was meant to unite all Native peoples—Barton's data was picking it all apart.[138]

His arrangement in the order of arrival supposedly allowed Barton to chart different peoples' relative knowledge of and attachment to place, and therefore the duration of their occupancy on the continent. Thus he claimed that the Southern or "Mexican" group—Creeks, Cherokees, Chickasaws, and Choctaws—"long resided in the same district of country" and that the Six Nations had also "for a great length of time, continued their improvements nearly in the same districts of the continent." The import of these two descriptions is not the same. Barton presumed "Northern peoples" to be less connected to the land than southern ones, even if northern groups had been "improving" the lands for a "great length of time." As Barton split communities based on linguistic differences, these divisions obscured real-life relational connections to each other and the land. Importantly, Barton's lists produced evidence that could be used to judge aboriginal claims. This data could also help to establish which group was of ancient enough standing to approve cessions and other transfers of title.

In addition to enabling the technicalities of land theft, Barton's migration historiography emphasized Native peoples' supposedly inherently nomadic dispositions. Any "change in the geographical situation of our tribes," US settlers could argue, would be part of a larger predilection to migration.[139] Barton himself predicted a future in which Native peoples would "retire"—in his words—"perhaps to begin new confederacies of war, and conquest, to the vast countries beyond the Mississippi."[140] President Jackson later used Barton's migration model to lobby support for trans-Mississippi deportation; however, settlers had been using it to assist Indigenous dispossession well before the 1830 Indian Removal Act.[141]

Learning of Earthshapers

After Barton published the first edition of *New Views* in the early summer of 1797 he fled Philadelphia to escape the miasma that had sickened him in previous years. Traveling to the Haudenosaunee lands then called Western New York, he stayed for some time with his friend and colleague Samuel Kirkland, the Presbyterian missionary to Oneidas living at Kanonwalohale (Oneida Castle). Kirkland had already corresponded with Barton regarding his research. In 1788, when Kirkland visited Seneca lands at the behest of speculators, he recorded information about earthworks located near the Genesee and Tonawanda Rivers, accounts of which he sent Barton in 1791.[142] At that time, Kirkland also recalled learning that all Five Nations maintained traditions "that their ancestors came originally from the west; and the Senecas say that [they] first settled in the country of the Creeks."[143] The missionary corrected this traditional version, writing that European histories maintained the Five Nations' origin on "the north side of the great lakes," from which they were driven by enemies and who themselves had "expelled the Satanas" when settling on the southern bank.[144]

In the early eighteenth century, after journeying up from an area then called New Bern, North Carolina, the Tuscarora Nation joined the Five Nations' Longhouse. War with the settlers had caused Tuscarora leaders to seek refuge with their northern kin; they were formally admitted as the sixth sibling of the Confederacy in 1721. At first, Tuscaroras lived on the upper Susquehanna near the multinational Oneida town of Oquaga; Shawnee and Lenape groups also lived on the upper Susquehanna at this time.[145] The latter Minsi (Munsee)

Lenape peoples had been expelled from their lands lower down the Lenapenwihìtàk (Delaware River); the Shawnees were kin who had returned north.[146] In the 1770s, after Loyalist forces burned Haudenosaunee towns—Oneida and Tuscarora had allied with the Patriots—the communities moved to more northerly lands near Kanonwalohale, which after the War was the closest Haudenosaunee village to the US settlements.[147] Oneida and Tuscarora volunteers fought alongside Patriot forces while other Longhouse Nations—Mohawk, Onondaga, Cayuga, and Seneca—allied with the British or attempted to remain neutral.[148] These nations were treated as conquered enemies after the war, and most of their lands were confiscated and turned into the "Central New York Military Tract."[149]

After the war, the US and New York State governments actively promoted the "settling" of central New York by whites, first by assigning the lands to veterans, and then by selling off the areas "left-over."[150] A decade later, the 1794 Treaty of Canandaigua "opened" lands east of the Genesee River to white settlement. After this, most of the northern Tuscaroras—about eight hundred people—moved from Oneida lands to Seneca territory on the Niagara River.[151] But Seneca leaders leased a majority of their lands to New York financier Robert Morris—who then sold them to the Holland Land Company—and arranged a treaty that confined Senecas (and Tuscaroras who had moved to Seneca territory) to reservations with the 1797 Treaty of Big Tree.[152] Indeed, whereas the Treaty of Greenville's reservations delimited settler space within Native lands, the Treaty of Big Tree created reservations to detain Haudenosaunee people on their own lands. Thus the 1797 treaty "opened" lands west of the Genesee as well, and these were the lands that Barton crossed to reach Kirkland.

At the same time that Barton was staying with Kirkland in the summer of 1797, a young Tuscarora student named David was also living with his Presbyterian tutor.[153] David Cusick—who had been born in Oneida country—would grow up to become a respected Haudenosaunee historian and antiquary in his own right.[154] Years later, in 1825–1826, Cusick recorded and self-published a version of "the ancient history of the Six Nations," one that he formulated from his life among different Indigenous and white communities.[155] It is possible that Barton learned some of these traditions during his time in Cusick's company.

In his *Sketches of the Ancient History of the Six Nations* (1827), Cusick recounted traditions of multiple large beings including the "Big Quisquiss"—which he suggests was the mammoth (although the Mohawk translation is closer to Big Boar)—Big Elk, and the Great Horned Serpent.[156] He also wrote of the

Ronnongwetowanca, the "Giants of the North" who warred on the family of the Five Nations when they lived along the Saint Lawrence River, and the Giant Bears who once threatened Onondaga.[157] He recounted that in the early days (roughly 250 CE), the families living along the Saint Lawrence were constantly in danger; at one point their habitations were largely destroyed by a "blazing star."[158] He relayed that "Perhaps about 1250 years before Columbus discovered the America . . . a powerful tribe of the wilderness, called Otne-par-heh, i.e., Stonish Giants* overrun the country," and they "were so ravenous that they devoured the people of almost every town in the country."[159] To this section he added a specific explanatory note:

> *It appears by the traditions of the Shawnees, that the Stonish Giants descent from a certain family that journeyed on the east side of [the] Mississippi River, went towards the northwest after they were separated, on account of the vine broke. The family was left to seek its habitation, and the rules of humanity were forgotten, and afterwards eat raw flesh of the animals. At length they practiced rolling themselves on the sand by means their bodies were covered with hard skin[. T]hese people became giants and were dreadful invaders of the country.[160]

Cusick's note harkens back to an earlier moment in his own narratives, in which members of the "Eagwehoewe" (or Ongweh'onweh, real people) were lost across the Mississippi. Here he recounts a similar Shawnee tradition of migration and kin lost over the Great River, one Lenape communities maintain as well.[161] Cusick, who had grown up around a community of Oneida and Tuscarora people—who had likely also lived with extended Shawnee and Lenape relations—included their traditions in his own history. However, settlers would contend that these traditions were evidence of prior non-Haudenosaunee occupation in New York.

Barton's tour to New York occurred just after the disastrous Treaty of Big Tree at Buffalo Creek and in the midst of a fractured Longhouse.[162] Disagreements over religion and politics—spurred by Christian missionaries and pressure for acculturation as well as constant violence—made for a difficult time on Haudenosaunee lands. For Barton, this meant that any information he recorded from Indigenous informants was shaded by this context of land theft, settler violence, and Christianity versus traditionalism.[163] Just a few years beforehand, even George Washington—notorious Town Destroyer—had decried the region's increasing anti-Indigenous violence—committed by "bad white men."[164] He likened their violence to the actions of the "bad Indians, and the outcast[s] of several tribes who reside at the Miamee Village, [who] have long continued their murders and depredations upon the frontiers laying along the Ohio" in an attempt to sway Seneca opinion against joining their western kin ("For the United States cannot distinguish the tribes to which bad Indians belong, and every tribe must take care of their own people").[165] To convince Six Nations members that Washington desired the "United States and the six nations should be truly brothers," US agents offered annuities and reiterated Six Nations reservation boundaries.[166] In 1790 Washington also recalled that, as part of their "friendship" with the United States, the Six Nations could not be forced to sell their lands. Moreover, he pledged to Seneca leaders Cornplanter, Half-Town, and Great Tree, the "general Government will never consent to your being defrauded—But it will protect you in all your just rights."[167] Nevertheless, the results of the private 1797 Treaty of Big Tree—which stole lands west of the Genesee River—forced Senecas to move onto a scattering of reservations across their traditional homelands, exemplifying the promises broken.[168] Thus, while Barton was busy collecting stories of migration in the past, the peoples around him were living with the experience and ongoing threat of migration in the present.

AT KANONWALOHALE BARTON asked the (unnamed) Oneida "principal chief" about large bones. To his disappointment, the "venerable old man . . . knew nothing concerning the Mammoth, but what he had heard from the Shawnanese, whose ancestors, he understood, had destroyed these monstrous animals."[169] To Barton, the response was itself an unspoken migration history: for why else would an elder have no memory of mammoths—when mammoth bones were embedded in Haudenosaunee lands—unless Oneidas had arrived in the country *after* mammoths had left? That Tuscaroras, like the Shawnees and Lenapes, told stories of battles with these great animals, Barton speculated, meant that they too must have brought memories of the mammoth with them when they migrated north.[170] Indeed, Barton wrote in his journal that he detected a similarity between Tuscaroras and Otomíes, as described by Clavijero (the description that also inspired Alzate to connect them with the Nuu-cha-nulth), and he was inclined to believe that the Tuscaroras had come north "from some part of the Mexican empire."[171] In particular, he noted the seeming coincidence that "the Mexicans, in their migration from the north, are known to have traversed a considerable tract of that very country in which the vestiges of the Mammoths have, in our times, been discovered, in very great abundance."[172] He reasoned that Tuscarora memories of living mastodons would by necessity have originated in "a very distant era—certainly far more remote than the sixth century of the Christian era—when the Mammoths inhabited, and even prevailed very generally in, the ancient territories of the Mexicans."[173]

Barton's understanding of Haudenosaunee, Shawnee, Lenape, as well as Mvskoke and Cherokee history all corroborated his idea that eastern Natives were really from elsewhere, and that some of the continent's oldest nations descended from groups who, after establishing themselves in Anáhuac, had returned northward. Moreover, his readings of Clavijero had convinced him that Mexica annals went back no further than the sixth century, and so in his mind this became the temporal horizon beyond which mammoths had overrun the "ancient territories of the Mexicans." Oneidas, therefore, must have arrived (from Asia) after that date; that Lenape, Shawnee, and Tuscarora groups also maintained similar oral traditions Barton attributed to the former groups' importation of "Mexican traditions."

"Proof" of his southern migration theory arrived in the form of a letter from the Moravian missionary John Heckewelder in March of 1797, in which Heckewelder recounted hearing Ohio traders relay that the Lenape name for Shawnee, "*Schawanno,* denoteth their origin *far* to the South." After this, Barton concluded that the "Shawnese formerly resided on the borders of Mexico."[174] His growing sense, encouraged by Heckewelder, was that Lenape (Delaware) was a common root language for many American peoples, and that "dialects of what I have called the Delaware language, were spoken within the limits of the Mexican empire."[175] He was convinced, for example, that Michoacán—"the name of one of the finest provinces of Mexico"—was "a Delaware word."[176] Additions to his 1798 *New Views* corroborated the language tables he had already published in the 1797 version: "I have lately been assured," Barton wrote in the 1798 edition, "that the Shawnees preserve a tradition, that they were driven by the Spaniards from the borders of Mexico."[177] He confidently predicted, "it will be found, that the Creeks are nearly related to the Talascallas, so celebrated in the history of the conquest of Mexico."[178] Combining his philological work with migration traditions he had been collecting for a decade, Barton became increasingly persuaded that, due to the "extensive wanderings of our Indians, through the continent... many of the northern tribes of America were driven from the borders of Mexico, by the successes of Cortez."[179] While Barton's language work had allowed him to analyze the migration traditions for their geographical and chronological data, Barton's 1798 confidence was supplied by something else altogether: giants.

Although Barton cautioned against believing in giants when he first published *New Views* in 1797, his journals indicate that he clearly had not stopped thinking about them, particularly in terms of migration. Indeed, Barton had started collecting megafaunal memories as data points much in the way he had once charted earthworks. In extracting more "Mexican" information for the 1798 *New Views*, Barton alighted on mentionings of a "race of giants" in multiple Spanish sources, such as José de Acosta's version of a Tlaxcala tradition in which the "mens bones of an incredible bigness" were identified as those of Chichimecas.[180] Bernal Díaz del Castillo had included the presentation of a large bone to Cortés by the leaders of Tlaxcala in 1519, supposed to be the remains of the "men and women of great size" defeated by their ancestors.[181] Antonio de Herrera y Tordesillas repeated Acosta's 1590 claim about Chichimeca bones in his influential *Décadas* (1601–1615). Also, Juan de Torquemada and Fernando de Alva Cortés Ixtlilxóchitl both referenced Mexica traditions recalling the earth-giants who created Teotihuacan. But Barton was cautious, his scientific mind not allowing him to put much stock in what he learned. In *New Views*, he even warned of "writers, who, building upon the tradition of the natives, and upon the discovery of bones, sculls, and entire skeletons of prodigious size . . . have imagine[d] that the first inhabitant of that country [New Spain] were giants."[182]

Barton knew his compatriots would be interested—perhaps too interested—in these traditions of giants from New Spain, for in the north there were also traditions "that a race of men had existed, in former times, of extraordinary height and bulk."[183] Indeed, early English settlers in the Americas—and their associates in Europe—had been fascinated by what were referred to in the Bible as "giants on the Earth, in those Dayes."[184] When a mastodon tooth emerged from the banks of the Muhheakkantuk (Hudson River) in 1705, it inspired the English poet Edward Tyler to pen an epic—drawing somewhat on Mahican and Minsi Lenape origin traditions—dedicated to the "Gyant of Claverack."[185] With rapid changes in population centers during the eighteenth century, megafaunal bones—and stories about them—began resurfacing at prodigious rates. The settlers' discussions, however, were refracted through Indigenous, biblical, and European literary frameworks, nothing meeting Barton's empirical requirements.[186]

More generally the Hudson River tooth was assumed to belong to the antediluvian Leviathan; it was believed to be a material trace of scriptural knowledge in the American soil (it emerged not far from where a complete mastodon skeleton would be unearthed by artist and impresario Charles Willson Peale in 1801).[187] Into the latter half of the century, as fossilized teeth and bones from the frontier made their way back to the East Coast, traders and travelers continued to hear stories of large ancient creatures from their Indigenous partners. The first article in the first issue of the *Columbian Magazine*, in September 1786, for example was dedicated to a "Description of BONES, &c. found near the RIVER OHIO" and brought to Philadelphia from "Big Bone Lick" in Kentucky.[188] An engraving of the bones, drawn by Peale, was included in the magazine; the specimens themselves were placed on display in the federal city, where Barton had ample opportunity to see them.[189]

Reading about the Mexican "race of giants" doubtless recalled the "Claverack Giant" and Big Bone Lick collection, but they also specifically reminded Barton of a 1789 article in the *Columbian Magazine*, in which the Moravian missionary Abraham Steiner recalled that Lenape, Ojibwe, and Wyandot inhabitants of Lake Erie's southern shore "assert that the bones which are found in the graves in the vicinity of both the fortifications are much larger than those of the tallest Indians, of our own times."[190] Although paying little attention to them at the time, after his 1797 trip upstate Barton realized that these memories of giants could be important historical resources, too.

Botanizing Indigenous Knowledges

Barton definitively established his botanical reputation when he brought forward one of the United States' "first great botanical textbook[s]," *Elements of Botany: Or, Outlines of the Natural History of Vegetables* (1803). In it, Barton described his methods for reconstructing past time specifically in terms of ecology, explaining that the "traditional knowledge of our Indians" about the environment contained much information about the past. In fact, *Elements* was a much updated and expanded version of a work he had published more than ten years before and for which he drew widely both from Indigenous oral traditions and non-Native ethnographies.[191] The textbook went through multiple editions in his lifetime, testifying to its wide influence, and solidified his reputation as a leading US scientist.

At the 1807 inaugural meeting of the Philadelphia Linnaean Society, Barton delivered a lecture in which he outlined important avenues for members' future research: "I would suggest the propriety of collecting, with sedulous care, the *traditional* knowledge of our Indians concerning the changes which the continent has undergone. I am far from insinuating, that such traditions should be received as *pure history*: but I am persuaded that, on some occasions, much interesting information might be deduced from them."[192] While Barton's new methodology included assembling oral traditions regarding megafauna, flora, and earthworks as useful supplements to "pure history"—rather than history itself—his results themselves increasingly registered as "scientific." That is to say, despite his own doubts as to the historicity of their contents, Barton relayed singular elements from traditional knowledge as more "fact" than "myth."

If the Steiner or Cusick "giant" narratives are a "distilled memory" of the People—as Yankton Dakota scholar Vine Deloria Jr. once referred to such traditions—then settlers like Barton were so fixated on human migration, civilizational seriality, and racial replacement that they could hardly recognize it.[193] Like histories of earthworks, most Indigenous oral traditions have usually been dismissed as "fable." Deloria contended that their rejection is part of the same epistemological paradigm rendering non-Natives incapable of entertaining alternative accounts of world histories without the categories "myth," "fable," or "fiction."[194]

Many Indigenous traditions feature the battles of extraordinary beings—Hobomok and Beaver, for example, or Flint and Skyholder. These Transformers and Earthshapers, as well as other large more-than-human beings, could all be described as "tall people."[195] Indigenous philosopher Nimachia Howe recalls that all creations are *persons*, including animals, plants, and rocks as well as Big Elk or Underwater Panther.[196] But because many traditions were recorded by antiquarian listeners who used metaphorics and frameworks that only made sense to (or for) white settlers, the truth of the stories—which carry teachings of right relation and balance as well as memories of ages past—was seldom captured, and they instead were dismissed as mythical.[197]

Barton, for example, was interested in what Native peoples knew about local flora, fauna, and changes in the climate because he believed he could use those answers to determine how long a population had been in a given area. His research, however, was aimed at bolstering the chronological theory of successive population, not describing Indigenous lifeworlds. He believed that ecological knowledge could help him determine which peoples were in an area first, where they had been before, and who were the subsequent arrivals: he used Indigenous knowledge to extinguish, not learn from, Indigenous intelligence.

Barton established his methods for reconstructing past time by looking at Native peoples' attentiveness to "agricultural rules" as reflected "in their calendars." These "Calendaria Florae"—that is, "the time of leafing, flowering, fruiting, &c., of vegetables"—Barton saw as particularly useful in tracking climate change and adaptation. In the original edition of *Elements*, Barton provided the following example, wherein "among our [Lenape] Indians,"

> some of the months are designated by circumstances derived from the state of vegetation in their country. These people [Lenapes] have a

'Strawberry-month,' a 'Mulberry month,' &c. . . . The Chikkasah and Choktah Indians called the Spring season, Otoolpha, from Oolpha, the name in their language for a bud, or to shoot out. The Cheerake-Indians denominate the autumn, Oolekhoste, 'the fall of the leaf.'[198]

As with individual entries for a specific plant's medicinal qualities, Barton isolated place, time, and growth pattern to produce a standardized "calendar" that "enable[s] us to compare the climate of different countries or places ... such as Florida and Palestine, Philadelphia and Pekin, New-York and Rome."[199] Barton imagined future historians looking to Indigenous ecological knowledge as an encapsulated past, as a future antiquity: "In the hands of future ages," he wrote, Calendaria Florae "will be deemed amongst the most precious monuments of natural history that can be bequeathed by an inquisitive and enlightened people."[200]

Standardized Indigenous calendars also helped Barton better understand the time-depth of migration in relation to Indigenous temporality. The updated version of *Elements of Botany*, written around 1811 and published in 1812, contains the following explanatory note on two Indigenous modes of time-keeping: "The Mexicans, we are informed, made a considerable change in their calendar, when, migrating from the northern Atztlan, they seated themselves in the milder and more southern and more happy clime of Anahuac."[201] To Barton's mind, his model answers the question of why Mexica and Haundenosaunee calendars do not match. "If, as I suppose," he wrote, "they came from the south-west, they must have altered, and accommodated, their calendar to the more northern regions of which they took possession."[202] In addition to what he had gleaned from Clavijero, Barton mainly learned about Indigenous timekeeping from reading León y Gama's *Descripción de las dos piedras* (1792)—a copy of which had been donated to the APS in 1802 by Spanish astronomer José Joaquín de Ferrer y Cafrangen—from which he learned that the Sun Stone was supposed to reveal Mexica dating conventions and calculations, providing the tools to reveal the exact year Mexica ancestors left their Aztlán homeland and therewith reverse calculate their path and extent of migration, also allowing scholars to coordinate biblical with Indigenous timekeeping.[203]

The fact that Barton's scholarship from this time almost exclusively registers as *botanical* rather than *historical* is largely due to a conventional reading of *Elements* as an individual scholarly undertaking, despite his continued commitment to investigating Indigenous traditions. Indeed, much of the information contained in *Elements* Barton did credit to Native informants, as well as to practices "particularly observed among the American Indians," such as the "proper time to plant the Indian-corn," which he had tracked.[204] He reported, for example, that turmeric "is said to be endued with useful medical powers" and that "Cassena, of our Southern Indians, is a very powerful diuretic. It is also one of the most interesting vegetable articles in the history of the American Indians."[205] In these anecdotes, Barton extracts from Indigenous teachings very specific information. But as ashkikiiwikwe (Anishinaabe medicine woman) Mary Siisip Geniusz explains, the knowledge held by plants must be accompanied by the stories through which they teach.[206] They cannot be extracted as stand-alone data points. This would mean the plants were not respected as members of Indigenous communities and teachers of ancient wisdom; pared down "facts" presented according to a non-Native system denies Indigenous intellectual sovereignty and colonizes Indigenous knowledges.[207]

Although the plants Barton described in *Elements* were indigenous—as in, they had been created in place—Native peoples, for Barton, were still migrants. It was only by living alongside the plants for so long that they had gained their intimate knowledge of place. While Barton saw Native peoples' "vegetable" chronologies as indicative of long duration on the land, he understood it in terms of stadial civilizationist conventions rather than ontology, only accounting for the knowledge of place as gained by dint of experience. What Barton did not realize is how intertwined the lives of Indigenous peoples are with the land: as Syilx Okanagan critic Jeannette Armstrong has advised, Indigenous worldviews are the result of many generations' "distinctive interaction with a geography."[208] The precision of that geography and the relations human and more-than-human geographies sustain (what Lisa Brooks calls "social geography") form not only a peoples' cosmovision and cultural expressions but also the People themselves.[209] In looking for "facts," Barton missed the much larger context and significance of the traditions he was studying.

Remembering Pre-Sunrise Time

In order to make the method of "dividing time among the Indians" useable to his own project, Barton attempted to calculate, standardize, and convert Indigenous time into settler time. Yet because Indigenous traditions rarely matched European timelines, Barton looked to other methods for corroboration and validation. In 1807 Barton counseled his fellow naturalists to look to plants and fossils—not tradition—as the only way "we shall ever be able to form a correct theory of our earth."[210] He encouraged dendrochronological analyses of trees in the West—where large oaks and other ancient trees had been seen growing atop the earthworks at Marietta only a few years before—suggesting that with this tree-borne data "our knowledge in regard to the state of our climate, might be carried much farther back."[211] Barton also spoke of the "petrifactions and impressions which are found upon many of our mountains" as forming "a most interesting subject of inquiry," mentioning the "large collection of such impressions, &c." in his possession.[212] He encouraged his fellow naturalists to spend their time on botany, mineralogy, and geology rather than Indigenous knowledge (even though he admitted that if understood, "like mines, among the rubbish of which we dig, with success, for the most precious metals," they too would yield treasure).[213] Although Barton's and other scholars' minds increasingly turned to fossils rather than oral tradition as a means for reconstructing the past, evidence of both approaches resurfaced in *Elements of Botany*, which contains traces of Barton's earlier, pre-archaeological version of time even while it hints at this move away from information existing *above* ground and toward that existing *below*.

Between 1805 and 1810, Barton wrote a series of letters to Cuvier and Jefferson on the subject of the American *incognitum* (mastodon) and other megafaunal fossils. Yet even as his methods shifted, Barton fiercely maintained his commitment to an anti-originality thesis: at the first Linnaean Society meeting (at which he was inaugurated president) Barton dismissed claims that "the Americans are really the Aborigines, or Autochthones, of the soil and regions in which they were discovered." Rather, Barton proclaimed, "[t]he Indian is, unquestionably, of Asiatic origin."[214] One reason he clung so closely to his anti-originality thesis had to do with a return to his 1790s research and his increasing interest in archaeology. Indeed, as the century changed, so did Barton's science: from natural history and linguistics to archaeology and geology. Prompted by a letter written by Bishop James Madison on the discovery of "mammoth" bones in Virginia—which Barton read aloud at the December 16, 1803, APS meeting—he reviewed the relations of giant bones and their fossilized tales of extinction, increasingly trusting the "facts" of bones over the "myths" of Native peoples.

The 1803 emergence of mammoth bones in Virginia recalled Barton's previous work on "tall ones" traditions in the late 1790s. Although Barton may have originally dismissed the Tlaxcalan giants, he did seemingly take to heart the idea of a distinct age of giants and their monuments: "It is *possible*," he wrote in *Archaelogiae Americana Telluris Collectanea et Specimina* (1814)—one of the last writings Barton published before his death—"that the wars of the Giants, of which the Mexican histories affect to preserve some memorials, may refer entirely to a very distant era—certainly far more remote than the sixth century of the Christian era—when the Mammoths inhabited, and even prevailed very generally in, the ancient territories of the Mexicans."[215] As Barton had already learned from criollo historiography, Mexica people understood the passage of time as a cycle of eras, each introduced by the rising of a new Sun and dawning of a new Age. The current era, the Fifth Sun, was the era of humans; the previous was one of giants. During the darkness after the setting of the Suns, the previous beings were vanished or petrified, leaving behind traces of their existence in fossils and gigantic architecture.[216] This understanding of the pre-Sunrise time of giants could apply to the mastodon bones, and, potentially, the western earthworks as well: as traces of a people and time gone by preserved in "some memorials [that] may refer entirely to a very distant era."[217] These "distilled memories" of mammoths, therefore, proved to Barton that current-day peoples *could not have* existed alongside the giant mammoths of antiquity; instead they were the memories of their ancestors, preserved through the sharing of oral tradition. Although Barton's method was different, this was largely a reiteration of his 1796 declaration on the "sameness" of the Moundbuilders and American indigenes, both still—stubbornly—Asian migrants.

Attending to Barton's oeuvre shows how archaeology came to supplant philology as a technique of historical reconstruction, moving between physical artifact and print and certainly away from orality and embodied knowledge. By revisiting the migration, linguistic, and botanical knowledge he had amassed in the 1790s alongside the revelations of archaeology and paleontology, Barton gained a base against which to develop additional empirical methods for historical reconstruction, which silently surfaced in the new edition of his *Elements of Botany* (1812) and again in *Archaelogiae Americana* (1814). Although Barton's conclusions are not terribly different from his observations in 1787 or views in 1797, his late work is particularly indicative of changes in antiquarian, historical, and scientific priorities during the early nineteenth century.[218]

While *Archaelogiae Americana* clearly is important to the archaeological shift in Barton's research, a potentially more influential source was León y Gama' 1792 pamphlet on the piedras antiguas, which had convinced Barton of the soundness of archaeological investigations. In 1805, the APS received another copy of the famous pamphlet, this one included in a shipment of "valuable books" that was part of an exchange between scientists in the United States and New Spain.[219] Recognizing the importance of the twice-donated publication, Barton wrote about it to Jefferson in September 1809:

You will, I think, be pleased to hear, that I have received from Mexico, a very important pamphlet on the Astronomy of the ancient Mexicans. It is not a fanciful work, such as an ingenious man might write in his closet, from the traditions of Indians, or the vague facts and reports of others. It is truly historical, and is principally founded upon the discovery of the "Mexican Century," a vast stone monument, which was discovered in Mexico, in the year 1790. The work is written by one Gama, a man of real learning; and will serve to overturn many an ingenious theory, the work of such historians and writers as Robe[r]tson, De Pauw &c.[220]

The "truly historical" pamphlet interested Barton so keenly, he explained, because it was based on the science of archaeology, rather than on "vague facts" or "ingenious theory." The former president, equally intrigued, replied that he looked forward to reading the work in translation.[221] Soon afterward, Barton commissioned an APS colleague, Dr. William E. Hulings—formerly US vice consul in New Orleans—to translate the pamphlet from Spanish into English. When it was returned, Barton sent a copy to a friend at the Royal Society in London (although seemingly not to Jefferson), in the hopes he could arrange for its publication abroad. Although Barton had wanted to publish his translation in Philadelphia—where there was already a large Spanish American exile community—he concluded that the "times were not that the taste of my native country would encourage it."[222] Barton also included in his transatlantic packet a notice of the "remains of four vast cities [that] have been discovered in the Spanish provinces of Campeachy, and the vicinity."[223] Both the "vast stone monument" and the ruins of "vast cities" were, for Barton, important evidence of American antiquity.[224] Yet he sought to contextualize and interpret the evidence only in terms of American, not Indigenous, origins.

In 1818, the "Mexican calendar" reappeared, this time bringing the mounds along with it. That year, William Hulings donated his translation of León y Gama's *Descripción* to the APS, which was slowly amassing other items from the Spanish Americas, as well as many which focused on the continent's natural and ancient history.[225] For context, he added translated excerpts from the autonomist newspaper *El Diario de México*, one of which included "reflections drawn from Various extracts of Antient Monuments, collected by the Chevalier Lorenzo Boturini Benaduci."[226] At the very end of his translation, Hulings appended the following note:

Query: May not the Mounds discovered in the western parts of our country which bear the appearances of regular fortifications, have been the works of some of the *Nations* since settled in Mexico; constructed during the *frequent stops* made by them in their journeys from their *country Aztlan*, which, in some places, were extended to a period of many years? This appears to me more than probably, and *Aztlan* is said to have been *some where* on the North West Coast of America; and peopled perhaps *Originally* from Asia, by the way of Bhering's Straits, or otherwise (19).

Hulings's attempt to account for the western earthworks indicates that the Mexica migration theory was still not nearly as widespread in the United States as in New Spain, despite Barton's work, but it also indicates the continued application of anti-originality to US continental expansion and inter-imperial competition.

Learning the Language of the Land

Barton continued working on a new version of *New Views* up until his death in 1815, but his will asked that the materials not be published posthumously. Instead, they were to be deposited with the newly organized American Antiquarian Society in Worcester, Massachusetts.[227] The secretary of the APS, Peter DuPonceau, was instructed to send all of Barton's manuscripts pertaining to *New Views*—including all of his language materials—north. However, by all accounts DuPonceau, himself a gifted linguist, kept Barton's papers for his own language project. They are still at the APS, along with a myaamiaataweenki vocabulary from Heckewelder and the one from Volney, Wells, and Mihšihkinaahkwa.[228] On Volney's vocabulary is a personal inscription to Jefferson, a reminder that the list was the collaborative production of once-living people within a wider settler project.[229]

In his *Tableau*, Volney wrote of Mihšihkinaahkwa as a "hero" who became "convinced at length that all opposition was fruitless" and who ultimately "had the wisdom to persuade his tribe to peaceable measures."[230] This wisdom was no doubt compounded by the special annuity paid him by the United States when he retired to kenapacomaqua, "Little Turtle's Town," in a house built with federal monies. As Little Turtle became increasingly friendly with the United States—largely out of necessity—he began to lose the trust of many Miamis, especially after the disastrous 1809 Treaty of Fort Wayne.[231] Soon the Ohio country was at war again, an outcome he had sought to avoid since 1795. Mihšihkinaahkwa died on July 14, 1812 and was buried at his old kiihkayonki home, already renamed Fort Wayne.[232] In August 1812 his son-in-law was killed by Potawatomi forces at the battle of Fort Dearborn while helping to evacuate US settlers.[233] The US suspected Wells and other allied Miami fighters of treachery, and this defeat triggered punitive anti-Indigenous campaigns across Miami and Potawatomi lands: a few months later, General William Henry Harrison ordered the destruction of all Miami villages within two days' march of Fort Wayne, including kenapacomaqua, although they left Little Turtle's house standing.[234] Many remaining Miami communities moved southward to join their kin on the forks of the waapaahšiki siipiiwi (Wabash River) and along the nimacihsinwi siipiiwi (Mississiniwa River)—near current-day Peru, Indiana—an area that had been their permanent home since the 1790s, when life elsewhere in their homelands became too dangerous.[235]

After years of dislocation and social pressure, the Miami language that Volney had heard spoken in Vincennes and Philadelphia began to go dormant. In 1895, Albert Gatschet of the Smithsonian Institution's Bureau of Ethnology recorded another, much more extensive, word list, which was continued by linguist Jacob Dunn the following decade.[236] It is thought that the last monolingual myaamiaataweenki speaker in Indiana (Mongosa or Polly Wildcat) died in 1917, and the last fluent Miami speaker there (Wapshingah or Ross Bundy) passed in 1963.[237] Yet myaamiaataweenki has not died; thanks to the dedicated revitalization work of Miami linguist David J. Costa—who reconstructed a living vocabulary based on the Gatschet-Dunn lists as well as the Volney list—and Miami scholar Daryl Baldwin—who used these alongside "old documents belonging to his grandfather"—a new generation of Miami people are once again speaking, and singing, their language.[238] So much of the work to revive myaamiaataweenki was done by Indigenous linguists consulting these very datasets of the "Moundbuilder archive" that were compiled to write them away.[239] Also on the lands currently called Indiana, myaamia people are reconnecting with the traditional knowledge that their homelands contain.[240] This resurgence method of history actively engages traditions, language, and place to recontextualize and recall the histories and languages of Miami lands and peoples.[241]

A particularly striking example of resurgence is a collaboration between the Smithsonian Institution and Miami University's Myaamia Center, founded in 2013, that focuses on teaching science and language to Miami youth through embodied knowledge of myaamionki.[242] Knowledge of the universe—the Earth and Sky—is taught in myaamiaataweenki on miaamionki, reawakening a location-based practice thousands of years old. Students learn the names of lands and waters, such as the ahseni siipiiwi (Great Miami River), of myaamionki.[243] Whereas Volney had recorded the word for "stone" as "sâné" ("ahsena"), the Miami learners are taught words specific to the "ahsena myaamionkonci" at a site not far from Fort Wayne.²⁴⁴ Students also learn that "eehsahsena" is any "rock with a shell in it" (fossil) and that "fossils are most commonly found in waapahsena" (limestone), a process that simultaneously teaches them about the relationships across water, animals, and stone.²⁴⁵ Another youth camp, focused on language acquisition and learning Miami heritage, is called "saakaciweeta," "emerge."²⁴⁶ Oklahoma-or Kansas-based students regain the myaamionki context for knowledge based in their old homelands, and they learn to see the continuities with current Miami life.²⁴⁷ The manifold increase in Miami-language speakers and renewal of cultural life is known as "myaamiaki eemamwiciki," "the Myaamia awaken."²⁴⁸ Today, groups of myaamiaataweenki speakers gather at traditional homeland sites—such as the repurchased aašipehkwa waawaalici, the limestone cliffs of the Seven Pillars along the Mississinewa near Peru—to recite stories and reengage traditional histories, reawaken Miami culture, and revivify Miami lands in their own words.²⁴⁹

BARTON AND HIS colleagues showed how the collection of words and phrases could provide the basis for an American origin story with no Indigenous origins, an anti-originality story now known as the "Moundbuilder myth."²⁵⁰ In this chapter, I have demonstrated that natural history at the turn of the nineteenth century—as it was narrowing into separate disciplines such as botany, geology, and archaeology—also separated Indigenous from settler knowledge. Indigenous knowledge in the form of songs and traditions became unreliable, unscientific "folklore" that was nonetheless extracted in the service of Moundbuilder mythology; this process "naturalized" settler control of science. The migration model of history disconnects the land from the language it formed, both as an aim and as a consequence, based on the extraction of data from living stories and active experience.

CHAPTER 5

Removal in the Antiquarian Archive

Present invisibility
need not concern.
My weight remains
heavy upon this land.

—Allison Adelle Hedge Coke, "Snake Mound 1," 2006

IN 1811, PITTSBURG RESIDENT Henry Marie Brackenridge became one of the first US citizens to write about the grand complex of earthworks across from St. Louis, which Kaskaskia chief Jean Baptiste Ducoigne had called the "palace of his ancestors" three decades earlier.[1] "I have no where read any description of it," Brackenridge remarked in a January 1811 article for the *Louisiana Gazette*, "yet I scarcely know of any curiosity in the western country, more worthy of such notice."[2] Although French maps had noted the "ruined castles" on the river's eastern bank—along with the nearby copper and lead mines—Brackenridge was shocked at the earthworks' seeming obscurity.[3] To rectify this, he included their description alongside his observations on the territory's economic potential ("In minerals," the area was "unquestionably the richest portion of the American territory").[4] He described platform pyramids, plazas, and former ball courts spread over a six-mile stretch, and identified the sites of two "cities, in the distance of five miles, on the bank of the cohokia, which crosses the American bottom at this place."[5] There, in addition to the "stupendous" main mound and a "great number of small elevations of earth," Brackenridge also noted that "pieces of obsidian or flint are found in great quantities... as in the case of the [Mexica] Teocalli."[6] From the architecture and artifacts he concluded "that a very populous town had once existed here, similar to those of Mexico."[7] Writing Thomas Jefferson two years later, he reported being "perfectly satisfied ... that cities similar to those of Ancient Mexico, of several hundred thousand souls have existed in this part of the country."[8] We "might even be warranted," he proposed, in considering "the mounds of the Mississippi more ancient than the Teocalli."[9] Perhaps, Brackenridge implied, the United States had its own Mexico City.

Brackenridge was not terribly far off: at its height around 1150 CE, the settlement—the site of which has come to be known as "Cahokia," named for the Tamaroa-Cahokia (Inoka/Peoria) people who were displaced by French settlers in the early eighteenth century—was indeed populous, hosting as many as twenty thousand people.[10] Cahokia is the largest complex of earthworks in the northern continent and still home to more than eighty mounds today: its largest earthwork boasts two levels of terraces with a view of water—and the St. Louis Arch—from the top.[11] Waves of prairie grass undulating in the wind—inspiring, in the 1830s, William Cullen Bryant's poem "The Prairies"—soften the mounds in their various conical and pyramidal aspects. A nearby sign describes the site as "America's Oldest City," "a metropolis that thrived more than five-hundred years before Jefferson was born."[12]

Brackenridge proposed that the structures at Cahokia had been made by the "Olmees" or "Toultees," who had "probably migrated from the Mississippi."[13] After all, he noted, "The distance from the large mound on Red River, to the nearest [Teocalli] in New Spain, is not so great but that they might be considered as existing in the same country."[14] He suggested Jefferson read about Cholula, Paplanta, Mitla, and the "Casas Grandees on the Rio Gila Intendency of Senora" to investigate the connection.[15] Brackenridge could only have known of the "large mound on Red River"—in current-day Lafayette County, Arkansas—from New Spanish maps and criollo descriptions.[16] His message to Jefferson reveals settler antiquaries' tendency to look southward, rather than locally, for hints to America's past.[17]

By the early 1810s, ancient Mexico had become the standard bearer of an American "civilization"—similar to that of ancient Egypt or Assyria—against which other Indigenous peoples were measured, and the chronology of American antiquity regularly reached back to the "Olmees" and "Toultees." Brackenridge's letter, however, points to lingering questions about the identity of the continent's most ancient people and their most ancient places, as well as how these should be ordered on Western timelines. "Who," he asked, "will pretend to speak with certainty as to the Antiquity of America—The races of men who have flourished and disappeared"?[18] By appropriating the language and imagery of criollo historians, early nineteenth-century US antiquaries prioritized pasts from Mexico over local Native ones, thereby constructing an imagined spatiotemporal geography that integrated western territory into the Republic while physically expelling its current Native inhabitants beyond the national frontier.

This type of antiquarianism aimed not just at proving a "civilized" ancient people had once flourished in the Americas, but also sought to surface the evidence of their alleged disappearance.[19]

Brackenridge, like many of the period's antiquaries, was an early member of the American Antiquarian Society (AAS), a nerve center for antiquarianism in the nineteenth-century United States. Founded in Massachusetts in 1812 by a group of well-connected nationalists, their goal was "the acquisition, description, and preservation of American Antiquities," and members were explicitly amassing materials they presumed would hold historical importance for future generations.[20] Whereas conventional antiquarianism had come to signify insatiable collecting to no real end, this more preservationist strain was explicit about its orientation toward the future. In an era of rapid material and demographic changes, preservationist antiquarianism sought both to explain as well as memorialize that which had come before. Yet exactly which "before" was being preserved depended on the antiquary's interpretation of who would live in its future. The usual result was the replacement of Indigenous futures with American ones.[21]

Preservationist antiquaries looked in their attics and libraries for antiquities they might save, but most of all they looked at, and in, the land. As fossil archaeology was developing with respect to paleontology and ichthyology, nationalists' attention to potsherds, stone tools, and other artifacts transitioned from mere curiosity to belief in their potential historical relevance. Whereas antiquarian collectors most often identified surface-level items as "Indian antiquities"—meaning that they held some resemblance, in settlers' eyes, to objects used by living Indigenous individuals—items excavated from the earth were deemed "ancient" and therefore not considered "Indian" at all. Brackenridge made this distinction clear in his description of Cahokia, where he discerned "the traces of two distinct races of people, or periods of population, one much more ancient than the other." One set "belong[ed] to the same race as existed in the country when the French and English effected their settlements on this part of the Continent" while another—the "extraordinary tumuli or mounds"—dated to a more "ancient period."[22] Repeating the common refrain that the "oldest Indians have no tradition as to their [the earthworks'] Authors, or the purposes for which they were originally intended"—and claiming that local Indigenous groups used the sites for their own purposes only "unconsciously"—Brackenridge transformed Cahokia into a memorial for people who had long ago "flourished and disappeared," their only traces lodged in the soil that was rapidly succumbing to the shovel of "progress."[23]

In correspondence with the AAS leadership, Ohio member Caleb Atwater described the earthworks as being "driven away before us like the aborigines, and like them will soon be no more."[24] Atwater pledged to "snatch from the destroying, ruthless hand of man" whatever he could and forward all of it to the society's headquarters in Massachusetts.[25] In the September 1819 issue of Kentucky's *Western Review*, "B."—likely editor William Gibbs Hunt, also a member of the AAS—suggested "rescu[ing] from oblivion all the monuments that remain" and moving them to safety elsewhere.[26] Other members followed suit. Indeed, thanks to the American Antiquarian Society's expanding network of members—stretching from Massachusetts to Lexington, St. Louis, New Orleans, and beyond—the society collected a large cabinet of "American antiquities" saved from "oblivion."[27] Atwater's and B.'s proposals to send away Indigenous materials demonstrate that grappling with Indigenous peoples and histories provided US antiquaries the means to actualize national success in ways at odds with the seemingly benign and paternalistic concepts of "collection" and "preservation."

Thanks to these early members, some of the AAS's cabinet's "antiquities" were the physical remains and funerary objects of Native peoples stolen from, beside, or beneath resting human bodies; these are to this day often overlooked in summary accounts of early US museum collections.[28] And although the "antiquities" that filled the society's early cabinet are now gone—having been deaccessioned at the turn of the twentieth century—their textual archive is ultimately more durable and better preserved.[29] Atwater himself proved crucial to the formation of the American Antiquarian Society's archive. His most well-known essay, "Description of the Antiquities Discovered in the State of Ohio and Other Western States," published in *Archaeologia Americana: Transactions and Collections of the American Antiquarian Society* (1820), is not infrequently cited as an origin point for US archaeology.[30]

It is no coincidence that by the time Atwater and B. were writing about antiquities preservation the ink was still drying on the first of the new "removal"-style treaties. Nor that at the opening session of the 1819 New York State Legislature, Governor DeWitt Clinton—also an AAS member—explicitly linked forced relocation to preservation when he claimed, in reference to Haudenosaunee communities: "I have never ceased to believe their departure is essential to their preservation."[31] The removal of Indigenous peoples from the US body politic—like the removal of Indigenous history materials to a "safe" and permanent place of deposit—was, to preservationist antiquaries, an extention of their "preservation" work. In fact, US antiquaries' calls for preservation—distinctly *not* calls to end either forced removal or settler expansion—were in reality calls to reframe and thereby naturalize the violence of political and cultural annihilation attendant upon the creation of American antiquity. Their redefinition of "departure" and "removal" as "preservation" allowed for the creation of US property out of the destruction (or attempted destruction) of Indigenous space and social geography.[32] Indeed, the mandate the AAS adopted in 1812—to "COLLECT and PRESERVE"—encapsulates the interdependence of preservationist antiquarianism and Native dispossession.[33]

Early nineteenth-century antiquarian preservationism thus depended on digging into the land's past to constitute a nationalist future, which meant first disassembling the existing Native past (and present) and then segregating any remaining traces of those pasts to a pre-or extra-national spatiotemporality. In this chapter, I propose that it is only in understanding the collection and preservation of "antiquities"—emblematized by the early AAS archive—as procedures of dispossession and destruction that the links between antiquities, expansion, and settler nationalism become clear.[34] Without placing the pristine printed pages and folders of yellowed manuscripts within the specific constitutive context of land theft and Indigenous extermination, the AAS's archival violence remains hidden and thus continues its work.[35]

In 1813, Brackenridge was not wrong in suggesting that parts of Cahokia were more ancient than México-Tenochtitlan. In evoking Olmeca and Tolteca histories, moreover, he signaled his willingness to consider a period even farther back than had been customary, a period of time that transcended contemporary policy questions.[36] He was not alone: as the developing sciences of paleontology, archaeology, and geology began to deepen the pool of the past, other US antiquaries sensed a chronological morass as well. Geology, established in European laboratories and lecture halls throughout much of the eighteenth century, did not become an explicit concern in the United States until after the century's turn.[37] But by 1809, the term "strata"—meaning layers of earth—was all over the country's most important scientific publications.[38] This meant that turn-of-the-century US naturalists and antiquaries (usually one and the same) were coming to envision the land as having been formed over time (not all at once) in layers comprised of fossilized fragments deposited over the originary soil of Creation. With the progressive accretion of time, the silted layers hardened into "strata." Antiquaries soon found the vocabulary provided by the earth sciences useful not just for describing layers of rocks and dirt but for describing the past as well.[39]

Stratigraphy—the current-day archaeological term that describes "the order and position of layers of archaeological remains"—and by extension "the analysis

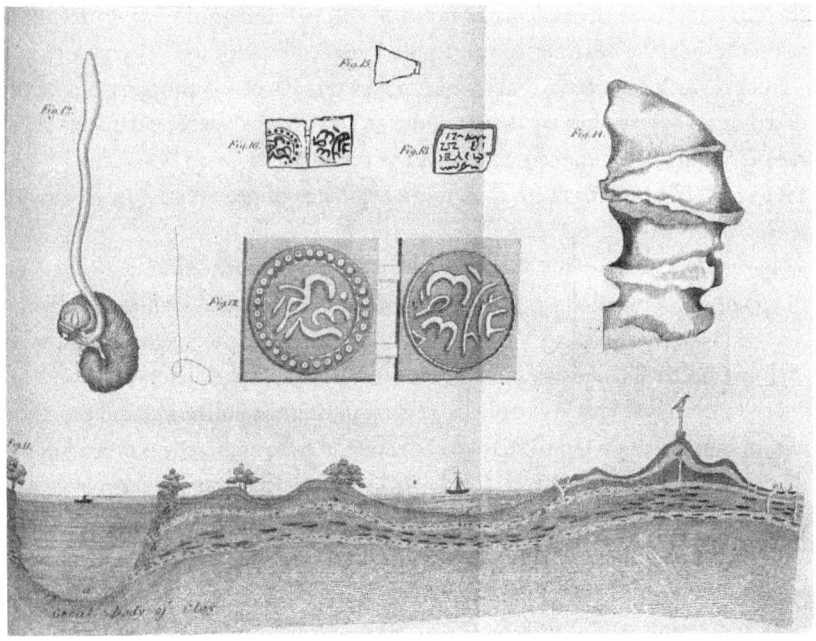

FIGURE 14. "Great Body of Clay," *Memoirs of the American Academy of Arts and Sciences* 3 (1809), f. 2. Courtesy of the Biodiversity Heritage Library and Missouri Botanical Garden. Lower third of the image is a cross-sectional depiction of the stratified landscape.

of these layers with regard to the relative chronology of artefacts and features found in them" operates according to a *logic* of *stratification* that conceptualizes time as separated spatially, wherein the objects occupying different strata are understood to have been deposited at different times. Preservationist antiquarianism relied on the visualization of layered geological time to impose "order"—including historical order—while enabling a synchronic assessment of the past as epitomized by the geological cross section.[40] Their legacy is seen in current-day diagrams of excavations, which continue to portray time as a horizontal spatialization in which depth of surface translates as depth of time, with time usually arrayed in separate layers or "strata."

In the absence of any real sense of the age or purpose of the remains before them, early nineteenth-century settler-scholars created an underground chronology that allowed them to envision the evidence of previous habitation as "ancient" or "antediluvian," that is, existing before the biblical Flood that receded to reveal the current earth, and separate from the present era. Visualizing time in terms of geological layers provided the tool that preservationist antiquaries needed to separate the ancient past from the national present. Indeed, this logic of temporal stratification—as refined through excavation and thus the destruction of Indigenous earthworks—I term "stratiology." A stratiological model of history, therefore, stresses the stratiform ordering of eras and peoples and is usually arranged in a vertical hierarchy from surface to depth, emphasizing layers or breaks between epochs and peoples.[41] Stratiology also serves to describe the habits of mind that prioritized the *spatial* separation of peoples, as in the "racial quarantine" maintained by the African emigration and Indian reservation programs.[42]

Unlike the transformative racial theories that undergirded Jeffersonian assimilation policies—structured by racial beliefs that literary scholar Katy Chiles describes as "external, flexible race"—nineteenth-century settlers' explanations of antiquity centered on the "rise and fall" of individual peoples arranged as a series of absolute substitutions or replacements, one after the next, each with "internal and fixed racial differences."[43] Ancient "Moundbuilders" thus gave way to recent "Indians," who gave way to Europeans, who in turn gave way to new Americans. But populations, wrote feminist critic Annette Kolodny, "are not 'exchanged' or 'replaced' unless as a result of genocidal planning. Rather they are subject to adaptation and change."[44] Narratives that sustained this fiction of seriality emphasized what Kolodny called "the drama of sudden displacement" and provided cover for violent assimilation.[45] Indeed, by emphasizing "displacement" in terms of layering and replacement, the very changes to the land—as well as the genocidal policies against Indigenous peoples—came to be understood as the natural, geological course of history.

This chapter places preservationist antiquarianism within a hemispheric project of scientific discourse on Indigenous dispossession to reveal the interdependence of preservation, forced removal, and replacement. It posits that during the first quarter of the nineteenth century US nationalist antiquaries developed an "excavatory" mode of looking through the landscape to the "natural resources" supposedly concealed within and thereby past the surface of the present. In this way, preservationists' excavatory visuality perpetuated the desecration of Native gravesites and Indigenous dislocation even after the landscapes they pillaged to "preserve" were far removed from their original purposes. I link stratiology to antiquaries' theorizations of time and space as based on the layers of humus, fossils, and minerals as well as the bodies of human ancestors and related funereal objects they disturbed from their resting places as they targeted Native sacred sites for excavation. In so doing, they also targeted Indigenous futures for destruction, because grave-digging literally robs descendants of their ancestors. These antiquaries' stratiological model of history depended on the visual as well as physical removal of Indigenous peoples and ancestors from their homelands in order to visualize their American past.

This chapter reveals that the antiquarian turn toward preservationism mapped onto a shift in US Indian policy away from "civilizationism" and toward a system of absolute temporal, visual, and physical segregation.[46] In particular, the chapter suggests that AAS member Caleb Atwater's contributions to the society's first scholarly publication, *Archaeologia Americana*—as well as his own conduct as a model antiquary—connects the stratiological model of history to contemporaneous US policies of Indian Removal. The continental, excavatory vision that Atwater and his peers adapted from a previous generation of settler-scholars and their stratiological model of history enabled not only the "progress" of US science but also the successful project of the expanded republic.

Seeing Excavation, Strata, and Space

As the new century turned, forces of the "historical trinity of U.S. imperialism—war, slavery, and territorial expansion"—were transforming a country whose population since 1783 had more than doubled and its territorial claims trebled.[47] Especially after the 1803 Louisiana Purchase the peoples who lived in the nation's "interior" changed: more laboring Europeans, more free and unfree Black residents, more Native peoples with multivariate sovereignties and alliances. 1803 was also the year that Ohio left the Northwest Territory and was admitted to the Union as the seventeenth state, testing the new regulations and strength of self-governance. Uprisings in Spanish America as well as the United States' wars with Britain, Tecumseh's Confederacy, Creeks, and Seminoles during the first two decades, moreover, renewed debates over citizenship, foreign policy, and Indian affairs, especially as related to the projection of US sovereignty over the lands it often still only nominally claimed.[48] Citizens of this rapidly growing and demographically-changing nation, where "preservation" was held in tension with "change," manifested contrasting approaches toward land: on the one hand, an attitude that saw the land as the repository of history; on the other, as a depository of future fortune.

Settlers and speculators saw the western lands, in the words of Thomas Paine, as "the real riches . . . and natural funds of America."[49] The lure of fertile soil, deposits of mineral wealth, and projected "internal improvements"—turnpikes, saltworks, canals—drew workers, farmers, and industrialists westward in large numbers.[50] Massachusetts-born attorney Caleb Atwater was drawn to Ohio, as were many "western emigrants," by the desire for a new start (although he had the added advantage of family who had moved there before him).[51] In 1814, Atwater was specifically seeking to escape a bad investment in the New York glass industry and so Ohio—with its promise of fascinating landscapes and a social network of fellow Freemasons—must have seemed like the perfect location for reinvention and—perhaps—prosperity.[52] When Atwater arrived from western New York to scout Ohio's prairielands in 1814, he saw in the long-grass meadows profitable opportunities for grazing, growing corn, gathering peat, and planting orchards.[53] Looking across the prairies he not only began to reimagine his future: Atwater began to see the past in a new way, too.[54]

US surveyors learned to identify earthworks as markers of choice lands and portents of prosperity, in the process also disturbing and destroying the physical traces of peoples who had come before the current migrants.[55] As the newcomers girdled, felled, and dug, they marked changes to the land with a mixture of optimism and regret. Settlers' "improving" aimed to reform the land according to the dominant ideas of progress that emphasized neatly tilled fields, fenced farmsteads with kitchen gardens, and urban nucleation over autonomous "backcountry" modes of living based on foraging, hunting, and seasonal movement.[56] As settler farmers domesticated the "raw wilderness" that had already been scarred by war and was littered with the detritus of prior settlements, their shovels and hoes revealed what they called "antiquities"—arrowheads, pottery fragments, pipe stems, and stone pounders—which they often brought into their homes. These collections index the temporal complexity revealed by the peeled-away layers of earth.[57]

As nineteenth-century settlers in the United States refigured the territory from "wilderness" to "civilization," what they consistently missed was the landscape of the present or even the recent past. In 1809, Jacob Cist, a correspondent to Philadelphia's *Port-Folio* suggested that because "the elements are daily combining with man to efface these monuments of art, science loudly demands that they should be preserved in some work not of an ephemeral cast."[58] As a start, he offered a sketch of the "Remains of an Ancient Work" located on the Scioto River. Yet Cist's skech of earthworks, located "on land belonging to colonel Worthington," preserves a shallow settler history only passing itself off as an ancient one and adds little to contextualize the "monuments of art."[59] Not even fifty years before Worthington and Cist, however, the lands hosting "ancient works" in the Scioto River Valley and nearby Pickaway Plains—a sandy, rocky, prairie created by the glacial retreat and named by settlers for the Pekowi division of Shawnees— had hosted important Shawnee villages such as Chillicothe and Wakatomica, many of which were abandoned or destroyed during Lord Dunmore's War and the Revolution.⁶⁰ The site that Cist portrayed in 1809—located on land purchased by Thomas Worthington (future Ohio governor)—was not far from his mansion built two years earlier. The view from his Adena estate today allegedly features on Ohio's official seal, "Adena" being a supposedly Hebrew (but actually fabricated) word Worthington believed to mean "paradise."⁶¹ In the twentieth century, this name would also be given to the archaeological "culture complex" epitomized by excavations at the site Cist described, creating by extension a new identity for the people who built the earthworks and lived there from 800 BCE to 100 CE, a people seemingly disconnected from Indigenous history—especially the recent Shawnee history—of the region.⁶²

Australian archaeologist Denis Byrne has written of the erasure of "Aboriginal visibility" in which non-Aboriginal Australians willfully ignore the "continued presence of Aboriginal people in the post-1788 landscape" to envision instead traces of a fanciful Indigenous past they are seemingly called to preserve.⁶³ Similarly, the processes of settler colonialism in North America have also "rendered invisible"—physically and discursively—traces of concurrent Indigenous presence and redirected settler attention to a past often more fantasy than fact.⁶⁴ Instead of seeing overgrown fields, abandoned village sites, and lonely hunting grounds as due to the relatively recent events of colonialism, settlers saw them as belonging to a layered past absolutely separate from their own present. Not only did this interpretation absolve settlers of personal and proximate roles in the annihilation of surrounding Indigenous communities, but it also enabled them to assert the security of their title by imagining themselves to exist on a land free of living claimants. Viewing the region's "fortifications" as "ancient," in other words, kept settlers from seeing their deep connection to and responsibility for the present. And it was that unique version of the past they wanted to bring into the future.⁶⁵

Amassing Atwater's Artifacts

In 1815, Caleb Atwater led his small family west along the Genesee Turnpike, relocating to Ohio's newly incorporated Scioto River town of Circleville.⁶⁶ According to Atwater's daughter Belinda many years later, her father had been drawn to Circleville "by hearing of the curious mounds and fortifications made there by the Indians of former days."⁶⁷ The first white settlers began moving to the Scioto River valley in the late 1790s—after the Treaty of Greenville ended the wars—but the new people of Chillicothe—who named their new town for the Shawnee one it replaced—did not regard the earthworks as features to preserve. Instead, they were largely only documented by travelers such as Cist,

Brackenridge, or Massachusetts minister Thaddeus Mason Harris, exciting more speculation in the East than in most Ohio towns.[68] Indeed, while the people of Marietta (1788)—located to the east, on the Muskingum—had taken pains to preserve the earthworks anchoring its contours, the new settler towns on the Scioto River—Chillicothe (1796), Columbus (1812), and Circleville (1813)—tended to commemorate their earthworks by replacement rather than preservation.[69]

In 1810, Circleville's site had been selected as the Pickaway County seat explicitly for its "most perfect . . . ancient works," and its grouping of square and circular mounds gave the town both physical and nominal shape.[70] The new town's unique design featured an octagonal courthouse placed at the center of two concentric "embankments," but the large mounds there had to be razed to make room. Townspeople used the stone and soil from those "perfect" earthworks to build their houses.[71] The bricks comprising the Atwater family home in "the Circle" neighborhood most certainly came from the formerly ten-foot high "square fort" in "the Circle" at the town's center.[72] Instead of keeping the Circle's mounds, the town kept the shape—for a short time—and the name.[73]

These Scioto Valley towns—at the center of Shawnee homelands—were founded during the years that Tecumtheth (Tecumseh) and his brother led the movement to take them back. In 1811, Tecumseh's forces fought Harrison and the US Army at Prophetstown on the Wabash and Tippecanoe Rivers; the Shawnee leader would continue to gather support and defend his homelands until his death in 1813 and defeat by Harrison's forces.[74] The constant settler emigration and town-building in the Ohio country during Tecumseh's War— i.e., Columbus in 1812 (incorporated 1816) and Circleville in 1813 (incorporated 1814)—amounted to a civilian front in the US war of occupation.

The expansion process—of which Atwater was a willing part—unfailingly produced new sites to "clear" and excavate and thus more antiquities to preserve. Yet excavations that became increasingly common in the places that became the states of Ohio, Indiana, and Illinois—in 1803, 1816, and 1818—consistently revealed that the "pioneer" settlers were no pioneers at all. An 1814 article in Columbus's *Western Intelligencer* describing the destruction of the large local mound, for example, asked "who the people were that once settled this fertile country, from whom or what nation they descended, or what cause could have so completely annihilated such a numerous race, that not a vestige of them can be found except their works."[75] An 1817 article in Philadelphia's *North American Review* described an Indiana excavation, reporting that the "immense tract of country, which has every mark of having been for centuries past a desolate wilderness," was revealed to have been "thickly inhabited at some former period by a warlike people, who had made much greater advances in the

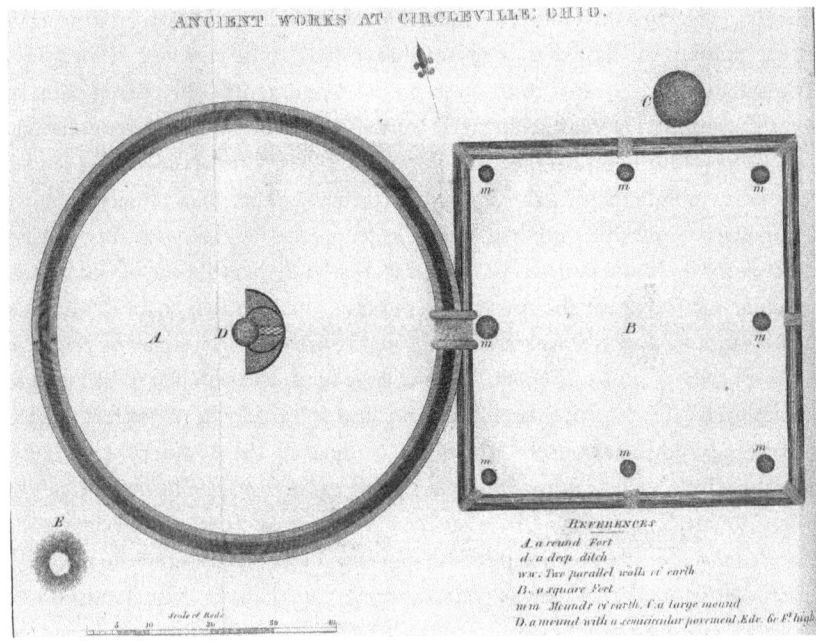

FIGURE 15. Caleb Atwater, "Ancient Works at Circleville Ohio," *Archaeologia Americana* (1820), pl. 4. Courtesy of the Library of Congress.

arts of civilized life, than any of the aboriginal inhabitants of North America."[76] All around, settlers detected messages left by populations they assumed to be long gone and disconnected from the Native peoples whose presence they wished away as well.

Watching the town grow, Caleb Atwater was certain all the "ancient works" would fall casualty to "progress": "Every brick maker has a kiln near one of these works," he wrote in August 1818, lamenting that the very materials used to build the nation's taverns, schoolrooms, and courthouses were drawn from the earthworks' mounded clay.[77] "All I could do," he wrote despairingly to AAS president Isaiah Thomas, "was to step down upon the beach of this ocean and there examine the fragments which, by time and accident have been cast upon the shore. This I have done with the mighty waves, which threaten soon to swallow up the rest, rolling in full view before me. What is left undone it will soon, soon be too late forever to do."[78] Atwater was determined to use "the only means within my power to perpetuate their memory"—that is, to retrieve the "few fragments of history which had fortunately been saved from the deluge of time."[79] Racing the tide, Atwater collected feverishly and exchanged faithfully.[80] Whatever he could—words, images, or antiquities—he promised to colleagues or added to his own collection.[81] From an earthwork dismantled in Circleville, for example, Atwater retrieved a plate of "isinglass" (sheet mica), some flint arrowheads, and a horn-handled knife, some of which he offered to send to the AAS.[82]

In the first decade of the society's existence, AAS members wrote each other, exchanged "specimens" for study or preservation, and penned essays published in eastern and western periodicals like the *American Monthly Magazine* and the *Western Review*, extending the terms of national unity into the past as well as westward and southward. After being appointed postmaster of Circleville, Atwater's own antiquarian network expanded to include correspondents in western towns like St. Louis and Shawneetown (now Old Shawneetown, Illinois), and his collection rapidly expanded "through the kindness of my friends in various parts of this Western county."[83] The expanding postal system, in particular, supported the AAS's mission, and the federal position provided Atwater with franked postage, ample access to the newest scientific publications, and a small but central venue where he could display his antiquarian finds.[84] Indeed, the expansion of the United States can be visualized through the corresponding networks of AAS membership (as well as postal routes), networks that made the mission of "deposit"—from Circleville and St. Louis, to St. Stephens and Mobile—possible.[85] Settlers' ability to move farther west and south after 1815—the end of the War of 1812—had been enabled by the decade of military campaigns as well as the resultant treaty negotiations granting trade, mail, and transport access across Indian Country.[86]

In 1818, Atwater boasted a personal collection "worth all others put together, on this side of the mountains."[87] It was, in his words, a "small cabinet of curiosities calculated to throw some light on our past leading through the dark ages of Antiquity."[88] Although by the early century many savants still depended on linguistic analysis to establish Indigenous migration paths and interconnections, Atwater was sure that a minute analysis of Ohio's antiquities themselves would yield better results.[89] A February 24, 1819 description of his antiquarian methodology is also a summary of his own antiquities collection:

> The fragments of history, as Bacon would say, which I examine, are the Geology and Botany of the country where the works are found-the skeletons of the people themselves; their medals and monuments intended to perpetuate the memory of important events in their history (the stone mounds etc) their dress; their weapons of offense and defense; their places of amusement, public resort and public worship, etc. and comparisons are

instituted between whatever belonged in common to this and other people wither of ancient or modern times; residing in this, or any other part of the world.[90]

Atwater's words reveal his neo-Baconian understanding that the objects called "antiquities" were really "fragments of history" waiting to be pieced back together. Like geologists for whom bits of sandstone literally represented eons past, Atwater understood uncovered artifacts as historical records dislodged from their proper chronological order, which was up to him to restore. All items—stones, fossil plants, ancestors, and artifacts—became, in Atwater's eyes, records against which he could compare other known peoples and times.[91]

And he had ample opportunity for comparison: by the time he became an Ohioan, Atwater was regularly corresponding with physician Samuel L. Mitchell in New York City, Professor Benjamin Silliman at Yale, and Bowdoin's professor Parker Cleaveland, as well as other "men of science" closer by, trying out on them all of his theories of Ohio history.[92] As early as 1817, Atwater had become enough of an expert on Ohio's antiquities that when President Monroe's summer tour passed through Circleville the two men conferred on the subject together.[93] The next year, Atwater submitted an account of their conversation to the *American Monthly Magazine* in New York; his article, "Aboriginal Antiquities in the West," brought the Ohioan to the attention of the American Antiquarian Society, which honored Atwater with membership that spring.[94]

Not only did Atwater amass collections of items removed from excavated mounds, he also collected the technical information of earthworks' dimensions and shape, often commissioning surveyors to make official plats, which he then elaborated and studied. Indeed, Atwater saw antiquities collection only as a part of the crucial work of surveying, documenting, and excavating the earthworks. In March of 1820, for example, Atwater wrote to AAS president Thomas to describe his learning process: "By obtaining survey of the ancient works . . . and by [completing] a thorough examination of them, as well as by collecting the articles found near them, new light may be afforded."[95] He longed to make "an accurate survey of all these ancient remains" before they were destroyed, he told Thomas, but antiquarian research was expensive. As early as July 1818 he reported laying out "$200 within one year past in collecting information," neglecting his professional duties as attorney and circuit judge to do so.[96] "Could I be well assured of anything like a remuneration for the labour and money which I should be obliged to expend," he hinted to AAS secretary Rejoice Newton in 1818, he would devote himself wholeheartedly to the work "for a year or two."[97]

Originally, Atwater had hoped to publish his findings as *Notes on the State of Ohio*—a project inspired by Jefferson but impelled by a circular he had received from New York governor DeWitt Clinton—but Atwater was seldom solvent and he despaired of ever being able to preserve—at least in print as Cist suggested— the antiquities around him.

For more than two years Atwater maintained a regular correspondence with Thomas, often asking for money and usually sending multiple letters a month.[98] In 1819 alone, Atwater's two-dimensional collection of antiquities—letters, descriptions, plats, and drawings—arrived in forty-four separate installments. Eventually, Thomas agreed to underwrite Atwater's research by publishing his essay on Ohio antiquities at the society's expense.[99] In exchange, Atwater would receive the support he needed to travel, hire surveying and excavating teams, and write what would eventually comprise his "Description of the Antiquities Discovered in the State of Ohio and other Western States," the 150-page essay that became the highlight of *Archaeologia Americana* (1820), the first volume of the "Transactions and Collections of the American Antiquarian Society."[100]

Sketching Images of American Antiquity

As with much contemporary scientific writing, it was not uncommon for naturalists to accompany their specimens and scientific reports with two-dimentional drawings. Difficulties of conveyance frequently meant that art was the most expedient way of transmitting information to the Atlantic seaboard from the West, and sketches often served as surrogates for artifacts not otherwise portable.[101] For this reason Atwater's drawings and plats were particularly valuable: illustration was the surest mode he had to circulate and compare his hypotheses, and the best way for him to exchange information across his network of antiquaries and scientists as well.

In 1820, the AAS opened its new headquarters in Worcester, Massachusetts: Antiquarian Hall. This was a purpose-built repository for members' donations, and in it "a place for every thing, and . . . everything in its place."[102] As a counterpart to this physical repository, the AAS also published its first volume of scholarship that year. *Archaeologia Americana* (its title self-consciously following the British model) functioned as an index to the kinds of antiquities the AAS sought to preserve in its own collection while also establishing the society's reputation as "the center of antiquarian studies in the 1820s."[103] Although it never sold well, the AAS's inaugural volume was widely circulated and almost immediately found an extensive readership beyond the context of the AAS.

FIGURE 16. Sarah Clifford, "Triune Idol" (c. 1820). Courtesy of the American Antiquarian Society. Atwater received this painting from colleague John Clifford in Lexington and shared it with the AAS for inclusion in *Archaeologia Americana*.

When *Archaeologia Americana* went to press in August of 1820, none of the physical antiquities Atwater had promised to send the society had yet arrived. Nonetheless, the society still had plenty of illustrations to choose from because the Ohioan had already sent so many sketches and surveys to Thomas during the last year. When Atwater's long-promised donation finally arrived at Antiquarian Hall it was promptly entered into the donation book for October, where the entry indicates it had already been "Described in the 1st Volume of Transactions."[104] And despite the fact that there were many "antiquities" held in the AAS Cabinet, those that received the most attention were ones that had been featured in two dimensions; indeed, the most lasting of Atwater's contribution to *Archaeologia Americana* is, arguably, its imagery. Ultimately eleven of the items that Atwater donated in 1820 appeared in *Archaeologia Americana,* either in images or words before they appeared "in place" at Antiquarian Hall. In fact, the eight items pictured in Atwater's essay—including a stone pestle, two stone axes, two "stone ornaments," and a fragment of sheet mica—were all present in the AAS collection as drawings before they were present as physical artifacts.[105] In this sense, *Archaeologia Americana* is not merely illustrative of the continued connections of excavation, expansion, and national consolidation; the volume and its images also continue to stand as fundamental materials of the nationalist archive in all its dispossessive power.

To Atwater, the accuracy of the volume's engravings was as important as that of its written descriptions: readers needed one to understand the other.[106] Accurate imagery was also important because much of Atwater's credibility derived from his description of mounds and artifacts. Already in the April 1819 issue of the *American Monthly Magazine* Atwater explained that the object of his current work was "to clear away the rubbish with which superficial and hasty travelers have covered over our antiquities, so that every object might be distinctly seen."[107] His opening sentence envisaged the work as a labor of excavation and highlighted the importance of visualizing "every object." It is not just that Atwater emphasized his status and authority as an eyewitness. His words certainly did that—as when he complained that most writing on antiquities "generally has been done by men who never saw one of the works themselves"—but Atwater was also equally, if not more, interested in reproducing the eyewitness experience in others.[108] However, the published engravings portrayed Atwater's items at a fraction of their actual size, making them seem much less impressive and rendering their details indistinct. Had the engraving of the "Triune Vessel" been printed at its full seven inches, it would have occupied an entire octavo page; as published, however, it covered just less than half of one. In the end, Atwater was disappointed by what he saw on the pages of *Archaeologia Americana*.

Despite their uniform appearance and roughly approximate size, the volume's engravings span vastly different geographies, from the lower Mississippi Valley to the Northeast. Printing Natchez effigies alongside Quinnipiac everyday utensils and Cherokee funerary items established them all as "manufactured in former time by the native Indians, and deposited in the Cabinet of the American Antiquarian Society," no matter their actual date of manufacture, use, or acquisition.[109] Moreover, removing the objects from their original context and graphically replacing them with homogenous "antiquities" further removed the proof of Native occupancy from lands across the continent. Portraying the items at a fraction of their actual size rendered their details indistinct and lent them a flattened, uniform appearance, while their visual and material similarity implied a homogeneity of people and technology across time and place. The history reproduced dispenses with context and forgets the details of Native life. In this way, the artifacts in the AAS collection were freed to become "American antiquities" rather than elements of Indigenous history.

Chronologizing Continental Indigeneity

The nineteenth century's transformative first decades sounded increasing calls to naturalize western expansion and cohere the national citizenry—through both incorporation and expulsion—with ancient continental history. To do so, US antiquaries relied on the writings of Francisco Javier Clavijero and Baron von Humboldt to lengthen the chronology of American history, and they pointed to the importance of Native materials in establishing timelines and genealogical patterns. The US antiquaries took special care to preserve the western fortifications because those were the best evidence of the link between ancient Native peoples north and south.

The same September 1819 issue of the *Western Review* that printed B.'s letter also contained the first of Kentucky antiquary John D. Clifford's eight essays on "Indian Antiquities." Clifford's contributions added a new facet to an old thesis: that America's first peoples migrated from Asia, were the "same race as the ancient Hindus," and eventually became the "Azticas."[110] He also suggested that "[a]s the Lenni Lenapes increased in power they gradually extended their bounds and finally forced all the Azticas or Mexican tribes from this side of the Mississippi."[111] In a subsequent essay, Clifford asserted that the earthworks were evidence that the "various nations which inhabited the country of Anahuac may be considered of the same origin" as those who made the "circumvallations and tumuli" in the West.[112] For proof, Clifford referred to Humboldt's "Tolticas" and "Azticas," who both "emigrated from the north, and must consequently have once possessed the country on both sides of the Mississippi."[113] He also compared supposed Hindu calendrics with those via records of Mexico City's "immense block of granite" excavated in 1790 that featured the "ancient zodiac, with the symbols of the days of the month, their periods of time, and cycles of years."[114] Although Clifford mistranslated and misunderstood much of what he related, his essays nonetheless indicate a deep familiarity with criollo historians' (and Humboldt's) words and images. Like Brackenridge, he also cited the similarity of pyramids at Teotihuacan, Cholula, Xochicalco, Papantla, and Tenochtitlan with Cahokia and others in the Ohio and Mississippi River valleys.[115]

Clifford found manifold material evidence for his theory: from the alleged similarity of "religious ideas" (including alleged human sacrifice), resemblance in the architecture of earth and stone-sided pyramids, and even feather clothing.[116] In contrast to popular belief he denied the "American Prehistoric Earthworks" were designed for defense, maintaining instead that they were temples for "the rites of that bloody religion, which existed in Mexico until the time of its conquest by Cortez."[117] With these details, Clifford "point[ed] out the affinity and consequently the decent from the ancient Hindus of the nations of Anahuac and the aborigines of this western country."[118] Constructing, in this way, aboriginality as physically retraceable, he also located it as continental and temporally anterior, as a process that had long been completed. Not only did his hypothesis have the advantage of racializing Indigenous and "aboriginal" Americans differently, but it also meant that "hieroglyphic" writings and stone statues in southern North America could be incorporated into American, not just Spanish or Mexican, history.

A colleague of Clifford's at Transylvania University, the naturalist Constantine Rafinesque, also published writings on "antiquities" in the December 1819 issue of the *Western Review*, prompted by a visit he and Clifford had made together to "an ancient Town of the Alleghawee Nation."[119] Used like Clifford's term "aboriginal," Rafinesque's "Alleghawee" was one of the many names he was developing for the continent's first people (he claimed to have taken the word from Lenape informants but had in fact adapted it from Heckewelder's recently published "Account").[120] In a series of open letters to Jefferson published in Lexington's *Kentucky Reporter* the following summer, Rafinesque outlined and described "the numberless and astonishing monuments of remote origin scattered through the western states," which he again attributed to the "Alleghawee."[121] Linking his theories to Clifford's, Rafinesque explained "the Alleghawians were the ancestors of the Anáhuacans, or real Mexican nations."[122] Clifford and Rafinesque wanted not only to identify the people who had created the antiquities across the Ohio Valley—and thereby find "the true path of remote historical knowledge"—but they also sought to arrange those peoples in the chronology of human history.[123] In so doing, they replaced real Indigenous peoples with mythical ones.

Atwater had similar goals and he too elaborated the Mexican mounds hypothesis in his "Description." After his exposure to Clifford's and Rafinesque's "evidence," Atwater constructed a hypothesis in which he identified the "authors of our antiquities" as belonging to one of the following three groups: "People of European origin, Indians, and lastly to that Scythian race of man who erected all our mounds."[124] His study of the "Triune Idol" painting sent by Clifford, Atwater explained, enabled him to "trac[e] the authors of our ancient works, from

India to North, and thence to South, America."[125] Like Clifford, Atwater also argued that the Ohio earthworks were likely the product of Asian migrants who ultimately settled in the Valley of Mexico.[126] To make the connection even more obvious, he borrowed from Humboldt "a drawing of the temple of Cholula" to show visually "the correspondence which exists between the Teocalli of the Mexicans, and the tumuli of the North Americans."[127] His resulting contribution to *Archaeologia Americana* would enable nearly one hundred more years of antiquarian interest in hemispheric ancient America.

It is no coincidence that public scholarly conversations about Mexican mounds were occurring at the same time as Mexico was fighting its war for independence from Spain, and as US settlers were exchanging their "Black Legend"-tinged prejudices against criollos for republican solidarity.[128] In 1819—before the end of the Mexican war—the US and Spain renegotiated its southern and western border, easing some tensions.[129] And ancient American history provided a means for conceptualizing the new republic within narratives of rising empires and godly experiments as well as guidance for the current expansionist project in the United States.

Building a Stratiological Chronology

In addition to surveying many of the earthworks located across Ohio lands, Atwater's essay advanced a theory of serial peopling bolstered by a reading of antiquities as a record of the stadial progression of eras. Separating the population of American history into three different groups—"Mexican," "Indian," and "European," one replacing the next—lies at the heart of Atwater's essay. What is more, the antiquary's explicit division between ancient and contemporary Indigenous peoples—and the expulsion of one at the hands of the other—paved the way for the segregationist Indian policy then in development.

Since arriving in Ohio, Atwater's research had convinced him that human history was layered like geological strata. He assumed that materials found closest to the surface were the newest, while materials buried farther down dated to an older era.[130] Therefore, even as he developed what would seem to be a linear chronology, Atwater was also beginning to understand time horizontally, that is, spatially as well. Analogous to the previous century's "Great Chain of Being," the most recent—and most "civilized"—populations of history were at the top, while the oldest and most "primitive" were at the bottom. If what Atwater called the "traditionary chronology of the aborigines"—that is to say, the oral traditions—did not always provide a clear timeline, this improved spatial chronology—"extended by our antiquarians and geologists"—would.[131]

Atwater's eyewitness examinations and his contributions to Silliman's *American Journal of Science* in 1819 and 1820 make clear the importance of paleontology, hydrology, and geology to his interpretation of history. Although previous scholars of American antiquity had tended to approach questions about the earthworks with a mixture of Native oral tradition and comparative ethnographic analysis, Atwater's relationship to natural history led him to prioritize an observational, taxonomic, "scientific" approach to "the fragments which, by time and accident have been cast upon the shore."[132] His method for analyzing this fragmentary evidence included examining "the Geology and Botany of the country where the works are found" as well as the earthworks' physical contents.[133] Reflecting on the past of the Pickaway Plains, he explained to Thomas, Atwater saw "nothing but one <u>vast cemetery</u> of the beings of past ages."[134] He was not referring to the fighting of the 1770s, '80s, or '90s: rather, Atwater's timescale was antediluvian. Water had once collected, preserved, and deposited the artifacts in their final resting places, and Atwater imagined the surrounding prairielands as an undifferentiated past space in which mammoth, bamboo, and Moundbuilder were synchronically "<u>all</u> found here reposing together." The "General deluge" had caused "<u>man</u> and <u>his works</u>, the Mammoth, the cassia tree, the bamboo, the Palm tree, and other <u>tropical</u> animals, and plants" to be "overwhelmed and buried here in the same strata."[135] The naturalist saw in their assemblage an eternal cemetery located just under the surface, and therefore American antiquity was undergound, too.

Sensing that more recent remains covered "ancient" ones, Atwater assumed a clear break between the "recent" ("Indian") remains at the mounds' top and the "ancient" (Moundbuilder) ones hidden underneath. In short, Atwater thought a more recent populace had replaced a previous one, their dead entirely covering over the predeceased. This layering allowed Atwater to separate out the superficial "Indian antiquities" from the ones that most held his interest: "I divide therefore, our antiquities into three kinds /to wit/ Those belonging to the Indians, those who originally erected our old forts [,] and those belonging to the French and other Europeans who first traversed this country."[136] Just as Clinton had determined in 1811 that the works in New York could be neither European nor Native but instead the work of "antient and exterminated nations," Atwater likewise detected in the antiquities of Ohio the presence of a non-Native aboriginal group who had been replaced by usurpers, leaving their evidence in the ground.[137]

Assuming the typical "Asiatic origins" thesis, Atwater charted the layers of successive American populations and dated artifacts based on the characteristics of the layer it apparently most resembled (the "European" layer, "Indian" layer, "Moundbuilder" layer). Beneath his new hometown, Atwater saw not the Mississauga, Odawa, Seneca, Lenape, Wendat, or Shawnee peoples who were and had been there long before his own arrival, but rather the mythical "Indians of former days."[138] Nor did Atwater see that expansionist and preservationist policies had transformed Ohio's Natives into the "former" rather than "present" population. Likewise, Atwater's geological framework produced histories for Ohio that both excluded Indigenous peoples from the land and from the present.[139]

What was particularly different about Atwater's stratiological time was the insistence that the destructive work had been done by nature (oceans, soil, etc.) rather than humans, despite evidence of war and conflict all around. As historically-minded writers and Indian Policy administrators struggled to place the continent's diverse population on equal footing with settler societies, their descriptions of the landscape and its antiquities—which continued to be taken from graves and former Native settlement sites—reflected that absolving geological shift and its concomitant excavatory vision.

Stealing from Sacred Grounds

It is no surprise that when Atwater looked at Ohio's prairies his mind turned not only to the layers under the soil's surface but also to the image of the cemetery: for the majority of his working knowledge, and his collection, came from graves. Antiquaries like Atwater knew that most of the earthworks they regularly disrupted were burial sites because they disturbed recognizeably human bones and witnessed the familiar evidence of purposeful interment. For example, Atwater listed the "antiquities" he took from an earthwork in Circleville—arrowheads, a horn knife, wood cinders, charred bricks, a mica mirror—and explained that at the mound's core were "Two human skeletons, lying on what had been the original surface of the earth."[140] This description makes clear that the foregoing items—some of which he had sent to the AAS—had originally been placed around the bodies, and likely they were specific possessions related to the interred persons. Similarly, Atwater identified another mound as "the common cemetery, as it contains an immense number of human skeletons, of all sizes and ages," although he dismissed its contents as "of little value, though very numerous; something being found near the head of almost every individual."[141] To retrieve those objects of "little value"—which he nonetheless did—Atwater had to take them out from under human heads.

Not only do Atwater's essay's words provide a direct account of excavation as a grave-robbing process, they also provide a detailed account of the relation between material object and formerly living person, demonstrating how objects were being asked to serve as historical surrogates and ultimately replace their human bearers. Such is the case in the essay's section about a destroyed Chilicothe mound, which Atwater begins by explaining had been made of "sand, and contained human bones, belonging to skeletons which were buried in different parts of it."[142] In his description of the excavation, Atwater wrote that removing the top layer of earth and a woven mat had revealed a human skeleton, "on the breast" of whom rested "what had been a piece of copper, in the form of a cross, which had now become verdigrise."[143] He continued:

> On the breast also, lay a stone ornament with two perforations, one near each end, through which passed a string, by means of which it was suspended around the wearer's neck. On this string, which was made of sinews, and very much injured by time, were placed a great many beads, made of ivory or bone; for I cannot certainly say which. With these facts before us, we are left to conjecture at what time this individual lived; what were his heroick achievements in the field of battle; his wisdom and eloquence in the councils of his nation. But his contemporaries have testified in a manner not to be mistaken, that among them, he was held in grateful remembrance.[144]

The repeated phrase "on the breast" and methodical description of string passing through ornament, bead passing onto string, and necklace passing over neck in Atwater's prose serves to reconstitute the skeleton's more fleshy form and recall the funereal moment. But although Atwater's words stage the excavation as opportunity for grieving, they showcase objects, not people. The stone ornament only seemed to speak in the voice of contemporary mourners; in no way did Atwater hear tell of the artifacts' spiritual or cosmic power. Moreover, the term "ornament" ignores that the "antiquities" he disinterred and sent away were powerful medicine objects, some of which show strong affinities to past and present Shawnee and Cherokee burial and renewal practices.[145] With the individual body imaginatively revivified, Atwater contemplates translating the "facts" of copper, stone, bone, and sinew—as objects—into written history; his evaluation of facts and data left no room for Indigenous humanity.

About two-thirds down the page with the cited passage appears an illustration of the so-called ornament—"The following is a correct drawing of the stone ornament, and saves me the trouble of a description of it"—its presence a jarring instrusion on a page otherwise lined with text.[146] The illustration's force draws the eye downward, hurrying it past the words and eliding possibilities for further narrative reanimation or heart-felt mourning. Its visual dominance communicates "object" rather than "person," shifting from an evocation of life lost and community grief to one of representational efficiency. In this visual and kinetic sense, the engraving frames the excavation vignette not as biography but rather as empirical, comparable, and exchangeable evidence. Moreover, the crosshatched lines seemingly project the ornament toward the reader, which almost asks to be picked up and reenact the process of extraction. Displaced and transformed, the "ornament" references other "antiquities" like it over the specificity of its burial in a grave along the Scioto River, or its value to wearer or loved one.

Examining the catalog of items Atwater sent to Thomas—not just their representations in *Archaeologia Americana*—reveals even more starkly the relationship of antiquities collections to Native bodies. The catalog, for example, lists a "fragment of an ancient brick found in a mound, formerly standing near the center of the round fort in Circleville, Ohio" and "a fragment of the large [mica] mirror, found in a tumulus in Circleville."[147] In the catalog, Atwater also included bones removed from that mound, likely those he had earlier described as "two human skeletons, lying on what had been the original surface of the earth."[148] Much of the time "Description" hinted that excavation sites were grave sites, but Atwater's papers in the AAS archive make it clear that almost all of the "antiquities discovered in the state of Ohio and other Western States" came from graves.[149]

Perhaps the most striking admission from Atwater came in the form of the link he made between drawings and desecrated graves in a letter to Thomas. In the same letter in which he promised to send "a small, but valuable cabinet" to the AAS, Atwater also promised to "endeavor to procure drawings of several articles as well as the skulls of the people beneath whose heads they were found."[150] Later, he apologized for sending none—although he did send a sketch of a skull at another time—because he had found that "they fall into pieces, soon after being exposed to the atmosphere."[151] In fact, of all the in-text engravings, only one definitively did *not* come from a Native grave. And while the question of whether stone axes are settlement detritus rather than grave goods is debatable, it is harder to argue that the "ornaments"—identified as such because of their position relative to a human skeleton—were not.[152]

In fact, unearthing burial sites had long been at the core of antiquarian science.[153] In the 1770s, Thomas Jefferson developed a technique for slicing into burial mounds, determining that the depth of layers held the key to their epoch of inhumation.[154] Dissecting an earthwork lengthways, he described the process layer by layer: "At the bottom, that is, on the level of the circumjacent plain," he wrote, "I found bones; above these a few stones, brought from a cliff a quarter of a mile off, and from the river one-eighth of a mile off; then a large interval of earth, then a stratum of bones, and so on."[155] The deeper Jefferson dug, the deeper he delved into time. Noting, dryly, that "[t]he different states of decay in these strata . . . seem to indicate a difference in the time of inhumation," he surmised that the bones at the surface (the ones "least decayed") were the newest.[156] In 1803 Thaddeus Mason Harris described gruesome excavations at Marietta and seeing other mounds in the Scioto Valley also "filled with bones" and "composed of strata . . . of bones in regular order, of full-grown people and of infants, in different stages of decay."[157] Also in 1803, Benjamin Smith Barton's friend Bishop James Madison, in the course of excavating mammoth bones in Virginia's Kanawha Valley, opened earthworks revealing "human bones, and Indian relicks."[158] Observing the "alternate strata of bones and earth, mingled with stone and Indian relicks" at the Kanawha Valley site, Madison explained finding "near the summit of those mounds articles of European manufacture, such as the tomahawk and knife," items that he never saw "at any depth in the mound." His chronology, which matched the supposedly serial settlement of ancient, Native, and European peoples on the continent, translated into a timeline of human migration that figured population change as stratiological, one arrival replacing another.[159] Harris's, Madison's, and Jefferson's experiences—as well as Atwater's—demonstrate the crucial position of objectified Native bodies to shifts in US historical thinking.

At the same time that Native communities were increasingly viewed by settlers as part of the distant past, early US settlers went looking for history in their burial grounds; this was despicably wishful, because all around—the wars, treaties, border disputes—were evidence that Native communities were not simply going away.[160] Although it is seldom recognized in current-day scholarship—perhaps a relic of settler "objectivity"—I emphasize that the items illustrating *Archaeologia Americana* did not just happen to be "found" in groves and backyards, fragments of a replaced past carelessly left behind. There is no question that these antiquaries knew they were disturbing resting places. Their eyes, however, had learned to detect a disconnected "ancient" existence and not a continuous modern one. They assimilated the information as "evidence"—of time, of technique, but never of life—and packed Indigenous relatives away with other "antiquities"—minerals, pottery, etc.—because they very literally did not *see* the bones as human bodies but rather as materials for measurement and preservation for further study.[161]

It has often been implied that grave robbing was an unfortunate but incidental activity, a practice not noteworthy at the time and only offensive to current-day sensibilities. Yet settler-collectors often made the choice to excavate despite knowledge that disinterring the dead had meaning—and produced pain—in the contemporary moment. In 1785, for example, Samuel H. Putnum told his soldiers not to excavate on the Great Miami River until after the Shawnee treaty council had finished, not wanting to insult the Indigenous attendants.[162] At the very least, settlers implicitly recognized that "antiquities" were funerary objects and body parts. Explicitly, though, they regularly identified these items as ownerless and inert. Their association with (often recently deceased) Native lives was obscured behind a term—"antiquity"—that denoted a distant, finite, and disconnected past.

It is obvious in Clifford's "Indian Antiquities" letters that he obtained most of his evidence from burial sites: he routinely detailed and analyzed the position of skeletons in burial mounds and described bracelets removed from arms and beads taken from around the necks of disinterred ancestors.[163] Almost every aspect he used to construct his argument came from a grave. Indeed, he was extremely interested in what was (and what was not) buried with individual bodies and how mass burials were arranged.[164] Not only did Clifford's grave-digging desecrate those buried, it also violated their relatives; his actions assumed—because he deemed the interred to be ancient, non-Native "aborigines"—that there were no descendants left to mourn or revere the sacred ground. According to Clifford, any mourners would have to have been in Mexico anyway. I call attention to this not to rehearse the descriptions of desecrated graves, but to reinvest the topic with humanity: to recall that both Atwater and Clifford were practicing arranging history with bones in their hands, arranging them in the same way they arranged bits of coal and quartz. The theory of antiquarian stratiological temporality—in addition to its material archive—has long been furnished from the graves that gave archaeology its form.

Illustrating Deep Disturbance

That all of the drawings in *Archaeologia Americana*—the correct portrayal of which troubled Atwater so deeply—portray material from graves should give us pause. In a sense, opening its pages is akin to reopening human graves. This should make us question the propriety of continuing to reproduce, as Atwater and Thomas did, these certainly pilfered and arguably sacred items. Remains taken unwillingly (or unknowingly) from descendant communities should not circulate without permission, whether in physical or visual form. Not only does their circulation represent the entrenched settler-colonial interests of early American antiquaries, their continued exposure reinscribes a particular disrespect for Native life that mirrors the translation of Native bodies into archival objects that outweighs the material and cosmological life of the Native peoples they also depict. Thus, in examining sensitive mortuary items—as I have done here—it should be a priority to support cultural continuities between ancestral and current Native peoples. This goal is particularly important in spaces like the Ohio country which, due in part to these settler nationalist archive-building practices, has come to seem as if it is not Native space.

For decades, Indigenous relatives have mourned and protested the disturbance of their ancestors' resting places. Activists and scholars have only gradually won victories and received recognition for their work; in 1989–1990 this translated to official assistance from the US government with the passage of the Native American Museum Act and the Native American Graves Protection and Repatriation Act (NAGPRA).[165] This federal legislation enabled the return of certified human remains, funerary items, and cultural heritage materials under specific conditions. Yet despite the healing enabled by the physical return and reburial of Indigenous ancestors, repatriation itself is not reconciliation. It does not alter the epistemological modes and historiographic methods that continue to cause the dispossession, erasure, and denial of Indigenous histories, knowledge, and humanity.[166] Nor does it call attention to the ongoing exploitation of Native burial and sacred grounds by private hands in the name of hobby and, at times, science.

Over the past quarter century, a palpable shift in approaches by archivists and museum professionals encouraged by activists as well as the example of tribal museums and increasing collaborations between non-Native cultural institutions and tribal nations has resulted in significant (if yet insufficient) changes in the ways that Indigenous materials are held, displayed, and interpreted by non-Indigenous institutions.[167] Indigenous professionals continue to outline specific access protocols and guidelines for change, which are being adopted unevenly.[168] In 2020, for example, the National Library of Australia redesigned its online search engine such that it now provides a "cultural advice" pop-up, with the stated goal of ensuring the "cultural safety of First Australians."[169] The American Philosophical Society (APS) now has a similar, if not as prominent, message, as does Harvard's Peabody Museum.[170] Even these actions, however, are aimed largely at mitigation and "sensitivity," not at reckoning with the concepts and practices of contemporary historiography and museology that have developed from the desecration of Native bodies and spaces.

Abenaki anthropologist Margaret Bruchac writes of the museum professional's imperative to repair and restore disturbances caused by acts of collection—physically, spiritually, and intellectually—deploying what she calls "restorative methodologies" to do so.[171] Likewise, Denis Byrne calls for an "ethos of return" to "reverse" the discursive processes that have erased Native presence from settler national presents.[172] All that said, NAGPRA has no provisions or advice for objects that exist in print, such as those featured in *Archaeologia Americana*. Images of ancestors and grave goods occupy a complicated space in art historical and anthropological, if not historical, scholarship and the ethics of representing sacred objects in museum or other exhibitions has been hotly debated over the past few decades.[173] However, the status of those same "objects" as *reproductions* has received little attention in the United States and indeed they continue to be widely circulated.[174]

This chapter has described, for the most part, a collection of archival objects—both physical and textual—with territorial if not ancestral connections to the three federally recognized Shawnee nations: the Shawnee Tribe, the Eastern Shawnee Tribe of Oklahoma, and the Absentee Shawnee Tribe of Indians of Oklahoma. That all of these nations are headquartered in Oklahoma is the legacy of violent deportation campaigns conducted by the state of Ohio and the United States government in the mid-nineteenth century but effected from the eighteenth century until the present day by the epistemological structures that dug up the resting places of Shawnee ancestors and their relatives, removing bodily and funereal remains to private and public collections elsewhere, and staking the emptied land—and the filled archives—in the name of preservation.[175] Reflecting that some Native traditions prohibit the discussion of death rituals and that these materials are by consequence not to be "voiced" or "recovered" by non-Native scholars should also provoke new thinking not only about recovery and continued reproduction but also the continued existence of these kinds of archival "objects," especially as used to narrate (early) American history.

Mapping Preservation

Despite his direct handling of deceased Indigenous relatives, Atwater seldom made an explicit link between "antiquities" and "Indians" except to say that the former usually excluded the latter. Yet, mid-project, Atwater made an odd decision: "I shall add to my Antiquities an appendix of 50 pages on our Indians in Ohio." This would include, he informed Thomas in May 1819, "their numbers-places of abode-their manners-customs-religions-opinions-vocabulary of their language-their names of places with their signification."[176] The proposed appendix would comprise information "from official sources by order of the General Government for my use expressly."[177] Although this gesture may seem to bring "antiquities" and "Indians" together, instead it exposes how the antiquarian strategies of "collection and preservation" supported the alienation of Indigenous land through a reservation policy that collected Native peoples together in one place and deposited them elsewhere for their own supposed preservation.

After the return of Native refugees from Tecumseh's War, US officials and settlers alike began to fear for their safety and the security of their newly claimed lands. As historian Karim M. Tiro has explained, sporadic attacks and killings served as "the most efficient means of rolling back the frontier," a defensive strategy well documented by Lisa Brooks among seventeenth-century Wabanaki protectors.[178] With a rising sense of panic in the 1810s and 1820s, the United States moved to create detention facilities for Indigenous inhabitants who found themselves surrounded by settlers.[179] Similar to the concurrent American Colonization Society's movement to relocate free Black people from the United States to the African continent, these Indian Reservations were meant to provide a space for Native bodies apart from the body of the Republic.

Atwater's "official" information for the appendix came from Indian Agent John Johnston, who like many in the Indian affairs system was convinced by the Jeffersonian civilizationist project, in which Christian conversion and US-style farming was meant to "relieve" Natives of their "excess" land and shift their economic models from geographically-extensive hunting and home-production to plow-style agriculture and manufactured goods.[180] This, they believed, would further condense the population and thereby enable future land cessions.[181] During and after the War of 1812, Johnston's family farm in Piqua, Ohio—just inside the US side of the old 1795 boundary line and on land that had once served as the Miami-French trading post Fort Pickawillany—addressed the needs of Ohio Shawnee populations as the Piqua Indian Agency. In 1816 Johnston explained his agency's goals to Secretary of War William Crawford, writing of his plan "to collect the Indians at one point, to build them a mill, and place one or two laboring men with them to assist in farming, they would then have no objection to parting with the surplus of their lands in an amicable way."[182] By this method, Johnston predicted, he could, "in four or five years procure a peaceable and willing transfer of the greater part of the Indian lands within the limits of this state of Ohio."[183]

Ahead of schedule, however, the 1817 treaty at Fort Meigs, the Foot of the Maumee Rapids, "extinguished" Native title across the state, adding over four million acres to Ohio's total.[184] At the negotiations, Michigan Territory's governor Lewis Cass—who had fought at the Battle of the Thames—suggested Ohio Natives move westward rather than consolidate themselves on the new reservations—fewer than two hundred thousand acres total—which many agreed were already too small. That time Cass's suggestion was rebuffed and all signatories elected to remain on the plots carved out of their homelands, albeit now alienable land they would hold in fee simple.[185] But this was only an intermediary step in the government's plan: as Cass wrote to Crawford in September 1818, "as our settlements gradually surround them, their minds will be better prepared" for concessions.[186] Changing the spatial arrangement of Native peoples within the new borders of Ohio would consist of confinement, concession, and eviction, all of which began soon afterward.

In 1818, the Wyandot leader Between-the-Logs led a delegation (including representatives from Shawnee and Seneca groups) to Washington to protest the size of the reserved lands assigned in 1817 and to request additional annuities.[187] In response, the US called additional "New Purchase" treaty councils, these to be held at the important portage between the Auglaize and St. Mary's rivers. Fort St. Mary's (formerly Girty's Town) had been built in 1795, its location a settler outpost across the Boundary Line. Now the fort would serve as the US's gateway to the west.[188] For although before the 1817 treaty only Odawa families were confined to reservations, after the 1818 renegotiations—in which the reservations and annuities were indeed augmented—all Native families in Ohio would be; the 1795 line itself would cease to exist.

When President Monroe had toured that corner of Indian County in the summer of 1817—after which he met with Atwater to discuss antiquities—he became eager to "extend our settlements from the uninhabited parts of the State of Ohio" and cement the connection with Michigan Territory and the West.[189] In order to do so, Monroe stated in his December 1817 address to Congress, "It is our duty to make new efforts for the preservation, improvement, and civilization of the native inhabitants."[190] These efforts included expulsion. Indeed, when Cass brought up removal again during negotiations at St. Mary's, representatives from Captain Anderson's Lenape band agreed to cede their remaining Ohio lands near the Upper Sandusky, where they had lived since the Revolutionary War.[191] This was in exchange for debt relief, an annuity, and guaranteed lands west of the Mississippi (until Anderson's band members left for Missouri in 1821, they stayed in Johnston's Piqua stockade).

Civilians as well as government agents were concerned with "preservation, improvement, and civilization." In January 1819 a group of Ohioans petitioned the US Senate's Committee on Public Lands, which had advised the 1817 and 1818 treaties, "praying the adoption of measures for the improvement of the Indians."[192] "Improvement," in these cases, usually meant assimilation along the "civilizationist" model. Yet despite Congress's passage in March 1819 of the "act making provision for the civilization of the Indian tribes, adjoining the frontier settlements"—which set aside monies to support agricultural training, primary school, and Christianization efforts for reservation residents—the 1817 and 1818 treaties presaged the end of the nation's commitment to an assimilationist Indian policy and the factory system, which was already beginning to fail due to the pressures of land-grabbing, "improvement," and preservationism.[193]

Reservations were only imagined as temporary, after all: for US sovereignty to remain unilateral, it demanded Native extermination. Reservations thus placed Native peoples and their lands in a position of no future, in a present already assumed to be anterior.[194] The settler public, for their part, already imagined Indian Country to be part of the past, as testified by their maps. For example, on the 1819 edition of John Kilbourn's popular *Ohio Gazetteer*, the section of the state map that had in previous editions been labeled "Indian Country" carried a note announcing the lands as "recently purchased of the Wyandott and other Tribes of Indians," implying imminent, although incomplete, annexation. By the 1821 edition, the entire space disappeared behind gridded lines, Indian Country completely eliminated from geopolitical space.[195] To fully transform Indian Country into national space, almost all of Ohio's Native peoples would need to be expelled.[196]

Ironically, even though Atwater's research was dependent on land dispossession, the bureaucratic processes of nationalizing Indian Country had the effect of slowing Atwater's preservation work. As the land-generating motives of US Indian policy dramatically increased the demand for Ohio land assessors in the late 1810s, Atwater could no longer work on his project. In a letter to Thomas on July 24, 1819, he explained needing to take a three-week hiatus because he had been left short-handed: "The surveyors are all gone to the late purchase from the Indians" at St. Mary's.[197] He had no way to survey, visualize, or excavate the newly "opened" lands because the resources were all tied up in selling the land. From 1812 to 1821, the Ohio land offices sold more than 375,000 acres of "extinguished" Indian title land, retaining much of the rest as "public lands" which became parks, school grounds, military bases, and other government sites.[198] Partly, the official actions to reserve, extinguish, and "dispose" of Indian Country were just catching up to what the settler public already imagined was true: that Ohio (and other US spaces) were sovereign and contiguous and that "Indians" only existed in the past.

Only a few months after Congress ratified the Treaty of St. Mary's, in early 1819, Johnston replied to a questionnaire from Atwater which, among other things, asked for information about "The Indians that formerly inhabited your country."[199] Rather than supplying Atwater with information about language, history, or the "monuments, forts, tumuli or mounds" amongst which he lived, Johnston offered a tallied "number of souls" then resident in the state. For the year 1819 he reckoned the total figure of "Wyandots, Shawnees, Senecas, Delawares, Mohawks, and Ottawas" at 2,407.[200] The ability to provide this information reflects the fact that, already by spring of 1819, most Native people in "Ohio" were living on reservations.[201] On July 21, 1819, Atwater copied out and transmitted Johnston's figures to Thomas for publication in his Appendix.[202]

The tally in *Archaeologia Americana* preserves Johnston's original organization and in this reveals contemporary reservation arrangements. Towns (reservations) are listed by national group: Wyandots at Upper Sandusky, Zanes, Mad River, Fort Finley, and Solomon's Town; "Shawanoese" at Wapakoneta, Hog Creek, and Lewis Town; Senecas also at Lewis Town and Seneca Town.[203] Most of Ohio's reservations centered on lands deeded to pro-US leaders, like the Shawnee chiefs Catecahassa (Black Hoof) at Wapakoneta and Quatawapea (Captain Lewis) at Hog Creek, with the calculated effect of dividing groups against each other to guard against the resurgence of something like Tecumseh's pan-tribal confederacy and deliberately confusing title concerns.[204] There was a Lenape group at Upper Sandusky and a Mohawk one at Honey Creek.[205] Those Odawas "whose residence is not stationary" (i.e., those not already confined to reservations in 1807) were located "about Miami Bay, and on the southern shore of Lake Erie," as well as at Blanchard's Fork, Little Auglaize, and Rock de Bouef.[206] Johnston's list serves to accentuate fractionalization and diminution. Down from the region's hundreds of villages and thousands of Indigenous inhabitants in the late eighteenth century, the diminishing numbers were also taken as signs of the success—to settler nationalists—of their western project.

Atwater added a map to accompany Johnston's information in his Appendix, the foldout "Map of the State of Ohio, including the Indian Reservations Purchased and Laid out into Counties and Townships in 1820," added just before the volume was published.[207] Despite the pastward focus of Atwater's essay, his inclusion of this Ohio map alongside Johnston's "Account of the present state of the Indian tribes inhabiting Ohio" is consistent with the larger way in which Atwater understood ancient American history as divided into three stages receding into the past: Europeans, "Indians," and the "people who raised our ancient forts and tumuli."[208]

FIGURE 17. Abner Reed, "Map of the State of Ohio, including the Indian Reservations Purchased and Laid out into Counties and Townships in 1820," detail, *Archaeologia Americana* (1820). Courtesy of the American Antiquarian Society. The 1795 border is still visible as a faint diagonal line crossing Shelby and Logan counties.

Settler sovereignty, explains historian Lisa Ford, includes the power of "ordering indigenous people in space."[209] For the most part, settler claims depended on the relatively novel assertion of the absence of Indigenous rights, claims that were aided by the fact that recent cessions and removals had eliminated previous claims of occupancy.[210] Maps, gazetteers, and state histories were all imperative to the fabrication of this "perfect territorial jurisdiction," an implicit technology for transforming Indigenous into national space. Publications like the *Western Gazetteer or Emigrant's Directory* (1817) became ways to see the land as "civilized" and "settled," consolidating geographical and intellectual images of the "new" states and bringing the unknown "west" into eastern knowability and, ultimately, territorial control. They also served to erase Native peoples and polities from US geography and history. A ghostly presence of this erasure remains on Atwater's 1820 map.

Because the model map that Atwater sent the engraver was from the *Ohio Gazetteer*'s most recent edition—which still indicated the 1795 treaty line and included place names from an earlier era—Atwater also sent specific instructions for updates. In order to add the "4 new counties erected in the Indian Country last winter," he directed, "All that was needed, was to fill up, a blank space, in the Indian Country."[211] But the changes came so late in the publication schedule that the former Greenville Line still appears as an after-image. Near St. Mary's—site of the 1818 treaty councils—a misprint in "Wapghkonetta" resulted in the inclusion of a nonexistant "Wassokonnetta Reserve." The Wyandot village identified on Johnston's chart as "Fort Finley" is completely gone.[212] The faded reservation lines and erased Indigenous towns reinforced the sense that Native peoples' presence in Ohio was an error to be corrected. On the whole the map visualized Native borders and Native peoples as if they were already subsumed by the state.

Atwater also applied his excavatory vision of time to the map by accentuating the topological and geological—over the antiquarian—contours of the state. "I want the Prairies & barrens, at upper Sandusky, and all the hills, [included] on the Map of Ohio," he instructed his engraver.[213] He insisted that the map contain the state's mineralogical information, with different colors used to indicate different substrates—"The blue is limestone you will recollect"—as well as up-to-date political figurations.[214] The only explicitly antiquities-related location was Grave Creek in Virginia (but the earthwork is not indicated), although its name is given as "Grove Creek." Rarely is a spatial visualization comprising geological time, antiquarian interest, and Indian policy so clear: but this appendix, which juxtaposes Atwater's antiquarian "Description" with documents displaying the contemporary effects of the United States' expansionist policies places into relief the material connections across antiquarianism, preservationism, and expansion.

Due largely to the map's errors and a protracted dispute over copyright, Atwater cut his ties to the AAS in 1821. Turning his talents to electoral politics instead, that year he was elected State Representative for Pickaway County. His signal causes were public education and the construction of an Ohio canal like the one being built in New York. While Atwater politicked, he continued to use antediluvian and ancient Ohio history to advance the nationalist cause.[215]

Assessing Atwater's Afterlives

Although he had originally proposed to travel across North America documenting antiquities for the AAS, Caleb Atwater stayed in Ohio until 1829, when President Jackson appointed him as US Commissioner of Indian Affairs and sent him to Michigan Territory.[216] Cherokee intellectual Elias Boudinot's anti-removal newspaper, the *Cherokee Phoenix*, announced Atwater's appointment in July 1829, reporting that the object of the proposed treaty "was said to be the purchase of the right of soil south of the Ouisconsin [Wisconsin] river, especially the lead region."[217] The last detail is not incidental: the upper Mississippi is rich in mineral deposits, something the people who have lived there for eons—Meskwaki (Fox), Sauk, Ho-Chunk, Dakota, Ojibwe, Odawa, Potawatomi and others—have long known. In the 1820s, however, a "lead rush" brought increasing numbers of US government agents and settlers to this area, and they immediately began to claim the lands and its contents as their own.[218] The "Red Bird Uprising" of 1827 was one of the outcomes: this was a series of Ho-Chunk-led tactics meant to defend against trespassing US miners and to answer for recent back-and-forth killings.[219] The conflict, which ended quickly in the short term due to an overwhelming show of US force, indicates the escalating intra-tribal and Native-settler tensions on the Upper Mississippi.[220] Atwater was being sent to Prairie du Chien (in what is currently Wisconsin) in 1829 to formalize de-facto land cessions caused by the lead miners' illegal settlements. That he was personally connected to treaties crucial to future forced removals in the Iowa, Wisconsin, and Illinois countries brings the relevance of Indian policy even closer to continental antiquarianism.

In August 1829 at Fort Crawford in Prarie du Chien—which had been built atop a mound—Atwater signed removal treaties with Ho-Chunk and Council of Three Fires (Ojibwe, Odawa, and Potawatomi) representatives in exchange for annuity payments and border guarantees.[221] The first signature on the Ho-Chunk treaty belongs to the Sauk leader "Hay-ray-tshon-sharp" or Black Hawk, who three years later would lead a resistance against US incursions onto his Rock River homelands. It was at the same Fort Crawford where Black Hawk would surrender to Colonel Zachary Taylor in 1832. After the treaties were finished, Atwater took them to Washington, bringing gifts exchanged at the councils, portraits painted by artists Peter Rindisbacher and James Otto Lewis, a sample of Ho-Chunk poetry and oration, and specimens from the nearby mines.[222] Curiously, Atwater did no excavating while he was at Fort Crawford, although the site now called "Effigy Mounds National Monument" is right across the river.[223]

On his way back home, Atwater stopped in Philadelphia, where he dined with the renowned physician Samuel G. Morton, with whom he would afterward maintain a correspondence.[224] Atwater also visited the American Philosophical Society (APS), where he examined "their great and interesting collection of objects . . . especially the antiquities of Mexico and Peru."[225] That year, former US minister to Mexico Joel R. Poinsett donated a large selection of manuscripts, "which he had collected, relating to early journeys made through portions of Mexico & certain antiquities," to the APS.[226] Two years earlier, Poinsett had given the society "models of two stones found in Mexico, one of which was said to be that of the ancient Mexican Calendar."[227] These were undoubtedly items that sparked Atwater's imagination. "It is quite possible," he remarked afterward, "that these fragments of Mexican and Peruvian history, may throw great light on the history of the man of the eastern continent."[228] He outlined these thoughts in the travel memoir he published in 1831, just one year before the climax of the devastating Black Hawk War.

In *Remarks Made on a Tour to Prairie du Chien* (1831), Atwater warned of the violence inherent in the US government's policy "to collect all the Indians, on this side of the Rocky Mountains, into one territory, as soon as possible."[229] He predicted that the US "collecting" policy would cause a war "which would cost millions of dollars, and rivers of blood," and turn "our whole frontier" into "one vast field of conflagration and butchery."[230] Atwater also despaired of future US-Native relations, "so long as the National Government has any thing to do with the Indians." Imagining that antiquaries and scholars would do a better job of it, Atwater recommended Congress leave Indian Affairs to the APS so "[t]he Indian would be saved from destruction, and the national honor preserved."[231] The antiquary—whose mind had not often turned to Natives during his years of studying "ancient" Ohio history—could finally articulate the connection between antiquarian preservationism and the United States' own "Indian collection." And after looking at the Mexican antiquities in Philadelphia, Atwater foresaw the future of preservationism not in the United States but further south.

In March of 1830, after Atwater was back at home in Circleville, he wrote Dr. Morton about some "specimens" in his possession, by which he meant human skulls.[232] Atwater had already donated skulls to the AAS, even including engravings of one in *Archaeologia Americana*—which was reprinted in multiple Atlantic antiquities texts over the next decades—but he was less interested in craniometry (skull science) than Morton. In fact, the Philadelphian had only turned his own attention to craniometry ten years before, but he was rapidly amassing what would become the largest collection of crania on record, with over eight hundred individuals locked in his storehouse.[233] Over the next decade, US correspondents—like geologist William Maclure—would send Morton skulls from Mexico, including those of four Mexican soldiers killed at the battle of San Jacinto in 1836, the clash that turned the tide for the US-backed Texians.[234] Using these donations, Morton would eventually argue that there was no apparent anatomical difference between the remains of Moundbuilders and Indigenous peoples, but not before he sorted his skulls into different "stocks," including "Toltecan" and "Barbarian" American races.[235] The former was represented by skulls from the "semi-civilized" peoples of Mexico (likely conscripted Indigenous soldiers), while the skulls disinterred from contemporary Native graves like the one Atwater sent Morton were identified as "Barbarian." He reached these racist conclusions thanks to existing paradigms regarding the difference between the ancient peoples of the US and Mexico.[236]

The AAS was also interested in skulls, but it remained interested in mounds as well: in the 1830s, AAS Secretary Christopher Columbus Baldwin proposed moving an entire mound from Illinois to Massachusetts for preservation.[237] Although the society did not publish its next volume of *Archaeologia Americana* until 1836, the second volume—like its first—was dedicated to the continent's "aboriginal inhabitants." During the the sixteen-year hiatus the AAS had intensified its preservationist language, increasingly believing the entire hemisphere's Indigenous population to be "rapidly passing away."[238]

The AAS would continue to encourage and fund antiquarian work for the rest of the century. Some members, like former Treasury Secretary Albert Gallatin, continued in the older tradition of writing universal histories based on language research and using conventions set by criollos. His 1845 essay "Notes on the Semi-Civilized Nations of Mexico, Yucatan, and Central America" even included images from the *Codex Boturini* and a summary of León y Gama's "Mexican almanac."[239] Other AAS members, like Increase Allen Lapham and Ephraim G. Squier, followed in Atwater's empiricist archeological footsteps.

A New Yorker who was briefly editor of the *Scioto Gazette,* Squier caught his first in-person glimpse of Ohio's antiquities when he moved to Chillicothe in 1845.[240] With local physician Edwin H. Davis, Squier co-authored the Smithsonian Institution's first volume of scholarship, *Ancient Monuments of the Mississippi Valley* (1848) (which Morton called "the most important contribution to the Archaeology of the United States that has ever been offered to the public") based on their research in Ohio.[241] In addition, much of the volume repurposed work by the previous generation of antiquaries including Atwater; indeed, among its more than 200 engravings of earthworks and antiquities are passages taken directly from Atwater's 1820 "Description."[242] However, unlike Atwater's essay, *Ancient Monuments* is considered the moment when archaeological excavation in the US became not the resort of the "parlor antiquarian"—curiously embodied by Atwater—but the "scientist."[243] The move to praise Squier and Davis while shunning Atwater is due in no small regard to

Atwater's direct embrace of the Moundbuilder myth and Mexican migration hypothesis. Yet even "scientists" like Squier relied on allegedly Mexican ideas of the past to understand American antiquity. *Ancient Monuments* inherited and expanded these theories: Squier and Davis repeatedly wrote of the "mysterious race of the mounds" and the "close resemblance to the Teocallis of Mexico" of Ohio's earthworks.[244] Indeed, Squier's papers at the Library of Congress today include a clipping of the "Mexican almanac" (Sun Stone) engraving from Gallatin alongside copies of Nahuatl iconic manuscripts and Dupaix's line drawings in Squier's own hand.[245]

Like Atwater, Squier and Davis also practiced stratiological history. In a chapter on "Sacrificial Mounds" beneath an illustration of "Mound City" near Chillicothe, a cross-section labeled "Figure 29" depicts what appears to be a cut-away mound, a rough half-circle with the highest part toward the middle of the page and tapering toward the edges.[246] The variegated shading runs in lines following the sinusoid outline of the whole. Along the left-hand side runs a scale that matches the intensity of shading to a labeled section, laying out a visual chronology of excavation: "Pebbles and coarse gravel" at the top, repeating layers of "Earth," "skeleton," "stratum of sand," and "calcined bones" on the layers down.[247] "Figure 29" is one of the first cross-sectional representations of an archaeological site, an excavatory envisioning that highlights the necessity of annihilation to the expansionist settler project in that it "preserves" the mound in the midst of its own destruction to prove continental aboriginality. These stratiological cutaways are one way that the citizens of the United States—in the nineteenth century and later—have learned to understand earthworks as visualizations of "prehistory" rather than as markers of Indigenous continuity. The Squier and Davis illustrations are still the preeminent source of earthworks images, and their engravings grace almost every museum and historic marker at earthwork sites.

IN JANUARY OF 2015, construction workers for the Guernsey Crossing shopping center in Chillicothe leveled an earthwork on its newly purchased property there, revealing a former burial site.[248] In what would soon become a parking lot, volunteer archaeologists immediately went to work excavating human bones, pottery fragments, and charred wood, warehousing everything in the state historical society, the Ohio History Connection (OHC).[249] Ten years before this the Chillicothe earthwork had been "a bump around 2 1/2 feet tall and quite easy to see," according to archaeologist Jarrod Burks, but in 2008 the site had been razed and went unreported in the purchase and planning processes.

Representatives for the developer said they had "no idea that any part of the site ... was considered sacred ground."[250] Under typical circumstances, Burks lamented, the mound would have been forgotten and "another important piece of Ohio history lost"; instead the developers granted Burks and volunteers three weeks to excavate. Both parties "agreed not to speak publicly about it until the Native American tribes could be told of the find."[251] When contacted, tribal leaders expressed their wishes to leave the burials "intact and honored," but this was not in the company's plans and so Burks conceded that in this case "preservation is the next best thing."[252] Thus, after the January 2015 dig, everything was collected and deposited at the OHC just up the Scioto River in Columbus, with the plan that the excavated objects would be cataloged for further study.[253] A year later, after the site—now named the "North Bridge Street Mound"—had been paved over, the developers installed an interpretive panel and reconstructed the mound so that visitors could "appreciate this nearly lost aspect of Chillicothe's unique Native American heritage."[254]

The interpretive panel at the new mound identifies the original two-thousand-year-old earthwork as made by "people of what archaeologists now refer to as the Adena culture," missing an opportunity to provide any information about local Indigenous history by naming Worthington's estate (and thereby the settler history of Chilicothe) but not mentioning any Shawnee relatives.[255] It also displays an engraving from *Ancient Monuments of the Mississippi Valley*—in which this specific mound was "first documented"—as well as photographs from the excavation and an artist's rendering of a prior structure "used for, among other things, rituals related to the dead." The disturbed burial site that has become the North Bridge Street Mound—the archive of which comprises a 1848 Squier and Davis engraving, a storeroom of skeletons, and a reconstructed model—exemplifies the ways in which Native lands have been consistently evacuated of their physical and discursive contents in the interest of "preservation," especially in the face of imminent destruction, whether by building shopping centers, plowing fields, or evicting residents. The well-intentioned preservation effort nonetheless proliferates invented identities and sidesteps the complexity inherent in naming a "piece of Ohio history" when the state's history itself was made possible by removing its earthworks and its Native residents. This style of antiquarian preservation of earthworks—which Atwater declared in 1819 as "the only means within my power to perpetuate their memory"—subordinates the vibrant circles and squares of earth to dehumanized "objects" taken from underneath the land and placed in the past.

FIGURE 18. North Bridge Street Mound, Chillicothe, Ohio. Author's photograph, 2018. Visitors read interpretive panel at the reconstructed burial mound, located in a strip mall parking lot.

The misrepresentation of Native history as Ohio's or Chillicothe's, as well as the characterization that depositing human remains and grave goods in a scholarly repository for "preservation" is "the next best thing"—despite explicitly betraying the wishes of the federally recognized Shawnee nations—relies on an acquisitive logic and possessive approach to the past that, at the very least, values US history more than "Native American heritage."[256] The newest mound in Chillicothe illustrates the casual violence of replacement that has filled the archive with Native ancestors, a constitutive part of "preservation" that persists to this day.

CHAPTER 6

An American Babylon in the Mexican Republic

Elaq'an chaqe
ri ulew, ri che', ri ja'.
Ri man e k'owinan taj
xa are ri', ri Nawal.
Man kekuwin ta wa'.

—Humberto Ak'abal, "Elaq'" (Stolen), 1996

IN SEPTEMBER 1819, AS Atwater was describing antiquities in Ohio, François "Juan Francisco" Corroy made his first excursion to see the casas de piedras (stone houses) near the town of Palenque in Chiapas. Corroy—a French physician who had lived in New Spain for almost twenty years—traveled inland over ninety miles from the lowlands of Tabasco to reach the dense cedar and mahogany rainforest concealing the ruins.[1] Readers in Mexico and across the Atlantic world would become more familiar with Palenque's "stone houses" three years later, when an illustrated translation of Antonio Del Río's 1787 report would be published in London. But Corroy had already caught a glimpse of the structures in sketches drawn by Luciano Castañeda who, along with Captain Guillermo Dupaix, had stayed with Corroy after the Royal Antiquities Expedition's visit to Palenque in 1808.[2] In his attempt to capture the French Société de la Géographie prize for information about the place "once inhabited by the Toltecan, or Toltequan nation," Corroy would ultimately make two more visits to Palenque during his lifetime.[3] In 1833, an article about these efforts appeared in the New York monthly *The Knickerbocker*.[4] Comprised of Corroy's letters to Samuel L. Mitchell and other members of New York's Lyceum of Natural History, the article described an "American Babylon in ruins," hidden in the jungles of Mexico.[5]

Corroy's hemispheric correspondence gives a good indication of how widespread Atlantic scholars' interest in Mexico's past had become in the early years of Mexican Independence. Once "the rubbish has been cleared away," wrote

Corroy in 1833, the ruins of Palenque would exhibit "evidences of a nation once existing there."[6] This past nation, Corroy was certain, had been "composed of Phenicians, Egyptians, Greeks, Asiatics, Arabs, and Chinese," an Eastern Imperium.[7] Antiquaries in the "Old World" had, at least since the Napoleonic Expeditions in Egypt, increasingly turned their eyes to focus on the Near East. In the 1810s and 1820s, agents of the British East India Company performed excavations at the sites of Babylon, Persepolis, and Ninevah, and their findings accelerated desires that ancient corollaries would be found in the New World.[8] For centuries, European and criollo settlers heard and repeated rumors of ancient civilizations and cities "lost" in the jungle, tales that called soldiers, scholars, and tourists in search of hidden wonders.[9] Indeed, much of the field of archaeology was built around the romantic allure of "ruins" and the narratives of declension they represented.[10]

In the 1820s and 1830s, the Republic of Mexico's "lost" Maya cities rewarded machete, paintbrush, and imagination. However, as antiquaries like Corroy or readers in the Atlantic world shook their heads at the "overgrown" sites, imagining who might have once lived there, local Indigenous residents were often using them: tending milpas (farm plots), respecting guardian spirits, and conducting renewal ceremonies.[11] Savants' calls to "clear away"—to discover, preserve, and rebuild—the cities, however, overrode the function that those structures continued to serve for the local communities. For Mexican antiquaries, the allegedly abandoned "wasteland" ("baldío") recalled Indigenous traditions of ancient calamity and extinction—especially the cycle of Suns—and opened space for a new, "mexicano" civitas to move in, one that was disconnected from the realities of Indigenous sovereignty on the ground.

It was not until the turn of the twenty-first century that archaeologists found a way to see through the foliage without clearing it out. Light Detection and Ranging (LiDAR) technology—pulsing laser beams sent from aircraft—has enabled three-dimensional maps of the landscape below the vegetation.[12] With this tool, archaeologists have visualized thousands of Indigenous-made structures otherwise concealed by the jungle. Dramatic headlines—like "Laser maps reveal 'lost' Mayan treasure in Guatemala jungle"—regularly feature in mainstream and scientific press venues.[13] In addition to revolutionizing archaeological and conservation work, LiDAR's visualizations have also revived the discourse of "lost cities," "hidden treasure," and the mysteriousness of the American past.

It is no coincidence that the ersatz lost cities of Mexico are usually located in areas least penetrated by state control, places largely outside the capital: the volcanic highlands, coastal lowlands, and subtropical basins. These are regions occupied, in the majority, by various Indigenous communities, the largest groups of which are Maya.[14] Before the twentieth century, "Maya" people rarely identified as such, instead referring to themselves by language, lineage, location, or in other ways; indeed, settlers frequently referred to "Maya" people by region (i.e., "Chipanese" from Chiapas) or polity (e.g., K'iche') in the Spanish colonial period.[15] Even today, most "Maya" do not employ the term, although it has picked up significance in Indigenous advocacy circles in the last quarter century.[16] The word is used much more frequently by archaeologists, the Mexican government, and by the state-supported "Rivera Maya" tourism industry.[17] The continued visualization of these spaces as "lost"—or even as "Maya"—is built on centuries-long histories of land and identity struggles that persist in Mexico today.

For the most part, early national politicians and letrados of Mexico City knew very little about Maya history. What they did know was largely centered on apocryphal narratives originating with Palenque, which they were always describing as "mysterious" or "hieroglyphic" (as in secret or hidden).[18] I gloss that sense of secrecy and concealment as the "glyphic" aspect of ancient American history. Shortened from the word "hieroglyphic"—which in the nineteenth century particularly referenced Mayan as well as Egyptian iconic writing—"glyphic" draws from the Early Modern understanding of Egyptian script as mysterious, hidden, or "secret knowledge." In Mexico, "glyph" became an indeterminately Indigenous index that always pointed to the past and usually indicated outsiders' imaginative interpretations of those pasts. The early Mexican identity, built upon the discourse of "ancient Mexican cities"—as emblematized by the "glyph"—was a tool of erasure and depopulation for the newly independent settler nation.

European and US scholars were attracted to the Maya past because it seemed to confirm transatlantic migratory models of history, and the "lost cities" theme operated similarly to that of archaeological stratiology, exchanging dirt for foliage. Both visualized hidden yet distinct layers of history. That is to say, the discourse of "lost cities" itself implies disconnection: founded by a people not linked—racially, relationally, culturally—to the people now living in the region. Mexicans, however, initially resisted incorporating Maya pasts into their national history because they did not confirm the migration hypotheses elaborated in the eighteenth century: descent from Aztlán. Indeed, Maya traditional teachings tend to emphasize autochthony rather than movement, which was less aligned with the political goals of americanos and mexicanos.

Foreigners were especially interested in Maya sites because of their locations on the periphery of the Mexican nation, where they could operate under the least surveillance. The US writer-diplomat-archaeologist John Lloyd Stephens described his 1839 visit to Palenque—which he knew was prohibited—as only possible because fighting on the Guatemala border and Indigenous uprisings in nearby Tabasco, Campeche, and Yucatán had not left "any spare soldiers to station there as a guard" to keep him out.[19] In his 1841 travel narrative, Stephens recalled his time in Palenque, writing that its ruins were "the first which awakened attention to the existence of ancient and unknown cities in America."[20] Other foreign travelers also concentrated on the "overgrown" areas where national control was weakest, explaining their almost singular focus on Chiapas and the Yucatán in the 1830s and 1840s.

In the 1950s, Mexican historian Juan A. Ortega y Medina argued that Stephens and those who followed him deployed Maya archaeological material from the Yucatán to create a monolithic "Indian" past in support of a US hemispheric imperialism he called "Monroísmo arqueológico."[21] More recently, literary scholar Robert Aguirre argued that nineteenth-century archaeology in Mexico and Central America—and the way it represented current-day Indigenous peoples as "hopelessly backward and unknowable"—was an important arm of British "informal" power in Latin America.[22] Adventuring for "hidden treasure" and "lost cities" in verdant "jungle" landscapes is practically canonical in archaeological history, although in the main the scholarship has focused on the ways in which an American archeological past—construct of the United States and Europe—aided the fiscal and political domination of Mexico.[23] Yet although foreigners often articulated the myths of lost (and found) cities and civilizations—especially Maya ones—the discourse was first produced by nineteenth-century Mexicans as a crucial component of national consolidation.[24]

In the mid-nineteenth-century United States, figurations of an imaginary "Aztec" past were used to rationalize the invasion of Mexico and legitimate continental Indigenous displacement; but before this, those histories had already been used in Mexico to justify displacing or occupying Indigenous communities, especially those resistant to Mexican national rule. In 1820s and 1830s Mexico, the past represented by visualizations of Palenque emerged as a powerful tool of national consolidation, pushing the country's identity southward (toward Guatemala) and westward (into Campeche and the Yucatán), rather than northward to the "barbarous" lands of Téjas, Nuevo México, and Alta California. National policies kept these southern and western territories within the central pull of the federal capital by attacking the Indigenous social structures that depended on specific relationships to place. This was not programmatic extermination but was instead based on eviction and acculturation. That is, the Mexican state prioritized dislocating Indigenous populations in terms of political as well as cultural difference. Support for the "lost cities" mythology—not dissimilar to the Moundbuilder myth in the United States—thereby disconnected current-day, usually Maya, Indigenous peoples from the lands and legacies of their ancestors. Ancient cities were both imaginatively and literally depopulated of Indigenous lives in order to create space—real and imaginative—for new Mexican citizens.

Mexican anthropologist Guillermo Bonfil Batalla once argued that the early national emphasis on Mexica—and eventually Maya—histories promoted an "imaginary Mexico" by ignoring the realities and heterogeneity of Indigenous groups. In this way, a Euro-American (white or mestizo) "mexicano" identity—produced via the central government's capital, land-owning, and cultural incentives that prioritized a white (i.e., American and European) settler indigeneity—simultaneously "de-Indianized"—to also use Bonfil Batalla's term—Mexica and Maya ancestors.[25]

Mexico's official "imaginary" Indigenous identity that took shape after the war with Spain not only manifested the ideological rupture but was itself an active instrument of Indigenous peoples' dispossession, erasure, and replacement. By adapting "rupture" or "displacement" narratives from the United States (i.e., no continuity of Indigenous communities over time), mexicanos become the imaginary inheritors of México-Tenochtitlan.[26] This chapter considers the ways that (non-Indigenous) Mexicans—in the face of considerable imperial threats during the Republic's early years and grappling with significant internal political, economic, and demographic changes—produced an imaginary "mexicano" past to strengthen their own hold on Mexico's lands, resources, and peoples.[27] I connect the legacy of "lost city" visuality to the first Mexican Republic's concerted efforts at de-Indigenization (desindianizar).

The political contexts within which nineteenth-century "Mexicanness" was produced and circulated reveal its role in cohering the settler citizenry. As the nation's elites—most formerly criollos-americanos—found themselves at the pinnacle rather than penultimate level of social hierarchy, their imagination of Mexicanness underwent the process of blanqueamiento (whitening), which in turn undergirded early national demographic and power shifts.[28] The invention of a civic, racially-unmarked mexicano (Mexican) cultural identity in the 1820s, 1830s, and 1840s—a precursor to the twentieth century's raza cosmica—was expurgatory and even genocidal to real Indigenous peoples, who were largely considered obstacles to republican national unity.

Nationalizing Ethnic Landscapes

Like their eighteenth-century counterparts, americanos of the early nineteenth century drew freely from Nahua—largely Mexica—histories to create their "mexicano" inheritance.[29] When the autonomist americano Fray José Servando Teresa de Mier, in exile during the Independence struggle, glossed New Spain as "formerly Anáhuac" in the title of his *Historia de la revolución de Nueva España, antiguamente Anáhuac* (1813), he was emphasizing that the Spanish had merely renamed an enduring former polity. In 1821, Fray Servando exhorted his "Anáhuacan countrymen" to honor their country's past by writing "Mexico" with an "x" rather than the Hispanicized "j," and more generally to "protest the suppression of the *x* in the Mexican or Aztec place names."[30] Preserving an orthography matching the original pronunciation—"the Indians do not say anything other than *Mescico*"—would help perpetuate an Indigenous, rather than Spanish, lineage for their new patria.[31] Historian Benjamin Keen has called this imagined continuity of independent Mexico and imperial Tenochtitlan the "revival of Anáhuac."[32]

When the insurgent leader José María Morelos convened the Congress of Chilpancingo—also known as the Congress of Anáhuac—in September 1813, he detailed the transfer of sovereignty to the People, acknowledged the supremacy of Catholicism, and affirmed the inviolability of property. He proclaimed: "We are about to re-establish the Mexican Empire [el imperio Mexicano]."[33] Links between the original imperio mexicano (1428–1521) and the short-lived Imperio Mexicano (1821–1823) were most obvious, but the invocations continued into the federal Republic (1824–1835). During those years, the elites in charge—especially the Federalist politician Lucas Alamán and Centralist Carlos María de Bustamante—also drew on the Mexica past regardless of political faction, both supporting projects to increase Anáhuacan patriotism through increasing the public's knowledge of Mexican antiquity.

Although the protection of landed property was long at the center of the movement for a new Mexican state, it was frequently hidden by this rhetoric of imperial antiquity. It is crucial to recall, however, that Anáhuac references territory not just temporality. Evoking the lands where the first Nahua families finally settled, "Anáhuac" not only indexes their migration history but also places Mexico in a specific, prophesized locale. Its Nahuatl name—"surrounded by water"—not only signals the five lakes of the altiplano where the Mexica and others settled—Lakes Texcoco, Zumpango, Xaltocán, Xochimilco, and Chalco—but also the waters of Aztlán and the oceans around the Mexican landmass.³⁴ Thus not just a synonym for the "Valley of Mexico" or even "New Spain," this term linked directly to Indigenous territory and the precedent of Nahua settlement.

Like "Anáhuac," the so-called "tierras mayas" (Maya lands)—as both a specific region and an abstract foil to Mexico's Nahua center—have deep roots running to the imaginative and political management of territory.³⁵ Unlike well-rehearsed Mexica history, however, little Maya history had circulated outside Chiapas and the Yucatán by the outbreak of the Mexican War for Independence in 1810.³⁶ Partly, this was because the lands on which Maya peoples live, even in the nineteenth century, are relatively removed from the nation's center. Furthermore, these peripheries were not rich in the gold and silver initially pursued by the Spanish invaders. (However, the settlers soon found that the lands were rich in space for cash crops and people for forced labor.) For this among other reasons, most non-Indigenous Mexicans in the 1820s continued to identify almost every aspect of Indigenous history and material culture as "Mexican" despite ample evidence that Nahua was not the only Indigenous group or history around.³⁷

It was not until the 1830s that outsiders began to recognize the Mexica-Maya division that had already been in use locally for centuries.³⁸ Although the commonplace that "Maya civilization" was "discovered" in the nineteenth century was developed particularly through the exploits John Lloyd Stephens, "Maya" identity was merely "invented" then for the rest of the world. In the early colonial period, the categories "Maya" and "Mexican" were spatial shorthand designating Indigenous populations by region: *mexicanos* lived west of the Isthmus of Tehuantepec while *mayas* lived east and south, even though many other Indigenous groups live within this geographical stretch as well.³⁹ Initially, "Maya" mainly applied to peoples living in the Yucatán, but this was eventually extended to other Mayan-language speakers in the highlands (e.g., Chiapas, Péten).

When Cortés and his assigns—who first disembarked on Maya lands and negotiated with Maya peoples—eventually asserted Spanish authority, it was through Nahua (mainly Mexica and Tlaxalteca) and Otomí force. Their subjugation of Maya highlanders in the 1520s even retraced some of the roads tread—and kingdoms vanquished—by the Triple Alliance.⁴⁰ Results of the Spanish invasion included immense loss of life, many Mayas sent into slavery, the destruction of cities, villages, and agricultural fields, and the creation of large numbers of refugees. Many lowland Mayas left their ancestral seats in the Yucatán and fled to the Selva Lacandona (Lakandon Jungle), which stretches across the lower Yucatán, middle of Chiapas, Guatemala, and Honduras. In the mid-sixteenth century, Dominicans pursued a policy of reducción (congregation), in which they rounded up disparate Indigenous converts and relocated them to new parish towns. The Spanish village of Santo Domingo de Palenque, for example, was founded in 1567 on Tzeltal and Ch'ol Maya lands to evangelize displaced Ch'ol families. By the end of the seventeenth century, after long and punishing campaigns of conquest—in which Maya peoples were subject to torture, murder, and other violence causing many to flee and thus changing the demography and ecology of the whole region—the Spanish proclaimed their control over the Maya lands and peoples.[41]

The ways in which "Maya lands" and "Maya" identity came to have meaning for the Spanish were deeply implicated in Indigenous conceptions of the past. Indeed, long before the Triple Alliance asserted its power to the southeast, Nahua and Maya peoples had interacted—through trade, kinship, war, and the exchange of ideas—for hundreds of years. By the time of Teotihuacan's dominance in central Mexico—c. 1–500 CE—Mayas were adopting Nahuatl loan words and adapting aspects of Teotihuacano material culture such as chacmool basins and tzompantli (skull racks). Likely this exchange accounts for the commonality of feathered serpents—embodied by Kukulcán, Q'uq'umatz, and Quetzalcoatl—across Mexica and Maya regions.[42] By the time the Spanish arrived, almost all the other Maya nobles, including those in the southeastern highlands, were marking these connections to Tolteca, Teotihuacano, and other pasts.[43]

In their campaigns for dominance, Spanish settlers adopted some of the chauvinism of their Nahua mercenaries. They learned, for example, that Nahuas considered Mayan speakers inferior: in the manuscript created under the direction of Fray Sahagún in the 1570s, the *Florentine Codex*, the scribes reported that elders called people from the Yucatán Peninsula nonouacat, the speechless.[44] Malinztin, Cortés's consort and interpreter—who had been purchased by Chontal Mayas and knew Yucatec Mayan as well—likely shared her own views as a cultural broker.[45] Nahua soldiers also told stories of the "lost city" of Mayapán, the twelfth-century power center of northwest Yucatán said to have been founded by the feathered serpent deity K'uk'ulkan and Itzá ancestors after the fall of Chichén Itzá. The Spanish misappropriated the city's name and the language spoken there—maaya t'aan—to refer to all the region's people.[46] Mayapán, in fact, was an important Toltec-Maya link that brought Maya and Nahua worlds together, although the Spanish had no real sense of this when they extended the "Maya" identity to all lowland and highland Mayan-speaking peoples and the places they lived.

Writing (Out) Maya Lands

To stamp out traditional Maya ways of life, the Spanish destroyed countless votive entities—including stone deities, World Tree effigies, and stone mounds—as well as "ancient paintings" or the bark-and-lime screenfold books inscribed in a phonetic and logographic script that settlers later called "hieroglyphics." The systematic devastation continued until at least the late seventeenth century: in 1690, for example, the Dominican friar Francisco Núñez de la Vega recalled ordering one particularly "dangerous" manuscript to be burned.[47] Today there are no highland Maya texts dating before the Spanish invasion (known to the general public) and only four from the Yucatán.[48] This process of cultural extermination was called "conquista pacifica" to disguise and distinguish it from other forms of violence against Indigenous peoples.[49] During those years, Maya individuals and communities guarded their ancient documents. Some Spanish priests even complained about their "secretiveness," all the while actively trying to root out the "devil"—traditional belief systems—in the communities they occupied.

Some Dominicans—whose order was founded to counter heresy and was in charge of the Inquisition—also attempted to document local histories: like their Franciscan counterparts in México, Dominicans worked with Christian Maya nobles to compile grammars and books of cosmology as well as to translate Catholic religious texts into local languages.[50] Due to the missionaries' presence, Maya leaders—who like their Nahua counterparts were looking to preserve their previous standing—gained familiarity with Spanish and a new alphabetic script and were thus—also like the Nahua caciques—able to protest land seizures, unjust levies, and other abuses in colonial courts.[51] They also produced documents to substantiate land claims—such as the *Título de Totonicapán*, created by Diego Reynoso in 1554—and tribute rights, some of which ended up in the Dominicans' collections as well.[52] Also in the 1550s, a selection of widely memorized sacred histories were set to paper in alphabetic K'iche' by three anonymous authors.[53] A century and a half later the Dominican friar Francisco Ximénez copied this manuscript, now called the *Popul Vuh*, and stored it among the other Indigenous documents amassed by the black-robed Preachers.[54]

At about the same time, Núñez de la Vega wrote that, as part of his Inquisition duties, he assembled "history booklets written in the Indian language," "painted blankets," calendars, and interrogation reports of "suspected nagualistas" or Chiapan "shapeshifters."[55] When Núñez de la Vega, who was bishop of Chiapas, read the *Popul Vuh* manuscript, one of the aspects that most interested him was its account of the voyage made by the K'iche' founders—the "Aj Toltecat" (Toltecs)—to visit their Nahua brothers at "Tulan," where these ancestors established the K'iche' lineage and received their patron deities.[56] Combining his previous research with biblical teachings and population hypotheses, Núñez de la Vega deduced that this was an account of Adamic descendants who had settled in Maya lands after the Flood, perhaps in the deep "selva" (jungle) of Chiapas.[57] He even went so far as to identify a Tzeltal (batzil'op) Maya deity, Votán—whom he claimed had witnessed the fall of the Tower of Babel—as Noah's nephew.[58] Although considerably more interested in eradicating evil than in understanding the K'iche' writings, Núñez de la Vega bequeathed his successors an enduring image of an Old World colony hidden somewhere in the dense rainforest homeland of the Lakandon Maya.

In 1773, when Chiapan guides led Friar Ramón Ordóñez y Aguiar to see the rumored casas de piedras in the jungle—in a location that "the succession of many centuries has erased from man's memory"—Núñez de la Vega's ideas resurfaced.[59] Ordóñez compiled all he could to explain the ruins, including a Tzeltal Maya lineage for Votán and the *Popol Vuh*, which he translated from K'iche' into Spanish in 1796.[60] Although the collected writings describe genealogies and deities—such as Q'uq'umatz, who helped to create humans out of maize—as well as cycles of destruction and rebirth—like Núñez de la Vega before him—Ordóñez focused most intently on supporting his conviction that Votán's ancestry proved the correspondence of American and biblical chronologies. In 1794 Paul Félix Cabrera in Guatemala City claimed that Palenque was the capital of "Amaguemecan," the alleged Toltec homeland, which apparently was also called Anáhuac.[61] Cabrera also drew on Núñez de la Vega, Ordóñez, Ximénez's *Popul Vul*, Del Río's 1787 report, and Clavijero to solve "the Grand Historical Problem" of America's original peopling.[62] All of this work was done to account for the same casas de piedras that Captain Guillermo Dupaix in 1807 attributed to "a race of men unknown to ancient or modern historians."[63]

"Discovering" the Stone Houses

The allegedly unknown peoples' stone houses were located about five miles outside the Spanish village of Santo Domingo de Palenque, at the site of the powerful former "city-state" now also called Palenque. Palenque had been founded by the ajaw (lord) K'uk' Bahlam I (reign 431–435 CE) and expanded under ajaw K'inich Kan Bahlam II (reign 684–702 CE). At the instigation of the latter, three large talud-tablero-style stone pyramids topped with temples were constructed at the site; inside, basalt blocks carved in relief depicted Palenque's dominant histories and teachings, including portraits and ancestral lineages that linked K'inich Kan Bahlam to the era of creation and Palenque's patron deities.[64] One particularly notable set of carvings there, now referred to as the "Cross Group," depicts not a Christian symbol but more probably a World Tree, representing the axis of Earth and Sky. After war and defeat to a rival city-state, Palenque declined; by the tenth century the former ruling line's adherents had largely abandoned it.[65] Although the site did not regain its influential political power or cultural reach, Maya individuals continued to live in and around old Palenque, using the land for maize milpas and structures for ceremony.

When Ordóñez reported his "discovery" of the stone houses in the 1770s a notice made its way into the hands of Royal Historian Juan Bautiza Muñoz who spread word of the "large city in Chiapas" in Spain.[66] The Crown deemed the news sufficiently important to order official explorations, of which there were three (1784, 1785, and 1787) in rapid succession.[67] The 1787 visit was conducted by criollo soldier Captain Antonio Del Río, who forwarded copies of his report to officials in Guatemala City and Madrid that year.[68] These included a sketch of the "Cross Group," which he described as pertaining to the "idolatry of the Phoenicians, the Greeks, and the Romans."[69]

The place Ordóñez "discovered" (after having been led there by Maya guides) was far from forgotten: on the third Royal expedition Del Río had even commandeered seventy-nine Maya laborers from the nearby village of Tumbala to guide him and clear the site—stripping and burning the brush—and to break off samples of the stone architecture for the Royal Cabinet.[70] For various reasons, the Crown did not send another expedition to Palenque until Dupaix and Castañeda visited as part of the Royal Antiquities Expedition.[71] And with the outbreak of war in Europe—and Dupaix's arrest as a supposed revolutionary—their reports and drawings remained in America, "forgotten" for another decade.

At the end of the Spanish era, Spanish and criollo scholars mapped information about Palenque and its peoples onto their existing interest in American origins. The suggestion that Maya peoples may have had ties to the Holy Land or ancient empires of North Africa gave the Americas a place within universal Christian history.[72] And if Palenque's supposed old-world origins indicated to criollos-americanos an initial transatlantic Indigenous population, that same history later proved to nationalist Mexicans that the continent's past was rooted in a Europeanized "Toltec" heritage. As in the United States, this belief vitiated contemporary Indigenous claims of American aboriginality. Moreover, the specific Toltec-Palenque connection would be elaborated contemporaneously by Benjamin Smith Barton and Baron von Humboldt, then later repeated by people like Corroy in the 1830s.[73] But it was not until well after Mexico became a Republic that Palenque's stone houses again found an important place in Mexico's historical discourse. During the Revolution and its aftermath, nationalists kept their attention on the "Aztec race."

That Spanish knowledge of Palenque was enabled by the violent displacement of Maya families farther into the Lakandon Jungle—likely also a factor that kept the casas de piedras' location largely unknown to the Spanish for two centuries—meant that understanding Maya history depended on understanding the difference between ancient and current Palenqueños in terms of colonialism. Spanish observers, however, took the difference as evidence of a lost colony. Their descriptions of it as such went far to enable the dismissal of contemporary residents' cultural and historic ties.

Uniting Anáhuac and Teaching Patriotism

Despite Mexico's new geographic unity after Independence, the country was otherwise politically fractured: partisan disagreements over the role of federal, state, and municipal governments, an economy on the verge of collapse, destroyed infrastructure, and a population exposed to epidemics and hunger created an environment of hardship and instability. Historian David Brading describes the earlier independence period as one determined by the deep ideological fissures of creole patriotism, insurgent nationalism, and liberal republicanism.[74] One of the deepest splits was between those who favored a centralized versus a federal (individual state-based) government, although their shared ideological commitment to the settler nation usually transcended faction.[75] There were also dissident actors with no interest in a united Mexico, among these guerilla bands in the central plateau's mountainous peripheries and Yaqui and Mayo defenders in Sonora.[76] Powerful caciques and wealthy merchants in the South and Southeast also threatened succession, and a constant state of quasi-war with Spain—Mexican independence was not officially recognized until 1836—as well as the prospect of invasion from France and the United States and defections to Central America made for a precarious confederation.[77]

Independence posed the challenge of creating a new national people from a patchwork fabric of castas, white, and Indigenous identities.[78] The politically powerful tended to come from the army and landowning classes, usually wealthy whites (formerly criollos) and elite mestizos.[79] Castas and Indigenous peoples—like the insurgents José Morelos and Vicente Guerrero—were hardly in the majority; and the few Indigenous politicians there usually maintained ties to the elite cacique class, whose politics were often at odds with those of the "masses."[80] The interests of the rural and Indigenous peoples calling for land reform and respect for pueblo autonomy—one of the major desires motivating Father Miguel Hidalgo's supporters in 1810—were also generally underrepresented in formulations of Mexico's, and Mexicans', future.[81]

At least a tenth of the colonial population perished during the war with Spain and much of the colonial infrastructure that supported the population—roads, aqueducts, mills, haciendas, etc.—was destroyed.[82] In a post-war attempt to recover its decimated finances, the Republic continued the practice of encouraging foreign investment by specifically allowing for joint Mexican-foreign holdings.[83] Britain particularly made a concerted political effort to involve itself in the recently opened markets and this was encouraged by government officials like Lucas Alamán. From a mining family himself, Alamán believed that mining was crucial to the economy.[84] Yet while this courting of foreign capital stimulated the economy, it all placed Mexico in a delicate relationship with predatory investors and resulted in a sizeable—and potentially seditious—foreign population.[85] Furthermore it opened Mexico to other kinds of predation: the United States, which recognized Mexican independence in 1822, concentrated less on encouraging (or regulating) private investment by its own citizens and more on exploiting its neighbor's weakened position to angle for territory along the US southern border. It looked to Mexico's lands (and to the Mexican polity) much as it had to other lands in the "west": as underutilized wasteland to be made productive under the stars and stripes. Thus Mexican officials were well aware of their nation's tenuous hold on the extractive industries of mining, manufacture, and agriculture and the importance of maintaining muscular control of the territory.

During the war, much of the demolition came at the hands of Indigenous and underclass insurgents looking for reform.[86] Indeed, the populist insurgency that led to Mexican independence had originally been motivated by the severe inequality of the Spanish colonial era, during which much of New Spain's economy had been powered by the extraction of mineral wealth and the export of crops such as cochineal, sisal, and Campeche wood. All of these industries were labor-heavy and depended on the colonial labor structure of the encomienda and hacienda systems.[87]

As Spain's colonial wealth had come from Indigenous peoples and their lands, the new nation's plans for an independent economy depended on Indigenous "resources" as well. Initially, wealth would be generated through the sell-off of communal land holdings, the civic transformation of displaced "indios" into laboring "campesinos" (peasants), and the reintroduction of taxation requirements. However, a series of droughts and famines as well as falling population and the casualties of war led to labor shortages in the countryside. For Indigenous communities in particular, the reduction of communal land-holdings and changes to the traditional tribute structure left many—especially those in decentralized areas such as Oaxaca, Chiapas, and Yucatán—in dire straits.[88] To survive, the newly "landless" were forced to work on haciendas and silver mines for wages rather than support themselves from the commons.[89] But as the market contracted during and after the war—especially the valuable cochineal market—and credit evaporated, Indigenous workers had to work for subsistence, not trade (their own or others'). Unable to find dayworkers for their plantations, the ruling-class-aligned merchants, lenders, and hacendados blamed the economic instability and inequality not on the war or market but on "Indian idleness."[90] In 1824 José María Luis Mora—the early Republic's representative to Congress from Mexico state—was so convinced that the solution to the nation's economic and political instability was Indigenous assimilation that he asked Congress to eliminate the very word "indio" from its legal vocabulary.[91]

If the politicians, hacendados, and capitalinos thought that the widespread poverty was due to cultural "backwardness," Euro-American visitors overwhelmingly attributed it to racialized traits. Largely barred from New Spain during the colonial era, foreign investors began traveling to Mexico en masse after 1821, especially encouraged by Humboldt's glowing—but outdated—words and the independent nation's market incentives.[92] During the 1820s, foreigners consistently commented on the nation's poverty. The anonymous author of *A Sketch of Customs and Society in Mexico, During the Years 1824, 1825, 1826* (1828), for example, noted the "strange mixture of squalor combined with luxury" that marked Mexico City homes.[93] William Bullock—an English silversmith and museum proprietor who traveled to Mexico in 1823 to take over the abandoned Del Bada silver mine but who only stayed for six months—contrasted the "poverty of the present Mexicans and the wealth of their ancestors."[94] Visitors also spread unflattering descriptions of Indigenous peoples in their portrayals of Mexican life.[95] Although commentators foreign and domestic seemed to trace the nation's ills to its Indigenous communities, few connected their immiseration to Mexican politician's attempts at "solving" the "problem" of Indigenous particularity.[96]

Like the Spanish Constitution of 1812, the Mexican Constitution of 1824 assumed the republican ideal that all citizens were equal and subject to the same laws. This was a de facto repudiation of the Laws of the Indies, whereby

Indigenous subjects of the Crown were endowed a different set of legal rights than those held by Spanish subjects. With these separate "rights"—which included separate political representation, some degree of self-government through the cacicazgo system, and the right of semi-autonomous pueblos to hold land in common (ejidos)—also came the responsibility to pay annual tribute and the inability to assume debt or participate in certain commercial transactions.[97] Certain Mexicans saw this separate set of laws as discriminatory; most non-Indigenous politicians agreed that they were damaging to the assimilationist goals of the nation. Doing away with the legal separation, as Representative Mora put it, would "hasten the fusion of the Aztec race with the general body of citizens."[98] Thus Mora, on one side, believed that the answer was to set "the white race"—rather than the Indigenous one—as "the concept that must shape the Republic."[99] On the other side, supporters of the Indigenous populations saw land redistribution as a form of ancestral restitution, although the more revolutionary calls for reform were thought to be redolent of race or caste war.[100] The problem of poverty began to be seen more and more as a characteristic intrinsic to Indigenous Mexicans and therefore one only "solvable" via "whitening"—in both physiognomic and cultural terms—and assimilation into the Republic.[101]

The early national politicians intent on transforming Indigenous peoples into capitalist workers and consumers were also operating under the assumption that if Indigenous Mexicans would disavow their traditional "usos y costumbres" (uses and customs), they would "mexicanizar" (become Mexican), which is to say, whiten.[102] According to eighteenth-century theories of racial degeneration it took at least three generations of "crossing" to "improve the race."[103] The early Republic's leaders were looking for a more rapid solution: they found it in dislocation and deterritorialization.

"Improving the Race" to Secure the Nation

The Mexican Republic did not just occupy the footprint of New Spain: its lands stretched from the southeastern border with Guatemala north to the United States and the Oregon Territory. But these borders were not stable. When Guatemala broke away from the Mexican Empire in 1823, the neighboring region of Chiapas followed. The minority community of criollo elite in Chiapas overwhelmingly expressed their desire for Mexican annexation, believing Chiapas would do better with economic ties to Mexico City. They were also swayed by concerns over Guatemala's supposed inability to control "Indian insurrection."[104] A month before the 1824 Constitution was promulgated, the Chiapas region—formerly part of the Kingdom of Guatemala—was annexed to Mexico and admitted as a "Free and Sovereign State." The new Constitution reserved for the General Congress the right to add or consolidate new states and territories, regulate borders, and maintain the peace both inside and outside national boundaries. Mexico's central government stationed military forces in Chiapas for three years in order to enforce the border and help with the region's "Mexicanization," which in this case meant both pacification and integration into the central economy. Yet even after annexation and military occupation, these Maya lands remained peripheral to the nation.[105]

At the end of the colonial period, Spain had still been recruiting Indigenous and Euro-American settlers to its northern borderlands, particularly those that became the state of Coahuila y Tejas, as a form of imperial occupation. In early 1821, lead-magnate Moses Austin was granted land on which to settle three hundred US families, a plan fulfilled by his son Stephen in 1825.[106] In terms of its reach into the Indigenous lands of what Mexico imagined as its northern frontier—"La Gran Chichimeca," as it had been called in colonial times—Mexico had inherited New Spain's spatial imaginary, as well as its system of border diplomacy.[107] During the war for independence, however, Spanish forces had been unable to uphold their diplomatic relations with northern Indigenous groups—especially Apache groups—and thus independent Mexico found itself with a particularly uncertain borderland. The Republic struggled to maintain control over the northern lands it claimed, especially Sonora y Sinaloa, the Californias, and Coahuila y Tejas.

Although some Mexican leaders such as Lorenzo de Zavala looked at US and European colonists as New Spain had—as salubrious influences—others, like Lucas Alamán, were not so sure.[108] Under the Mexican Empire, this problem had been addressed by a law explicitly requiring immigrants to become Catholic and only provided naturalization upon marriage to a Mexican citizen. This was supposed to guarantee that Anglo settlers in Tejas would remain loyal to Mexico and to "Latin" (i.e., Roman Catholic) culture.[109] The point was for Hispanicized white settlers to serve as a buffer to the United States and to absorb conflicts with Indigenous groups—mainly Apaches and Comanches—along the northern border. In 1822, Mexican diplomat and Tejas colonization enthusiast Simón Tadeo Ortíz wrote of the disturbing violence on the borderlands and his concern for the "integrity of the national territory," warning that the north risked "being lost if there is not a change in the system."[110] The next year, Foreign Minister Lucas Alamán specifically addressed the necessity of "calming" the "barbarous tribes" then "infesting our northern borders," recommending a reenergized federal militia along the northern presidial line.¹¹¹ A strengthened missionary presence, he also predicted, would "civilize and establish a more peaceful kind of life" and help residents in the north become "useful members of our Nation."¹¹² Additionally, concerns about the border increased immigration as a technique of national security, for colonization schemes were punitive and militarily strategic as well. After the Yaqui uprising in Sonora (1825–1832), for example, the governor of Occidente issued tax incentives to promote white settlement among the Yoeme (Yaquis), whose common lands the government privatized.¹¹³ White colonization was explicitly meant as a technique for addressing the ongoing violence between settlers and Indigenous peoples in the borderlands, not dissimilar from New Spain's policy of settling "friendly" Nahuas on its frontiers in the sixteenth century.

The 1824 General Colonization Law also established new rules for territory that the national government termed "wasteland," enticing colonists with promises of guaranteed land grants.¹¹⁴ This followed Alamán's suggestion of the previous year, in which he advocated for the distribution of Indigenous lands ("freed" as a result of missionary reducciones) so as to establish emigrant colonies.¹¹⁵ Yet Mexico's officials were suspicious of pockets of foreigners such as those forming in the central mining towns; thus, the new law also placed an encomium on Mexicanization. Moreover, the 1824 law also prioritized *internal* colonization; that is to say, it encouraged the movement of (Hispanicized) Indigenous groups and other Mexicans from central Mexico to the peripheries. It aimed at incorporating these peripheral lands and residents—especially Indigenous residents—into the larger "Mexican family."¹¹⁶

Possessing Patrimony as Mexico's Property

As another technique of national security and unity, Republican nationalists prioritized an Anáhuacan "Mexican" identity. This homogenized, common civic identity they invented drew from previous iterations of an idealized Tenochca-Mexica past, which they took pains to teach to Mexico's non-Indigenous citizens. But Indigenous citizens, believed Foreign Minister Lucas Alamán, needed a different kind of education to "de-Indigenize" them ("desindianizarlos") before they would be receptive to civic instruction: first, they required lessons focused on the idealization of a white European cultural—and private property—base.¹¹⁷

When Alamán returned to Mexico after spending much of the war away on the "grand tour" of Europe—visiting the great museums of Madrid, Paris, and London—one of his early actions was to survey the nation's cultural and scientific institutions.[118] After an inventory of the remaining Boturini materials, he learned that many of the famous documents—including the *Codex Boturini*—were gone; those that remained were deteriorating.[119] In his initial speech to Congress in 1823, Minister Alamán revealed that "many very valuable monuments of Mexican antiquities have disappeared," and he urged the legislators to take action.[120] He proposed a National Museum, a model for which letrado Isidro Rafael Gondra had already established as the small Museo de Antigüedades in the library of the university.[121] A space to educate and cohere the national citizenry, the National Museum of Mexico would become a site to inculcate a new, civic "mexicanidad" while also sidelining past and present Indigenous political particularity by transforming Indigenous items, places, and peoples into entirely historic objects of national instruction. In a sign of Mexico's continuing commitment to the past—even as the city faced an uncertain future—Alamán's plan to found a national antiquities museum was eventually approved by President Guadalupe Victoria in 1825.

Of the two projects meant to mark the establishment of the National Museum in the 1820s—a catalog as well as a longer publishing project—both were based on the contention that Mexican citizenship and mexicanidad could be taught. In 1823 Alamán had also recommended the new government establish a system of public instruction—from primary school to university—and open public reading rooms.[122] He advised Congress to retain the collection of Classical statues and drawings at the shuttered Academia de San Carlos de las Nobles Artes—"which had been the font of good taste in our Nation"—and to send young Mexican artists to Rome for further training. A national museum, library, and archives would be connected to the revitalized hospital and botanical garden to create a nucleus of learning.[123] This centralized venue would provide visual examples of "good" (i.e., European) taste as well as the curriculum for producing a free, liberal, and united Mexican citizenry. The former viceregal complex on the Plaza Mayor would become a place in which Mexicans could learn to be Mexicans.[124]

Installed within the new National Palace, the museum's very collection would facilitate the nationalists' narrative of a selectively continuous Indigenous past, one that was disconnected from living aspects of indigeneity in Mexico. It would contain three categories of objects: "Mexican monuments from prior to or contemporary with the Spanish invasion"; "Monuments from ancient people of other continents, and the other American nations"; and "Statues, paintings, hieroglyphics, etc., according to the taste and use of the Indigenous peoples."[125]

This collection policy's insistence on keeping "ancient people" separate from "Indigenous peoples" hints that the museum was expected to serve as a reference for the temporal segregation between "ancient" and "modern" Mexicans. Material would be amassed from locations all across the nation, lending an expansive territorial and cultural vision to the "modern" version of ancient Mexico.

In addition to physical monuments, the museum would also house the "drawings and antiquities of Dupeé [Dupaix] yet to be published."[126] The preeminence that Alamán and others placed on Dupaix's archive attests to the fact that Mexico was committed to nationalizing all kinds of Crown property, not just Mexica sculpture or mapas. Remarkably, however, the monuments so celebrated in the 1790s hardly figured in the new museum's plan at all. In fact, Coatlicue would remain buried in the University's courtyard into the 1830s (although unearthed for Humboldt and Bullock), and the Sun Stone would stay cemented to the Cathedral until 1886. Their omission from the museum project signals that the unifying work of ancient Mexico in the 1820s was wholly distinct from the exceptionalizing work it had performed for turn-of-the-century americanos.[127]

Elite Mexicans like Alamán, who now considered items of Mexican antiquity—"statuary, paintings, hieroglyphs"—as vital to the prosperity of the young Republic, were increasingly concerned about the removal of archaeological objects from Mexico. Although the drain across the Atlantic had begun long before—at least with Cortés's first shipment to the Hapsburgs—the condition worsened without the patrol of Spain's navy. For years, Indigenous and non-Indigenous residents had sold notable items—clay figurines, for example, or stone carvings—to "idol men" who then hawked them to more upscale clientele. After the war, the clients were increasingly from overseas.[128] In emphasizing the citizenry's patriotic duty to protect Mexico's Indigenous heritage, Alamán's program also indicated a change in the way antiquities would be valued by the Republic: Indigenous materials were now a part of Mexico's patrimony, a valuable inheritance from its ancestors.[129] Drawing from what he had learned in Europe—especially France, where the concept of "patrimoine" had been consolidated under Napoleon—Alamán transformed items that had formerly been the property of the Crown into national treasure.[130] That nationalists placed so much importance on formerly Spanish-held Indigenous materials demonstrates the value of Indigenous pasts to the imaginative processes of nation building in the first years of the Mexican Republic. At the same time, it exposes the fact that another competing group of people—namely foreigners—also considered those Indigenous items valuable, although not in patrimonial terms.

Indeed, in the 1820s, foreign arrivals began to sense in ancient Mexico a more lucrative investment opportunity than those presented by the struggling markets of modern Mexico. Moreover, as Spanish subjects left the country during and after the war—some by force—many took their collections of antiquities with them.[131] First, in 1822, an illustrated English translation of Del Río's 1787 Palenque report was published in London, *Description of the ruins of an ancient city discovered near Palenque, in the Kingdom of Guatemala*.[132] The official report and original sketches—now thirty-five years old—had been spirited away from the Guatemalan archives during the war, stolen in reaction to what the publisher called "the jealousy entertained by that nation [Spain] with regard to their possessions in Mexico."[133] After learning of these events, an incensed group of citizens in Mexico City unsuccessfully demanded the manuscripts' return.[134] What is more, the following year it became clear that William Bullock had stolen the precious *Codex Boturini* and taken it to London. He only surrendered the document thanks to Alamán's intercession.[135] But when Dupaix's documents and antiquities were sold at auction in 1824—to a French buyer who had outbid the English competition—there was little Mexico's General Congress could do.[136] Ultimately, however, this export problem lent support to the museum's establishment.

In a country so divided and insolvent, the thefts and exports were more than just an insult to patriotic spirit: they endangered a key national resource—the past—and challenged the new nation's jurisdictional reach. Finally, in 1827 Congress passed a law explicitly prohibiting the exportation of "monumentos y antigüedades mexicanas," along with the export of three other national treasures: gold and silver specie and cochineal bugs.[137] Like Mexico's major natural resources, Mexico's nationalists considered monuments and antiquities strategic to the nation's patriotic strength and political development.

Unfortunately, however, the National Museum itself had few resources to seize, purchase, or relocate antiquities, especially before 1827.[138] As a solution, the museum's leaders encouraged private citizens to contribute their own collections and deposit any newly uncovered antiquities with government agents. Wealthy capitalinos opened their cabinets and extramuros hacendados ordered Indigenous workers to excavate and transport items to the federal capital. This directive not only concerned the nation's elite: in 1825, for example, Mexico City's "honest old plumber" Diego de la Rosa y Landa gave to the museum, among other items, a coiled feathered serpent figure carved of deep green stone.[139] The message both implicitly and explicitly was that all antiquities by right were property of the Republic, a reversal of the doctrine of private property that the same nationalists contemporaneously preached to Indigenous citizens in communal pueblos. The patriotic donation program worked so well that the director received enough donations in the spring of 1825 to make separate inventories for March, May, and July.[140]

With its growing collection, in 1825 the Museo Nacional—forerunner of today's Museo Nacional de Antropologiá e Historia in Chapultepec Park—was opened in a suite of rooms at the nationalized University.[141] There, the first director Ignacio Cubas—as historian Miruna Achim has summarized—sought to "bring together as many things as possible" as based on eighteenth-century Enlightenment protocols of knowledge-as-domination.[142] Some of the first items installed were from the defunct Academia de San Carlos, including four Mexica statues recovered in the 1790s from beneath a house of the Mayorazgo de la Mota (these had formerly been housed at the fine arts academy, where they had been seen and sketched by Dupaix in 1794).[143] Most of the other items came from the university or the former viceroyal secretariat. The new museum contained antiquities as well as documents, engravings and paintings, mineralogical and zoological specimens, mummies, and suits of armor.[144] The natural history cabinet at the College of Mines—which had consisted "principally of copper and stone adzes, spears, arrow-heads, &c." as well as much of Dupaix's antiquities—was also absorbed into the national collection.[145] To provide for acquisitions, the federal government sent collecting teams alongside military and diplomatic outfits, such as the 1828 Comisión de Limites expedition meant to set the border with the United States.[146] By 1828, Mexico's prime minister claimed that the museum contained "600 paintings and drawings on the history of indigenous peoples, 200 stone and 400 clay 'monuments,' 60 manuscripts, 42 paintings by Mexican artists, 200 kinds of shells and minerals, wood samples, maritime productions, and extraordinary bones."[147]

Although some criticized its eccentricity and seeming lack of order, there was a clear nationalist logic behind this diverse collection. Individual contributions from different states visually reinforced the Federalists' vision of a successful federal union, transcending geographical division.[148] Another large selection of objects came from as far away as the Isla de Sacrificios in the Gulf and in 1829 officials in Alta California dispatched "a feather-lined tunic . . . an 'exquisite' leather belt; the model of a canoe with rowers and huntsman, a harpoon handle, and an impermeable shirt of bear intestine. . . and a bow, strung with nerve fibers, and arrows, used by the Indians of California."[149] Combining minerals, shells, fish, and megafaunal bones with paintings, antiquities, and mapas, the National Museum exemplified a composite past for a sprawling country. This unified heterogeneity was useful in cohering "Mexico" as itself a distinct collection of objects, lands, and peoples. Although for years it would seem to visitors that the National Museum had no real order, in fact it was this *Mexicanizing* effect of its heterogeneous contents, not their arrangement, that was important.[150]

While the National Museum was presumed to comprise "antigüedades mexicanos," its actual holdings included items created by many peoples, over many times, from across many regions. Moreover, because most items were recovered from areas surrounding Mexico City, the antiquities were all largely assumed to be Mexica, whether or not that was truly the case. They were functionally, if not *ethnically*, Mexica in the minds of early nationalists. For example, the inventory of two house altars, two clay figurines, a coral amulet, and a carved-agate figure purchased from hacendado Martín Corchado, which were all noted as coming from Santiago Tlatelolco—a formerly Indigenous-only neighborhood of Mexico City and once host to the altepetl's large market—were likely of Toltec, Zapotec, and Tlatilco artisanry.[151] The effect is that all Indigenous-made objects were presented as belonging to the same "mexicano" people, a homogenizing transformation by which all antiquities became "Mexican."[152]

Despite the government's attempt to monopolize its antiquities, the anti-exportation laws were notoriously disrespected. Representative Carlos María de Bustamante was so concerned about the ongoing loss of antiquities that in 1829 he proposed and helped pass additional protective legislation.[153] Yet at times, the federal government facilitated international exchanges.[154] It is worth considering this antiquities traffic in the context of inter-imperial US-Mexico politics rather than—as it is usually conceived—a struggle between the US and Britain highlighted by the Monroe Doctrine. For President James Monroe did not just warn Europe off the Western hemisphere; his declaration to the emerging republics was that the US would be the hemispheric hegemon. Occasional US-Mexico diplomacy was even performed via antiquities: "in return for manuscripts and idols of little value," US Minister Joel R. Poinsett gave the National Museum "the attire of natives from New Mexico, an engraving of the American Declaration of Independence, and the portraits of six US presidents."[155] In 1825 Monroe had offered to purchase the disputed Sabine-Red River lands and when that offer was rejected, he sent the botanist-diplomat Poinsett back to Mexico City to negotiate a new border treaty.[156] While this exchange did not settle the border, it did cause some Mexicans to look more favorably on the neighboring settler nation for seemingly recognizing Mexico's cultural parity.[157]

Championing Private Property

Originally, the Mexican elite had "envisioned a republic composed of yeoman farmers cultivating small plots of land," and their debates over national and private property—in terms of real estate—were at the heart of discussions for "modernizing" Mexico.[158] Like their northern neighbor, Mexican elites imagined that their nation's progress "could only come from the 'individual interest' of a numerous class of proprietary farmers."[159] Centralist liberals—like Fray Servando Teresa de Mier, Carlos María de Bustamente, and Lorenzo de Zavala—pushed a "radical" republican solution that emphasized individual self-interest and centered on the importance of personal property. After spending the years 1829–1831 in exile in the United States, Zavala became particularly impressed by what he saw as the "grand majority of [US] inhabitants [being] landowners," and he thought the United States provided an apt model for how Mexico might grow to be its own regional power.[160]

The liberals saw the massive plantations (haciendas) and large Church holdings, as well as the pueblos, as obstacles to economic "progress." But to seize Church funds would require liquidating private collateral (in the form of property) and potentially destabilize an entire swath of mortgage-holding citizens, to which the more conservative representatives objected.[161] Liberals also maintained that the integration of Indigenous farmers into the central market—as producers and consumers—was necessary for an economically healthy new nation.[162] Others, like Alamán, believed the nation needed an independent banking system first. The push for civic equality meant the political specificity of Indigenous ethnicity—although not day-to-day racial discrimination—was erased with the goal of breaking up communal pueblos and encouraging a more self-interested, agrarian citizenry, a compromise that suited them all. But in order to create a united citizenry of farmers, Mexico first had to remove the farmers already there.[163]

To advance their agenda, Congress passed a series of land reform laws from 1826 to 1832 that focused on parceling out communal landholdings, a process called "desmortización" (confiscation).[164] These reforms gave the state the right to break up ejidos as well as to market "terrenos baldíos" (wastelands)—where Indigenous individuals often lived without colonially sanctioned title—to private landowners. For the right to continue working their milpas, Indigenous individuals—who eventually became known as "baldíos" themselves—owed rent or labor to the new owners.[165] In addition, in 1827 Congress passed an anti-vagrancy "Servitude Law," allowing for "vagrants"—i.e., adults "without steady employment"—to be pressed into labor contracts or conscripted into the military.[166] As a result, many Indigenous residents not only lost their lands but also found themselves in conditions of servitude either as baldíos or soldiers for an unforeseeable period of time.

Nationalists saw the more peripheral areas like the Yucatán, Chiapas, and the south (i.e., Oaxaca, Guerrero, parts of Veracruz, and southern Puebla state) as a challenge to their unifying project because those lands remained majority Indigenous. For years, the nation would attempt to change the demographics of all these areas, pulling them closer to the center and attempting to integrate their resources into the Mexican economy. In response, individual states enacted desmortización legislation as well: Veracruz state passed a confiscation law in 1826; Michoacán in 1827; Puebla in 1828.[167] These confiscated lands were then slated for grants to immigrants from Europe or the United States.[168] Nonetheless, Indigenous farmers in more isolated areas were better able to avoid state surveillance and therefore stay put, their presence not always registering with those who sold or bought their lands.

A second federal colonization law in 1828 was meant even more explicitly to entice European colonists to Mexico's "under-populated" territories. It made land grants of three hundred square leagues and defrayed starting costs under the condition that entrepreneurs establish vineyards, olive groves, silk farms, and other prescribed agrarian activities.[169] This was an attempt to combat the challenge to Mexican economic and ethnic power that the European mining colonies represented. The colonization policies of the first Republic all were aimed at increasing agricultural (as opposed to mining) output and integrating outlying areas of the country as well as "Mexicanizing" the citizenry.[170] Besides highlighting a contradictory immigration policy that desired emigrant settlers but suspected foreign interference—in a country that was already fighting its own battles against national disunity—the legislative emphasis on Mexicanization reveals another aim as well: immigration was not only meant for security, finances, or to increase the country's population, but to "whiten" it as well. Blanqueamiento—in terms of "mejorar la raza" (improving the race)—is often dated to the late nineteenth century in Mexico and is thought to underlie the twentieth-century celebration of mestizaje and cultural pluralism, but these policies have their precedent in this earlier moment.[171]

France took particular advantage of the new colonization laws, still looking to Mexico for investment—it was already Mexico's third most important trading partner—and as a "Latin" (i.e., Roman Catholic) sibling. A telling example is the case of the French Goazacalco Colony.[172] In 1828, two years after Veracruz passed its confiscation orders, the state awarded a large plot of land to the French lawyer Jean François Giordan and his associate, the politician Gabriel-Jacques Laisné de Villévêque.[173] The grant was on the Isthmus of Tehuantepec (near present-day Coatzacoalcos) where Simon Tadeo Ortíz de Ayala was already planning to establish a colony and inter-oceanic canal.[174] After receiving their grant, the two Parisians quickly founded the Society for the Goazacalco Colony and recruited an eager priest named Henri Baradère as a scout.[175] Giordan met with Baradère in Mexico City, where the two solidified their plans.

At the same time that he was scouting for Giordan, Baradère also managed to visit the site of Palenque from his base in Veracruz, and he collected a large number of antiquities. Knowing of the anti-export laws, Baradère approached Isidro Ignacio Icaza of the National Museum to arrange a trade: in exchange for permission to excavate and take away "anything worth presenting in a museum" and export half of whatever he collected from Palenque, Baradère would leave the other half with the National Museum.[176] While there he also purchased copies of the Castañeda drawings and arranged for Icaza to send him, in three months' time, copies of Dupaix's reports and itinerary from 1805–1807. Icaza was particularly protective of the latter and made Baradère swear not to share copies with just anyone. The General Congress was called to approve this arrangement, which it did in November 1828.[177] The following summer the Society for the Goazacalco Colony began soliciting colonists. Baradère wrote a prospectus filled with exaggerated claims and misinformation: "All the Indians near the concession [grant] are sweet, civilized, and farmers," he promised. "They will help the new colonists, even at low salaries."[178] His words doing their work, from November 1829 to June 1830 the society sent three ships from Le Havre, bringing a total of 328 French immigrants to "Goazacoalcos."[179] By 1831, however, the French colony had failed miserably and Baradère came under considerable scrutiny for his role in the scheme.[180] As Baradère's case demonstrates, foreign investment in Mexico was not limited to financial and colonization ventures but instead frequently overlapped or amplified interest in the Mexican past.

Dislocating Indigenous Identity

To complement the explicitly anti-Indigenous property legislation of the late 1820s, the new National Museum deployed multiple methods prioritizing Indigenous assimilation and annihilation. For one, its catalog made a clear point of separating ancient Mexicans from contemporary indios. Using words from

Dupaix, one page reminds the viewer of "the knowledge and perfection that the Mexicans had achieved in geometry, architecture, and sculpture," and contrasts this with "the rough simplicity that characterizes the miserable huts of mild and uneducated peoples" ("los pueblos salvajes é incultos") in current-day Mexico.[181] Indeed, the only people whose objects and histories were selected for inclusion in the catalog were the noble, intelligent "antiguo pueblo mexicano," whose beginnings trace back to "the old continent." For example, the catalog identifies a large "Clay Vessel" as a "doubtless Etruscan" piece that proves "the logical idea put forth by a distinguished savant who derives for the ancient Mexicans a Carthaginian origin."[182] Similarly, the catalog's title page models a "civilized" Mediterranean-American past through its imagery depicting a Mexican eagle grasping a cactus and perching upon an easel draped with a garland of grapes set atop a pedestal decorated with leonine and human heads. The unusual composition blends neoclassical and Indigenous aesthetics that are the publication's hallmark: the eagle and cactus pay homage to the flag of the First Republic while the swag recalls Hellenistic and Roman statuary; the pedestal is a nod to the Phoenician sphinx. The imagery provides an interpretive framework that dislocated current Indigenous peoples from their own pasts by moving those pasts into the realm of European myth.

In addition, the museum also dislocated Indigenous communities from their particularized place-identity (altepetl, tlaxilacalli, pueblo, ejido, etc.), which nationalists saw as competing with national allegiance, through its collecting program.[183] Among the museum's "200 stone and 400 clay 'monuments'" were those identified in the catalog as "gods called [Dii] Penates by the Romans," a definition marking them as a "special protector of the family."[184] These votive objects or god images—usually labeled "idols"—had responsibilities to a community (like an altepetl) and community members owed reciprocal responsibilities to their patron god-image (e.g., performing ceremony). Within Nahua philosophy, figural "objects" like god images or other patron deities are not representations but instead are inhabited by the real presence and power of the deity.[185] As such, the god images provide not only protection but also cosmic, ethnic, and socio-spatial identity.[186] Excavating, collecting, and displaying those "idols," however, alters spatiotemporal as well as interpersonal coordinates and as a result also alters the relationship of people, place, and power. That is, when the "idol" leaves the community the power it enjoyed in relation to its people and the community's sense of order goes with it.[187] Their removal (intentionally or not) therefore decenters the Indigenous communities they anchor. In this sense, removing votive objects from the locations in which they were imbued with power was also a means of removing Indigenous identities from those communities.

An American Babylon in the Mexican Republic

FIGURE 19. Title page, *Colección de las antigüedades mexicanos* (1827). Courtesy of the Newberry Library. Designed by Waldeck.

There is some indication that the curators understood a certain sense of the ritual power conducted by some of the objects in their care, if not the consequences of their collection. Indeed, the fact that the National Museum possessed hundreds of examples of votive figurines and family altars described as "household gods" meant that the curators at least understood them to be the loci of Indigenous cultural memory and community cohesion.[188] Moreover, the catalog's evocation of Rome signals that any belief in the "power" of the "idols" should best be left in the "pagan" past, sounding distinct echoes of the early colonial period. As sixteenth-century Spanish missionaries had believed that removing "idols" would destroy the "idolatry" that kept Indigenous peoples from becoming Christians, the National Museum's consolidation of "idols" and their recoding as national property similarly targeted Indigenous particularity for destruction.[189] The very accumulation of these "idols" in the national collection is a pointed method of Indigenous dislocation.[190]

These cosmic removals are akin to what anthropologist Patrick Wolfe termed the "elimination of the Native," or what social scientist Eva Sanz Jara and historian Inmaculada Simón Ruiz have termed "la negación de lo indio" (the disavowal/negation of the Indian).[191] While elimination or rejection can be effected by overt genocidal acts, it is also accomplished through the transformation of Indigenous places and peoples—politically and cosmically—into national ones. Thus, the museum's collection and preservation of social objects like god-images was an explicit destruction of Indigenous social structures as well as a depopulation of Indigenous places. In effect, the processes of collecting—collecting for public consumption, not just as private scholarly resources—transformed ordinary and sacred items of Indigenous life into mere historic objects. These processes—and the resultant collections—were instruments of cosmic and social, if not physical, displacement, deterritorialization, and thereby de-Indigenization.

Writing Alphabets and Reading Glyphs

At the same time that the National Museum was consolidating a Mexica identity through its Indigenous collection, two similar but distinct processes of objectification and dislocation were taking place: the first was the catalog, which would allow Mexicans to learn by sight. Whereas previously only a select few had be able to access the materials now in the national collection, a catalog would figuratively open it to everyone who could read or—if the illustrations were good enough—see the images.[192] The second was a project aimed to place "Mexican history" directly in the hands of literate Mexican citizens: publishing the colonial-era manuscripts that had long been held in the viceregal offices. This democratizing move would demonstrate that Mexica history was not intrinsically mysterious but only that it had been deliberately hidden from the people for political gain during the colonial period. Initially, Minister Alamán and Oaxaca's Representative Bustamante assumed the job of locating and republishing the colonial-era texts. Eventually Bustamante, who had been conducting research into the Mexica past for at least a decade, worked on it alone.[193] Thanks to him, Mexico's history would be alphabetic, that is to say, written in Spanish and alphabetized Nahuatl script.

Bustamante's publication project was squarely rooted in the criollo archive.[194] The first volume he produced was criollo antiquary Mariano Fernández de Echeverría y Veytia's unpublished *Tezcoco en los últimos tiempos de sus antiguos reyes* (1826), which he compiled from Fernando de Alva Cortés Ixtlilxóchitl's materials in the 1770s. This was followed shortly by the seventeenth-century

Franciscan Manuel de la Vega's *Historia del descubrimiento de la América Septentrional por Cristobal Colón* (1826), with notes by his contemporary Chimalpahin Quauhtlehuanitzin, as well as Francisco López de Gómara's *Historia de las conquistas de Hernando Cortés*, rewritten by Chimalpahin.[195] In 1829, Bustamante published Ixtlilxóchitl's seventeenth-century memoir, *Horribles crueldades de los conquistadores de México*.[196] After that, he brought forth three volumes of Bernardino de Sahagún's *Historia general de las cosas de Nueva España* (1829–1830 and 1831), another multiauthor, seventeenth-century, criollo-Nahua text.[197] With these self-consciously Nahua *and* criollo texts, Bustamante's project anchored an identifiably Euro-American-Indigenous—Mexican—historical canon.[198]

Bustamante was particularly interested in training a generation of young Mexican men who would grow into their adulthood as Mexican citizens rather than colonial subjects. To do so, however, posed the question of whose histories were prioritized in Mexico's initial creation of its past. Because the alphabetic histories of the sixteenth and later centuries were almost exclusively made by conquistadors, clerics, or Nahua elite, the selection of materials from which Bustamante drew inevitably emphasized Nahua-and "Azteca"-centric accounts, and these are the ones that Bustamante deemed most important for the new generation of Mexicans to access. His publishing program thus exposed the bifurcation of indigeneity in Mexican nationalist discourse: overexposure of "ancient Mexicans" but erasure of other Indigenous peoples living in the "new" Mexico.[199] This bifurcation also reveals how different approaches to the past can be more or less advantageous to the expression of imperial—including settler-colonial—power.

In the 1820s, Mexica history served to define a successfully unified *nación* comprised of disparate inhabitants. But as portended by the Mediterranean-American past projected by the National Museum's catalog, the Republic's growing fracture lines called for an alteration to Anáhuacan exclusivism and demanded instead a Mexican inclusivism that not only grouped various Indigenous histories under the "Mexican" umbrella but also rooted Mexico itself in traditional universalist history as signified by Classical antiquity. For a nation in disunity, an implied connection with the biblical world was a useful device for consolidating *and* whitening Mexico's past.

Foreigners and Mexican nationalists were not the only ones to call upon versions of the Indigenous past for help. In 1825, for example, renewed anti-occupation efforts in Sonora and Sinaloa were forwarded by the Yaqui leader Juan Bandaras, who carried a standard featuring the Virgin of Guadalupe and Motecuhzoma, attracting other Indigenous groups to his cause.[200] The military officer and later president Vicente Guerrero—who claimed descent from

Texcoco nobility—also evoked Motecuhzoma in his quest for equality and land reform.²⁰¹ Some historians have suggested that these Indigenous and populist uprisings were reasons why nationalists began to abandon their previous admiration for Mexican antiquity, especially after Guerrero's rise in 1828.²⁰² Yet Tlaxcala's persistent autonomy, the Chumash Revolt in 1824, ongoing negotiations and violence with Comanche and Apache communities in the north, and Indigenous resistance in Chiapas, Tabasco, and the Yucatán also contributed to a growing sense among the elite that traditional representations of indigeneity and Mexicanness did not mix. Certainly the 1825–1832 resistance campaigns in the north led by Bandaras as well as the presidency of Guerrero—from 1829 until his execution in 1831—contributed to the sense that appeals to a strictly Mexica past were less useful for national cohesion than they had been previously.

Revealing the Hieroglyphic Past

In 1827, the two curators of the National Museum, Icaza and Gondra, approached artist and engineer Jean-Frédéric Waldeck to make the lithographs for their catalog. Having struggled to find support for their project, the curators hoped that Waldeck's fame would help attract subscribers. Waldeck had been the in-house illustrator for the London bookseller who commissioned the English edition of Del Río's 1787 Palenque report in 1822. When copies of the report and Almendáriz's original sketches arrived in London, Waldeck drew the line lithographs for the volume.²⁰³ The translated and illustrated *Description* was the talk of the town; Waldeck received so much attention that a Mexico City advertisement later announced him as "Waldeck, whose talent we well know."²⁰⁴ Although Waldeck would not reach Palenque in person until 1832, later in life he admitted that ever since 1822 he had aimed at "nourish[ing] the secret desire to see them [Palenque's structures] for myself," and soon after the 1822 publication was finished he made his way to Mexico.²⁰⁵

When Waldeck was hired, José Luciano Castañeda was technically still the museum's illustrator. Castañeda had traveled with Dupaix on the Royal Antiquities Expedition two decades beforehand, and when Dupaix died in 1817 he left his papers to his longtime collaborator.²⁰⁶ Castañeda kept most of the sketches, manuscripts, and objects until 1824, when he sold them at auction, although he did retain a few copies. At least one set was sold abroad while the museum kept another, which it had hoped to publish (but never did).²⁰⁷ Along with the earlier loss of the Del Río materials and the stream of foreigners now visiting Palenque, hiring Waldeck was one of the few ways the museum could secure its own claim to the Chiapas site.

The National Museum's catalog had been planned as a serial imprint, and initially Waldeck was responsible for drawing copies of two Mexica mapas to be included in each number, as well as producing "historical paintings" and portraying the museum objects.[208] Eventually, however, he became responsible for most of the publication's content, including its interpretive essays. Surprisingly, he was never tasked with reproducing any of the Palenque imagery that had made him famous. Despite this, Waldeck still brought a version of the "hieroglyphic" history he had first seen in London to viewers in Mexico City. Indeed, the catalog's title page makes this clear: for when compared against the prior Castañeda and Almendáriz illustrations, Waldeck's unusual leonine and human heads as well as the sphinxlike pedestal are revealed to be stylized renderings of a sculptured panel from Palenque that he had drawn five years earlier. Palenque made it into the catalog after all.

Indeed, Palenque's shadowy presence insinuates a glyphic past that unites the peoples of the Mexican Republic within a historical narrative that combined the worlds of Mediterranean, Mexica, and Maya antiquity between one paper cover. Many of the items Waldeck depicted—such as the carved lizard found "on the wall of an old home near the *Camino Real de México*"—were objects that, by the time the stones for the first number were inked, had already been lost to collectors abroad.[209] Waldeck's lithographs, however, based on memory and previous publications, made the statement that these objects—while now hidden from the public—were nonetheless still important national property. The images emphasized the cypher-like quality of Mexico's Indigenous past by creating images that were both familiar and inaccessible.

Foreigners tended to be interested in Mexico's "mystified" Maya past because they believed the ruined structures at Palenque and its "hieroglyphs" represented a cognate to European Classical heritage. Although scholars in New Spain, Mexico, and the United States had been drawing connections between Mexico and Egypt for hundreds of years, the specific context of post-Napoleonic Egyptiana tended to place more of an emphasis on the graphic similarities of Mayan to Egyptian "hieroglyphic writing," especially after Champollion's Rosetta Stone breakthrough in 1822.[210] As a testament to this event's significance, the following year the Parisian committee awarding the Prix Volney—a legacy left by the comte—was focused on the study of "hieroglyphic" languages.[211] Alongside Champollion, much credit for the renewed Mexico-Egypt connection in the 1820s goes to William Bullock, whose "ancient Mexico" exhibit in London (at which he displayed his ill-gotten lithograph of the *Codex Boturini*) was held, appropriately, in Piccadilly's Egyptian Hall.[212] Whereas in the earlier colonial period "Aztec writing" had been considered "hieroglyphic," by the nineteenth century Nahuatl had been written in alphabetic (Latin) letters for over three centuries, and it was "Maya writing"—usually (but not always) in the form of stone inscriptions—that were considered to be mysterious because they were seemingly unreadable. This transformation of inscribed Mayan script and sculptured histories into "hieroglyphs" was predominantly performed by scholars in the United States and Europe.[213]

In Mexico City the National Museum's catalog—*Colección de las antigüedades mexicanos* (1827)—debuted the hieroglyph, visually and verbally, as something that could be useful for developing a Mexican past.[214] Like much of its contents, however, the "hieroglyphic" aspect of "ancient Mexico" that circulated throughout the Atlantic scholarly sphere in the late 1820s and 1830s was largely produced at the hands of non-Mexicans who were introduced to the subject by way of Palenque. Indeed, Waldeck's own "glyphic" contributions helped cultivate an enigmatic, spectacular version of Mexican history that would come to dominate representations of Mexico in the middle of the century.[215]

Identifying Palenque from the outside in

In 1826, Paris's elite Société de la Géographie announced a grand prize for "the most complete and exact description yet possessed of the ruins of the ancient city of Palenque," to be submitted before January 1, 1830.[216] At almost the same time—and after Waldeck was already in Mexico City—the new owner of the Dupaix collection, who was a French antiquary from New Orleans named François Latour-Allard, submitted descriptions and images of the over one hundred eighty Mexican objects and one hundred twenty drawings to Parisian and London periodicals as part of a marketing campaign.[217] The already extensive attention abroad, the Geographic Society prize, and now this exposure promised increasing competition for Mexico's national property.[218] Indeed, it was not long before Palenque called to the foreigners already living in Mexico. When Waldeck saw the announcement for the Palenque prize in a July 1827 issue of *El Aguila Mexicana*, he was likely the person with the best knowledge of Palenque outside of Chiapas.[219] But that did not stop Francisco Corroy in Tabasco, who also had his eyes on the award. And in Mexico City, Henri Baradère, a priest from the southwest of France, also began to dream of claiming the prize as well.[220]

FIGURE 20. Ricardo Almendariz, *Colección de estampas copiadas de las figuras originales* (1787), pl. 23. Courtesy of the Kislack Collection, Library of Congress. Waldeck drew the 1822 Del Rio illustrations from these images.

After learning of the sale and export of the Dupaix materials to France, Poinsett assured Stephen Duponceau—secretary of the American Philosophical Society (APS)—that he would "endeavor to obtain some drawings and some account of the Ruins of Palenque in the province of Chiapas" for the society.[221] That same year, 1827, Constantine Rafinesque—the prolific scholar and nemesis of Caleb Atwater—sent an open letter to Philadelphia's *Saturday Evening Post* concerning so-called Mexican hieroglyphs. Over the next six years, Rafinesque continued to send letters about Mayan script to the *Post*, thereby bringing even more attention to the subject of Maya glyphs to readers in the United States. Meanwhile Duponceau—a French-born US citizen—submitted a winning response for the Volney Prize in 1828 based on samples of "Mexican" writing that had first appeared in Humboldt's 1810 *Vues* and again in the 1822 Del Río: that is to say, Mexican writing that was actually Mayan iconic script.[222] In 1829 the Baltimore antiquary James Haines M'Culloh reprinted the Del Río hieroglyphs in his *Researches, Philosophical and Antiquarian, Concerning the Aboriginal*

History of America and identified them as "Guatemalan" (when Del Río's report was made in the 1780s, Palenque was indeed located within the Kingdom of Guatemala).[223] He also wrote that the "civilization of the Guatemalans could be fairly derived from the Toltecas alone." In 1830, with no little delight, Duponceau accepted from Poinsett a donation of a large number of Dupaix's notes, which Poinsett seems to have procured from the National Museum.[224] These papers included a detailed tracing of a "cross" from one of Palenque's "temples."

In 1831, the Hispano-Irish military officer John "Juan" Galindo—then living in Guatemala and serving as governor of Péten—sent an account of his Palenque "discovery" to the *Literary Gazette* in London, only one year before Waldeck would move into the same ruins.[225] Also at that time in London the Castañeda illustrations made their publishing debut in volume four of Lord Kingsborough's luxe series *Antiquities of Mexico: comprising fac-similes of ancient Mexican paintings and hieroglyphics...* (1830–1848), although its extreme expense meant few could afford to see them.[226] In Philadelphia, Rafinesque printed a selection of glyphs from the APS materials in his self-published *Atlantic Journal and Friend of Knowledge* (1832–1833) on a chart comparing African or "Lybian" and American or "Otolum" (Palenque) languages in 1832.[227]

Attempts to understand Palenqeño writings and identity were long running: Humboldt himself had called the Palenque inscriptions "Mexican" although he later corrected himself; he had also noted that the ruins there "prove[d] the predilection of the peoples of the Toltec and the Aztec race for architectural detail."[228] These words reveal a subtle, but important difference in Mexican and non-Mexican (neither one Indigenous) figurations of the ancient past.

Non-Mexicans like Humboldt only began to understand that there *was* a difference between Mexica and Maya (or Mexica and any other group) people in the nineteenth century. A crucial figure in this differentiation was the "Toltec." For centuries, rumors that Christian apostles had visited the Americas and met (or became) Toltecs was part of the attraction of the mythology: because conquistadors supposedly witnessed "crosses" in the Yucatán, this was assumed to be evidence that a "lost" population there had accepted apostolic evangelization.[229] Poinsett's gift of the Palenque "Table Cross" sketch, therefore, went a long way toward advancing the theory of Palenque's connections to the Old World. The Philadelphia craniologist Samuel G. Morton even identified the circulating Palenque imagery as "Toltecan sculpture."[230]

Evocations of Toltecas, in this context, recall the Domincans' hypotheses based on misread K'iche' genealogies but also provide a separately racialized set of ancestors for Mayas (Toltecs) and Mexicans (Aztecs).[231] Thus when Humboldt

FIGURE 21. "Table Cross." Courtesy of the American Philosophical Society. Likely by Castañeda but resembles Waldeck's 1822 lithograph.

wrote of the "peoples of the Toltec and the Aztec race," he was expressing a racialized difference that was more important to scholars in the United States and Europe than to those in Mexico. By the 1830s, Toltecs—thanks to Palenque—had come to be associated with the Moundbuilders in the United States. In fact, in 1839 Morton even used skull measurements to "prove" that Moundbuilders were members of the "Toltecan Family" rather than the "American Family," which was comprised of the continent's "Barbarous Nations."[232]

Nationalist Mexicans, who were so well steeped in Nahua histories—especially those narratives of origin and migration—knew that Toltecs were avowedly Mexica ancestors but not necessarily Maya ones.[233] Although few concretely understood the capacious way in which Toltecas related (and continued to relate) to Nahuatl-and Mayan-speaking peoples—both ancestrally and historically—Mexican nationalists at least understood that there *was* a difference between "Toltecs" and "Mayas," whereas foreigners—who tended to treat Toltecs as purely historical subjects—readily confused the two.[234] When Bustamante reissued León y Gama's *Descripción histórica y cronológica de las dos piedras* in 1832—including the unpublished second volume from 1794 (along with previously unseen watercolors by criollo Francisco Agüera)—this reframing of

Mexica "hieroglyphic" inscriptions rerouted the nationalist Mexican gaze from Palenque and back to Nahua ancestors: that is, back to the country's mixed and multilayered—but *Mexican*—pasts.

Consolidating Glyphic Pasts

In July of 1834, after he finished the first eight numbers of his folio album *Antiquités mexicaines*, Baradère sent a complimentary set to Mexico's federal Congress.[235] Baradère's gift, in fact, was the fulfillment of an agreement made with Congress six years before.[236] Writing from his sylvan retreat in Tacubaya outside the capital in December 1834, President Antonio López de Santa Anna thanked him and expressed his approval of Baradère's centralized vision of a ruins-strewn "country of Anáhuac." Santa Anna was evidently so pleased that he pledged an extravagant order of ten copies—which would have totaled 32,000 francs—for Mexico's new National Library.[237] He praised the sumptuously-colored "monuments that come to life" and proclaimed them "worthy of marching alongside the pyramids of Egypt."[238] *Antiquités mexicaines*, he explained, would "testify to the world" the greatness of the "ancient civilization of the country of Anáhuac" by "rais[ing] the veil" that had long covered a past "glorious to the Mexican nation."[239] With Dupaix's reports translated into Spanish and copies of Castañeda's sketches—borrowed from the National Museum—*Antiquités mexicaines* was a joint Mexican and French venture that would also prove useful to Mexico's nationalists in their campaign of whitening and Mexicanization at home.[240] Santa Anna's invocation of a refigured Anáhuac included all residents living under Mexico's banner, including Indigenous groups and heterogeneous white, mestizo, African, and immigrant populations. Projecting Mexican hegemony in the face of competing claims for lands and sovereignty, the Anáhuac of *Antiquités mexicaines* located the Republic in an enduring conception of "ancient Mexican peoples."

Santa Anna's Anáhuacan boosterism casually places Maya history inside Mexican space. Indeed, despite its title, Baradère's *Antiquités mexicaines* is mainly focused on sites associated with ancient Maya rather than Mexica peoples: the two highlighted locations are Palenque and Mitla, sites located, respectively, in the southeastern states of Chiapas and Oaxaca. Neither was built, or majority inhabited, by Nahua ancestors. A map that outlines the three itineraries of Dupaix's antiquarian expeditions gives a hint of this focus. Outlined in green, blue, and red, the itineraries all start in Mexico City and crawl eastward, visualizing the federal district's centripetal pull.[241] Baradère's map makes Mexico's territorial and historical project clear: that is, to indexically consolidate all of the territory as nationally—if not ethnically—Mexican. Depicting a nation arching from Michoacán and Guanajuato across Veracruz and Oaxaca to meet Chiapas, Tabasco, and Yucatán and ending at the Sea of the Antilles on the far right, the cropped map is undoubtedly oriented toward the Atlantic. Watery gulfs above and below emphasize the slender Tehuantepec Isthmus, cracked halfway by the Coatzacoalcos River—its route the shortest overland passage from the Atlantic to the Pacific—to revive Europeans' centuries-long dream of circumnavigation. By centering Tehuantepec, the majority Maya state of Chiapas and the largely Mixtec and Zapotec state of Oaxaca are drawn into the Mexican national space. The volume's popularization of "Maya" pasts as "Mexican" ones thus facilitates a visual Mexican occupation of all Indigenous lands within Mexico's claimed boundaries. The descriptor "mexicain," therefore, refers to the Mexican patria—and implied whitened patrimony—rather than to specific Nahua, Maya, Zapotec (Ben' Zaa), or Ñuudzahui (Mixtec) pasts.

In 1834, Santa Anna's government suspended the 1824 Constitution and replaced it with a set of laws centralizing power in Mexico City. The next year, Santa Anna's administration began increasing federal military forces in "rebellious" states—such as Zacatecas, Oaxaca, and Coahuila y Tejas—that protested his centralizing changes. Areas that resisted were punished: the state of Aguascalientes, for example, was split off from Zacatecas in 1836 in reprisal for resistance battles there the year before. Tejas, Tabasco, and Yucatán would eventually declare their independence from Mexico altogether, as would Nuevo León, Tamaulipas, Coahuila, and Tabasco. In the shadow of the Texas War (1835–1836) and other conflicts in the north, elites' unexpected privileging of a "glyphic" representation of Mexican history became a new way of asserting an essential, centralized "Mexicanness."[242]

In the 1830s, a hybrid Mexica/Toltec/Mediterranean "glyphic" history became useful to the strengthening central state. This was especially true as the associations with both Maya and Mexica peoples shifted away from the former tendency to contrast Mexica peoples as urbane yet superannuated nobles versus mystical and elusive Maya rustics and toward one in which Mexica (or Nahua) peoples were seen as more aggressive, whereas Mayas, with their "lost cities," were more sophisticated and pacific.[243] But after the violence in the Yucatán turned into what was perceived as a "race war" of Mayas against white Yucatecos in 1847—the Caste War—nationalists in Mexico City again turned away from the glyphs of Maya Lands and returned to the histories of Aztlán.[244]

IN 2018, THE volunteer advocacy group *The Decolonial Atlas* circulated a post on its Facebook page with the following caption: "The great cities of Maya civilization were 'discovered' under dense jungle. They were given names like Copán and Palenque. But their original names were never lost. #RenameReclaimDecolonize."[245] The post featured a list of forty-four glyphic place names with alphabetic translations, explaining: "All of the words written in the [L]atin alphabet are indeed from 'discoverer's' languages. The original names are the Maya Emblem Glyphs." Although the accuracy of some of the pictured glyphs and alphabetic names came under scrutiny, the larger point—about considering glyphic writing as language and not something that needed to be "discovered," deciphered, or translated to have meaning—stood.[246] The "great cities of Maya civilization" existed long before they were assigned alphabetic names or three-dimensional renderings, before it was discovered that they were "lost."

A half century before this post, Mexican historian Juan A. Ortega y Medina argued that US interest in the "lost" Maya past was an extension of what he called "Monroísmo arqueológico," that is, US hemispheric aggression.[247] The Old World-New World debate resurrected by Waldeck, Baradère, Stephens, and others was a sign of this cultural-territorial struggle between European diffusionists and American "autochthonists."[248] Yet the imperial power struggles of "Monroism" have tended to obscure the ways in which Mexican nationalists also deployed the forces of empire within their own settler state. Moreover, the so-called autochthonists were never as singularly opposed to European diffusionism as it may appear; this is not to say that Mexican nationalists consented to the imperialist attempts against Mexican sovereignty, but rather to propose that they used multiple approaches to guarantee their *own* aboriginality, and with it, the success of the Mexican settler nation. In addition, Mexican theories about Indigenous origins recirculating in Bustamante's books, about the disconnection of Comanches and Apaches from "Mexican Indians" and about "idolatrous," "lost," or violent Mayas assisted in the cultural justification for the United States' annexation of Texas but rejection of the Yucatán.[249] This is not to blame Mexico for US aggression or racism: instead, it is to point out a continuity of settler-colonial techniques deployed in both places but with different, yet interconnected, histories.

EPILOGUE

After American History

And our struggle is a beautiful, righteous struggle that is our collective gift to Indigenous worlds, because this way of living necessarily continually gives birth to ancient Indigenous *futures in the present.*

—Leanne Betasamosake Simpson, 2017

For Native Americans, there can be no better remedy for the theft of land than land.

—David Truer, 2021

IN THE YEARS BEFORE the US war with Mexico (1846–1848), the circulation of "Aztec" pasts in the US reinforced a view of Mexico as "Indian Country" open for conquest.[1] "It is matter of congratulation," craniologist Samuel G. Morton wrote in 1839, "that the time is rapidly approaching when the Anglo Saxon race will control the destinies of Mexico, and throw open her buried monuments to the scrutiny of art and science."[2] Indeed, the US increasingly claimed Mexico's monuments, territory, and history, although not its peoples. Aztlán reappeared in a 1843 Philadelphia edition of Southey's poems and in William H. Prescott's monumental *History of the Conquest of Mexico* (1843). Mexican travelogues dominated US bookshelves: first John Lloyd Stephens's wildly successful pair of *Incidents* (1841; 1843), then B. A. Norman's *Rambles in Yucatán* (1842), followed by Brantz Meyer's *Mexico as It Was and as It Is* (1844). Mexico's scholars, so frustrated by Prescott's interpretation of "their" history—which was nonetheless popular even in English—produced multiple "corrected" translations in 1844–1846.[3] After the Battle of Chapultepec in 1847, the commanding general of the US Army General Winfield Scott and some US Marines carried copies of the Prescott version into the "Halls of the Montezumas." Wartime reporting and veterans' accounts continued the US focus on Mexico's

Indigenous past.[4] And ultimately the prospect of an indefinite occupation was rejected along lines largely pointing to indigeneity: US Senator John C. Calhoun famously protested that "more than half of the Mexicans are Indians, and the other [half] is composed chiefly of mixed tribes," swearing that his country "never dreamt of incorporating into our Union any but the Caucasian race—the free white race."[5] For precedent, the slaveholding senator cited the previous wars, forced removals, and expulsionist reservation policy.[6] To end the war, the US seized millions of acres of Indigenous homelands, including those long sought as locations for Aztlán. As with so many of the confrontations between settlers and Natives over the previous centuries, the peace between the US and Mexico hinged on territory.

Part of the 1848 cession includes the region currently referred to as the "Four Corners." There, on lands sacred to Ute, Diné (Navajo), Ndé (Apache), and Pueblo peoples, a majestic promontory rises out of the surrounding green valley. Carved from the high plateau by the nearby river eons ago, the eighty-four-hundred-foot escarpment towers over miles of canyon and bottomlands. The sky-high mesas and sandstone cliffs shelter remnants of homes built and lives lived roughly a millennium ago. Today, many Indigenous groups in the region count the People Who Lived Up High among their ancestors. Whereas Hopi people call the strikingly beautiful area Towtoyka—the Place of the Songs—on US maps part of Towtoyka is called Mesa Verde National Park.[7] The park is near the sleepy city of Cortez, within the Colorado county of Montezuma. Not far away, Aztec Ruins National Monument in New Mexico gives a good sense of how well the nineteenth-century US settlers listened to Hopi and other Puebloan peoples when they arrived to occupy the former space of "Old Mexico." These settlers' ideas of the past also misappropriated Indigenous traditions and produced nationalist myths that helped secure the mesas, canyons, and trails that now bear their names.

After 1848, fantasies of Aztec originality in the new West ran on a parallel track to Moundbuilder intrigue in the East; at points, such as in the 1864 novel *Centeola: Maid of the Mounds* or the work of Western photographer William Henry Jackson, they converged.[8] But US settlers' historical imaginations increasingly focused on southwestern sites as the years passed. So remarkable were they, wrote one author in the December 1878 issue of *Scribner's*, that the "mysterious mound-builders fade into comparative insignificance before the grander and more ancient cliff-dwellers, whose castles lift their towers amid the sands of Arizona and crown the terraced slopes of the Rio Mancos..."[9] In the 1880s, a family of ranchers began excavating the adobe, stone, and wooden structures of Mesa Verde, exporting pottery and mummified ancestors to museums and exhibits out East, bringing the region even more attention.[10] As it had been for their Moundbuilder counterparts, the real thrill of the vanished "Cliff Dwellers" was as a newly revealed "prehistoric race"—"whose crumbling habitations are their only headstones"—and in the combination of disappearance and "progress."[11] In the halls of Washington D.C., concern that looters and vandals were destroying sites of national significance provoked the Congressional action that eventually led to the 1906 American Antiquities Act.[12]

Within the Act's first two years, President Theodore Roosevelt had designated almost two million acres of "public land" as National Monuments, all of which was located in the western states of California, Arizona, New Mexico, Utah, Montana, Wyoming, and South Dakota.[13] He was able to do so because the legislation transferred the plenary power of Congress over "public lands" to the Executive in the interest of preserving "historic landmarks, historic and prehistoric structures, and other objects of historic or scientific interest that are situated upon the lands owned or controlled by the Federal Government."[14] Among the first National Monuments were New Mexico's stunning butte "El Morro"—where Juan de Oñate scribbled over the rock's inscriptions in 1605— and "Montezuma Castle," located in the Hopi and Yavapai ancestral lands of central Arizona (Mesa Verde, oddly, fell under separate National Parks legislation, which extended federal authority over all archaeological sites in the area including those on the nearby Ute Mountain Ute Reservation).[15] Unlike the similar Ley sobre Monumentos Arqueológicos passed in Mexico in 1897—which explicitly protected antiquities everywhere in Mexico and prohibited any excavations without the express permission of the Executive—the US law only protected sites of "prehistoric," "historic," or "scientific" import that were located on US public lands.[16] Of course, what merited protection depended considerably on the foundation for thinking about the past set by the antiquities searches of the previous centuries.

The "vanishing" mythology that contributed to the 1906 statute—and shaped the "Turn and Learn" story at Aztalan—remains powerful at Mesa Verde today. In the summer of 2021, tomes at the park's bookstore proclaimed the so-called Anasazi a "vanished civilization" and evoked the area's "unsolved mystery."[17] As so many times before, this narrative does not match local Indigenous knowledge that teaches "the people who live among but not with us"—called Anaa'sází by Diné, Mokwic by Ute and Paiute, and Hisatsinom by Hopi peoples—still inhabit their homelands.[18] When TJ Atsye—a Laguna Pueblo woman and former Park Ranger—visits Mesa Verde, for example, she experiences the continuity: it "still feel[s] like home when you walk into a dwelling... even on top of the Mesa, you're walking on sacred ground." Like Atsye, Puebloan and other descendant peoples periodically "return home" to the powerful mesas and cliffs to become re-energized and centered.[19] Yet as on so many sacred Indigenous landscapes, returning home still means visiting on settler terms.[20]

When the forty-fifth US president reduced the size of various national parks and monuments dedicated by his predecessor—chief among these Bears Ears in southeastern Utah—the outdoor apparel company Patagonia and conservationist association Sierra Club responded in outrage, launching a campaign with the name "The President Stole Your Land."[21] Yet this indignation over a misuse of "public lands" was embarrassingly disconnected from any curiosity as to why those lands are "public" in the first place, or from Indigenous reclamation movements such as LandBack.[22] Not only about mineral exploitation, the rescission was also about Indigenous disempowerment and dispossession, although unnoted by the conservationists. Even though the lands had been seized by the US long ago, the reversal in status revoked the shared administrative power of the Bears Ears Commission and its tribal members. Without a call for the restoration of Indigenous oversight or stewardship, the well-intentioned campaign was revealed to be, at heart, only meant to protect and restore—to settlers—Indigenous lands where "public" access to "historic landmarks, historic and prehistoric structures, and other objects of historic or scientific interest" were at stake.

Before the 2016 US presidential election, the protests at Standing Rock, the COVID-19 pandemic, and the 2020 murder of George Floyd, the epilogue to this book might have scrutinized the Antiquities Act and its legacy more closely. Or it might have discussed how, in 1857, the Smithsonian Institution finally decided to support a national museum, admitting that one "appears to be a necessary establishment at the seat of government of every civilized nation" (unlike the "civilized" United States, Mexico had already founded its National Museum in 1825).[23] The new national museum in Washington, DC, had many predecessors, including the Indian Office's collection of portraits made at treaty councils—which allowed visitors to "indulge in reflections on these scenes which are past"—and the National Gallery at the Patent Office, established in 1841 by Secretary of War Poinsett and his associates.[24] Its first donations included a tarantula from Texas, a "Piece of an Indian's coffin, from the big Mound, near St. Louis," and "Three boxes, containing fragments of ruined temples from Central America," physically bringing natural history, expansionism, Indigenous graves, and lost cities together in a location expressly meant to preserve American history.[25] In 1850 José Fernando Ramírez, conservator of Mexico's

National Museum, wrote his colleague Isidro Gondra to complain about his institution's progress in archaeology versus the Smithsonian's, which—along with the American Antiquarian Society and some Ivy League schools—supported the efforts of US adventurer-archaeologists in Mexico, Central America, and across the United States.[26]

But the challenges of the twenty-first century make reckoning with the past in the present—especially in the context of ongoing conflicts over land and water rights, the right to self-determination, and the basic right not to be killed—too dangerous, like unremoved statues and namesakes, not to address.[27] Burial places and sacred landscapes continue to be scraped away so that settlers may literalize the border, dominate the skies, and water the desert.[28] Women, girls, Two Spirit, and femme people across North America are not just missing or murdered but disappeared, even their deaths ignored or unknown. Thousands still mourn the Indigenous school children who never made it home, whose passing was never marked.[29] Assertions of Indigenous sovereignty have been met with all-too-familiar violence at Standing Rock and Maunakea, on Wet'suwet'en and Navajo lands, in Michoacán and Chiapas.[30] Hnähñu women protest centuries of violence in Mexico City while migrants from the Northern Triangle weigh the risk of leaving home; O'odham activists leverage their bodies against the machines threatening ha:sañ (ancestral saguaro cactuses) while transnational Indigenous groups lock arms to protect water, manoomin (wild rice), and treaty rights.[31] All the while, settlers reiterate and "normalize" the epistemological and spatial structures of Indigenous annihilation and dispossession by their ignorance and disavowal of this everyday violence.[32]

As in the nineteenth century, stories of conquest, loss, and mystery continue to characterize much of what passes for settler interest in the Indigenous past, exemplifying the lasting power of ancient history to "destroy to replace."[33] To make a change, settlers need to tell new stories that are not replacement or extinction narratives, drawn from a repertoire of epistemic moves that invent aboriginal pasts, erase Indigenous presence, and abet white supremacy. These new American histories must start, as Chickasaw scholar Jodi Byrd has suggested, by "activating indigenous presences as the point of critical inquiry."[34] One way to do this is for settlers to start hearing Native stories as they are voiced on and in Native lands, in the present tense. Another is to stop misappropriating or trying to "prove" them. Indeed, even as settler scientists and philosophers increasingly turn to Indigenous traditions and peoples for guidance in the Sixth Extinction, they frequently focus on "corroborating" Indigenous knowledges with methods that recenter settler beliefs rather than learning from Indigenous teachings.[35]

EARTHWORKS CONTINUE TO tell their stories: the old mounds at Grave Creek, Miamisburg, and Cahokia watch over struggling post-industrial cities. "Sugarloaf Mound"—its name encapsulating the entangled forces of settler colonialism and enslaved labor at the heart of the US national project—is the last earthwork still intact in St. Louis, formerly "Mound City."[36] In 2009 the Osage Nation purchased the land on which the earthwork stands, with plans to rehabilitate it and build an education center nearby. Their fundraising poster reminds area residents of a storied past embedded in the land long before 1804: "Before you built the arch, we built the mounds." New mounds tell of pasts, too: the Mound Building in Okmulgee, Oklahoma—seat of the Muscogee (Creek) Nation's government—calls back to eastern homelands; Oklahoma City's First Americans Museum, with its large earthen mound and circles of steel and glass aligned with the stars, heals an abandoned oil field and brings together thirty-nine Native nations. Up the Mississippi, Indigenous futurist artist X (Koasati and Hacha'maori) builds new earthworks in Zhekagoynak (Chicago), working to "restor[e] Indigenous place-making" and create "new monuments for new cities."[37] His Pokto Činto (Serpent Twin Mound) reverberates with the energy of the earthen doodemag around the Great Lakes. These earthworks all hold Indigenous futures as well as pasts, presencing the world before—and after—American history.[38]

NOTES

Preface

1. I am inspired by Abenaki scholar Lisa Brooks's articulation of "Native space" as "a network of relations and waterways containing many different groups of people as well as animal, plant, and rock beings that was sustained through the constant transformative 'being' of its inhabitants" (*Common Pot*, 3). For place-worlds see Basso, *Wisdom*, 6.
2. "Who Built the Mound and Why Did They Build It?" Miamisburg Mound, Dayton, Ohio, September 2011.
3. Barker, "Territory," 135.
4. Barker, "Territory," 135.
5. Tuck and Yang, "Decolonization," 2, 3.
6. Tuck and Yang, "Decolonization," 31.
7. Tuck and Yang, "Decolonization," 3; Veracini, "Decolonizing Settler Colonialism."
8. Simpson, "Land as Pedagogy."
9. Tuck and Yang, "Decolonization," 3.
10. Vimalassery et al., "On Colonial Unknowing." Their definition is worth reiterating: "Colonial unknowing endeavors to render unintelligible the entanglements of racialization and colonization, occluding the mutable historicity of colonial structures and attributing finality to events of conquest and dispossession" (n.p.).
11. Tlostanova and Mignolo, *Learning to Unlearn*, 31–59.

A Note on Terminology and Method

1. Lockhart, *Nahuas*, 1.
2. For a careful explanation of some of these differences see Howey, *Mound Builders*.

Introduction

1. During the Black Hawk War (1832) some Ho-Chunk and Three Fires fighters allied with the United States against Sauk leader Black Hawk and his Sauk, Meskwaki, Kickapoo, and Ho-Chunk forces. See Trask, *Black Hawk*; Owens, *Mr. Jefferson's Hammer*. In 1836, Wisconsin was split off from Michigan Territory in preparation for Michigan statehood; it comprised areas now known as Wisconsin, Minnesota, Iowa, and the Dakotas. See Saler, *Settlers' Empire*. In 1837 Secretary of War Joel R. Poinsett negotiated a new set of treaties to seize more Dakota lands (Westerman and White, *Mni Sota Makoce*, 148–63).

2. Aztalan State Park, Aztalan, Wisconsin. April 2016.

3. This map was copied from I. A. Lapham's *Antiquities of Wisconsin* (1855).

4. For the "vanishing Indian" trope see Dippie, *Vanishing*, also Bieder, *Science Encounters*; Deloria, *Playing Indian*; O'Brien, *Firsting and Lasting*.

5. With the Treaties of September 26 and 27, 1833, the "United Chippewa, Ottawa, and Potawatomi Nation" ceded the lands that are currently the states of Illinois and Wisconsin. This revoked the "Indian Boundary" set after the 1816 Treaty of St. Louis, which followed the forty-second parallel (set as the northernmost reach of the Spanish West by the 1819 Adams-Onís Treaty). See Tanner, *Atlas*, 139–57.

6. *Milwaukee Advertiser*, July 13, 1836; October 20, 1836; February 11, 1837.

7. Hyer, "Letter to the Editor," 2. Hyer claimed to have first seen the "citadel" in October 1836; his initial report ran in the January 1837 *Chicago American* and appeared in the major East Coast outlets as well as papers from Chillicothe and New Orleans to Richmond and Raleigh. However, the February 25, 1837 *Milwaukee Advertiser* article contained much more detail.

8. In the rest of the book I use "Mexica," the word for the Nahuatl-speaking people of Tenochtitlan, but use "Aztec" here for clarity. See "Note on Terminology."

9. Humboldt, *Vues*, pl. 7; Clavijero, *Storia*, t. 2 pl. 1.

10. Cass, "Article XII," 243. In Ralph Waldo Emerson's 1841 essay "History," the pyramids of Egypt and Mexico, ruins at Pompeii and Herculaneum, Stonehenge, and "the Ohio Circles" all stand as remains of antiquity (*Essays*, 241).

11. It would not become a museum piece until the 1880s (Achim, "National Museum," 23).

12. See Alarcón, *Aztec Palimpsest*; Clendinnen, "Fierce and Unnatural Cruelty"; Keen, *Aztec*. Many Latin American Indigenous activists articulate a decolonizing, rather than a recognition-based stance on sovereignty. See for example Nash, *Mayan Visions* and Castillo, *Histories and Stories*; for critiques of recognition in the north, see Coulthard, *Red Skins* and Simpson, *Mohawk*. For Latin Americanist discussions of de-coloniality and decolonization, see Quijano, "Coloniality of Power"; Mignolo, "Introduction" and *Darker Side*.

13. 25.7 million people self-identified as Indigenous in 2015 according to Mexico's National Institute of Statistics and Geography ("Indigenous World 2020," IWGIA. May 11, 2020. https://www.iwgia.org/en/mexico/3625-iw-2020-mexico.html).

14. Haiti, the first nation formed by formerly enslaved peoples, has a markedly different relationship to settlement than Mexico or the United States. The Dominion of Canada was created in 1867.

15. See, for example, the Ancient One/Kennewick Man controversy (Thomas, *Skull Wars* and Williams, "From Whence"). For American anthropology and indigeneity, see Barnhart, *American Antiquities* and *Squier*; Gunn, *Empire*; see also Pagden, *Fall of Natural Man*.

16. Typically, settler nations are exemplified by the former British colonies of Australia, Canada, Aotearoa New Zealand, South Africa, and the United States. Even as

scholars have begun looking to the operations of settler colonialism worldwide, Latin America is often absent from these discussions. Shannon Speed's work is a notable exception ("Structures"). See Faragher, "Commentary;" Johnston and Lawson, "Settler Colonies"; Mamdani, "Settler Colonialism"; Saranillio, "Settler Colonialism"; Simpson and Smith, "Introduction"; Veracini, *Settler Colonialism* and *Settler Colonial Present*; Wolfe, "Settler Colonialism."

17. This view of mestizaje is a conventional oversimplification. See Castañeda, "We are not Indians"; Chorba, *Mestizo to Multicultural*; Forbes, *Aztecas Del Norte*; Lomnitz, *Deep Mexico*; MacLachlan and Rodríguez O., *Cosmic Race*; Martínez, *Genealogical Fictions*, 143–52; Pérez-Torres, *Mestizaje* and "Miscegenation"; Saldívar, "It's Not Race."

18. Paz, *Labyrinth*, 89.

19. Guidotti-Hernández, *Unspeakable Violence*, 22.

20. Deloria, *Playing Indian*; O'Brien, *Firsting and Lasting*.

21. The vast historiography on American "invented" pasts typically begins with O'Gorman's *Invention of America* (1961). For a selection, see Greenblatt, *Marvelous Possessions*; Greene, *Intellectual Construction of America*; Hulme, *Colonial Encounters*; Rabasa, *Inventing America*; Slotkin, *Regeneration*; Florescano, *Myth*.

22. Greer contends that nineteenth-century Mexico perceived its "Indian problem" as *internal* to the nation, while the United States pursued policies to prove it *external* (*Property*, 424–32).

23. For discussions of transamerican elite networks, see Lazo, *Filadelfia* as well as Gruesz, *Ambassadors* and Brickhouse, *Transamerican*.

24. Blackhawk, *Violence*, 1, 8–10; Guidotti-Hernández, *Unspeakable Violence*, 4. See also Nemser, "Eviction and the Archive," 124; Mt. Pleasant et al., "Materials and Methods," 424.

25. Veracini, *Settler Colonialism*, 4.

26. DeLay's 2008 *War of a Thousand Deserts* is a standout exception.

27. Brooks, *Common Pot*, 3. Reflecting my own orientation as a scholar in and of the United States, the scales predictably tilt northward, an imbalance itself partly due to the structures of dominance developed in the era under study. Scholars within American literary studies have attempted this balance, to greater or lesser successs, especially in the early twenty-first century: for overviews see Bauer, "Hemispheric Studies" and Sadowski-Smith and Fox, "Theorizing."

28. Priest, *American Antiquities*, vii–viii.

29. Priest, *American Antiquities*, 25–26, 40. On Priest, see Sloan, *Crimsoned Hills*, 86–104.

30. Kovach, *Indigenous Methodologies*, 13. See also Tuck and Yang, "Decolonization" and Vimalassery et al., "On Colonial Unknowing."

31. Vimalassery et al., "On Colonial Unknowing." I use "dispossessive" as a modifier based on Veracini's "dispossessive logic," which is the structure serving to "uproot and destroy the place-based autonomies of Indigenous peoples" (*Settler Colonialism*, 4).

32. Saunt, *Unworthy Republic*, xviii, 318.

33. Brooks, "Awikhigawôgan," 265–67 and *Our Beloved Kin*, 4. For additional examples of NAIS and/or Indigenous historiographical methods, including land-based, iconic, and embodied forms of record-keeping, see Carroll, *Roots of Our Renewal*; Cruikshank, "Glaciers"; Echo-Hawk, "Ancient History;" Miller and Riding-In, *Native Historians Write Back*; Silva, "'Moʻolelo and Mana." The collection *Sources and Methods in Indigenous Studies* edited by Anderson and O'Brien is indispensable.

34. This usage dates to the 1820s ("Art. 2...Mr. Webster"; Yates and Moulton, *History*). "Pre-colonial" is from a later period ("pre-colonial, adj.," *OED Online*).

35. Van Tassel, *Recording*, 177; 171–79. H.H. Bancroft, Francis Parkman, and Justin Winsor in particular relied on the earlier "amateur" work.

36. The Instituto Nacional de Antropología e Historia (INAH) was created in 1939 to manage the holdings of the former Museo Nacional de Arqueología, Historia y Etnografía. Today, these Indigenous manuscripts are held by the INAH library (Biblioteca Nacional de Antropología e Historia or BNAH), not housed with the "Fondo de Origen" collection (of "books printed in Europe between 1501 and 1859") at the Biblioteca Nacional de México ("Antecedentes," Biblioteca Nacional de México. UNAM, Instituto de Investigaciones Bibliográficas. https://bnm.iib.unam.mx/index.php/quienes-somos/antecedentes). Recently INAH/BNAH has undertaken a rigorous digitization campaign of this collection.

37. Burton, "Introduction," 7. NAIS scholars have counseled early Americanists to confront the sites and sources created "to facilitate scholarship that served national and imperial frameworks" (Mt. Pleasant et al., "Methods and Materials," 416). Kovach specifically critiques settler scholars as "adept at ignoring, forgetting, and often reproducing the colonial past, when in fact that very complex colonial past influences daily Indigenous life" (*Indigenous Methodologies*, 13). See also Schweitzer, "Afterlives" and O'Neal, "Immemorial." For a counter example, see Doyle et al., "Indigenization of Knowledge Organization."

38. Bruchac, "Lost and Found," 150, 156.

39. Kauanui, "A Structure." Coulthard writes of settler colonialism as "structured dispossession" (*Red Skin*, 7). The Indigenous modalities that Cherokee linguist Ellen Cushman has explained as necessary to a "decolonial archive" are story, place, meaning, and perseverance ("Letters and Characters"). For selected NAIS approaches to decolonization, see Lonetree, *Decolonizing the Museum*; O'Neal, "Respect, Recognition, and Reciprocity;" Powell, "Protocols for the Treatment of Indigenous Materials;" Schweitzer and Henry, *Digital Afterlives*.

40. Conn, *History's Shadow*, 9.

41. Delafield, "Propose," 5, 4. On March 8, 1845, an anonymous writer in New York's Latter Day Saints newspaper *The Prophet* reproduced some of this imagery to argue that Aztalan was explained by the Book of Mormon. The writer had excavated there in 1839.

42. See Beckett, *Writing Local History* and Swann, "Countryside." For manuscript antiquarianism see Yale, "With Slips."

43. Trigger, *Archaeology*, 56. Johann Winckelmann demonstrated a technique for dating statuary in *Geschichte der Kunst des Altertums* (1764) by locating their inscriptions in Classical texts.

44. For archaeology and Hapsburg collections, see Blix, *Paris*; Findlen, *Early Modern Things* and *Possessing Nature*; Miller, "Writing Antiquarianism"; Russo, "Cortés's Objects"; Schapp, *Discovery of the Past*; Spitta, *Misplaced Objects*.

45. Trigger, *Archaeology*, 60. The *Accademia Ercolanese di Archeologia* began releasing illustrated volumes of the Herculaneum, Stabiae, and Pompeii artifacts in 1757; *Le antichità di Ercolano esposte* would eventually comprise eight volumes (1757–1792).

46. Ross argues that "historicism"—"the doctrine that all historical phenomena can be understood historically, that all events in time can be explained by prior events in historical time"—was not present in history writing in the United States until the 1880s ("Historical Consciousness," 910). For history writing in British North America, see Van Tassel, *Recording;* for New Spain, Florescano, *Myth* and *National Narratives*.

47. Fabian traces the word to its Greek root, "stoppage" (*Time and the Other*, 4). The *OED* dates its meaning as a "distinctive period" to 1673 ("epoch, n, 2a.," *OED Online*). According to Chakrabarty, "[i]n the awakening of this sense of anachronism lies the beginning of modern historical consciousness" (*Provincializing*, 238).

48. Callcott marks a "transition in historical thinking" between the works of William Robertson and Edward Gibbon of the 1780s and the "flowering" of literary histories in the 1820s and 1830s (*History*, 20–21). See also Pagden, *Fall of Natural Man* and *European Encounter*.

49. Furthermore, settlers' prioritization of (settler-defined) "civilization" has resulted in ancient histories overemphasizing built-up settlements—such as the "cities" at Cahokia, Canyon de Chelly, Tenochtitlan, or the Classic Maya kingdoms—and deemphasizing the interconnected and interdependent groupings of peoples across the continent. This tendency toward isolationism and parochialism is an obstacle in colonial American history that the movement toward a "Vast Early America" has meant to address. See Barr and Countryman, *Contested Spaces*; Mt. Pleasant et al., "Methods and Materials," 421.

50. Marcocci writes elegantly about the "disharmony of chronology" in sixteenth-century Europe and New Spain ("Inventing the Antiquities" 115, 128).

51. See Blix, *Paris*.

52. Franciscans and criollo antiquaries published inventories and compilations such as Cortés's letters and Francisco Hernández de Toledo's seventeenth-century herbal (Lorenzana, *Historia*; Gómez Ortega, *Francisci Hernandi*). Archbishop Lorenzana's Cortés edition featured illustrations adapted from Indigenous manuscripts with Spanish glosses as well as a 1769 map by José Antonio de Alzate y Ramírez. British colonists like Cotton Mather, Benjamin Franklin, James Logan, and Thomas Jefferson filled large personal and corporate libraries with "antiquities" that included colonial chronicles, bills of mortality, treaty council minutes, and bills of sale after the English antiquarian model (Yale, "With Slips.")

53. "Aborigine, n. and adj.," *OED Online*.

54. American antiquities became major artillery in transatlantic intellectual battles after Buffon proposed that America had recently emerged from the oceans and its inhabitants only just arrived. See Gerbi, *Dispute*.

55. Although the US initially conducted its Indian affairs by treaty and contract, this process—which theorhetically recognized Indigenous "aboriginal title"—was expensive. On "aboriginal title," see McNeil, *Common Law* and Banner, *How*.

56. Quoted in Coulthard, "Place," 79.

57. Wilson, *Research Is Ceremony*, 80.

58. "territory, n.1," *OED Online*.

59. Wolfe, "Settler Colonialism," 388. The nuance is mine.

60. Wolfe, "Settler Colonialism," 388.

61. Nichols, *Theft*, 6.

62. Nichols, *Theft*, 8.

63. Indigenous peoples can assert possession (as stewardship and responsibility) and nonetheless be stripped of "original possession" or "aboriginal title" by settler states (Nichols, *Theft*, 6).

64. Simpson, *Mohawk*, 74.

65. Territory's "irreducible element" is sovereignty (Foucault, *Security*, 11–12, 20). With the shift from singular sovereign power to the diffused sovereignty of the state—according to Foucault—governance shifted from power over territory to power over populace. See also Morgensen, "Biopolitics."

66. Barker, "Territory," 31.

67. See Lipsitz, *Possessive Investment*; he borrows from Black legal scholar Cheryl I. Harris.

68. Kazanjian, *Colonizing Trick*, 2, 20. In Marx's *Capital*, vol. 1, exchange value disguises relationships between people as relationships between commodities: the "trick" (I prefer Kazanjian's term taken from David Walker to Marx's "fetish") is the disingenuous presentation of one thing as another, the disguise.

69. Speed, 'Structures," 784–85; Wolfe, "Land."

70. Florescano, *Myth*, 192. See Gonzálba Aizpuru, "La trampa"; Israel, *Race, Class, and Politics*; Jackson, *Race, Caste, and Status*; Vinson, *Before Mestizaje*; Wade, *Race and Ethnicity*.

71. For archaeology in the Porfiriato, as well as indigenismo after the Mexican Revolution, see Bueno, *Pursuit*; Garrigan, *Collecting Mexico*; Vailant, *Ornamental*.

72. MacLachlan and Rodríguez O., *Cosmic Race*. See also Blackwell, "Indigeneity," 101–2.

73. Forbes, *Aztecas del Norte*.

74. Chorba writes of Mexico's "mestizophile ideology" (*Mexico*, 2). See also Miner, *Creating Aztlán*; Peréz-Torres, *Mestizaje*.

75. Saldaña-Portillo, *Revolutionary Imagination*, 292. See also Gabilondo, "Genealogía"; Loewe, *Maya or Mestizo*; Saldaña-Portillo, "No country."

76. See Dippie, *Vanishing*; O'Brien, *Firsting and Lasting*. James Fenimore Cooper's novels are paradigmatic of the "lasting" trope's power.

77. Byrd, *Transit*, xxvi.

78. There is growing scholarship on Blackness and Indigeneity, such as Infante, "Magical and Paradigmatic"; King et al., *Otherwise Worlds*; Leroy, "Black history."

79. Basso, *Wisdom*, 6.

80. Basso, *Wisdom*, 6.

81. Other scholars have suggested "medieval," "early Modern," or "ancient" for these years. While encompassing the periods when Indigenous ancestors built Mesa Verde, Etzanoa, Cahokia, and Tenochtitlan, "distant" does not rely on an urban-centric, civilizational hierarchy. "Distant" also avoids associations with Classical antiquity, European periodization, or Mesoamericanist chronologies that articulate pre-Classic, Classic, and post-Classic timelines based on a culture area's "golden age" (i.e., Palenque is a Classic-era Maya city because it reached its "height" in the seventh century). I likewise avoid "culture area" chronologies that resulted from searching for Moundbuilders (i.e., Adena, Hopewell, Oneota, etc.), which tend to emphasize difference over continuity.

82. Echo-Hawk, "Ancient," 270, 286, 288. Round writes of "employing a deep time perspective" and "recovering the deep time continuum of Native spaces" when writing Native history ("Mississippian," 458, 468). See also Mackenthun and Mucher, *Decolonizing*.

83. I strive to counteract deterministic temporal terminologies such as "pre-Contact," "pre-Hispanic," "pre-Columbian," and especially "prehistoric."

84. Simpson, *Always Done*, 2.

85. Warrior, *People*, 182. Multitemporality is conventional in many northern Indigenous teachings—i.e., the time of the Thunderers or Corn Mother—as well as in "Mesoamerican" ones (e.g., pre-Sunrise time).

86. Lyons, *X-Marks*, 16, 13.

87. Witgen, *Infinity*, 33. See also Basso, *Wisdom*. Non-Native histories, of course, are also constructed according to the needs of the present, as Hayden White and Michel de Certeau have argued.

88. Gniadek, "Times of Settler Colonialism"; Kauanui, "A structure, not an event"; Wolfe, "Structure and Event."

89. Saldaña-Portillo, *Indian Given*, 9, 6, 3–6. See also Grande, "American Indian Geographies."

90. Because the Indigenous population is numerically larger in the highlands than in central Mexico, Indigenous peoples are perceived to live largely in nonurban, non-acculturated areas such as Chiapas or the Yucatán (Bonfil Batalla, *México Profundo*, 47). These population percentages, however, obscure the Indigenous communities across Mexico's lands and participate in the vanishing discourse of mestizaje, wherein indigeneity disappears through cultural admixture and adaptation. In the US, non-Natives too frequently believe that Indigenous peoples exist(ed) only in some unspecified, premodern moment (Deloria, *Indians in Unexpected Places*).

91. Barker, "Territory," 33.
92. On the "givenness" of settler colonialism see Rifkin, "Settler common sense."
93. I try to emphasize Brooks's process of "awikhigawôgan" (mapping/writing) and "ôjmowôgan" (history-making), which results in "pildowi ôjmowôgan," a recursive history or cyclical recalling (*Our Beloved Kin*, 4).
94. The epigraphs from Indigenous writers are meant as a gesture of relationship and responsibility in a book that otherwise focuses on settler histories and where Native voices can be hard to hear (Doerfler et al., "*Bagijige*," xv.)
95. Levin Rojo, *Return*, 2, 39.
96. See Foucault, *Archaeology*, especially part 3. In terms of the archive as textual and embodied, see González Echevarría, *Myth and Archive;* Richards, *Imperial Archive;* Taylor, *Archive and the Repertoire*.
97. For resurgence, see Simpson, *Always Done*.

Chapter 1

1. Warhus, *Another America*, 28. For Oñate's Plains entrada, see Craddock, *Quivira*.
2. Weber, *Spanish Frontier*, 79; Levin Rojo, *Return*, 84.
3. Levin Rojo, *Return*, 33, 66–68.
4. This site is currently called Paquimé.
5. Levin Rojo, *Return*, 33–34, 40, 61, 71.
6. Weber, *Spanish Frontier*, 77–87; Levin Rojo, *Return*, 81–86.
7. Details from Craddock, *Quivira*, 5–8, 52, 99, 185–91 and Blakeslee, "Miguel Map," 67–71.
8. Blakeslee, "Miguel Map," 70. Under the Spanish "castas" system Indigenous peoples were categorized in ways that ignored ethnic, geographic, or political differences for bureaucratic efficiency: i.e., "indios" (Indigenous people), "mestizos" (people of Indigenous and Spanish heritage), "ladinos" (Hispanicized Indigenous people or mestizos), "zambos" (people of Indigenous and African heritage), "indios bárbaros" ("unpacified" Indigenous peoples who generally did not live in permanent villages). See Wade, *Race and Ethnicity* and Albero and Gonzalbo Aizpuru, *La sociedad novohispana*.
9. Craddock, *Quivira*, 186; "Mapa diseñado por Miguel, indio de Quivira, en 1602," reproduced in Craddock, *Quivira*, 206–8. See also Vehik, "Oñate's Expedition."
10. Correia, *Properties of Violence*, 15. The map is held in Spain's Archivo General de Indias (mapas y planos, México 50).
11. See Foreman, "Journal of the Proceedings."
12. Cossins, "Missing City"; Benson et al., "Possible Impacts."
13. According to the *LA Times*, "Town leaders are hoping for a UNESCO World Heritage site designation" (Kelly, "Archaeologists").
14. Kelly, "Archaeologists."
15. Kelly, "Archaeologists." See also Russell, "Lost City of Etzanoa Found," and McAdams, "Etzanoa."

16. The Wichita and Affiliated Tribes are involved, to an extent, with the Etzanoa Conservancy. See "Department Reports," *Wichita Tribal News*, February 2018, 7.

17. More refers to Sigüenza y Gongora's "Creole archive," while Villella calls it the "cacique-criollo" archive (More, *Baroque Sovereignty*, 164–69; Villella, *Indigenous Elites*, 10). See also Higgins, *Constructing* and Townsend, *Annals*.

18. Levin Rojo, *Return*, 56.

19. Quoted in Levin Rojo, *Return*, 123.

20. Glass, "Boturini Collection." Anthropologist John B. Glass is responsible for "nearly everything we know of Boturini" (Schroeder, "Foreward," xiii).

21. He sought the testimonies and documents created two centuries prior to defend the ancestry of Isabel Moctezuma (daughter and heir to Motecuhzoma II) and establish her encomienda rights (Levin Rojo, *Return*, 176). Note the Hispanicized spelling of the family name.

22. Levin Rojo, *Return*, 2. Villella detects a "distinct indigenous role in the creole projects to imagine a Mexican nationhood emphasizing native roots" (*Indigenous Elites*, 4).

23. For "Mexica," see León-Portilla, "Los Aztecas" and Lee, "Aztec Triple Alliance" as well as my Notes on Terminology.

24. Lockhart, *Nahuas*, 22; 14–58. The altepetl is primarily a Nahuatl-speaking peoples' arrangement that denotes an ethno-religious-cosmic orientation and forms the basis for wide-ranging political arrangements and organization for tribute and labor collection (Simpson, *Encomienda*, 56–64). Both individual and collective identity were derived from the altepetl, calpolli—a smaller social unit of extended kin—and its constituent unit, the tlaxilacalli (Kranz, *Tlaxcalan*, 9).

25. See Lee, "Aztec Triple Alliance."

26. Rama, *Lettered City*, 1; 1–16. See also Mundy, *Mapping*, 1–28.

27. Gibson, *Aztecs*, 157–62, 266.

28. Gibson, *Aztec*, 224–26, 231–32. See also Simpson, *Encomienda* and Lockhart, "Encomienda."

29. Gibson, *Aztec*, 157–62, 166–93.

30. Nemser, *Race*, 102.

31. Nemser, *Race*, 21, 58, 59; Lockhart, *Nahuas*, 44–45. See also Cline, "Civil Congregations" and Gerhard, "Congregaciones," 347–48.

32. Nemser, *Race*, 56–62.

33. Weber, *Bárbaros*, 104; Adams, "Embattled," 206. By the eighteenth century other Indigenous groups—such as the Lipan Apaches, who were being pushed out of their homelands by Comanches and Comanche allies—became the principle targets of New Spanish aggression.

34. Nemser, *Race*, 35, 38–29. Nemser argues that this physical consolidation coincided with the conceptual consolidation of "indio" as a racialized identity (*Race*, 25–64, especially 27, 58–59).

35. In the case of Nuevo México, Oñate's and his associates' murderousness had created some of those ruins, as had Coronado at "Cíbola," the destroyed Zuni pueblo of Hawikuh.

36. For European ideas of "barbarians" see Pagden, *Fall of Natural Man*, 15–26.

37. López Austín and López Luján, *Past*, 200. "Chichimecas" were usually represented on iconic Nahua records as "dressed in animal skins, carrying bows and arrows, [and living] in arid environments symbolized by caves, mesquite trees, and prickly-pear and barrel cacti" (López Austín and López Luján, *Past*, 201).

38. Gibson, *Aztecs*, 10. Nonetheless, some Franciscans compiled "Otomí" grammars and vocabularies and worked with Hnähñu (Otomí) students. Interestingly, "otoncuicatl" (Otomí song) is a form of Nahua poetry (Lastra, *Los Otomíes*).

39. See Chapter 6 for settlers collecting materials in Maya lands.

40. Adams, "Embattled," 206; 206n2.

41. Similarly, the transformation of "mythic" Toltecs into "heroic" Mexicas was crucial to the power of the Mexica-Culhua dynasty (Gradie, "Chichimecas," 69).

42. Purchas wrote: "The first inhabitants of New Spain were very barbarous and savage, which lived only by Hunting, and for this reason were called Chichimecas . . . They seem to have learned the Savage nature of the wilde Beastes, of whom and with whom they live. By this meanse it came to passe, that this wilde Mountainous people left the best and most fertile part of the Countrey unpeopled, which certaine remote Nations possessed, whom they called Navatalcas [Nahuatecas], for their civility. These came from those Northerne parts, which now they call New Mexico. The Navatalcas paint their beginning and first Territory in manner of Caves (because of their seven Tribes) and men coming out of them" (*Hakluytus Posthumus*, 15: 236).

43. For other histories of Mesoamerican Indigenous writing practices see Marcus, *Mesoamerican Writing*; Boone, *Stories* (especially 3–63); Boone and Mignolo, *Writing without Words*; Boone and Urton, *Their Way of Writing*; Leibsohn, *Script and Glyph*.

44. DiCesare, *Sweeping*, 6–7; Bennett, "Bundles."

45. The category of "manuscript" is not formally straightforward in early modern European book history either; see Yale, "With Slips."

46. Purchas, *Hakluytus Posthumus*, 15: 305. Another of the "Mexican Bookes" likely sent to Charles V by Cortés was the *Dresden Codex*, which is in fact a Mayan text (Thompson, *Dresden Codex*, 17). Two Ñuudzahui (Mixtec) documents, now called *Codex Vindobonensis Mexicanus I* and *Codex Zouche-Nuttall*, were also likely part of that shipment. For objects (and people) displayed in Europe at that time, see Russo, *Untranslatable Image*.

47. See Glass, "Survey."

48. "tlapohualli," *Online Nahuatl Dictionary*, edited by Stephanie Wood. Wired Humanities Projects, 2020. https://nahuatl.uoregon.edu/content/tlapohualli.

49. Mexica documents relating to time and history came in many forms, but Europeans largely assumed they were only round. An excellent example is *Calendario Mexicano, Veytia no. 7* (c. 1701–1720) at INAH.

50. Purchas, *Hakluytus Posthumus*, 15: 369, 418–20. The c. 1540s–1550s manuscript is now housed at Oxford's Bodleian Library. Bleichmar has suggested that Purchas's reproduction "may well be the single most reproduced non-Western manuscript in early

modern publications" ("History," 696). See also Bleichmar, "Painting." For circulation, see Alpert-Abrams, "Unreadable Books," 82–88.

51. Motolinía wrote of the xiuhtlapohualli (year-count book) used in Tenochtitlan and described the New Fire ceremony (Elson and Smith, "Archaeological deposits," 158). See also Townsend, *Annals*.

52. Acosta, *History of the Indies*, 331, 331–33.

53. Mendieta and Sahagún quoted in DiCesare, *Sweeping*, 9.

54. DiCesare, *Sweeping*, 7–9. See also Boone and Mignolo, *Writing without Words*.

55. Townsend, *Fifth Sun*, 9.

56. For Mexica time, see Levin-Rojo, *Return*, 254–55n104, and Townsend, *Annals*, 4–6. For another "calendar account" see Kruell, "Algunas precisions," 142–44, 158.

57. "Calli" (house) is signified by a mound-like sign (see Figure 6) that evokes the joining of "tepetl" (mountain) and "atl" (water). Different from the Sky or Below Worlds, this is the Water-and-Earth middle space of human life (See Carrasco, *Religions*, 70). For "altepetl" as sacred mound structures, see Megged, *Social Memory*, 154.

58. See Umberger, "Notions." While some feasts and celebrations must occur on certain days, moveable feasts "occur on dates with particular cosmic resonance" (Umberger, "Notions," 96).

59. Kruell has traced the confusion over Nahuatl terms to choices made by León y Gama ("Algunas precisions," 148–49, 159).

60. The Tlatelolco colegio was built on a former calmecac and served many of the same students (Calneck, "Calmecac," 170, 169). A multilingual ethnographic project by students from Tlatelolco led by Fray Bernardino de Sahagún in the 1550s–1570s has proved to be the most complete archive of this period.

61. Durán and Torquemada also collected oral testimony and consulted Indigenous scholars, amassing a large "Indian" archive. The writings of Fray Andrés de Olmas, Motolinía, and Sahagún are believed to contain the earliest translated Indigenous sources (Douglas, *Palace*, 7). See also Townsend, *Annals* and Higgins, *Constructing*.

62. For "pictorial" texts produced by Nahua scribes I use the term "iconic" to emphasize the communicative—rather than verisimilar—aspects of the script.

63. Florescano, *Myth*, 185, See also Mundy, *Mapping*, 61–89; Schwaller, "Brothers"; McDonough, *Learned Ones*; Townsend, *Annals*.

64. Douglas, *Palace*, 6, 12.

65. The pueblos retained some autonomy through the cacicazgo (Indigenous governorship system) but were still obliged to pay tribute to the Crown (Lockhart, *Nahuas*, 22).

66. The *Mapa de Oztoticpac* depicts lands Ixtlilxóchitl I may have given to Don Carlos Chichimecatecatl of Texcoco in 1539; it was likely made by the historian Ixtlilxóchitl's sons to reclaim the lands ("The Oztoticpac lands map." [1540] Library of Congress Geography and Map Division. https://www.loc.gov/item/88690436/).

67. In exchange for Sigüenza's help Juan de Alva Ixtlilxóchitl gave him his father's library (Brading, *First America*, 365; More, *Baroque Sovereignty*, 154, 155–57).

68. Florescano, *Myth*, 185; Douglas, *Palace*, 6.

69. The *Crónica Mexicayotl* (c. 1598) by Alvarado Tezozómoc, grandson of Motecuhzoma Xocoyoltzin, is a bilingual account of the Mexica ruling lineage through the early Spanish period. It is now at the National Library of France (BNF), along with Muñoz Camargo's *Historia de Tlaxcala*. See Higgins, *Constructing*; Velazco, *Visiones de Anáhuac*; Ward, "Emerging Notion."

70. The name used by Ixtlilxóchitl—whose ancestor Fernando Ixtlilxóchitl II had allied with Cortés—recalls his dual Mexica and Spanish nobility. See Brian, *Native Archive* and Brokaw and Lee, *Ixtlilxóchitl and His Legacy*.

71. Schroeder, *Chimalpahin*, 27–30, 27; Lockhart et al., *Annals of His Time*, 11.

72. Levin, *Return*, 117.

73. Villella, *Indigenous Elites*, 19.

74. The earliest extant post-invasion Nahua iconic texts are those used to make patrimonial land claims in the Indian Courts (Douglas, *Palace*, 7).

75. Yannakakis, *In-Between*, 14, 30. For the first few decades of colonial rule Indigenous residents had exceptional access to the courts. See Ruiz Medrano et al., *Reshaping* and Ruiz Medrano, *Indigenous Communities*, 2.

76. Ruiz Medrano, *Indigenous Communities*, 96–98; Villella, *Indigenous Elites*, 9, 10.

77. Ruiz Medrano, *Indigenous Communities*, 31–32.

78. Lockhart, *Nahuas*, 149.

79. Lockhart, *Nahuas*, 149.

80. Douglas, *Palace*, 5; Boone, *Stories*, 248. The provenance of these anonymously authored mapas is based on their appearance (Navarrete, "Aztlán to Mexico).

81. Ruiz Medrano, *Indigenous Communities*, 13–14.

82. Lockhart, *Nahuas*, 362.

83. Lockhart, *Nahuas*, 353, 355. For "questions of land or houses" even mainly alphabetic documents rely on iconic script and stylistic conventions to represent land (i.e., they include line drawings, rectangular-shaped plots, household name glyphs).

84. Indigenous communities continued to produce records to navigate the legal landscape through the nineteenth century. The Tlaxcalan case is the most well known: see Martínez Baracs, *Tlaxcala*; Portillo, *Fuero indio*. For the Mixteca region, see Menegus, *La Mixteca Baja*, and "Cacicazgos y repúblicas."

85. The *Mapa de Ecatepec-Huitziltepec* (*Codex Quetalecatzin*), which had likely been in the possession of Sigüenza and is now at the Library of Congress, is an excellent example of a mapa made to preserve colonial-era land claims. It depicts the de León family genealogy and their descent from Lord-11 Quetzalecatzin (Hessler, "Codex Quetzalcatzin").

86. Townsend, *Fifth Sun*, 155–79; Flint, "Treason or Travesty."

87. Lockhart, *Nahuas*, 1, 10; Douglas, *Palace* 6, 8; Florescano, *Myth*, 195n30.

88. See Brading, *First America*, 363, 366–67.

89. More, *Baroque Sovereignty*, 56; Villella, *Indigenous Elite*, 3. For changes in reception, see Cañizares-Esguerra, *How to Write*, 60–129.

90. Nemser, *Race*, 101–7. C.f. Pagden, *Spanish*, 97.

91. More, *Baroque Sovereignty*, 149–50. See also Peraza-Rugeley, *Llámenme el mexicano*. Sigüenza saved the viceregal archives from destruction during the 1692 uprisings,

after which he became official geographer and mapped Pensacola Bay in 1693 (More, *Baroque Sovereignty*, 158–201; 243).

92. Clavigero, *History of Mexico*, xxii. This translation is henceforth cited as "Clavijero, 1787."

93. Nemser, "Archaeology," 204; Pagden, *Spanish*, 93–97. Sigüenza also tried to link ancient Mexico to St. Thomas the Apostle (More, *Baroque Sovereignty*, 77).

94. Lockhart et al., *Annals of His Time*, 12; Burrus, "Clavigero," 63. Villella argues that the Sigüenza-Boturini collection initiated a "new era" in "creole historiography" (*Indigenous Elites*, 267).

95. More, *Baroque Sovereignty*, 147, 156; Schávelzon, "La primera excavación"; Brading, *First America*, 363–67. He also included an engraving of a manuscript described as "the road the antient Mexicans travell'd when they came from the Mountains to inhabit the Lake, call'd at present of Mexico," copied from the *Mapa Sigüenza*. On the *Mapa Sigüenza*, see Castañeda de la Paz, *Pintura*.

96. Boturini, *Idea*, 169. *New General History* is a 2015 English translation of Boturini's 1746 *Idea*. In subsequent citations, *New* refers to the 2015 English translation and *Idea* the 1746 Spanish original. Doña Manuela de Oca Silva y Moctezuma engaged Boturini to collect the unpaid monies on her behalf (Schroeder, "Foreword," xii; Poole, "Introduction," 4). These patrimonial lands still technically belong to the family (González Acosta, "Los herederos," 152)

97. Boturini only completed one volume of his *Historia general de la América septentrional*, in 1749, which remained unpublished until 1948 (Poole, "Introduction," 8).

98. "Monumento," Terrreros y Pando, *Diccionario*, 2: 646: "Las piezas, ó especies de historias, que nos han quedado de los antiguos, acerca de los sucesos pasados."

99. Boturini, *New*, 62–63.

100. Boturini, *New*, 147, 146–47.

101. "Mapa," *Diccionario de Autoridades*, 4: 493: "Qualquiera cosa sobresaliente y bizarra en su línea."

102. Poole, "Select Glossary," 17.

103. Boturini, *Idea*, 41, 42.

104. Boturini, *New*, 214. Screenfolds such as this were reminiscent of "books" to Europeans, and therefore, were regularly identified as "codices." The *Codex Boturini* covers the period 1168–1355 CE (Aguilar-Moreno, *Handbook*, 267–68).

105. Boturini, *New*, 214. His collection comprised eighteen mapas, fourteen manuscripts "by Indian authors," and various "sueltos" (Boturini, *New*, 214–21). Clavijero (and later Josiah Priest) would reproduce details from Gemelli's *Mapa Sigüenza* engraving.

106. This is held at INAH's Biblioteca Nacional de Antropología e Historia (BNAH).

107. This is held at the BNAH.

108. Now called "Plano parcial de la Ciudad de México," it is at the BNAH. See Mundy, *Death*, 77–79.

109. Boturini, *New*, 216. This depicts an area largely dominated by private landholders. Altepetl land was managed at the level of the calpolli; the tlatoani typically determined the calpolli tasks (Lockhart, *Nahuas*, 16–19, 43–44; 142–76).

110. Mundy, *Death*, 77. Other mapas that depicted "ancestral lands of different lords" and the "lands won in war" performed multiple functions as well (Boturini, *New*, 215, 216).

111. Boturini, *New*, 123, 128.

112. Boturini, *New*, 67. This kind of temporality was not altogether unfamiliar to Spanish scholars: medieval Christianity, after all, had set the world into six ages, each roughly divided into millennia, and their yearly calendars also revolved around days devoted to saints and specific—and sometimes moveable—feasts.

113. Boturini, *New*, 62–63, 65.

114. Boturini must have been concerned because he wrote a disclaimer to reassure the Inquisitors: "Although on the occasion of writing this *Idea of a History*, I have had to meditate on the secret and scientific plans of the Indians and to use ... their own concepts in order to explain it, nevertheless, I am so far from separating myself in the least way from the purity of the Catholic religion, in which I was born, that rather I am prepared to die for it" (*New*, 58).

115. For descriptions of these materials, see Townsend, *Fifth Sun*, 215–31 and *Annals*. In addition to Nahua documents, Boturini collected Hnähñu (Otomí) and possibly Matlatzinca and Hñatho (Mazahua) mapas. He lamented not collecting Purépecha materials from Michoacán (Boturini, *New*, 227).

116. Boturini, *New*, 209.

117. Cañizares-Esguerra, *How to Write*, 148. On the "reliability" of Indigenous sources to Europeans, see More, *Baroque Sovereignty*, 90 and Cañizares-Esguerra, *How to Write*, 60–129.

118. More, *Baroque Sovereignty*, 257.

119. Mignolo, *Darker Side*.

120. Carrasco, *Religions*, 14–15.

121. Cañizares-Esguerra, *How to Write*, 130–203.

122. On the "subjectivity of seeing" the Virgin see Favrot Peterson, *Visualizing Guadalupe*, x, 10, 259–274). See also Conover, "Reassessing," 256, 254, 272–73.

123. Cañizares-Esguerra, *How to Write*, 136–137.

124. Boturini, *Idea*. These were Indigenous-authored "manuscritos" written in alphabetic Nahuatl, Otomìta, or Spanish as well as iconic mapas (Boturini, *New*, 209, 209n7).

125. With the neoclassical vogue came a renewed interest in the "Museum" as a space intended for the Muses and their related arts. By extension, "museum" came to signify the diverse objects gathered within such a place and often served as a synonym for "collection" (cf. "museum, n., 1a; 2a, b.," *OED Online*). Boturini's collection is a museum because it is a diverse collection of Indigenous historical materials gathered with the approval of the Muses (Boturini, *New*, 43).

126. Boturini's museum was explicitly devoted to "Indian History" rather than the "Historic Indian" (so "Indian" modifies "Historical Museum"). He also held a small collection of artifacts, some perhaps from Teotihuacan (*New*, 97–98).

127. Burrus, "Clavigero," 69; Glass, *Boturini in Spain*, 155, 24; Cañizares-Esguerra, *How to Write*, 300.

128. For Boturini's interpretive accomplishments, see Cañizares-Esguerra, *How to Write*, 133–55.
129. See Endfield, "*Pinturas*" and Yannakakis, "Witnesses."
130. The historical tendency to consider disease the primary genocidal agent removes attention from enslavement and violence.
131. See Schroeder, *Pax Colonial*.
132. Boturini, *New*, 203, 229.
133. Boturini, *Idea*, 260.
134. Boturini, *New*, 199.
135. Boturini, *New*, 63.
136. Boturini, *New*, 63.
137. Boturini, *New*, 65. Douglas, *Palace*, 14.
138. Boturini, *New*, 159.
139. Boone, "Aztec Pictorial Histories," 52–53, 70. Boone uses "cartographic history" to describe Mexica origin histories (Boone, *Cycles*, 49–51; *Stories*, 61). See also Mundy, "Mesoamerican Cartography."
140. The first arrival of the Nahua ancestors on the American continent "is depicted at the town of *Culhuacan*, which means *the town of the serpent*, which is the first on the continent" (Boturini, *New*, 167).
141. Boturini, *New*, 156; López Austín and López Luján, *Past*, 200, 202.
142. This was also how he viewed the Casas Grandes ruins. See Boturini, *New*, 221n25, and Ives, "Reconstruction."
143. Boturini, *New*, 214.
144. Boturini, *New*, 156.
145. Boturini, *New*, 178, 180.
146. Boturini, *New*, 175.
147. Boturini, *New*, 180. This group "set out from the remote areas toward Michoacan and penetrated the lands of the Toltecs, founding the 'Chichimeca empire'" (Boturini, *New*, 180). Boturini is careful to distinguish between the "settled Chichimeca nation" and the "nomadic Chichimecas who ... make continuous raids against peaceful Indians ['indios de paz'] and Spaniards" (amplifying the connotation of barbarism with a mention of cannibalism) (*New*, 180).
148. Boturini, *New*, 181; Gradie, "Chichimecas," 69.
149. López Austín and López Luján, *Past*, 202.
150. Gradie, "Chichimecas," 69.
151. Boturini, *New*, 183.
152. The people of Xicalanco, historically Nahuatl speakers, are from Isla del Carmen, Campeche, a Maya-Nahua contact zone.
153. Park, "Spanish Indian Policy," 327.
154. Weber, *Bárbaros*, 92.
155. See Blackhawk, *Violence*, 16–54 and Hämäläinen, *Conquest*, 68–140.
156. Boturini, *New*, 221. Boturini mentioned possessing Kino's original "daily accounts ... of the discovery of the Río Grande, adjacent to the Sea of California, and

of the peaceful state of the provinces of Pimería and Sonora" as well as an unpublished manuscript by Captain Juan Mateo Manje, who had been on expeditions in Sonora in the early 1700s.

157. Boturini, *New*, 167.

158. While Boturini's predecessors were under the presumption that Indigenous writings were historical records—albeit ones difficult to understand—his successors believed the documents merely demonstrated the capacities of their creators (Cañizares-Esguerra, *How to Write*, 63). In this shift, Cañizares-Esguerra detects a "major change in European perception of the reliability of non-alphabetical scripts in keeping historical records" (*How to Write*, 60).

159. By 1786, Gálvez's *Instrucciones* for achieving "Indian control" called for an extensive system of forced relocation onto "establecimientos" (reservations) and the concerted destruction of cultural specificity through vicious campaigns of "Hispanicization" (Park, "Spanish," 330, 341, 340; Weber, *Bárbaros*, 156–59; Moorhead, *Apache Frontier*, 125, 229 and "Deportation," 205, 212; Babcock, *Apache*, 61, 2). Galvez argued that the "nomadic" Apache and other "indios bárbaros" needed to Hispanicize or face annihilation (Babcock, *Apache*, 8).

160. After attempting to shut down Wazhazhe (Osage) trade outlets and arm Caddoes and Wichitas, Spain began encouraging the relocation of allied Native groups (Rollings, *Osage*, 10, 185; McEnroe, *Colony*, 39–40; 22–56; Park, "Spanish," 338, 336). Spain also actively cultivated Miami, Lenape, Shawnee, Cherokee, and Chickasaw groups to act as buffers between itself and the Osage as well as the British (and later American) colonies, looking to eastern Native peoples—as it had to Tlaxcalans and other Nahuas in earlier times—as allied "vassal" polities to pit against "barbarous" enemies (Rollings, *Osage*, 12, 186; Morrow, "William Gilliss," 20–21).

161. Babcock, *Apache*, 62.

162. Teodoro de Croix encouraged Spanish agents to make alliances against the Lipan Apaches who, proclaimed the new viceroy Bernardo de Gálvez (nephew of José), "are our real enemies in the *Provincias Internas*" (Park, "Spanish," 335, 337; Gálvez, *Instructions*, 197).

163. Although the Crown ordered a cease to outright offensives in 1779—as its military powers were being absorbed by the Anglo-American war with Britain—individual governors and agents continued to encourage anti-Apache alliances and launch anti-Apache attacks (Park, "Spanish," 336).

164. Park, "Spanish," 330. Weber, *Bárbaros*, 146–51. The uprising in Michoacán from 1766–1767, for example, Spain ruthlessly crushed (Gutiérrez Cruz, "Granados," 290).

165. See Gutiérrez Cruz, "Granados," 288, 292, 295.

166. Granados y Gálvez, *Tardes Americanas* 1, 56.

167. See Blackhawk, *Violence*; Delay, *War*; Hämäläinen, *Comanche Empire*. Most continued to live as the equestrian rulers of Kónitsaahii gokíyaa (Gran Apachería), which overlapped Comanchería. In the eighteenth century, these comprised the spaces that are currently Texas, New Mexico, eastern Arizona, and portions of Coahuila, Nueva Viscaya, and Sonora (Babcock, *Apache*, 5).

168. Cañizares-Esguerra, *How to Write*, 132, 173.

169. Winterer, *Enlightenments*, 78, 82, 84, 86. In his *History of America*, William Robertson returned to what original sources he could: studying not only sixteenth-century publications—most notably Purchas's reproduction of the *Codex Mendoza*—but also arranging to have new copies made from originals in Rome and Berlin (Winterer, *Enlightenments*, 76–88).

170. Robertson, *History*, 2: 484.

171. Almeida, *Reimagining*, 20. It was banned in Spanish America.

172. Nemser, "Eviction," 131; 131–32.

173. Muñoz, *Historia*, 1: xlviii–xlx. See also *Catálogo Muñoz*; Slade, "Enlightened" and "Imperial," and Nemser, "Eviction."

174. Muñoz, *Historia*, 1: xlviii–xlx.

175. Muñoz *Historia*, 1: vi–vii.

176. In fact, his volume contained nothing of ancient American history, which he deemed unnecessary because, "it does not appear that any of them [Indigenous Americans] ever attained to a sufficient number of general and abstract ideas, or scarce ever tasted the blessings of a tranquil government, so as to rise from that depth of obscurity to the light of true knowledge" (Muñoz, *Historia*, 1: 76).

177. Clavigero, 1787, xxx.

178. They were kept in the Real Caja from 1743–1745 then held at the university. In 1787 they were transferred to the Convento de San Francisco in preparation for their passage to Spain, but some were waylaid in Veracruz (Cañizares-Esguerra, *How to Write*, 136–37).

179. In Italy, he was in the company of other exiled criollos such as Abate Juan Ignacio Molina and Juan Pablo Viscardo y Guzmán (Almeida, *Reimagining*, 33). See Reynoso, *Clavigero*.

180. Clavigero, 1787, xxiv, xxviii–xxiv. He consulted materials at the university as well as the Vatican libraries and the archives in Hapsburg Vienna. The Vatican library houses, among others, the *Codex Borgia*, *Codex Ríos*, *Codex Vaticanus B*, and *Codex Mexicanus 1*. The *Codex Cospi* (formerly held in the Museo Cospiano) is now at the University of Bologna.

181. The English title omits "antiquity," giving it a different temporal signification. The German *Geschichte von Mexico* (Leipzig, 1789–1790) does the same. A Spanish translation was published in London in 1826 and Mexico City in 1844.

182. Quoted in Almeida, *Reimagining*, 40, 49. The Italian version was first noticed in Britain's *Critical Review* of July 1781.

183. Robertson, *History*, 2: xx; Cañizares-Esguerra, *How to Write*, 235–36. Clavijero's premature death in 1787 precluded a response.

184. Clavigero, 1787, vii.

185. Clavigero, 1787, vii.

186. Clavigero, 1787, xvii.

187. Clavigero, 1787, xxxi. See Pagden, *Spanish*, 101–16; Almeida, *Reimagining*, 23; Winterer, *Enlightenments*, 89.

188. By routinely referring to the years before and including the era of the Triple Alliance as "ancient," Clavijero emphasized "antiquity" as a political (i.e., the time

before Spanish rule) rather than temporal category. For Clavijero, "ancient" history was Nahua-specific. Periodizing this history in the same way as that of Greece and Rome was an act of American equality.

189. Clavigero, 1787, xvii.

190. On European timelines, the "ancient" period occurred before the fifth century, while later events are "modern" (or "medieval"). "Ancient history" also means "early in the world's history," although in the eighteenth century it tended to reference the time before the fall of Rome ("ancient history, n.," *OED Online*). See also "modern, adj.": "Characteristic of the present time, or the time of writing."

191. He signaled by name, for example, his use of a "History of the Conquest" written by Taddeo de Niza, "a noble Indian of Tlascala," as well as those "Historical Commentaries" written "in the Mexican language" by Gabriel d'Ayala, "a noble Indian of Texcuco" (Clavigero, 1787, xvii).

192. See chapter ten of Veytia's *História Indiana de México* (1836) and Cañizares-Esguerra, *How to Write*, 204–65.

193. Boturini, *New*, 63.

194. Clavigero, 1787, 112. Although Clavijero's reliance on iconic manuscripts is rarely announced, it is implied when he discusses altepetl names, as in the examples of Colhuacan and Tlatilolco (1787, 121, 121m, 124).

195. Clavigero, 1787, xxii; 112. See Kirchhoff, "Aztlán" and García-Zambrano, "Ancestral Rituals."

196. The word is a demonym for "Aztlán," written in alphabetic Nahuatl underneath the calli in the *Codex Aubin* and also featuring in the *Codex Azcatitlan* (as "Ascatilta"). The synonymous usage of "Azteca" for "Mexican" is retained in English; in fact, "Azteca" was first introduced into the English language in this context ("Aztec, n. and adj.," *OED Online*). "Azteca" does not appear in the Spanish Royal Academy's dictionary until 1884.

197. Clavigero, 1787, 124. The terms are often grouped, revealing their synonymous relationship, as in "Aztechi o Messicanai"; "Messicani o Aztechi"; "Aztechi, ovvero Messicani" (Clavigero, 1787, 10, 24a, 124). He uses "Aztechi" to name the "Mexican" people thirteen times.

198. Clavigero, 1787, xxiv.

199. Confusingly, he described having "acquired the Mexican language [Nahuatl]" and "conversed with the Mexicans," which could mean any Nahuas or any Mexico City residents (Clavigero, 1787, vii).

200. The presidial line recognized the de facto frontier between Spanish and Indigenous lands, even if the Crown claimed sovereignty north of it.

201. Clavigero, 1787, 114, 115f. When Clavigero elaborates the migration route through "Pimería," he apologizes for a relative dearth of information on the "Casas Grandes," writing: "We should wish to have a plan of their form and dimensions; but now it would be very difficult to be obtained, the whole of that country being depopulated by the furious incursions of the Apachas and other barbarous nations" (1787, 114, 115f.)

202. Clavigero, 1787, 112.

203. Clavigero, 1787, 112d. See Ives, "Reconstruction"; Kino, *Kino's Historical Memoir*; Burrus, *Kino*. Kino's 1701 map first appeared in the *Jesuit Relations* in 1705 and *Philosophical Transactions* in 1708.

204. Boturini, *New*, 214.

205. Clavigero, 1787, 114–15. See Ives, "Reconstruction." Robertson also included information about "Casas Grandes" (now called Paquimé) located at "lat. N 30. 46 longit. 258. 24. From the Island of Teneriffe, or 460 leagues NNW from Mexico" (Robertson, *History*, 2: 484). The ancestral desert-dwelling peoples who built and lived at Paquimé are conventionally, but mistakenly, referred to as "Hohokum"; their descendants live among O'odham, Hopi, and Zuni communities. See Hinsley and Wilcox, "Arizona's First Sacred Site." Boturini and Clavijero identified "Casas Grandes" (Paquimé) as a Mexica site due to the "earthen pots, dishes, and jars, and little looking-glasses of the stone Itztli [obsidian]" there (Clavigero, 1787, 114–15).

206. Clavigero, 1787, 115. Boturini believed "Case grandi" to be unlike the settlements of nearby Indigenous peoples, by which he presumably meant Pueblo and ancestral Puebloan dwellings.

207. The Franciscan mission town built in 1580 was destroyed and reestablished a century later. The military base there was a center of conflict and negotiation with Apache and other Indigenous groups. For more on the anti-Apache campaign, see Quintero Saravia, *Bernardo de Gálvez*, 21–61

208. Clavigero, 1787, 115. Clavijero identifies this as Culicán, then in Nueva Galicia (1787, 114e).

209. Clavigero, 1787, 116. He identifies trenches near Nayarit not as Mexica but as "made by the Cor[a] [náayerite], to defend themselves from the Mexicans in their route from Huicilhuacan to Chicomoztoc" (1787, 115).

210. Clavigero, 1787, 115; 115–16.

211. Quoted in Williams, *Madoc*, 15.

Chapter 2

1. Belknap [Varenius, pseud.], "Thoughts," 7–8. The pseudonym alluded to Bernhard Varenius, author of *Geographia generalis* (1650). Belknap would found the Massachusetts Historical Society in 1791.

2. Belknap, "Thoughts," 7–8. On eighteenth-century humoral and environmental thinking see Parrish, *Curiosity*, 78–79; Lafleur, *Natural History*, 4–5, 32–62. On Jefferson and the environment see Chiles, *Transformable*, 64–106; Pamela Regis, *Describing Early America*, 79–105.

3. See Gerbi, *Dispute* and Pratt, *Imperial Eyes*.

4. Belknap, "Thoughts," 8.

5. Belknap, "Thoughts," 8.

6. Belknap draws from Samuel Stanhope Smith's 1787 essay and Blumenbach's continental race theory, on which see Horsman, *Race*, 98–157; Stanton, *Leopard's Spots*; Jordan, *White over Black*; Dain, *Hideous Monster*. On natural history and race see Meyers and Pritchard, *Empire's Nature*; Schiebinger and Swan, *Colonial Botany*; Winterer, *Enlightenments*; Parrish, *American Curiosity*; Murphy, "Translating"; Iannini, *Fatal Revolutions*; Strang, *Frontiers of Science*.

7. Hill's argument for the centrality of husbandry to whiteness has profoundly affected my thinking ("Blood"). See also Martínez-San Miguel and Arias, *Routledge Companion*.

8. Belknap, "Thoughts," 8.

9. Webster, "Letter 1," 11.

10. McClure, *Diary*, 92. A devotee of Eleazer Wheelock, McClure directed Moor's Charity School and went to Oneida with Joseph Johnson (Peters, *Diary*, v). From 1743–1758 Chiningue (Logstown, Pennsylvania) was an intertribal village and trading post (Tanner, *Atlas*, 41, 44, 47).

11. McClure, *Diary*, 91–92. In 1772 Joseph Tomlinson Jr.—a slave-owning Marylander who claimed four hundred acres on the Virginia side of the Ohio River—found he had built his stockade cabin (which he called Fort Tomlinson) only a stone's throw away from a sixty-foot-tall mound (Fenton, *Fruitful Valley*, 8–9, 19). The family evacuated in 1777 but returned in 1784.

12. Cresswell, *Journal*, 71; Delf, *Mammoth Mound*, 10.

13. Cresswell, *Journal*, 123. He was accompanied by George Rogers Clark.

14. Martinko, "So Majestic," 32.

15. Webster, "Letter 1," 12.

16. Hunter calls this the "multiple-migration displacement scenario" (*Place of Stone*, 12–13, 112–29). Kolodny calls it a "rupture" narrative ("Competing Narratives").

17. Levin Rojo, *Return*, 7–12. For essential work on the "Moundbuilder myth" see Silverberg, *Moundbuilders* and Barnhardt, *American Antiquities*. Other key texts include Hay, "Moundbuilder Ecology"; Kennedy, *Hidden Cities*; Kolodny, "Fictions"; Martinko, "So Majestic"; Sayre, "Mound Builders"; Watts, *Colonizing*; Williams, *Fantastic Archaeology*. See also Galloway, "Medievalism"; McGuire, "Archeology"; Miller, "Soil."

18. O'Brien uses "firsting" in reference to white settlers in the Northeast but I find it useful in this context as well (*Firsting*).

19. O'Brien, *Firsting*, xxi, xv.

20. The "Doctrine of Discovery" altered but did not upend title. See Cheyfitz, *Poetics of Imperialism* and Ben-zvi, *Native Land*.

21. Rifkin, "Settler common sense." On seriality see Ross, "Historical." See also White, *Backcountry*.

22. See Williams, "From Whence Came" and Watts, *Colonizing*.

23. Browne and Lafleur have argued in other contexts that racialization is a strategy for producing difference in the service of governance, for which I am in their debt (Browne, *Dark Matter*, 12–16; Lafleur, *Sexuality*, 20). See also Morgensen, "Biopolitics of Settler Colonialism."

24. See Rifkin, "Making Peoples."

25. Martinko, "So Majestic," 32; Shannon, "Ohio Company."

26. Martinko, *Historic*, 16, 18; also "So Majestic."

27. I.e., William Bartram, Thomas Jefferson, and Benjamin Smith Barton.

28. Watts, *Colonizing*; Mann, "Intruding"; Mann, *Archaeologists*.

29. This is "happiness" in the sense articulated by the First Continental Congress in 1774.

30. Foucault, *Security*, 98–99.

31. Quoted in Greene, *Science*, 343.

32. Jefferson, *Writings*, 223.

33. Adair, *History*, 194–95.

34. Jefferson called them "barrows" likely because he thought of them as tombs and thus "monuments." Kennedy argues that Jefferson did not call them "monuments" until after 1799 ("Jefferson," 111).

35. Jefferson, *Writings*, 223; Cf. "monument, n." *OED Online*. Robertson's similar conclusion—that the Mexican structures were "monument[s] of American industriousness"—followed directly from eighteenth-century European discussions of American abilities, taking the phrase itself from Diderot and d'Alembert's *Encyclopédie* (quoted in Winterer, *Enlightenments*, 83; "Mexico, ville de," in Diderot and d'Alembert, *Encyclopédie*, 10: 480).

36. Bartram, *Travels*, 37.

37. "Account of the Short Creek Settlement," 410.

38. Heart, "A Letter," 215.

39. See Pateman, "Settler Contract," 35–78 on "vacant land" and sovereignty.

40. Smith, *Lectures*, 14–16; Pocock, *Barbarism*, 309–29. See also Pagden, "Defense" and Berry, *Social Theory*, especially 61–73, 93–99. Gibbon's theory of rising and falling civilizations is a version of stadialism (Pocock, "Gibbon"). On stadial theory, see Jordan, *White over Black*, 218–91.

41. Martinko, *Historic*, 5. Similarly, Buffon had proposed peoples' dominance over nature as a sign of civilization (Buffon, *Histoire Naturelle*, 5: 225–54).

42. Hodgen, *Early Anthropology*, 272–76.

43. Although "Asiatic origins" was most popular, the transatlantic hypothesis also gained many adherents. In the 1780s a "tidal wave of Welsh Indian stories" broke on Atlantic shores, sending travelers out to find Welsh-speaking "white aborigines" or "White Paducas" (Williams, *Madoc*, 37; McCulloh, *Researches*, 217; Watts, *Colonizing*, 29). See also Watts, *Colonizing*, 23–53. Williams argues these fantasies of "sanitized contact" were meant to justify national expansion (*Madoc*, 23).

44. Carver, *Travels*, 211. He believed "America received its first inhabitants from the northeast" by separate migrations "from Tartary, China, Japon, or Kamchatka" (*Travels*, 210).

45. Fisher, "Cartography," 574. See also Mucher, "Born of the Soil."

46. Nor did the term "native" necessarily refer to the peoples otherwise called "Indians." During the US War of Independence, "Native American" was used to distinguish Patriots from Loyalists ("native," adj., *OED Online*). See Horsman, *Race*.

47. "Aborigine, n. and adj.," and "indigenous, adj.," *OED Online*. Humboldt uses "Indian" and "indigenous" synonymously in his 1808 *Essai Politique*. Barton once planned to write of "indigenous vegetables" (quoted in Ewan and Ewan, *Barton*, 463).

48. "aboriginal title, n." *OED Online*. See also McNeil, *Common Law*.

49. Spencer, "Two Unpublished," 571; Stanton, *Leopard*, 65–72; Chiles, *Transformable*, 91–106. Polygenesis would take off in the US after Abraham Bradley's 1801 *New Theory of the Earth* (Spencer, "Two Unpublished," 570, 570n20).

50. Barton, *New Views*, iv, vi–vii.

51. Byrd, *Transit*, 202.

52. Dain, *Hideous Monster*, 1–80. Barton spent much of *Observations* refuting Kames.

53. Lafleur argues for the connection between natural history and settler colonialism (*Sexuality*, 155–58). For antiquarianism's centrality to US race thinking, see Stanton, *Leopard's Spots*, 1–15.

54. Barton, *Elements*, 10, 70, 111. Cf. "indigenous, adj." *OED Online*. Linnaeus began distinguishing subspecies in his tenth edition of *Systema naturae* (1758): Homo sapiens Ferus, Americanus, Europaus, Asiaticus, Afercanus, Monstruosus. On taxonomy, see Schiebinger, *Nature's Body*, 14, 44–47.

55. For race thinking in the early United States, see Chiles, *Transformable*; LaFleur, *Sexuality*; Dain, *Hideous Monster*. On transatlantic racial thinking see Schiebinger, *Nature's Body*; Wheeler, *Complexion*.

56. Hodgen, *Early Anthropology*, 272–76.

57. Jefferson, *Writings*, 264–65.

58. Chiles, *Transformable*, 64–106. See also Hill, "Blood."

59. See Onuf, *Jefferson's Empire*; Taylor, "Jefferson's Pacific"; Kehoe, "Manifest Destiny."

60. Greene, *Science*, 320–42; Stanton, *Leopard's Spots*; Horsman, *Race*. Curran suggests degenerationist arguments about racial mutability were outmoded by the 1780s and replaced by stadial theory (*Anatomy*, 169, 194).

61. Calloway, *Victory*, 39.

62. Adams, *Papers*, 16: 205–6.

63. Adams, *Papers*, 16: 205–6; Wallace, *Death and Rebirth*, 151–55.

64. *Continental Congress* 1783, 25: 677–95; Horsman, *Expansion* 16–20.

65. Washington, *Papers*, 2: 141.

66. Washington, *Papers*, 2: 141.

67. Jefferson, *Papers*, 6: 581–617. In a 1784 letter to Madison expanding on the act "ceding the lands North of Ohio," Jefferson references giant bones surfaced in North and South America (*Papers* 6: 544–45, 547).

68. Jefferson, *Papers*, 7: 10.

69. Jefferson, *Papers*, 7: 10.

70. Jefferson, *Papers*, 7: 9–11.

71. Cayton, *Frontier Republic*, 7–9; Rohrbaugh, *Land Office*, 15–16; Saler, *Settlers' Empire*, 41–55. See also Hindraker, *Elusive Empire*; Furstenberg, "Trans-Appalachian." After the Continental army disbanded following the Revolutionary War, Fort McIntosh—a former French blockhouse below the falls of Big Beaver Creek—became home to the new nation's standing army, the First American Regiment.

72. *Treaties*, 6–7. The assembled Native representatives "acknowledge[d] themselves and all their tribes to be under the protection of the United States and of no other sovereign whatsoever" (*Treaties*, 7).

73. Madison, *Papers*, 8: 309–11. Signed in January 1786, the Treaty of Fort Finney was never ratified by the US Senate. On the treaty council, see White, *Middle Ground*, 417, 435–39.

74. Quoted in Taylor, *History*, 454, 449–50. Clark, who had been fighting Shawnees since 1774, was a particularly insulting addition.

75. Quoted in Brooks, *Common Pot*, 126.

76. Quoted in Taylor, *History*, 455–56.

77. *Treaties*, 18–20. The United States "allot[ed] to the Shawanee nation, lands within their territory to live and hunt upon, beginning at the South line of the land allotted to the Wyandots and Delaware nations" (*Treaties*, 18). In the following century, the movement supporting Tecumseh fought to reclaim these homelands.

78. *Continental Congress* 1785, 28: 375–86. See Calloway, *Victory*, 35–60 for an overview of this treaty-making and land-division process.

79. The federal government kept every eighteenth and thirty-sixth lot as "public land."

80. Calloway, *Victory*, 39. The legacy of the US Public Land Survey is reflected in straight lines drawn across the United States.

81. Tanner, *Atlas*, 44.

82. Barton, *Observations*, 1787.

83. See Shannon, "Ohio Company," 393–413.

84. Shannon, "Ohio Company," 400.

85. Quoted in Sayre, "Mound Builders," 227. See Cayton, "Marietta," 103–105.

86. See Calloway, *George Washington*; Hindraker, *Elusive Empire*; Cayton, *Frontier Republic*; Hurt, *Ohio Frontier*, Hatter, *Citizens*; Harper, *Unsettling*.

87. Quoted in Barnhart, *American Antiquities*, 55; Evans, *An Analysis*, 13.

88. Filson, *Kentucke*, 80, 8.

89. Adair, *History*, 185n. He recounted a Chickasaw elders' report of a group from "the old Chikkasah nation" who came north from Mexico around 1700, "in quest of their brethren" reportedly killed or expelled by French soldiers (*History*, 196–97).

90. Quoted in Barnhardt, *American Antiquities*, 75.

91. McClure, *Diary*, 108. Lenape and Six Nations fighters battled Catawbas in the 1720s–1730s.

92. Quoted in Barnhart, *American Antiquities*, 67; Zeisberger, "Zeisberger's History," 30–31; De Schwenitz, *Life*, 371–72, 433, 436; Gill and Curtis, *Man Apart*, 52.

93. Filson, *Kentucke*, 73, 26.
94. Filson, *Kentucke*, 74.
95. Jones, "A Plan," 29.
96. Jones, "A Plan," 29. See also Martinko, *Historic*, 22.
97. Jones, "A Plan."
98. Rufus Putnam was also supposed to join the surveying party but could not.
99. Madison, *Papers*, 8 : 410–13.
100. Barton, "Journals," 61. APS; McAtee, "Journals," 28. APS.
101. Wellenreuther and Wessel, *Zeisberger*, 614. It is close to current-day Akron, Ohio.
102. Barton, "Journals," 95. APS; McAtee, "Journals," 42. APS.
103. Barton, *Observations*, 22.
104. Tanner, *Atlas*, 43–67. Much of the tangle of peoples, languages, lands, and histories was a result of post-invasion upheavals, but some stretched to time immemorial.
105. Barton, "Journals," 95. APS; McAtee, "Journals," 42. APS.
106. The consequences of the 1774 "Yellow Creek Massacre"—when Virginia settlers ambushed and killed relatives of Ohio Seneca-Cayuga leader Chief Logan—triggered "Lord Dunmore's War," pitting Virginia (and therefore Kentucky) colonial forces against Ohio Seneca, Shawnee, and Lenape ones. See Harper, *Unsettling*, 61–66; Hindraker, *Elusive Empire*, 185–226; McConnell, *Country Between*. After this Shawnees lost their confidence in Lenape peace-making abilities (Fur, *Women*, 205).
107. Hurt, *Ohio Frontier*, 10. The Shawnees underwent a long period of migration and coalescence, settling as far as the Delaware, Susquehanna, and Savannah River valleys by the 1690s. See Warren, "Greatest Travelers," *Worlds*; Lakomäki, *Gathering Together*; Spero, "Stout, Bold, Cunning."
108. Tanner, *Atlas*, 44.
109. Evans, "A General Map. . ."; the Eries, defeated by the Five Nations in the long wars, were forced to leave their lands by 1656 and joined Huron/Wendat kin (Tanner, *Atlas*, 30).
110. Ironstrack, "Crooked Trail"; Anderson, *Crucible*, 22–32; Edmunds, "Pickawillany"; Tanner, *Atlas*, 44–45. See also White, *Middle Ground*, 94–222.
111. The Seven Years' War decimated "middle ground" relationships (White, *Middle Ground*, 317).
112. Dowd, *Spirited*, 33.
113. See Tanner, *Atlas*, 44; Sleeper-Smith, *Indigenous Prosperity*, 244; White, *Middle Ground*.
114. Olmstead, *Blackcoats*; Marsh, *Hannah Freeman*.
115. White, "Cahokia"; Layton, "Transformation."
116. See Dubcovsky, *Informed Power*; Ethridge, *Chicaza to Chickasaw* and *Creek Country*; Ethridge and Shuck-Hall, *Mapping*; Layton, "Indian Country"; Shuck-Hall, *Journey to the West*; White, "After Cahokia."
117. See White, *Middle Ground*; McConnell, *Country Between*; Hurt, *Ohio Frontier*; Warren, *Worlds*; Lakomaki, *Gathering Together*, Nichols, *Peoples*.

118. Brooks, *Our Beloved Kin*, 221. See Hindraker, *Elusive Empires*.
119. On Zane's claim see Winsor, *Westward Movement*, 69.
120. McClure, *Diary*, 69; Harper, *Unsettling*, 39–45; 51–56.
121. Brooks, *Our Beloved Kin*, 216, 222; Mt. Pleasant, "Contexts for Critique," 533–36.
122. See Hintzen, *Border Wars*.
123. Barton, "Journals," 95. APS; McAtee, "Journals," 42. APS.
124. Barton, "Journals," 95. APS; McAtee, "Journals," 42. APS. Barton referred to the cradleboard as "one of those curious machines in which the women carry their you[ng] children."
125. Hitakonanu'laxk, *Grandfathers*, 17.
126. Barton, "Journals," 95. APS; McAtee, "Journals," 42. APS.
127. White, *Middle Ground*, 368; Hindraker, *Elusive Empires*, 238–42; Mintz, *Seeds*, 86–155; Harper, *Unsettling*, 119–44.
128. On the war and its aftermath, see White, *Middle Ground*, 366–412.
129. Tanner, *Atlas*, 81.
130. Tanner, *Atlas*, 81–83; Heckewelder, "Account," 49n1; Dowd, *Spirited*, 65–89.
131. Hitakonanu'laxk, *Grandfathers*, 27–30; see also Harper, *Unsettling* and Hurt, *Ohio Frontier*.
132. Griffin, "Reconsidering," 11–31.
133. White, *Middle Ground*, 368.
134. See Schutt, *Peoples*; White, *Middle Ground*; Haskins, "Shawnee and Delaware."
135. See Brook, *Common Pot*, 3–8 and 106–62.
136. *American State Papers, Class 2: Indian Affairs* (Hereafter *ASP2*), 1: 9. Brooks, *Common Pot*, 121–26. Both Thayendanegea and Degonwadonti (Molly Brant) were in attendance, but the Brants' imbrication in the William Johnson circle (as well as Joseph Brant's willingness to sell land)—made for lasting divisions with members of the Haudenosaunee Confederacy (Hall, *American Empire*, 387).
137. Quoted in Brooks, *Common Pot*, 124; Hall, *American Empire*, 386. This is from Brant's 1793 letter to McKee. He continued: "If we saw that such a part of the country belongs to one nation and such a part to another, the union cannot subsist and we cannot more effectually serve our enemies, whose whole aim has been to divide us" (quoted in Brooks, *Common Pot*, 124).
138. Quoted in Brooks, *Common Pot*, 124; White, *Middle Ground*, 411.
139. *ASP2*, 1: 8–9; Brooks, *Common Pot*, 292n65; White, *Middle Ground*, 417, 435–39, 443–47.
140. *ASP2*, 1: 8; *Middle Ground*, 413–68; Calloway, *Victory*.
141. *ASP2*, 1: 9.
142. *ASP2*, 1: 9.
143. *ASP2*, 1: 243; 243–45. For an account of the 1790–1794 period, see Calloway, *Victory*.
144. Jefferson, *Papers*, 9: 476–78; see also Parsons, "Discoveries."
145. Jefferson, *Papers*, 10: 316; 9: 476–78.

146. Jefferson, *Papers*, 10: 316.
147. Höpfl, "Scotsman," 20; 31–32; Shapiro, *Culture of Fact*. Lewis, *Democracy of Facts*, 72–106. On "progress" in American history writing, see Callcott, *History*, 160–66.
148. On colonial analogy see Greenblatt, *Marvelous Possessions*.
149. Brown, "Eighteenth-Century Historian"; Smitten, "Impartiality"; Winterer, *Enlightenments*.
150. Robertson, *History*, 2: 280.
151. For US uses of Classical antiquity, see Winterer, *Mirror*; Shelav, *Rome*.
152. Robertson, *History*, 2: 286, 297. These structures were copied from the Mixtec *Codex Mexicanus*.
153. Robertson, *History*, 2: 485.
154. Jefferson, *Papers*, 11: 323–24. Robertson, *History*, 2: 271–72.
155. Robertson, *History*, 2: 271–72.
156. Robertson, *History*, 2: 293, 271, 272. Robertson relied heavily on Adair, who presumed a similarity between the "primitive Chikkasah" and people the Spanish writers "stile Chichemicas, and whom they repute to have been the first inhabitants of Mexico" (*History*, 196–97).
157. Robertson, *History*, 2: 482, 485.
158. Symmes, *New-York*, 234–35. Emphasis mine.
159. Symmes, *New-York*, 234–35.
160. The first US edition, published by Dobson in Philadelphia, was advertised in the January 1804 *Monthly Anthology* (Dobson also published Barton's *Papers* in 1796). Jefferson owned the 1780 Italian original.
161. Clavijero, *Storia*, 1: 267–68. Curiously, Clavijero's engraving of Tenochtitlan's Templo Mayor came from Torquemada's *Monarquía Indiana* (1615), not an Indigenous source.
162. Sargent, "Plan," 29. The drawings were made at Sargent's request; Sargent sent a stylized map to the American Academy of Arts and Sciences in 1787. See also Martinko, *Historic*, 15–39.
163. Heart, "Account," 427.
164. Heart, "Letter," 215.
165. Heart, "Plan."
166. Smith, *Mapping of Ohio*, 35–37. Martinko suggests Freemasonry led Putnam to see pyramids (*Historic Real Estate*, 24, 232n51). The sketch Thaddeus Mason Harris provided in his 1805 *Journal* clearly depicted "Conus" as a pyramid.
167. Holmes devoted one note to "Mexican History," copying Clavijero to explain that the "Mexicans lived in Aztlan, a country situated to the north of California, until about AD 1160; when they commenced their migration toward the country of Anahuac" (*American Annals*, 482–83).
168. Jefferson, *Papers*, 14: 698.
169. Morse, *Geography*, 577, 580, 715; Coram, *Political Inquiries*, 12.

170. Harris, *Journal*, 163, 103.
171. Harris, *Journal*, 158–59.
172. Leon-Portilla, "Aztecas," 307–13.
173. Robertson, *History*, 2: 271–72.
174. "Account of the Short Creek Settlement," 411.
175. Robertson, *History*, 2: 289.
176. Cutler, "American Antiquities," 1.
177. Cutler, "American Antiquities," 1. Cutler also extended this to the "present natives," between whom and the ancient Mexicans he suspected some resemblance.
178. Cutler, "American Antiquities," 1.
179. Harper, *Unsettling*, 119–44.
180. *ASP2*, 1: 12, 13.
181. See Jefferson, *Papers,* 6: 60–64.
182. *ASP2*, 1: 12, 13.
183. Carolina whites tried to establish the "State of Franklin" and committed "many unprovoked outrages . . . against the Cherokees" (*ASP2*, 1: 36).
184. *ASP2*, 1: 52.
185. See Rockwell, *Indian Affairs* and Horsman, *Expansion*.
186. This would be the site of Sarah Josepha Hale's *Genius of Oblivion* (1823).
187. The pope specified that refusing conversion made "heathens" into eternal enemies liable to be conquered in "just war." See Greer, *Possession*; Seed, *Ceremonies*; Jones, *License for Empire*.
188. *ASP2*, 1: 9, 53. Congress's Resolve of July 2, 1788, conceded "the Indian right to the lands they possess" and planned "to appropriate a sum of money solely for the purpose of extinguishing the Indian claims to lands they had ceded to the United States, and for obtaining regular conveyances of the same." On Knox see Prucha, *Great Father*.
189. See Rockwell, *Indian Affairs*.
190. *ASP2*, 1: 53.
191. Johnson v. M'Intosh (1823) later obviated the right with the device of "occupation" as opposed to "possession."
192. *ASP2*, 1: 53. Knox contended that Indigenous nations ought to be considered "foreign nations," which resulted in the 1790 Indian Trade and Intercourse Act.
193. Vattel, *Le droit des gens*, 1: 35. The Black Legend is operative here. See Greer et al., *Rereading the Black Legend* and DeGuzmán, *Long Shadow*.
194. Vattel, *Le doit des gens*, 1: 35; Wertheimer, *Imagined*, 27–28. Vattel's book was staple reading for Franklin, Washington, and Jefferson (Ossipow and Gerber, "Reception").
195. Vattel, *Le doit des gens*, 1: 34–35.
196. Lucius, "Observations," 1. The letter was widely reprinted and included in the *American Museum* in February 1789.
197. Farrell, *Counting Bodies*, 6, 2, 7; Nelson, *Who Counts*, 17, 25–26. See also Hoppit, "Political Arithmetic."

198. A century earlier, Lenni Lenape ("ordinary people" or "human beings") were spread across Lenapehoking ("land of the people") in autonomous villages and bands loosely grouped by geography, language, and clans or divisions (Fur, *Women*, 5, 6).

199. For linguistics and Indian policy see Harvey, *Native Tongues*.

200. Byrd, *Transit*, xx, 126, 148.

201. Lee describes waves of "first" and "second" migrations, but I avoid this metaphor to deemphasize teleology and stress continuity within change (*Middle Waters*).

202. Ironstrack, "Myaamia Beginning" and "Walking Myaamionki."

203. They became known to Inoka/Peoria (Illinois) and Myaamia peoples as "Arkansa" or "kaanseenseepiiwi" (Dorsey, "Migrations," 215; "kaanseenseepiiw-[n.inan] Ohio River," *Myaamia-Peewaalia Dictionary*. Miami-Illinois Indigenous Languages Digital Archive, Miami Tribe of Oklahoma. https://mc.miamioh.edu/ilda-myaamia/dictionary/).

204. Lee, *Middle Waters*, 23; McMillan, "Migration Legends," 15–16; Dorsey, "Migrations"; Pauketat, "America's First," 20–21. After living on the Missouri River's western edge, the upriver families separated again, with Kansa, Ponca, Omaha groups traveling to three separate waters.

205. Lee, *Middle Waters*, 9; Burns, *Osage*, 3–22; Vehik, "Dhegiha Origins," 232; Henning, "Adaptive," 253, 260–62.

206. For kinship and captivity, see Snyder, *Indian Slavery*. For 1540–1720, see Ethridge and Shuck-Hall, *Mapping*.

207. Reilly, "People of Earth," 125–38. See also Anderson, "Monumentality"; King, "Historic Period."

208. "Abandonment" overlooks push and pull factors and thus Indigenous agency or strategy in favor of "disappearance" (cf. Cobb and Butler, "Vacant," 636–38). For archaeological dissent, see Lewis, "Late Prehistory"; for Mississippian cycling see Anderson, "Savannah River Chiefdoms."

209. See, for example, Shoemaker, "How Indians" and Safir, "Global" and *Measuring*.

210. Brooks, *Common Pot*, 109–11; Oakley, "Center of the World," 4.

211. Brown, "Cahokian Expression," 118–19 and "Birdman"; Diaz-Granados, "Marking Stone"; Dye, "Art," 198, 203; Hall, "Cahokia," 98–100, 102–3; Kelly, "Redefining Cahokia"; Seeman, "Hopewell Art," 57; Pauketat, *Cahokia*.

212. Howe, *Retelling Trickster*, x, 7.

213. Hill, *Clay*, 3.

214. Hill, *Clay*, 5.

215. Cusick, *Sketches*, 13.

216. Howe, *Retelling Trickster*, 13, 1. In a Niitsítapiiksi world, Howe relays, "beings are known by the way they move" (*Retelling Trickster*) 29.

217. Gunn, *Empire*, 40, and Dain, *Hideous Monster*, 226–37.

218. Round, "Mississippian," 469. See also Hahn, "Cussita Migration" and Piker, *Acorn Whistler*.

219. For storied lands see Basso, *Wisdom*; Fair, "Inupiat Naming," and Goeman, "From Place to Territories."

220. Howe, *Retelling Trickster*, 12.
221. Lyons, *X-Marks*, 3–5.
222. Trowbridge, *Shawanese Traditions*, 55. See also Warren and Noe, "Greatest Travelers," and Spero, "Stout, Bold, Cunning."
223. Shuck-Hall, *Journey to the West*, 27–29.
224. Costa, *myaamia neehi peewaalia aacimoona*, 53.
225. Volney, *Tableau*, 2: 439; "mihtohseeni-(n.an) Human, Person," *Myaamia-Peewaalia Dictionary*. Miami-Illinois Indigenous Languages Digital Archive, Miami Tribe of Oklahoma. https://mc.miamioh.edu/ilda-myaamia/dictionary/.
226. Galloway, *Choctaw Genesis*, 324–336, 320. Galloway recounts Creeks, Cherokees, Chickasaws, and Choctaws all emerging from the Mother Mound (Galloway, *Choctaw Genesis*, 335). Adair learned Choctaws "called those old fortresses *Nanne Yah*, 'the hills or mounts of God'" (*History*, 377–77).
227. Howe, *Hunger Pots*, 1. Indigenous theorists have argued that earthworks are alive, acting and creating place for their people as living beings (Howe, "Embodied Tribalography"; Hedge Coke, *Blood Run*; Allen, *Trans-Indigenous*, 193–247; Mojica, "In Plain Sight"). Howe views mounds as "embodied stories that Natives carry expressing our duration here as ever-alive and ever-returning" ("Embodied Tribalography," 89). See also Allen, "Earthworks," "Performing" and "Serpentine Figures"; Saunders, "Early Mounds."
228. Cutler, "American Antiquities," 1.
229. Cobb and Butler, "Vacant Quarter," 625.
230. Tuck and Yang, "Decolonizing," 3.
231. For a summary of the eleventh to seventeenth centuries, see Lee, *Middle Waters*, 18–31.
232. McCoy et al., *ašiihkiwi neehi*, 70–71.
233. "The Newark Earthworks: An American Indian Sacred Site," Great Circle Earthworks Museum (Ohio History Connection). Newark, Ohio, August 2018. In 2019 the OHC adopted an "American Indian Policy" and started partnering with forty-five descendant nations—including the Eastern Shawnee Tribe of Oklahoma, Delaware Nation of Oklahoma, Stockbridge-Munsee Community, Wyandotte Nation, Pokagon Band of Potawatomi Indians, and Seneca Nation of Indians—in repatriation efforts and in stewarding many of the "American Indian Sites" that OHC maintains.
234. Silverberg, *Moundbuilders*, 19. After colonial invasion, some Sauk, Mesquakie (Fox), and Ho-Chunk groups started moving southward along the Mississippi River, while Ojibwe communities regrouped in Mni Sota Makoce, a result of fur-trade expansion and the Ojibwe-Dakota Wars (Tanner, *Atlas*, 29–35, 42–47).
235. The "Gentleman of Elvas" mentioned a chief's house "upon a very high mount made by hand for defense; at the other end of the town was a temple, on the top of which perched a wooden fowl with gilded eyes" (quoted in Silverberg, *Moundbuilders*, 10). An account compiled by El Inca Garcilasco in 1605 also described elevated sites built "from twenty-eight to forty-two feet in height (quoted in Silverberg, *Moundbuilders*, 12).
236. Silverberg, *Moundbuilders*, 22, 23.
237. Lee, *Middle Waters*, 233.

238. This was different from Barlow's and Freneau's interest in the Columbian "discovery" (Wertheimer, *Imagined*, 17–90).

239. Kirkland, *Journal*, 56.

240. Clark's letter was reprinted in Schoolcraft, *Historical*, 4: 133–36.

241. Trowbridge, *Shawanese Traditions*, 57.

242. In 1790 an invented "Indian Tradition" about mammoths and earthworks appeared in Carey's *American Museum* and was taken as authentic (quoted in Schoolcraft, *Historical*, 4: 133–136).

243. Steiner, "Account," 543.

244. Steiner, "Account," 544.

245. Barton, "Journals," 62. APS; McAtee, "Journals," 29. APS. Steiner noted that his Ojibwe, Lenape, and Wendat hosts were "of the opinion that these works, and many others, were formerly made by Indians, before any white people came to the country, at a time when the nations always were at war with each other" (Steiner, "Account," 544).

246. Watts, *Colonizing*, 95–137.

247. On the Madoc myth, see Williams, *Madoc*.

248. For an archaeologist's survey of origin theories, see Williams, "From Whence Came."

249. According to Lepper, "nearly all the elements of the [Moundbuilder] myth were derived from American Indian oral traditions" ("Earthworks history").

250. Lyons, *X-Marks*, 3.

251. Lyons, *X-Marks*, 4. For example, "Inscription Rock Petroglyphs" on Kelleys Island in Lake Erie.

252. Lyons, *X-Marks*, 3.

253. Lee, *Middle Waters*, 23.

254. Williams, *Fantastic Archaeology*, 52. See also Marsh, *Hannah Freeman*, 100; White, *Middle Ground*; Witgen, *Infinity*.

255. Barton, *Observations*, iv–v. He forbade a reissuance of *Observations* at the end of his life (Ewan and Ewan, *Barton*, 876).

256. Quoted in Spencer, "Two Unpublished," 568.

257. Quoted in Spencer, "Two Unpublished," 568.

258. Barton, *Observations*, 15, 11, 17.

259. Beside mentioning Fort Harmar, *Observations* betrays little of his western journey.

260. Barton, *Observations*, 30. He attested that the map, identified only as "TOWN," was accurate.

261. Barton, *Observations*, 33, 32, 74nQ. He describes "large eminences" along the Mississippi seen by his countryman James Boyd of Lancaster, who also remarked on the dearth of traditions held by the country's inhabitants, "concerning their antiquity—their use,—or the people, by whom they were constructed" (Barton, *Observations*, 21).

262. Barton, *Observations*, 19, 20.

263. The conclusion is usually more implied than explicit. See Greene, *American Science*, 346; Sayre, "Moundbuilders," 227.

264. Barton, *Observations*, 60; Ewan and Ewan, *Barton*, 126. Other than Clavijero's translation, Barton's *Observations* was the first use of "Tolteca" in English.

265. Barton, *Observations*, 60.

266. Barton, *Observations*, 60.

267. Barton, *Observations*, 60. Barton's muddled instinct to connect the earthworks that were later called "Hopewellian" with those called "Mississippian" anticipated the move in twentieth-century archaeology. The "Hopewell" name comes from the farm owned by Confederate veteran Mordecai Hopewell, where "Hopewell culture" items were recovered in the 1890s.

268. Barton, *Observations*, 65, 67.

269. Barton, *Observations*, 61. Barton's 1803 *Hints on the Etymology* expanded on his earlier comparison between American and Welsh languages.

270. Barton, *New Views* 1797, xxiii; also xciv, xcv, 83.

271. Bartram, *Travels*, 17, 54, 38. The results circulated privately but were not published until 1853, when they were edited by Squier (reprinted in Waselkov and Braund, *William Bartram*). See Williams, "Manuscript."

272. Quoted in Bartram "Observations," 134.

273. Burkhart, "Physics," 40–41.

274. Barton, "Proposals for printing," Barton Papers, Series 1, APS.

275. *ASP2*, 1: 12, 13.

276. *ASP2*, 1: 139–40; White, *Middle Ground*, 448–54.

277. See Bohaker, "Reading" and "Nindoodemag."

278. Quoted in Hall, *American Empire*, 394. From Simon Pokagen's recounting of Tecumseh's 1809 speech ("gwanaajiwi" is "beautiful" in Ojibwemowin). Ohi:yo' is a Seneca name for the Ohio-Allegheny-Susquehanna waterway that settlers called the Allegheny River.

279. Howe, "Embodied Tribalography," 81, 76. As the Indigenous playwright Monica Mojica writes: "The land is our archive, and our embodied relationship to the land defines indigenous identities, history, science, cosmology, literature—and our performance" (Mojica, "In Plain Sight, 219").

280. Knight, "Symbolism." The ceremonial square-ground mounds "are rebuilt each year in connection with a purification rite, the sweeping of the ground" (Knight, "Symbolism," 425).

281. Mann, "Ohio Valley," 444.

282. Hìtakonanu'laxk, *Grandfathers*, 48. Màxaxkuk battled Kichichax'hàl (Great Toad).

283. Hìtakonanu'laxk, *Grandfathers*, 51.

284. The shortest portage between the Ohio-flowing and Great Lakes-flowing rivers is a one-mile carrying place between the Tuscarawas and Cuyahoga, protected by the town Barton visited in 1785 (Tanner, *Atlas*, 41, 44).

285. Hìtakonanu'laxk, *Grandfathers*, 44, 50. The different Lenape orthographies are taken from Hìtakonanu'laxk and the *Lenape Talking Dictionary*. Delaware Tribe of Indians. https://www.talk-lenape.org.

Chapter 3

1. León y Gama, *Descripción*, 2; "Hallazgo del los monolitos" panel, Museo del Templo Mayor (INAH), Mexico City, July 2016.
2. Villela et al., "Introduction," 4; León y Gama, *Descripción*, 1.
3. León y Gama, *Descripción*, 8–9.
4. Most accounts date autonomous movements to the 1790s (Lazo, *Filadelfia*, 162). See also Rodríguez O., *Independence* and Fitz, *Our Sister Republics*.
5. On Enlightenment science and the Spanish Empire, see Engstrand, *Spanish Scientists*; Dew and Delbourgo, *Science and Empire*; Barrera-Osorio, *Experiencing Nature*. See also Bleichmar, *Visible Empire* and Puig-Samper, "Illustrators of the New World."
6. See Rama, *Lettered City*.
7. Lazo, *Filadelphia*, 3, 72–73; Rodríguez O., *Independence*. See also Berruezo León, *La lucha* and McFarlane, "Science and Sedition."
8. Brading, *First America*, 464; León y Gama, *Descripción* 3, 2. See also Pagden, "Identity" and *Spanish Imperialism*; Cañizares-Esguerra, *How to Write*.
9. Brading, *First America*, 388–390; Bauer and Mazzotti, *Creole Subjects*, 6–8, 52–55; Lynch, *Spanish-American Revolutions*, 16–19. In the Carribean context, see Goudie, *Creole America*.
10. Cañizares-Esguerra, *How to Write*, 204–65, 209.
11. Carrera, *Imagining Identity*, 80.
12. Humboldt *Views*, 400; Villela and Miller, "Researches," 82; Pratt, *Amerindian Images*, 584; see also Jaksic, *Hispanic World*.
13. Rodríguez-Alegría, *Archaeology and History*.
14. Lazo, *Filadelfia*, 77–78, 79–80, 81. I use "americano" rather than "criollo" following Lazo. According to Humboldt, criollos regularly began referring to themselves as "Americans" in 1789 (Brading, *First America*, 530).
15. See Farago, "Understanding Visuality." In Nahuatl, writing and painting are expressed with the same word, differentiated by surface: i.e., writing (painting) on paper is tlahcuiloa and on metal (printing) is tepoztlacuiloa (Karttunen, *Dictionary*, 261; Lockhart, *Nahua*, 273).
16. A Spanish dictionary from 1786 reiterated the word's artistic nuance: "To represent something with the brush, burin, pen, or speech . . . according to some, the same as copying or writing, although not in common usage." "Describir, v. a.," *Diccionario* 1780, 334.
17. For a deep exploration of Mexica/Nahua visualizations of the city, see Mundy, *Death*.
18. Hamann, "Social Life," 353.
19. Townsend, *Fifth Sun*, 122–124.
20. González Acosta, "Los herederos," 152; Townsend, *Fifth Sun*, 132–134.
21. Townsend, *Fifth Sun*, 160. They had to labor and supply food and goods in lieu of encomienda (for indios outside the city) or tribute obligations.
22. Quoted in O'Hara, "Stone," 658.

23. Townsend, *Fifth Sun*, 159, 165–75. After the Indigenous uprisings in the sixteenth and seventeenth centuries the restored plaza became even more important as the locus of Spanish power (Nemser, *Race*, 102). See also Exbalin, "Riot."

24. According to tradition, the Virgin appeared to Nahua peasant Juan Diego atop Tepeyac hill (already consecrated to the Mexica earth deity Tonantzin) in 1531. This narrative, first recorded in 1648, sparked the "cult of the Virgin of Guadalupe," which was especially popular in Mexico City but had spread across New Spain by the late eighteenth century (Peterson, "Virgin," 39, 44). In 1578 Sahagún complained: "native worshipers consistently referred to Guadalupe as Tonantzin" (Peterson, "Virgin," 40). See also Peterson, *Visualizing Guadalupe*.

25. Peterson, "Virgin," 40.

26. O'Hara, *Flock Divided*, 96–100. Ethnic enclaves persisted even after parish desegregation (Carrera, *Imagining Identity*, 38–39).

27. Cañizares-Esguerra, *How to Write*, 55–59, 125–29.

28. Because the scope of this study is the settler use and perception of "Indian" (not Indigenous) history, I refer to the "Indigenous archive"—the Indigenous-created, Indigenous-serving material of the past—sparingly.

29. Townsend, *Fifth Sun*, 19, 20; Pool, *Olmec Archaeology*, 118. See also Diehl, *Olmecs* and Justeson and Kaufman, "Decipherment."

30. Townsend, *Fifth Sun*, 9. Toward the Gulf, peoples the Spanish eventually called "Mayas" built grand stone pyramids, used a similar calendar, and recorded their histories on monumental stone slabs. See Evans, *Ancient Mexico* and Spence, "Tzintzuntzan to Paquimé."

31. I follow Townsend in this translation (*Fifth Sun*, 21). See also Carrasco, *Religions*.

32. Townsend, *Fifth Sun*, 46–48.

33. Matthew, *Becoming*, 40–41, 42.

34. MacLachlan and Rodriguez, *Cosmic Race*, 29, 32–33; León-Portilla, *Cantares mexicanos*, 1: 173.

35. Diaz del Castillo described it as enchanting and marvelous. See León-Portillo, *Los antiguos mexicanos*, 10–11; Townsend, *Fifth Sun*, 106.

36. Hamann, "Social Life," 351, 351n2. For Aztec "archaeology," see Matos Moctezuma, *Teotihuacan*, 100–105.

37. Mundy, *Death*, 28; Maffie, *Aztec Philosophy*, 23. See also Bassett, *Earthly Things*. On teotl more expansively, see Maffie.

38. Umberger, "Aztec Sculptures," 23–24. I propose this because the basalt for the Sun Stone came from Mount Xitle.

39. Umberger, "Aztec Sculptures," 19.

40. Florescano, *Myth*, 58, 57. After a great flood in 1449, Motecuhzoma I (reign 1440–1453) had Tenochtitlan rebuilt to emphasize Tenochca-Mexica dominance, with likenesses of Mexica rulers called teixiptlameh (s. teixiptla) carved into the cliffs of Chapultepec along with name and date glyphs to fix memorable events in stone. See Umberger, "Aztec Sculptures," 14, 30.

41. Coe and Koontz, *Mexico*, 61; MacLachlan and Rodriguez O., *Cosmic Race*, 22.

42. Quoted in Aguilar-Moreno, *Handbook*, 403. See also León-Portilla, *Los antiguos mexicanos*, 33.

43. Quoted in Coe and Koontz, *Mexico*, 59; León-Portilla, *Los antiguos mexicanos*, 23–24.

44. Toltec settlement in Cholula is recalled in both the *Anales de Cuauhtinchan* and *Historia Tolteca-Chichimeca*.

45. Quoted in Aguilar-Moreno, *Handbook*, 403; León-Portilla, *Los antiguos mexicanos*, 33.

46. The change in ages is explained as an ongoing cosmic struggle across four powerful Tezcatlipocas (Coe and Koontz, *Mexico*, 205–6, 206–7). The Mexica cosmos is organized under a principle of balanced dualism and ever-moving power, teotl. See Maffie, *Aztec Philosophy* and Carrasco, *Religions*.

47. Bassett, "Bundling."

48. See León-Portilla, *Los antiguos mexicanos*, 16–18. This part of the *Anales* is also known as the *Codex Chimalpopoca*, or "Legend of the Five Suns," a manuscript that supposedly belonged to Ixtlilxóchitl (Townsend, *Fifth Sun*, 220–21).

49. Umberger, "Notions," 90.

50. *Florentine Codex*, 7: 4–7.

51. Umberger, "Notions," 90. Coatlicue had already borne over four hundred children. Huitzilopochtli was conceived with a quetzal feather and born on 1 Tecpatl in the year 2 Acatl.

52. Townsend, *Fifth Sun*, 3–4.

53. Umberger, "Notions," 91; Elson and Smith, "Archaeological deposits."

54. Hamann, "Social Life," 354. The ceremony commences at dusk before Huitzilopochtli's birthday and is marked by extinguishing all sacred and household fires. At midnight a new fire is kindled in a sacrificed human body (like Nanahuatzin) and the flame distributed throughout the land in welcome.

55. Townsend, *Fifth Sun*, x.

56. Townsend, *Fifth Sun*, 4.

57. Umberger, "Notions," 91.

58. Umberger, "Antiques," 83; Hamann, "Social Life," 356.

59. Umberger, "Aztec Sculptures," 28. The Mexica and Acolhua of Texcoco had previously allied against the Tepaneca; the union with Culhuacán—believed to be a mighty Toltec city—allowed the Mexica to claim a connection to the powerful Toltecs.

60. Hamann, "Social Life," 351.

61. As early as 1536, a Nahua man was put on trial for possessing allegedly idolatrous texts (Ruiz Medrano, *Indigenous Communities*, 31).

62. Hamann, "Chronological Pollution"; Mundy, *Death*.

63. Nemser, *Race*, 102–3. It was quite usual to have broken god images built into exterior walls, although some were reportedly installed intact indoors—away from Spanish eyes—as well (Hamann, "Chronological Pollution," 810).

64. Hamann, "Chronological Pollution"; Villella, *Indigenous Elites*, 306.

65. Pagden, *Fall of Natural Man*; Keen, *Aztec Image*, 71–137; Moffitt and Sebastián, *O Brave*.
66. Schávelzon, "La primera excavación."
67. Brading, *First America*, 366–67.
68. López Luján, "El Tajín," 23; Blix, *Paris*, 11–12.
69. Alzate, "Origin," 82. The pagination is out of order in the Newberry Library's copy, cited here.
70. Alzate, "Origin," 82, 84, 82.
71. Alzate, "Origin," 82.
72. Eguiara y Eguren's *Biblioteca Mexicana*, for example, lists Mexica documents but does not use them to construct meaning for colonial Mexico, whereas Boturini, Clavijero and Veytia did.
73. Originally, with the designation of the traza as Spanish-only some out-lying neighborhoods (barrios) were also designated as Indigenous-only. Parishes were equally divided into Spanish (and castas-) serving and Indigenous-serving congregations, the latter known as "doctrinas de indios." See Cope, *Limits* and Estrada Torres, "Fronteras."
74. O'Hara, "Stones," 653. While Indigenous laborers moved into the traza during the seventeenth century—prompting the new "segregación" system designed by Carlos Sigüenza y Gongora and Agustín de Vetancurt in the 1690s—the separate doctrinas and their ethnic makeup remained largely intact over the next century. See Nemser, *Race*; Silva Prada, "Impacto"; Seed, "Social Dimensions."
75. Mundy, *Death*, 41.
76. Mundy, "Place-Names," 349 and *Death*, 135, 137.
77. Mundy, "Place-Names," 342, 344.
78. Mundy, *Death*, 137.
79. Mundy, "Place-Names," 354n44.
80. He published the map in 1768 but altered it the following year and again in 1772 (Alzate, *Nuevo Mapa* and "Plano"). See Valverde and Lafuente, "Space Production," 205–6.
81. The closest mention of "Tierra havitada de los Yndios enemigos" (note past tense) is in Coahuila, just south of the Rio Grande. All named Indigenous peoples are implicitly "Yndios enemigos."
82. O'Hara, "Stones," 665. This explains why he and his cohort believed the doctrinas were irrelevant.
83. Nemser, *Race*, 132; Mundy, "Images," 67 and *Death*, 221. In the 1690s, Sigüenza allegedly compiled Vetancurt's toponymic information onto a map likely meant to help restore the Indigenous-only barrios under the resegregation system; while I do not have concrete evidence that Alzate consulted the Vetancurt records and Boturini's *Plano*, the materials would have been accessible to him and is research typical of his work. Vetancurt was pastor of San José de los Naturales for forty years.
84. Mundy, "Place-Names," 339, 340. In fact, he advocated for the retention of Nahuatl plant names even as the "modern" Linnaean system was Latinizing them (Lafuente and Valverde, "Linnaean Botany," 161n18, 161n19; Alzate, "Carta de Edimburgo,"

20–22). In 1786 the Crown tasked Alzate with working on Hernández's writings; Spanish botanist Casimiro Gómez Ortega published a version of the work in 1790. See also Nemser, *Race*, 132–34.

85. Mundy, "Images"; Nemser, "Archaeology."

86. Mundy, "Place-Names," 340. Alzate's map is held at the BNF. He had planned it for a Spanish-language translation of Clavijero's *History* (which never happened).

87. Mundy, "Place-Names," 339.

88. He recorded them as follows: Moyotla, Teopan ó Xochimilca, Atzalcoalco, Quepopan ó Tlaquechiuhcan.

89. For more on the use of color, see Magaloni Kerpel, "Traces" and *Colors*.

90. The southeastern quarter, San Pablo Teopan, included the center temple complex and the "Mixiuca" (where women give birth). Coatlan, "place of the serpents," is located in San Sebastián Atzalcoalco (Mundy, *Death*, 27, 38).

91. Mundy, *Death*, 21–36.

92. The tecpan (seat of governance), temple, and market were closely located, demonstrating the hallmark "urban nucleation" of Azteca cities. See Lockhart, *Nahuas*, 15, 18–20.

93. Tlatílco, "this is heaps of earth" or "place of earthquakes," is number sixteen (Mundy, *Death*, 52). The Yopico temple in Moyotlan took over in importance from one in Tlatelolco in the 1540s (Mundy, *Death*, 110).

94. Mundy, "Place-Names," 339.

95. For the most part, Alzate seems to have recorded geographical rather than cosmological place names. Although many tlaxilacalli names are "geographically descriptive," usually designating important buildings or referring to historical events or uses, their geography is also cosmic. Mundy explains, "both 'Mixiuca' (where women give birth) and 'Temazcaltitlan' (next to the sweat baths) in the parcialidad of San Pablo Teopan relate to the history of [cosmic] foundation" (*Death*, 27).

96. In fact, many of the Nahuatl names—like Chichimecapan and Cuezcontitlan—are left untranslated, perhaps because Indigenous neighbors were not safe to share their knowledge.

97. Alzate missed that Nahuas were creating new names for spaces both new and old (Mundy, "Place-Names," 345, 350).

98. O'Hara calls these buildings and their contents "polyvocalic" symbols of "social belonging"; he argues that despite the re-arrangement of parish membership the "sacred property" was still "symbolically strong" as "visual mnemonics" of "a collective identity based on 'Indianness'" ("Stones," 650).

99. O'Hara, "Stones," 657.

100. O'Hara, "Stones," 658. Altepeme were host to specific ethnic gods (Lockhart, *Nahuas*, 16–17, 25).

101. Levin Rojo, *Return*, 124; Lockhart, *Nahuas*, 24–25. Nahua migration narratives feature accounts of the "sibling" constituents of the original altepetl of Aztlán. After Tenochtitlan was founded, the migratory constituent parts (called either "tlaxilacalli" or "calpolli") also translated into the constituent parts of the four altepeme (Lockhart,

Nahuas, 16–17). Tezozómoc recorded fifteen "ethnic" calpolli by the early fourteenth century, each with its own "ethnic divinity," ruler, and altepetl territory. Mundy has studied the ceremonial processions that reenacted migration history across the city's topography (*Death*, 169–80).

102. Mundy, *Death*, 137. In the colonial era, tlaxilacalli toponyms were frequently appended to Indigenous residents' personal names, connecting person to place and maintaining the city's former shape in the current day. See Mundy, "Place-Names."

103. Because Tenochtitlan was originally constructed upon an island, both the Mexica and colonial city were subject to flooding.

104. Pietschman, "Protoliberalismo," 27–65. See also Llombart, *Campomanes*. Lafuente and Valverde call these new systems of population management "imperial biopolitics" ("Linnaean Botany," 138, 140).

105. On the 1682 uprising see More, *Baroque Sovereignty*, 158–201 and Exbalin, "Riot."

106. Uribe-Uran, "Birth"; Clark, "Read All About"; Deans-Smith, "Colonial Subject," 175–82.

107. Brading, *First America*, 473–76, 477. The king also opened the Colegio de Arte y Oficinas para Mujers de las Vizcaínas (1767), the Royal College of Surgery (1768), a Royal Public Library (1778)—stocked with libraries from expelled Jesuits—and the Royal Academy of the Three Fine Arts of San Carlos (1783). His successor, Carlos IV (reign 1788–1808), opened the Public Academy of Medicine and Royal Botanical Garden (1788) and the Royal College of Mines (1792).

108. After 1776, criollos were limited to a third of court and clerical positions in Spanish America; the rest were reserved for peninsulares. See Cañizares-Esguerra, *How to Write*, 300; Brading, *First America*, 444–83, Rama, *Lettered City*, 20.

109. On Malaspina see Bleichmar, *Visible Empire*.

110. Florescano, *Myth*, 193; Koch, *John Lloyd Stephens*, 92; Estrada de Gerlero, "Carlos III," 79; Constantino, "José Longinos Martínez," 3. See also Rickett, *Royal Botanical*.

111. On Martínez and Mociño see Engstrand, "Spanish California."

112. Bleichmar, "Geography of Observation," 377. See also Safier, *Measuring*.

113. Like Spanish naturalist Baltasar Boldo, who worked in Cuba (Strang, *Frontiers of Science*, 172–73).

114. Daston, "Empire of Observation," 81.

115. Villella, *Indigenous Elites*, 24–25, 273.

116. Clark, "Gazeta de Literatura." *La Gazeta de México*, begun in 1784 and printed by Manuel Antonio Valdés Murguía y Saldaña—an associate in the printing firm of Felipe de Zúñiga y Ontiveros—was considered a "semiofficial" publication of the Viceroyalty.

117. Cañizares-Esguerra, *How to Write*, 282–84. León y Gama reportedly castigated Alzate in 1772 for sloppy astronomical observations, implying he had brought shame to criollos by leading foreigners to see them as "savages" (Cañizares-Esguerra, *How to Write*, 281).

118. Florescano, *Myth*, 197.

119. Alzate, "Prologo," 3.

120. Mundy, "Place-Names," 344. See Moreno, *Un ecclesiastico* and Preset, "La Naturaleza."

121. Alzate, "Prologo," 3.

122. Quoted in Earle, *Return*, 136. Humboldt included Alzate's 1791 illustrations of Xochicalco in *Vues* (1810).

123. Glass, *Boturini in Spain*, xlvii–xlx. Boturini's collection was inventoried by Vicente de la Rosa y Saldívar in 1791 and again in 1795.

124. Cañizares-Esguerra, *How to Write*, 301, 303.

125. Two Franciscans created the thirty-two volume *Colección de memorias de Nueva España* from 1790 to 1792 (Cañizares-Esguerra, *How to Write*, 303).

126. Glass, "The Boturini Collection," 24; Cañizares-Esguerra, *How to Write*, 304, 303.

127. Burrus, "Clavijero," 70; quoted in Burrus, "Clavijero," 70. See also Achim, *Idols*.

128. "Historia" panel, Museo Nacional de las Culturas (INAH), Mexico City, July 2016.

129. Crary described a shift in European "regimes of vision" by the 1820s in terms of the reorganization of knowledge and emphasized the European observer "who sees within a proscribed set of possibilities, one who is embedded in a system of convention and limitation" (*Techniques*, 5–6).

130. Bleichmar, *Visible Empire*, 9.

131. León y Gama, "Quaderno," 380.

132. "Mexico" and "Observación sobre esta noticia," *Gazeta de México*, March 10, 1784, 43–46; 45. The author claimed that there was "no tusk of equal size" to be found in any of the Viceroyalty's "copious Natural history cabinets" (45–46).

133. "Paplanta," *Gazeta de México*, July 12, 1785, 349–51; 349. He lamented that the "native [Totonaca] Indians of el Tajín were not ignorant of it [the site], although they never revealed it to Spain" (351). See López Luján, "El Tajín."

134. "Paplanta," *Gazeta de México*, July 12, 1785, 349.

135. Dupaix visited the site in 1805 and 1807, expecting to write a book on El Tajín/Paplanta. Some of his papers are at the APS in the collection "Notes on Mexican Antiquities" (Mss.913.72.N84).

136. Alzate, *Suplemento*.

137. His 1769 map, refitted to emphasize Cortés's voyages, appeared in Lorenzana's *Historia* (Alzate, "Plano.")

138. Alzate, *Nuevo Mapa*. Alzate's 1768 map includes political and ethnographic information later used by Humboldt (Sherwood, "Cartography," 99–110). Source maps for the northern portions were made by Francisco Álvarez Barreiro in the 1720s (Sherwood, "Cartography," 100). Alzate located several "mancions" (houses) allegedly made by the migrants on their way south, which had also appeared on earlier colonial maps.

139. Alzate, "Origin," 80. Although the longitude measurement is impossible, the context makes clear that his coordinates were supposed to allude to the disputed Nootka Sound territory (the following paragraph referenced descriptions of Nuu-chah-nulth peoples and their homes as portrayed in Cook's *Voyage*). Teguyo/Teguayo/Tehuallo as

a name for the "Great Salt Lake" dates to the Domínguez-Escalante expedition of 1776, during which Alzate's 1768 map was used for reference (Russon, "Trail Guide," 33). See also Cline, *Exploring*, 18–32, 50–55 and Tyler, "Myth of the Lake."

140. Alzate, "Origin," 81, 81e; Cook, *Voyage to the Pacific*.
141. Alzate, "Origin," 83.
142. Alzate, "Origin," 83.
143. Alzate, "Origin," 80.
144. Alzate, "Origin," 81.
145. Alzate, "Origin," 83.
146. Alzate, "Origin," 81. A 1913 introduction to *Noticias de Nutka* cites Alzate but provides N 41°33', W 127° as the intended coordinates for Nootka (Carreño, lxxxviin1).
147. Pilling, "Yurok," 140.
148. Quoted in Williams, *Madoc*, 15.
149. Alzate, *Suplemento*, 2.
150. Alzate, "Se ha estrañado," *Gazeta de Literatura*, December 13, 1790, 66.
151. "Hallazgo del los monolitos" panel, Museo del Templo Mayor (INAH), Mexico City. July 2016.
152. Alzate, "Se ha estrañado," *Gazeta de Literatura*, December 13, 1790, 66.
153. Alzate, "Se ha estrañado," *Gazeta de Literatura*, December 13, 1790: 66. These interpretations would have been bolstered by Spanish chroniclers like Lopez de Gómara, who (like Clavijero) incorrectly identified the patrons as Huitzilopochtli and Tezcatlipoca, instead of Huitzilopochtli and Tlaloc (Boone, "Templo," 16). León y Gama's correction was not printed until 1832 (Boone, "Templo," 27).
154. León y Gama, *Descripción*, 3.
155. León y Gama, *Descripción*, 4.
156. León y Gama, *Descripción*, 4.
157. León y Gama, *Descripción*, 8. See Boone, "Templo," 19; Florescano, *Myth*, 193, 148; Díaz-Andreu, *World History*, 120–24; Alcina Franch, *Arqueólogos*, 120–24; Matos Moctezuma, *Tríptico*, 30–33.
158. Alzate, "Se ha estrañado. . .," *Gazeta de Literatura*, December 13, 1790, 66.
159. Alzate, "Con el motivo de haberse escabado. . .," *Gazeta de Literatura*, January 11, 1791, 82.
160. Alzate, "Se ha estrañado. . .," *Gazeta de Literatura*, December 13, 1790, 66.
161. Alzate, "Se ha estrañado. . .," *Gazeta de Literatura*, December 13, 1790, 66.
162. That same December the Viceroy announced a Royal Order to increase expertise in Indigenous "hieroglyphics" (Cañizares-Esguerra, *How to Write*, 306). Criollo lawyer José Ignacio Borunda, one of the earliest to take up the call, began writing his "Key to the Hieroglyphics," which he finished in 1792. It was not published, however, for another century (*Clave*).
163. Tecuilhuitzintli, "Carta," 378, 379. Cf. Boturini, *New*, 74. Poole translates "bulto" as "bundle" and "Vulte de obscuridad" (or rather, "Bulto cenciciento, bulto de obscuridad y neblina" in Boturini) as "ash-colored bundle, bundle of darkness and low-lying clouds" (*New*, 74n115). See also Bassett, "Bundling."

164. Tecuilhuitzintli, "Carta," 379.
165. Tecuilhuitzintli, "Carta," 378.
166. Boturini, *New*, 253.
167. Tecuilhuitzintli, "Carta," 377. "Triadecaterida" is a technical term Boturini used to describe the thirteen-day week (or trecena).
168. Hajovsky, *On the Lips of Others*, 49, 139; Bassett, *Earthly Things*.
169. See Christin, "Visible/legible" and Cummins, "From Many into One."
170. León y Gama, "Quaderno," 380. He wrote a second volume in 1794 that was not published until the 1830s.
171. León y Gama, "Quaderno," 380.
172. Tecuilhuitzintli, "Carta," 378.
173. Alzate replied the following month ("Respuesta").
174. Despite his feud with Alzate, extra copies of the small pamphlet were stocked at the offices of the *Gazeta de Literatura* that summer.
175. A third statue, uncovered in December 1791 and identified as a "sacrificial stone" (cuauhxicalli), was laid face up in the Cathedral gardens, its round surface exposed "to the merited insult of every passenger" (Bullock, *Catalogue*, 22).
176. By the time it was published he had secured over seventy subscribers.
177. León y Gama, *Descripción*, 3; "Quaderno," 380.
178. León y Gama, *Descripción*, 3, 19–20, 20n1–3.
179. León y Gama, *Descripción*, 13.
180. León y Gama, *Descripción*, 3–4, 7. Boone, "Templo," 19; Cañizares-Esguerra, *How to Write*, 273–77.
181. De León, "Coatlicue," 284. She argues that the meaning of the Coatlicue statue's iconography would have been clearest to those with access to mapas (De León, "Coatlicue," 278, 262).
182. León y Gama, *Descripción*, 8.
183. León y Gama, *Descripción*, 5.
184. Poinsett, *Notes on Mexico*, 83; Cañizares-Esguerra, *How to Write*, 268; Díaz-Andreu, *World History*, 56.
185. Hamann, "Chronological Pollution."
186. Quoted in Leask, *Curiosity*, 278.
187. Klein, "New Interpretation." See also López Luján, "El ídolo sin pies."
188. Villela et al., "Introduction," 4.
189. Coatlicue reemerged on August 13, 1790, or 1 Miquiztli 1 Miquiztli 12 Tochtli (1 Skull of the 1 Skull trecena in year 12 Rabbit), a day significant to the transition between life and death, beginnings and endings.
190. León y Gama, *Descripción*, 8.
191. Brading, *Mexican Phoenix*, 202.
192. Quoted in Brading, *Mexican Phoenix*, 202.
193. She was sanctioned in 1754; Mexico City took her as its patron in 1746. See Peterson, *Visualizing Guadalupe*.
194. Quoted in Brading, *Mexican Phoenix*, 202.

195. Le Brun-Ricalens et al., "Guillaume Joseph Dupaix" and "Luxembourgeois de Vielsalm."

196. Florescano, *Myth*, 194.

197. *Gazeta de México,* April 27, 1790; August 24, 1790; October 19, 1790; Bernal, *Museum*, 133; Cañizares-Esguerra, *How to Write*, 302.

198. The private collections of Dupaix, Ciriaco González de Carvajal, José Mariano Sanchez y Mora (ex-Conde del Peñasco), and José Gomez (ex-Conde de la Cortina) were also particularly notable at the turn of the nineteenth century.

199. López Luján shows that of the total nineteen objects, sixteen were from Tenochtitlan, two from Coyoacán, and one remained at "Cerro Moctezuma." Sixteen are in the possession of the INAH today.

200. López Luján, *Descripción*. The manuscript, now at the BNAH, is twenty-two pages (with one page lost). It was engraved by Agüera Bustamante.

201. These are now at the BNF (MS Mexicain 97). See Omont, *Catalogue*, 17n97. The Stone of Tizoc statue was also kept in the public eye, resting against the cathedral. Tizoc was tlatoani from 1481–1486.

202. Dupaix later produced a series of descriptions of historical sites and attempted to clarify the iconic script ("Explicación" and "Descripción iconográfica").

203. Achim, *Idols*, 25.

204. With his companion, Aimé Bonpland, Humboldt spent five years traveling the Americas, eleven months of which—from 1803–1804—were spent in New Spain.

205. Humboldt, *Views*, 400.

206. Throughout his work, Humboldt relied on the descriptive work of criollos León y Gama, Alzate, Clavijero, Boturini, and Sigüenza.

207. Pratt writes that he spent much time in the archives (*Imperial Eyes*, 115, 129). The first of Humboldt's writings from his trip were published as the phenomenally successful *Ensayo político sobre el reino de la Nueva España* (1808), in which Humboldt first discussed the astronomical calculations made by the scholar he called "Gama" (Florescano, *Myth*, 204).

208. Humboldt had it from a "very trustworthy person . . . that the cathedral foundations are surrounded by countless idols and reliefs" (Humboldt, *Views*, 154).

209. Pratt, "Humboldt," 592; Stoetzer, "Humboldt."

210. Moxó, *Cartas mejicanas*, 214–15. Moxó's antiquities were reportedly presented to him by the Indigenous residents of Tlatelolco (Keen, *Aztec Image*, 315).

211. "Reflections drawn from Various extracts of Antient Monuments, collected by the Chevalier Lorenzo Boturini Benaduci" was printed in Carlos María de Bustamante's *Diario de México* on August 5 and 6, 1806. The passage addressed Aztlán and the "arrival of the Indians at Chapultepec."

212. The arrangement self-consciously replicates some Mexica elements of spatiality-as-power.

213. "Hallazago del los monolitos" panel, Museo del Templo Mayor (INAH), Mexico City, July 2016. The panel is located in "Sala 1: Antecedentes arqueológicos." English translation provided.

214. "Historia" panel, Museo Nacional de las Culturas (INAH), Mexico City, July 2016.

Chapter 4

1. Ewan and Ewan, *Barton*, 446. For Humboldt's visit see Walls, *Passage to the Cosmos* and De Terra, "Studies."
2. Dunbar and Hunter ascended the Ouachita in 1804–1805; Freeman and Custis ascended the Red River in 1806. Pike went to the Rockies and Southwest in 1807, using Humboldt's map. See Berry, "Ouachita River" and Berry et al., *Forgotten Expedition*. Lewis carried with him Barton's copy of Le Page du Pratz's *Histoire de la Louisiane*—which contained the 1757 map—as well as a copy of *Elements of Botany*.
3. The 1757 map was supposedly based on the Yazoo traveler Moncacht-apé's voyage to the Pacific (Sayre, "A Native American"). The 1803 map by Arrowsmith was highly flawed ("Chart"). See Allen, "Humboldt's Critique."
4. De Terra, "Motives," 314; "Studies," 560–62.
5. Friis, "Humboldt's Visit," 34. Some Humboldt purchased at the auction of León y Gama's estate.
6. APS, *Proceedings*, 358. He returned via Lancaster to meet the surveyor Andrew Ellicott; Charles Willson Peale was one of his guides.
7. Friis, "Baron," 22, 26. See De Terra, "Humboldt's Correspondence."
8. Humboldt, "General Chart."
9. In the 1811 *Atlas*, "Sierra de Timpanogos" is replaced by the "Lac Timpanogos," which Humboldt supposed was Lake Teguayo, "des bords du quel, d'apres quelques Historiens, les Aztèques passèrent au Rio Gila" (from the banks of which, according to some historians, the Aztecs went to the Gila River).
10. De Terra, "Motives," 314; "Studies," 563.
11. APS, *Proceedings*, 384. The donation is filled with annotations in Barton's hand.
12. "Mr. Thomas Dobson," *Monthly Anthology* 1, no. 3 (January 1804): 142.
13. Bedini, *Jefferson Stone*; Greene, *Science*, 147. When De Ferrer's donation was received at the APS in July 1802, the gift was recorded as "sketches of two supposed Mexican Monuments" rather than explicitly noted as an astronomical treatise.
14. Jefferson, *Papers*, 4: 555–57.
15. I.e., Ewan and Ewan, *Barton* and Greene, *Science*. Harvey and Rivett, "Colonial-Indigenous" is a major exception, especially in its consideration of "graphic pluralism" and Latin American scholarship (457n31).
16. See Porter, *Eagle's Nest*, especially 1–40.
17. Valauskas, "Benjamin Smith Barton."
18. Jefferson was president of the APS and the United States concurrently.

19. Harvey, *Native Tongues*; Murray, "Vocabularies."

20. I am deeply indebted to Indigenous ethnobotanists Mary Siisip and Wendy Makoons Geniusz for their explanations of Anishinaabeg plant knowledges. See *Our Knowledge* and *Plants Have So Much to Give* as well as Kimmerer, *Braiding Sweetgrass*.

21. Cajete, *Native Science*, 57–83, 177–213; Hereniko, "Indigenous Knowledge"; Round, "Mississippian Contexts," 450. See also Little Bear, *Naturalizing*; Burkhart, "Physics"; TallBear, *DNA*; Tinker "Stones."

22. Before 1787 he collected information "sufficiently numerous to serve as DATA"—data that mapped Native ancestors out of Native lands—but many of the "facts and observations" he sought were filtered through "conjecture" and "myth" (Barton, *Observations*, 20).

23. This was the conventional application of philology and ethnology (Harvey, *Native Tongues*, 65–79, 185–94; Harvey and Rivett, "Colonial-Indigenous," 463, 465).

24. Kolodny wrote: "it may not be merely coincidental that this theory appears to have been articulated first in 1797, just two years after the Treaty of Greenville" ("Fictions," 705).

25. Bartram, "Observations," 139–141; Ewan and Ewan, *Barton*, 113.

26. Bartram, "Observations," 142.

27. Bartram, "Observations," 140.

28. Bartram, "Observations," 140; *New Views*, xci.

29. Bartram, "Observations," 140.

30. Bartram, "Observations," 143.

31. Barton, *New Views*, lxviii.

32. Bartram, "Observations," 141, 140. McGillivray apparently told Barton that Creeks were more recently established in the country than Cherokees (Barton, *New Views*, xlv). Hawkins requested a copy of Bartram's *Travels* when he arrived at his post in 1798 (Waselkov and Braund, "Significance," 211).

33. Sargent and Barton, *Papers*, 26. Barton also compares the "quantity of issing-glass" (mica) at Marietta with the "little looking-glasses of the stone Itzli" (obsidian) Clavijero referenced at the "Case-grandi, in California" (*Papers*, 28).

34. Barton, "Ancient Tumulus," 184, 188, 197, 183; Sargent and Barton, *Papers*, iii.

35. Barton, "Ancient Tumulus," 191–97.

36. Pratt, *Imperial Eyes*, 20.

37. Pratt calls Humboldt a type "herbolizer" (*Imperial Eyes*, 7).

38. "data, n.," *OED Online*. These served as what Pratt has called "civic description," that is, empirical information enabling natationalist audiences to better know and exploit their countries (*Imperial Eyes*, 20–21).

39. Ewan and Ewan, *Barton*, 274.

40. Ewan and Ewan, *Barton*, 282. This was contained in Hakluyt's *Virginia Richly Valued* (1609).

41. Bartram, *Travels*. See also Waselkov and Braund, *William Bartram*.

42. Ewan and Ewan, *Barton*, 280. A proposal for the volume is held in Barton's papers at the APS.

43. Ewan and Ewan, *Barton*, 125.

44. R., "Fortifications," 23. When the travelers asked "the surrounding Onandagoes and other nations" about the earthworks, they concluded that "the natives themselves had never noticed it" (R., "Fortifications," 24).

45. Ewan and Ewan, *Barton*, 130; Heart, "A Letter." Heart had created the account and map published in the May 1787 *Columbian Magazine*.

46. Quoted in Ewan and Ewan, *Barton*, 123. Morgan would afterward plat and recruit US settlers to New Madrid (Morrow, "New Madrid").

47. Sargent and Barton, *Papers*, 1. Sargent, who would go on to become governor of Mississippi Territory in 1798, kept up his interest in antiquities even after he left Marietta for Natchez.

48. Sargent and Barton, *Papers*, 7.

49. Sargent and Barton, *Papers*, 12.

50. Barton, "Ancient Tumulus," 211; Sargent and Barton, *Papers*, 8.

51. Barton, *Observations*, 16.

52. Barton, "Ancient Tumulus," 188. In *New Views*, Barton returned to his previous Toltec theories without insisting on their Danish (Viking) origins (Barton, *New Views*, 84, 83, 87).

53. Sargent and Barton, *Papers*, 7. This latter reference is to Clavijero's notes on Casa Grande/Casas Grandes.

54. Sargent and Barton, *Papers*, 7.

55. Barton, "Ancient Tumulus," 197.

56. Barton, "Ancient Tumulus," 185.

57. Barton, "Ancient Tumulus," 185.

58. At the end of the eighteenth century the areas that have come to be called Alabama, Mississippi, and Florida were largely controlled by an alliance of Creek and Seminole leaders who triangulated support across British, Spanish, and US associates (Saunt, *West of the Revolution*, 169–208). See also Dubcovsky, "Creek Information Networks"; Ethridge, *Creek Country*; Saunt, *New Order*; Waselkov, *Conquering Spirit*. The expanse known as the "Yazoo lands" was disputed by Georgia and Spain in addition to Choctaws, Creeks, Chickasaws, Cherokees, and others who lived there (Kennedy, "Pinch of Snuff"; Sammons, "Fruit"; Hobson, *Great Yazoo*).

59. Although the United States officially took control of Mississippi Territory in 1798, Spain retained control of New Orleans, the Mississippi River, and much of the Gulf coast until 1803. See Rosen, *Border Law*, 11–39.

60. Washington, *Papers*, 2: 86–98. He wrote, "the touch of a feather, would turn them any way" (92).

61. Haskins, "Shawnee and Delaware," 35.

62. When Knox suspected "Creeks on the Alabama and Apalacicola Rivers" of waging war against Georgians in 1789 he negotiated with McGillivray for purchase of the land (*ASP2*, 1: 36).

63. *ASP2*, 1: 8–16, 25–34. Wars with Chickamauga Cherokees were largely ended with the 1794 Treaty of Tellico Blockhouse.

64. *ASP2*, 1: 80. See Greer, *Property*; Banner, *How*; Saunt, *Unworthy Republic*.

65. Waselkov, *Conquering Spirit*, 19. See also Dowd, *Spirited Resistance*, 90–103. This treaty resulted in the cession of disputed Oconee lands—which Georgia was selling illicitly—in return for goods and an annuity payment. Creeks were also required to give notice "of any designs, which they may know or suspect to be formed in any neighboring tribe, or by any person whatever against the peace and interests of the United States."

66. In 1792, other southern nations—especially Chickamauga Cherokees and Upper Town Creeks—were also signing treaties of protection with the Spanish governors of Louisiana and West Florida.

67. Hamilton, *Papers*, 26: 548–49. The articles were not made public until 1848 (Appleton and Ward, "Secret Articles"; Saunt, *New Order*, 78–82, 196–97). Like McGillivray, Cherokee leaders also received special payments (e.g., the 1792 Treaty of Philadelphia).

68. The act states that the United States could not guarantee claims made before passage of the Constitution. From 1796 to the mid-1840s, the United States did not oversee or approve of any of the New York State sponsored "treaties" (Starna, "United States," 33). See Hauptman, *Conspiracy*.

69. Saunt, "Financing"; Kennedy, "Yazoo Land Sale." In 1802 Georgia "sold" its Mississippi land claims to the United States—much of which had already been organized into the Mississippi Territory—for a cash settlement and clear title. See also Saunt, *Unworthy Republic*.

70. This became painfully obvious during the Jackson administration.

71. Lakomäki, *Gathering Together*, 12. Harmar invaded the Miami towns at kiihkayonki in 1790 but was out maneuvered and overpowered by the Western Confederacy forces. Knox encouraged St. Clair to attack the stronghold again, and the United States suffered an immense loss (Calloway, *Victory*, 17–19; Brooks, *Common Pot*, 106–62). See also Bergmann, *Early West*. Chickamauga fighters joined Little Turtle and Blue Jacket (Calloway, *Victory*, 108).

72. Calloway, *Victory*, 149.

73. *ASP2*, 1: 562–683. For more on the war, see Calloway, *Victory* and Sword, *Indian War*.

74. Harrison, "Wampum Diplomacy," 210; *ASP2*, 1: 576, 570–71. For the treaty council, see Mann, "Greenville Treaty" and Shriver, "Four Versions."

75. Quoted in Brooks, *Common Pot*, 137–38. These are Aupaumut's words to Pickering in 1793. See also Aupaumut, "Narrative."

76. *ASP2*, 1: 528.

77. "Treaty of Greenville," Record Group 11, National Archives Records Administration. https://catalog.archives.gov/id/299800.

78. Also spelled Kekionga.

79. Rafert, *Miami of Indiana*, 60; *ASP2*, 1: 570; Calloway, *Victory*, 6–8. Piankashaw and Kaskaskia signatories assented later (Harrison, "Wampum Diplomacy," 211n2).

80. Samuel Ogden (great uncle to David) bought land along the northern border. In 1796 David's father Abraham negotiated the Treaty of New York with the Seven Nations of Canada, as a result of which the Seven Nations relinquished their claims in New York state. David Ogden was counsel to the Holland Land Company and founded the Ogden Land Company in 1810. See Hauptman, *Conspiracy*.

81. The treaty assured that Spain would not lend military assistance to Native peoples in formerly disputed Spanish-US lands.

82. Strang, *Frontiers*, 136. From 1797–1799 Andrew Ellicott (Barton's acquaintance from the Seven Ranges Survey) led an expedition to draw the US boundary with East and West Florida at the thirty-first degree line, right through the "Yazoo lands." In 1802, the Georgia Compact explicitly extinguished aboriginal title to the "Yazoo lands." This legislation served as the inspiration for a similar law meant to "clear" title in the Ohio and Indiana Territories and push US hegemony through to the Mississippi's eastern bank. Meanwhile, in 1802, Joseph Ellicot (with whom Barton took his 1785 walking tour) was buying Haudenosaunee land for the Holland Land Company.

83. Tanner, *Atlas*, 87–104; Calloway, *Victory*, 75–77.

84. Cazier, *Surveys*, 37–45.

85. Sword, *Indian War*, 335–36. Two distinct factions emerged, one headed by the Wyandot leader Tarhe (The Crane) and the other by Little Turtle. The latter would represent the "Nine nations" who found the agreement wanting. See Harrison, "Wampum Diplomacy"; Shriver, "Four Versions."

86. Little Turtle, "Speech."

87. Little Turtle, "Speech."

88. Hutton, "William Wells," 204.

89. Volney's betrays an understanding of language as a reflection of the "primitive." See Pagden, *European Encounter*, 126–40 and Schreyer, "Savage Languages." See also Axtell, "Babel of Tongues"; Erben, *Harmony of the Spirit*; Rivett, "Empirical Desire."

90. "To the Citizens of the United States," *Boston Gazette*, March 26, 1798, 1; Rafert, *Miami of Indiana*, 62; Young, *Little Turtle*, 146; Sword, *Indian War*, 335–36.

91. For the eighteenth and nineteenth centuries, see Harvey, *Native Tongues*; for the seventeenth century, see Rivett, "Empirical Desire" and "Learning to Write."

92. Volney, *View*, 363. On language and race see Gray, *New World*; Harvey, *Native Tongues*, 19–48; Murray, "Vocabularies"; Rivett, *Science*, 125–72.

93. Volney, *View*, 421.

94. Volney, *View*, 423. This references the 1804 English translation. *Tableau* is the 1803 French original.

95. Quoted in Mundy, "Place-Names," 340.
96. Sayre, "Mound Builders," 245; Harvey, *Native Tongues*, 58–65; 71–79. See also Looby, "Concentration" and Thompson, "Judicious Neology."
97. Jefferson, *Writings*, 227. Under Jefferson, the APS became a major philological center; its "Committee for History, the moral Sciences, & general Literature" was founded in 1815. See Morris, "Jefferson"; Greene, "Early Scientific" and *Science*; Smith, "Interest"; Harvey, *Native Tongues*.
98. Barton, *New Views* 1798, xiv–xv; xv, xii–xiii; xi–xxii.
99. Barton, *New Views*, xi, xiii. Unless noted otherwise, the reference is to the 1797 *New Views*.
100. Barton, *New Views*, xii.
101. For language study as a technique of empire, see Harvey and Rivett, "Colonial Indigenous." On early New World language collections, see Pollack, "Native American Words," especially 204–44.
102. Barton, *New Views* 1798, xxv; Barton, *New Views*, xc. Many Indigenous intellectuals today—including Burkhart and Alfred—describe the function of languages in this way.
103. Harvey, *Tongues*, 53–57, 93–96; APS, *Proceedings*, 246.
104. Barton, *New Views*, xi.
105. Ewan and Ewan, *Barton*, 275–78.
106. Quoted in Ewan and Ewan, *Barton*, 280.
107. Harvey, *Native Tongues*; Murray, "Vocabularies."
108. Volney, *View*, 427; Volney, "Extrait de Barton," Morgan Library.
109. Volney, *View*, 433.
110. Volney, *View*, 420.
111. Swan, "Report," 18. Barton Papers, Series 3. APS.
112. Swan, "Report," 22. Barton Papers, Series 3. APS.
113. Waselkov and Braund, "Significance," 190; Saunt, *New Order*, 72.
114. "Barton to McGillivray, 29 July 1792." Barton Papers, Series 2. APS. Among Knox's papers is a document likely written by William Bartram (signed "WB") around the time of the 1790 New York Treaty. Waselkov and Braund suggest Knox obtained it through the Quaker community ("Significance," 187–88).
115. Barton to McGillivray, 29 July 1792, Barton Papers, Series 2. APS. Barton's letter was delivered via Knox.
116. Barton, *New Views*, viii, viii–ix.
117. He claimed to have heard the following languages: Chippewa, Mahican, Munsee, Shawnee, Potawatomi, Miami, Mohawk, Seneca, Wyandot, Miami, Creek, Chickasaw, Choctaw, and Cherokee. I imagine he heard words in Creek, Chickasaw, Choctaw, and Cherokee from Bartram and McGillivray. His Miami likely came from Volney (via Wells and Little Turtle). Zeisberger sent an Onondaga vocabulary, likely the source of the "Flower Calendar."
118. Barton, *New Views*, xxv.

119. Barton, *New Views*, xxvi.

120. Barton, *New Views*, 7–9.

121. Aupaumut, for example, explained in 1791 that "the Shawanees are my younger brothers—the Miamie my fathers—the Delawares my grandfathers—the Chippewas my grandchildren—and so on," a speech likely heard by Kirkland (quoted in Taylor, "Captain," 437). Kirkland and Aupaumut, as well as Kirkland and Barton, were in correspondence in July and November 1791, respectively. See Kirkland's papers at Hamilton College (138c, 141a).

122. This tracks with eighteenth-century Six Nations diplomatic protocols (Richter, *Longhouse*; Ruediger, "Tributary Subordination"). To Barton, it only translated as a reference to the 1784 Treaty of Fort Stanwix, at which he believed the confederacy had "assumed the right of selling lands to the Whites" (Barton, *New Views*, xxv). This arrangement reinforced the recent proceedings at the Treaty of Greenville, which also followed Six Nations diplomatic protocol, and at which the principal peacemaker was Tarhe, although Little Turtle represented a sizeable dissident faction (Harrison, "Wampum Diplomacy").

123. Barton, *New Views*, xxxi.

124. Jefferson, *Papers*, 9: 372–373.

125. Foucault, *Order of Things*, 131; 217–31.

126. Burkhart, "Physics," 40; Simpson, *Always Done*, 20.

127. Little Bear, "Rethinking."

128. Lyons similarly describes Ojibwemowin as "constituted by verbs on the move" (*X-Marks*, 4).

129. Murray, "Vocabularies," 592.

130. Quoted in Burkhart, "Physics," 39; Alfred, *Wasáse*, 33.

131. The influence of the "language of the Delawares" was "evinced by the [Lenape] Indian names of many of the waters, the mountains, and the vallies of the country" (Barton, *New Views*, lx).

132. Barton, *New Views*, lxx, xc.

133. Barton, *New Views* 1798, 1–133.

134. On word analysis, see Murray, "Vocabularies."

135. Barton, *New Views*, xxv.

136. Barton, *New Views*, xxv.

137. These groupings follow those that became conventional later in the nineteenth century. On Gallatin, an important point of synthesis and continuity, see Harvey, *Native Tongues*; Strang, "Scientific Instructions"; Wisecup, "Entangled."

138. See Brooks, *Common Pot*, 106–62.

139. Barton, *New Views* 1798, 11.

140. Barton, *New Views* 1798, 11; Barton, *New Views*, lx.

141. Harvey, *Native Tongues*, 57–79, especially 66–71.

142. Kirkland was there at the behest of land speculators Phelps and Gorham.

143. Clinton "Discourse," 56.

144. Clinton "Discourse," 56. Decades later the white Seneca adoptee and Indian Agent Horatio Jones explained that "when the ancestors of the Senecas spr[a]ng into existence, the country, especially about the lakes, was thickly inhabited by a race of civil, enterprising, and industrious people, who were totally destroyed, and whose improvements were taken possession of by the Senecas" (Yates, *New York*, 40; quoted in Seaver, *Mary Jemison*, 157–59).

145. Calloway, *American Revolution*, 108–28.

146. Hitakonanu'laxk, *Grandfathers*, 5–6, 20–21. The Minisi were explicitly expelled after 1742 and settled in that area with Oneida and Cayuga consent (Hitakonanu'laxk, *Grandfathers*, 21).

147. Wallace, *Tuscarora*, 72–74; Brooks, *Common Pot*, 121.

148. Graymont, *Iroquois*, 192–97.

149. New York reached a settlement with the Onondaga and Cayuga nations—whom it dispossessed—to settle the boundaries of the Military Tract (today the Finger Lakes area) in 1788 and 1789; surveying was completed in 1793. Hundreds of Stockbridge, Brothertown, and Mahican peoples also had their Massachusetts-New York border-area lands forcibly alienated from them; many left to join the Oneida, and some would eventually move to Wisconsin.

150. In 1788 speculators Phelps and Gorham purchased Massachusetts's "preemption rights" to Cauyga and Onondaga lands; in 1792 and 1793 the Holland Land Company bought much of the Phelps-Gorham purchase.

151. Tiro, *Standing Stone*, 68; Wallace, *Tuscarora*, 75. Of the three parcels comprising the Tuscarora Reserve: one was granted by the Senecas in 1797, another deeded by the Holland Land Company, and the last purchased in 1804 with proceeds of North Carolina land sales (Wallace, *Tuscarora*, 76).

152. Violating the 1790 Act, Morris exchanged stock in the Bank of North-America for Seneca land, which he gave to the US president to hold in trust (Senecas were to be paid a six percent annuity, which did not happen). Horatio Jones was an official interpreter at the Treaty of Big Tree. These proceedings created a precedent for the later Ohio reservations (Stockwell, *Other Trail*, 73).

153. Hamilton Academy opened in 1798, by which time Cusick had already lived with Kirkland for four years and would remain there until at least the spring of 1800 (Nicholas Cusick to Kirkland, 17 March 1800; David Cusick to Kirkland, Jr., 22 March 1800. Samuel Kirkland Papers, Special Collections. Hamilton College).

154. In the 1820s his home on the Tuscarora Reservation would see any number of white visitors looking for the kind of traditions Cusick had kept safe. See Stansbury's account of his visit in 1821 (*Pedestrian Tour*, 98).

155. Cusick, *Sketch*, 4.

156. Cusick, *Sketch*, 10; Bonaparte, *Creation*, 43.

157. Cusick, *Sketch*, 8–10, 14–15. Bonaparte notes a similar Anishinaabe tradition of giants (*Creation*, 43).

158. Cusick, *Sketch*, 11.

159. Cusick, *Sketch*, 14.

160. Cusick, *Sketch*, 14.

161. Hìtakonanu'laxk, *Grandfathers*, 9. The current-day Lenape elder and storyteller Hìtakonanu'laxk recounts the migration and tensions it caused, which eventually erupted in war: "Great battles were fought, and many warriors fell on both sides... One battle took place in which hundreds fell, who were afterward buried together in heaps and covered over with earth" (*Grandfathers*, 8).

162. The council fire had been moved to Buffalo Creek after it was extinguished at Onondaga during the Revolutionary War.

163. By the 1790s most Christian Tuscaroras lived at Kanonwalohale while Ganaghsaraga—between Oneida and Onondaga—had become an important traditionalist settlement (Mt. Pleasant, *Whirlwind*, 48, 59; Tiro, *Standing Stone*, 21, 89).

164. On Washington and the Sullivan-Clinton Campaign see Mintz, *Seeds of Empire*; Mt. Pleasant, *Whirlwind* and "Revisiting Representations."

165. Washington, *Papers*, 7: 146–50.

166. In 1792, for example, Kanatsoyh (Nicholas Cusick) was the designated recipient for US monies paid to the Tuscarora Nation; Kirkland and Captain Hendrick received funds for Oneida and Stockbridge, respectively (Pickering, Timothy. "Appropriations of money to Indian tribes," 1790. https://wardepartmentpapers.org/s/home/item/42872). Kanatsoyh was an important ally of the Patriots during the Revolution and was close with the Brant-Johnson family.

167. Washington, *Papers*, 7: 146–50.

168. In 1798, Holland Land Company agent Joseph Ellicot fixed the boundaries of the "Mile Strip" along the Niagara (Hauptman, *Conspiracy of Interests*, 9). In the mid-1810s, the idea of removing the "New York Indians"—a plan championed by the Ogden Land Company—began to gain traction in American political circles (Hopkins, "Clinton I," 113–43 and "Clinton II," 213–41; Mt. Pleasant, *Whirlwind*, 158).

169. Barton, *Archaeologiae Americanae*, 57. Barton Papers, Series 2. APS.

170. Barton, "Journal of Tuscaroras." Barton Papers, Series 2. APS.

171. Barton, "Journal of Tuscaroras." Barton Papers, Series 2. APS.

172. Barton, *Archaeologiae Americanae*, 59. Barton Papers, Series 2. APS.

173. Barton, *Archaeologiae Americanae*, 59. Barton Papers, Series 2. APS.

174. Barton, *New Views 1798*, 9. He failed to understand that "southern" was relative, not absolute.

175. Barton, *New Views 1798*, 2. Heckewelder had begun working for the War Department in 1792.

176. Barton, *New Views 1798*, 3.

177. Barton, *New Views* 1798, 3.
178. Barton, *New Views* 1798, 3.
179. Barton, *New Views* 1798, 10–11.
180. Quoted in Mayor, *Fossil*, 364n3. See also Grafton, *Defenders*, 146–45, 207–8.
181. Quoted in Mayor, *Fossil*, 34.
182. Barton, *New Views*, 84c, 83.
183. Barton, "Journals," 61. APS; McAtee, "Journals," 28. APS.
184. Morris, "Geomythology," 701. For Cotton Mather on Genesis 6:4, see Semonin, *American Monster*, 29–32.
185. Taylor, "Description," 59–60; Morris, "Geomythology," 707, 708; Semonin, *American Monster*, 3.
186. Morris, "Geomythology," 702.
187. The Claverack tooth was later connected to a frozen elephantine animal recovered from Siberia called the "mammoth"; it evoked comparisons to elephants from Africa and Asia (Semonin, *American Monster*, 2). Also noteworthy is Catsby's 1726 account of teeth and tusks found by enslaved Africans at Stono, near Charleston (Semonin, *American Monster*, 86).
188. In 1739, Baron de Longueuil Le Moyne's expedition against the Chickasaw came upon oversized bones at a swamp that became known as "Big Bone Lick." Knowledge of this place and its remains circulated during the Seven Years' War and beyond (Semonin, *American Monster*, 84–85, 87).
189. Wistar, "Description."
190. Steiner, "Account," 544; McAtee, "Journals," 28. APS.
191. This reference is to his *Observations* (1787) and *Fragments of the Natural History of Pennsylvania* (1799).
192. Barton, *Discourse*, 59–60.
193. Deloria, *Red Earth*, xiv, 36.
194. Deloria, *Red Earth*, 82.
195. Bruchac, "Earthshapers."
196. Howe, *Retelling Trickster*, 12.
197. Deloria, *Red Earth*, 139. For current-day science looking to corroborate (or disprove) Indigenous traditions, see Mackenthun and Mucher, *Decolonizing "Prehistory."*
198. Barton, *Elements*, 249–50. This refers to the 1803 edition.
199. Barton, *Elements*, 300.
200. Barton, *Elements*, 300.
201. Barton, *Elements* 1812, 428.
202. Barton, *Elements* 1812, 428.
203. De Ferrer to Vaughan, 15 July 1802, Barton Papers, Series 2. APS; APS, *Proceedings*, 384. The Sun Stone itself does not depict dates as much as it describes the cosmos in a manner that legitimized Mexica political power; yet as this escaped León y Gama, so too did it escape Barton.

204. Barton, *Elements*, 16, 298, 10.

205. Barton, *Elements*, 69, 16. See also Ewan and Ewan, *Barton*, 268–69.

206. Geniusz, *Plants*, 3.

207. For decolonized botanical teachings, see Geniusz, *Our Knowledge*.

208. Armstrong, "Land Speaking," 178–79; Fitzgerald, *Native Women*, 25. See also Belt and Bender, "Speaking Difference."

209. Brooks, *Common Pot*, 144. Simpson explains a similar concept wherein Nishnaabemowin radically transforms and recreates, not just revitalizes, the People (*Always Done*, 6, 50).

210. Barton, *Discourse*, 53.

211. Barton, *Discourse*, 88. In 1798, Cutler noted the "only possible *data* for forming any probable conjecture respecting the antiquity of the works . . . must be derived from the [tree] growth upon them" ("American Antiquities," 1).

212. Barton, *Discourse*, 53.

213. Barton, *Discourse*, 59–60.

214. Barton, *Discourse*, 16–20.

215. Barton, *Archaeolegiae Americanae*, 58–59. Barton Papers, Series 2. APS. Cuvier made a formal case for extinction in 1796 (O'Connor, *Earth On Show*, 34). On species extinction see Rudwick, *Bursting*, 239–376.

216. Hamann, "Social Life."

217. Barton, *Archaeolegiae Americanae*, 59. Barton Papers, Series 2. APS.

218. Barton, *Archaeologiae Americanae*, v. Barton Papers, Series 2. APS.

219. Donated by mineralogist Andrés del Río in Mexico City.

220. Jefferson, *Papers*, 4: 520–22.

221. Jefferson, *Papers*, 4: 555–57. He sent Barton one of the recovered Lewis manuscripts, a Pawnee vocabulary.

222. Quoted in Ewan and Ewan, *Barton*, 254–55.

223. Quoted in Ewan and Ewan, *Barton*, 254; Barton, "A Discovery," 491. Alejandro Ramírez y Blanco, secretary of the Junta of Guatemala and APS member, had included the announcement with del Río's gift (Ewan and Ewan, *Barton*, 254).

224. While his account of Palenque's "discovery" was widely and immediately circulated, as late as 1813, León y Gama's work, which Barton thought "is of the first importance in the view of American history," still seemed to him equally "wholly unknown in Britain" (quoted in Ewan and Ewan, *Barton*, 254–55).

225. [Hulings,] "An historical and chronological description," Mss. 913.72.L55. APS.

226. *El Diario de México* was the short-lived newspaper founded by Carlos María de Bustamante in 1805.

227. There are no records of this donation at the AAS. See instead Duponceau's donation, "A Comparative Vocabulary of Indian Languages (1798-1821), Mss. 497.B28. APS.

228. "The Miamis words are principally copied from a MS vocabulary [. . .from] the late Mr. Sam Colesworth (of Boston)" (Barton, *New Views*, xii).

229. Volney, "Vocabulary." In fact, while Little Turtle and Volney did occasionally speak directly, Volney mainly conversed with Wells. Volney recorded his disappointment not at missing Little Turtle at Vincennes, but in not finding Wells, the "only person in America capable of giving me the aid I wanted" (*View*, 356).

230. Volney, *View*, 356–57.

231. Rafert, *Miami of Indiana*, 68.

232. His remains were disturbed in 1911 and funerary goods sold on the private market. Many ended up at the Allen County-Fort Wayne Historical Society (Rafert, *Miami of Indiana*, 201; Young, *Little Turtle*, 169–77).

233. Rafert, *Miami of Indiana*, 74.

234. Rafert, *Miami of Indiana*, 74; Young, *Little Turtle*, 165.

235. Rafert, *Miami of Indiana*, 63. In 1846, most Miamis were forced west to Kansas and Oklahoma; their descendants comprise the Miami Nation of Oklahoma. A few families remained behind on the Mississiniwa reserves where their relatives—including some of Little Turtle's family—remain today as the Miami Nation of Indiana, whose "federal status" was terminated in 1897.

236. Rafert, *Miami of Indiana*, 193–94; Zaveri, "Indigenous Languages."

237. Rafert, *Miami of Indiana*, 192, 186, 254. That Bundy was the last Miami speaker in Indiana is Rafert's claim.

238. Costa, "Historical Phonology," 367. See also Costa, "Redacting."

239. For a Canadian perspective on language resurgence, see Booth, "Role of Archives." See also Hinton, *Bringing*, and Hinton et al., *How to Keep*.

240. Harvey and Rivett, "Colonial-Indigenous," 471–72.

241. On resurgence, see Simpson, *Always Done*.

242. Ironstrack, "eehkwa mihtelowe."

243. "ahseni siipiw-(n.inan) Great Miami River (Ohio)," *Myaamia-Peewaalia Dictionary*. Miami-Illinois Indigenous Languages Digital Archive, Miami Tribe of Oklahoma. https://mc.miamioh.edu/ilda-myaamia/dictionary/.

244. Volney, "Vocabulary of the Miami Indians," American Indian Vocabulary Collection, Mss.497.V85. APS.

245. McCoy et al., *ašiihkiwi neehi*, 26. The root "ahsena" (stone) is inanimate but the nouns for "fossil," (eehsahsena) and "limestone" (waapahsena) are animate ("ahsen-[n.inan] Stone, rock"; eehsahsen-[n.an] Fossil; "waapahsen-[n.an] Limestone," *Myaamia-Peewaalia Dictionary*. Miami-Illinois Indigenous Languages Digital Archive, Miami Tribe of Oklahoma. https://mc.miamioh.edu/ilda-myaamia/dictionary/.)

246. "Eemamwiciki Summer Youth Educational Experience," Miami Tribe of Oklahoma, updated summer 2021. https://www.miaminationsm.com/eewansaapita.

247. Ironstrack, "eewansaapita kiihkayonki."

248. See Strack, *myaamiaki*.

249. McCoy et al., *ašiihkiwi aeehi*, 30. In the 1980s, the Miami Nation of Indiana bought thirty-five acres of traditional homelands along the Mississiniwa, where the Seven Pillars are located (Rafert, *Miami of Indiana*, 288).

250. Watts, *Colonizing*; Timmerman, "Contested."

Chapter 5

1. *Louisiana Gazette*, January 9, 1811, 3; quoted in Schoolcraft, *Historical*, 133–34.

2. Quoted in Hammes, "Cantine Mounds," 149.

3. Jefferson, *Papers*, 6: 322–30; Brackenridge, "Population," 158. The letter was read aloud at the APS in October 1813 and printed almost verbatim in the 1818 *Transactions* (APS, *Proceedings*, 441).

4. The article was reprinted widely, appearing, for example, in the *New Hampshire Patriot and State Gazette* in April 1811.

5. Jefferson, *Papers*, 6: 324.

6. Brackenridge, "Population," 158. In *Views* he adds "earthen vessels" (189).

7. Brackenridge, *Views*, 189.

8. Jefferson, *Papers*, 6: 324.

9. Brackenridge, "Population," 158. About the number of mounds Brackenridge witnessed on his travels, Jefferson replied: "I never before had an idea that they were so numerous" (Jefferson, *Papers*, 6: 518).

10. Benson et al., "Possible Impacts" and "Boom and Bust."

11. A trio of Franco-American businessmen ran a canteen atop "Monks Mound" throughout the Revolutionary war, but they abandoned it in 1784 because "the Indians grew too troublesome" (Chappell, *Cahokia*, 74; Hammes, "Cantine Mounds"). The river there still bears the name. See the description of Monk's Mound in the November 18, 1837 *Wisconsin Democrat* (quoted in Arjona, "Sublime perversions," 197).

12. "Cahokia Mounds: the road to America's Oldest City," Cahokia State Park, Collinsville, Illinois. July 2021. The Cahokia Mounds Interpretive Center, built in 1988–1989, sits over the location of "over eighty houses and storage buildings" constructed from 1050–1275 CE. See *Cahokia: City of the Sun* for the museum's interpretation.

13. Brackenridge, "Population," 158.

14. Brackenridge, "Population," 156.

15. Jefferson, *Papers*, 6: 330.

16. For earthworks on a map from Domingo de Terán de los Rios's 1691–92 entrada into the "Provincia de Texas," Caddo country, see McKinnon, *Battle Mound*. The Red River divides Oklahoma, Texas, and Arkansas; in 1813 it served as the US-New Spain/Mexico border.

17. Jefferson, *Papers*, 6: 326–27. For Cahokian diaspora, see Ethridge and Shuck-Hall, *Mapping*. In 1764 French trappers established a trading fort on Wazhazhe land that they named for Saint Louis, which became a profitable center for French and Osage groups.

French-allied Kaskaskias, Peorias, and other members of the Inoka/Illinois Confederacy relocated to be closer to allies (Tanner, *Atlas*, 92; DuVal, *Native Ground*, 120–21, 172; Aron, *American Confluence,* 88–90). The powerful Grand Osages sent multiple diplomatic envoys to Washington; New York City physician Samuel L. Mitchell later recorded a selection of poetry recited when Osage leaders came to Washington in 1804 ("Communications," 315–17).

18. Brackenridge, "Population," 158.

19. Martinko defines an "historic" built environment as that which is "invested with the capacity to connect present and future viewers with the past" (Martinko, *Historic*, x).

20. AAS, *Proceedings*, 33.

21. Hinsley, "Digging for Identity," 189.

22. Jefferson, *Papers*, 6: 324.

23. Jefferson, *Papers*, 6: 323. Brackenridge's tremendous circling of the square creates a material set of differences creating and separating one "race" from another. He uses contemporary traditions regarding earthworks as proof that the later population—Osage or Peoria groups, for example—had wholly usurped a prior, disappeared one.

24. Atwater to Newton, 21 August 1818, Caleb Atwater Letters and Drawings, 1818–1835. American Antiquarian Society. Hereafter referred to as "Atwater Papers."

25. Atwater to Thomas, 4 October 1819, Atwater Papers. AAS.

26. B., "Review," 66–67.

27. For an overview of the AAS collecting program and members, see Snead, *Relic Hunters*, especially 18–52. Classic histories include Shipton, "Museum" and Joyce, "Antiquarians."

28. Lewis, *Facts*, 94; LaVaque-Manty, "There Are Indians." An important exception is Kertész, "Family Affair." See also DeLucia, "Fugitive Collections"; Midtrød, "Vengeance"; Wisecup, "Meteors, Ships."

29. Most of the "ethnographic" items went to the Smithsonian Institution and Harvard's Peabody Museum (AAS, *Proceedings*, 72; AAS Acquisition Files. Peabody Museum).

30. Reps, *Urban America*, 487. Conn argues that Atwater's book marked the beginning of the "hunt for the Mound Builders" (*History's Shadow*, 120).

31. Quoted in Hopkins, "Clinton I," 137. On initial discussions of Haudenosaunee removal see Hopkins, "Clinton I," 113–43 and "Clinton II," 213–41; Mt. Pleasant, *Whirlwind*, 158.

32. Martinko, *Historic*, 4.

33. *Archaeologia Americana*, 1: 39; AAS, *Proceedings*, 1–5. Documents 1813, AAS Records. AAS.

34. Burton writes: "archives do not simply arrive or emerge fully formed; nor are they innocent of struggles for power in either their creation or their interpretive applications" ("Introduction," 6).

35. This underlines Guidotti-Hernández's and Blackhawk's point about the ubiquity of violence. I thank Elizabeth Bacon Eager for thinking this over with me.

36. Of course, the Ohio country earthworks were even older than that, some more than two millennia.

37. See Hutton, *Theory of the Earth* and Cuvier, *Theory of the Earth*.

38. The 1809 volume included William Maclure's explanation of his geological map of the US (APS, *Transactions,* 4: 411–28).

39. On the creation of geological time, see Rudwick, *Earth's Deep History*. For "deep history," see Shryock and Smail, *Deep History*.

40. I follow Martinko, who suggests that preservation was an instrument for "dispossession and spatial control" (*Historic*, 8). In this sense, preservationism was constitutive of expansionist violence.

41. This is close to the change Yablon detects in the meanings of "fortune" and *translation imperii* (*Ruins*, 28, 33, 35). Allen calls the visualizations of history in the chronographies made by Elizabeth Peabody, Sarah Pierce, and Emma Willard "stratigraphical" (Allen, *A Republic in Time*, 168; Baym, *Women Writers*, 52–53). See also Grafton and Rosenberg, *Cartographies* and Burnett, "Mapping Time."

42. Warren, *Neighbors*, 60.

43. Chiles, *Transformable*, 29.

44. Kolodny, "Competing Narratives," 44.

45. Kolodny, "Competing Narratives," 33; 32–38.

46. Horsman, *Expansion*, 170–72. As early as 1802, Ohio had begun to claim lands properly designated Indian Country. After the Treaty of Detroit (1807) Ohio began forming reservations for Odawa communities near the mouth of the Maumee River. See Stockwell, *Other Trail*, 66–70, 73, 78–80.

47. Doolan, *Fugitive Empire*, xv; Rohrbough, *Land Office*.

48. Rosen, *Border Law*; Waselkov, *Conquering*; Onuf, *Jefferson's Empire*, 109–46. See also Connolly, "Panic" and Saunt, "Financing."

49. Quoted in Saler, *Settlers' Empire*, 17; on post-1795 migration, see 56–60.

50. Calloway, *Victory*, 39.

51. Foster, *Strange*, 27.

52. *History of Franklin and Pickaway*, 227; Foster, *Strange*, 23, 26.

53. Atwater, "On the Prairies," 121 and "Prairies in Ohio," 87–88.

54. Pickaway Historical Society, *Pickaway County*, 4–5.

55. "Antiquities of Western America," 2; Brackenridge, *Views*, 184; Wade, *Urban Frontier*.

56. White, *Backcountry*, 131–37.

57. Many settlers discovered their antiquarian passion while working to make expansion possible: cutting roads, marking surveys, scouting for mineral resources, leading armies, riding circuits.

58. Cist, "Ruins," 419.

59. Cist, "Ruins," 418a, 419.

60. Hindraker, *Elusive Empires*, 185–226; Dowd, *Spirited*, 90–122. See also Warren and Noe, "Greatest Travelers" and Spero, "Stout, Bold, Cunning."

61. "Ohio Coat of Arms," Adena Mansion & Gardens, Chillicothe, 2018. In Worthington's diary, he wrote: "Adan, Aden, or Adena signifying (in the Hebrew language)

pleasure. That name was given to places remarkable for the delightfulness of their situations considered either in themselves or comparatively with the adjoining country" (Adena Mansion).

62. Webb and Snow, *Adena People*, 8. Curator of the Ohio State Archaeological and Historical Society (now Ohio History Connection) William Mills published on his "Adena Mound" excavations in the first decade of the twentieth century but the label "Adena People" was not adopted until the 1930s. Stratigraphy was identified as an important element of the "Adena mounds"—usually burial mounds—best visualized by making "a complete vertical slice through it" (Webb and Snow, *Adena People*, 37). The mounds in Enon, Grave Creek, and Miamisburg Ohio are all identified as "Adena."

63. Byrne, "Ethos," 73.

64. Byrne, "Ethos," 74.

65. Byrne, "Ethos," 76.

66. Foster, *Strange*, 26; Brown, "Brown Family," 229.

67. Foster, *Strange*, 29–30.

68. E.g., Harris, *Journal of a Tour*, 147–63. See Dunlop, "Curiosities," 257.

69. Martinko, *Historic*, 37.

70. Foster, *Strange*, 29; Martinko, *Historic*, 37. In the summer of 1816 periodicals across the nation carried notices of the Circleville's "ancient" features: e.g., Campbell, "Of The Aborigines," 6–7; "Topographical: Circleville," 2.

71. Atwater, "Aboriginal Antiquities," 333; Foster, *Strange*, 29; Smith, *Mapping*, 34–35.

72. Foster, *Strange*, 32.

73. In mid-century the town changed to a grid layout in a process called "squaring the circle" (*History of Pickaway County*, 34).

74. After Johnston replaced Wells as Fort Wayne's Indian Agent in 1809, he facilitated a treaty in which the Miamis were forced to share payment for ceded lands. This was one factor driving Miami support to Tecumseh and Tenskwatawa at Prophetstown (Hutton, "William Wells," 214).

75. "Antiquities of Western America," 2.

76. "Indian Antiquities," 136–37.

77. Atwater to Newton, 21 August 1818, Atwater Papers. AAS.

78. Atwater to Thomas, 4 October 1819, Atwater Papers. AAS.

79. Atwater to Thomas, 4 October 1819, Atwater Papers. AAS.

80. Atwater to Thomas, 4 October 1819, Atwater Papers. AAS.

81. Atwater to Thomas, 4 October 1819, Atwater Papers. AAS.

82. Atwater, "Aboriginal Antiquities," 333. Harris also described an excavated body with "a quantity of isinglass on his breast" (*Journal of a Tour*, 152).

83. Atwater to Newton, 13 July 1818, Atwater Papers. AAS; AAS, *Proceedings*, 131.

84. Prechtel-Kluskens, "Postmasters," 84.

85. From 1816 to 1819 the territories of Indiana, Illinois, Mississippi, Missouri, and Alabama were all admitted to the Union as new states. In 1818 there was a short-lived attempt to form two new territorial governments: one at Prairie du Chien in Ho-Chunk

territory and another stretching from disputed lands south of the Red River to Galveston Bay (see article reprinted from the *Saint Louis Enquirer* as "New States" in Chillicothe's October 23, 1818 *Scioto Gazette*). Instead, Arkansas Territory (west of the Mississippi to the negotiated Spanish border) was formed in 1819. After the Panic of 1819, New Spain's Florida and Tejas attracted entreprenures with flexible commitments to nation, like Moses Austin and the Creek leader William Bowles (Waselkov, *Conquering*, 44, 57, 59; Rosen, *Border Law*, 20–26; Mongey, *Rogue Revolutionaries*, 9–37; Weeks, *John Quincy Adams*; Owsley and Smith, *Filibusters*).

86. See Henkin, *Postal Age* and Dubcovsky, *Informed Power*.

87. Atwater to Newton, 13 July 1818, Atwater Papers. AAS; AAS, *Proceedings*, 131; Atwater to Thomas, 14 October 1820, Atwater Papers. AAS. Dorfeuille's museum purchased Atwater's collection; according to Belinda, it was destroyed by fire (Foster, *Strange*, 48).

88. Atwater to Newton, 13 July 1818, Atwater Papers. AAS.

89. Gunn, *Empire*, 17–51; Harvey, *Native Tongues*, 80–112; 145–81.

90. Atwater to Thomas, 24 February 1819, Atwater Papers. AAS.

91. Atwater to Thomas, 24 February 1819, Atwater Papers. AAS.

92. Hopkins and Spring, *Williams College*, 47, 57, 100–101; Atwater, "Circular," Caleb Atwater Papers, 12 August 1818. VFM 769. OHC. Mitchell was president of New York City's Lyceum of Natural History.

93. Waldo, *Tour*, 272–78.

94. Atwater, "Aboriginal Antiquities"; Atwater to Newton, 13 July 1818, Atwater Papers. AAS; AAS, *Proceedings*, 20.

95. Atwater to Thomas, 13 March 1820, Atwater Papers. AAS.

96. Atwater to Newton, 21 August 1818, Atwater Papers. AAS.

97. Atwater to Newton, 21 August 1818, Atwater Papers. AAS; Atwater to Thomas, 20 May 1819, Atwater Papers. AAS.

98. He promised to "survey and examine these Antiquities, all the way to the Gulf of Mexico and in to the Province of Texas" if his benefactors would support him, grumbling that even "With my slender means, poor, embarrassed and afflicted with several years sickness, I have done more than was ever done by any other person in North America and have never recd one cent, as yet, by way of assistance" (Atwater to Thomas, 4 March 1820, Atwater Papers. AAS).

99. Atwater to Thomas, 20 May 1819. AAS; Atwater to Thomas, 24 February 1819, Atwater Papers. AAS.

100. Atwater to Thomas, 24 February 1819. AAS; Atwater to Thomas, 2 October 1819, Atwater Papers. AAS.

101. For specimen drawings in Latin America, see Podgorny, "Portable."

102. *Archaeologia Americana*, 1: 43–44; Goodwin, *Address*, 17. "Every thing in its place" recalls Enlightenment regimes of order and Lancastrian education (Foucault, *Order of Things*, 131, 135). For regimes of order in terms of anthropologizing Native peoples see Beider, "Representation."

103. Lewis, *Facts*, 100.

104. AAS, *Donation Book*, AAS Records, 140.
105. Atwater, "Description," 232, 232–35.
106. Atwater to Thomas, 30 August 1819, Atwater Papers. AAS.
107. "Art. 4 Atwater's Notes on Ohio." See *Philanthropist*, February 18, 1819, 154; *American Monthly Magazine*, March 1819, 389; *Philadelphia Register*, June 12, 1819, 400.
108. "Art. 4. Atwater's Notes on Ohio," 445; Atwater to Thomas, 4 March 1820, Atwater Papers. AAS.
109. Atwater, "Description," 235.
110. Clifford, "Letters," 21. On AAS members see Snead, *Relic Hunters*, 82–126.
111. Clifford, "Letters," 27. He believes that Lenape history recorded by Heckewelder, in which the "Alligewi are mentioned as finally emigrating to the south and west, whence they never returned," provides the missing narrative (Clifford, "Letters," 7).
112. Clifford, "Letters," 1, 7, 9. The next month, B. reviewed the Philadelphia edition of Clavijero's *History*, Atwater weighed in from Circleville, and Clifford published another letter.
113. Clifford, "Letters," 7, 8.
114. Clifford, "Letters," 58–59. He named many of the months and days of the Mexica calendar and explained the five ages and the "Binding of the Years" ceremony ("Letters," 53–54, 56, 50).
115. Clifford, "Letters," 61.
116. Clifford, "Letters," 18, 19, 10, 42.
117. Clifford, "Letters," 2.
118. Clifford, "Letters," 10, 19, 21.
119. Quoted in Clifford, "Letters," 135n14. From textual evidence in Atwater's 1820 essay it is clear that he read Clifford's series with enthusiasm, although Boewe points out that Clifford's influence on Atwater has gone mostly unnoticed (Atwater, "Letter," 177–79; Boewe *Indian Antiquities*, 135n12, 144). For Clifford-Rafinesque-Atwater exchanges, see Snead, *Relic Hunters*, 61–76.
120. In a July 1820 letter to Atwater, Rafinesque wrote that "All the various monuments, scattered through the western states by that ancient and populous nation, the Alleghawian, (as we find it called by the Lennape tribes) are very far from being thoroughly and accurately known" (Rafinesque, "Letter," 53). An excerpt of Heckewelder's "Account of the History, Manners, and Customs of the Indian Nations, Who Once Inhabited Pennsylvania and the Neighboring States," published by the APS, was included in *The Western Review* in September 1819.
121. "Rafinesque to Jefferson, 1 August 1820," *Founders Online*, National Archives.
122. "Rafinesque to Jefferson, 1 August 1820," *Founders Online*.
123. "Rafinesque to Jefferson, 1 August 1820," *Founders Online*. Atwater warned Thomas of "sheer Indian fabrication" in Heckewelder's "Account," slighting Rafinesque: "Since the publication of that absurd tale, every whimsical writer, is telling tales about Allegawean monuments &c" (Atwater to Thomas, 29 September 1820, Atwater Papers. AAS).
124. Atwater to Thomas, 24 February 1819, Atwater Papers. AAS.

125. Atwater, "Description," 248, 250.
126. As evidenced in 1817 "On the Peopling" and Campbell's 1816 "Of the Aborigines" in *The Port-Folio*. Barnhart's *American Antiquities* (especially 1–152) provides an excellent overview. See also Williams, *Fantastic*; Greene, *Science*; Silverberg, *Moundbuilders*.
127. Atwater, "Description," 251; Atwater to Thomas, 2 December 1819, Atwater Papers. AAS.
128. Lazo, *Filiadelfia*, 30–31.
129. The forty-second parallel was set by the 1819 Adams-Onís Treaty. President Adams offered to purchase the disputed Sabine-Red River lands in 1825.
130. Atwater to Newton, 21 Aug 1818, Atwater Papers. AAS.
131. Atwater to Newton, 30 May 1819, Atwater Papers. AAS.
132. Atwater to Thomas, 24 February 1819; 4 October 1819, Atwater Papers. AAS.
133. Atwater to Thomas, 24 February 1819, Atwater Papers. AAS.
134. Atwater to Thomas, 19 May 1820, Atwater Papers. AAS.
135. Atwater to Thomas, 19 May 1820, Atwater Papers. AAS.
136. Atwater to Newton, 21 Aug 1818, Atwater Papers. AAS.
137. Clinton, "Discourse," 61.
138. Tanner, *Atlas*, 99, 101.
139. Kolodny, "Fictions," 705.
140. Atwater, "Description," 178.
141. Atwater, "Description," 180.
142. Atwater, "Description," 181.
143. Atwater, "Description," 182.
144. Atwater, "Description," 182.
145. Wheeler-Voegelin, *Mortuary*; Mann, *Native Americans*, 217–19.
146. Atwater, "Description," 182.
147. Atwater to Thomas, 13 March 1820, Atwater Papers. AAS; Atwater Catalog, March 26, 1820, Atwater Papers. AAS.
148. Atwater, "Description," 178; AAS, *Donation Book*, AAS Records, 127, 140–42.
149. These items were on display until 1895 (AAS, *Proceedings* 49, 45–50, 72). See also AAS Acquisition Files. Peabody Museum.
150. Atwater to Thomas, 24 February 1820, Atwater Papers. AAS.
151. Atwater to Thomas, 13 March 1820, Atwater Papers. AAS.
152. Atwater, "Description," 181, 180, Atwater Papers. AAS.
153. Thomas, *Skull Wars*, 52–63, 123–32; Mann, *Native Americans*, 5–104. See also Conn, *History's Shadow*.
154. Jefferson, *Writings*, 224.
155. Jefferson, *Writings*, 224–25.
156. Jefferson, *Writings*, 225. On Jefferson's excavation see Atalay, "Indigenous Archaeology," 285–88.
157. Harris, *Journal of a Tour*, 152, 159.
158. Madison, "A Letter," 132–42.

159. Madison, "A Letter," 136–37. See Barnhart, *American Antiquities*, 152–53.

160. Bruchac, "Lost and Found," 150.

161. "Whenever you see a number of holes in the earth, without any regard to regularity, of about a foot and a half in diameter, there, by digging a few feet, you may find an Indian's remains" (Atwater, "Circleville," 443–44).

162. Parsons, "Discoveries," 124.

163. Clifford, "Letters," 43, 45.

164. Clifford, "Letters," 25.

165. See Deloria, *God Is Red*, 13–18; Echo-Hawk and Echo-Hawk, *Battlefields*; Fine-Dare, *Grave Injustice*; Lonetree, *Decolonizing Museums*, 12–19; Mihesuah, *Repatriation Reader*; Riding-In, "Our Dead" and "Repatriation"; Riding-In et al., "Protecting"; Thomas, *Skull Wars*, 198–208; Trope and Echo-Hawk, "Native American Graves," 135–38; Vizenor, "Bone Courts." See also Colwell-Chanthaphonh and Nash, *Museum Anthropology*; Cooper, *Spirited Encounters*; Colwell, *Plundered Skulls*; King, *Legible Sovereignties*; Sleeper-Smith, *Contesting Knowledge*.

166. Klesert and Powell, "Perspective"; Mihesuah, "American Indians."

167. See Bruchac, "Lost and Found"; Lonetree, *Decolonizing Museums*; Poremski, "Voicing," 8.

168. See, for example, "Protocols for Native American Archival Materials," Northern Arizona University Libraries, 2006. https://www2.nau.edu/libnap-p/. For specific archival interventions see O'Neal, "From Time Immemorial" and "The Right to Know."

169. "Cultural Sensitivity," *Trove*, National Library of Australia. Accessed July 13, 2020. https://www.trove.nla.gov.au/partners/partner-services/adding-collections-trove/enrich-your-data/cultural-sensitivity.

170. "Open Access Policy," American Philosophical Society, November 2018. https://www.amphilsoc.org/reference-requests#paragraph–719. The Peabody Museum's message is on its Collections page (https://www.peabody.harvard.edu/collections).

171. Bruchac, "Lost and Found," 150, 156.

172. Byrne, "Ethos," 73.

173. Trope and Echo-Hawk, "Native American Graves," 127. I am not advocating for a total prohibition on reproductions of grave goods but rather policies reflective of context. Items such as Catholic relics, for example, owe much of their spiritual and cultural power to circulation and display (I thank Andrew McClellan for this point).

174. For example, presentations that reproduce images of the "Kentucky mummy." See Kertész, "Family Affair."

175. Mann has documented some of the most disturbing personal collections (*Native Americans*, 253–54). Pothunters and hobbyists persist, largely undeterred (Mallouf, "Unravelling Rope"; Pember, "Made for TV"; Yang, "Southern California"). See also Erdrich, "eBay Bones."

176. Atwater to Thomas, 20 May 1819, Atwater Papers. AAS.

177. Atwater to Thomas, 20 May 1819, Atwater Papers. AAS.

178. Tiro, "Piqua," 31; Brooks, *Our Beloved Kin*.

179. Warren, *Neighbors*, 60.

180. See Horsman, *Race*; Sheehan, *Seeds*.

181. Johnston served during the wars in Ohio under General Anthony Wayne. He became factor at Wayne's fort not long afterward and was present at the 1803 Treaty of Fort Wayne that set the boundaries of the "Vincennes Tract" around Fort Vincennes and "all the lands adjacent to which the Indian titles had been extinguished" (7 Stat. 74, June 7, 1803). Wells is listed as an interpreter and Hendrick Aupaumut was also present.

182. Quoted in Hill, *John Johnston*, 95.

183. Quoted in Hill, *John Johnston*, 95.

184. Warren, *Neighbors*, 56; *ASP2*, 2: 149.

185. Stockwell, *Other Trail*, 77–84; *ASP2*, 2: 137–140. Jackson had similar instructions for his July 8, 1817 treaty with the Cherokees (Stockwell, *Other Trail*, 77; *ASP2*, 2: 140–44).

186. Quoted in Miller, "Treaties," 145n74; *ASP2*, 2: 177. See Hurt, *Ohio Frontier*, 364. This was similar to the contemporaneous treaty policy in the southeast.

187. Stockwell, *Other Trail*, 84; 88–96. See also *ASP2*, 2: 149–71.

188. Although white settlers had moved to St. Mary's by 1820, the white town was not founded until 1823. Nearby land was flooded in 1845 to create a resevoir for the Miami-Erie Canal (built 1831–45).

189. Quoted in Stockwell, *Other Trail*, 84; 75–76.

190. Hamilton, *Writings of Monroe*, 6: 38; 33–43.

191. *Treaties*, 255–56. With this they sold Captain Pipe's Town along the Tymochtee Creek as well as their Indiana lands along the White River (Stockwell, *Other Trail*, 134).

192. *Senate Journal*. 15th Cong., 2nd sess., 21 January 1819, 173; *Annals of Congress*, Senate, 15th Congress, 2nd Session, 170. A petition from the region's Quakers had been submitted the previous month (*Senate Journal*. 15th Cong., 2nd sess., 23 December 1819, 96).

193. *House Journal*. 15th Cong., 2nd sess., 3 March 1819, 343; *Bills and Resolutions*, House of Representatives, 15th Cong., 1st sess., 21 January 1818; *ASP2*, 2: 325.

194. Rifkin, *Manifesting*, 13–14; Snyder, "Rise and Fall," 387.

195. Kilbourn, *Ohio Gazetteer* 1819, 8–9 interleaf; Kilbourn, *Ohio Gazetteer* 1821, foldout. Cf. Kilbourn, *Ohio Gazetteer* 1816, 72–73; Kilbourn, *Ohio Gazetteer* 1817, 28–29 interleaf.

196. Shawnees were expelled to Kansas from 1831 to 1833; the Ohio Seneca in 1831 and Odawa in 1833; the Wyandot in 1843. That year Ohio officially "extinguished" aboriginal title. Johnston was particularly involved in the Wyandot negotiations.

197. Atwater to Thomas, 8 July 1819, Atwater Papers. AAS.

198. Rohrbough, *Land Office*, 131; Van Atta, *Securing*, 41–42, 45–46.

199. Atwater, "Circular." Caleb Atwater Papers, 12 August 1818, VFM 769. OHC.

200. Atwater to Thomas, 9 May 1819; 2 October 1819, Atwater Papers. AAS. Most were living on reserved lands or at Johnston's Piqua agency.

201. Atwater, "Description," 271.

202. He enclosed not only Johnston's figures but also "remarks on the welch and Jewish Indians" (Atwater to Thomas, 21 July 1819, Atwater Papers. AAS).

203. Atwater, "Description," 270.

204. Atwater, "Description," 270. This arrangement, which favored pro-US leaders, consolidated former towns into reservation-based political bands (Warren, *Neighbors*, 57).

205. Atwater, "Description," 270.

206. Atwater, "Description," 270.

207. Kilbourn's map identified "Grave Creek" and "Mammoth Mound."

208. Atwater, "Description," 111.

209. Ford, *Settler Sovereignty*, 1, 3.

210. Ford, *Settler Sovereignty*, 18.

211. Atwater to Thomas, 18 April 1820; 20 June 1820, Atwater Papers. AAS. These counties were made from Non-County Area 6: Mercer, Paulding, Van Wert, Williams. When the Northwest Territory became "extinct" on August 15, 1796, all "unorganized federal territory" became known as "Non-County Areas," which is to say Native lands clamed but not administered by the US (*Territorial Papers* 2: 567–58; 3: 447). In 1820, the Ohio Assembly eliminated all "Non-County Areas," meaning there were no "unincorporated" regions left within the state (thanks to the 1817 and 1818 treaties).

212. Atwater, "Description," 270; Atwater to Thomas, 30 August 1820, Atwater Papers. AAS. "Fort Findlay" (now Findlay, Ohio) briefly housed Wyandot families after the War of 1812 and was at the site of a Wyandot town. Located on the Upper Sandusky, "Fort Stephenson" (now Fremont, Ohio) was the site of an important 1813 battle.

213. Atwater to Thomas, 28 July 1820, Atwater Papers. AAS.

214. Atwater to Thomas, 18 April 1820, Atwater Papers. AAS.

215. In an 1825 address to the Freemasons in Circleville, Atwater evoked the antiquity of the land as evidence of the brotherhood's own antiquity (Atwater, "Address," 117, 113).

216. Foster, *Strange*, 48.

217. *Cherokee Phoenix*, July 8, 1829. Only a few days after Atwater completed the deals at Prairie du Chien, Jackson hatched a plan to buy Texas from Mexico.

218. *Treaties*, 371–79. Prairie du Chien is located on an island in the Mississippi, just north of the Wisconsin River's mouth.

219. See Hall, *Uncommon*; Jung, *Black Hawk*; Trask, *Black Hawk* for accounts of the 1832 war.

220. In response, the US would step in with treaties and more military power until declaring "Wisconsin Territory" a state and ejecting its Native residents.

221. Hall, *Uncommon*, 91; Jung, *Black Hawk*, 46.

222. Atwater, Caleb. "Indian Poetry," US Mss 7E, Box 1, WHS. Foster, *Strange*, 48–49; Atwater, *Remarks*, 190. Atwater donated art and wrote of his experiences to Lyman

Draper in 1854 (3, 24 July; 13, 14 August, 1854. Draper-Wisconsin Historical Society Correspondence, 4).

223. William H. Keating had noted the site in his 1824 *Narrative*. From 1850–1852 Increase Allen Lapham mapped the Wisconsin mounds (including Aztalan) for the AAS, and his work was published by the Smithsonian Institution as *The Antiquities of Wisconsin* (1855).

224. Atwater, *Remarks*, 244.

225. Atwater, *Remarks*, 243.

226. APS, *Proceedings*, 587, 600.

227. APS, *Proceedings*, 581; Fauvet-Berthelot et al., "Dupaix," 470.

228. Atwater, *Remarks*, 243.

229. Atwater, *Remarks*, 145.

230. Atwater, *Remarks*, 145.

231. Atwater, *Remarks*, 146.

232. Atwater to Samuel G. Morton, 29 March 1830, Morton Papers, Mss.B.M843. APS.

233. Fabian, "Curious Cabinet." See also Thomas, *Skull Wars* and Fine-Dare, *Grave Injustice*.

234. See *Freeman Guide* 2212 and 2215. Morton proposed that the populations belonged to two separate races: "Toltecan" and "Barbarous Indians" (*Inquiry*, 4, 13).

235. See Armstrong-Fumero, "Even the Most Careless"; Brace, "The Roots."

236. Morton's research has had a long tail, notably with debates around biology, race, and IQ (Gould, *Mismeasure*). See Fabian, *Skull Collectors*, for a full history.

237. In 1832 Baldwin wrote: "I want the skulls of that unknown forgotten people who built the mounds and forts" (*Diary*, ix–x). See also Bieder, "Representations."

238. *Archaeologia Americana*, 2: vii. An important indication of the southward direction of AAS members' attention was the contribution by Juan Galindo, military governor of Petén, who conducted work with the support of the AAS. See Aguirre, *Informal Empire*, 72–74.

239. "Notes on Indian Tribes of Mexico and Adjacent Regions," Gallatin Papers, Library of Congress.

240. Barnhart, *American Antiquities*, 27, 30; Kincheloe, "Squier," 5.

241. Quoted in Kincheloe, "Squier," 4.

242. Squier and Davis, *Monuments*, 7. This denotes the 1998 reprint; *1848* denotes the original. For its publishing history see Gunn, *Empire*, 225n22.

243. Kincheloe, "Squier," 4; Warren, *Rafinesque*, 140.

244. Squier and Davis, *Monuments*, 7, 3; also 45, 55, 74, 104, 118–19, 301, 306. The 1998 anniversary edition's introduction describes the volume as "one long argument that the moundbuilders were a numerous, widespread, and homogenous race . . . [who] bore unmistakable traces of a deep historic connection to the semi-civilized peoples of Mexico and Peru" (Meltzer, *Monuments*, 36).

245. E. G. Squier Papers, Reel 10. Library of Congress.

246. Squier and Davis, *1848*, 144.

247. Squier and Davis, *1848*, 144 ff29.

248. Kent, "Site preparations."
249. Turner, "Mall construction."
250. Zachariah, "Developers"; Turner, "Mall construction."
251. A later report noted that the excavation "was conducted with the consultation of the federally-recognized Indian Tribes whose homeland included southern Ohio" ("Developer Honored").
252. Zachariah, "Developers."
253. Lepper, "Archaeology Blog."
254. Heartland Earthworks Conservancy, "Last weekend, the HEC officially recognized. . ." *Facebook*. May 22, 2016. https://m.facebook.com/HeartlandEarthworks-Conservancy/posts/last-weekend-the-hec-officially-recognized-the-cincinnati-based-firm-that-built-/978009215600922/. The interpretive panel is exemplary in that it prominently identifies the area's "ancient mounds and earthen enclosures" as "built by the ancestors of today's Native Americans" which, it adds, nearly all "contain human burials" ("North Bridge Street Mound" Interpretive Panel, Chillicothe, 2017. Courtesy of Fred Straub of the Thomson Company).
255. "North Bridge Street Mound." See "Map of a section of twelve miles of the Scioto Valley with its Ancient Monuments," *1848*, 3f. This is far from the only "reconstructed" mound across the state.
256. For an example of dispossession at a different Ohio site, see MacDonald, "Whose Earthworks?"

Chapter 6

1. Diaz, "Sombras," 24–26.
2. Diaz, "Sombras," 30.
3. Ackerly, "Antiquities," 373.
4. Ackerly, "Antiquities," 374.
5. Ackerly, "Antiquities," 371.
6. Ackerly, "Antiquities," 376.
7. Ackerly, "Antiquities," 373–74.
8. See Claudius Rich, *Memoir on the Ruins of Babylon* (1815).
9. I.e., Meyer and Gallenkamp, *The Mystery of the Ancient Maya* (1985); Bourbon, *The Lost Cities of the Mayas* (2000); Lourie, *Mystery of the Maya: Uncovering the Lost City of Palenque* (2001); the National Geographic television series *Lost Treasures of the Maya* (2018).
10. For an overview, see Díaz-Andreu, *World History*. On the "archaeological sublime," see Harvey, *American Geographics*.
11. In 1787 Del Río identified "accumulated heaps of rubbish, sand, and small stones" concealing some of Palenque's structures (*Description*, 12, 15). I suspect that some were ancestral shrines or prayer mounds. See Farriss, "Remembering," and Picas, "Plurivocality."
12. Devereux et al., "Visualisation"; Chase et al., "Geospatial revolution."

13. Davis, "Laser maps"; Kamrani, "Maya Megalopolis"; Graham-Harrison, "Archaeologists."

14. See Lovell, "Surviving Conquest." Most sites are in Yucatán, although the "oldest and largest Maya structure" so far—a mile-long, three thousand-year-old site of earthen mounds called Aguada Fénix—is in Tabasco, about eighty miles east of Palenque (Inomata et al., "Aguada Fénix"; "Oldest and largest," *Reuters*). In 2011, LiDAR images of a massive Purépecha complex of pyramids and plazas in Michoacán served as a reminder that not all of Mexico's history is Maya- or Mexica-made (Davis, "Laser scanning").

15. Maya communities trace to various lineages including (but not limited to) K'iche,' Tz'utujil, Mam, Kaqchikel, Lakadon, Q'eqchi,' Ch'orti', and Yukatek.

16. Sheedy, "Everyday," 27. Two such groups in the Yucatán are Múuch Xíinbal and Múul Meyaj ("Everyday," 32n20). Sheedy notes that Xocén people more readily describe themselves as "máasewáalo'ob" (ordinary Maya people) as opposed to "¢'ùulo'ob" (white Yucatecos) ("Everyday," 30–31). See also Castañeda, "We Are Not Indigenous!"

17. Castañeda, "Transcultural," 264; Juarez, "Struggles."

18. "hieroglyphic, n., adj. *OED*.

19. Stephens, *Incidents*, 2: 36, 252.

20. Stephens, *Incidents*, 2: 294–95.

21. Ortega, "Monroísmo arqueológico." Evans and Harvey expand on these ideas.

22. Aguirre, *Informal Empire*, xvi. See also Williams, "Collecting."

23. I.e., Aguirre, *Informal*; Evans, *Romancing*; Harvey, *American Geographics*.

24. This connection was inherent to the argument for americano sovereignty (Brading, *First America*, 602).

25. "Mestizo" is not the same as "mestizaje," a process of whitening (Hill, *Blood*).

26. Bonfil Batalla, *México Profundo*, 105, 41–58. For "rupture narratives," see Kolodny, "Competing Narratives."

27. For the "invention" of Maya culture, see Castañeda, *Museum*.

28. "Mexican" came to signify what "criollo" had before: middling-to-elite Americas-born *white*.

29. Brading, *First America*, 581; Florescano, *Myth*, 198, 217, 220, 250n56.

30. Quoted in O'Gorman, *Mier*, 7–9.

31. He explained: "the Spanish pronounced 'Mexico' as *Méjico* [Me-hi-co], even though the Indians do not say anything other than *Mescico*" (quoted in O'Gorman, *Mier*, 7–9). Later deployments of "Mexico" versus "Mejico" and related "x" words would recall this preference for an Indigenous over Spanish (or Hispanicized) identity.

32. Keen, *Aztec Image*, 317.

33. Quoted in Brading, *First America*, 581. Bustamante wrote Morelos's speech.

34. The word "cem anáhuac," explains historian Davíd Carrasco, signified "land surrounded by water" to the Mexica, who used the demonym "anahuaca" for themselves, the people who lived in that island place (Carrasco, *Daily Life*, 1, 264).

35. See Castañeda, *Museum*, and Picas, "Plurivocality."

36. Juarros's *Compendio*, a little-known report on Palenque was published in Guatemala City in 1810. Morton later cited it in *Crania Americana*.

37. There are more than sixty separate Indigenous "ethnicities" in Mexico, which is nonetheless an inadequate measure of Indigenous presence today.

38. Gollnick, *Reinventing*, 70; cf. Castañeda, *Museum*, 12, 8. For examples of the "discovery" discourse, see Preston, "America's Egypt," and Carlsen, *Jungle of Stone*. On Stephens and "Maya culture" see Mucher, "Collecting."

39. Matthew, *Conquest*, 16.

40. See Rosenswig et al., "Lidar Data," and Rosenswig et al. "Izapa and Soconusco."

41. Highland refugee groups include Itzá, Kejacje, and Kowoj Mayas. Even after 1697, resisters continued to be persecuted and deported to Guatemala. See Restall and Asselbergs, *Invading Guatemala*.

42. Schele and Mathews, *Code*, 201; Sharer and Trexler, *Ancient*, 166; Mathew, *Conquest*, 29.

43. Christenson, *Popul Vuh*, 28–29. There is ample evidence of a material relationship between Chichén Itza and Tula, but ancestral claims also operate in terms of fictive kinship and power, as they did for the Mexica (Roys, *Chumayel*, 88–89).

44. *Florentine Codex*, 10: f149 Christenson, *Popul Vuh*, 27.

45. Townsend, *Malinztin*, 24–26.

46. Matthew, *Conquest*, 16. The word comes from "maaya' t'áan," the language spoken at Mayapán (Sheedy, "Everyday," 26, 28).

47. León Cazares, "La presencia," 53.

48. In the lowlands, Maya communities reconstituted their histories into *The Books of Chilam Balam*.

49. Hanks, *Converting*, 1.

50. For the Yucatán see Hanks, *Converting*, 25–58.

51. Christenson, *Burden*, 84.

52. Christenson, *Burden*, 73. See also Carmack, *Título*, 28–29, and Tedlock, *Popul Vuh*, 56. Hanks mentions Mayan alphabetic documents from the Yucatán in the 1550s as well (*Converting*, 338).

53. See "Popol Wuj Online," Ohio State University Libraries. https://www.library.osu.edu/projects/popolwuj.

54. This copy is now held by the Newberry Library (Ayer Vault MS 1515), which has recently begun receiving visits from Maya delegations (personal conversation, Seonaid Vailant, May 2016).

55. Núñez de la Vega, *Constituciones*. "Nagualista," a shapeshifter who takes Jaguar form, is a powerful cosmic intermediary conventionally denigrated as a "witch" and associated with the Christian devil.

56. Christenson, *Popol Vul*, 80n102, 230–32, 257–60. It tells of the arrival of a group of outsiders from the east (Mathew, *Conquest*, 29). See also Carmack, *Quiché*, 43–74.

57. León Cazares, "La presencia," 55.

58. Núñez de la Vega, *Constituciones*, 74; Humboldt, *Views*, 92.

59. Quoted in Luján, *Cultura maya*, 135. Sometimes his name is written "Ordóñez y Aguilar." He identified Palenque as located in the "Tzendal [Tzeltal] Province."

60. A reproduction of the "Probanza de Votan" is held at the Newberry (Ayer MS 1564).

61. Del Río, *Description*, 54, 91.

62. Del Río, *Description*, 24, 25, 30–34, 33, 110. Cabrera's 1794 *Teatro Critico Americano* was included in the 1822 Del Río edition.

63. Quoted in Evans, *Romancing*, 24, 166n31.

64. For discussions, see Tedlock, *1000 Years*.

65. Sharer and Traxler, *Ancient Maya*, 472, 451.

66. Evans, *Romancing*, 16, 164n12. Del Río was accompanied by Guatemalan artist Ricardo Almendáriz (Florescano, *Myth*, 193; Koch, *Stephens and Catherwood*, 92). Almendáriz's original sketches were unearthed in Madrid and are now at the Library of Congress (Cline, "Apocryphal," 297). See Figure 20.

67. Evans, *Romancing*, 17.

68. Del Río, *Description*, 11.

69. Del Río, *Description*, 19.

70. Del Río, *Description*, 2.

71. Del Río, *Description*, 14; Estrada de Gerlero, "Carlos III," 79.

72. Dominican Fray Gregorio García wrote about the continent's Carthaginian origins in his 1607 *Origen de los indios del nuevo mundo* (Brading, *First America*, 196, 198).

73. Humboldt, *Views*, 69. Cervantes gave Humboldt the sketch, which he had engraved in Rome (*Views*, 67).

74. Brading, *First America*, 565, 581 663, 667. A complex mix of competing influences—from the Church, Monarchists, Freemasons, Rousseauians, and others—made for a tumultuous political beginning.

75. Federalists in early Mexico advocated a weak central government that deferred to states' rights, while Centralists wanted to reduce the power of individual states in favor of national power centralized in Mexico City. Centralism won out and Mexico today uses "federal" much in the same way that the United States does.

76. Brading, *First America*, 581.

77. Anna, *Forging*.

78. Bonfil Batalla, *México Profundo*, 63; 110–46. Arrizón, "Mestizaje"; Cottrol, *Long, Lingering*; Hill, "Blood." See Gonzalbo Aizpuru, "La trampa," 17–154; Restall, *Beyond*; Seed, "Social Dimensions"; Twinam, *Purchasing*. See also Bauer, "Hemispheric Genealogies," and Martínez, *Genealogical Fictions*.

79. Murray, "Church" 46; Guardino, *Peasants*, 5–6.

80. Villella, *Indigenous Elites*.

81. In 1810 the insurgent priest Hidalgo halted the leasing of Indigenous lands and urged respect for traditional boundaries; in 1813 Morelos exclaimed that property should only be owned by Americans (Brading, *First America*, 563, 577).

82. Gregory, *Brute*, 133, 149.

83. Gregory, *Brute*, 149; Gilmore, "Henry George Ward," 38.
84. Gilmore, "Henry George Ward," 36, 39. Alamán had been managing director of the British United Mexican Mining Association (Lamar, "Alamán," 90).
85. Barker, *French Experience*, 10, 14; Gregory, *Brute*, 148, 149.
86. Hamnett, "Dye Production," 70. Workers sacked the estates.
87. See Lockhart, "Encomienda."
88. Including the 1804 "consolidations" of Church property and 1813 decree that ordered the division of all communal lands except ejidos (De la Maza, *Código*, 148).
89. Hamnett, "Dye Production," 70, 75. Similar circumstances existed in the Yucatán.
90. Quoted in Hamnett, "Dye Production," 74.
91. Sanz and Simón, "Desamortización," 99.
92. See Poinsett, *Notes*, 254, 265–66.
93. Quoted in Gregory, *Brute*, 137; Penny, *A Sketch*, 89.
94. Bullock, *Six Months*, 133.
95. See also Beaufoy, *Mexican Illustrations*; Tayloe, *Journal*. For more, see Gregory, *Brute*.
96. In an 1829 letter to Henry Clay, Poinsett pinpointed Mexico's problem as its citizens' "constant intercourse with the aborigines, who were and still are degraded to the very lower class of human beings" (quoted in Gregory, *Brute*, 138).
97. Brading, *First America*, 653, 568.
98. Quoted in Brading, *First America*, 654.
99. Hale, *Mora*, 119; quoted in Sanz and Simón, "Desamortización," 93, 91.
100. Brading, *First America*, 579–80.
101. Sanz and Simón, "Desamortización," 92.
102. The Austrian visual artist Nina Hoechtl describes racialized capitalism in Mexico as "el delirio güero" ("white delusion"), the performance of consuming whiteness, which she traces to this early national moment ("Delirio Güero," 161, 169). Her film *Delirio Güero White Delusion 1825, 2018, 2211 and back* (2019/2211) explicitly examines Waldeck. I thank the artist for sharing her film with me.
103. Hill, "Blood." Although it was possible to make "petitions for whiteness" (gracias al sacar) as a mode of social mobility (major casta), Hill detects the erasure of Black castas categories as an expression of deep anti-Blackness ("Blood," 84). On anti-Blackness in Mexico, see Restall, *Beyond* and Aguirre Beltrán, *La población negra*.
104. Benjamin, *Rich Land*, 7–8. In 1825, the small Pacific region of Soconusco—also contested by Guatemala and the short-lived state of Los Altos (de Chiapas)—was also claimed by Mexico.
105. Bobrow-Strain, *Intimate Enemies*, 252.
106. Hernández, "Colonization," 313. Moses had already become a Spanish subject in 1798 when he formed a settlement in Spanish Louisiana.
107. Frye writes about how ruralness and traditionalism signify "indio" in a small community that used to be a "pueblo de indio" but now sees itself as a mestizo city (*Mexicans*, 4, 9). See also Bonfil Batalla, *México Profundo*, 46–47.

108. Lamar, "Alamán," 88; Zavala, *Viage*.
109. De la Maza, *Código*, 172.
110. Quoted in Hernández, "Colonization," 311, 312; Ortiz, *México*. See Kelly and Hatcher, "Tadeo Ortiz de Ayala."
111. Alamán, "Memoria 1823," 67, 84.
112. Alamán, "Memoria 1823," 67, 84, 67.
113. Folsom, *Yaquis*, 209.
114. De la Maza, *Código*, 355.
115. Alamán, "Memoria 1823," 85.
116. Hernández, "Colonization," 322.
117. Sanz and Simón, "Desamortización," 91, 100; Brading, *First America*, 654.
118. He sent questionnaires asking about "monuments of antiquity" to every state governor (Achim, *Idols*, 26, 30).
119. The inventory was made in 1823 by Junta de Antigüedades member Ignacio Cubas (GSS, Box 82, File 20, AGN).
120. Alamán, "Memoria 1823," 90–91.
121. This museum went through as many names as reorganizations; following Achim's lead, I refer to it as the National Museum (*Idols*).
122. Alamán, "Memoria 1823," 91.
123. Alamán, "Memoria 1823," 86–88; 91; Achim, *Idols*, 30–31.
124. Alamán, "Memoria 1825," 142, 146–47, 149.
125. Lombardo and Solís, *Antecedentes*, 39.
126. Alamán, "Memoria 1823," 86–88.
127. Achim, "National Museum," 23.
128. Rozental, "Material Ecologies," 191–92.
129. Alamán, "Memoria 1823," 90–91; "patrimony, n.," *OED Online*.
130. On the development of French patrimoine, see Poulot, "Heritage."
131. Gilmore, "Henry George Ward," 37. Mexico issued three Spanish expulsion orders between 1821 and 1836.
132. Its provenance is still murky and may have involved a man named McQueen (Cline, "Apocryphal," 299; Evans, *Romanticizing*, 166n45). McQueen & Co. were Berthoud's lithographers; Diaz writes the name as McQuy (Diaz, "Sombras," 31).
133. Del Río, *Description*, viii.
134. Baradère, *Antiquités*, 1: vii.
135. When Icaza and historian Manuel Orozco y Berra learned of this they pressured the authorities for its return. Bullock complied but not before taking a lithographic copy for himself (Achim, *Idols*, 42). The APS (and Delafield) copy appears to have been made from the Bullock lithograph.
136. Fauvet-Berthelot et al., "Real Expedición," 468, 466–67. The recommendation that Mexico buy back the collection for an astounding 145,000 francs was met with empty coffers. Adrien de Longpérier's exhibit of American antiquities at the Louvre the

following year was enabled by this acquisition. Most of it is at the Musée du quai Branly in Paris today.

137. Lombardo and Solís, *Antecedentes*, 40. A 1827 circular reported that two cases of Mexican antiquities had been found on the French ship *Joven Emilia* leaving from Vera Cruz for France (Lombardo and Solís, *Antecedentes*, 46).

138. Achim, "National Museum," 17; López Luján, "El capitán," 76.

139. *Memoria economica*, 113; "Antiguedades Mexicanas," *El Sol*, 18 May 1825, 3–4.

140. Achim, *Idols*, 49, 50, 263n84, 263n85. General de Brigade Juan Pablo de Anaya even sent manuscripts and artifacts from Chiapas, including a 1792 letter by Ordóñez y Aguiar; it was printed in *El Aguila Mexicana* in 1825.

141. Castillo Ledón, *Colección*, i; Keen, *Aztec Image*, 321.

142. Achim, *Idols*, 49.

143. López Luján, "El capitán."

144. Achim, "National Museum," 14.

145. Bullock, *Six Months*, 331.

146. Swiss naturalist Jean-Louis Berlandier botanized and recorded ethnographic notes along the "borderland" (but kept most of the materials for himself). See Berlandier, *Texas in 1830*.

147. Achim, "National Museum," 17–18.

148. Shelton, "Dispossessed," 75.

149. Achim, "National Museum," 15–16; quoted in Achim, "National Museum," 16.

150. Achim, "National Museum," 14; "Rosa Isídica," *El Sol* (November 4, 1827), 3–4. Achim believes this was an anagram for Gondra.

151. Icaza and Gondra, *Colección*, 2: 4. In Number 2, the origins of figures 2, 3, and 9 are potentially Toltec (noting especially the "butterfly motif" on 2 and 9 as well as the talud-tablero-style altars); for 4, Tlatilco (or El Arbolillo or Zacatenco) because it resembles an "Olmec-style" jaguar baby and Mexica for 7 and 8. The clay funereal figure (5) looks potentially Zapotec.

152. Quoted in Sanz and Simón, "Desamortización," 91.

153. Bustamante, *Mañanas*, n.p.

154. Aguirre, *Informal Empire*, 29–30. Bullock claimed his antiquities collection had been "formed with the sanction and through the aid of the present Mexican Government" (*Descriptive catalogue*, iii).

155. Achim, "Art of the Deal," 218, 228n10.

156. Lamar, "Alamán," 91. Even after the 1819 Adams-Onís treaty, sovereignty over the territories of Tejas y Coahuila as well as the Sabine-Red River lands were points of dispute. Mexico successfully negotiated a new treaty and sent a commission to survey it in 1828 (Lamar, "Alamán," 93). See also St. John, *Line*.

157. Lamar, "Genesis."

158. Hernández, "Colonization," 302.

159. Brading, *First America*, 562, 562–63.

160. Zavala, *Viage*, 353.

161. The church had long served as the temporary "trustee" for Indigenous lands ("temporalidades"), which Indigenous communities paid for the ability to live on with their labor.

162. Sanz and Simón, "Desamortización," 102; Brading, *First America*, 562, 562–63, 642, 641.

163. Bonfil Batalla, *México Profundo*, 46–47; Guardino, *Peasants*.

164. Sanz and Simón, "Desamortización, 101. These included Chihuahua and Jalisco in 1825, Veracruz in 1826, Michoacán in 1827, and Mexico in 1830. See de la Maza, *Código*, 148.

165. Mucher, "Collecting," 26. See also Wasserstrom, *Class*.

166. Benjamin, *Rich Land*, 13, 14.

167. Sanz and Simón, "Desamortización," 101.

168. Sanz and Simón, "Desamortización," 98.

169. Duval, *Les colonies*, 104.

170. Duval, *Les colonies*, 104.

171. See for example Arrizón, "Mestizaje," 133, and Chorba, *Mexico*.

172. There were approximately twenty other European colonization schemes at the time.

173. Maison, *Précis*, 5. The land was granted July 3, 1828, and received in Giordan's name by Edmond Chedehoux, a naturalized Mexican citizen (Mansion, *Précis*, 92). Chedehoux was supposed to receive government grants in Goatzacoalcos or Texas, where Giordan planned to found a Fourier-inspired commune (Maison, *Précis*, 92; Barker, *French Experience*, 12).

174. Alamán, "Memoria," 1823, 158. Along with Diego Barry and Felipe O'Reilly, Ortíz de Ayala planned to settle ten thousand Irish and Canary Island immigrants in Texas and break Texas away from Spain (Ortíz de Ayala, *México*; Kelly and Hatcher, "Tadeo Ortíz de Ayala"). Giordan moved into Ortíz de Ayala's home in the "Indian hamlet" of Minatitlan, Veracruz, and apparently made a (failed) deal to pay him in taxidermy birds, prepared by Baradère (Achim, "Art of the Deal," 230n36). After a stint as Mexican consul in Bordeaux from 1830–1831, Ortíz de Ayala's colonization designs shifted back to Texas.

175. Maison, *Précis*, 93. With his links to France's Southwest—an important source of emigrants during the eighteenth and nineteenth centuries—Baradère was an important asset to the Goazacoalco project.

176. *Bulletin de la Société de Géographie*, December 1829, 48. It was dated September 4 and signed November 7, 1828.

177. Baradère returned with copies of Dupaix's reports and Castañeda's drawings as well as three iconic manuscripts from Boturini's collection and many antiquities (Edison, "Prospecting").

178. Maison, *Précis*, 108.

179. Maison, *Précis*, 1.

180. See Laisné de Villevèque et al., *Colonie du Goazacoalco*, and Giordan, *Réponse*.
181. Icaza and Gondra, *Colección*, 1: 1–2.
182. Icaza and Gondra, *Colección*, 1: 2. Waldeck wrote this description.
183. Conventionally, criollos understood Mexican "temples" as the home of objects of veneration, which they usually termed "idols" (Humboldt, *Views*, 46, 42). The first engraving in Humboldt's *Views* was a representation of an "Azteque Priestess," a small Water or Corn god-image, copied from a Dupaix sketch (6).
184. Icaza and Gondra, *Colección*, 2: f2. The ancient Romans believed Dii Penates were the protectors of the household, the "domestic gods" ("penates, n." *OED Online*).
185. See Bassett, "Bundling."
186. Hamman, "Social Life," 354, 353; Lockhart, *Nahuas*, 16–17. See McAnny, *Ancestors*; Monaghan, *Covenants*, 99–104; Watanabe, *Saints*, 74–96.
187. Hamman, "Social Life," 354. I thank James Maffie for guidance here.
188. Icaza and Gondra, *Colección*, 2: f3.
189. In 1652, Bishop de Landa held his infamous Inquisition investigations and auto-da-fé in the Yucatán town of Mani, in which he ordered all of the "wooden idols" and "hieroglyphical" manuscripts burnt. Landa, indeed, instigated such a campaign of torture and other anti-Maya violence—against the peoples and their cosmologies—that his efforts led to the migration of many lowland (Yucatán) Mayas into the highlands of Chiapas and Péten (Christenson, *Burden*, 21–22).
190. Those "objects" were the "property" of the pueblo—just as the land was the pueblo's property—but property in this sense is more about identity and social balance and less about liberal tenets of ownership. See O'Hara, "Stones."
191. Wolfe, "Settler Colonialism"; Sanz and Simón, "Desamortización," 91.
192. It was designed as a fundraiser to be issued as a serial and the first number appeared at the end of September (Waldeck, *Journal*, Ayer MS 1261. Newberry Library; Achim, *Idols*, 71–72). It contained a historical painting—which Waldeck claimed was inspired by a Boturini document—as well as an episode from a Nahua genealogical codex and two plates depicting items from Dupaix's expedition.
193. Castillo Ledón, *Colección*, n.p. Bustamante was out of office from 1825–1828.
194. See Higgins, *Criollo Archive*; Townsend, *Annals*; More, *Baroque Sovereignty*.
195. For the Gómara-Chimalpahin text, see Schroeder et al., *Chimalpahin's Conquest*. On Chimalpahin, see Lockhart et al., *Annals of His Time*.
196. On Ixtlilxóchitl, see Brian, *Native Archive*.
197. Keen, *Aztec Image*, 322.
198. Keen, *Aztec Image*, 321.
199. As Nahua histories written in European alphabetic letters were made accessible in the late 1820s and early 1830s, Maya (and Zapotec-Mixtec, among others) histories were ignored altogether. Yucatecan Maya notaries, however, were transcribing and recopying their own oral and iconic histories into alphabetic script at this time (Mignolo, "Signs," 308). See also Hanks, *Converting*.
200. Folsom, *Yaquis*, 211–212, 213. He allied with the Opata leader Dolores Gutiérrez.

201. Brading, *First America*, 642.

202. Guerrero, an Afro-Indigenous man from Tixtla who grew up speaking Nahuatl, had encouraged land redistribution (Brading, *First America*, 658, 641).

203. Berthoud (sometimes Berthon) timed the launch of his edition to coincide with a display of the originals at his Piccadilly Circus bookstore.

204. Baradère *Antiquités*, 1: viii; Flyer reprinted in Castillo Ledón, *Colección*, n.p.

205. Quoted in Evans, *Romancing*, 36. In 1825, after an English mining company purchased the rights to a mine in Tlalpujahua, Michoacán—arranged with the help of Mexico's Minister to the UK—Waldeck was appointed as agent. Waldeck had turned to staging phantasmagorias and painting portraits in the capital city by 1826.

206. See Guillermo Dupaix Papers, G373 Ms. Nettie Lee Benson Latin American Collection, University of Texas Libraries, University of Texas at Austin. His objects were stored at the Royal College of Mines.

207. Dupaix, *Expediciones*. The 1820 copy was used for the Kingsborough edition and eventually ended up in Seville; the other was later lent to Baradère.

208. Waldeck, *Journal*, Ayer MS 1261. Newberry Library. The first engraving is a "historical painting" by Waldeck portraying "el ray de los Aztlanecas," Huitzíhuitl (Icaza and Gondra, *Colección*, 1:1).

209. Icaza and Gondra, *Colección*, 2: f2; 2:4. Of the Dupaix objects, the museum kept a stone ring from Tlahuac, a wooden drum from Tepoyango, Tlaxcala, and a Zapotec stone sculpture from Zaachila, Oaxaca (Fauvet-Berthelot et al., "Real Expedición," 479n7). The report that the items were in France by 1825 is a mistake: not only did Waldeck record seeing them in Mexico City in January 1826, Latour-Allard also wrote in July 1826 that the items had arrived "in Paris a few weeks ago" (quoted in Fauvet-Berthelot et al., "Real Expedición," 471). See also Achim, "Art of the Deal," 223, and Podgorny, "Portable" 586–89.

210. See Trafton, *Egypt Land*.

211. See Duponceau, "Essai."

212. Latour-Allard sold Kingsborough the Castañeda drawings, his publications reportedly inspired by Bullock's *Exhibition* (Baradère, *Antiquités*, 1: ix). Kingsborough used them to argue a Lost Tribes hypothesis.

213. Rasmussen has described the ethnocentrism of alphabetic writing as a "possessive investment in writing as a marker of reason and civilization" (*Queequeg*, 19). See also Boone and Mignolo, *Writing without Words*.

214. Waldeck spent years collecting information for a never-achieved *Encyclopédie archaéologique* (1829–1832). His 1838 *Voyage pittoresque et archéologique* still included some of the illustrations from the 1827 *Colección* (Bernal, *History*, 109).

215. Achim, "Art of the Deal," 219.

216. Diaz, "Sombras," 32. The year before, Warden had translated Del Río's report into French and presented it to the Society's membership, to great interest. See *Bulletin de la Société de Géographie* (1825): 308–10; (1826): 595–96; Warden, "Recherches."

217. Fauvet-Berthelot et al., "Real Expedición.".

218. The prize did not seem to motivate many Mexicans, despite the French-focused elite. This may have been due to the country's very real political turmoil, which included the Fredonia rebellion in Tejas (1826–1827), a quasi-civil war that led to a civilian lock-down in Mexico City during the summer of 1827, and the Spanish invasion of Tampico in 1829.

219. Waldeck, *Journal*, Ayer MS 1261. Newberry Library, 198.

220. By 1829, Baradère was back in Paris and defending the authenticity of his borrowed documents. See Edison, "Prospecting" and Achim, "Art of the Deal."

221. Quoted in Freeman, "Manuscript Sources," 532; Fauvet-Berthelot et al., "Real Expedición," 470.

222. Duponceau, "Essai," 64.

223. M'Culloh, *Researches*, 300. In 1829, Corroy was planning his second trip to Palenque and in Paris Barradère was exhibiting his Mexican antiquities (including some from Palenque) in front of the Société de la Géographie. Waldeck compared notes with Corroy in 1832 (Priego, "Corroy," 4). See also Luján, *Cultura maya*, 24.

224. Freeman, "Manuscript Sources," 531–32; APS, *Proceedings*, 587, 600.

225. Galindo, "Peten."

226. Fauvet-Berthelot et al., "Real Expedición," 474. Volumes 1–5 were published in 1830 by Augustine Aglio; Kingsborough died in 1837 before all nine volumes were released.

227. Rafinesque, *Atlantic Journal* (Autumn 1832), 38. The "Glyphs" of "Otolum" match those on the APS's "Table Cross." Rafinesque and Duponceau would ultimately share the Prix Volney in 1835, and Americans and Europeans continued to be particularly involved in the quest to "decode" Maya writing for the next two centuries.

228. Fauvet-Berthelot et al., "Real Expedición," 470; Humboldt, *Views*, 324.

229. Some Spanish chroniclers and later observers also noted "crosses" in Maya carvings (Brading, *First America*, 163, 198).

230. Morton, *Crania Americana*, 145.

231. M'Culloh, *Researches*, 338.

232. Morton, *Crania Americana*, 6, 63; 65; 83. Morton's iteration of Mexican history is noteworthy for his reproduction of the migration chronology (*Crania Americana*, 141–43). See Fabian, *Skull Collectors*.

233. In fact, ancestral claims between the Itzá (Maya Ancient Ones) and Tula's Toltecs also operate in terms of fictive kinship and power (Roys, *Chumayel*, 88–89).

234. People like Mier, for example, believed that the Yucatán had been visited by St. Thomas in the guise of Quetzalcoatl/Kukulcán; for him, this was about Maya and Mexica history (Brading, *First America*, 583).

235. The two copies at the Newberry Library are bound slightly out of order (Ayer 500.A105 B22 1834 and Ayer 500.A105 B22 1834b).

236. See Dupaix, *Expediciones*, for a twentieth-century reproduction of the Madrid copy. Ultimately, the images in Baradère's volume made Palenque's "hieroglyphic" inscriptions explicit in ways seldom seen outside Chiapas or Guatemala City before 1822; even then, the London Del Río version was only in black-and-white.

237. This does not appear to have happened. There are at least two copies in Mexico, one at the Biblioteca Nacional de Mexico and the other at the Monterrey Institute of Technology.

238. Baradère, *Antiquités Mexicaines*, 79.

239. Baradère, *Antiquités Mexicaines*, 79.

240. Baradère, *Antiquités Mexicaines*, n.p. (bound in Newberry Library folio vol. 1, Ayer 500 A105.B22 1834).

241. The green line stops in Veracruz and the blue in Oaxaca; the red line stretches from Mexico City to the far side of "Chiapa" that was in the Kingdom of Guatemala when Dupaix visited.

242. E.g., the incorporation of hieroglyphs into both of the Spanish-language translations of Prescott's *History* published in Mexico City from 1844–1846 (Achim, "National Museum," 21).

243. The relative abundance of elite-focused visual iconography in Maya sculpture and painting led nineteenth-century foreign archaeologists to valorize the relative "complexity" of Maya society (i.e., hierarchized) vis-à-vis their apparently "inferior" Nahua counterparts (Matthew, *Conquest*, 27). This would reverse during the Caste War.

244. The scholarship on the Caste War is vast: for a start see Rugeley, *Maya Wars*, and Joseph, "United States."

245. Decolonial Atlas, "The great cities of Maya Civilization..." *Facebook*. April 30, 2018. https://www.facebook.com/decolonialatlas/photos/pb.371492386351172.-2207520000.1525989549./992787127555025/?type=3&theater.

246. The post was notably critiqued by Indigenous anthropologist and activist Juliana K'abal-Xok Willars.

247. Mucher, "Collecting," 27n11.

248. Ortega, "Monroísmo," 55.

249. For the racial politics at play, see Kazanjian, *Colonizing*.

Epilogue

1. Byrd, *Transit*, 148. Byrd writes that the figure of the "enemy Indian" has served as the "transit of empire" for the United States, which is to say, has facilitated US imperial conquest.

2. Morton, *Crania Americana*, 149n. On Morton see Achim "Skulls and Idols," 23–44 and Fabien, *Skull Collectors*.

3. Achim, *Idols*, 178 and "National Museum," 21.

4. For this history and the cultural legacy of the war, see Johannsen, *To the Halls*.

5. Calhoun, *Papers*, 25: 64.

6. "We have conquered many of the neighboring tribes of Indians, but we never thought of holding them in subjection—never of incorporating them into our Union.

They have either been left as an independent people among us, or been driven into the forests" (Calhoun, *Papers*, 25: 64).

7. Mesa Verde Voices Podcast, 4.5: "Where Did They Go?" 2021. https://www.mesaverdevoices.org/wheredidtheygo

8. Thompson, *Centeola*; Snead, *Ruins and Rivals*, 7.

9. Hardacre, "Cliff-Dwellers."

10. Rothman, *Preserving*, 18, 19, 22, 23; Snead, *Ruins and Rivals*, 3-64.

11. Hardacre, "Cliff-Dwellers."

12. "An act for the preservation of American antiquities," June 8, 1906, 34 *Stat*. 225.

13. Rothman, *Preserving*, 233–34.

14. Act of June 8, 1906, ch. 3060, *Stat*. 225.

15. "An Act Creating Mesa Verde National Park," 29 June 1906. 34 *Stat*. 616. Sellers, "Very Large," 299–300. See also Noble, *Legacy of Distrust*.

16. Palacios, *Maquinaciones neoyorquinas*. In Mexico legislation protecting antiquities stretched back to 1827—and earlier if Crown prohibitions are considered—although these laws were unevenly enforced. See also Bueno, *Pursuit*.

17. E.g., Craig Childs, *House of Rain* (2008); David E. Stuart, *Anasazi America* (2014); Gustaf Nordenskiold, *Cliff Dwellers of Mesa Verde* ([1893] 1990).

18. McPharson, *Viewing the Ancestors*, 16. According to a sensationalist headline in a 2015 article in *Nature*, "nearly 30,000 people disappeared" from the Four Corners region in the mid-1200s, which was the "greatest vanishing act in prehistoric America" (Monastersky, "Greatest Vanishing Act").

19. Mesa Verde Voices Podcast, 4.5: "Where Did They Go?" 2021. https://www.mesaverdevoices.org/wheredidtheygo.

20. See *National Park Service and American Indians, Alaska Natives and Native Hawaiians: Excerpts and identified sections from Management Policies* (2008). https://www.nps.gov/history/tribes/documents/npsmanagementpolicy.pdf.

21. Andrews, "The President Stole Your Land"; Pinsker, "Patagonia, REI."

22. White House, "Presidential Proclamation Modifying the Bears Ears National Monument," December 4, 2017. https://www.whitehouse.gov/presidential-actions/presidential-proclamation-modifying-bears-ears-national-monument.

23. Smithsonian Institution, *Annual Report*, 2: 151.

24. Quoted in Saunt, *Unworthy Republic*, 102; 101–2. Until 1857, most of the objects that Poinsett hoped to protect were housed at the APS or Peale's Philadelphia Museum. Afterward, collections resulting from exploring expeditions—particularly the Wilkes squadron—came under the Smithsonian's purview (*Annual Report*, 2: 121).

25. "List of Donations to the National Institute, November 14, 1842," National Institute Accession Records, 1840–1848, SNRU007058. Smithsonian Institute Archives. The temple fragments are not attributed, but I have reason to believe they came from Stephens (*Yucatan*, 2: 179). See also Record Unit 7084, William Henry Holmes Papers, Image No. SIA2011-2772. Smithsonian Institution Archives.

26. Achim, *Idols*, 171–209, esp. 174–76. In 1857 the Mexican National Museum produced a new inventory and catalog with lithographs showing some of the objects. On the Smithsonian in Central America, see Barnhart, *Squier*.

27. Associated Press, "Clemson to strip name"; Campbell and Opilo, "Christopher Columbus statue"; Suliman and Diogo Mateus, "Statue of Christopher Columbus."

28. Bruno, "Tribe Says Border-Wall."

29. "Reclaiming Power and Place: The Final Report of the National Inquiry into Missing and Murdered Indigenous Women and Girls," National Inquiry into Missing and Murdered Indigenous Women and Girls. https://www.mmiwg-ffada.ca/.

30. Nelson, "This land."

31. See, for example, Devereaux, "We are still here" and "Welcome Water Protectors," Honor the Earth, https://www.honorearth.org/welcome_water_protectors.

32. In 2017, the AGN in Mexico celebrated its 225th anniversary (1792–2017), its website interestingly dating the *national* archive's creation prior to that of the *nation* state.

33. Wolfe, "Settler Colonialism," 388.

34. Byrd, *Transit*, 229.

35. I.e. Hall, *Plants as Persons* or Rutherford, *Brief History*.

36. Apparently someone once believed it resembled the pyramidal block of white sugar that epitomized the eighteenth-century Atlantic economy.

37. Carrigan, "One Mound at a Time"; Rockett, "A Serpent and Mounds."

38. Pokto Činto, along the Chicago and Des Plaines Rivers, was opened to the public on Indigenous Peoples' Day, 2019.

BIBLIOGRAPHY

Archives and Special Collections

American Antiquarian Society (AAS), Worcester, Massachusetts
    AAS Records
        Correspondence 1812–1819
            Samuel Mitchell, Box 2, Folder 15
        Correspondence 1820–1829
        Documents 1813
            Thomas Manuscripts, October–December, Box 1, Folder 2
        Donation Book, 1813–1829
        Caleb Atwater Letters and Drawings, 1818–1835
        Isaiah Thomas Papers, 1748–1874
Archivo General de la Nación (AGN), Mexico City
    GSS Box 82, File 20
American Philosophical Society (APS), Philadelphia, Pennsylvania
    American Philosophical Society Archives
    American Philosophical Society Historical and Literary Committee
        American Indian Vocabulary Collection
    Benjamin Smith Barton Journals; notebooks, 1785–1806
    Guillermo Dupaix, Viages Sobre las Antiquedades Mejicanas
    Notes on Mexican Antiquities
    Samuel George Morton Papers
    Violetta Delafield-Benjamin Smith Barton Collection
        Benjamin Smith Barton Papers, Series I. Correspondence
        Benjamin Smith Barton Papers, Series II. Indian Materials
        Benjamin Smith Barton Papers, Series III. Bound Volumes
Hamilton College Special Collections, Clinton, New York
    Samuel Kirkland Papers
Library of Congress, Washington, DC
    Albert Gallatin Papers, 1783–1847
    E. G. Squier Papers, 1809–1888
Missouri Historical Society, St. Louis, Missouri
    William Clark Papers
Morgan Library, New York, New York
Newberry Library, Chicago, Illinois

Edward E. Ayer Collection
Edward E. Ayer Manuscript Collection
  Waldeck Journals England and Mexico, 1825–1837
  Waldeck Papers, 1825–1827,
  Waldeck Papers, 1827–1853,
Ohio History Connection, Columbus, Ohio
  Caleb Atwater Papers, 1818 VFM 769
  Caleb Atwater Papers, 1819–1821
  Oversized Materials Collection
Peabody Museum of Archaeology & Ethnology, Harvard University
  AAS Acquisition Files
Smithsonian Institution Archives, Washington, DC
  National Institute Accession Records, 1840–1848
  William Henry Holmes Papers
Wisconsin Historical Society, Madison, Wisconsin
  Indians of North America Miscellaneous Material, 1909–1917

Cited Sources

Achim, Miruna. "The Art of the Deal, 1828: How Isidro Icaza Traded Pre-Columbian Antiquities to Henri Baradère for Mounted Birds and Built a National Museum in Mexico City in the Process." *West 86th: A Journal of Decorative Arts, Design History, and Material Culture* 18, no. 2 (2011): 214–31.

———. *From Idols to Antiquity: Forging the National Museum of Mexico*. Lincoln: University of Nebraska Press, 2017.

———. "The National Museum of Mexico: 1825–1867." *Museum History Journal* 9, no. 1 (January 2016): 13–28.

Acosta, José de. *Natural and Moral History of the Indies*. Edited by Jane E. Mangan and translated by Frances López-Morillas. Durham, N.C.: Duke University Press, 2002.

[Ackerly, Samuel.] "American Antiquities." *Knickerbocker* 2, no. 5 (November 1833): 371–82.

Adams, David. "Embattled Borderland: Northern Nuevo León and the Indios Bárbaros, 1686–1870." *Southwestern Historical Quarterly* 95, no. 2 (October 1991): 205–20.

Adair, James. *The History of the American Indians; Particularly Those Nations adjoining to the Mississippi, East and West Florida, Georgia, South and North Carolina, and Virginia: Containing An Account of their Origin, Language, Manners, Religious and Civil Customs [. . .]*. London: Printed for Edward and Charles Dilly, 1775.

Adams, John. *The Adams Papers*. Vol. 16, *February 1784–March 1785*, edited by Gregg L. Lint, C. James Taylor, Robert Karachuk, Hobson Woodward, Margaret A.

Hogan, Sara B. Sikes, Sara Martin, Sara Georgini, Amanda A. Mathews, and James T. Connolly. Cambridge, Mass.: Harvard University Press, 2012.

Aguilar-Moreno, Manuel. *Handbook to Life in the Aztec World*. New York: Oxford University Press, 2007.

Aguirre Beltrán, Gonzalo. *La población negra de México, 1519–1810*. Mexico City: Ediciones Fuente Cultural, 1946.

Aguirre, Robert D. *Informal Empire: Mexico and Central America in Victorian Culture*. Minneapolis: University of Minnesota Press, 2005.

Alamán, Lucas. "Memoria Presentada a las dos Cámaras del Congreso General de la Federación por el Secretario de Estado y del Despacho de Relaciones Esteriores é Interiores, al abrirse las sesiones del año de 1825, sobre el estado de los negocios de su ramo." *Documentos Diversos (Inéditos y muy raros)*. Vol. 1, edited by Rafael Aguayo Spencer. 115–61. Mexico City: Editorial Jus, 1945.

———. "Memoria que El Secretario de Estado y del Despacho de Relaciones Esteriores e Interiores Presenta al Soberano Congreso Constituyente sobre los negocios de la Secretaria de su cargo, leída en la sesión de 8 de noviembre de 1823" In *Documentos Diversos (Inéditos y muy raros)*. Vol. 1, edited by Rafael Aguayo Spencer, 57–106. Mexico City: Editorial Jus, 1945.

Alarcón, Daniel Cooper. *The Aztec Palimpsest: Mexico in the Modern Imagination*. Tucson: University of Arizona Press, 1997.

Alcina Franch, José. *Arqueólogos o anticuarios: Historia de la arqueología antigua americana*. Barcelona: Editorial Planeta, 1994.

Allen, Chadwick. "Earthworks as Indigenous Performance." In *In the Balance: Indigeneity, Performance, Globalization*, edited by Helen Gilbert, Dani Phillipson, and Michelle Raheja, 291–308. Liverpool: University of Liverpool Press, 2017.

———. "Performing Serpent Mound: A Trans-Indigenous Meditation." *Theatre Journal* 67, no. 3 (October 2015): 391–411.

———. "Serpentine Figures, Sinuous Relations: Thematic Geometry in Allison Hedge Coke's *Blood Run*." *American Literature* 82, no. 4 (December 2010): 807–34.

———. *Trans-Indigenous: Methodologies for Global Native Literary Studies*. Minneapolis: University of Minnesota Press, 2012.

Allen, David Y., "Alexander von Humboldt's Critique of Aaron Arrowsmith's 1810 Map of Mexico." *Imago Mundi* 68, part 2 (2016): 232–36.

Allen, Thomas M. *A Republic in Time: Temporality and Social Imagination in Nineteenth-Century America*. Chapel Hill: University of North Carolina Press, 2008.

Almeida, Joselyn M. *Reimagining the Transatlantic, 1780–1890*. London: Routledge, 2016.

Alpert-Abrams, Hannah Rachel. "Unreadable Books: Early Colonial Mexican Documents in Circulation," PhD diss., University of Texas-Austin, 2017.

Alzate y Ramírez, José Antonio de. "Carta de Edimburgo 10 de Mayo, 1786." *Gazeta de México* (1788): 20–22.

———. "Del origen de los Indios Mexicanos." *Gazeta de Literatura de México* 11 (February 8, 1790): 81–84.

———. *Nuevo Mapa Geographico De La America Septentrional, Perteneciente al Virreynato de Mexico.* Madrid: Calle de Atocha, frente la casa de los Gremios, 1768.

———. "Plano de la Nueva España en que se señalan los Viages que hizo el Capitán Hernán Cortés así antes como después de conquistado el Imperio Mexicano." In *Historia de Nueva-España. Escrita por su Esclarecido Conquistador Hernán Cortés. Aumentada con otros documentos, y notas* [...], edited by Francisco Antonio Lorenzana y Buitrón. Mexico City: Hogal, 1770.

———. "Prologo." *Gazeta de Literatura de México* 1, no. 1 (January 15, 1788): 1–7.

———. "Respuesta del Autor de la Gazeta Literatura á la Carta que se publicé por la nuestra en la de 16 del pasado, escrita por un Anónime." *Gazeta de México* 4, no. 42 (September 13, 1791): 395–96.

———. *Suplemento a la Gazeta de Literatura. Descripcion de las antiguedades de Xochicalco. Dedicada a los señores de la actual expedicion marítima al rededor del orbe.* [...]. Mexico City: Zúñiga y Ontiveros, 1791.

American Antiquarian Society. *Archaeologia Americana: Transactions and Collections of the American Antiquarian Society.* Vol 1. Worcester, Mass.: William Manning, 1820.

———. *Archaeologia Americana: Transactions and Collections of the American Antiquarian Society.* Vol 2. Cambridge, Mass.: Printed for the Society at the [Harvard] University Press, 1836.

———. *Archaeologia Americana: Transactions and Collections of the American Antiquarian Society.* Vol 3. Cambridge, Mass.: Printed for the Society at the [Harvard] University Press, 1857.

———. *Proceedings of the American Antiquarian Society, 1812–1849.* Worcester, Mass.: The Society, 1912.

American Philosophical Society. *Proceedings of the American Philosophical Society.* Part 3: *Early Proceedings of the American Philosophical Society for the Promotion of Useful Knowledge, Compiled by One of the Secretaries, from the Manuscript Minutes of Its Meetings from 1744–1838* 22, no. 119 (1885).

American State Papers. Class 2: *Indian Affairs, 1st Cong.–19th Cong., May 25, 1789–Mar. 1, 1815,* selected and edited under the authority of Congress by Walter Lowrie and Matthew St. Clair. Vol. 1. Washington, D.C.: Gales & Seaton, 1834.

American State Papers. Class 2: *Indian Affairs, 1st Cong.–19th Cong., May 25, 1789–Mar. 1, 1815,* selected and edited under the authority of Congress by Walter Lowrie and Matthew St. Clair. Vol. 2. Washington, D.C.: Gales & Seaton, 1834.

Anderson, Chad, and Jean O'Brien, eds. *Sources and Methods in Indigenous Studies.* New York: Routledge, 2017.

Anderson, David G. "Monumentality in Eastern North America during the Mississippian Period." In *Early New World Monumentality*, edited by Richard L. Burger and Robert M. Rosenswig, 78–108. Gainesville: University Press of Florida, 2012.

———. *The Savannah River Chiefdoms: Political Change in the Late Prehistoric Southeast*. Tuscaloosa: University of Alabama Press, 1994.

Anderson, Fred. *Crucible of War: The Seven Years' War and the Fate of Empire in British North America, 1754–1766*. New York: Alfred A. Knopf, 2000.

Andrews, Travis M. "'The President Stole Your Land': Patagonia, REI blast Trump on National Monument Rollbacks." *Washington Post*, December 5, 2017.

Anna, Timothy E. *Forging Mexico, 1821–1835*. Lincoln: University of Nebraska Press, 1998.

[Anonymous.] "Account of the Short Creek Settlement." *Columbian Magazine* (July 1789): 410–11.

[Anonymous.] "Antigüedades americanas." *Aguila Mexicana* 239, August 27, 1827, 2.

[Anonymous.] "Antiquités mexicaines de M. Latour-Allard," *Revue encyclopédique III* 31, no. 93 (1826): 848–51.

[Anonymous.] "Antiquities of Western America." *Poulson's American Daily Advertiser* (November 4, 1814), 2.

[Anonymous.] Art. 2 "A Discourse deliverd at Plymouth, December 22, 1820, in commemoration of the first settlement of New England. By Daniel Webster." *North American Review* 11, no. 36 (July 1822): 21–51.

[Anonymous.] "Art. 4 Atwater's Notes on Ohio." *American Monthly Magazine and Critical Review* 4, no. 6 (April 1819): 439–41.

[Anonymous.] "Developer Honored for Archeology Preservation," *iheart.com* May 15, 2016.

[Anonymous.] "Indian Antiquities." *North American Review* 6, no. 16 (November 1817): 136–38.

[Anonymous.] "On the Peopling of America: Whence Come the Men and Animals of America?" *Port Folio* 6, no. 1 (July 1815): 7–10.

[Anonymous.] "Topographical: Circleville, Ohio." *Daily National Intelligencer*. (June 16, 1816), 2.

Appleton, J. L., and R. D. Ward. "Albert James Pickett and the Case of the Secret Articles: Historians and the Treaty of New York of 1790." *Alabama Review* 51 (January 1998): 3–36.

Arista, Noenoe. *The Kingdom and the Republic: Sovereign Hawai'i and the Early United States*. Philadelphia: University of Pennsylvania Press, 2019.

Arjona, Jamie M. "Sublime perversions: Capturing the uncanny affects of queer temporalities in Mississippian ruins." *Journal of Social Archaeology* 16 No. 2 (2016): 189–215.

Armstrong, Jeanette. "Land Speaking." In *Speaking for the Generations: Native Writers on Writing*, edited by Simon J. Ortiz, 174–94. Tucson: University of Arizona Press, 1998.

Arrizón, Alicia. "Mestizaje." In *Keywords for Latina/o Studies*, edited by Deborah R. Vargas, Nancy Raquel Mirabal, and Lawrence La Fountain-Stokes, 133–36. New York: New York University Press, 2017.

Arrowsmith, Adam. "Chart of the West Indies and Spanish Dominions in North America." London: Jones & Smith, 1803.

Armstrong-Fumero, Fernando. "Even the Most Careless Observer": Race and Visual Discernment in Physical Anthropology from Samuel Morton to Kennewick Man." *American Studies* 53, no. 2 (2014) 5–29.

Associated Press, "Clemson to strip name of John C Calhoun from honors college." *The Guardian Online.* Jun 13, 2020. https://www.theguardian.com/us-news/2020/jun/13/clemson-john-c-calhoun-slavery-honors-college.

Atalay, Sonya. "Indigenous Archaeology as Decolonizing Practice." *American Indian Quarterly.* 30, nos. 3–4 (Summer/Fall 2006): 280–310.

Atwater, Caleb. "Aboriginal Antiquities in the West—Addressed to his Excellency James Monroe, President of the United States. Circleville, Pickaway County, Ohio, Jan. 1, 1818." *American Monthly Magazine and Critical Review* 2 (March 1818): 333–36.

———. "An Address, Delivered on the 25th June, A. L. 5821, before Pickaway Lodge, No. 23, at Circleville, Ohio, it being the Festival of St. John the Baptist; by brother Caleb Atwater, a member of said lodge." *Masonic Casket* 2, no. 8 (July 1821): 113–19.

———. "Circleville, Feb. 13th, 1819. To the Editor of the American Monthly Magazine." *American Monthly Magazine and Critical Review* 4, no. 6 (April 1819): 441–50.

———. "Description of the Antiquities Discovered in the State of Ohio and Other Western States." *Archaeologia Americana: Transactions and Collections of the American Antiquarian Society* 1 (1820): 105–267.

———. "Observations on the Remains of Civilization and Population, Extant on the Vast Plains Situated South of the North-American Lakes." *American Monthly Magazine and Critical Review* 2 (March 1818): 332–33.

———. "On the Prairies and Barrens of the West." *American Journal of Science* 1, no. 2 (1819): 116–24.

———. "Prairies in Ohio [draft]" *Western Medical and Physical Journal, Original and Eclectic* 1, no. 2 (May 1827): 85–92. Oversized Materials Collection, OVS 1414, Ohio History Connection.

———. *Remarks Made on a Tour to Prairie du Chien; Thence to Washington City in 1829.* Columbus, Oh.: Isaac N. Whiting, 1831.

———. *Writings of Caleb Atwater.* Columbus, Oh.: Published by the Author, 1833.

Aupaumut, Hendrick. "Narrative of an Embassy to the Western Indians [1791]," edited by B. H. Coates. *Memoirs of the Historical Society of Pennsylvania* 2, part 1 (1827): 63–131.

Axtell, Peter. "Babel of Tongues: Communicating with the Indians in Eastern North America." In *The Language Encounter in the Americas, 1492–1800: A Collection of Essays*, edited by Edward G. Gray and Norman Fiering, 15–60. New York: Berghahn Books, 2000.

B. [Hunt, William Gibbs.] "Review of Heckewelder's Account." *Western Review and Miscellaneous Magazine* (Sept 1819): 66–67.

———. "The History of Mexico [...]." *Western Review and Miscellaneous Magazine* 1, no. 3 (October 1819): 128–42.

Babcock, Matthew. *Apache Adaptation to Hispanic Rule*. New York: Cambridge University Press, 2016.

Baldwin, Christopher Columbus. *A Place in My Chronicle: A New Edition of the Diary of Christopher Columbus Baldwin, 1829–1835*. Edited by Caroline Sloat and Jack Larkin. Worcester, Mass.: American Antiquarian Society, 2010.

Banner, Stuart. *How the Indians Lost Their Land: Law and Power on the Frontier*. Cambridge, Mass.: Harvard University Library, 2007.

Baradère, Abbé Henri. *Antiquités mexicaines. Relation des trois expéditions du capitaine Dupaix, ordonnées en 1805, 1806, et 1807,* [...]. Paris: Bureau des Antiquités Mexicaines, impr. de J. Didot l'aîné, 1834.

Barker, Joanne. "Territory as Analytic: The Dispossession of Lenapehoking and the Subprime Crisis." *Social Text* 36, no. 2 (2018): 19–39.

Barker, Nancy Nichols. *The French Experience in Mexico, 1821–1861*. Chapel Hill: University of North Carolina Press, 1979.

Barnhart, Terry A. *American Antiquities: Revisiting the Origins of American Archaeology*. Lincoln: University of Nebraska Press, 2016.

———. *Ephraim George Squier and the Development of American Anthropology*. Lincoln: University of Nebraska Press, 2005.

Barr, Juliana, and Edward Countryman, eds. *Contested Spaces of Early America*. Philadelphia: University of Pennsylvania Press, 2014.

Barrera-Osorio, Antonio. *Experiencing Nature: The Spanish American Empire and the Early Scientific Revolution*. Austin: University of Texas Press. 2006.

Barton, Benjamin Smith. *Archaeologiae Americanae Telluris Collectanea et Specimina, or, Collections, with Specimens, for a Series of Memoirs on Certain Extinct Animals and Vegetables of North-America: Together with Facts and Conjectures Relative to the Ancient Condition of the Lands and Waters of the Continent*. Philadelphia: Printed for the author by John Bioren, 1814.

Barton, Benjamin Smith. *A Discourse on Some of the Principal Desiderata in Natural History, and on the Best Means of Promoting the Study of this Science, in the United-States: Read Before the Philadelphia Linnean Society, on the tenth of June, 1807*. Philadelphia: Denham & Town, 1807.

———. "A Discovery of the Remains of Four Large Cities in South America." In *Sketches of a Tour to the Western Country*, edited by Zadock Cramer, 491. Pittsburgh: Cramer, Spear & Eichbaum, 1810.

———. *Elements of Botany, or, Outlines of the Natural History of Vegetables*. Philadelphia: Printed for the author, 1803.

———. *Elements of Botany, or, Outlines of the Natural History of Vegetables*. 2nd ed. Philadelphia: Printed for the author, 1812.

———. *Hints on the Etymology of Certain English words: And on their Affinity to Words in the Languages of Different European, Asiatic, and American (Indian) Nations in a Letter from Dr. Barton to Dr. Beddoes*. [Philadelphia: s.n., 1803].

———. "Journal on Tuscaroras." Unpublished manuscript in Violetta Delafield-Benjamin Smith Barton Collection, Mss.B.B284d, Series 2. Philadelphia, American Philosophical Society.

———. "Journals and Notebooks from the Historical Society of Pennsylvania." Unpublished manuscripts in Benjamin Smith Barton journals; notebooks, 1785–1806, Mss B B284.1. American Philosophical Society, Philadelphia, Pa.

Barton, Benjamin Smith. *New Views of the Origin of the Tribes and Nations of America*. Philadelphia: Printed for the author by John Bioren, 1797.

———. *New Views of the Origin of the Tribes and Nations of America*. 2nd ed. Philadelphia: Printed for the author by John Bioren, 1798.

———. "Observations and Conjectures concerning Certain Articles Which Were Taken out of an Ancient Tumulus, or Grave, at Cincinnati, in the County of Hamilton, and Territory of the United-States, North-West of the River Ohio: In a Letter from Benjamin Smith Barton, M. D. to the Reverend Joseph Priestley, L. L. D. F. R. S. &c." *Transactions of the American Philosophical Society* 4 (1799): 181–215.

———. *Observations on Some Parts of Natural History: To which is Prefixed an Account of Several Remarkable Vestiges of an Ancient Date, which Have been Discovered in Different Parts of North America*. Part 1. London: Printed for the author [1787].

———. "Proposals for printing, by subscription, An Historical and philosophical inquiry into the original, nature, and design of various remains of antiquity, which have been discovered in America [1790]." Violetta Delafield-Benjamin Smith Barton Collection, Mss.B.B284d. Philadelphia: American Philosophical Society.

Barton, Benjamin Smith, and Winthrop Sargent. "A Drawing of Some Utensils, or Ornaments, Taken from an Old Indian Grave, at Cincinnati, County of Hamilton, and Territory of the United-States, North-West of the River Ohio, August 30th 1794. By Colonel Winthrop Sargent. Communicated by Benjamin Smith Barton, M. D." *Transactions of the American Philosophical Society* 4 (1799): 179–80.

Bartlett, Robert. *The Making of Europe: Conquest, Colonization, and Cultural Change, 950–1350*. Princeton, N.J.: Princeton University Press, 1993.

Bartram, William. "Observations on the Creek and Cherokee Indians." In *William Bartram on the Southeastern Indians*, edited by Gregory A. Waselkov and Kathryn E. Holland Braund, 133–86. Lincoln: University of Nebraska Press, 1995.

———. *Travels Through North & South Carolina, Georgia, East & West Florida, the Cherokee Country, the Extensive Territories of the Muscogulges, or Creek Confederacy, and the Country of the Chactaws; Containing An Account of the Soil and Natural Productions of Those Regions, Together with Observations on the Manners of the Indians*. Philadelphia: James & Johnson, 1791.

———. *William Bartram, Travels and Other Writings*, edited by Thomas Slaughter. New York: The Library of America, 1996.

Bassett, Molly H. "Bundling Natural History: Tlaquimilolli, Folk Biology, and Book 11." In *The Florentine Codex: An Encyclopedia of the Nahua World in Sixteenth-Century Mexico*, edited by Peterson, Jeanette Favrot and Kevin Trerraciano, 139–51. Austin: University of Texas Press, 2019.

———. *The Fate of Earthly Things: Aztec Gods and God-Bodies*. Austin: University of Texas Press, 2015.

Basso, Keith. *Wisdom Sits in Places: Landscape and Language among the Western Apache*. Albuquerque: University of New Mexico Press, 1996.

Bauer, Ralph. "The Hemispheric Genealogies of 'Race': Creolization and the Cultural Geography of Colonial Difference across the Eighteenth-Century Americas." In *Hemispheric American Studies*, edited by Caroline Levander and Robert Levine, 36–56. New Brunswick, N.J.: Rutgers University Press, 2007.

Bauer, Ralph, and José Antonio Mazzotti. Introduction to *Creole Subjects in the Colonial Americas: Empires, Texts, Identities*, edited by Ralph Bauer and José Antonio Mazzotti, 1–49. Chapel Hill: University of North Carolina Press, 2009.

Bauer, Ralph, and José Antonio Mazzotti, eds. *Creole Subjects in the Colonial Americas: Empires, Texts, Identities*. Chapel Hill: University of North Carolina Press, 2009.

Baym, Nina. *American Women Writers and the Work of History, 1790–1860*. New Brunswick: Rutgers University Press, 1995.

Beaufroy, Mark. *Mexican Illustrations, Founded Upon Facts: Indicative of the Present Condition of Society, Manners, Religion, and Morals among the Spanish and Native Inhabitants of Mexico*. London: Carpenter and Son, 1828.

Beckett, John. *Writing Local History*. Manchester, U.K.: Manchester University Press, 2007.

Bedini, Silvio A. *Jefferson and Science*. Charlottesville: Thomas Jefferson Foundation, 2002.

Belknap [Varenius, pseud.], "Thoughts on the Colour of the native Americans and the recent population of this continent." *American Magazine* 8 (July 1790): 7–8.

Belt, Thomas, and Margaret Bender, "Speaking Difference to Power: The Importance of Linguistic Sovereignty." In *Foundations of First Peoples' Sovereignty: History, Education, and Culture*, edited by Ulrike Weithaus, 187–96. New York: Peter Lang, 2007.

Benjamin, Thomas. *A Rich Land, a Poor People: Politics and Society in Modern Chiapas*. Rev. ed. Albuquerque: University of New Mexico Press, 1996.

Bennett, Richard E. "'A Nation Now Extinct,' American Indian Origin Theories As of 1820: Samuel L. Mitchell, Martin Harris, and their New York Theory." *Journal of the Book of Mormon and Other Restoration Scripture* 20, no. 2 (2011): 30–41.

Benson, Larry V., Timothy R. Pauketat, and Edward R. Cook. "Cahokia's Boom and Bust in the Context of Climate Change." *American Antiquity* 74, no. 3 (2009): 467–83.

Benson, Larry V., Michael S. Berry, Edward A. Jolie, Jerry D. Spangler, David W. Stahle, Eugene M. Hattori, "Possible impacts of early-11th-, middle-12th-, and late-13th-century droughts on western Native Americans and the Mississippian Cahokians." *Quaternary Science Reviews* 26, nos. 3–4 (2007): 336–50.

Ben-zvi, Yael. *Native Land Talk: Indigenous and Arrivant Rights Theories*. Hanover, N.H.: Dartmouth College Press, 2018.

Bergmann, William H. *The American National State and the Early West*. New York: Cambridge University Press, 2012.

Berlandier, Jean Louis. *The Indians of Texas in 1830*. Edited by John C. Ewers and translated by Patricia Reading Leclercq. Washington: Smithsonian Institution Press, 1969.

Bernal, Ignacio. *A History of Mexican Archaeology: The Vanished Civilizations of Middle America*. London: Thames & Hudson, 1980.

Berry, Christopher J. *Social Theory of the Scottish Enlightenment*. Edinburgh: Edinburgh University Press, 1997.

Berry, Trey. "The Expedition of William Dunbar and George Hunter along the Ouachita River, 1804–1805." *Arkansas Historical Quarterly* 62 (Winter 2003): 386–403.

Berry, Trey, Pam Beasley, and Jeanne Clements, eds., *The Forgotten Expedition, 1804–1805: The Louisiana Purchase Journals of Dunbar and Hunter*. Baton Rouge: Louisiana State University Press, 2004.

Berruezo León, María Teresa. *La lucha de Hispanoamérica por su independencia en Inglaterra 1800–1830*. Madrid: Ediciones de Cultura Hispánica, 1989.

Bieder, Robert E. "The Representations of Indian Bodies in Nineteenth-Century American Anthropology." In *Repatriation Reader: Who Owns American Indian Remains?* edited by Devon Abbot Mihesuah, 19–36. Lincoln: University of Nebraska Press, 2000.

———. *Science Encounters the Indian, 1820–1880: The Early Years of American Ethnology*. Norman: University of Oklahoma Press, 1986.

Blackhawk, Ned. *Violence over the Land: Indians and Empires in the Early American West*. Cambridge, Mass.: Harvard University Press, 2006.

Blackwell, Maylei. "Indigeneity." In *Keywords for Latina/o Studies*, edited by Deborah R. Vargas, Nancy Raquel Mirabal, and Lawrence La Fountain-Stokes, 100–105. New York: New York University Press, 2017.

Blakeslee, Donald. "The Miguel Map Revisited." *Plains Archaeologist* 63, no. 245 (February 2018): 67–84.

Bleichmar, Daniela. "The Geography of Observation: Distance and Visibility in Eighteenth-Century Botanical Travel." In *Histories of Scientific Observation*, edited by Lorraine Daston and Elizabeth Lunbeck, 373–95. Chicago, Ill.: University of Chicago Press, 2011.

———. "History in Pictures: Translating the *Codex Mendoza*." *Art History* 38, no. 4 (September 2015): 682–701.

———. "Painting the Aztec Past in Early Colonial Mexico: Translation and Knowledge Production in the *Codex Mendoza*." *Renaissance Quarterly* 72, no. 4 (2020): 1362–415.

———. "A Visible and Useful Empire: Visual Culture and Colonial Natural History in the Eighteenth-Century Spanish World." In *Science in the Spanish and Portuguese Empires, 1500–1800*, edited by Daniela Bleichmar, Paula De Vos, Kristin Huffine, and Kevin Sheehan, 290–310. Stanford, Calif.: Stanford University Press, 2009.

———. *Visible Empire: Botanical Expeditions and Visual Culture in the Hispanic Enlightenment*. Chicago, Ill.: University of Chicago Press, 2012.

———. *Visual Voyages: Images of Latin American Nature from Columbus to Darwin*. New Haven, Conn.: Yale University Press, 2017.

Blix, Göran. *From Paris to Pompeii: French Romanticism and the Cultural Politics of Archaeology*. Philadelphia: University of Pennsylvania, 2009.

Bobrow-Strain, Aaron. *Intimate Enemies: Landowners, Power, and Violence in Chiapas*. Durham, N.C.: Duke University Press, 2007.

Boewe, Charles, ed. *John D. Clifford's Indian Antiquities: With Related Material by C. S. Rafinesque*. Knoxville: University of Tennessee Press, 2000.

Boewe, Charles. Introduction to *John D. Clifford's Indian Antiquities: With Related Material by C. S. Rafinesque*, edited by Charles Boewe, ix–xxxi. Knoxville: University of Tennessee Press, 2000.

Bohaker, Heidi. "*Nindoodemag*: The Significance of Algonquian Kinship Networks in the Eastern Great Lakes Region, 1600–1701." *William and Mary Quarterly* 63, no. 1 (2006): 23–42.

———. "Reading Anishinaabe Identities: Meaning & Metaphor in Nindoodem Pictographs." *Ethnohistory* 57, no. 1 (2010): 11–33.

Bonfil Batalla, Guillermo. *México Profundo: Reclaiming a Civilization*, translated by Philip A. Dennis. Austin: University of Texas Press, 1996.

Boone, Elizabeth Hill. "Aztec Pictorial Histories: Records Without Words." In *Writing Without Words: Alternative Literacies in Mesoamerica and the Andes*, edited by Elizabeth Hill Boone and Walter Mignolo, 50–76. Durham, N.C.: Duke University Press, 1994.

———. *Cycles of Time and Meaning in the Mexican Books of Fate*. Austin: University of Texas Press, 2007.

———. *Stories in Red and Black: Pictorial Histories of the Aztecs and Mixtecs*. Austin: University of Texas Press, 2001.

———. "Templo Mayor Research, 1521–1978." In *The Aztec Templo Mayor*, edited by Elizabeth Hill Boone, 5–70. Washington, D.C.: Dumbarton Oaks Research Library and Collection, 1987.

Boone, Elizabeth Hill, and Walter Mignolo, eds. *Writing without Words: Alternative Literacies in Mesoamerica and the Andes*. Durham, N.C.: Duke University Press, 1994.

Boone, Elizabeth Hill, and Gary Urton, eds. *Scripts, Signs, and Pictographies in Pre-Columbian America*. Cambridge, Mass.: Harvard University Press, 2011.

Booth, Samantha. "The Role Of Archives In Indigenous Language Maintenance and Resurgence." Master's thesis, University of Winnipeg, 2020.

Borunda, José Ignacio. *Clave general de jeroglíficos americanos de Ignacio Borunda; manuscrit inédit publié par le Duc de Loubat*. Rome: J.P. Scotti, 1889.

Boturini Benaduci, Lorenzo. *Idea of a New General History: An Account of Colonial Native Mexico*. Translated and edited by Stafford Poole. Norman: University of Oklahoma Press, 2015.

———. *Idea de una nueva historia de la America septentrional*. Madrid: Juan de Zuniga, 1746.
Bourbon, Fabio. *The Lost Cities of the Maya: The Life, Art, and Discoveries of Frederick Catherwood*. Vercelli, Italy: White Star Publishers, 1999.
Brading, David A. "Creole Nationalism and Mexican Liberalism." *Journal of Interamerican Studies and World Affairs* 15, no. 2 (1973): 139–90.
———. *The First America: The Spanish Monarchy, Creole Patriots, and the Liberal State 1492–1866*. New York: Cambridge University Press, 1991.
———. *Mexican Phoenix: Our Lady of Guadalupe: Image and Tradition across Five Centuries*. New York: Cambridge University Press, 2001.
Brace, Loring C. "The Roots of the Race Concept in American Physical Anthropology." In *A History of American Physical Anthropology, 1930–1980*, edited by Frank Spencer, 11–30. New York: Academic Press, 1982.
Brackenridge, H. H. [*Sic*, Henry Marie]. "On the Population and Tumuli of the Aborigines of North America. In a Letter from H. H. Brackenridge, Esq. to Thomas Jefferson." *Transactions of the American Philosophical Society* 1 (1818): 151–59.
Brackenridge, Henry Marie. *Views of Louisiana; Together with a Journal of a Voyage up the Missouri River, in 1811*. Pittsburgh: Cramer, Spear and Eichbaum, 1814.
Brian, Amber. *Alva Ixtlilxochitl's Native Archive and the Circulation of Knowledge in Colonial Mexico*. Nashville: Vanderbilt University Press, 2016.
Brickhouse, Anna. *Transamerican Literary Relations and the Nineteenth-Century Public Sphere*. New York: Cambridge University Press, 2005.
Brokaw, Galen and Jongsoo Lee, eds. *Fernando de Alva Cortés Ixtlilxóchitl and His Legacy*. Tucson: University of Arizona Press, 2016.
Brooks, Lisa. "Awikhigawôgan ta Pildowi Ôjmowôgan: Mapping a New History." *William and Mary Quarterly* 75, no. 2 (2018): 259–94.
———. *The Common Pot: The Recovery of Native Space in the Northeast*. Minneapolis: University of Minnesota Press, 2008.
———. *Our Beloved Kin: Remapping A New History of King Philip's War*. New Haven, C.T.: Yale University Press, 2018.
Brown, James A. "The Cahokian Expression." In *Hero, Hawk, and Open Hand: American Indian Art of the Ancient Midwest and South*, edited by Richard F. Townsend, 118–19. New Haven, Conn.: Yale University Press, 2004.
———. "On the Identity of the Birdman within Mississippian Period Art and Iconography." In *Ancient Objects and Sacred Realms: Interpretations of Mississippian Iconography*, edited by F. Kent Reilly III and James F. Garber, 56–106. Austin: University of Texas Press, 2007.
Brown, Lewis. "The Brown Family." In *The Atwater Family, or Truth Is Stranger Than Fiction*, edited by Lucy Atwater Brown, 168–241. Indianapolis: s.n., 1915.
Brown, Stewart J. "An Eighteenth-Century Historian on the Amerindians: Culture, Colonialism and Christianity in William Robertson's History of America." *Studies in World Christianity* 2 (Autumn 1996): 204–22.

Browne, Simone. *Dark Matters: On the Surveillance of Blackness*. Durham: Duke University Press, 2015.

Bruchac, Margaret. "Earthshapers and Placemakers: Algonkian Indian Stories and the Landscape." In *Indigenous Archaeologies: Decolonizing Theory and Practice*, edited by Claire Smith and Martin Wobst, 52–74. New York: Routledge, 2005.

———. "Lost and Found: NAGPRA, Scattered Relics, and Restorative Methodologies." *Museum Anthropology* 33, no. 2 (September 2010): 137–56.

Bruno, Bianco. "Tribe Says Border-Wall Construction Is Trashing Burial Sites," *Courthouse News Service*. September 2019. https://www.courthousenews.com/tribe-says-border-wall-construction-is-trashing-burial-sites/amp/.

Bueno, Christina. *The Pursuit of Ruins: Archaeology, History, and the Making of Modern Mexico*. University of New Mexico Press, 2016.

Buffon, Georges Louis Leclerc, comte de. *Histoire naturelle, général et particulièr avec la description du Cabinet du Roi*. Supplement. Vol. 5: *1778*. Paris: L'imprimerie royale, 1749–1804.

Bullock, William. *A Descriptive Catalogue of the Exhibition, entitled Ancient and Modern Mexico*[. . .]. London: Printed for the proprietors, 1824.

———. *Six Months' Residence and Travels in Mexico, Containing Remarks on the Present State of New Spain, Its Natural Productions, State of Society, Manufactures, Trade, Agriculture, and Antiquities, &c*. London: John Murray, 1824.

Burkhart, Brian Yazzie. "The Physics of the Spirit: The Indigenous Continuity of Science and Religion." In *The Routledge Companion to Religion and Science*, edited by James W. Haag, Gregory R. Peterson, Michael L. Spezio, 34–42. New York: Routledge, 2011.

Burnett, Graham D. "Mapping Time: Chronometry on Top of the World." *Daedalus* 132, no. 2 (Spring 2003): 5–19.

Burns, Louis F. *A History of the Osage People*. Tuscaloosa: University of Alabama Press, 2004.

Burrus, Ernest J. *Kino and the Cartography of Northwestern New Spain*. Tucson: Arizona Pioneers' Historical Society, 1965.

———. "Clavigero and the Lost Sigüenza y Góngora Manuscripts." *Estudios de Cultura Náhuatl* 1 (1959): 59–90.

Burton, Antoinette M. "Introduction: Archive Fever, Archive Stories." In *Archive Stories: Facts, Fictions, and the Writing of History*, edited by Antoinette M. Burton, 1–24. Durham, N.C.: Duke University Press, 2005.

Bustamante, Carlos María de. *Mañanas de la Alameda de México*. Mexico City: Impr. de la Testamentaria de Valdés, 1835.

Byrd, Jodi A. *The Transit of Empire: Indigenous Critiques of Colonialism*. Minneapolis, University of Minnesota Press, 2011.

Byrne, Denis. "The Ethos of Return: Erasure and Reinstatement of Aboriginal Visibility in the Australian Historical Landscape." *Historical Archaeology* 37, no. 1 (2003): 73–86.

Cahokia: City of the Sun. Prehistoric Urban Center in the American Bottom. Rev. ed. Collinsville, Ill.: Cahokia Mounds Museum Society, 1999.

Cajete, Gregory. *Native Science: Natural Laws of Interdependence.* Santa Fe, N.M.: Clear Light Publishers, 2002.

Calhoun, John C. *The Papers of John C. Calhoun,* Vol. 25, edited by Clyde N. Wilson and Shirley Bright Cook. Columbia: University of South Carolina Press, 1959.

Calloway, Colin G. *American Revolution in Indian Country: Crisis and Diversity in Native American Communities.* Cambridge, U.K.: Cambridge University Press, 1995.

——. *The Indian World of George Washington.* New York: Oxford University Press, 2018.

——. *One Vast Winter Count: The Native American West before Lewis and Clark.* Lincoln: University of Nebraska, 2003.

——. *The Victory with No Name: The Native American Defeat of the First American Army.* New York: Oxford University Press, 2015.

Calneck, Edward. "The Calmecac and Telpochcalli in Pre-Conquest Tenochtitlan." In *The Work of Bernardino de Sahagún: Pioneer Ethnographer of Sixteenth-Century Aztec Mexico,* edited by J. Jorge Klor de Alva, H. B. Nicholson, Eloise Quiñones Keber, 169–77. Albany: SUNY Albany Institute for Mesoamerican Studies, 1988.

Campbell, Colin and Emily Opilo, "Christopher Columbus statue near Little Italy brought down, tossed into Baltimore's Inner Harbor." *Baltimore Sun.* July 4, 2020. https://www.baltimoresun.com/maryland/baltimore-city/bs-md-ci-columbus-statue-20200705-xc4bhthfhjaflifz72org2lrhy-story.html.

[Campbell, John P.] "Of the Aborigines of the Western Country." *Port Folio* 1, no. 6 (June 1816): 457–463.

——. "Of the Aborigines of the Western Country." *The Port Folio* 2, no.1 (July 1816): 1–8.

Cañizares-Esguerra, Jorge. *How to Write the History of the New World: Histories, Epistemologies, and Identities in the Eighteenth-Century Atlantic World.* Stanford, Conn.: Stanford University Press, 2001.

Carlsen, William. *Jungle of Stone: The True Story of Two Men, Their Extraordinary Journey, and the Discovery of the Lost Civilization of the Maya.* New York: William Morrow, 2016.

Carmack, Robert M. *The Quiché Mayas of Utatlán: The Evolution of a Highland Guatemala Kingdom.* Norman: University of Oklahoma Press, 1980.

Carmack, Robert M., and James L. Mondloch. *Título de Totonicapán.* Mexico City: Universidad Nacional Autónoma de México, 1983.

Carrasco, Davíd. *Religions of Mesoamerica: Cosmovision and Ceremonial Centers.* New York: Harper and Row, 1990.

Carrasco, Davíd, and Scott Sessions. *Daily Life of the Aztecs: People of the Sun and Earth.* Westport, Conn.: Greenwood Publishing Group, 1998.

Carreño, Alberto M. "El Br. D. Jose Mariano Moziño y la Expedicion Cientifica del Siglo XVIII." In *Noticias de Nutka*, edited by Joseph Mariano Moziño Suárez de Figueroa, v–cix. Mexico City: Imprenta y fototipia de la Secretaría de Fomento, 1913.

Carrera, Magali M. *Imagining Identity in New Spain: Race, Lineage, and the Colonial Body in Portraiture and Casta Paintings*. Austin: University of Texas Press, 2003.

———. *Traveling from New Spain to Mexico: Mapping Practices of Nineteenth-Century Mexico*. Durham, N.C.: Duke University Press, 2011.

Carrigan, Margaret. "One mound at a time: Native American artist Santiago X on rebuilding Indigenous cities." *Art Newspaper* 315 . September 2019. https//:www.theartnewspaper.com/the-art-newspaper/315-september–2019.

Carroll, Clint. *Roots of Our Renewal. Ethnobotany and Cherokee Environmental Governance*. Minneapolis: University of Minnesota Press, 2015.

Carver, J[onathan]. *Travels Through the Interior Parts of North America, in the Years 1766, 1767, and 1768*. London: Printed for the author, 1778.

Cass, Lewis. "Article XII—Archaeologia Americana. Transactions and Collections of the American Antiquarian Society." *North American Review and Miscellaneous Journal* 12 (April 1821): 225–46.

Castañeda, Quetzil E. *In the Museum of Maya Culture: Touring Chichén Itzá*. Minneapolis: University of Minnesota Press, 1996.

———. "Heritage and Indigeneity: Transformations in the Politics of Tourism." *Cultural Tourism in Latin America. The Politics of Space and Imagery*, edited by M. Baud and A. Ypeij, 263–95. London: Brill, 2009.

———. "The 'Past' as Transcultural Space: Using Ethnographic Installation in the Study of Archaeology." *Public Archaeology* 8, nos. 2–3 (2009): 262–82.

———. "'We Are Not Indigenous!': An Introduction to the Maya Identity of Yucatan." *Journal of Latin American Anthropology* 9, no. 1 (2004): 36–63.

Castañeda de la Paz, María. *Pintura de la peregrinación de los Culhuaque-Mexitin, mapa de Sigüenza: Análisis de un documento de origen Tenochca*. Zinacantepec: El Colegio Mexiquense, 2006.

Castillo, R. Aída Hernández. *Histories and Stories from Chiapas*. Translated by Martha Pou. Austin: University of Texas Press, 2001.

Castillo Ledón, Luis. Foreword to *Colección de las antigüedades mexicanas que ecsisten en el Museo nacional, y dan a luz. Isidro Icaza é Isidro Gondra. Litografiadas por Federico Waldeck*. Mexico City: Museo Nacional de Arqueología, Historia y Etnografía, 1927.

Catálogo de la colección de D. Juan Bautista Muñoz. Vol. 3: *Indice General Documentos de Don Juan Bautista Muñoz*. Madrid: Real Academia de la Historia, 1956.

Cayton, Andrew R. L. "The Contours of Power in a Frontier Town: Marietta, Ohio, 1788–1803," *Journal of the Early Republic* 6, no. 2 (Summer 1986): 103–5.

———. *The Frontier Republic: Ideology and Politics in the Ohio Country*. Kent, Oh.: Kent State University Press, 1986.

Cazier, Lola. *Surveys and Surveyors of the Public Domain, 1785–1975*. Washington D.C.: Government Printing Office, 1978.

Chakrabarty, Dipesh. *Provincializing Europe: Postcolonial Thought and Historical Difference*. Princeton, N.J.: Princeton University Press, 2000

Cheyfitz, Eric. *The Poetics of Imperialism: Translation and Colonization from "The Tempest" to "Tarzan."* Rev. ed. Philadelphia: University of Pennsylvania Press, 1997.

Chiles, Katy. *Transformable Race: Surprising Metamorphoses in the Literature of Early America*. New York: Oxford University Press, 2014.

Chorba, Carrie C. *Mexico, from Mestizo to Multicultural: National Identity and Recent Representations of the Conquest*. Nashville, Tenn.: Vanderbilt University Press, 2007.

Christenson, Allen J. *The Burden of the Ancients: Maya Ceremonies of World Renewal from the Pre-Columbian Period to the Present*. Austin: University of Texas, 2016.

Christin, Anne-Marie. "Visible/legible: An Iconic Typology of Writing." In *Sign and Design: Image as Script in a Cross-Cultural Perspective (300–1600 CE)*, edited by Brigitte Bedos-Rezak and Jeffrey Hamburger, 19–29. Washington, D.C.: Dumbarton Oaks and Harvard University Press, 2016.

C[ist], J[acob]. "Ruins of an Ancient Work on the Sciota," *The Port-Folio* 2, no. 5 (November 1809): 418a–19.

Clark, Fiona. "'Read All About It': Science, Translation, Adaptation, and Confrontation in the Gazeta De Literatura De México, 1788–1795." In *Science in the Spanish and Portuguese Empires, 1500–1800*, edited by Daniela Bleichmar, Paula De Vos, Kristin Huffine, and Kevin Sheehan, 147–77. Stanford, Calif.: Stanford University Press, 2009.

———. "The Gazeta de Literatura de México (1788–1795): The Formation of a Literary-Scientific Periodical in Late-Viceregal Mexico." *Dieciocho: Hispanic Enlightenment* (2005): 7–32.

Clavigero, Abbé D. Francesco Saverio. *The History of Mexico: Collected from Spanish and Mexican Historians, from Manuscripts, and Ancient Paintings of the Indians. Illustrated / by Charts, and Other Copper Plates*. Translated from the Italian by Charles Cullen, Esq. 2 vols. London: Printed for G. G. J. and J. Robinson, 1787.

———. *Geschichte von Mexico* [...]. Leipzig: Schwickertschen Verlage, 1789–1790.

———. *Storia antica del Messico* [...]. Cesena: G. Biasini, 1780–1781.

Clavigero, Franciso J. *Historia antigua de México y de su conquista* [...]. Traducida del italiano por J. Joaquín de Mora. Mexico City: Impr. de Lara, 1844.

———. *Historia antigua de Mégico:* [...]. Traducida del italiano por Jose Joaquin de Mora. London: Rudolf Ackerman, 1826.

Clendinnen, Inga. "'Fierce and Unnatural Cruelty': Cortés and the Conquest of Mexico." *Representations* 33 (Winter 1991): 65–100.

Clifford, John D. "Letters I–VIII." In *John D. Clifford's Indian Antiquities: With Related Material by C. S. Rafinesque*, edited by Charles Boewe, 1–64. Knoxville: University of Tennessee Press, 2000.

Cline, Gloria Griffen. *Exploring the Great Basin.* Norman: University of Oklahoma Press, 1963.

Cline, Howard F. "The Apocryphal Early Career of J.F. Waldeck, Pioneer Americanist." *Acta Americana* 5 (1947): 278–300.

———. "Civil Congregations of the Indians in New Spain, 1598–1606." *Hispanic American Historical Review* 29, no. 3 (August 1949): 349–69.

Cline, Howard F., ed. *Handbook of Middle American Indians,* Volume 14/15: *Guide to Ethnohistorical Sources.* Parts 3 and 4. Austin: University of Texas Press, 1975.

Cobb, Charles R., and Brian M. Butler, "The Vacant Quarter Revisited: Late Mississippian Abandonment of the Lower Ohio Valley." *American Antiquity* 67, no. 4 (2002): 625–41.

Coe, Michael, and Rez Koontz. *Mexico: From the Olmecs to the Aztecs.* New York: Thames & Hudson, 2013.

Cohen, Matt, and Jeffrey Glover, eds. *Colonial Mediascapes: Sensory Worlds of the Early Americas.* Lincoln: University of Nebraska Press, 2014.

Colwell, Chip. *Plundered Skulls and Stolen Spirits: Inside the Fight to Reclaim Native America's Culture.* Chicago: University of Chicago, 2017.

Colwell-Chanthaphonh, Chip, and Stephen Nash, eds. *Museum Anthropology* 33, no. 2 (September 2010).

Conn, Stephen. *History's Shadow: Native Americans and Historical Consciousness in the Nineteenth Century.* Chicago: University of Chicago Press, 2008.

Connolly, Emilie. "Panic, State Power, and Chickasaw Dispossession." *Journal of the Early Republic* 40, no. 4 (2020): 683–89.

Conover, Cornelius. "Reassessing the Rise of Mexico's Virgin of Guadalupe, 1650s–1780s." *Mexican Studies/Estudios Mexicanos* 27, no. 2 (2011): 251–79.

Constantino Ortiz, María Eugenia. "José Longinos Martínez: un expedicionario, dos gabinetes de historia natural." *Corpus* 5, no. 2 (June–December 2015): 1–34.

Cook, James. *A Voyage to the Pacific Ocean, undertaken by the Command of His Majesty, for Making Discoveries in the Northern Hemisphere [. . .].* London: W. and A. Strahan for G. Nicol and T. Cadell, 1784.

Cooper, Karen Coody. *Spirited Encounters: American Indians Protest Museum Policies and Practices.* Lanham, Md.: AltaMira Press, 2007.

Cope, R. Douglas. *The Limits of Racial Domination: Plebian Society in Colonial Mexico City, 1660–1720.* Madison: University of Wisconsin Press, 1994.

Coram, Robert. *Political Inquiries: To which is Added, a Plan for the General Establishment of Schools Throughout the United States.* Wilmington, Del.: Andrews and Brynberg, in Market-Street, 1791.

Correia, David. *Properties of Violence: Law and Land Grant Struggle in Northern New Mexico.* Athens: University of Georgia Press, 2013.

Cossins, Daniel. "The Missing City on the Plains." *New Scientist* 240, no. 3206 (December 2018): 40–43.

Costa, David J. "The Historical Phonology of Miami-Illinois Consonants." *International Journal of American Linguistics* 57 no. 3 (July 1991): 356–93.

———. "Redacting Premodern Texts without Speakers: the Peoria Story of Wiihsakacaakwa." In *New Voices for Old Words: Algonquian Oral Literatures*, edited by David J. Costa, 34–89. Lincoln, Neb.: University of Nebraska Press, 2015.

Costa, David J., ed. *myaamia neehi peewaalia aacimoona neehi aalhsoohkana-Myaamia and Peoria Narratives and Winter Stories*. Translated by David Costa. Oxford, Oh.: Miami Tribe of Oklahoma and the Peoria Tribe of Oklahoma, 2010.

Coulthard, Glen. "Place Against Empire: Understanding Indigenous Anti-Colonialism." *Affinities: A Journal of Radical Theory, Culture, and Action* 4, no. 2 (Fall 2010): 79–83.

———. *Red Skin, White Masks: Rejecting the Colonial Politics of Recognition*. Minneapolis: University of Minnesota Press, 2014.

Craddock, Jerry R. "Juan de Oñate in Quivira: The Valverde Interrogatory." *Romance Philology* 56 (2002): 51–164.

Craddock, Jerry, ed. *The Expedition of Juan de Oñate to Quivira in 1601 as Narrated in the "True Report" and the "Valverde Interrogatory."* Translated by John H. R. Polt. Cíbola Project, University of California, Berkeley, 2013. https://escholarship.org/uc/item/7162z2r1p.

Cresswell, Nicholas. *The Journal of Nicholas Cresswell, 1774–1777*. New York: The Dial Press, 1924.

Cruikshank, Julie. "Are Glaciers 'Good to Think With'? Recognising Indigenous Environmental Knowledge." *Anthropological Forum* 22, no. 3 (2012): 239–50.

———. *Do Glaciers Listen? Local Knowledge, Colonial Encounters, and Social Imagination*. Vancouver, B.C.: University of British Columbia, 2005.

Cuming, F[ortiscue]. *Sketches of a Tour to the Western Country*. Edited by Zadoc Cramer. Pittsburgh: Cramer, Spear & Eichbaum, 1810.

Cummins, Thomas B. F. "From Many into One: The Transformation of pre-Columbian Signs into European Letters in the Sixteenth-Century," in *Sign and Design: Image as Script in a Cross-Cultural Perspective (300–1600 CE)*, edited by Brigitte Bedos-Rezak and Jeffrey Hamburger, 85–107. Washington, D.C.: Dumbarton Oaks and Harvard University Press, 2016.

Curran, Andrew. *The Anatomy of Blackness: Science and Slavery in an Age of Enlightenment*. Baltimore: Johns Hopkins University Press, 2011.

Cushman, Ellen. "Letters and Characters: Letter from Walter Duncan to Dollie Duncan from the OK State Penitentiary." Unpublished paper presented at Hidden Literacies Conference, Trinity College, Hartford, Conn. April 5, 2019.

[Cusick, David.] *David Cusick's Sketches of ancient history of the Six Nations* [. . .]. Tuscarora Village, Lewiston, N.Y.: Printed for the author, 1827.

[Cusick, David.] *David Cusick's Sketches of ancient history of the Six Nations* [. . .]. Tuscarora Village, Lewiston, Niagara Co., N.Y.: s.n., 1828.

Cutler, Manassas. "American Antiquities." *Rural Magazine* 1, no. 39 (November 10, 1798): 1.

Cuvier, Georges. *Essay on the Theory of the Earth* [...]. Translated by Robert Kerr. Edinburgh: William Blackwood, John Murray, and Robert Baldwin, 1813.
Dain, Bruce R. *A Hideous Monster of the Mind*. Cambridge, Mass.: Harvard University Press, 2009.
Daston, Lorraine. "The Empire of Observation, 1600–1800." In *Histories of Scientific Observation*, edited by Lorraine Daston and Elizabeth Lunbeck, 81–113. Chicago, Ill.: University of Chicago Press, 2011.
Davis, Nicola. "Laser maps reveal 'lost' Mayan treasure in Guatemala jungle." *Guardian*, April 30, 2019.
———. "Laser scanning reveals 'lost' ancient Mexican city 'had as many buildings as Manhattan.'" *Guardian*, February 15, 2018.
Deans-Smith, Susan. "Creating the Colonial Subject: Casta Paintings, Collectors, and Critics in Eighteenth-Century Mexico and Spain." *Colonial Latin American Review* 14, no. 2 (2005): 169–204.
DeGuzmán, María. *Spain's Long Shadow: The Black Legend, Off-Whiteness, and Anglo-American Empire*. Minneapolis: University of Minnesota Press, 2005.
Delafield, John. *An Inquiry into the Origin of the Antiquities of America*. Cincinnati: N. G. Burgess & Co., 1839.
———. "Propose To Publish a Volume, Entitled A New View Of The Origin Of The Antiquities Of America." New York: Colt, Burgess, & Co., 1839.
Delay, Brian. *War of a Thousand Deserts: Indian Raids and the U.S.-Mexican War*. New Haven, Conn.: Yale University Press, 2008.
De León, Ann. "Coatlicue or How to Write the Dismembered Body." *MLN* 125, no. 2 (March 2010): 259–86.
Delf, Norona. *Moundsville's Mammoth Mound*. Moundsville: West Virginia Archaeological Society, 1957.
Deloria, Vine, Jr. *Custer Died for Your Sins: An Indian Manifesto* [1969]. Norman: University of Oklahoma Press, 1988.
———. *God Is Red: A Native View of Religion* [1973]. 2nd ed. Golden, Co.: Fulcrum Publishing, 1992.
———. *Red Earth White Masks: Native Americans and the Myth of Scientific Fact*. Golden, Co.: Fulcrum Publishing, 1995.
Deloria, Philip J. *Indians in Unexpected Places*. Lawrence: University of Kansas, 2004.
———. *Playing Indian*. New Haven, Conn.: Yale University Press, 1998.
Del Río, Antonio. *Description of the ruins of an ancient city: discovered near Palenque, in the kingdom of Guatemala, in Spanish America translated from the original manuscript report of Captain Don Antonio del Rio; followed by Teatro critico americano, or, A critical investigation and research into the history of the Americans by Doctor Paul Felix Cabrera, of the City of New Guatemala*. London: Henry Berthoud, no. 65, Regent's Quadrant, Piccadilly, 1822.
DeLucia, Christine. "Fugitive Collections in New England Indian Country: Indigenous Material Culture and Early American History Making at Ezra Stiles's Yale Museum." *William & Mary Quarterly* 75, no. 1 (January 2018): 109–150.

De Schwenitz, Edmund. *The Life and Times of David Zeisberger: The Western Pioneer and Apostle of the Indians*. Philadelphia: J. B. Lippincott & Co., 1871.

De Terra, Helmut. "Alexander von Humboldt's Correspondence with Jefferson, Madison, and Gallatin." *Proceedings of the American Philosophical Society* 103 (1959): 783–806.

———. "Motives and Consequences of Alexander Von Humboldt's Visit to the United States (1804)." *Proceedings of the American Philosophical Society* 104, no. 3 (1960): 314–16.

———. "Studies of the Documentation of Alexander Von Humboldt: The Philadelphia Abstract of Humboldt's American Travels Humboldt Portraits and Sculpture in the United States." *Proceedings of the American Philosophical Society* 102, no. 6 (1958): 560–859.

Devereux, B. J., Amable, G. S. & Crow, P. "Visualisation of LiDAR terrain models for archaeological feature detection." *Antiquity* 82 no. 316 (2008): 470–79.

Devereaux, Ryan. "'We are still here': Native Activists in Arizona Resist Trump's Border Wall." *The Intercept*. November 24, 2019. https://www.theintercept.com/2019/11/24/arizona-border-wall-native-activists/.

Dew, Nicholas and James Delbourgo, eds. *Science and Empire in the Atlantic World*. New York: Routledge, 2008.

Díaz-Andreu, Margarita. *A World History of Nineteenth-Century Archaeology: Nationalism, Colonialism, and the Past*. New York: Oxford University Press, 2007.

Diaz-Granados, Carol. "Marking Stone, Land, Body, and Spirit." In *Hero, Hawk, and Open Hand: American Indian Art of the Ancient Midwest and South*, edited by Richard F. Townsend, 143–147. New Haven, Conn.: Yale University Press, 2004.

Diaz Perrera, Miguel Ángel. "Sombras y Luces sobre un misterioso anticuario franco-mexicano. François Corroy, 'Tabasqueño por adopción,' 1777–1836." *Revista Oficio de Historia e Interdisciplina* 9 (July–December 2019): 23–40.

DiCesare, Catherine R. *Sweeping the Way: Divine Transformation in the Aztec Festival of Ochpaniztli*. Louisville: University Press of Colorado, 2009.

Diderot D., and J. d'Alembert, eds. *Encyclopédie ou dictionnaire raisonné des sciences, des arts et des métiers*. Vol. 10. Paris: Briasson, David, Le Breton, Durand, 1765.

Diehl, Richard. *The Olmecs: America's First Civilization*. New York: Thames & Hudson, 2004.

Dippie, Brian. *The Vanishing American: White Attitudes and U.S. Indian Policy*. Middletown: Wesleyan University Press, 1982.

Doerfler, Jill, Niigaanwewidam James Sinclair, and Heidi Kiiwetinepinesiik Stark. "Bagijige: Making an Offering." In *Centering Anishinaabeg Studies: Understanding the World Through Stories*, edited By Jill Doerfler Jill, Niigaanwewidam James Sinclair, and Heidi Kiiwetinepinesiik Stark, xv–xxviii. Lansing: Michigan State University Press, 2013.

Doolan, Andy. *Fugitive Empire: Locating Early American Imperialism*. Minneapolis: University of Minnesota Press, 2005.

Dorsey, James Owen. "Migrations of Siouan Tribes." *American Naturalist* 20, no. 3 (1886): 214–22.

Douglas, Eduardo. *In the Palace of Nezahualcoyotl: Painting Manuscripts, Writing the Pre-Hispanic Past in Early Colonial Period Tetzcoco, Mexico.* Austin: University of Texas Press, 2012.

Dowd, Gregory Evans. *A Spirited Resistance: The North American Indian Struggle for Unity, 1745–1815.* Baltimore: Johns Hopkins University Press, 1992.

Doyle, Ann M., Kimberly Lawson, and Sarah Dupont, "Indigenization of Knowledge Organization at the Xwi7xwa Library," *Journal of Library and Information Studies* 13, no. 2 (December 2015): 107–34.

Dubcovsky, Alejandra. "Defying Indian Slavery: Apalachee Voices and Spanish Sources in the Eighteenth-Century Southeast." *William and Mary Quarterly* 75, no. 2 (April 2018): 295–322.

———. *Informed Power: Communication in the Early American South.* Cambridge, Mass.: Harvard University Press, 2016.

Dupaix, Guillermo. "Descripción iconográfica de la Antigua y famosa pirámide [...] de Paplanta." Unpublished manuscript in Viages Sobre las Antiquedades Mejicanas collection, Mss.913.72.D92v, American Philosophical Society, Philadelphia.

———. *Expediciones acerca de los antiguos monumentos de la Nueva España, 1805–1808*, edited by José Alcina Franch. Madrid: Ediciones J. Porrúa Turanzas, 1969.

———. "Explicación de Algunos geroglíficos." Unpublished manuscript in Viages Sobre las Antiquedades Mejicanas collection, Mss.913.72.D92v, American Philosophical Society, Philadelphia.

Duval, Jules. *Les colonies et la politique coloniale de la France [...] Avec deux cartes du Sénégal et de Madagascar dressées par M. V. A. Malte-Brun.* Paris: A. Bertrand, 1864.

Duval, Kathleen, *The Native Ground: Indians and Colonists in the Heart of the Continent.* Philadelphia: University of Pennsylvania Press, 2006.

Dye, David H. "Art, Ritual, and Chiefly Warfare in the Mississippian World." In *Hero, Hawk, and Open Hand: American Indian Art of the Ancient Midwest and South*, edited by Richard F. Townsend, 191–207. New Haven, Conn.: Yale University Press, 2004.

Earle, Rebecca. *The Return of the Native: Indians and Myth-Making in Spanish America, 1810–1930.* Durham, N.C.: Duke University Press.

Echo-Hawk, Roger C. "Antiquity History in the New World: Integrating Oral Traditions and the Archaeological Record in Deep Time." *American Antiquity* 65, no. 2 (2002): 267–90.

Echo-Hawk, Roger C., and Walter R. Echo-Hawk. *Battlefields and Burial Grounds: The Indian Struggle to Protect Ancestral Graves in the United States.* Minneapolis, Minn.: Lerner, 1994.

Echo-Hawk, Roger, and Larry J. Zimmerman. "Beyond Racism: Some Opinions about Racialism and American Archaeology." *American Indian Quarterly* 30, nos. 3–4 (2006): 461–85.

Edison, Paul N. "Colonial Prospecting in Independent Mexico: Abbé Baradère's Antiquités Mexicaines (1834–36)." *Western Society for French History* 32 (2004). https://hdl.handle.net/2027/spo.0642292.0032.012.

Edmunds, R. David. "Pickawillany: French Military Power Versus British Economics." *Western Pennsylvania Historical Magazine* 58, no. 2 (1975): 169–84.

Eguiara y Eguren, Juan José de. *Bibliotheca mexicana* [. . .]. Mexico City: s.n., 1755.

Elson, Christine M., and Michael E. Smith. "Archaeological Deposits from the Aztec New Fire Ceremony." *Ancient Mesoamerica* 12, no. 2 (2001): 157–74.

Emerson, Ralph Waldo. *Essays & Lectures*. New York: Library of America, 1996.

Endfield, G. H., "Pinturas, Land and Lawsuits: Maps in Colonial Mexican Legal Documents." *Imago Mundi* 53 (2001): 7–27.

Engstrand, Iris H. W. "The Eighteenth Century: Enlightenment Comes to Spanish California." *Southern California Quarterly* 80, no. 1 (Spring 1998): 3–30.

———. *Spanish Scientists in the New World: The Eighteenth-Century Expeditions*. Seattle: University of Washington Press, 1981.

Erben, Patrick M. *A Harmony of the Spirits: Translation and the Language of Community in Early Pennsylvania*. Chapel Hill: University of North Carolina Press, 2012.

Erdrich, Heid. "eBay Bones." *Museum Anthropology* 33, no. 2 (September 2010): 251.

Erdrich, Louise. *Books and Islands in Ojibwe Country: Traveling Through the Land of My Ancestors*. Washington, D.C.: National Geographic, 2003.

Estrada de Gerlero, Elena Isabel. "Carlos III y los Estudios Anticuarios en Nueva España." In *1492–1992: V Centenario arte e historia*, edited by Xavier Moyssen and Louise Noelle. Mexico: Universidad Nacional Autónoma de México, 1993: 61–92.

———. "La Real Expedición Anticuaria de Guillermo Dupaix." *Mexico en el mundo de las colecciones de arte* 4 (1994): 168–82.

Estrada Torres, María Isabel. "Fronteras imaginaries en la ciudad de México: Parcialidades indígenas y traza española en el siglo XVII." In *Las ciudades y sus estructuras: Población, espacio y cultura en México, siglos XVII y XIX*, edited by Luis Pérez Cruz, Sonia Pérez Toledo, and René Eliazalde Salazar, 93–108. Mexico City: UAM-Iztapalapa, 1999.

Ethridge, Robbie. *Creek Country: The Creek Indians and Their World*. Chapel Hill: University of North Carolina Press, 2003.

———. *From Chicaza to Chickasaw: The European Invasion and the Transformation of the Mississippian World, 1540–1715*. Chapel Hill: University of North Carolina Press, 2010.

Ethridge, Robbie, and Sheri M. Shuck-Hall, eds. *Mapping the Mississippi Shatter Zone: The Colonial Indian Slave Trade and Regional Instability in the American South*. Lincoln: University of Nebraska Press, 2009.

Evans, Brad T. *Romancing the Maya: Mexican Antiquity in the American Imagination, 1820–1915*. Austin: University of Texas Press, 2004.

Evans, Lewis. *An Analysis of a General Map of the Middle British Colonies*. Philadelphia: Benjamin Franklin, 1755.

Evans, Susan Toby. *Archaeology of Ancient Mexico and Central America, an Encyclopedia*. New York: Garland Publishing, Inc., 2001.

Ewan, Joseph, and Nesta Dunn Ewan. *Benjamin Smith Barton, Naturalist and Physician in Jeffersonian America,* edited by Victoria C. Hollowell, Eileen P. Duggan, and Marshall R. Crosby. St. Louis: Missouri Botanical Garden Press, 2007.

Exbalin, Arnaud. "Riot in Mexico City: A Challenge to the Colonial Order?" *Urban History* 43, no. 2 (2016): 215–31.
Fabian, Ann. "The Curious Cabinet of Dr. Morton." in *Acts of Possession: Collecting in America*, edited by Leah Dilworth, 112–37. New Brunswick: Rutgers University Press, 2003.
———. *The Skull Collectors: Race, Science, and American's Unburied Dead*. Chicago: University of Chicago Press, 2010.
Fabian, Johannes. *Time and the Other: How Anthropology Makes Its Object*. New York: Columbia, 1983.
Fair, Susan W. "Inupiat Naming and Community History: The Tapqaq and Saniniq Coasts near Shishmaref, Alaska." *Professional Geographer* 49, no. 4 (1997): 466–80.
Faragher, John Mack. "Commentary: Settler Colonial Studies and the North American Frontier," *Settler Colonial Studies* 4, no. 2 (2014): 181–91.
Farago, Claire. "Understanding Visuality." In *Seeing Across Cultures in the Early Modern World*, edited by Dana Leibsohn and Jeanette Favrot Peterson, 239–56. Burlington, Vt.: Ashgate, 2012.
Farrell, Molly, *Counting Bodies: Population in Colonial American Writing*. New York: Oxford University Press, 2016.
Farriss, Nancy. "Remembering the Future, Anticipating the Past: History, Time, and Cosmology Among the Maya of Yucatán." *Comparative Studies in History and Society* 29, no. 3 (July 1987): 566–93.
Fauvet-Berthelot, Marie-France, Leonardo López Luján and Susana Guimaraes. "The Real Expedición Anticuaria Collection," in *Fanning the Scared Flame: Mesoamerican Studies in Honor of H. B. Nicholson*, edited by Matthew A. Boxt and Brian Dervin Dillon, 461-485. Boulder: University Press of Colorado, 2012.
Fenton, Elizabeth R., ed. *Fruitful Valley: A Chronicle of Williamstown, West Virginia* [1886] Marietta, Oh.: Williamstown Historical Committee, 1976.
Filson, John. *The Discovery, Settlement and Present State of Kentucke* [...]. Wilmington, Del.: John Adams, 1784.
Findlen, Paula, ed. *Early Modern Things: Objects and their Histories, 1500–1800*. New York: Routledge, 2012.
Findlen, Paula. *Possessing Nature: Museums, Collecting, and Scientific Culture in Early Modern Italy*. Berkeley: University of California Press, 1994.
Fine-Dare, Kathleen S. *Grave Injustice: The American Indian Repatriation Movement and NAGPRA*. Lincoln: University of Nebraska Press, 2002.
Fisher, Raymond H. "The Early Cartography of the Bering Strait Region." *Arctic* 37, no. 4 (1984): 574–89.
Fitz, Caitlin. *Our Sister Republics: The United States in an Age of American Revolutions*. New York: W. W. Norton & Company, 2016.
Fitzgerald, Stephanie. *Native Women and Land: Narratives of Dispossession and Resurgence*. Albuquerque: University of New Mexico Press, 2015.
Flint, Shirley Cushing. "Treason or Travesty: The Martín Cortés Conspiracy Reexamined." *The Sixteenth Century Journal* 39, no. 1 (Spring 2008): 23–44.

Florescano, Enrique. "Creation of the Museo Nacional de Antropologia of Mexico and Its Scientific, Educational, and Political Purposes." In *Collecting the Pre-Columbian Past: a Symposium at Dumbarton Oaks, 6th and 7th October 1990*, edited by Elizabeth Hill Boone, 81–103. Washington D.C.: Dumbarton Oaks Research Library and Collection, 1993.

———. *Memory, Myth, and Time in Mexico: From the Aztecs to Independence*. Translated by Albert G. Bork with Katherine R. Bork. Austin: University of Texas Press, 1994.

Folsom, Raphael Brewster. *The Yaquis and the Empire: Violence, Spanish Imperial Power, and Native Resilience in Colonial Mexico*. New Haven, Conn.: Yale University Press, 2014.

Forbes, Jack. *Aztecas Del Norte: The Chicanos of Aztlan*. Greenwich, Conn.: Fawcett, 1973.

Ford, Lisa. *Settler Sovereignty: Jurisdiction and Indigenous People in America and Australia, 1788–1836*. Cambridge, Mass.: Harvard University Press, 2011.

Foreman, Grant, ed. "The Journal of the Proceedings at Our First Treaty with the Wild Indians." *The Chronicle of Oklahoma* 14 (December 1936): 393–413.

Foster, Belinda Atwater. *The Atwater Family, or Truth Is Stranger Than Fiction*, edited by Lucy Atwater Brown. Indianapolis: s.n., 1915.

Foucault, Michel. *The Archaeology of Knowledge & The Discourse on Language* [1969]. Translated by Alan Sheridan. New York: Pantheon Books, 1972.

———. *The Order of Things: An Archaeology of the Human Sciences*. New York: Pantheon Books, 1970.

———. *Security, Territory, Population: Lectures at the College de France, 1977–78*, translated by Graham Burchell. Basingstoke, U.K.: Palgrave MacMillan, 2007.

Freeman, John Finley. "Manuscript Sources on Latin American Indians in the Library of the American Philosophical Society." *Proceedings of the American Philosophical Society* 106, no. 6 (1962): 530–40.

Freeman, John F., and Murphy D. Smith. *A Guide to Manuscripts Relating to the American Indian in the Library of the American Philosophical Society*. Memoirs of the American Philosophical Society 65. Philadelphia: The Society, 1966.

Friis, Herman R. "Baron Alexander von Humboldt's Visit to Washington, D. C., June 1 through June 13, 1804." *Records of the Columbia Historical Society, Washington, D.C.* 60/62 (1960/1962): 1–35.

Frye, David. *Indians into Mexicans: History and Identity in a Mexican Town*. Austin: University of Texas Press, 1996.

Fur, Gunlög. *A Nation of Women: Gender and Colonial Encounters among the Delaware Indians*. Philadelphia: University of Pennsylvania Press, 2009.

Furstenberg, François. "The Significance of the Trans-Appalachian Frontier in Atlantic History." *American History Review* 113 (2008): 647–77.

Gabilondo, Joseba. "Genealogía de la 'raza latina': para una teoría atlántica de las estructuras raciales hispanas." *Revista Iberoamericana* 75, no. 228 (July–September 2009): 795–818.

Galindo, Juan. "A Short Account of Some Antiquities Discovered in the District of Peten, Central America [...]. [1831]." In *Archaeologia Americana: Transactions and Collections of the American Antiquarian Society*. Vol. 2 (1836): 450–543.

Galloway, Andrew. "William Cullen Bryant's American Antiquities: Medievalism, Miscegenation, and Race in 'The Prairies.'" *American Literary History* 22, no. 4 (Winter 2010): 724–51.

Galloway, Patricia. *Choctaw Genesis, 1500–1700*. Lincoln: University of Nebraska Press, 1995.

Gálvez, Bernardo de. *Instructions for Governing the Interior Provinces of New Spain, 1786*. Edited and translated by Donald E. Worcester. Berkeley: University of California Press, 1951.

García-Zambrano, Angel. "Ancestral Rituals of Landscape Exploration and Appropriation amongst Indigenous Communities in Early Colonial Mexico." In *Sacred Gardens and Landscapes: Ritual and Agency*, edited by Michel Conan, 1–27. Washington D.C.: Dumbarton Oaks, 2007.

Garrigan, Shelley E. *Collecting Mexico: Museums, Monuments, and the Creation of National Identity*. Minneapolis: University of Minnesota Press, 2012.

Geniusz, Mary Siisip. *Plants Have So Much to Give Us, All We Have to Do Is Ask: Anishinaabe Botanical Teachings*. Edited by Wendy Makoons Geniusz. Minneapolis: University of Minnesota Press, 2015.

Geniusz, Wendy Makoons. *Our Knowledge Is Not Primitive: Decolonizing Botanical Anishinaabe Teachings*. Syracuse, N.Y.: Syracuse University Press, 2009.

Gerbi, Antonello. *Dispute of the New World*. Pittsburgh: University of Pittsburgh Press, 1973.

Gerhard, Peter. "Congregaciones De Indios En La Nueva España Antes De 1570." *Historia Mexicana* 26, no. 3 (1977): 347–95.

Gibson, Charles. *The Aztecs Under Spanish Rule: A History of the Indians of the Valley of Mexico, 1519–1810*. Stanford, Calif.: Stanford University Press, 1964.

Gill, Harold B., Jr., and George M. Curtis, III. *A Man Apart: The Journal of Nicholas Cresswell, 1774–1781*. Lanham, Md.: Lexington Books, 2009.

Gilmore, N. Ray. "Henry George Ward, British Publicist for Mexican Mines." *Pacific Historical Review* 32, no. 1 (February 1963): 35–47.

Giordan, Jean François. *Réponse au libelle intitulé Précis historique sur la colonie du Goazacoalco, de Hippolyte Mansion*. Paris, Imprimerie de Auguste Auffray, 1831.

Glass, John. "A Survey of Native Middle American Pictorial Manuscripts." In *Handbook of Middle American Indians*. Vol. 14/15: *Guide to Ethnohistorical Sources*, Parts 3 and 4, edited by Howard F. Cline, 3–80. Austin: University of Texas Press, 1975.

———. *Boturini in Spain*. Lincoln Center, Mass: Conemex Associates, 2005.

———. "The Boturini Collection." In *Handbook of Middle American Indians*. Vol. 14/15: *Guide to Ethnohistorical Sources*, Parts 3 and 4, edited by Howard F. Cline, 473–86. Austin: University of Texas Press, 1975.

———. *The Boturini Collection and the Council of the Indies, 1780–1800*. Lincoln Center, Mass: Conemex Associates, 1976.

Gniadek, Melissa. "The Times of Settler Colonialism." *Lateral: Journal of the Cultural Studies Association* 6, no. 1 (Spring 2017). http://www.csalateral.org/issue/6-1/forum-alt-humanities-settler-colonialism-times-gniadek/.

Goeman, Mishuana R. "Disrupting a Settler-Colonial Grammar of Place: The Visual Memoir of Hulleah Tsinhnahjinnie." In *Theorizing Native Studies*, edited by Audra Simpson and Andrea Smith, 235–65. Durham, N.C.: Duke University Press, 2014.

———. "From Place to Territories and Back Again: Centering Storied Land in the Discussion of Indigenous Nation-Building." *International Journal of Critical Indigenous Studies* 1, no. 1 (2008): 23–34.

Gollnick, Brian. *Reinventing the Lacandón: Subaltern Representation in the Rain Forest of Chiapas.* Tucson: University of Arizona Press, 2008.

Gómez Ortega, Casimiro, ed. *Francisci Hernandi [. . .]. Opera: cum edita, tum inedita, ad autographi fidem et integritatem expressa, impensa et jussu regio.* Matriti [Madrid]: Ex Typografia Ibarrae Heredum, 1790.

Gonzalbo Aizpuru, Pilar. "La trampa de las castas." In *La sociedad novohispana: estereotipos y realidades,* edited by Solange Alberro and Pilar Gonzalbo Aizpuru, 11–191. Mexico City: México, El Colegio de México, 2013.

González Acosta, Alejandro. "Los herederos de Moctezuma." *Boletín Millares Carlo* 20 (2001): 151–58.

González Echevarría, Roberto. *Myth and Archive: A Theory of Latin American Narrative.* New Haven, Conn.: Yale University Press, 1990.

Goodwin, Isaac. *An Address, Delivered at Worcester, August 24, 1820. Before the American Antiquarian Society, at the Opening of the Antiquarian Hall, that Day Received as a Donation from the President of the Society.* Worcester: Manning & Trumbull, September 1820.

Goudie, Sean X. *Creole America: The West Indies and the Formation of Literature and Culture in the New Republic.* Philadelphia: University of Pennsylvania Press, 2006.

Gould, Stephen Jay. *Mismeasure of Man.* Rev. ed. New York: W. W. Norton & Company, 1996.

Gradie, Charlotte M. "Discovering the Chichimecas." *Americas* 51, no. 1 (July 1994): 67–88.

Grafton, Anthony. *Defenders of the Text: The Traditions of Scholarship in an Age of Science, 1450–1800.* Cambridge, Mass.: Harvard University Press, 1994.

Grafton, Anthony, and Rosenberg, Daniel. *Cartographies of Time: A History of the Timeline.* Princeton, N.J.: Princeton Architectural Press, 2010.

Graham-Harrison, Emma. "Archaeologists discover remains of vast Mayan palace in Mexico." *Guardian*, December 27, 2019.

Granados y Gálvez, Joseph Joaquin. *Tardes Americanas: gobierno gentil y catolico: breve y particular noticia de toda la historia indiana: Sucesos, casos notables, y cosas ignoradas, desde la entrada de la Gran Nacion Tulteca a esta tierra de Anahuac, hasta los presentes tiempos. Trabajadas por un indio, y un espanol.* Mexico City: Felipe de Zuniga y Ontiveros, 1778.

Grande, Sandy Marie Anglas. "American Indian Geographies of Identity and Power: At the Crossroads of Indigena and Mestizaje." *Harvard Educational Review* 70, no. 4 (Winter 2000): 467–98.

Gray, Edward G. *New World Babel: Languages and Nations in Early America*. Princeton, N.J.: Princeton University Press, 1999.

Greenblatt, Stephen. *Marvelous Possessions: The Wonder of the New World*. Chicago, Ill.: University of Chicago Press, 1991.

Greene, Jack P. *The Intellectual Construction of America: Exceptionalism and Identity from 1492 to 1800*. Chapel Hill: University of North Carolina Press, 1993.

Greene, John C. *American Science in the Age of Jefferson*. Ames: Iowa State Press, 1984.

———. "Early Scientific Interest in the American Indian: Comparative Linguistics." *Proceedings of the American Philosophical Society* 104, no. 5 (1960): 511–17.

Greer, Allan. *Property and Dispossession: Natives, Empires and Land in Early Modern North America*. New York: Cambridge University Press, 2017.

Greer, Margaret, Walter J. Mignolo, and Maureen Quilligan. Introduction to *Rereading the Black Legend*, edited by Margaret Greer, Walter J. Mignolo, and Maureen Quilligan, 1–26. Ithaca, N.Y.: Cornell University Press, 2007.

Gregory, Desmond. *Brute New World: Rediscovery of Latin America in the Early 19th Century* London: Bloomsbury, 1992.

Griffin, Patrick. "Reconsidering the Ideological Origins of Indian Removal: The Case of the Big Bottom 'Massacre.'" In *The Center of a Great Empire: The Ohio Country in the Early Republic*, edited by Andrew Clayton and Stuart D. Hobbs, 11–35. Athens: Ohio University Press, 2005.

Gruesz, Kirsten Silva. *Ambassadors of Culture: The Transamerican Origins of Latino Writing*. Princeton, N.J.: Princeton University Press, 2002.

Guidotti-Hernández, Nicole M. *Unspeakable Violence: Remapping U.S. and Mexican National Imaginaries*. Durham, N.C.: Duke University Press, 2011.

Gunn, Robert L. *Ethnology and Empire: Languages, Literatures, and the Making of the North American Borderlands*. New York: New York University Press, 2015.

Guardino, Pater F. *Peasants, Politics, and the Formation of Mexico's National State: Guerrero, 1800-1857*. Stanford, Calif.: Stanford University Press, 1996

Gutiérrez Cruz, Sergio Nicolás. "Granados y Gálvez, José Joaquín, *Tardes Americanas* [1778] [. . .]." *Relaciones* [Colmich, Zamora] 13, no. 51 (1992): 286–96.

Hahn, Steven C. "The Cussita Migration Legend: History, Ideology, and the Politics of Mythmaking." In *Light on the Path: The Anthropology and History of the Southeastern Indians*, edited by Thomas J. Pluckhahn and Robbie Ethridge, 57–93. Tuscaloosa: University of Alabama Press, 2006.

Hale, Charles A. *Mexican Liberalism in the Age of Mora, 1821–1853*. New Haven, Conn.: Yale University Press, 1968.

[Hale, Sarah Josepha.] *Genius of Oblivion; and Other Original Poems*. Concord, N.H: J. B. Moore, 1823.

Hall, Anthony J. *American Empire and the Fourth World: The Bowl with One Spoon*. Part 1. Montreal, Q.C.: McGill-Queen's University Press, 2003.

Hall, Matthew. *Plants as Persons: A Philosophical Botany*. Albany: State University of New York Press, 2011.

Hall, Robert L. "The Cahokia Site and Its People." In *Hero, Hawk, and Open Hand: American Indian Art of the Ancient Midwest and South*, edited by Richard F. Townsend, 93–104. New Haven, Conn.: Yale University Press, 2004.

Hajovsky, Patrick Thomas. *On the Lips of Others: Moteuczoma's Fame in Aztec Monuments and Rituals*. Austin: University of Texas, 2015.

Hakluyt, Richard. *Virginia richly valued, by the description of the maine land of Florida* [. . .]. London: Printed by Felix Kyngston for Matthew Lownes, 1609.

Hämäläinen, Pekka. *The Comanche Empire*. New Haven, Conn.: Yale University Press, 2008.

Hamann, Byron L. "Chronological Pollution: Potsherds, Mosques, and Broken Gods Before and After the Conquest of Mexico." *Current Anthropology* 49, no. 5 (2008): 803–36.

———. "The Social Life of Pre-Sunrise Things: Indigenous Mesoamerican Archaeology." *Current Anthropology* 43, no. 3 (2002): 351–82.

Hammes, Raymond H. "The Cantine Mounds of Southern Illinois: The First Published Report of Their Existence and an 1811 Eyewitness Account of the Monks Who Lived There." *Journal of the Illinois State Historical Society* 74, no. 2 (1981): 145–46.

Hamnett, Brian R. "Dye Production, Food Supply, and the Laboring Population of Oaxaca, 1750–1820." *Hispanic American Historical Review* 51, no. 1 (Feb 1971): 71–78.

Hanks, William F. *Converting Words: Maya in the Age of the Cross*. Berkeley: University of California Press, 2010.

Hardacre, Emma C. "The Cliff-Dwellers." *Scribner's Monthly* 12 (1878): 266–276.

Harjo, Joy. *A Map to the Next World: Poems and Tales*. New York: W. W. Norton & Company, 2000.

Harper, Rob. *Unsettling the West: Violence and State Building in the Ohio Valley*. Philadelphia: University of Pennsylvania Press, 2018.

Harris, Thaddeus Mason. *The Journal of a Tour into the Territory Northwest of the Alleghany Mountains, Made in the Spring of the Year 1803 with a Geographical and Historical Account of the State of Ohio*. Boston: Manning & Loring, 1805.

Harrison, Daniel F. "Change amid Continuity, Innovation within Tradition: Wampum Diplomacy at the Treaty of Greenville, 1795." *Ethnohistory* 64, no. 2 (April 2017): 191–215.

Harvey, Bruce A. *American Geographics: U.S. National Narratives and the Representation of the Non-European World, 1830–1865*. Stanford, Calif.: Stanford University Press, 2001.

Harvey, Sean P. *Native Tongues: Colonialism and Race from Encounter to the Reservation*. Cambridge, Mass.: Harvard, 2015.

Harvey, Sean P., and Sarah Rivett. "Colonial-Indigenous Language Encounters in North America and the Intellectual History of the Atlantic World." *Early American Studies, An Interdisciplinary Journal* 15, no. 3 (Summer 2017): 442–73.

Hauptman, Laurence M. *Conspiracy of Interests: Iroquois Dispossession and the Rise of New York State*. Syracuse: Syracuse University Press, 1999.

Haskins, Sarah. "The Shawnee and Delaware Indians in early Missouri, 1787–1832." Master's thesis, University of Missouri, Columbia, 2005.

Hatter, Lawrence. *Citizens of Convenience: The Imperial Origins of American Nationhood on the U.S.-Canadian Border*. Charlottesville: University of Virginia Press, 2016.

Hay, John. "A Poet of the Land: William Cullen Bryant and Moundbuilder Ecology." *ESQ* 61, no. 3 (2015): 475–511.

Heart, Jonathan. "A Letter from Major Jonathan Heart, to Benjamin Smith Barton, M.D. Containing observations on the Ancient Worlds of Art, the Native Inhabitants, &c. of the Western Country." *Transactions of the American Philosophical Society* 3 (1793): 214–22.

———. "Account of some Remains of Ancient Works, on the Muskingum, with a Plan of these Works. By J. Heart, Capt. in the first American regiment." *Columbian Magazine* 1 no. 9 (May 1787): 425–27.

———. "Plan of the Remains of some Ancient Works on the Muskingum." *Columbian Magazine* 1, no. 9 (May 1787): 424–25.

Heckewelder, John Gottlieb E. "An Account of Some Uncommonly Large Human Bones Found on the River Huron [...] Gnadenhutten, (Muskingum, Ohio) 3 Feb. 1810." In Fortiscue Cuming, *Sketches of a Tour to the Western Country*, edited by Zadoc Cramer, 453–55. Pittsburgh: Cramer, Spear & Eichbaum, 1810.

———. "An Account of the History, Manners, and Customs, of the Indian Nations, Who Once Inhabited Pennsylvania and the Neighboring States." *Transactions of the Historical & Literary Committee of the American Philosophical Society* 1 (1819): 351–450.

Hedge Coke, Allison Adelle. *Blood Run: Free Verse Play*. Cambridge, U.K.: Salt Press, 2006.

Henkin, David M. *The Postal Age: The Emergence of Modern Communications in Nineteenth-Century America*. Chicago, Ill.: University of Chicago Press, 2008.

Henning, Dale R. "The Adaptive Patterning of the Dhegiha Sioux." *Plains Anthropologist* 38, no. 146 (1993): 253–64.

Hereniko, Vilsoni. "Indigenous Knowledge and Academic Imperialism." In *Remembrance of Pacific Pasts: An Invitation to Remake History*, edited by Robert Borofsky, 78–91. Honolulu: University of Hawai'i Press, 2000.

Hernández, José Angel. "From Conquest to Colonization: Indios and Colonization Policies after Mexican Independence." *Mexican Studies/Estudios Mexicanos* 26, no. 2 (2010): 291–322.

Hessler, John. "The Codex Quetzalecatzin comes to the Library of Congress." *Worlds Revealed: Geography & Maps at the Library of Congress* (blog). November 21, 2017. https://blogs.loc.gov/maps/2017/11/the-codex-quetzelecatzin/.

Higgins, Antony. *Constructing the Criollo Archive: Subjects of Knowledge in the Bibliotheca Mexicana and the Rusticatio Mexicana*. West Lafayette, Ind.: Purdue University Press, 2000.

Hill, Leonard Uzal. *John Johnston and the Indians: In the Land of the Three Miamis*. Piqua, Oh.: Stoneman Press, 1957.

Hill, Ruth. "How Long Does Blood Last? Degeneration as Blanqueamiento in the Americas." In *The Eighteenth Century: Global Networks of Enlightenment*, edited by David T. Gies and Cynthia Wall, 72–94. Charlottesville: University of Virginia Press, 2018.

Hill, Susan M. *The Clay We Are Made Of: Haudenosaunee Land Tenure on the Grand River*. Winnipeg: University of Manitoba Press, 2018.

Hindraker, Eric. *Elusive Empires: Constructing Colonialism in the Ohio Valley, 1673–1800*. Cambridge, U.K.: Cambridge University Press, 1997.

Hinsley, Curtis M. "Digging for Identity: Reflections on the Cultural Background of Collecting." *American Indian Quarterly* 20, no. 2 (1996): 180–96.

———. "In Search of the New World Classical." In *Collecting the Pre-Columbian Past: A Symposium at Dumbarton Oaks, 6th and 7th October 1990*, edited by Elizabeth Hill Boone, 105–21. Washington D.C.: Dumbarton Oaks Research Library and Collection, 1993.

Hinsley, Curtis M., and David R. Wilcox. "Arizona's First Sacred Site: The Mystique of the Casa Grande, 1848–1889." *Bilingual Review/ La Revista Bilingüe* 25, no. 2 (2000): 129–45.

Hinton, Leanne. *Bringing Our Languages Home: Language Revitalization for Families*. Berkeley: University of California Press, 2013.

Hinton, Leanne, Matt Vera, and Nancy Steele. *How to Keep Your Language Alive*. Berkeley: University of California Press, 2002.

Hintzen, William. *The Border Wars of the Upper Ohio Valley, 1769–1794*. Manchester, Conn.: Precision Shooting, 1999.

History of Franklin and Pickaway Counties, Ohio, with Illustrations and Biographical Sketches of Some of the Prominent Men and Pioneers. [Cleveland, Oh.:] Williams Bros., 1880.

Hìtakonanu'laxk. *The Grandfathers Speak: Native American Folk Tales of the Lenape People*. New York: Interlink Books, 1994.

Hobson, Charles F. *The Great Yazoo Lands Sale: The Case of Fletcher v. Peck*. Lawrence: University of Kansas Press, 2016.

Hoechtl, Nina. "A Visual Glossary: Deliro Güero (White Delusion)." In *Sharpening the Haze: Visual Essays on Imperial History and Memory*, edited by Giulia Carabelli, Miloš Jovanović, Annika Kirbis, and Jeremy F. Walton, 159–76. London: Ubiquity Press, 2020.

Holmes, Abiel. *American Annals; or A Chronological History of America from its Discovery in MCCCXCII to MDCCCVI*. Cambridge, Mass.: W. Hilliard, 1805.
Höpfl, H. M. "From Savage to Scotsman: Conjectural History in the Scottish Enlightenment." *Journal of British Studies* 17, no. 2 (Spring 1978): 19–40.
Hopkins, Mark, and Leverett Wilson Spring. *A History of Williams College*. Boston: Houghton Mifflin, 1917.
Hopkins, Vivian C. "DeWitt Clinton and the Iroquois (Concluded)." *Ethnohistory* 8, no. 3 (Summer 1961): 213–41.
Hopkins, Vivian C. "DeWitt Clinton and the Iroquois." *Ethnohistory* 8, no. 2 (Spring 1961): 113–43.
Hoppit, Julian. "Political Arithmetic in Eighteenth-Century England." *Economic History Review* 49, no. 3 (1996): 516–40.
Horsman, Reginald. *Expansion and American Indian Policy, 1783–1812*. Norman: University of Oklahoma Press, 1992.
———. *Race and Manifest Destiny: The Origins of American Racial Anglo-Saxonism*. Cambridge, Mass.: Harvard University Press, 1986.
Howe, LeAnne. "Embodied Tribalography: Mound Building, Ball Games, and Native Endurance in the Southeast." *Studies in American Indian Literature* 26, no. 2 (June 2014): 75–93.
Howe, LeAnne, and Padraig Kirwan, eds. *Famine Pots: The Choctaw-Irish Gift Exchange, 1847–Present*. East Lansing: Michigan State University Press, 2020.
Howe, Nimachia. *Retelling Trickster in Naapi's Language*. Louisville: University Press of Colorado, 2019.
Howey, Meghan C. L. *Mound Builders and Monument Makers of the Northern Great Lakes, 1200–1600*. Norman: University of Oklahoma Press, 2012.
[Hulings, William, trans.] "An Historical and Chronological Description of Two Stones Found Underground, in the Great Square of the City of Mexico, in the years 1790" [1818]. Unpublished manuscript, Mss.913.72.L55, American Philosophical Society, Philadelphia.
Hulme, Peter. *Colonial Encounters: Europe and the Native Caribbean, 1492–1797*. New York: Routledge, 1992.
Humboldt, Alexander von. "Carte Generale Du Royaume De La Nouvelle Espagne [. . .]." In *Atlas geographique et physique du royaume de la nouvelle-espagne, fonde sur des observations astronomiques, des mesures trigonometriques et des nivellemens barometriques*. Paris: Chez F. Schoell, 1811.
———. *Essai politique sur le royaume de la Nouvelle Espagne: ouvrage qui présente des recherches sur la géographie du Mexique*. Paris: Chez F. Schoell, 1808.
———. *Political Essay on the Kingdom of New Spain*. Translated by John Black. London: Longman, Hurst, Rees, Orme & Brown, 1811.
———. *Researches, Concerning the Institutions & Monuments of the Ancient Inhabitants of America, with Descriptions & Views of Some of the Most Striking Scenes in the*

Cordilleras! Translated by Helen Maria Williams. London: Longman, Hurst, Rees, Orme & Brown, J. Murray & H. Colburn, 1814.

———. *Views of the Cordilleras and Monuments of the Indigenous Peoples of the Americas: A Critical Edition*. Edited by Vera M. Kutzinski and Ottmar Ette. Chicago, Ill.: University of Chicago Press, 2012.

———. *Vues des Cordillères, et monumens des peuples indigènes de l'Amérique*. Paris: F. Schoell, 1810.

Hunter, Douglas. *The Place of Stone: Dighton Rock and the Erasure of America's Indigenous Past*. Chapel Hill: University of North Carolina Press, 2017.

Hurt, R. Douglas. *The Ohio Frontier: Crucible of the Old Northwest, 1720–1830*. Indianapolis: Indiana University Press, 1996.

Hutton, James. *Theory of the Earth, with Proofs and Illustrations*. Edinburgh: Messrs. Cadell, Junior, and Davies, 1795.

Hutton, Paul A. "William Wells: Frontier Scout and Indian Agent." *Indiana Magazine of History* 74, no. 3 (September 1978): 183–222.

Iannini, Christopher P. *Fatal Revolutions: Natural History, West Indian Slavery, and the Routes of American Literature*. Chapel Hill: Published for the Omohundro Institute of Early American History and Culture, Williamsburg, Virginia, by the University of North Carolina Press, 2012.

Icaza, Isidro, and Isidro Gondra, *Colección de las antigüedades mexicanas que ecsisten en el Museo nacional, y dan a luz. Isidro Icaza é Isidro Gondra. Litografiadas por Federico Waldeck*. Mexico City: P. Robert, 1827.

Infante, Chad B. "The Magical and Paradigmatic Intimacy of Blackness and Indianness in *The Brief Wondrous Life of Oscar Wao*." In *The Palgrave Handbook of Magical Realism in the Twenty-First Century*, edited by Richard Perez and Victoria A. Chevalier, 397–418 New York: Palgrave Macmillan, 2020.

Inomata, T., Daniela Triadan, Verónica A. Vázquez López, Juan Carlos Fernandez-Diaz, Takayuki Omori, María Belén Méndez Bauer, Melina García Hernández, Timothy Beach, Clarissa Cagnato, Kazuo Aoyama, and Hiroo Nasu. "Monumental architecture at Aguada Fénix and the rise of Maya civilization." *Nature* 582 (2020): 530–33.

Ironstrack, George. "eehkwa mihtelowe peepamihkaweewaaci/Their Footprints Are Still Visible: Landscape, Stories, and Myaamia 'Miami Indian' Language and Culture Revitalization." Unpublished Myaamia Center Presentation, September 22, 2017. http://www.miamialum.org/s/916/blank2.aspx?sid=916&gid=1&pgid=5467.

———. "eewansaapita Kiihkayonki: Earth and Sky in Fort Wayne, Indiana." *aatotankiki myaamiaki*, Summer 2015. http://www.miamination.com/sites/default/files/pdfs/newspaper_archive/mto_summer_news_2015.pdf.

———. "A Myaamia Beginning." *Aacimotaatiiyankwi* (blog), August 13, 2010. http://www.aacimotaatiiyankwi.org/2010/08/13/a-myaamia-beginning/.

———. "waakihsenki miiwi pinkwaawilenionkiši. The Crooked Trail to Pickawillany (1747–1752)." *Aacimotaatiiyankwi* (blog), April 19, 2012. http://www.aacimotaatiiyankwi.org/2012/04/19/the-crooked-trail-to-pickawillany–1747–1752/.

———. "Walking a Myaamia Trail." *Aacimotaatiiyankwi* (blog), April 4, 2011. http://www.aacimotaatiiyankwi.org/2011/04/04/walking-a-myaamia-trail/.

———. "Walking Myaamionki." *Aacimotaatiiyankwi* (blog), December 16, 2010. http://www.aacimotaatiiyankwi.org/2010/12/16/walking-myaamionki/.

Israel, J. I. *Race, Class, and Politics in Colonial Mexico, 1610–1670*. Oxford, U.K.: Oxford University Press, 1975.

Ives, Ronald L. "Father Kino's 1697 Entrada to the Casa Grande Ruin in Arizona: A Reconstruction." *Arizona and the West* 15, no. 4 (Winter 1973): 345–70.

Jackson, Robert H. *Race, Caste, and Status: Indians in Colonial Spanish America*. Albuquerque: University of New Mexico Press, 1999.

Jaksic, Ivan. *The Hispanic World and American Intellectual Life, 1820–1880*. London: Palgrave Macmillan, 2012.

Jefferson, Thomas. *Notes on the State of Virginia*. London: J. Stockdale, 1787.

———. *The Papers of Thomas Jefferson, Retirement Series, Volume 1, 4 March 1809–15 November 1809.*, edited by J. Jefferson Looney. Princeton: Princeton University Press, 2004.

———. *The Papers of Thomas Jefferson, Retirement Series, Volume 6: 11 March to 27 November 1813*, edited by J. Jefferson Looney. Princeton: Princeton University Press, 2010.

———. *The Papers of Thomas Jefferson, Volume 7, 2 March 1784 – 25 February 1785*, edited by Julian P. Boyd. Princeton: Princeton University Press, 1953

———. *The Papers of Thomas Jefferson, Volume 9, 1 November 1785 – 22 June 1786*, edited by Julian P. Boyd. Princeton: Princeton University Press, 1954.

———. *The Papers of Thomas Jefferson, Volume 11, 1 January–6 August 1787.*, edited by Julian P. Boyd. Princeton: Princeton University Press, 1955.

———. *The Papers of Thomas Jefferson, Volume 12, 7 August 1787 – 31 March 1788*, edited by Julian P. Boyd. Princeton: Princeton University Press, 1955.

———. *The Papers of Thomas Jefferson, Volume 14, 8 October 1788 – 26 March 1789*, edited by Julian P. Boyd. Princeton: Princeton University Press, 1958.

———. *Writings*. Edited by Merrill D. Peterson. New York: Library of America, 1984.

Johannsen, Robert W. *To the Halls of the Montezumas: The Mexican War in the American Imagination*. New York: Oxford University Press, 1985.

Johnston Anna, and Alan Lawson. "Settler Colonies." In *A Companion to Postcolonial Studies*, edited by Henry Schwarz and Sangeeta Ray, 361–62. Oxford, U.K.: Blackwell, 2005.

Jones, Dorothy V. *License for Empire: Colonialism by Treaty in Early America*. Chicago: University of Chicago Press, 1982.

[Jones, David.] "A Plan of an old Fort and Intrenchment in the Shawanese Country, Taken on Horse Back, by Computation only. October 17, 1772." *Royal American Magazine* 2, no. 1 (January 1775): 29–32.

Jordan, Winthrop D. *White Over Black: American Attitudes Toward the Negro, 1550–1812*. New York: Penguin Books, 1969.

Joseph, Gilbert M. "The United States, Feuding Elites, and Rural Revolt in Yucatan, 1836–1915." In *Rural Revolt in Mexico*, edited by Daniel Nugent, 173–206. Durham: Duke University Press, 1998.

Journals of the Continental Congress, January 11, 1785 to June 30, 1785. Vol. 28. Washington, D.C.: Government Printing Office, 1933.

Joyce, William C. "Antiquarians and Archaeologists: The American Antiquarian Society, 1812–1912." *Proceedings of the American Antiquarian Society* 91 (October 1981): 301–17.

Juarez, Ana M. "Ongoing Struggles: Mayas and Immigrants in Tourist Era Tulúm." *Journal of Latin American Anthropology* 7, no. 1 (2002): 34–67.

Juarros, Domingo. *Compendio de la historia de la ciudad de Guatemala*. Guatemala City: I. Beteta, 1810.

Jung, Patrick J. *The Black Hawk War of 1832*. Norman: University of Oklahoma Press, 2007.

Justeson, John and Terrence Kaufman. "A Decipherment of Epi-Olmec Hieroglyphic Writing." *Science* 259 (1993): 1703–11.

Kalttunen, Karen. "Grounded Histories," *William and Mary Quarterly* 68, no. 4 (October 2011): 513–31.

Kamrani, Kambiz. "Maya 'Megalopolis' Found After LiDAR Scanning the Guatemalan Jungle." Anthropology.net, February 2, 2018. https://www.anthropology.net/2018/02/02/maya-megalopolis-found-after-lidar-scanning-the-guatemalan-jungle/.

Karttunen, Frances E. *Between Worlds: Interpreters, Guides, and Survivors*. New Brunswick, N.J.: Rutgers University Press, 1994.

Karttunen, Frances E. *An Analytical Dictionary of Nahuatl*. Austin: University of Texas Press, 1983.

Kauanui, J. Kēhaulani. "A Structure, Not an Event": Settler Colonialism and Enduring Indigeneity." *Lateral: Journal of the Cultural Studies Association* 5, no. 1 (Spring 2016) http://www.csalateral.org/issue/5-1/forum-alt-humanities-settler-colonialism-enduring-indigeneity-kauanui/.

Kazanjian, David. *The Colonizing Trick: National Culture and Imperial Citizenship in Early America*. Minneapolis: University of Minnesota Press, 2003.

Keen, Benjamin. *The Aztec Image in Western Thought*. New Brunswick, N.J.: Rutgers University Press, 1971.

Kehoe, Alice Beck, "Manifest Destiny as the Order of Nature" in *Nature and Antiquities: The Making of Archaeology in the Americas*, edited by Philip L. Kohl,

Irina Podgorny, and Stefanie Gänger, 186–201. Tucson: University of Arizona Press, 2014.

Kelly, David. "Archaeologists explore a rural field in Kansas, and a lost city emerges." *Los Angeles Times*, August 19, 2018. http://www.latimes.com/nation/la-na-kansas-lost-city-20180819-htmlstory.html.

Kelly, Edith Louise, and Mattie Austin Hatcher, eds. "Tadeo Ortiz de Ayala and the Colonization of Texas, 1822–1833." *Southwestern Historical Quarterly* 32 (July 1928): 74–86.

Kelly, Edith Louise, and Mattie Austin Hatcher, eds. "Tadeo Ortiz de Ayala and the Colonization of Texas, 1822–1833." *Southwestern Historical Quarterly* 32 (April 1929): 311–43.

Kelly, John E. "Redefining Cahokia: Principles and Elements of Community Organization." *Wisconsin Archeologist* 77 (1996): 97, 106–14.

Kennedy, Brenden. "'Not Worth a Pinch of Snuff': The 1789 Yazoo Land Sale and Sovereignty in the Old Southwest." *Georgia Historical Quarterly* 101, no. 3 (September 2017): 198–232.

Kennedy, Roger G. *Hidden Cities: The Discovery and Loss of Ancient North American Cities*. New York: Free Press, 1994.

Kennedy, Roger. "Jefferson and the Indians." *Winterthur Portfolio* 27, nos. 2–3 (1992): 105–21.

Kent, Matthew. "Site preparations begin at Guernsey Crossing." *Chillicothe Gazette*, January 5, 2015.

Kertész, Judy. "History, Memory, and the Appropriation of the American Indian Past: A Family Affair," *Dublin Seminar for New England Folklife Annual Proceedings* (2004): 199–207.

Kilbourn, John. *The Ohio Gazetteer, or Topographical Dictionary* [. . .]. 2nd ed. Columbus: J. Kilbourn, 1816.

Kilbourn, John. *The Ohio Gazetteer, or Topographical Dictionary* [. . .]. 3rd ed. Columbus: J. Kilbourn, 1817.

Kilbourn, John. *The Ohio Gazetteer, or Topographical Dictionary* [. . .]. 6th ed. Columbus: J. Kilbourn, 1819.

Kilbourn, John. *The Ohio Gazetteer, or Topographical Dictionary* [. . .]. 7th ed. Columbus: J. Kilbourn, 1821.

Kimmerer, Robin Wall. *Braiding Sweetgrass: Indigenous Wisdom, Scientific Knowledge, and the Teachings of Plants*. Minneapolis, Minn.: Milkweed Editions, 2013.

Kincheloe, John W. "Yours Very Respectfully, E.G. Squier." *Ohio Archaeologist* 48 (November 1998): 4–12.

King, Adam. "The Historic Period Transformation of Mississippian Societies." In *Light on the Path: The Anthropology and History of the Southeastern Indians*, edited by Thomas J. Pluckhahn and Robbie Ethridge, 179–95. Tuscaloosa: University of Alabama Press, 2006.

King, Lisa Michelle. *Legible Sovereignties: Rhetoric, Representations, and Native American Museums*. Corvallis: Oregon State University Press, 2017.
King, Tiffany Lethabo, Jenell Navarro, and Andrea Smith. *Otherwise Worlds: Against Settler Colonialism and Anti-Blackness*. Durham, N.C.: Duke University Press, 2020.
King, Thomas. "How I Spent My Summer Vacation: History, Literature, and the Cant of Authenticity." In *Landmarks: A Process Reader*, edited by Roberta Birks, Tomi Eng, Julie Walchli, 248-54. Scarborough, Or.: Prentice Hall and Bacon, 1998.
———. *The Inconvenient Indian: A Curious Account of Native People in North America*. Minneapolis: University of Minnesota Press, 2012.
Kingsborough, Edward King, Viscount. *Antiquities of Mexico* [...]. London: Robert Havell and Conaghi, 1831–1848.
Kino, Eusebius Francisco. "A Passage by Land to California Discover'd by ye. Rev. Fathr. Eusebius Francis Kino, Jesuite between ye Years 1698 & 1701. Based on Father Kino's map." *Philosophical Transactions* 2, no. 5 (1700–1720): 192.
Kino, Father Eusebius Francisco. *Kino's Historical Memoir of Pimería Alta: A Contemporary Account of the Beginnings of California, Sonora, and Arizona, 1683–1711*, edited by Herbert Eugene Bolton. Berkeley: University of California, 1919.
Kirchhoff, Paul. "Se Puede Localizar Aztlán?" *Anuario de Historia* (1961): 59–67.
Kirkland, Samuel. *The Journals of Samuel Kirkland: 18th Century Missionary to the Iroquois, Government Agent, Father of Hamilton College*, edited by Walter Pilkington. Clinton, N.Y.: Hamilton College, 1980.
Klein, Cecelia. "A New Interpretation of the Aztec Statue Called Coatlicue." *Ethnohistory* 55, no. 2 (2008): 229–50.
Klesert, Anthony L., and Shirley Powell. "A Perspective on Ethics and the Reburial Controversy." In *Repatriation Reader: Who Owns American Indian Remains?* edited by Devon Abbot Mihesuah, 200–210. Lincoln: University of Nebraska Press, 2000.
Knight, Vernon James, Jr., "Symbolism of Mississippian Mounds." In *Powhatan's Mantle: Indians in the Colonial Southeast*, edited by Gregory A. Waselkov, Peter H. Wood, and M. Thomas Hatley, 421–34. Lincoln: University of Nebraska Press, 2006.
Koch, Peter O. *John Lloyd Stephens and Frederick Catherwood: Pioneers of Archaeology* Jefferson, N.C.: McFarland, 2013.
Kolodny, Annette. "Competing Narratives of Ancestry in Donald Trump's America and the Imperatives for Scholarly Intervention." In *Decolonizing 'Prehistory': Deep Time and Indigenous Knowledges in North America*, edited by Gesa Mackenthun and Christen Mucher, 23–40. Tucson: University of Arizona Press, 2021.
———. "Fictions of American Prehistory: Indians, Archeology, and National Origin Myths." *American Literature* 75, no. 4 (December 2003): 693–721.
———. *In Search of First Contact: The Vikings of Vinland, the Peoples of the Dawnland, and the Anglo-American Anxiety of Discovery*. Durham, N.C.: Duke University Press, 2012.

Kovach, Margaret. *Indigenous Methodologies: Characteristics, Conversations, and Contexts.* Toronto: University of Toronto Press, 2009.

Kranz, Travis Barton. *The Tlaxcalan Conquest Pictorials: The Role of Images in Influencing Colonial Policy in Sixteenth-Century Mexico.* Los Angeles: University of California Press, 2001.

Kruell, Gabriel Kenrick. "Algunas precisiones terminológicas sobre el calendario náhuatl." *Estudios de Cultura Náhuatl* 54 (July–Dec 2017): 135–64.

LaFleur, Greta. *The Natural History of Sexuality in Early America.* New Haven, C.T.: Yale University Press, 2018.

Lafuente, Antonio and Nuria Valverde. "Linnaean Botany and Spanish Imperial Biopolitics." In *Colonial Botany: Science, Commerce, and Politics in the Early Modern World*, edited by Londa Schiebinger and Claudia Swan, 134–47. Philadelphia: University of Pennsylvania Press, 2005.

Laisné de Villevêque, Gabriel-Jacques, Jean François Giordan, H. Baradère, and J. Tastu. *Colonie du Guazacoalco.* Paris: Imprimerie de J. Tastu, 1829.

Lakomäki, Sami. *Gathering Together: The Shawnee People through Diaspora and Nationhood, 1600–1870.* New Haven, Conn.: Yale University Press, 2014.

Lamar, Curt. "Genesis of Mexican-United States Diplomacy: A Critical Analysis of the Alaman-Poinsett Confrontation, 1825." *Americas* 38, no. 1 (1981): 87–110.

Lamar, Quinton Curtis. "The Role of Lucas Alamán in Mexican-United States Relations, 1824–1853." PhD diss., Louisiana State University, 1971.

LaVaque-Manty, Danielle. "There are Indians in the Museum of Natural History." *Wicazo-Sa Review* 15, no. 1 (2000): 71–89.

Layton, Brandon. "Indian Country to Slave Country: The Transformation of Natchez During the American Revolution." *Journal of Southern History* 82 (February 2016): 27–48.

Lazo, Rodrigo. *Letters from Filadelfia: Early Latino Literature and the Trans-American Elite.* Charlottesville: University of Virginia Press, 2020.

Leask, Nigel. *Curiosity and the Aesthetics of Travel Writing, 1770–1840: From an Antique Land.* Oxford: Oxford University Press, 2002.

Le Brun-Ricalens, Foni, Leonardo López Luján, Marie-France Fauvet-Berthelot, and Elodie Richard. "Guillaume Joseph Dupaix (1746–1818) alias Guillermo Dupaix: un Luxembourgeois méconnu aux origines de l'archéologie précolombienne et mexicaine." *Archaeologia luxemburgensis* 1 (2014): 130–51.

Lee, Jacob F. *Masters of the Middle Waters: Indian Nations and Colonial Ambitions along the Mississippi.* Cambridge, Mass.: Belknap Press, 2019.

Lee, Jongsoo. "The Aztec Triple Alliance: A Colonial Transformation of the Prehispanic Political and Tributary System." In *Texcoco: Prehispanic and Colonial Perspectives,* edited by Jongsoo Lee and Galen Brokaw. 63–91. Louisville: University Press of Colorado, 2014.

Leibsohn, Dana. *Script and Glyph: Pre-Hispanic History, Colonial Bookmaking and the Historia Tolteca-Chichimeca.* Washington, D.C.: Dumbarton Oaks Research Library and Collection, 2009.

León Cazares, María del Carmen. "La presencia del demonio en las Constituciones Diocesanas de fray Francisco Núñez de la Vega." *Inicio* 13, no. 13 (1993): 41–71.
León-Portilla, Miguel. *Los antiguos mexicanos a través de sus crónicas y cantares* [1961]. Mexico City: Fondo de Cultura Económica, 2005.
León-Portilla, Miguel. "Los Aztecas. Disquisiciones Sobre un Gentilicio." *Estudios de Cultura Náhuatl* 31 (2000): 275–81.
León-Portilla, Miguel, ed. *Cantares Mexicanos,* vol. 1. Mexico City: Universidad Nacional Autónoma de México, 2011.
León y Gama, Antonio de. *Descripción histórica y cronológica de las dos piedras que con ocasión del nuevo empedrado que se esta formando en la plaza principal de México, se hallaron en ella el año de 1790. Explícase el sistema de los calendarios de los Indios ... Noticia ... á que se añaden otras curiosas [...] sobre la mitología de los Mexicanos, sobre su astronomia, y sobre los ritos y ceremonias [...] en tiempo de su gentilidad.* Mexico City: Zúñiga y Ontiveros, 1792.
[León y Gama.] "Se héa concluido un Quaderno." *Gaceta de México* 4, no. 40 (August 16, 1791): 380.
Le Page du Pratz, Antoine-Simon. *Histoire de la Louisiane, Contenant la Decouverte de ce vaste pays.* Paris: Bure, Delaguette, and Lambert, 1758.
Lepper, Bradley. "Archaeology Blog: Archaeology staff assists with Salvaging History." *Ohio History Connection*, January 31, 2015.
———. "Earthworks History Remains Muddled." *Columbus Dispatch*, June 6, 2011.
Levin Rojo, Danna. *Return to Aztlán: Indians, Spaniards, and the Invention of Nuevo México.* Norman: University of Oklahoma Press, 2014.
Lewis, Andrew J. *A Democracy of Facts: Natural History in the Early Republic.* Philadelphia, University of Pennsylvania Press, 2011.
Linnæi [Linnaeus], Caroli. *Systema naturae per regna tria naturae, secundum classes, ordines, genera, species, cum charateribus, differentiis, synonymis, locis [...].* 10th ed. Holmiae: Impensis L. Salvii, 1758–49.
Lipsitz, George. *The Possessive Investment in Whiteness: How White People Profit from Identity Politics.* Rev. ed. Philadelphia: Temple University, 2006.
Llombart, Vicent. *Campomanes, economist y politico de Carlos III.* Madrid: Alianza Editorial, 1992.
Little Bear, LeRoy. *Naturalizing Indigenous Knowledge: Synthesis Paper.* Saskatoon, Sask.: Canadian Council on Learning. Aboriginal Learning Knowledge Centre, 2009.
———. "Rethinking Our Sciences: Blackfoot Metaphysics Waiting in the Wings." *IEI Online Seminar*, May 28, 2020.
Lockhart, James. "Encomienda and Hacienda: The Evolution of the Great Estate in the Spanish Indies." *Hispanic American Historical Review* 49, no. 3 (August 1969): 411–29.
———. *The Nahuas After the Conquest: A Social and Cultural History of the Indians of Central Mexico, Sixteenth Through Eighteenth Centuries.* Stanford, Calif.: Stanford University Press, 1992.

Lockhart, James, Susan Schroeder, and Doris Namala, eds. and trans. *Annals of His Time: Don Domingo de San Antón Muñón Chimalpahin Quauhtlehuanitzin*. Stanford, Calif.: Stanford University Press, 2006.
Loewe, Ronald. *Maya or Mestizo? Nationalism, Modernity, and its Discontents*. Toronto, Ont.: University of Toronto Press, 2010.
Lombardo de Ruiz, Sonia, and Ruth Solís Vicarte, eds. *Antecedentes de las leyes sobre Monumentos Históricos (1536–1910)*. Mexico City: INAH, 1988.
Lomnitz, Claudio. *Deep Mexico, Silent Mexico: An Anthropology of Nationalism*. Minneapolis: University of Minnesota Press, 2001.
Lonetree, Amy. *Decolonizing Museums: Representing Native America in National and Tribal Museums*. Chapel Hill: University of North Carolina Press, 2012.
Looby, Christopher. "The Concentration of Nature: Taxonomy as Politics in Jefferson, Peale, and Bartram." *Early American Literature* 22, no. 3 (1987): 252–73.
López Austin, Alfredo, and Leonardo López Luján. *Mexico's Indigenous Past*. Norman: University of Oklahoma Press, 2001.
López Luján, Leonardo. *Descripción de Monumentos antiguos Mexicanos o Álbum Arqueológico de 1794*. Mexico City: Instituto Nacional de Antropología e Historia, 2015.
———. "'El adiós y triste queja del Gran Calendario Azteca': el incesante peregrinar de la Piedra del Sol." *Arqueología Mexicana* 16, no. 91 (2008): 78–83.
———. "El capitán Guillermo Dupais y su Álbum Arqueologico de 1794." *Arqueologia Mexicana* 19, no. 109 (2011): 71–81.
———. "El ídolo sin pies ni cabeza: la Coatlicue a fines del siglo XVIII." *Estudios de Cultura Náhuatl* 42 (August 2011): 203–32.
———. "El Tajín en el siglo XVIII. Dos Exploraciones Pioneras en Veracruz." *Arqueología Mexicana* 89 (January–February 2008): 74–81.
Lorenzana y Buitrón, Francisco Antonio, ed. *Historia de Nueva-España. Escrita por su Esclarecido Conquistador Hernán Cortés. Aumentada con otros documentos, y notas* [...]. Mexico City: Hogal, 1770.
Lovell, George W. "The Maya of Guatemala in Historical Perspective." *Latin American Research Review* 23, no. 2 (1988): 25–47.
Luján Muñoz, Luis, ed. *La Cultura maya: antología de textos clásicos*. Mexico City: Publicaciones Cruz O., S.A., 1990.
Lucius [Melancton Smith]. "A Few Observations on the Western and Southern Indians." *Connecticut Courant, and Weekly Intelligencer* (December 8, 1788), 1.
Lynch, John. *The Spanish American Revolutions, 1808–1826*. New York: W. W. Norton & Company, 1973.
Lyons, Scott Richard. *X-Marks: Native Signatures of Assent*. Minneapolis: University of Minnesota Press, 2010.
MacDonald, Mary. "Whose Earthworks? Newark and Indigenous Peoples." In *Newark Earthworks: Enduring Monuments, Contested Meanings*, edited by Lindsay Jones and Richard D. Shiels, 230–41. Charlottesville: University of Virginia Press, 2016.

Mackenthun, Gesa, and Christen Mucher. Introduction to *Decolonizing "Prehistory": Deep Time and Indigenous Knowledges in North America*, edited by Gesa Mackenthun and Christen Mucher, 3–22. Tucson: University of Arizona Press, 2021.

MacLachlan, Colin M., and Rodríguez O., Jaime E. *The Forging of the Cosmic Race: A Reinterpretation of Colonial Mexico*. Berkeley: University of California Press, 1980.

Madison, Bishop James. "A Letter on the Supposed Fortifications of the Western Country, from Bishop Madison of Virginia to Dr. Barton." *Transactions of the American Philosophical Society* 6 (1809): 132–42.

Madison, James. *The Papers of James Madison*. Vol. 8: *10 March 1784 – 28 March 1786*, edited by Robert A. Rutland and William M. E. Rachal. Chicago, Ill.: University of Chicago Press, 1973.

Maffie, James. *Aztec Philosophy: Understanding a World in Motion*. Boulder: University Press of Colorado, 2014.

Magaloni Kerpel, Diana. *The Colors of the New World: Artists, Materials, and the Creation of the Florentine Codex*. Los Angeles: Getty Research Institute, 2014.

———. "The Traces of the Creative Process: Pictorial Materials and Techniques in the Beineke Map." In *Painting a Map of Sixteenth-Century Mexico City: Land, Writing, and Native Rule*, edited in Mary Miller and Barbara Mundy, 74–91. New Haven: Yale University Press, 2012.

Maison, Hyppolite. *Précis historique sur la colonie française au Goazacoalcos (mexique): avec la réfutation des prospectus publiés par MM. Laisné de Villeveque, Giordan et Baradère: suivi de plusieurs lettres autographes de MM. Laisné et Giordan, et d'une épitre en vers a M. Laisné de Villeveque*. London: Davidson et fils, 1831.

Mallouf, Robert J. "An Unraveling Rope: The Looting of America's Past." In *Repatriation Reader: Who Owns American Indian Remains?* edited by Devon Abbot Mihesuah, 59–73. Lincoln: University of Nebraska Press, 2000.

Mamdani, Mahmood. "Settler Colonialism: Then and Now." *Critical Inquiry* 41, no. 3 (Spring 2015): 596–614.

Mange, el Capitán Juan Matheo. *Luz de Tierra incógnita en la América Septentrional: y diario de las exploraciones en Sonora*. Edited by Francisco Fernández del Castillo. Mexico City: Talleres graficos de la Nacion, 1926.

Mann, Barbara Alice. "The Greenville Treaty of 1795: Pen-and-Ink Witchcraft in the Struggle for the Old Northwest." In *Enduring Legacies: Native American Treaties and Contemporary Controversies*, edited Bruce E. Johansen, 135–202. Westport, Conn.: Praeger, 2004.

———. *Native Americans, Archaeologists, and the Mounds*. New York: Peter Lang, 2003.

———. "Ohio Valley Mound Culture." *Encyclopedia of American Indian History*. Vol. 2, edited by Bruce E. Johansen and Barry M. Pritzker, 444–48. Santa Barbara, Calif.: ABC-Clio, 2008.

Marcocci, Giuseppe. "Inventing the Antiquities of New Spain" Motolinía and the Mexican Antiquarian Tradition." In *Antiquarianism: Contact, Conflict,*

Comparison. *Joukowsky Institute for Archaeology 8*, edited by Benjamin Anderson and Felipe Rojas, 109–133. Oxford, U.K.: Oxbow Books, 2017.
Marcus, Joyce. *Mesoamerican Writing Systems: Propaganda, Myth, and History in Four Ancient Civilizations*. Princeton, N.J.: Princeton University Press, 1992.
Marsh, Dawn G. *A Lenape Among Quakers: The Life of Hannah Freeman*. Philadelphia: University of Pennsylvania Press, 2014.
Martínez, María Elena. *Genealogical Fictions: Limpieza de Sangre, Religion, and Gender in Colonial Mexico*. Stanford, Calif.: Stanford University Press, 2008.
Martínez Baracs, Andrea. U*n gobierno de indios: Tlaxcala, 1519–1750*. México, Fondo de Cultura Económica: 2009.
Martínez-San Miguel, Yolanda, and Santa Arias, eds. *The Routledge Hispanic Studies Companion to Colonial Latin America and the Caribbean (1492–1898)*. London: Routledge, 2020.
Martinko, Whitney. *Historic Real Estate: Market Morality and the Politics of Preservation in the Early United States*. Philadelphia: University of Pennsylvania Press, 2020.
———. "'So Majestic a Monument of Antiquity': Landscape, Knowledge, and Authority in the Early Republican West." *Buildings and Landscapes* 16, no. 1 (Spring 2009): 29–61.
Marx, Karl. *Capital: Volume 1: A Critique of Political Economy*. New York: Penguin Books, 1992.
Matos Moctezuma, Eduardo. *Teotihuacan: The City of the Gods*. New York: Rizzoli, 1990.
———. *Tríptico del pasado: discurso de ingreso*. Mexico City: Colegio Nacional, 1993.
Matos Moctezuma, Eduardo, and Leonardo López Luján. *Escultura Monumental Mexico*. Mexico City: Fundación Conmemoraciones, 2009.
Matthew, Laura E. *Memories of Conquest: Becoming Mexicano in Colonial Guatemala*. Chapel Hill: University of North Carolina, 2012.
Mayor, Adrienne. *Fossil Legends of the First Americans*. Princeton, N.J.: Princeton University Press, 2007.
Mays, Kyle T. "Blackness and Indigeneity." In *400 Souls: A Community History of African America, 1619–2019*, edited by Keisha Blain and Ibram Kendi, 123–25. New York: Random House, 2021.
Maza, Francisco de la. *Código de colonización y terrenos baldíos de la República Mexicana, años de 1451 a 1892*. Mexico City: Secretaría de Fomento, 1893.
McAdams, Gary. "Etzanoa, The Great Settlement." *Wichita Tribal News*, July 2015, 11.
McAnny, Patricia. *Living With the Ancestors: Kinship and Kingship in Ancient Maya Society*. Austin, University of Texas Press, 1995.
McAtee, Waldo. "Journals and Note-books of Benjamin Smith Barton, 1785–1806." B284.2, Unpublished Manuscript in Benjamin Smith Barton journals; notebooks, 1785–1806, Mss B B284.1. American Philosophical Society, Philadelphia, Pa.
McClure, David. *Diary of David McClure, Doctor of Divinity, 1748–1820*. New York: Knickerbocker Press, 1899.

McConnell, Michael N. *A Country Between: The Upper Ohio Valley and Its Peoples, 1724–1774*. Lincoln: University of Nebraska Press, 1992.

McCoy, Tim, George Ironstrack, Daryl Baldwin, Andrew J. Strack, and Wayne Olm, *ašiihkiwi neehi kiišikwi myaamionki: Earth and Sky, the Place of the Myaamiaki*. Miami, O.K.: Miami Tribe of Oklahoma, 2011.

McCulloh, J. H. *Researches, Philosophical and Antiquarian, Concerning the Aboriginal History of America*. Baltimore: Fielding Lucas, Jr., 1829.

McDonough, Kelly S. *The Learned Ones: Nahua Intellectuals in Postconquest Mexico*. Tucson: University of Arizona Press, 2014.

McEnroe, Sean F. *From Colony to Nationhood in Mexico: Laying the Foundations, 1560–1840*. New York: Cambridge University Press, 2012.

McFarlane, Anthony. "Science and Sedition in Spanish America: New Granada in the epoch of the Atlantic revolutions, 1776–1810." *Boletin de Historia y Antiguedades* 96, no. 844 (2009): 83–104.

McGuire, Randall H. "Archeology and the First Americans." *American Anthropologist*, New Series 94, no. 4 (1992): 816–36.

McKinnon, Duncan. *The Battle Mound Landscape: Exploring Space, Place, and History of a Red River Caddo Community in Southwest Arkansas*. Fayetteville: Arkansas Archaeological Survey, 2017.

McMillan, R Bruce. "Migration legends and the Origins of Missouri's Siouan-speaking Tribes." *Missouri Archaeologist* 75 (2014): 5–47.

McNeil, Kent. *Common Law Aboriginal Title*. Oxford, U.K.: Clarendon Press, 1989.

McPharson, Robert S. *Viewing the Ancestors: Perceptions of the Anaasází, Mokwic, and Hisatsinom*. Norman: University of Oklahoma Press, 2014.

Megged, Amos. *Social Memory in Ancient and Colonial Mesoamerica*. New York: Cambridge University Press, 2010.

Meltzer, David J. Introduction to *Ancient Monuments of the Mississippi Valley*, edited by David J. Meltzer, 1–95. Washington D.C.: Smithsonian Institution, 1998.

Memoria Economica de la Municipalidad de Mexico, Formada de Porden del Exmo. Ayuntamiento [. . .]. Mexico City: Martin Rivera, 1830.

Menegus Bornemann, Margarita. "Cacicazgos y repúblicas de indios en el siglo XVI. La transformación de la propiedad en la Mixteca." In *Configuraciones territoriales en la Mixteca*. Vol 1: *Estudios de historia y antropología*, edited by Manuel Herman Lejarazu, 205–20. Mexico City: CIESAS, 2016.

———. *La Mixteca Baja entre la Revolución y la Reforma. Cacicazgo, territorialidad y gobierno, siglos XVIII-XIX*. Oaxaca: Universidad Autónoma Benito Juárez, 2009.

Meyers, Amy R. W. and Margaret Beck Pritchard, eds. *Empire's Nature: Mark Catesby's New World Vision*. Chapel Hill: University of North Carolina Press, 1998.

Midtrød, Tom Arne. "'Calling for More Than Human Vengeance': Desecrating Native Graves in Early America." *Early American Studies: An Interdisciplinary Journal* 17, no. 3 (2019): 281–314.

Mignolo, Walter D. *The Darker Side of Western Modernity: Global Futures, Decolonial Options*. Durham, N.C.: Duke University Press, 2011.

———. "Introduction: Coloniality of Power and De-Colonial Thinking." *Cultural Studies* 21, nos. 2–3 (2007): 155–67.

———. "Signs and Their Transmission: The Question of the Book in the New World." In *Writing Without Words: Alternative Literacies in Mesoamerica and the Andes*, edited by Mignolo Walter D. and Boone Elizabeth Hill, 220–70. Durham, N.C: Duke University Press, 1994.

Mihesuah, Devon A. "American Indians, Anthropologists, Pothunters, and Repatriation: Ethical, Religious, and Political Differences." In *Repatriation Reader: Who Owns American Indian Remains?* edited by Devon Abbot Mihesuah, 95–105. Lincoln: University of Nebraska Press, 2000.

Mihesuah, Devon A., ed. *Repatriation Reader: Who Owns American Indian Remains?* Lincoln: University of Nebraska Press, 2000.

Miller, Angela. "'The Soil of an Unknown America': New World Lost Empires and the Debate over Cultural Origins." *American Art* 8, nos. 3–4 (1994): 9–27.

Miller, Peter N. "Writing Antiquarianism: Prolegomenon to a History." In *Antiquarianism and Intellectual Life in Europe and China, 1500–1800*, edited by Peter N. Miller and François Louis, 27–47. Ann Arbor: University of Michigan Press, 2012.

Miller, Robert J. "Treaties Between the Eastern Shawnee Tribe and the United States: Contracts Between Sovereign Governments." In *The Eastern Shawnee Tribe of Oklahoma: Resilience Through Adversity*, edited by Stephen Warren, 107–48. Norman: University of Oklahoma Press, 2017.

Miller, Susan A., and James Riding-In, eds. *Native Historians Write Back: Decolonizing American Indian History*. Lubbock: Texas Tech University Press, 2011.

Miner, Dylan A. T. *Creating Aztlán: Chicano Art, Indigenous Sovereignty, and Lowriding Across Turtle Island*. Tucson: University of Arizona Press, 2014.

Mintz, Max. *Seeds of Empire: The American Revolutionary Conquest of the Iroquois*. New York: New York University Press, 1999.

Mitchell, Samuel L. "Communications from Dr. Samuel L. Mitchell, L.L. D. &c." *Archaeologia Americana: Transactions and Collections of the American Antiquarian Society* 1 (1820): 313–55.

Moffitt, John, and Santiago Sebastián. *O Brave New People: The European Invention of the American Indian*. Albuquerque: University of New Mexico Press, 1996.

Mojica, Monique. "In Plain Site: Inscripted Earth and Invisible Realities." In *New Canadian Realisms: New Essays on Canadian Theatre*. Vol. 2, edited by Roberta Barker and Kim Solga, 218–42. Toronto, On.: Playwrights Canada Press, 2012.

Monaghan, John D. *The Covenants with Earth and Rain: Exchange, Sacrifice, and Revelation in Mixtec Society*. Norman: University of Oklahoma Press, 1995.

Mongey, Vanessa. *Rogue Revolutionaries: The Fight for Legitimacy in the Greater Caribbean*. Philadelphia: University of Pennsylvania Press, 2020.

Monastersky, Richard "The greatest vanishing act in prehistoric America: Seven centuries ago, tens of thousands of people fled their homes in the American Southwest: Archaeologists are trying to work out why." *Nature.* 527 (7576): 26–29.

Moorhead, Max. *The Apache Frontier: Jacob Ugarte and Spanish-Indian Relations in Northern New Spain, 1769–1791.* Norman: University of Oklahoma Press, 1968.

———. "Spanish Deportation of Hostile Apaches: The Policy and the Practice." *Arizona and the West* 17, no. 3 (Autumn 1975): 205–20.

Morgensen, Scott Lauria. "The Biopolitics of Settler Colonialism: Right Here, Right Now." *Settler Colonial Studies* 1, no. 1 (2011): 52–76.

More, Anna. *Baroque Sovereignty: Carlos de Siguenza y Gongora and the Creole Archive of Colonial Mexico.* Philadelphia: University of Pennsylvania Press, 2013.

Moreno, Evelyn. "Northwest Portage Walking Museum: Connecting Visitors to Illinois' Natural and Cultural History," NPS.gov, November 22, 2019. http://www.nps.gov/articles/northwest-portage-walking-museum-connecting-visitors-to-illinois-natural-and-cultural-history.htm.

Moreno, Roberto. *Un ecclesiastico criollo frente al estado Borbón.* Mexico City: Universidad Nacional Autónoma de México, 1980.

Morris, Amy. "Geomythology on the Colonial Frontier: Edward Taylor, Cotton Mather, and the Claverack Giant." *William and Mary Quarterly* 70, no. 4 (2013): 701–24.

Morris, Mabel. "Jefferson and the Language of the American Indian." *Modern Language Quarterly* 6, no. 1 (1945): 31–34.

Morrow, Lynn. "New Madrid and its Hinterland: 1783–1826." *Bulletin of the Missouri Historical Society* 36, no. 4 (1980): 241–50.

———. "Trader William Gilliss and Delaware Migration in Southern Missouri." In *The Ozarks in Missouri History: Discoveries in an American Region*, edited by Lynn Morrow, 19–36. Columbia: University of Missouri Press, 2013.

Morse, Jedidiah. *The American geography; or, A view of the present situation of the United States of America:* [. . .]. Elizabethtown, N.J.: Printed by Shepard Kollock for the author [1789].

Morton, Samuel G. *Crania Americana; Or a Comparative View of the Skulls of Various Aboriginal Nations of North and South America; To Which Is Prefixed an Essay on the Varities of the Human Species. Illustrated with Seventy-Eight Plates and a Colored Map.* Philadelphia: J. Dobson, 1839.

———. *An Inquiry into the Distinctive Characteristics of the Aboriginal Race of America.* 2nd edition. Philadelphia: John Pennington, 1844.

Moxó y Francolí, Benito María de. *Cartas mejicanas escritas por D. Benito María de Moxó en 1805.* Genova: Pellas, 1837.

Mt. Pleasant, Alyssa. "After the Whirlwind: Maintaining a Haudenosaunee place at Buffalo Creek, 1780–1825." PhD diss., Cornell University, 2007.

———. "Contexts for Critique: Revisiting Representations of Violence in *Our Beloved Kin*," *American Historical Review* 125, no. 2 (April 2020): 533–36.

Mt. Pleasant, Alyssa, Caroline Wigginton, and Kelly Wisecup. "Materials and Methods in Native American and Indigenous Studies: Completing the Turn." *William and Mary Quarterly* 75, no. 2 (2018): 207–36.

Mucher, Christen. "Antiquity, Prehistory, Culture: American Narratives of the Distant Past, 1787–1867." PhD diss., University of Pennsylvania, 2012.

———. "Born of the Soil: Demography, Genetic Narratives, and American Origins." In *Decolonizing "Prehistory": Deep Time and Indigenous Knowledges in North America*, edited by Gesa Mackenthun and Christen Mucher, 51–70. Tucson: University of Arizona Press, 2021.

———. "Collecting Native America: John Lloyd Stephens and the Rhetoric of Archaeological Value." *Journal of Transnational American Studies* 9, no. 1 (2018). https://www.escholarship.org/uc/item/23h3n9w9.

Mundy, Barbara. *The Death of Aztec Tenochtitlan: The Life of Mexico City*. Austin: University of Texas Press, 2015.

———. "The Images of Eighteenth-Century Urban Reform in Mexico City and the Plan of José Antonio Alzate." *Colonial Latin American Review* 21, no. 1 (2012): 45–75.

———. *The Mapping of New Spain: Indigenous Cartography and the Maps of the Relaciones Geográficas*. University of Chicago Press, 1996.

———. "Mesoamerican Cartography." In *The History of Cartography*. Vol. 2, Book 3: *Cartography in the Traditional African, American, Arctic, Australian, and Pacific Societies*, edited by David Woodward and G. Malcolm Lewis, 183–256. Chicago: University of Chicago Press, 1998.

———. "Place-Names in Mexico-Tenochtitlan." *Ethnohistory* 61, no. 2 (Spring 2014): 329–55

Muñoz, Juan Bautista de. *Historia del Nuevo-Mundo* [. . .]. Madrid: La Viuda de Ibarra, 1793.

Murphy, Kathleen S. "Translating the Vernacular: Indigenous and African Knowledge in the Eighteenth-Century British Atlantic." *Atlantic Studies* 8, no. 1 (2011): 29–48.

Murray, Laura J. "Vocabularies of Native American Languages: A Literary and Historical Approach to an Elusive Genre." *American Quarterly* 53, no. 4 (2001): 590–623.

Murray, Paul V. "The Church and the First Mexican Republic, 1822–1830." *Records of the American Catholic Historical Society of Philadelphia* 48, no. 1 (1937): 1–89.

Nash, June C. *Mayan Visions: The Quest for Autonomy in an Age of Globalization*. New York: Routledge, 2001.

Navarrete, Federico. "The Path from Aztlán to Mexico: On Visual Narration in Mesoamerican Codices." *RES: Anthropology and Aesthetics* 37 (Spring 2000): 31–48.

Nelson, Cody. "'This land is all we have left': tribes on edge over giant dam proposal near Grand Canyon." *The Guardian Online*. August 12, 2020. https://www.theguardian.com/us-news/2020/aug/12/navajo-nation-dams-big-canyon-pumped-storage-project.

Nelson, Diane M. *Who Counts: The Mathematics of Death and Life After Genocide*. Durham, N.C.: Duke University Press, 2015.
Nemser, Daniel. "Archaeology in the Lettered City." *Colonial Latin American Review* 23, no. 2 (2014): 197–223.
———. "Eviction and the Archive: Materials for an Archaeology of the Archivo General de Indias." *Journal of Spanish Cultural Studies* 16, no. 2 (2015): 123–41.
———. *Infrastructures of Race: Concentration and Biopolitics in Colonial Mexico*. Austin: University of Texas Press, 2017.
Nichols, David Andrew. *Peoples of the Inland Sea: Native Americans and Newcomers in the Great Lakes Region, 1600–1780*. Athens: Ohio University Press, 2018.
Nichols, Robert. *Theft Is Property! Dispossession and Critical Theory*. Durham, N.C.: Duke University Press, 2019.
Nuñez de la Vega, D. Fr. Francisco. *Constituciones dioecesanas del obispado de Chiappa, hechas y ordenadas por su señoria illustriss*. Rome: C. Zenobi, 1702.
Oakley, Christopher Aaris. "The Center of the World: The Principle People and the Great Smoky Mountains." In *Landscapes of Origin in the Americas: Creation Narratives Linking Ancient Places and Present Communities*," edited by Jessica Joyce Christie, 3–14. Tuscaloosa: University of Alabama Press, 2009.
O'Brien, Jean. *Firsting and Lasting: Writing Indians Out of Existence in New England*. Minneapolis: Minnesota University Press, 2010.
O'Connor, Ralph. *The Earth On Show: Fossils And The Poetics Of Popular Science, 1802–1856*. Chicago, Ill.: University of Chicago Press, 2007.
O'Gorman, Edmundo. *The Invention Of America: An Inquiry Into The Historical Nature Of The New World And The Meaning Of Its History*. Bloomington: Indiana University press, 1961.
O'Gorman, Edmundo, ed. *Fray Servando Tereda de Mier: selección, notas y prólogo*. Mexico City: Impr. Universitaria, 1945.
O'Hara, Matthew D. *A Flock Divided: Race, Religion, and Politics in Mexico, 1749–1857*. Durham, N.C.: Duke University Press, 2010.
"Oldest and largest Maya structure discovered in Southern Mexico." *Reuters*, June 3, 2020.
Olmstead, Earl P. *Blackcoats among the Delaware: David Zeisberger on the Ohio Frontier* Kent, Oh.: Kent State University Press, 1991.
Omont, Henri. *Catalogue des manuscrits mexicains de la Bibliothèque nationale*. Paris: E. Bouillon, 1899.
O'Neal, Jennifer R. "From Time Immemorial: Centering Indigenous Traditional Knowledge and Ways of Knowing in the Archival Paradigm." *Afterlives Of Indigenous Archives, Essays In Honor Of The Occom Circle*, edited by Ivy Schweitzer and Gordon Henry, 45–49. Hanover, N.H.: Dartmouth College, 2019.
———. "The Right to Know: Decolonizing Native American Archives." *Journal of Western Archives* 6, no. 1 (2015): 1–17.
Onuf, Peter S. *Jefferson's Empire: The Language of American Nationhood*. Charlottesville: University Press of Virginia, 2000.

Ortega y Medina, Juan Antonio. "Monroísmo arqueológico: Un intent de compensacíon de americanidad insuficiente." In *Ensayos, tareas y estudios históricos*, 37–86. Xalapa: Universidad Veracruzana, 1953.

Ortiz de Ayala, Tadeo. *México considerado como nacion independiente y libre, ó sean algunas indicaciones sobre los deberes mas esenciales de los mexicanos*. Burdeos [Bordeaux]: C. L. Sobrino, 1832.

Ossipow, William, and Dominik Gerber. "The Reception of Vattel's Law of Nations in the American Colonies: From James Otis and John Adams to the Declaration of Independence." *American Journal of Legal History* 57, no. 4 (2017): 1–35.

Ostler, Jeffrey. *Surviving Genocide: Native Nations and the United States from the American Revolution to Bleeding Kansas*. New Haven, Conn.: Yale University Press, 2019.

Owens, Robert M. *Mr. Jefferson's Hammer: William Henry Harrison and the Origins of American Indian Policy*. Norman: University of Oklahoma Press, 2007.

Pagden, Anthony. "The 'Defence of Civilization' in Eighteenth-Century Social Theory." *History of the Human Sciences* 1, no. 1 (May 1988): 33–45.

———. *European Encounters with the New World: From Renaissance to Romanticism*. New Haven: Yale University Press, 1993.

———. *The Fall of Natural Man: The American Indian and the Origins of Comparative Ethnology*. Cambridge, U.K.: Cambridge University Press, 1982.

———. "Identity Formation in Spanish America." In *Colonial Identity in the Atlantic World, 1500–1800*, edited by Nicholas Canny and Anthony Pagden, 51–93. Princeton: Princeton University Press. 1987.

———. *Spanish Imperialism and the Political Imagination: Studies in European and Spanish-American Social and Political Theory 1513–1830*. New Haven, Conn.: Yale University Press, 1990.

Palacios, Guillermo. *Maquinaciones neoyorquinas y querellas porfirianas: Marshall H. Saville, El American Museum of Natural History de Nueva York y los debates en torno a las leyes de Protección del Patrimonio Arqueológico Nacional, 1896–1897*. Mexico City: Colegio de Mexico, 2014.

Park, Joseph F. "Spanish Indian Policy in Northern Mexico, 1765–1810." *Arizona and the West* 4, no. 4 (Winter 1962): 325–44.

Parrish, Susan Scott. *American Curiosity: Cultures of Natural History in the Colonial British Atlantic World*. Chapel Hill: University of North Carolina Press, 2006.

Parsons, [Samuel Holden]. "Discoveries Made in the Western Country." *Memoirs of the American Academy of Arts and Sciences* 2, no. 1 (1793): 119–27.

Pateman, Carole. "The Settler Contract." In *Contract and Domination*, edited by Carole Pateman and Charles W. Mills, 61–91. Cambridge: Polity Press, 2018.

Pauketat, Timothy R. "America's First Pastime." *Archaeology* 62, no. 5 (2009): 20–25.

———. *Cahokia: Ancient Americas; Great City on the Mississippi*. New York: Penguin, 2009.

Paz, Octavio. *Labyrinth of Solitude: Life and Thought in Mexico*. New York: Grave Press, 1961.

Peale, Albert Charles Peale. "Ancient Ruins of the Far West," *Illustrated Christian Weekly*. (October 9, 1875), 464–85.

———. "Ancient Ruins of the Far West," *Illustrated Christian Weekly*. (October 23, 1875): 509–10.

Pember, Mary Annette. "A Made for TV-Style Crime Probe into the Looting of Ancestral Remains." *Daily Yonder,* November 13, 2019. http://www.dailyyonder.com/a-made-for-tv-style-crime-probe-into-the-looting-of-ancestral-remains/2019/11/13/.

[Penny, Edward B.] *A Sketch of Customs and Society in Mexico, During the Years 1824, 1825, 1826.* London: Longman and Co., 1828.

Peraza-Rugeley, Margarita. *Llámenme el mexicano: Los almanaques y otras obras de Carlos de Sigüenza y Góngora.* New York: Peter Lang Publishing, 2013.

Pérez-Torres, Rafael. *Mestizaje: Critical Uses of Race in Chicano Culture.* Minneapolis: University of Minnesota Press, 2006.

———. "Miscegenation Now!" *American Literary History* 17, no. 2 (July 2005): 369–380.

Peters, John P. Preface to *Diary of David McClure, Doctor of Divinity, 1748–1820.* New York: Knickerbocker Press, 1899.

Peterson, Jeanette Favrot. "The Virgin of Guadalupe Symbol of Conquest or Liberation?" *Art Journal* 51, no. 4 (Winter 1992): 39–47.

———. *Visualizing Guadalupe: From Black Madonna to Queen of the Americas.* Austin: University of Texas Press, 2014.

Peterson, Jeanette Favrot and Kevin Trerraciano, eds. *The Florentine Codex: An Encyclopedia of the Nahua World in Sixteenth-Century Mexico.* Austin: University of Texas Press, 2019.

Picas, Mathieu. "The Plurivocality of Tulum: "Scientific" Versus Local Narratives About Maya Sites in Quintana Roo." In *Decolonizing 'Prehistory': Deep Time and Indigenous Knowledges in North America,* edited by Gesa Mackenthun and Christen Mucher, 211–30. Tucson, University of Arizona Press, 2021.

Pickaway Historical & Genealogical Society. *Pickaway County: History and Families, 1810–2005.* [Evansville, Ind.:] M.T. Publishing Company, 2005.

Pietschman, Horst. "Protoliberalismo, reformas borbónicas y revolucíon: la Nueva España en el ultimo tercio del siglo XVIII." In *Interpretaciones de siglo XVIII mexicano: El impacto de las reformas bórbonicas,* edited by Josefina Zorida Vásquez, 27–65. Mexico City: Editorial Patria, 1992.

Piker, Joshua. *The Four Deaths of Acorn Whistler: Telling Stories in Colonial America.* Cambridge, Mass.: Harvard University Press, 2013.

Pilling, Arnold. "Yurok." In *Handbook of North American Indians.* Vol 8: *California,* edited by Robert Heizer, 137–54. Austin: University of Texas Press, 1978.

Pinsker, Joe. "Patagonia, REI, and the Politics of 'The President Stole Your Land.'" *The Atlantic.* December 5, 2017

Pocock, J. G. A. *Barbarism and Religion*. Vol. 2: *Narratives of Civil Government*. Cambridge, U.K: Cambridge University Press, 1999.

———. "Gibbon and the Shepherds: The Stages of Society in the Decline and Fall." *History of European Ideas* 23 (1981): 193–202.

Podgorny, Irina. "Portable antiquities: Transportation, Ruins, and Communications in Nineteenth-century Archeology." *História, Ciências, Saúde* 15, no. 3 (July–September 2008): 577–95.

Poinsett, Joel R. *Notes on Mexico: Made In The Autumn Of 1822, Accompanied By A Historical Sketch Of The Revolution*. Philadelphia: H. C. Carey and I. Lea, 1824.

Popol Vuh: The Definitive Edition of the Mayan Book of the Dawn of Life and the Glories of Gods and Kings. Rev. ed. Translated by Dennis Tedlock. New York: Simon & Schuster, 1996.

Popol Vuh: Sacred Book of the Quiché Maya People. Translated by Allen J. Christenson. Norman: University of Oklahoma Press, 2007.

Poremski, Karen M. "Voicing the Bones: Heid Erdrich's Poetry and the Discourse of NAGPRA." *Studies in American Indian Literatures* 27, no. 1 (2015): 1–32.

Portillo, José María. *Fuero indio: Tlaxcala y la identidad territorial entre la monarquía imperial y la república nacional 1787–1824*. Mexico City: El Colegio de México, 2013.

Porter, Charlotte M. *The Eagle's Nest: Natural History and American Ideas, 1812–1842*. Birmingham: University of Alabama Press, 1986.

Pool, Christopher A. *Olmec Archaeology and Early Mesoamerica*. New York: Cambridge University Press, 2007.

Poole, Stafford. Introduction to *Idea of a New General History: An Account of Colonial Native Mexico*, by Lorenzo Boturini Benaduci, 3–18. Translated and edited by Stafford Poole. Norman: University of Oklahoma Press, 2015.

Poulot, Dominique. "The Birth of Heritage; 'le moment Guizot.'" *Oxford Art Journal* 11, no. 2 (1998): 40–46.

Powell, Timothy. "The American Philosophical Society Protocols for the Treatment of Indigenous Materials." *Departmental Papers (Religious Studies)* 16 (2014) https://repository.upenn.edu/rs_papers/16.

———. "Where Do Indigenous Origin Stories and Empowered Objects Fit into a Literary History of the American Continent?" In *Textual Distortion*, edited by Elaine Treharne and Greg Walker, New edition, 98–116. Boydell & Brewer, 2017.

Pratt, Mary Louise. "Humboldt and the Reinvention of America." In *Amerindian Images and the Legacy*, edited by René Jara and Nicholas Spadaccini, 584–606. Minneapolis: University of Minnesota Press, 1992.

———. *Imperial Eyes: Travel Writing and Transculturation*. New York: Routledge, 1992.

Prechtel-Kluskens, Claire. "Birthplace and Compensation of Postmasters in Ohio, 1816–1823." *Report* 33 (1993): 79–97, 134.

Preset, José Luis. "La Naturaleza Como Símbolo en la obra de José Antionio de Alzate." *Asclepio* 39, no. 2 (1987): 285–95.

Preston, Richard. "America's Egypt: John Lloyd Stephens and the Discovery of the Maya," *Princeton University Library Chronicle* 53, no. 3 (1992): 143–63.

Priest, Joseph. *American Antiquities, And Discoveries In The West: Being An Exhibition Of The Evidence That An Ancient Population Of Partially Civilized Nations, Differing Entirely From Those Of The Present Indians, Peopled America Many Centuries Before Its Discovery By Columbus: And Inquiries Into Their Origin, With A Copious Description Of Many Of Their Stupendous Works Now In Ruins: With Conjectures What May Have Become Of Them:* . . . Albany: Hoffman & White, 1833.

Prucha, Francis Paul. *The Great Father: The United States Government and the American Indians.* Lincoln: University of Nebraska Press, 1995.

Puig-Samper, Miguel Ángel. "Difusión institucionalización de la sistema lommeo en España y América." In *Mundialización de la ciencia y cultura nacional: actas del Congreso Internacional "Ciencia, Descubrimiento y Mundo Colonial,"* edited by Antonio Lafuente, Alberto Elena, and M. L. Ortega, 349–49. Madrid: Doce Calles, 1993.

———. "Illustrators of the New World. The Image in the Spanish Scientific Expeditions of the Enlightenment." *Culture & History Digital Journal* 1, no. 2 (2012): m102. https://doi.org/10.3989/chdj.2012.m102.

Purchas, Samuel. *Hakluytus posthumus, or Purchas his Pilgrimes: contayning a history of the world in sea voyages and lande travells by Englishmen and others.* London: Printed by William Stansby for Henrie Fetherstone, 1625.

Quijano, Aníbal. "Coloniality of Power, Eurocentrism, and Latin America." *Nepantla: Views from the South* 1, no. 3 (2000): 533–80.

R. "Newly Discovered Indian Fortifications." *New-York Magazine* (January 1, 1793): 23–24.

Rabasa, José. *Writing Violence On The Northern Frontier: The Historiography Of Sixteenth-Century: New Mexico And Florida And The Legacy Of Conquest.* Durham, N.C.: Duke University Press, 2000.

Rafert, Stewart. *The Miami Indians of Indiana: A Persistent People, 1654–1994.* Indianapolis: Indiana Historical Society, 1996.

Rafinesque, C. S. *Ancient History, or, Annals of Kentucky: With a Survey of the Ancient Monuments of North America, and a Tabular View of the Principal Languages and Primitive Nations of the Whole Earth.* Frankfurt, K.Y.: Printed for the author, 1824.

———. *The Ancient Monuments Of North And South America.* Philadelphia: Printed for the author, 1838.

———. *Atlantic Journal, and Friend Of Knowledge, in Eight Numbers, Containing about 160 Original Articles and Tracts on Natural and Historical Sciences.* Philadelphia: s.n., 1832–1833.

———. "Letter to Caleb Atwater, of Circleville: On the Upper Alleghawian Monuments of North Elkhorn Creek, Fayette County, Kentucky." *The Western Review*

and *Miscellaneous Magazine, a Monthly Publication, Devoted to Literature and Science* 3, no. 1 (August 1820): 53–47.
Rama, Angel. *The Lettered City*. Translated by John Charles Chasteen. Durham, N.C.: Duke University Press, 1996.
Rasmussen, Birgit Brander. *Queequeg's Coffin: Indigenous Literacies & Early American Literature*. Durham, N.C.: Duke University Press, 2012.
Real academia española, *Diccionario de la lengua castellana: en que se explica el verdadero sentido de las voces, su naturaleza y calidad* [. . .] Vol. 4. Madrid: F. Del Hierro, 1734.
Regis, Pamela. *Describing Early America: Bartram, Jefferson, Crevecoeur, and the Influence of Natural History*. Philadelphia: University of Pennsylvania Press, 1999.
Reps, John William. *The Making of Urban America: A History of City Planning in the United States*. Princeton, N.J.: Princeton University Press, 1965.
Restall, Matthew. *Beyond Black and Red: African-Native Relations in Colonial Latin America*. University of New Mexico Press, 2005.
Restall, Matthew and Florine Asselbergs. *Invading Guatemala: Spanish, Nahua, and Maya Accounts of the Conquest Wars* State College: Penn State Press, 2007.
Reynoso Bolaños, Arturo. *Francisco Xavier Clavigero: el aliento del espíritu*. Mexico City: Fondo de Cultura Económica, 2018.
Rickett, Harold William. *The Royal Botanical Expedition to New Spain, 1788–1820: As Described in Documents in the Archivo General De La Nación, Mexico*. Rev. ed. Waltham, Mass.: Chronica Botanica Co., 1947.
Riding-In, James. "Our Dead Are Never Forgotten: American Indian Struggles for Burial Rights and Protections." In *"They Made Us Many Promises": The American Indian Experience, 1524 to the Present*, edited by Philip Weeks, 291–323. Wheeling, Ill.: Harlan Davidson, 2002.
Riding-In, James, Cal Seciwa, Suzan Shown Harjo, and Walter Echo-Hawk. "Protecting Native American Human Remains, Burial Grounds, and Sacred Places: Panel Discussion." *Wicazo-Sa Review* 19, no. 2 (2004): 169–83.
Rifkin, Mark. *Beyond Settler Time: Temporal Sovereignty and Indigenous Self-Determination*. Durham, N.C.: Duke University Press, 2017.
———. "Making Peoples into Populations: The Racial Limits of Tribal Sovereignty." *Theorizing Native Studies*, edited by Audra Simpson and Andrea Smith, 149–87. Durham, N.C.: Duke University Press, 2014.
———. *Manifesting America: The Imperial Construction of U.S. National Space*. New York: Oxford University Press, 2009.
———. "Settler common sense." *Settler Colonial Studies*, 3 nos. 3-4 (2013): 322–340.
———. *Settler Common Sense: Queerness and Everyday Colonialism in the American Renaissance*. Minneapolis: University of Minnesota Press, 2014.
Richards, Thomas. *The Imperial Archive: Knowledge and the Fantasy of Empire*. New York: Verso, 1993.
Rivett, Sarah. "Empirical Desire: Conversion, Ethnography, and the New Science of the Praying Indian." *Early American Studies* 4, no. 1 (2006): 16–45.

———. "Learning to Write Algonquian Letters: The Indigenous Place of Language Philosophy in the Seventeenth-Century Atlantic World." *William and Mary Quarterly* 71, no. 4 (2014): 549–88.

———. *The Science of the Soul in Colonial New England*. Chapel Hill: University of North Carolina Press, 2011.

Robertson, William. *The History of America*. London: Printed for W. Strahan, T. Cadell, 1777.

Rockett, Darcel. "A Serpent and Mounds." *Chicago Tribune*, October 14, 2019.

Rockwell, Stephen J. *Indian Affairs and the Administrative State in the Nineteenth Century*. Cambridge, U.K.: Cambridge University Press, 2010.

Rodríguez O., Jaime E. *The Independence of Spanish America*. Cambridge, U.K.: Cambridge University Press, 1998.

Rodríguez-Alegría, Enrique. *The Archaeology and History of Colonial Mexico: Mixing Epistemologies*. New York: Cambridge University Press, 2016.

———. *The Oxford Handbook of the Aztecs*. New York: Oxford University Press, 2016.

Rohrbough, Malcolm J. *The Land Office Business: The Settlement and Administration of American Public Lands, 1789–1837*. Oxford, U.K.: Oxford University Press, 1968.

Rollings, Willard H. *The Osage: An Ethnohistorical Study of Hegemony on the Prairie-Plains*. Columbia: University of Missouri Press, 1992.

Rosen, Deborah A. *Border Law: The First Seminole War and American Nationhood*. Cambridge, Mass.: Harvard University Press, 2015.

Ross, Dorothy. "Historical Consciousness in Nineteenth-Century America." *The American Historical Review* 89, no. 4 (October 1984): 909–928.

Rothman, Hal. *Preserving Different Pasts: The American National Monuments*. Urbana: University of Illinois Press, 1989.

Round, Phillip H. "Mississippian Contexts for Early American Studies." *Early American Literature* 53, no. 2 (2018): 445–473.

Roys, Ralph L. *The Book of Chilam Balam of Chumayel*. Norman: University of Oklahoma Press, 1973.

Rozental, Sandra. "In the Wake of Mexican Patrimonio: Material Ecologies in San Miguel Coatlinchan." *Anthropological Quarterly* 89, no. 1 (Winter 2016): 181–219.

Rudwick, Martin J. S. *Bursting the Limits of Time: The Reconstruction of Geohistory in the Age of Revolution*. Chicago, Ill.: University of Chicago Press, 2005.

———. *Earth's Deep History: How It Was Discovered and Why It Matters*. Chicago, Ill.: University of Chicago Press, 2014.

Rugeley, Terry. *Maya Wars: Ethnographic Accounts from Nineteenth-Century Yucatan*. Norman: University of Oklahoma Press, 2001.

Ruiz Medrano, Ethelia. *Mexico's Indigenous Communities: Their Lands and Histories, 1500–2010*. Translated by Russ Davidson. Louisville: University Press of Colorado, 2010.

Ruiz Medrano, Ethelia, Julia Constantino, and Pauline Marmasse. *Reshaping New Spain: Government and Private Interests in the Colonial Bureaucracy, 1535–1550*. Louisville: University Press of Colorado, 2006.

Russell, Steve. "Lost City of Etzanoa Found." *Indian Country Today*, May 25, 2017. http://www.newsmaven.io/indiancountrytoday/archive/lost-city-of-etzanoa-found-jjfT-SVjZEqdAZoFgmGfCQ/.
Russo, Alessandra. "Cortés's objects and the Idea of New Spain: Inventories as Spatial Narratives." *Journal of the History of Collections* 23, no. 2 (2011): 229–52.
Russo, Alessandra. *Untranslatable Image: A Mestizo History of the Arts in New Spain, 1500–1600*. Austin: University of Texas Press, 2014.
Russon, Robert S. "A Trail Guide to the Dominguez-Velez de Escalante Expedition 1776." Master's thesis, Utah State University, 1973.
Rutherford, Adam. *A Brief History of Everyone Who Ever Lived: The Stories in Our Genes*. London: Orion, 2016.
Safier, Neil. "Global Knowledge on the Move: Itineraries, Amerindian Narratives, and Deep Histories of Science." *Isis* 101, no. 4 (2010): 133–45.
———. *Measuring the New World: Enlightenment Science and South America*. Chicago: University of Chicago Press, 2008.
Sahagún, Fray Bernardino de. *The Florentine Codex: General History of the Things of New Spain*. Book 7: *The Sun, the Moon and Stars, and the Binding of the Years*, translated by Arthur J. O. Anderson and Charles E. Dibble. Salt Lake City: University of Utah Press, 2012.
———. *The Florentine Codex: General History of the Things of New Spain*. Book 10: *The People*, translated by Arthur J. O. Anderson and Charles E. Dibble. Salt Lake City: University of Utah Press, 2012.
———. Libro decimo de los vicios y virtudes desta gente indiana [. . .] Manuscript, Medicea Laurenziana Library, Florence. http://www.teca.bmlonline.it/TecaViewer/index.jsp?RisIdr=TECA0001504065.
Saldaña-Portillo, María Josefina. *Indian Given: Racial Geographies across Mexico and the United States*. Durham, N.C.: Duke University Press, 2016.
———. "'No Country for Old Mexicans': The Collision of Empires on the Texas Frontier." *Interventions: International Journal of Postcolonial Studies* 13, no. 1 (2011): 67–84.
———. *The Revolutionary Imagination in the Americas and the Age of Development*. Durham, N.C.: Duke University Press, 2003.
Saldívar, Emiko. "'It's Not Race, It's Culture': Untangling Racial Politics in Mexico." *Latin American and Caribbean Ethnic Studies* 9, no. 1 (2014): 89–108.
Saler, Bethel. *The Settlers' Empire: Colonialism and State Formation in America's Old Northwest*. Philadelphia: University of Pennsylvania Press, 2015.
Sammons, Franklin. "'The Fruit of the Yazoo Compromise'': Mississippi Stock and the Panic of 1819." *Journal of the Early Republic* 40, no. 4 (Winter 2020): 671–76.
Sanz Jara, Eva, and Inmaculada Simón Ruiz. "La Desamortización Como Instrumento Para El Blanqueamiento En El Pensamiento Mexicano (Siglo XIX)." In *Fiscalidad, Integración Social Y Política Exterior En El Pensamiento Liberal Atlántico (1810–1930)*, edited By Pérez Herrero Pedro and Sanz Jara Eva, 89–106. Madrid: Marcial Pons, 2015.

Saranillio, Dean Itsuji. "Settler Colonialism." In *Native Studies Keywords*, edited by Stephanie Nohelani Teves, Andrea Smith, and Michelle H. Raheja, 284–300. Tucson: University of Arizona Press, 2014.

Sargent, Winthrop. "A Letter from Colonel Winthrop Sargent, to Dr. Benjamin Smith Barton, Accompanying Drawings and Some Account of Certain Articles, Which Were Taken out of an Ancient Tumulus, or Grave, in the Western-Country." *Transactions of the American Philosophical Society* 4 (1799): 177–78.

———. "Plan of an Ancient Fortification at Marietta, Ohio (With a Plate)." *Memoirs of the American Academy of Arts and Sciences* 5, New Series (1853): 29–48.

Sargent, Winthrop, and Benjamin Smith Barton. *Papers Relative to Certain American Antiquities*. Philadelphia: Thomas Dobson, 1796.

Saunders, Joe. "Early Mounds in the Lower Mississippi Valley." In *Early New World Monumentality*, edited by Richard L. Burger and Robert M. Rosenswig, 25–42. Gainesville: University Press of Florida, 2012.

Saunt, Claudio. "Financing Dispossession: Stocks, Bonds, and the Deportation of Native Peoples in the Antebellum United States." *Journal of American History* 106 (September 2019): 315–37.

———. *A New Order of Things: Property, Power, and the Transformation of the Creek Indians, 1733–1816*. Cambridge, U.K.: Cambridge University Press, 1999.

———. *Unworthy Republic: The Dispossession of Native Americans and the Road to Indian Territory*. New York: W. W. Norton & Company, 2020.

———. *West of the Revolution: An Uncommon History of 1776*. New York: W. W. Norton & Company, 2014.

Sayre, Gordon. "The Mound Builders and the Imagination of American Antiquity in Jefferson, Bartram, and Chateaubriand." *Early American Literature* 33, no. 3 (Fall 1998): 225–49.

———. "A Native American Scoops Lewis and Clark: The Voyage of Moncacht-apé." *Common-place* 5, no. 4 (June 2005).

Schapp, Alain. *The Discovery of the Past: The Origins of Archaeology*. London: British Museum Press, 1996.

Schávelzon, Daniel. "La primera excavación arqueológica de América: Teotihuacan en 1675." *Anales de Antropologia* 20, no. 1 (1983): 121–34.

Schiebinger, Londa L. *Nature's Body: Gender in the Making of Modern Science*. New Brunswick, N.J.: Rutgers University Press, 1993.

Schiebinger, Londa and Claudia Swan. *Colonial Botany Science Commerce & Politics in the Early Modern World*. Philadelphia: University of Pennsylvania Press, 2007.

Schoolcraft, Henry R. *Historical and Statistical Information Respecting the History, Condition, and Prospect of the Indian Tribes of the United States [...]*. Philadelphia: Lippincott, 1852.

Schele, Linda and Peter Mathews. *The Code of Kings: The Language of Seven Sacred Maya Temples and Tombs*. New York: Scribner, 1998.

Schreyer, Rudiger. "'Savage' Languages in Eighteenth-Century Theoretical History of Language." In *Language Encounter in the Americas, 1492–1800: A Collection of Essays*, edited by Edward G. Gray and Norman Fiering, 293–326. New York: Berghahn Books, 2000.

Schroeder, Susan. *Chimalpahin and the Kingdoms of Chalco*. Tucson: University of Arizona Press, 1991.

———. Forward to *Idea of a New General History: An Account of Colonial Native Mexico*, by Lorenzo Boturini Benaduci, xi–xiv. Translated and edited by Stafford Poole. Norman: University of Oklahoma Press, 2015.

Schroeder, Susan, ed. *Native Resistance and the Pax Colonial in New Spain*. Lincoln: University of Nebraska Press, 1998.

Schroeder, Susan, Anne J. Cruz, Cristián Roa-de-la-Carrera, David E. Tavárez, eds. *Chimalpahin's Conquest: A Nahua Historian's Rewriting of Francisco Lopez de Gomara's La conquista de Mexico*. Stanford, Calif.: Stanford University Press, 2010.

Schutt, Amy. *Peoples of the River Valleys: The Odyssey of the Delaware Indians*. Philadelphia: University of Pennsylvania Press, 2007.

Schwaller, John F. "The Brothers Fernando de Alva Ixtilxochitl and Bartolomé de Alva: Two 'Native' Intellectuals of Seventeenth-Century Mexico." In *Indigenous Intellectuals: Knowledge, Power, and Colonial Culture in Mexico and the Andes*, edited by Gabriela Ramos and Yanna Yannakakis, 39–49. Durham, N.C.: Duke University Press, 2004.

Schweitzer, Ivy. "Introduction: The Afterlives Of Indigenous Archives." *Afterlives Of Indigenous Archives, Essays In Honor Of The Occom Circle*, edited by Ivy Schweitzer and Gordon Henry, 2–20. Hanover, N.H.: Dartmouth College, 2019.

Schweitzer, Ivy and Gordon Henry, Jr. *Afterlives of Indigenous Archives: Essays in Honor of The Occom Circle*. Hanover, N.H: Dartmouth College Press, 2019.

Seed, Patricia. *Ceremonies of Possession in Europe's Conquest of the New World, 1492–1640*. New York: Cambridge University Press, 1995.

———. "The Social Dimensions of Race: Mexico City, 1753." *Hispanic American History Review* 62 (1982): 549–606.

Seeman, Mark F. "Hopewell Art in Hopewell Places," In *Hero, Hawk, and Open Hand: American Indian Art of the Ancient Midwest and South*, edited by Richard F. Townsend, 57–72. New Haven, Conn.: Yale University Press, 2004.

Sellers, Richard West. "A Very Large Array." *National Resources Journal* 47 (Spring 2007): 267–328.

Semonin, Paul. *American Monster: How the Nation's First Prehistoric Creature Became a Symbol of National Identity*. New York: New York University Press, 2000.

Shannon, Timothy J. "The Ohio Company and the Meaning of Opportunity in the American West, 1786–1795." *New England Quarterly* 64 (September 1991): 393–413.

Shapiro, Barbara. J. *A Culture of Fact: England, 1550–1720*. Ithaca, N.Y.: Cornell University Press, 2000.

Sharer, Robert J., and Loa P. Traxler. *The Ancient Maya*. 6th ed. Stanford, Calif.: Stanford University Press, 2006.

Sheedy, Crystal A. "The Everyday Sacred: A Symbolic Analysis of Contemporary Yucatec Maya Women's Daily Realities." PhD diss., State University of New York at Albany, 2019.

Sheehan, Bernard W. *Seeds of Extinction: Jeffersonian Philanthropy and the American Indian*. Chapel Hill, N.C.: University of North Carolina Press, 1974.

Shelav, Eran. *Rome Reborn on Western Shores: Historical Imagination and the Creation of the American Republic*. Charlottesville: University of Virginia Press, 2009.

Shelton, Anthony. "Dispossessed Histories: Mexican Museums and the Institutionalisation of the Past." *Cultural Dynamics* 7, no. 1 (1995): 69–100.

Sherwood III, Robert M. "Cartography of Alexander Von Humboldt: Images of the Enlightenment in America." PhD diss., University of Texas at Arlington, 2008.

Shoemaker, Nancy. "How Indians Got to Be Red." *American Historical Review* 102, no. 3 (1997): 625–44.

Shriver, Cameron (camshriver). "Four Versions of a Little Turtle Speech at Greenville, 1795." *aacimotaatiiyankwi* (blog). April 13, 2021. http://www.aacimotaatiiyankwi.org/2021/04/13/four-versions-of-a-little-turtle-speech-at-greenville-1795/.

Shuck-Hall, Sheri Marie. *Journey to the West: The Alabama and Coushatta Indians*. Norman: University of Oklahoma Press, 2008.

Shyrock, Andrew and Daniel Lord Smail, eds. *Deep History: The Architecture of Past and Present*. Berkeley: University of California Press, 2011.

Silva, Noenoe. "'Moʻolelo and Mana: The Transmission of Hawaiian History from Hawai'i to the United States, 1836–1843." *Journal of the Early Republic* 38, no. 3 (Fall 2018): 415–43.

Silva Prada, Natalia. "Impacto de la migración urbana en el proceso de 'separación de repúblicas': El caso de dos parroquias indígenas de la parcialidad de San Juan Tenochtitlán, 1688–1692." *Estudios de historia novohispana* 24 (2001): 77–109.

Silverberg, Robert. *The Moundbuilders of Ancient America: The Archaeology of a Myth*. Greenwich, Conn.: New York Graphic Society, 1968.

Simpson, Audra. *Mohawk Interruptus: Political Life Across the Borders of Settler States*. Durham, N.C.: Duke University Press, 2014.

Simpson, Audra, and Andrea Smith. Introduction to *Theorizing Native Studies*, edited by Audra Simpson and Andrea Smith, 1–30. Durham, N.C.: Duke University Press, 2014.

Simpson, Leanne Betasamosake. *As We Have Always Done: Indigenous Freedom Through Radical Resistance*. Minneapolis: Minnesota University Press, 2017.

———. "Land as Pedagogy: Nishnaabeg Intelligence and Rebellious Transformation." *Decolonization: Indigeneity, Education, and Society* 3, no. 3 (2014): 1–25.

Simpson, Lesley B. *The Encomienda in New Spain: The Beginning of Spanish Mexico*. Berkeley: University of California Press, 1950.

Shipton, Clifford K. "The Museum of the American Antiquarian Society." In *A Cabinet of Curiosities: Five Episodes in the Evolution of American Museums*, edited by Whitfield J. Bell Jr., 35–48. Charlottesville: University of Virginia Press, 1967.

Slade, David F. "An Imperial Knowledge Space for Bourbon Spain: Juan Bautista Muñoz and the Founding of the Archivo General de Indias." *Colonial Latin American Review* 20 (2011): 195–212.

Slade, David F. "Enlightened Archi-Textures: Founding Colonial Archives in the Hispanic Eighteenth Century." PhD diss., Emory University, 2005.

Sleeper-Smith, Susan. *Contesting Knowledge: Museums and Indigenous Perspectives*. Lincoln: University of Nebraska Press, 2009.

———. *Indigenous Prosperity and American Conquest: Indian Women of the Ohio River Valley, 1690–1792*. Chapel Hill: University of North Carolina Press, 2018.

Sloan, DeVillo. *The Crimsoned Hills of Onondaga: Romantic Antiquarians and the Euro-American Invention of Native American Prehistory*. Amherst, N.Y.: Cambria Press, 2008.

Slotkin, Richard. *Regeneration through Violence: The Mythology of the American Frontier, 1600–1860*. Middletown: Wesleyan University Press, 1973.

Smith, Adam. *Lectures on Jurisprudence*, edited by R. L. Meek, D. D. Raphael, and P. G. Stein. Indianapolis: Liberty Classics, 1982.

Smith, Linda Tuhiwai. *Decolonizing Methodologies: Research and Indigenous Peoples*. London: Zed Books, 1999.

Smith, Raoul N. "The Interest in Language and Languages in Colonial and Federal America." *Proceedings of the American Philosophical Society* 123, no. 1 (1979): 29–46.

Smith, Thomas H. *The Mapping of Ohio*. Kent, Oh.: Kent State University Press, 1977.

Smithsonian Institution. *Annual Report of the Board of Regents of the Smithsonian* [...]. *Report of the U.S. National Museum*. Part 2. Washington D.C.: Government Printing Office, 1897.

Smitten, Jeffrey. "Impartiality in Robertson's History of America." *Eighteenth-Century Studies* 19 (1989): 56–77.

Snead, James E. *The Relic Hunters: Archaeology and the Public in Nineteenth-Century America*. New York: Oxford, 2018.

———. *Ruins and Rivals: The Making of Southwest Archaeology*. Tucson: University of Arizona Press, 2001.

Snyder, Christina. *Slavery in Indian Country: The Changing Face of Captivity in Early America*. Cambridge, Mass.: Harvard University Press, 2010.

———. "The Rise and Fall and Rise of Civilizations: Indian Intellectual Culture during the Removal Era." *Journal Of American History* 104, no. 2 (September 2017): 386–409.

Spence, Michael. "From Tzintzuntzan to Paquimé: Peers or Peripheries in Greater Mexico." In *Mesoamerica: The Archaeology of West and Northwest Mexico*, edited by Michael Foster and Shirley Gorenstein, 255–61. Salt Lake City: University of Utah, 2000.

Spencer, Frank. "Two Unpublished Essays on the Anthropology of North America by Benjamin Smith Barton." *Isis* 68, no. 4 (December 1977): 567–73.

Spero, Laura Keenan. "'Stout, Bold, Sunning and the Greatest Travellers in America': The Colonial Shawnee Diaspora." PhD diss., University of Pennsylvania, 2010.

Spitta, Silvia. *Misplaced Objects: Migrating Collections and Recollections in Europe and the Americas*. Austin: University of Texas Press, 2009.

Squier, E. G. "New Mexico and California." *North American Review* 2, no. 5 (November 1848): 503–28.

Squier, E. G., and E. H. Davis. *Ancient Monuments of the Mississippi Valley*. Washington D.C.: Smithsonian Institution, 1848.

———. *Ancient Monuments of the Mississippi Valley*. Edited by David J. Meltzer. Washington D.C.: Smithsonian Institution, 1998.

Stanton, William R. *The Leopard's Spots: Scientific Attitudes Toward Race in America, 1815–49*. Chicago: University of Chicago Press, 1960.

Starna, William A. "'The United States Will Protect You': The Iroquois, New York, and the 1790 Nonintercourse Act." *New York History* 83, no. 1 (2002): 4–33.

Steiner, Abraham G. "Account of some Old Indian Works, on Huron Rover, With a Plan of them, taken the 28th of May, 1789." *Columbian Magazine* 3, no. 9 (September 1789): 543.

Stephens, John Lloyd. *Incidents of Travel in Central America, Chiapas, and Yucatan*. New York: Harper & Brothers, 1841.

———. *Incidents of Travel in Yucatan*. New York: Harper & Brothers, 1843.

St. John, Rachel C. *Line in the Sand: A History of the Western U.S.-Mexico Border*. New York: Oxford University Press, 2011.

Stockwell, Mary. *The Other Trail of Tears: The Removal of the Ohio Indians*. Yardley, Penn.: Westholme Publishing, 2016.

Stoetzer, Carlos. "Humboldt: Redescubridor del Nuevo Mundo." *Americas* 11, no. 6 (1959): 2–8.

Strack, Andrew J. *myaamiaki iši meehtohseeniwiciki/How the Miami People Live*, edited by Marry Tippmann, Meghan Dorey, and Daryl Baldwin. Miami, Oh.: Miami University Myaamia Project, 2010.

Strang, Cameron. *Frontiers of Science: Imperialism and Natural Knowledge in the Gulf South Borderlands, 1500–1850*. Chapel Hill: University of North Carolina Press, 2018.

[Swan, Caleb.] "Caleb Swan's Report to Henry Knox on Creeks, 2 May 1791." Unpublished manuscript in Violetta Delafield-Benjamin Smith Barton Collection, Mss.B.B284d. Series 3, Vol. 23, American Philosophical Society, Philadelphia.

Swann, Marjorie. *Curiosities and Texts: The Culture of Collecting in Early Modern England*. Philadelphia: University of Pennsylvania Press, 2001.

Sword, Wiley. *President Washington's Indian War: The Struggle for the Old Northwest, 1790–1795*. Norman: University of Oklahoma Press, 1985.

Symmes, John Cleve. "Letter to Charles Tompson, April 1787." *New-York Historical Society Collection* 11 (1878): 233–39.

TallBear, Kimberly. *Native American DNA: Tribal Belonging and the False Promise of Genetic Science*. Minneapolis: University of Minnesota Press, 2013.

Tanner, Helen Hornbeck, eds. *Atlas of Great Lakes Indian History*. Norman: Published for the Newberry Library by the University of Oklahoma Press, 1987.

Tayloe, Edward Thornton. *The Journal and Correspondence of Edward Thornton Tayloe*, edited by Harvey C. Gardiner. Chapel Hill: University of North Carolina Press, 1959.

Taylor, Alan. "Jefferson's Pacific: The Science of a Distant Empire, 1768–1811." In *Across the Continent: Jefferson, Lewis and Clark, and the Making of America*, edited by Douglas Seefeldt, Jeffrey L. Hantman, and Peter S. Onuf, 16–44. Charlottesville: University of Virginia Press, 2006.

Taylor, Diana. *The Archive and the Repertoire: Performing Cultural Memory in the Americas*. Durham, N.C.: Duke University Press, 2003.

Taylor, Edward. "The Description of the Great Bones dug up at Claverack on the Banks of Hudson's River, AD 1705." Reprinted in *New York History* 40 (1959): 59–60.

Taylor, James W. *History of the State of Ohio*. Cincinnati, Oh.: H. W. Derby & Company, 1854.

Taylor, Melanie Benson. Foreword to *Afterlives Of Indigenous Archives, Essays In Honor Of The Occom Circle*, edited by Ivy Schweitzer and Gordon Henry, ix–xiv. Hanover, N.H.: Dartmouth College, 2019.

Tecuilhuitzintli, Ocelotl. "Carta al Autor de la Gaztea de Literatura." *Gaceta de México* 4, no. 40 (August 16, 1791): 377–79.

Tedlock, Denis. *1000 Years of Mayan Literature*. Berkeley: University of California Press, 2011.

Terreros y Pando, Esteban de. *Diccionario castellano: con las voces de ciencias y artes y sus correspondientes en las tres lenguas francesa, latina e italiana*. Vol. 2. Madrid, 1787 [1767].

The Territorial Papers Of The United States. Vol. 2: *The Territory Northwest Of The River Ohio, 1787–1803*, edited by Clarence Edwin Carter. Washington D.C.: U.S. Government Printing Office, 1934.

Thomas, David Hurst. *Skull Wars: Kennewick Man, Archaeology, and the Battle for Native American Identity*. New York: Basic Books, 2000.

Thompson, John Eric Sydney. *A Commentary on the Dresden Codex: A Maya Hieroglyphic Book*. Philadelphia: American Philosophical Society, 1972.

Thompson, Peter. "'Judicious Neology': The Imperative of Paternalism in Thomas Jefferson's Linguistic Studies." *Early American Studies: An Interdisciplinary Journal* 1, no. 2 (2003): 187–224.

Timmerman, Nicholas A. "Contested Indigenous Landscapes: Indian Mounds and the Political Creation of the Mythical 'Mound Builder' Race." *Ethnohistory* 67 (January 2020): 75–95.

Tinker, George E. "The Stones Shall Cry Out: Consciousness, Rocks, and Indians." *Wicazo Sa Review* 19, no. 2 (2004): 105–25.

Tiro, Karim M. *The People of the Standing Stone: The Oneida Nation from Revolution through the Era of Removal.* Amherst, Mass.: University of Massachusetts Press, 2011.

———. "The View from Piqua Agency: The War of 1812, the White River Delawares, and the Origins of Indian Removal." *Journal of the Early Republic* 32, no. 1 (Spring 2015): 25–44.

Tlostanova, Madina V., and Walter D. Mignolo. *Learning to Unlearn: Decolonial Reflections from Eurasia and the Americas.* Columbus: Ohio State University Press, 2012.

Townsend, Camilla. *Annals of Native America: How the Nahuas of Colonial Mexico Kept Their History Alive.* Oxford University Press, 2017.

———. *The Fifth Sun: A New History of the Aztecs.* Oxford University Press, 2020.

———. *Matlintzin's Choices: An Indian Woman in the Conquest of Mexico.* Albuquerque: University of New Mexico Press, 2006.

Trask, Kerry A. *Black Hawk: The Battle for the Heart of America.* New York: Henry Holt and Company, 2006.

Trigger, Bruce G. *A History of Archaeological Thought.* 2nd edition. Cambridge, U.K.: Cambridge University Press, 2006.

Trope, Jack F., and Walter R. Echo-Hawk. "The Native American Graves Protection and Repatriation Act: Background and Legislative History." In *Repatriation Reader: Who Owns American Indian Remains?* edited by Devon Abbot Mihesuah. Lincoln: University of Nebraska Press, 2000.

Trowbridge, C. C. *Shawanese Traditions.* Edited by Vernon Kinietz and Erminie Voegelin. Ann Arbor: Museum of Anthropology, University of Michigan Press, 1939.

Truer, David. "Return the National Parks to the Tribes." *The Atlantic* (May 2021): n.p. http://www.theatlantic.com/magazine/archive/2021/05/return-the-national-parks-to-the-tribes/618395/.

Tuck, Eve, and K. Wayne Yang, "Decolonization is not a Metaphor." *Decolonization: Indigeneity, Education & Society* 1 no. 1 (2012): 1–40.

Turner, Caitlin. "Mall construction unearths American Indian mound." *Chillicothe Gazette*, January 30, 2015.

Twinam, Ann. *Purchasing Whiteness. Pardos, Mulattos, and the Quest for Social Mobility in the Spanish Indies.* Stanford, Calif.: Stanford University Press, 2015.

Tyler, S. Lyman. "The Myth Of The Lake Of Copala and Land Of Teguayo." *Utah Historical Quarterly* 20, no. 4 (1952): 313–29.

Umberger, Emily. "Antiques, Revivals, and References to the Past in Aztec Art." *RES: Anthropology and Aesthetics* 13 (Spring 1987): 62–105.

———. "Aztec Sculptures, Hieroglyphs, and History." PhD diss., Columbia University, 1981.

———. "Notions of Aztec History: The Case of the Great Temple Dedication." *RES: Anthropology and Aesthetics* 42 (Autumn 2002): 86–108.

[United States Commissioner of Indian Affairs.] *Treaties Between the United States of America and the Several Indian Tribes, from 1778 to 1837* [...] Washington D.C.: Langtree and O'Sullivan, 1837.

[United States Congress.] *The Debates and Proceedings in the Congress of the United States, Fifteenth Congress, Second Session.* Vol 1. Washington, D.C.: Gales & Seaton, 1855.

Uribe-Uran, Victor M. "The Birth of a Public Sphere in Latin America during the Age of Revolution." *Comparative Studies in Society and History* 42, no. 2 (2000): 425–47.

Vailant, Seonaid. *Ornamental Nationalism: Archaeology and Antiquities in Mexico, 1876–1911* Leiden: Brill, 2017.

Valauskas, Edward J. "Benjamin Smith Barton and the flowering of early American natural history." *Chicago Botanic Garden*, January 2015. http://www.chicagobotanic.org/library/stories/benjamin_smith_barton.

Valverde, Nuria and Antonio Lafuente. "Space Production and Spanish Imperial Geopolitics." In *Science in The Spanish And Portuguese Empires, 1500–1800*, edited By Daniela Bleichmar, Paula De Vos, Kristin Huffine, And Kevin Sheehan, 198–216. Stanford, Calif.: Stanford University Press, 2009.

Van Atta, John R. *Securing the West: Politics, Public Lands, and the Fate of the Old Republic, 1785–1850.* Baltimore, Md.: Johns Hopkins University Press, 2014.

Vattel, M. [Emer] de. *Le droit des gens ou Principes de la loi naturelle appliqués à la conduite et aux affaires des nations et des souverains.* London: s.n., 1758.

Vehik, Susan C. "Dhegiha Origins and Plains Archaeology," *Plains Anthropologist* 38, no. 146 (1993): 231–52.

———. "Oñate's Expedition to the Southern Plains: Routes, Destinations, and Implications for Late Prehistoric Cultural Adaptations." *Plains Anthropologist* 31 (1986): 13–34.

Velazco, Salvador. *Visiones de Anáhuac: reconstrucciones historiografías y etnicidades emergentes en el México colonial: Fernando de Alva Ixtlilxóchitl, Diego Muñoz Camargo y Hernando Alvarado Tezozómoc.* Guadalajara, Mex.: Universidad de Guadalajara, 2003.

Veracini, Lorenzo. "Decolonizing Settler Colonialism: Kill the Settler in Him and Save the Man." *American Indian Research Journal* 41, no. 1 (2017): 1–18.

———. "Introducing Settler Colonial Studies," *Settler Colonial Studies* 1, no. 1 (2011): 1–12.

———. *Settler Colonialism: A Theoretical Overview.* New York: Palgrave MacMillan, 2010.

———. *The Settler Colonial Present.* New York: Palgrave MacMillan, 2012.

Veytia, D. Mariano. *Historia antigua de México.* Mexico City: Juan Ojeda, 1836.

Villela, Khristaan D., and Mary Ellen Miller, eds. "Researches Concerning the Institutions and Monuments of the Ancient Inhabitants of America, with Descriptions and Views of Some of the Most Striking Scenes in the Cordilleras! (1810) Alexander von Humboldt." In *The Aztec Calendar Stone*, edited by Khristaan D. Villela and Mary Ellen Miller, 81–89. Los Angeles: Getty Publications, 2010.

Villela, Khristaan D., Matthew H. Robb, and Mary Ellen Miller. Introduction to *The Aztec Calendar Stone*, edited by Khristaan D. Villela and Mary Ellen Miller, 1–41. Los Angeles: Getty Publications, 2010.

Villella, Peter. *Indigenous Elites and Creole Identity in Colonial Mexico, 1500–1800*. New York: Cambridge University Press, 2016.

Vimalassery, Manu, Juliana Hu Pegues, and Alyosha Goldstein. "Introduction: On Colonial Unknowing." *Theory & Event* 19, no. 4 (2016): n.p.

Vinson, III, Ben. *Before Mestizaje: The Frontiers of Race and Caste in Colonial Mexico*. New York: Cambridge University Press, 2017.

Vizenor, Gerald. "Bone Courts: The Rights and Narrative Representation of Tribal Bones." *American Indian Quarterly* 10, no. 4 (1986): 319–31.

Volney, C.-F. "Extrait de Barton," *Autograph Manuscript*, MA 8013.8 (Portfolio), Morgan Library.

———. *Tableau du climat et du sol des États-Unis d'Amérique* [. . .]. Paris: Courcier et Dentu, 1803.

———. *A View of the Climate and Soil of the United States of America* [. . .]. Translated by C. B. Brown. Philadelphia: J. Conrad and Co., 1804.

———. "Vocabulary of the Miami Indians [March 1798]." Unpublished manuscript in the American Philosophical Society Historical and Literary Committee, American Indian Vocabulary Collection, Mss.497.V85. American Philosophical Society, Philadelphia.

Wade, Peter. *Race and Ethnicity in Latin America*. Chicago, Ill.: University of Chicago Press, 1997.

Wade, Richard C. *The Urban Frontier: The Rise of Western Cities, 1790–1830*. Cambridge, Mass.: Harvard University Press, 1959.

Waldeck, Frédéric de. *Voyage pittoresque et archéologique dans la province d'Yucatan (Amérique Centrale), pendant les années 1834 et 1836*. Paris: B. Dufour et Co, 1838.

Waldo, Samuel Putnam. *The Tour of James Monroe, President of the United States, Through the Northern and Eastern States, in 1817*. Hartford: Silus Andrus, 1819.

Wallace, Anthony F. C. *The Death and Rebirth of the Seneca*. New York: Vintage Books, 1972.

———. *Tuscarora: A History*. Albany: State University of New York Press, 2012.

Walls, Laura Dassow. *The Passage to Cosmos: Alexander Von Humboldt and the Shaping of America*. Chicago, Ill.: University of Chicago Press.

Ward, Thomas. "From the 'People' to the 'Nation': an Emerging Notion in Sahagún, Ixtlilxóchitl and Muñoz Camargo." *Estudios de Cultura Náhuatl* 32 (2001): 223–34.

Warden, David Bailie. *Recherches sur les antiquités de l'Amérique Septentrionale*. Paris: Everat, 1827.

Warhus, Mark. *Another America: Native American Maps and the History of Our Land*. New York: St. Martin's Press, 1997.

Warren, Leonard. *Constantine Samuel Rafinesque: A Voice in the American Wilderness*. Lexington: University of Kentucky Press, 2004.

Warren, Stephen. *The Shawnee and their Neighbors 1795–1870*. Urbana: University of Illinois Press, 2005.

———. *The Worlds the Shawnees Made: Migration and Violence in Early America*. Chapel Hill: University of North Carolina Press, 2014.

Warren, Stephen, ed. *The Eastern Shawnee Tribe of Oklahoma: Resilience Through Adversity*. Norman: University of Oklahoma Press, 2017.

Warren, Stephen, and Randolph Noe. "The Greatest Travelers in America: Shawnee Survival in the Shatter Zone." In *Mapping the Mississippi Shatter Zone: The Colonial Indian Slave Trade and Regional Instability in the American South*, edited by Robbie Ethridge and Sheri M. Shuck-Hall, 163–87. Lincoln: University of Nebraska Press, 2009.

Warrior, Robert. *The People and the Word: Reading Native Nonfiction*. Minneapolis: University of Minnesota Press, 2005.

Waselkov, Gregory A. *A Conquering Spirit: Fort Mims and the Redstick War of 1813–1814*. Tuscaloosa: University of Alabama Press, 2009.

Waselkov, Gregory A., and Kathryn E. Holland Braund. "The Significance of William Bartram's Writings on the Southeastern Indians." In *William Bartram on the Southeastern Indians*, edited by Gregory A. Waselkov and Kathryn E. Holland Braund: 199–214. Lincoln: University of Nebraska Press, 1995.

———. "William Bartram and the Southeastern Indians: An Introduction." In *William Bartram on the Southeastern Indians*, edited by Gregory A. Waselkov and Kathryn E. Holland Braund: 1–24. Lincoln: University of Nebraska Press, 1995.

Waselkov, Gregory A., and Kathryn E. Holland Braund, eds. *William Bartram on the Southeastern Indians*. Lincoln: University of Nebraska Press, 1995.

Washington, George. *The Papers of George Washington, Confederation Series, vol. 2, 18 July 1784–18 May 1785*. Edited by W. W. Abbot. Charlottesville: University of Virginia Press, 1992.

———. *The Papers of George Washington, Presidential Series, vol. 7, 1 December 1790–21 March 1791*. Edited by Jack D. Warren, Jr. Charlottesville: University of Virginia Press, 1998.

Wasserstrom, Robert. *Class and Society in Central Chiapas*. Berkeley: University of California Press, 1983.

Watanabe, John M. *Maya Saints and Souls in a Changing World*. Austin: University of Texas Press, 1992.

Watts, Edward. *Colonizing the Past: Mythmaking and Pre-Columbian Whites in Nineteenth-Century American Writing*. Charlottesville: University of Virginia Press, 2020.

Webb, William S., and Charles E. Snow. *The Adena People* [1945]. Rev. ed. Knoxville: University of Tennessee Press, 1988.

Weber, David J. *Bárbaros: Spaniards and Their Savages in the Age of Enlightenment*. New Haven: Yale University Press, 2005.

———. *The Spanish Frontier in North America*. New Haven: Yale University Press, 1992.
Webster, Noah. "Letter 1." *American Museum, or, Universal Magazine* [...] 6, no. 1 (July 1790): 11–12.
Weeks, William Earl. *John Quincy Adams and American Global Empire*. Lexington: University Press of Kentucky, 1992.
Wellenreuther, Hermann, and Carola Wessel, eds., *The Moravian Mission Diaries of David Zeisberger, 1772–1781*. Translated by Julie T. Weber. University Park: Pennsylvania State University Press, 2005.
Wertheimer, Eric. *Imagined Empires: Incas, Aztecs, and the New World of American Literature, 1771–1876*. New York: Cambridge University Press, 1999.
Westerman, Gwen, and Bruce White. *Mni Sota Makoce: The Land of the Dakota*. Minnesota: Minnesota Historical Society Press, 2012.
Wheeler, Roxann. *The Complexion of Race: Categories of Difference in Eighteenth-Century British Culture*. Philadelphia: University of Pennsylvania Press, 2000.
Wheeler-Voegelin, Erminie. *Mortuary Customs of the Shawnee and Other Eastern Tribes*. Indianapolis: Indiana Historical Society, 1944.
White, A. J., Samuel E. Munoz, Sissel Schroeder, and Lora R. Stevens. "After Cahokia: Indigenous Repopulation and Depopulation of the Horseshoe Lake Watershed, AD 1400–1900." *American Antiquity*, 85 (April 2020): 263–78.
White, Ed. *The Backcountry and the City: Colonization and Conflict in Early America*. Minneapolis: University of Minnesota Press. 2005.
White, Hayden. *The Content of the Form: Narrative Discourse and Historical Representation*. Baltimore: Johns Hopkins University Press, 1987.
White, Richard. *The Middle Ground: Indians, Empires, and Republics in the Great Lakes Region, 1650–1815*. Cambridge, U.K.: Cambridge University Press, 1991.
Williams, Elizabeth. "Collecting and Exhibiting Pre-Columbiana in France and England, 1870–1930." In *Collecting the Pre-Columbian Past: A Symposium at Dumbarton Oaks, 6th and 7th October 1990*, edited by Elizabeth Hill Boone, 123–40. Washington D.C.: Dumbarton Oaks Research Library and Collection, 1993.
Williams, Glyn. *Madoc: The Making of a Myth. The Legend of the Welsh Discovery of America* [1979]. Rev. ed. New York: Oxford University Press, 1988.
Williams, Mark. "E.G. Squier's Manuscript Copy of William Bartram's *Observations on the Creek and Cherokee Indians*." In *Fields of Vision: Essays on the Travels of William Bartram*, edited by Kathryn E. Holland Braund and Charlotte M. Porter, 169–79. Tuscaloosa: University of Alabama Press, 2010.
Williams, Stephen. *Fantastic Archaeology: The Wild Side of North American Prehistory*. Philadelphia: University of Pennsylvania Press, 1991.
———. "'From Whence Came those Aboriginal Inhabitants of America." In *New Perspectives on the Origins of Americanist Archaeology*, edited by David L. Browman and Stephen Williams, 30–49. Tuscaloosa: University of Alabama Press, 2001.

Wilson, Shawn. *Research Is Ceremony: Indigenous Research Methods.* Halifax, N.S.: Fernwood Publishing, 2008.

Winsor, Justin. *The Westward Movement: The Colonies and the Republic West of the Alleghanies, 1763–1798.* New York: Houghton, Mifflin, 1897.

Winterer, Caroline. *American Enlightenments: Pursuing Happiness in the Age of Reason.* New York: Oxford, 2016.

———. *The Mirror of Antiquity: American Women and the Classical Tradition, 1750–1900.* Ithaca, N.Y.: Cornell University Press, 2007.

Wistar, Caspar. "A Description of the Bones Deposited, by the President, in the Museum of the Society, and Represented in the Annexed Plates." *Transactions of the American Philosophical Society* 4 (1799): 526–31.

Wisecup, Kelly. "Entangled Archives: Cherokee Interventions in Language Collecting" in *Afterlives Of Indigenous Archives, Essays In Honor Of The Occom Circle*, edited by Ivy Schweitzer and Gordon Henry, 120–38. Hanover, N.H.: Dartmouth College, 2019.

———. "Meteors, Ships, Etc.: Native American Histories of Colonialism and Early American Archives." *American Literary History* 30, no. 1 (Spring 2018): 29–44.

Witgen, Michael. *Infinity of Nations: How the Native New World Shaped Early North America.* Philadelphia: University of Pennsylvania Press, 2011.

Wolfe, Patrick. "Land, Labor and Difference: Elementary Structures of Race." *American Historical Review* 106 (2001): 866–905.

———. "Settler Colonialism and the Elimination of the Native." *Journal of Genocide Research* 8, no. 4 (2006): 387–409.

———. "Structure and Event: Settler Colonialism, Time, and the Question of Genocide." In *Empire, Colony, Genocide: Conquest, Occupation, and Subaltern Resistance in World History,* edited by A. Dirk Moses, 102–32. New York: Berghahn Books, 2008.

Yablon, Nick. *Untimely Ruins: An Archaeology of American Urban Modernity, 1819–1919.* Chicago, Ill.: University of Chicago Press, 2009.

Yale, Elizabeth. "With Slips and Scraps: How Early Modern Naturalists Invented the Archive." *Book History* 12 (2009): 1–36.

Yang, Debra W. "Southern California Man Pleads Guilty to Selling 200-Year-Old Native Hawaiian Skull on eBay." U.S. Department of Justice, January 14, 2005. http://www.justice.gov/archive/usao/cac/Pressroom/pr2005/010.html.

Yannikakis, Yanna. *The Art of Being In-Between: Native Intermediaries, Indian Identity, and Local Rule in Colonial Oaxaca.* Durham, N.C.: Duke University Press, 2008.

———. "Witnesses, Spatial Practices, and a Land Dispute in Colonial Oaxaca." *The Americas* 65 (2008): 161–92.

Yates, John and Joseph Moulton. *History of New York Including the Aboriginal And Colonial Annals.* Vol. 1. New York: A.T. Goodrich, 1824.

Young, Calvin M. *Little Turtle (Me-she-kin-no-quah) the Great Chief of the Miami Indian Nation; Being a Sketch of His Life, Together with that of William Wells and Some Noted Descendants.* Indianapolis, In.: Sentinel Ptg. Co., 1917.

Zachariah, Holly. "Developers allow dig of sacred site in Chillicothe." *Columbus Dispatch*, January 30, 2015.

Zavala, Lorenzo de. *Viage a los Estados-Unidos del Norte de America*. Paris: Impr. de Decourchant, 1834.

Zaveri, Mihir. "With Indigenous Languages in Decline, Summer Camps offer Hope." *New York Times*, April 7, 2019. http://www.nytimes.com/2019/04/07/us/native-languages-decline.html?rref=collection%2Fsectioncollection%2Feducation.

Zeisberger, David. "David Zeisberger's History of the Northern American Indians." *Ohio State Archaeological and Historical Society Publication* 19 (1910): 128–41.

INDEX

Abenaki, 8–9, 192, 249n1
"aboriginal title," 12, 55, 59, 78–79, 132, 138, 254n55, 254n63, 294n82, 310n196
Achim, Miruna, 225, 319n150
Acoma Pueblo, 20
Adena (anthropological term), 203, 255n81, 305n62
Adena (estate), 174, 304n61
Aguirre, Robert, 208
Alamán, Lucas, 210, 217, 220–23, 227, 232, 317n84
Allegheny River (Ohi:yo'), 279n278
Alta California, 50, 108, 208, 225
Alzate y Ramírez, José Antonio de, 18, 93, 102, 106, 142, 253n52
American Colonization Society, 193
American Museum, 53–54, 77, 275n196, 278n242
American War of Independence, 64, 66, 84, 194, 271n71, 298n162, 302n11
Anáhuac Valley, 49, 51, 72
Anishinaabeg, 2, 17, 67–68, 70, 77, 84, 158, 291n20, 298n157
anthropology, 5, 9, 13, 16, 192, 209, 232, 250n15, 257n20, 324n246
antiquaries, 8–12, 103, 111, 124, 166–71, 179, 182, 186, 189, 191, 200–201, 206, 253n52
antiquities, xiv, 11–13, 28, 54, 56–57, 102, 114, 124–27, 130–31, 173, 177–84, 186–90, 194, 198–201, 223–26, 229, 238, 253n52, 289n210, 292n47, 306n98, 318–19nn136–37, 319n154, 320n177;

American, 5, 7–10, 13, 86, 136, 167–68, 254n54, 325n12; American Antiquities Act, 245–46; Indian, 167, 182, 185, 192–93; Mexican, 3, 9, 110, 200, 222, 226, 323n223; preservation, 168–69, 175; Royal Antiquities Expedition, 205, 215, 234
Apalachicola River, 77, 293n62
Archaeologia Americana, 18, 160, 168, 172, 176, 179–81, 184, 188–90, 192, 196–97, 200–201
archaeology, 98, 131, 133, 159–61, 164, 167–69, 190, 201, 206, 208, 247, 279n267
architecture, 11, 54, 97, 103, 165, 215, 230; earthen, xiii, xxii, 1, 58, 183; Mexican, 72–73; monumental, 72, 104, 107, 160
Arizona, 42, 50, 52, 244–45, 264n167
Arkansas River, 20, 52, 129
Atwater, Caleb, 168, 172–81, 183–88, 190, 192, 194–203, 205, 237, 303n24, 306n98, 307n120
Austin, Moses, 220
Aztalan (WI), 1–3, 5, 7–8, 245, 252n41, 312n223
Aztecas, xxi, 41, 47–51, 137
Aztec Calendar Stone, 3, 5. *See also* Piedra del Sol
Aztec Empire. *See* Triple Alliance
Aztec Ruins National Monument, 244
Aztlán, xxi, 2, 7, 20, 23, 34, 40–42, 47, 49, 51–52, 84, 100, 114, 118, 129, 137, 157, 162, 207, 210, 241, 243–44, 266n196, 274n167, 284n101, 289n211

Baja California, 49, 129
Bancroft, George, 9
Bandaras, Juan, 233–34
Baradère, Henri, 229, 236, 240, 242, 320nn174–75, 322n207, 323n220
Barton, Benjamin Smith, 18, 55–56, 64, 66–67, 69–70, 85–88, 128–37, 139, 142–61, 216, 270n47, 273n124, 291n32, 294n82, 296nn121–22, 299n203, 300n224
Bartram, William, 18, 58, 88, 133–34, 136, 144, 295n117
Bautista de Anza, Juan, 50
Beaver River, 62, 66–68
Benavente, Toribio de (Motolinía), 23, 95, 259n51, 259n61
Black Hawk (Ma-ka-tai-me-she-kia-kiak), 199, 249n1
Black Hawk War (1832), 1, 200, 249n1
Blackness, 16, 60, 255n78, 317n103
blanqueamiento, 15, 209, 228
Bodega y Quadra, Juan Francisco de la, 114
Boone, Daniel, 65
botany, 88, 131, 147, 155, 157, 159–60, 164, 177, 185
Boturini Benaduci, Lorenzo, 10, 17–18, 23, 33–42, 44–45, 47–49, 72, 92, 102, 111, 116, 118, 126, 129, 161, 201, 222, 224, 236, 261nn96–97, 262n115, 263n147, 263n156, 264n158, 283n72, 288n167, 289n206, 289n211, 321n192
Brackenridge, Henry Marie, 165–67, 169, 174, 182, 302n9
Britain, 51, 61, 69, 77, 86, 111, 113–14, 139–41, 172, 217, 226, 264n163, 300n224; British colonies, 250n16, 253n46, 253n52, 264n160, 292n58; British East India Company, 206; British people, xxi, 10–11, 22, 52, 59, 62–63, 67–70, 77–78, 108, 140, 150, 179, 208
Brown, Charles Brockden, 144

Bruchac, Margaret M., 9, 192
Buckeye Lake, xiii
Bustamente, Carlos María de, 210, 226, 232–33, 239, 300n226, 314n33, 321n193

cabecera, 24, 29
cacicazgo, 24, 219, 259n65
Cahokia, 1, 21, 68, 83, 90, 166–67, 169, 182, 248, 253n49, 255n81, 302n17
California, 42, 48, 220, 245, 274n167
Cañizares-Esguerra, Jorge, 92, 264n158, 265n178
Carlos III, 11, 43, 108
Carlos IV, 108, 124
Carlos V, 258n46
cartography, 21, 263n139
Carver, Jonathan, 59
Casa Grande Ruins National Monument, 49–50, 114, 129, 166, 292n53
Casas Grandes (Paquimé), 20, 49, 72, 114, 263n142, 266n201, 267n205, 292n53
Cass, Lewis, 3, 194
Castañeda, José Luciano, 205, 215, 229, 234–35, 238–39
Cedar Bog, xiii
Champlain, Samuel de, 143
Chapultepec, 4, 41, 97, 125, 225, 281n40, 289n211; Battle of, 243
Chassebœuf, Constantin François, 141–44, 146, 162–63, 295n117, 301n229
Cherokee, xvii, 58, 67, 77, 89, 134–35, 138–39, 142, 148, 153, 181, 187, 198–99, 252n39, 264n160, 275n183, 277n226, 291n32, 292n58, 293n63, 293nn66–67, 295n117
Chiapas, 97, 129, 205, 207–8, 211, 213–15, 218–20, 228, 234–37, 240–41, 247, 255n90, 317n104, 319n140, 321n189, 323n236
Chichimecas, 23, 26, 40–41, 43, 73, 154, 258n37, 258n42, 263n147

Chickasaw, 15, 57, 60, 68, 89, 133–34, 138–39, 142, 148, 247, 264n160, 271n89, 295n117, 299n188
Chihuahua, 20, 26, 49–50, 129, 320n164
Chippewa. *See* Ojibwe
Choctaw, 53, 68, 81, 89, 134, 138–40, 143, 148, 295n117
Cholula, 2–3, 40, 72–74, 87, 95, 103, 136, 166, 182, 184, 282n44
Christianity, 7, 12, 42, 65, 76, 123, 137, 153, 159, 215, 238; and conversion, 94, 193, 195; and cosmology, 24; and Mayas, 213; medieval, 262; Mexica, 123; and missionaries, 151; and scripture, 59; and Tuscaroras, 298
chronology, 11–12, 27, 32, 35–36, 50, 53, 55, 87, 90, 118, 128, 133, 166, 170, 182–85, 189, 202, 253n50, 323n232
Cíbola, 20, 113, 257n35
Cincinnati, 10, 63. *See also* Society of the Cincinnati
Circleville (OH), 174–78, 186, 188, 200, 305n70, 307n112, 311n215
citizenship, 5, 172, 222
civilization, 21, 43–44, 47, 52, 54, 57–58, 61, 72, 77–79, 166, 173, 194–95, 206, 208, 211, 238, 240, 242, 245, 253n49, 269nn40–41, 322n213
civilizationism, 7, 172, 193
Clark, George Rogers, 63, 70, 83, 268n13
Clavijero, Francisco Javier, 18, 23, 45–51, 53, 57, 72–75, 87, 92–93, 103, 112–13, 116, 118, 131, 136, 144, 152–53, 157, 182, 214, 261n105, 265n188, 266n201, 267n205, 267n208, 274n167, 283n72, 287n153, 289n206, 291n33
Clifford, John D., 182–84, 190, 307n119
Coatlicue, 100, 107, 115, 120–23, 125, 127, 223, 282n51, 288n181, 288n189
Codex Azcatitlan, 35, 266n196
Codex Boturini, 10, 34, 40, 42, 47, 49, 201, 222, 224, 236, 261n104

Codex Mendoza, 28, 265n169
Codex Sigüenza, 73
colonialism, 5, 8, 45, 67, 216. *See also* settler colonialism
"colonial unknowing," xv, 8, 249n10
Colorado River, 42, 50, 113
conquest, 5, 19, 77–79, 92, 121–22, 140, 149, 153, 183, 212, 243, 247, 249, 266n191, 324n1
continental race theory, 54, 268n6
Cook, James, 59
Coronado, Francisco Vázquez de, 20, 25, 257n35
Corroy, François "Juan Francisco," 205
Cortés, Hérnan, 19, 24, 30, 36, 94, 95–96, 102, 154, 211, 233, 258n46, 260n70
Council of Three Fires, 67, 199, 249n1
credit, xiii, 61, 218
Creek. *See* Mvskoke
creole, xxi, 6, 12, 15, 22, 52, 56, 85, 92, 109, 216, 257n17, 257n22, 261n94
criollos, xxi, 5, 18, 22, 28, 35, 43, 47–48, 50–51, 85, 92–94, 96, 98, 101, 103, 108–13, 115, 117–18, 120–27, 144–45, 184, 201, 209, 215–16, 265n178, 280n14, 285n108, 285n117, 289n206, 321n183
Crockett, Davy, xiii
Curiosa Americana, 10
Cusick, David, 80, 150–51, 297nn153–54
Cusick, Nicholas (Kanatsoyh), 297n153, 298n166

Dakota, 1, 13, 16, 156, 199, 249n1, 277n234
decolonization, xiv–xv, 250n12, 252n39
Delafield, John, 10
Delaware. *See* Lenape
Delaware River (Lenapewihìtàk), 150
Del Río, Antonio, 205, 215
Diné (Navajo), 244–45, 247
displacement, xiv, 6, 41, 85, 171, 208–9, 216, 232, 268n16

dispossession, 6–9, 13–17, 24–25, 29–30, 39, 41, 49, 57, 90, 96, 128, 132, 139, 149, 169, 171, 191, 195, 209, 246–47, 249n10, 252n39, 304n40, 313n256
domination, xiii, 41, 61, 208, 225
Dresden Codex, 258n46
Dupaix, Guillermo, 93, 124–25, 129, 205, 214–15, 223, 225, 229, 234, 236–37, 286n135

earthworks, xxi–xxii, 1, 5–7, 9, 18, 54–56, 58, 61, 64–67, 69, 71–76, 81–90, 131–37, 143, 149, 154–56, 159–60, 162, 165–68, 171, 173–76, 178, 182–86, 189, 201–3, 248, 277n227, 278n242, 279n267, 292n44, 302n16, 303n23, 303n36
Echo-Hawk, Roger, 16
encomienda, 15, 23–24, 30, 217, 257n21, 280n21
English property law, 12
ethnology, 7, 163, 291n23
Etzanoa, 20–21, 255n81, 257n16
Evans, Lewis, 64, 68

Florentine Codex, 99, 212
forts: Fort Atkinson, 1; Fort Crawford, 199; Fort Dearborn, 162; Fort Defiance, 139; Fort Findlay, 311n212; Fort Finley, 196, 198; Fort Finney, 63, 71, 271n73; Fort Harmar, 64, 73, 136, 278n259; Fort McIntosh, 63–64, 66, 71, 271n71; Fort Meigs, 193; fort of Niagara, 62; Fort Oswego, 136; Fort Ouiatenon, 141; Fort Pickawillany, 63, 68, 193; Fort Pitt, 66–67, 70; Fort Stanwix, 72, 141, 296n122; Fort Stephenson, 311n212; Fort St. Mary's, 194; Fort Tomlinson, 268n11; Fort Vincennes, 141–42, 310n181; Fort Wayne, 140–41, 162–64, 305n74, 310n181

Four Corners region, 52, 244, 325n18
France, 43, 62, 77, 92, 111, 140, 216, 223, 228, 236–37, 322n209
frontier, 38, 152, 154, 166, 193, 195, 200, 220–21, 266n200; colonies, 26; lands, 43; Ohio, 76

Galindo, John "Juan," 238, 312n238
Gazeta de Literatura de México, 92, 110, 112, 115, 124
Gazeta de México, 92, 112, 115, 117–18, 285n116
General Colonization Law (1824), 221
Geniusz, Mary Siisip, 158, 291n20
geography, 35, 49, 51–52, 54, 59–60, 79, 129, 158, 169, 197, 276n198, 284n95
Gila River, 49–50, 113–14, 129, 166, 290n9
Grave Creek, 54, 73–74, 86–87, 89–90, 136, 198, 248, 305n62
Great Plains, 21–22, 52, 79
Grito de Delores, 15
Guatemala, 40–41, 48, 108, 118, 129, 206, 208, 211, 219–20, 224, 238, 324n241; Junta of, 300n223
Guatemala City, 214–25, 315n36, 315n41, 317n104, 323n236
Gulf of California, 42, 47, 49, 73, 113–14

Haudenosaunee, 67, 70, 77, 80, 141, 149–53, 168, 273n136, 294n82, 303n31. See also Six Nations Confederacy
Hawikuh (Cíbola), 113, 257n35
Herrera y Tordesillas, Antonio de, 154
Hidalgo, Miguel, 217, 316n81
Hispanicization, 15, 26, 38, 264n159
Historia Indiana, 43
Ho-Chunk (Winnebago), 1, 80, 85, 199, 249n1, 277n234, 305n85
Hopewell (anthropological term), 255n81, 279n267
Hopi, 244–45, 267n205

Huitzilopochtli, 48, 98–100, 105, 107, 115–16, 122, 282n51, 282n54, 287n153
Humboldt, Alexander von, 4, 93, 124–25, 128–30, 182, 184, 216, 218, 223, 237–38, 280n14, 286n138, 289nn204–8, 290n2, 290n9, 316n73, 321n183
Hyer, Nathaniel F., 2–3, 7, 10, 250n7

"idols," 27, 76, 101–2, 125, 226, 230–31, 289n208, 321n183, 321n189
Illinois (people, also Inoka), 68, 77, 276n203, 303n17
Illinois (place), 7, 68, 83, 175, 177, 199, 201, 250n5, 305n85
Indiana, 63, 68, 141, 163, 175, 294n82, 301n235, 302n249, 305n85, 310n191
indigeneity, xv, 4–5, 8, 17, 96, 182, 209, 222, 233–34, 244, 250n15, 255n78, 255n90
Indigenous artifacts, 5, 9–11, 13, 18, 97, 103, 111, 124–25, 165, 167, 174, 178–79, 181–82, 185–87, 262n126, 319n140
Indigenous eviction, xiii, 194, 209. *See also* dispossession
Indigenous homelands, xiv, xvii, 18, 25, 56, 88, 114, 138–40, 148, 152, 163–64, 172, 175, 194, 199, 244–45, 248, 257n33, 271n77, 302n249
Itzcoatl, 35, 100
Ixtlilxóchitl, Fernando de Alva Cortes, 30, 36, 43, 109, 154, 259nn66–67, 260n70, 282n48

Jefferson, Thomas, 9, 18, 55, 57–58, 60–62, 71–72, 74, 128–30, 142–43, 146, 159–62, 165–66, 177, 179, 183, 188–89, 193, 253n52, 267n2, 269n34, 270n67, 274n160, 290n18, 295n97, 302n9
Johnston, John, 193, 196, 305n74, 310n181, 310n196
Johnston Indian Agency, xiii, 193, 310n200

Kanawha Valley, 189
kenapacomaqua (Little Turtle's Town), 162–63
kin, 67–68, 70, 80, 97, 134, 149–52, 163, 257n24, 272n109
kinship, xiii, 82, 145–47, 212, 276n206, 315n43, 323n233
Kirkland, Samuel, 83, 136, 149–50, 296n121, 297n142, 297n153, 298n166
Kitikiti'sh (Wichita), 20–22, 264n160. *See also* Wichita and Affiliated Tribes
Knox, Henry, 76–78, 144, 148, 275n192, 283n62, 293n71, 295n114

labor, xiii, 5, 15, 24–25, 57–58, 104, 215, 257n24, 320n161; colonial labor structure, 217–18, 227, 280n21, 283n74; contracts, 227; enslaved, 248; extractive, 6, 103; forced, 211, 248; management, 108; rights, 30; shortage, 218
latifundio, 15
Lenape (Delaware), xiv, xvii, 17, 54, 62–70, 82, 84, 89, 140, 143, 145–51, 153–56, 183, 186, 194, 196, 264n160, 271n91, 272n106, 276n198, 278n245, 279n285, 296n131, 298n161, 307n111
León y Gama, Antonio de, 18, 93, 110, 115, 119
letrados, 6, 92, 207
Lewis, James Otto, 199
Lewis Town, 196
Little Turtle (Mihšihkinaahkwa), 139–42, 146, 162–62, 293n71, 294n85, 296n122, 301n229, 301n235
Llano Estacado, 20
Lockhart, James, 24
London, 11, 33, 46, 73, 92, 161, 205, 222, 224, 234–36, 238, 265n181
López Austín, Alfredo, 25
López Luján, Leonardo, 25

Madrid, 9, 37, 45, 92, 108–9, 111, 115, 138, 215, 221, 316n66, 323n236
Mahican, 67–68, 134, 146, 148, 154, 295n117, 297n149
Mann, Barbara Alice, 175n309
mapas, 32, 34–37, 39–40, 42, 47, 50, 55, 97, 101, 109, 111, 116, 122, 127, 223, 225, 235, 260n80, 261n105, 262n110, 262n115, 262n124, 288n181
mapping, 7, 38, 51, 64, 105, 113, 192, 256n93
Mather, Cotton, 10, 253n52
Maya, 26, 206–9, 214–15, 238–42, 253n49, 255n81, 281n30, 314nn14–15, 315n48, 321n189, 321n199, 323n234, 324n243; antiquity, 235; and Guatemala, 41, 48, 206; hieroglyphics, 18, 207, 235–37, 323nn227–29; identity, 212; lands, 211–14, 220, 241; languages, 211; and Mayapán, 212; and Spanish invaders, 27, 216
McGirt v. Oklahoma, 14
Medrano, Ethelia Ruiz, 31
Menominee, 2
Mesa Verde, 245, 255n81
Mesa Verde National Park, 244–45
mestizaje, 5, 15, 228, 251n17, 255n90, 314n25
mestizo, 15–16, 29–30, 209, 216, 240, 254n74, 256n8, 314n25, 317n107
Mexica, 2, 7, 75, 92, 125, 129, 210, 233, 244, 250n8, 266n196, 284n92, 290n9; antiquarianism, 98; origins, 113; past, 3–4, 10, 18, 23, 208, 243; race, 216, 219, 238–39
Mexican antiquity, 7, 94, 210, 223, 234
Mexican migration thesis, 136, 202; Nahua, 26; narratives, 42–43, 47–48, 55, 132–33, 284n101; and New Spain, 38; and oral tradition, 131; patterns, 137; racialized, 56, 61; routes, 49–51, 134–35, 177; serial, 60–61; Toltec, 137; traditions, 113, 131, 134, 143, 146, 151, 153; trans-Mississippi migration thesis, 134

Mexico, Valley of, 25–27, 41, 73, 97, 184, 211
Mexico City, 2–4, 18, 20, 25, 32, 35, 37–38, 43, 45–46, 48, 91–92, 94, 96, 101–5, 109–13, 118, 120, 124–27, 130, 142, 166, 182, 207, 218–19, 224, 226, 229, 234–36, 240–41, 247, 265n18, 266n199, 281n24, 288n193, 316n75, 322n209, 323n218, 324nn241–42
migration, 7, 18, 48, 53–55, 59–60, 73–77, 81, 83–84, 87–88, 90, 104, 132, 134, 138–40, 145, 147, 149, 152–53, 156–57, 160, 164, 189, 207, 239, 266n201, 268n16, 270n44, 272n107, 274n167, 276n201, 298n161, 321n189, 323n232; Azteca, 20, 129, 137; Great Migration (Ojibwe), 81, 84–85; histories, 22–23, 26, 32, 50, 72, 118, 144, 152, 210, 285n101; mapping, 113, 133; Mexica, 35, 42–43, 47–48, 50–52, 55, 107, 118, 126, 132, 137, 162
Minsi Lenape (Munsee Delaware), 65, 68, 148–50, 154
Mississinewa River, 163–64, 302n249
Mississippi River, 21, 51, 68, 70–71, 79–83, 85, 89, 133–34, 136–40, 151, 199, 248
Missouri River, 51–52, 80, 129, 276n204
Mitchell, Samuel L., 178, 205, 303n172, 306n92
Moctezuma family inheritance, 23, 257n21, 261n96
Mohawk, 14, 71, 80, 141, 147–48, 150, 190, 295n117
Monticello, 9
Moravian Lenape (Christian Delaware), 66, 68, 70, 84
Morris, Robert, 150
Morton, Samuel G., 199–201, 238–39, 243, 312nn232–36, 315n36, 323n232
Motecuhzoma Xocoyotzin, 18, 23, 31, 33, 95, 97–98, 100–101, 103, 105, 116, 124, 233–34, 257n21, 260n69, 261n96, 281n40

Moundbuilder myth, 18, 55–57, 60, 75, 84, 86–87, 131–33, 164, 202, 209, 268n17, 278n239
Mundy, Barbara, 35, 106, 284n95, 285n101
Muñoz y Ferrandis, Juan Bautista, 45, 215
Museo Nacional de Antopologìa, 4, 127, 225, 252n36
Muskingum River, 64, 68, 136
Myaamia (Miami), xiii, xvii, 9, 63, 67–68, 70, 76–77, 79, 81–82, 136, 139–42, 144, 148, 162–64, 190, 193, 196, 264n160, 293n71, 295n117, 296n121, 301n228, 301n235, 301n243, 305n74
Mvskoke (Creek), 14, 58, 67–69, 77, 79, 86, 89, 133–35, 138–40, 144, 148–49, 153, 172, 248, 277n226, 291n32, 292n58, 293n62, 293n65, 295n117, 306n85

NAGPRA (Native American Graves Protection and Repatriation Act), 191–92
Nahua, xvii, xxi, 20, 22–23, 29–30, 34–36, 39–40, 46–49, 51–52, 57, 85, 96–98, 101, 107, 117, 121–23, 148, 210–14, 221, 230, 233, 240–41, 259n62, 260n74, 262n115, 263n140, 264n160, 266n188, 266n199, 280n17, 281n24, 282n61, 284n101, 321n192, 324n243; archive, 27, 94, 96; history, 56, 239, 321n199
Nahuatl, 26, 29–30, 35, 37, 41–42, 46–48, 97, 105–7, 116–17, 202, 212, 232–33, 236, 239, 250n8, 257n24, 258n37, 259n59, 262n124, 263n152, 266n196, 280n15, 283n84, 284n96, 322n202
NAIS (Native American and Indigenous studies), xv, xix, 8, 252n33, 252nn37–39
Natchez (people), 68, 80, 86, 133–35, 181
Natchez (place), 87, 292n47
National Library (Mexico), 9, 240
National Museum (Mexico), 9, 222, 224–26, 229, 231–36, 238, 240, 246–47, 326n26
national project, 5, 8–9, 15, 248

Native elimination, 8, 13–14, 232
natural history, xiii, 18, 55, 60, 85–88, 124, 131, 135, 145, 155, 157, 159, 164, 185, 205, 225, 246, 268n6, 270n53
Ndé (Apache), 16, 26, 41, 43, 244
Nebel, Karl, 3–4
New Mexico, 20, 42, 48–52, 226, 233, 244–45, 258n42, 264n167
New Spain, 5, 9, 18, 20, 22–26, 32–33, 38–40, 42–45, 48–49, 51–52, 56–57, 77, 90, 92–94, 96, 102, 104, 108–10, 113, 115, 118, 121, 123–26, 129–31, 137, 154, 160, 162, 166, 205, 210–11, 217–21, 235, 253n50, 258n42, 281n24, 289n204, 302n16, 306n85
New World, 5, 12, 22, 57, 59, 75, 109, 130, 145, 147, 206, 242, 295n101
New York, 4, 7, 52, 62, 136, 138, 144, 149–51, 157, 168, 173, 178–79, 185, 198, 201, 205, 252n41, 293n68, 294n80, 297n149, 303n17, 306n92
North Carolina, 77, 135, 149, 275n183, 297n151
Northwest Territory, 71, 73, 136, 140, 172, 311n211
Notes on the State of Virginia, 57, 60, 142
Nuevo León, 41, 241

Ohio, xiii–xiv, 65, 73, 75, 81, 84, 89, 133, 138, 141–42, 177, 179–80, 191–94, 272n106, 294n82, 297n152, 304n46, 310n181, 311n211, 313n251; antiquities, 177–78, 185, 201, 205; canal, 198; earthworks, 136, 184, 202, 303n36; emigration from, 70; Indiana border, 63; and Indigenous peoples, 72, 76, 186, 195–96; and Mihšihkinaahkwa, 162; and Northwest Territory, 172; and settlers, 69, 172; statehood, 172, 175; Tecumseh's War, 175
Ohio River, 62–64, 66, 71–72, 77, 79, 88–89, 112, 136, 139–40, 155, 182, 268n11
Ohio River Valley, 18, 54, 67–68, 71, 82–83, 85–88, 129, 148, 183

Ohio Seneca, 68, 272n106, 310n196
Ojibwe, xvii, 16–17, 55, 63, 67, 81, 84, 140, 148, 155, 199, 250n5, 277n234, 278n245, 295n117, 296n121
Oklahoma, 19, 21, 164, 192, 248, 277n233, 301n235
Oñate, Juan de, 19–20, 25, 52, 245, 256n1, 257n35
oral tradition, 31, 131–33, 143–44, 153, 155–56, 159–60, 184–85, 278n249
Orozco y Berra, Manuel, 9, 318n135

Pacific islands, 53, 108
Pacific Ocean, 49, 51–52, 59, 61, 104, 113–14, 128, 241, 290n3, 317n104
Palenque, 205–8, 212, 214–16, 224, 229, 234–40, 242, 255n81, 314n14, 315n36, 316n59, 323n223. *See also* Santo Domingo de Palenque
Paquimé. *See* Casas Grandes
Paris, 33, 61, 71, 92, 139, 221, 319n136, 322n209, 323nn220–23
Parsons, Samuel Holden, 63–64, 71–72, 74
past-making, 6, 8, 17, 103, 133
Paz, Octavio, 5
Peale, Charles Wilson, 154–55, 290n6
Peale's American Museum, 129, 325n24
Pennsylvania, 62, 65–66, 68–70, 147, 307n120
Peru, 10, 21, 40, 53–54, 78, 133, 199–200, 312n244
Peru (IN), 163–64
Philadelphia, 9, 53, 61, 64, 67, 88, 92, 109, 128–29, 135, 141–42, 144, 149, 155, 157, 161, 163, 199–200, 238, 243, 274n160, 307n112
Piedra del Sol (Sun Stone), 3–8, 18, 118, 120–23, 125–27, 157, 202, 223, 281n38, 299n203
piedras antiguas, 92, 96, 108, 117–18, 120–23, 125–27, 129, 160
pildowi ôjmowôgan, 8, 256n93

Plains Indian Sign Language (PISL), 20–21
Potawatomi, xvii, 67, 82, 140, 148, 162–63, 199, 250n5, 277n233, 295n117
Pratt, Mary Louise, 135
Priest, Josiah, 7, 10, 25, 43, 261n105
Puebla, 2, 40–41, 97, 228
Puebla-Tlaxcala Valley, 41
Purchas, Samuel, 28, 258n42, 258n50, 265n169
Putnam, Rufus, 64, 86, 272n98, 274n166
Pyramids of the Sun and Moon, 2, 102, 122

Quivira, 20, 25, 52, 113

race, xxi, 10, 54–56, 59–60, 65, 79, 154–55, 167, 171, 175, 182–83, 202, 214, 216, 219, 228, 238–39, 241, 243–45, 268n6, 270n53, 297n144, 303n23, 312n236, 312n244
race-making, 15
racialization, 60, 249n10, 269n23
racialized capitalism, 317n120
racialized Indian identity, 44, 257n34
racialized landscapes, 17
racialized migration, 56, 61
Rafinesque, Constantine, 128, 183, 237–38, 307nn119–23, 323n227
reservations, 14, 140, 150, 152, 194–97, 264n159, 297n152, 304n46
Robertson, William, 45–46, 49, 72–73, 75, 86, 253n48, 265n169, 267n205, 274n156
ruins, 20, 50, 52, 72, 98, 108, 129–30, 161, 205–6, 208, 214, 224, 236–38, 240, 250n10, 257n35, 263n142
Ruiz, Diego, 112
Ruiz, Simón, 232
Ruiz Cañete, José Francisco, 102–3

Santa Anna, Antonio López de, 240
Santo Domingo de Palenque, 108, 214

science, 92–93, 108, 159, 164, 169, 173, 191, 200, 243, 279n279, 280n5, 299n197; antiquarian, 188; archaeological, 133, 161, 163; Atlantic, 59; earth, 7; empirical, 131; Mexica, 130; US, 18, 109, 130, 172
Scioto River, 70, 139
Scioto River Valley, 173–75, 189, 313n255
Sea of California, 42, 263n156
Seneca, 54, 64, 68, 82–83, 134, 136, 141, 148–50, 152, 186, 194, 196, 272n106, 277n233, 279n278, 295n117, 297n144, 297nn151–52
settlement, 2, 7, 9, 20–22, 24–26, 38–39, 41, 47, 51, 55–56, 64–65, 67, 69, 71, 75–77, 82, 84, 134, 150, 166–67, 173, 186, 188–89, 194–95, 199, 211, 221, 250n14, 253n49, 267n206, 282n44, 298n163, 317n106
settler archive, 9, 17, 21–22
settler colonialism, 8–11, 13–15, 17, 137, 174, 248, 251n16, 252n39, 256n92, 270n53
settler histories, 8, 16–17, 256n94
settler nationalism, 5, 14, 16, 18, 169, 216
settler scholarship, xv, 12, 22, 72, 85, 131, 170, 172, 252n37
Seven Years' War, 66, 68, 272n111, 299n188
Shawnee, xiii, xvii, 54, 62–63, 65, 67–68, 70, 81–83, 89, 140, 148–53, 173–75, 177, 186–87, 190, 192–94, 196, 203–4, 264n160, 271n74, 272nn106–7, 277n233, 295n117, 310n195
Sigüenza y Góngora, Carlos, 10, 32–33, 36, 40, 45, 47, 101, 105, 257n17, 259n67, 260n85, 261n93, 283n74, 283n83, 289n206
Simpson, Audra, 14
Simpson, Leanne Betasamosake, 16, 146, 243
Six Nations Confederacy, 62, 134, 141, 145–48, 150, 152, 271n91, 296n122. *See also* Haudenosaunee

slavery, 5, 60, 172, 211
Society of Antiquaries (London), 11
Society of the Cincinnati, 64
South Carolina, 135, 275n183
Southey, Robert, 84, 243
sovereignty, 5–6, 12–16, 18, 31, 41, 44, 49–51, 56, 61, 78, 96, 123, 133, 138, 140, 158, 172, 195, 197, 206, 210, 240, 242, 247, 250n12, 254n65, 266n200, 314n24, 319n156
Spanish Empire, 11, 44–45, 47, 92, 137, 280n5
Spanish property law, 12
Squier, Ephraim G., 201–3, 279n271
St. Mary's River, 140, 194–95, 198
Susquehanna River, 68, 149, 272n107
Susquehannock (Conestoga), 68

Tardes Americanas, 43–44
Tecuilhuitzintli, 115–18, 120
Tejas, 3, 41, 70, 208, 220, 241, 306n85, 319n156, 323n218
Tennessee River, 89
Tenochtitlan, xxi, 3, 13, 21, 24–26, 29, 35, 48, 72–74, 87, 91, 94–95, 97–98, 104–7, 124, 169, 182, 209–10, 250n8, 253n49, 255n81, 259n51, 281n40, 284n101, 285n103, 289n199
Teotihuacan, 2–3, 97, 99–100, 102, 112, 122, 154, 182, 212, 262n127
Tepeyac Hill, 95, 112, 123, 281n24
"territoriality," 13–14
Texcoco, xxi, 24, 29, 49, 97, 113, 210, 234, 259n66, 282n59
Thayendanegea (Joseph Brant), 71, 146, 148, 273n136
Tlacopan, xxi, 24, 97
Toltec, 36, 41, 52, 55, 75, 97–100, 112, 120, 137, 143, 147, 212, 214–16, 226, 238–39, 241, 282n44, 282n59, 292n52, 319n151
Toluca Valley, 40–41
Tonawanda River, 149
Torquemada, Juan de, 46, 154

Towtoyka, 244. *See* Mesa Verde
treaties: Treaty of Big Tree (1797), 150–52, 297n152; Treaty of Canandaigua (1794), 141, 150; Treaty of Fort Finney (1786), 271n73; Treaty of Fort Wayne (1803, 1809), 162, 310n181; Greenville Treaty (1795), 140–41, 174, 291n24, 296n122; Treaty of Holston (1791), 138; Treaty of Hopewell (1785), 77; Treaty of New York (1790), 138; Treaty of Paris (1783), 61, 63, 139; Treaty of St. Louis (1816), 250n5; Treaty of St. Mary's (1818), 196
Triple Alliance, xxi, 13, 24, 26, 48, 97, 101, 211–12, 257n23, 265n188
"Turn and Learn," 1–2, 245
Tuscarawas River, 66, 68, 70, 84, 279n284
Tuscarora (people), 134, 141, 149–53

United Indian Nation, 70–71, 148
unsettlement, xiv–xv, 8
US Indian policy, 18, 134, 138, 141, 145, 172, 184, 186, 193, 195, 198–200, 244, 277n233
US-Mexican War, 6, 243–44
Ute, 244–45

viceregal palace, 45, 91, 95, 114
violence, xiv, 6, 9, 14, 17, 41, 44, 51, 63, 67–70, 76, 81, 89, 138, 151, 169, 200, 204, 212–13, 220–21, 234, 241, 247, 263n130, 303n35, 304n40, 321n189

Virginia, 68–69, 75, 89, 128, 159, 189, 198, 268n11, 272n106
Virginia Richly Valued, 135
Virgin of Guadalupe, 33, 110, 123, 233, 262n122, 281n24
Volney, comte de. *See* Chassebœf, Constantin François

Waldeck, Jean-Frédéric, 234–39, 242, 317n102, 321n192, 322n205, 322n209, 322n214
Washington, George, 62, 76, 151–52, 194
Wendat (Wyandot), 63, 66–68, 70, 82, 140, 145, 148, 155, 186, 194, 198, 272n109, 278n255, 294n85, 295n117, 310n196, 311n212
Wichita and Affiliated Tribes, 20, 21, 257n16
Wilson, Shawn, 13
Wisconsin, 7, 10, 199, 249n1, 250n5, 297n149; mounds, 312n223; Territory, 2, 311n220
Wisconsin River, 311n218
Worthington, Thomas, 173–74

Yazoo lands, 139–40, 292n58, 294n82
Yazoo River, 136
Yucatán, 40–41, 48, 201, 208, 211–13, 218, 228, 234, 238, 241–43, 255n90, 314nn14–16, 315n52, 317n89, 321n189, 323n234

WRITING THE EARLY AMERICAS

The Sun of Jesús del Monte: A Cuban Antislavery Novel
Translated and edited by David Luis-Brown

Letters from Filadelfia: Early Latino Literature and the Trans-American Elite
Rodrigo Lazo

Sifilografía: A History of the Writerly Pox in the Eighteenth-Century Hispanic World
Juan Carlos González Espitia

Creole Drama: Theatre and Society in Antebellum New Orleans
Juliane Braun

The Alchemy of Conquest: Science, Religion, and the Secrets of the New World
Ralph Bauer